# 2002
# GUIDE TO
# *Literary*
# AGENTS

*Put the odds of publication*
*IN YOUR FAVOR!*

EDITED BY
**RACHEL VATER**
ASSISTED BY
**ROBERT LEE BREWER**

**WRITER'S DIGEST BOOKS**
CINCINNATI, OH

Managing Editor, Annuals Department: Doug Hubbuch
Editorial Director, Annuals Department: Barbara Kuroff
Supervisory Editor: Kirsten Holm
Production Editor: Robert Lee Brewer

Writer's Digest Books website: www.writersdigest.com and www.writersmarket.com

**2002 Guide to Literary Agents.** Copyright © 2001 by Writer's Digest Books.
Published by F&W Publications, 1507 Dana Ave., Cincinnati, Ohio 45207. *Address after March 1, 2002:* 4700 E. Galbraith Rd., Cincinnati OH 45207. Printed and bound in the United States of America. All rights reserved. No part of this book may be reproduced in any form or by any electronic or mechanical means including information storage and retrieval systems without written permission from the publisher, except by reviewers who may quote brief passages to be printed in a magazine or newspaper.

International Standard Serial Number 1078-6945
International Standard Book Number 1-58297-075-0

Cover illustration by Darryl Ligasan

**Attention Booksellers:** This is an annual directory of F&W Publications.
Return deadline for this edition is April 30, 2003.

# contents at a glance

# Contents

## LITERARY AGENTS

Agents listed in this section generate 98 to 100 percent of their income from commission on sales. They do not charge for reading, critiquing, editing, marketing, or other editorial services.

### ◢ *insider* **reports**

## SCRIPT AGENTS: NONFEE-CHARGING & FEE-CHARGING

### Working with Script Agents

## INDEPENDENT PUBLICISTS

### Working with Independent Publicists

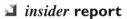 *insider* **report**

## WRITERS' CONFERENCES

*insider* **report**

## RESOURCES

## INDEXES

# From the Editor

While writing is a solitary endeavor, publishing is not. It takes a network of people to transform a manuscript into a book, from agents to editors to publicists, not to mention the printers, marketing people, accounting department, and graphic designers. And a script may be handed to an agent, a manager, a director, a producer and actors before it ever begins production. A writer soon finds out that what began as a solitary endeavor soon involves many others before it can reach the bookstore browsers or cinema viewers.

So how can you get your manuscript the attention it needs to set these wheels in motion? A literary agent is your key to unlocking the industry and getting your book through the doorway to the editors and negotiating you a fair contract. In this book, you'll find over 600 literary and script agents looking for manuscripts to represent. The next one could be yours.

A publicist can help promote your book to give it the attention and circulation it needs to be profitable and memorable. It's a common idea that "you're only as good as the sales of your last book," and publicists can help boost the numbers by creating media attention to give your book the spotlight it needs to succeed.

And wouldn't it be nice to step out of your solitude to meet the movers and shakers of the industry in person? With our listings of conferences, meeting the right people to help you on your way has never been so easy. We've also included articles with tips for approaching an agent—whether in person or through the mail. You'll read about success stories from agents and authors, inspirational and informative interviews with the people who've gone before you who can offer insights they've found to help you on your way.

Much more than just contact information, each listing includes a complete profile to help you find the best match possible:

- Look for the key icon ( **o┅** ) in agency listings to quickly obtain fundamental information about an agency. Here agents list their specialties, including their areas of strength and other services they provide for their clients. You'll also be able to determine if your manuscript fits the current needs of the agency of if your subject is one the agent is not interested in reading.
- Other time-saving features are included to expedite your search. Openness icons ( ▢ ◲ ◳ ◉ ⊘ ) let you immediately assess how receptive an agent is to new clients. Bold-faced phrases like **Considers these nonfiction areas:** and **Considers these fiction areas:** can help you determine the agency's full range of interests. And numerous indexes lead you to the right agent for your specific needs.
- To reduce the time and expense of mailing out material, we've also added, under the subhead **How to Contact:**, information indicating if an agent accepts e-mail and fax queries or permits multiple queries and submissions.

The information is in your hands. Now is the time to step out of your isolation and get your manuscript to the people who can make it happen for you too.

*Rachel Vater*

literaryagents@fwpubs.com
www.writersdigest.com

# Quick Start Guide to Using Your Guide to Literary Agents

Starting a search for a literary agent can seem overwhelming whether you've just finished your first book or you have several publishing credits on your résumé. You are more than likely eager to start pursuing agents—anxious to see your name on the spine of a book. But before you go directly to the listings of agencies in this book, take a few minutes to familiarize yourself with the way agents work and how you should approach agents. By doing so, you will be more prepared for your search, and ultimately save yourself time and unnecessary grief.

## Read the articles

The book divides agents into two sections: nonfee-charging literary agents and script agents. Each section begins with feature articles that give advice on the best strategies for contacting agents and provide perspectives on the author/agent relationship. The articles about literary agents are organized into four sections appropriate for each stage of the search process: **Before You Start, Narrowing Your List, Contacting Agents**, and **Before You Sign**. You may want to start by reading through each article, then refer back to relevant articles as you approach each new stage.

Because there are many ways to make that initial contact with an agent, we've provided Insider Reports throughout the book. These personalized interviews with agents and published authors offer both information and inspiration for any writer hoping to find representation.

## Decide what you're looking for

An independent publicist can promote your work—before or after an agent or publisher has taken an interest in it. Often publicists can drum up media time for their clients and help them get the exposure they need to make a sale or increase the number of copies sold.

A literary or script agent will actually present your work directly to editors or producers. It's his job to get his client's work published or sold and to negotiate a fair contract. In the nonfee-agents and script agents section, we list each agent's contact information and explain what type of work they represent and how to submit it for consideration.

For face-to-face contact, many writers prefer to meet agents at conferences. In this way, writers can assess an agent's personality and usually have a chance to get more feedback on their work than they can by submitting their work through the mail and waiting for a response. The section for writers' conferences is divided into regions and lists only those conferences where agents will be in attendance. In many cases, private consultations can be arranged, and agents attend with the hope of finding new clients to represent.

## *Frequently asked questions about the* Guide to Literary Agents

**Why do you include agents who are not currently seeing clients?**
We provide some information on well-known agents who have not answered our request for information. Because of these agents' reputations, we feel the book would be incomplete without an acknowledgement of their companies. Some agents even ask that their listings indicate they are currently closed to new clients.

**Why have you excluded fee-charging agents this year?**
There is a great debate in the publishing industry about whether literary agents should charge writers a reading or critiquing fee. There are fee-charging agents who make sales to prominent publishers. However, we have received a number of complaints in the past year regarding fees and therefore we've chosen to list only those agents who do not charge fees to writers.

**Why are some agents not listed in the *Guide to Literary Agents*?**
Some agents may have not returned our request for information. We have taken others out of the book because we received very serious complaints about that agency. Refer to the index to see why an agency in last year's book isn't in this edition.

**Do I need more than one agent if I write in different genres?**
More than likely not. If you have written in one genre and want to switch to a new style of writing, ask your agent if he is willing to represent you for your new endeavor. Most agents will continue to represent clients no matter what genre they use. Occasionally an agent may feel he has no knowledge of a certain genre and will make recommendations to his client. Regardless, you should always talk to your agent about any potential career move.

**Why don't you list foreign agents?**
Most U.S. agents have relationships with agents in other countries, called "foreign co-agents." It is more common for a U.S. agent to work with a co-agent to sell a client's book abroad, than for a writer to work directly with a foreign agent. We do, however, list agents in England and Canada who sell to both U.S and foreign publishers.

**Do agents ever contact a writer who is self-published?**
Occasionally. If a self-published author attracts the attention of the press or if her book sells extremely well, an agent might approach the author in hopes of representing her.

**Why won't the agent I queried return my material?**
An agent may not return your query or manuscript for several reasons. Perhaps you did not include a self-addressed, stamped envelope (SASE). Many agents will throw away a submission without a SASE. Or, the agent may have moved. To avoid using expired addresses, use the most current edition of the *Guide to Literary Agents*. Another possibility is that the agent is simply swamped with submissions. Agents can be overwhelmed with queries, especially if the agent has recently spoken at a conference or has been featured in an article or book.

# Reading the Listings
# in the *Guide to Literary Agents*

You could send a mass mailing to all the agencies listed in this book, but doing so will be apparent to agents and will likely turn them off. Instead, use the organizational tools in this book to help determine a core list of agents who are appropriate for you and your work.

First, determine whether you want a nonfee-charging agent, or an independent publicist. The best way to make your decision is by reading the articles in this book. Then, depending on the type of material you write and whether you write fiction or nonfiction, start your search with the following indexes:

## Agents specialties index

Striped for quick reference, this index immediately follows each section of listings and should help you compose a list of agents specializing in your areas. For literary agents, this index is divided by nonfiction and fiction subject categories. For script agents, this index is divided into various subject areas specific to scripts. Cross-referencing categories and concentrating on agents interested in two or more aspects of your manuscript might increase your chances of success. Some agencies are open to all topics and are grouped under the subject heading "open" in each section.

## Agencies indexed by openness to submissions

This index lists agencies and independent publicists according to their receptivity to new clients.

## Geographic index

For writers looking for an agent close to home, this index lists agents state-by-state and by country. Also included is a regional listing of independent publicists.

## Agent index

Often you will read about an agent who is an employee of a larger agency and you may not be able to locate her business phone or address. We asked agencies to list the agents on staff, then we've listed the agents' names in alphabetical order along with the name of the agency they work for. Find the names of the persons you would like to contact and then check their listings.

## Listing index

This index lists all agencies, conferences, and independent publicists appearing in this book.

## HOW TO READ THE LISTINGS IN THIS BOOK

Once you have searched the various indexes and compiled a list of potential agents or independent publicists for your manuscript, you should read the listings for each agent on your list, eliminating those who seem inappropriate for your work or your individual needs. Before approaching any of the agents listed in this book, be sure to read the various articles in this book to fully understand the etiquette of contacting agents.

LEVEL OF OPENNESS    AGENCY'S SPECIALIZATIONS    WHAT DO I SEND?    WHO DO I SEND TO?    PROFESSIONAL MEMBERSHIPS

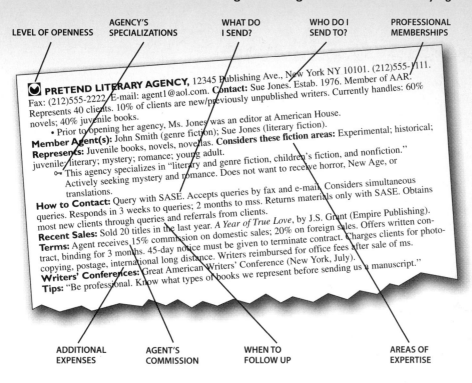

**PRETEND LITERARY AGENCY,** 12345 Publishing Ave., New York NY 10101. (212)555-1111. Fax: (212)555-2222, E-mail: agent1@aol.com. **Contact:** Sue Jones. Estab. 1976. Member of AAR. Represents 40 clients. 10% of clients are new/previously unpublished writers. Currently handles: 60% novels; 40% juvenile books.
• Prior to opening her agency, Ms. Jones was an editor at American House.
**Member Agent(s):** John Smith (genre fiction); Sue Jones (literary fiction).
**Represents:** Juvenile books, novels, novellas. **Considers these fiction areas:** Experimental; historical; juvenile; literary; mystery; romance; young adult.
➥ This agency specializes in "literary and genre fiction, children's fiction, and nonfiction." Actively seeking mystery and romance. Does not want to receive horror, New Age, or translations.
**How to Contact:** Query with SASE. Accepts queries by fax and e-mail. Considers simultaneous queries. Responds in 3 weeks to queries; 2 months to mss. Returns materials only with SASE. Obtains most new clients through queries and referrals from clients.
**Recent Sales:** Sold 20 titles in the last year. *A Year of True Love,* by J.S. Grant (Empire Publishing).
**Terms:** Agent receives 15% commission on domestic sales; 20% on foreign sales. Offers written contract, binding for 3 months. 45-day notice must be given to terminate contract. Charges clients for photocopying, postage, international long distance. Writers reimbursed for office fees after sale of ms.
**Writers' Conferences:** Great American Writers' Conference (New York, July).
**Tips:** "Be professional. Know what types of books we represent before sending us a manuscript."

ADDITIONAL EXPENSES    AGENT'S COMMISSION    WHEN TO FOLLOW UP    AREAS OF EXPERTISE

The following is a sample agency listing. Study it to understand what the information provided in it means. You also may want to refer to the brief introductions before each section of agency listings for other information specific to that particular section. For specific information on independent publicists, read the introduction to that section on page 259.

## SUBHEADS FOR QUICK ACCESS TO INFORMATION

Each listing is broken down into subheads to make locating specific information easier. The following are descriptions of the information found in each subhead and details indicating how you can use this information in your search for an agent.

### Contact and basic information

In the first paragraph, you'll find the information you'll need to contact each agency, including where to send your query letter and who to send it to. You'll also learn if the agency belongs to any professional organization. If an agent is a member of the Association of Authors' Representatives (AAR), they are prohibited from charging reading or evaluating fees. If they are a member of the Writers Guild of America (WGA), they are not permitted to charge a reading fee to WGA members, but are allowed to do so to nonmembers. An explanation of all organizations' acronyms is available on page 320. An agent's willingness to work with new or previously unpublished writers is indicated by the percentages given here. The total number of clients an agency represents can also suggest what your status might be in the agency.

### Member agents

Often different agents within an agency will have specific specialties. Listed here are agents and their individual specialties to help you know the best agent to query for your work.

## Quick Reference Icons

At the beginning of each listing, you will find one or more of the following symbols to help you quickly identify features particular to that listing.

- **N:** Agency new to this edition.
- ☑ Change in address, contact information or phone number from last year's edition.
- 🛢 Agents who charge fees to previously unpublished writers only.
- ▣ Agents who make sales to electronic publishers.
- ✦ Canadian agency.
- ⊕ International agency.

## Level of Openness

Each agency has an icon indicating its openness to submissions. Before contacting any agency, check the listing to make sure it is open to new clients.

- ◻ Newer agency actively seeking clients.
- ◪ Agency seeking both new and established writers.
- ◕ Agency prefers to work with established writers, mostly obtains new clients through referrals.
- ◎ Agency handling only certain types of work or work by writers under certain circumstances.
- ◙ Agency not currently seeking new clients. We include these agencies to let you know they are currently not open to new clients. *Unless you have a strong recommendation from someone well respected in the field, our advice is to avoid approaching these agents.*

For quick reference, a chart of these icons and their meanings is printed on the inside covers of this book.

## Represents

To expedite your search for an agent, only query agents who represent the type of material you write. Under this subhead, agents list what types of manuscripts they are interested in receiving. To help you find those agents more quickly, check the **Agents Specialties Index** immediately following each section of agency listings.

Look for the key icon ( ⚷ ) to quickly learn an agent's areas of specializtion or specific strengths (i.e., editorial or marketing experience, sub-rights expertise, etc.). For agents open to a wide-range of subjects, we list the nonfiction and fiction areas they are actively seeking as well as subjects they do *not* wish to receive.

## How to contact

Most agents open to submissions prefer initially to receive a query letter briefly descriging your work. (For tips on and sample queries, read "Queries That Made It Happen" on page 47.) Some agents ask for an outline or sample chapters, but you should send these only if ou are requested to do so. Agents indicate here if they are open to fax or e-mail queries, as well as if they consider simultaneous submissions. Always send a self-addressed, stamped envelope (SASE) or postcard for reply. If you have not heard back from an agent within the approximate reporting time given (allowing for holidays and summer vacations), a quick, polite phone call to ask when it will be reviewed would be in order. Also listed is the agent's preferred way of meeting new clients.

## Recent sales

Another way to determine if an agent is appropriate for your manuscript is to look at other titles sold by that agent. Looking at the publisher of those titles can also tell you the caliber of publishing contacts the agent has developed. To give you an idea of how successful an agent has been, we also list the number of titles an agent sold last year. If an agency lists no sales information, we explain why.

## Terms

Here you'll find the agent's commission, whether a contract is offered and for how long, and possible office expenses clients may have to pay (i.e., postage, photocopying, etc.). Most agents receive a 10 to 15 percent commission for domestic sales and a 15 to 20 percent commission for foreign or dramatic sales, with the diference going to the co-agent who places the work.

## Writers' conferences

The conferences agents attend also give an idea of their professional interests and provide a way for writers to meet agents face-to-face. For more information about a specific conference, check the **Writers' Conference** section starting on page 287.

## Reading list

Learn what magazines and journals agents read to discover potential clients.

## Tips

This subhead contains direct quotes from agents revealing even more specifics about what the agent wants and giving you a better sense of the agent's personality.

## OTHER RESOURCES AVAILABLE IN THIS BOOK

If you don't recognize a symbol or abbreviation, refer to the **Key to Symbols** on the front and back inside covers or the **Table of Acronyms** on page 320. For definitions of unfamiliar words or expressions, check the **Glossary** in the back of the book.

Starting on page 316 are additional resources available for writers including a list of **Professional Organizations** for writers, **Books & Publications of Interest** to further your knowledge about agents, and **Websites of Interest** to guide you to the best sites availablel for writers on the Internet.

# Do I Need an Agent?

If you have a book ready to be published, you may be wondering if you need a literary agent. Making this decision can be tough; therefore, we've included this article with the information you need to make an educated choice about using an agent.

## WHAT CAN AN AGENT DO FOR YOU?

An agent will believe in your writing and know an audience interested in your writing exists. As the representative for your work, your agent will tell editors your manuscript is the best thing to land on her desk this year. But beyond being enthusiastic about your book, there are a lot of benefits to using an agent.

For starters, today's competitive marketplace can be difficult to break into. Many larger publishing houses will only look at manuscripts from agents. In fact, approximately 80 percent of books published by the major houses are sold to them by agents.

But an agent's job isn't just getting your book through a publisher's door. In reality, that's only part of what an agent can do for you. The following describes the various jobs agents do for their clients, many of which would be difficult for a writer to do without outside help.

### Agents know editors' tastes and needs

An agent possesses information on a complex web of publishing houses and a multitude of editors to make sure her clients' manuscripts are placed in the hands of the right editors. This knowledge is gathered through relationships she cultivates with acquisition editors—the people who decide which books to present to their publisher for possible publication. Through her industry connections, an agent becomes aware of the specializations of publishing houses and their imprints, knowing that one publisher only wants contemporary romances while another is interested solely in nonfiction books about the military. By networking with editors over lunch, an agent also learns more specialized information—which editor is looking for a crafty Agatha Christie-style mystery for the fall catalog, for example.

### Agents track changes in publishing

Being attentive to constant market changes and vacillating trends is also a major requirement of an agent's job. He understands what it may mean for clients when publisher A merges with publisher B and when an editor from house C moves to house D. Or what it means when readers—and therefore editors—are no longer interested in westerns, but instead can't get their hands on enough Stephen King-style suspense novels.

### Agents get your manuscript read faster

Although it may seem like an extra step to send your manuscript to an agent instead of directly to a publishing house, an agent can *prevent* writers from wasting months sending manuscripts to the wrong places or being buried in someone's slush pile. Editors rely on agents to save them time as well. With little time to sift through the hundreds of unsolicited submissions arriving weekly, an editor is naturally going to prefer a work that has already been approved by a qualified reader. For this reason, many of the larger publishers accept agented submissions only.

### Agents understand contracts

When publishers write contracts, they are interested in their own bottom line over the best interests of the author. Writers unfamiliar with contractual language may find themselves bound to a publisher with whom they no longer want to work or unable to receive royalties on their first book until they have written several books. An agent uses her experience to negotiate a contract that benefits the writer while still respecting some of the publisher's needs.

## Agents negotiate—and exploit—subsidiary rights

Beyond publication, a savvy agent keeps in mind other opportunities for your manuscript. If your agent believes your book will also be successful as an audio book, a Book-of-the-Month club selection, or even a blockbuster movie, he will take these options into consideration when shopping your manuscript. These additional mediums for your writing are called "subsidiary rights"; part of an agent's job is to keep track of the strengths and weaknesses of different publishers's subsidiary rights offices to determine the deposition of these rights to your work. After the contract is negotiated, the agent will seek additional money-making opportunities for the rights he kept for his client. For more information on specific subsidiary rights, see "Subsidiary Rights: Much More Than a Book" on page 60.

## Agents get escalators

An escalator is a bonus agents can negotiate as part of the book contract. It is commonly given when a book appears on a bestseller list or if a client appears on a popular television show. For example, a publisher might give a writer a $50,000 bonus if she is picked for Oprah's Book Club™. Both the agent and the editor know such media attention will sell more books, and the agent negotiates an escalator to ensure the writer benefits from this increase in sales.

## Agents track payments

Because an agent only receives payment when the publisher pays the writer, it is in her best interests to make sure the writer is paid on schedule. Some publishing houses are notorious for late payments. Having an agent distances you from any conflict over payment and allows you to spend your time writing instead of on the phone.

## Agents are strong advocates

Besides standing up for your right to be paid on time, agents can ensure your book gets more attention from the publisher's marketing department, a better cover design, or other benefits you may not know to ask for during the publishing process. An agent can also provide advice during each step of this process as well as guidance about your long-term writing career.

# WHEN MIGHT YOU NOT NEED AN AGENT?

Although there are many reasons to work with an agent, an author can benefit from submitting his own work. For example, if your writing focuses on a very specific field, you may want to work with a small or specialized publisher. These houses are usually open to receiving material directly from writers. Smaller houses can often give more attention to a writer than a large house, providing editorial help, marketing expertise, and other advice directly to the writer.

Some writers use a lawyer instead of an agent. If a lawyer specializes in intellectual property, he can help a writer with contract negotiations. Instead of giving the lawyer a commission, the lawyer is paid for his time only. If you know your book will only appeal to a small group of readers, working with a lawyer is an option to consider.

And, of course, some people prefer working independently instead of relying on others to do their work. If you are one of these people, it is probably better to shop your own work instead of constantly butting heads with an agent. And despite the benefits of working with an agent, it is possible to sell your work directly to a publisher—people do it all the time!

# Three Editors Offer Differing Views on Agents

## BY WILL ALLISON

Do you really need an agent to help you sell your book? The answer depends in part upon the kind of publisher you're seeking. If, for instance, you want to send your science fiction novel to Del Rey Books, you'll need an agent just to get your foot in the door. On the other hand, if you're shopping a collection of poetry to small publishers or university presses, an agent may be unnecessary.

As a rule of thumb, the smaller the publishing house, the smaller the contracts. Since agents generally work on commission, it's often not profitable for them to handle small deals. Likewise, when there is little money at stake, authors run less of a risk in representing themselves. (See "Do I Need an Agent?" on page 8 for a more detailed discussion on the pros and cons of hiring an agent.)

## THE PUBLISHING HOUSES

The editors in the following interview represent three different types of publishing houses: a small publisher (Sarabande Books), a large publisher (Ballantine Books, a division of Random House), and a university press (University of Iowa Press).

Sarabande Books, an award-winning literary press in Louisville, Kentucky, specializes in poetry and short fiction, publishing only eight books a year. Editors Sarah Gorham and Kirby Gann say they occasionally deal with agents, but most of the submissions they receive—and most of the books they buy—come directly from authors.

The same is true at the University of Iowa Press, according to director Holly Carver. Like many university presses, Iowa primarily publishes the work of academics and independent scholars, plus a small selection of poetry, literary nonfiction, and fiction (including the annual Iowa Short Fiction Award story collection).

By contrast, an agent is involved in virtually every deal inked by Ballantine Books, which publishes more than 120 books each year. This is no coincidence: Ballantine accepts agented manuscripts and proposals only. According to senior editor Steve Saffel, exceptions to this policy are rare.

## THE EDITORS

Sarah Gorham is editor-in-chief of Sarabande Books, which she co-founded with Jeffrey Skinner in 1994. Books she has edited include Mary Ann Taylor-Hall's *How She Knows What She Knows About Yo-Yos*, Molly McQuade's *Stealing Glimpses: Of Poetry, Poets, and Things in Between*, Brenda Miller's *Season of the Body*, Jane Mead's *The Lord and the General Din of the World*, Dick Allen's *Ode to the Cold War*, and Baron Wormser's *When*. Gorham is also the

---

**WILL ALLISON** *is editor at large for* Zoetrope: All-Story, *former executive editor of* STORY, *and former editor of* Novel & Short Story Writer's Market. *He is the recipient of an Ohio Arts Council grant for fiction, has published short stories in* American Short Fiction, Florida Review, *and* Kansas Quarterly/Arkansas Review, *and owns an impressive collection of rejection slips.*

author of *Don't Go Back to Sleep* and *The Tension Zone*, which won the 1996 Four Way Books Award in Poetry. Her work has appeared in *Poetry, Paris Review, Grand Street, Antaeus, Ohio Review, Southern Review, Kenyon Review,* and *Missouri Review,* among other places.

Kirby Gann is fiction editor at Sarabande. Books that Gann has edited include Becky Hagenston's *A Gram of Mars,* Heather Sellers's *Georgia Under Water,* Judith Slater's *The Baby Can Sing and Other Stories,* and Brock Clarke's *What We Won't Do.*

Steve Saffel, a senior editor at Ballantine Books, specializes in science fiction, fantasy, alternate history, and media-related projects. His Del Rey list includes authors David Gemmell, J. Gregory Keyes, John Shirley, James Clemens, Harry Turtledove, and Toni Anzetti, as well as the Lovecraftian trade paperback anthologies. His media-related projects include *Star Wars* nonfiction, *Babylon 5* fiction and nonfiction, and the *X-Men* movie-related fiction. His authors for media-related books include Peter David, Academy Award winner Ben Burtt, Kristine Kathryn Rusch, Dean Wesley Smith, and Stephen Sansweet. Saffel also works with Ballantine's editor for military nonfiction titles, focusing primarily on personal accounts of combat duty. This list features books such as Gary Linderer's *Phantom Warriors,* Wynn Goldsmith's *Papa Bravo Romeo,* and Kregg Jorgenson's *LRRP Company Command* and *Very Crazy.*

Holly Carver has worked in university-press publishing for almost thirty years, both at the University of Texas Press and at the University of Iowa Press, where she has been director since 1999. Current and forthcoming titles include Ray A. Young Bear's *The Rock Island Hiking Club,* Donald Anderson's *Fire Road,* Sohrab Homi Fracis's *Ticket to Minto,* Janet Burroway's *Embalming Mom: Essays on Love and Letters,* and *Visiting Emily: Poems Inspired by the Life and Works of Emily Dickinson,* edited by Sheila Coghill and Thom Tammaro.

## Do you prefer to work with authors who represent themselves or with agents?

*Gorham* (pictured at right) *and Gann:* Sarabande does both, and there are advantages and disadvantages to each. An agent will likely retain most subsidiary rights, and, therefore, we'll lose valuable revenue potential. As well, they often ask for significant advances. We'd much rather spend our money producing and marketing the book, and we have a good list of contacts for sub-rights ourselves, so naturally we have some preference for dealing with authors directly. At the same time, there are talented writers who simply do not know how to present themselves professionally. They suffer for this, though we make an effort to read everything that comes across our desk.

*Saffel:* At the submission stage, I prefer agented manuscripts, but when it comes to the acquisition stage or the editorial process, I have no particular preference. In acquisition, the advantage in dealing with an agented author is that the agent bringing me the manuscript likely has experience negotiating a deal and navigating a contract. Thus the author is more likely to feel all of the contract points have been addressed thoroughly and to her satisfaction. Agents rarely become involved in the editorial process, so by that stage it's pretty much between the author and me.

*Carver:* I much prefer to work directly with authors who represent themselves. Since many of our authors are academics or independent scholars—theatre historians or prairie restorationists or Shakespeare specialists—who would seldom be represented by an agent, I deal with very few agents. However, the winners of our Iowa Short Fiction Awards are often represented by agents, as are some of our prize-winning poets and some of our authors of literary nonfiction. I sometimes find it frustrating to work with an agent who is not familiar with the limited resources of university press publishing. Our conversations seem adversarial; contract negotiations can be tense; and I feel that the author begins his association with us under a cloud.

### What's the value of an agent to you as editor?

*Gorham and Gann:* I think it's really the other way around—Sarabande is of considerable value to an agent who is having difficulty knowing what to do with an author who has written a collection of stories, but who has plans to produce a novel. We have launched many a career—discovered a new writer who then published a novel with a larger house. But to be fair, we value the service agents provide enormously—they sometimes, though not always, send us more accomplished work, serving as a kind of screening system. It's nice to establish ongoing relationships with agents who begin to know what sort of book you are looking for.

*Saffel* (pictured at right): When a submission comes in from an agent, I know another person has screened the manuscript and found it to be of professional caliber. If the agent and I have similar tastes, I may give the manuscript particular attention, since it's more likely to be my cup of tea. And if the agent and I have differing tastes, but I trust the agent's judgment in choosing quality clients, then I will consider it an opportunity to expand my horizons (and my list). At the negotiation stage, I count on the agent to know the business side of publishing and to be able to work with our contracts department to successfully iron out any wrinkles that may appear.

*Carver:* I do appreciate the feedback of an enthusiastic agent, one who sincerely values her authors' writing, and not just the financial rewards of her authors' writing. (I say "her" because the best agents I have worked with, Christy Fletcher of Carlisle & Company and Frances Kuffel of the Jean V. Naggar Literary Agency, have been female.) These agents have a warmth and an admiration for their clients that lend energy to our efforts. If I worked with agents more consistently, I'm sure I would have many more positive experiences.

### From an editor's perspective, what are the drawbacks of an agent?

*Gorham and Gann:* Most of these we have already mentioned.

*Saffel:* Drawbacks appear if the agent has trouble screening his or her client list, in which case I won't necessarily be able to count on that agent to bring me professional-caliber authors. It's also extremely helpful if an agent is looking at the long-term view, planning what's best for the author down the road, as his or her career grows and evolves. If the agent is looking only for short-term benefits, then it may become a drawback as I try to form an appropriate publishing plan for the author in question.

*Carver:* Publishing with a university press is often less immediately profitable, and it's certainly less glamorous, compared to publishing with a commercial house. I sometimes sense that an agent favors the commercial world and discourages authors from considering the university press world. The University of Iowa Press may not be able to compete financially—the few advances we are able to offer are insultingly small; our royalty arrangements can be depressing; and, furthermore, we pay royalties on net rather than on list prices. However, we have attractive benefits compared to some of the trade houses: We pay careful attention to copyediting, proof-reading, and design; we print our books on acid-free paper; and we can keep our backlist titles in print for decades. I think the best agents emphasize these advantages, but others seem to discount them.

**Do agented and unagented book proposals and/or manuscripts receive the same treatment at your publishing house?**

*Gorham and Gann:* We treat all manuscript submissions seriously. But if an author is agented, that author has already achieved a certain level of accomplishment for that author, and we tend to make an extra effort, even if subconsciously. Of the last twenty prose collections (short story, novella, novel, essay) we have signed, only three came to us directly through an agent. Several were agented contest submissions for our Mary McCarthy Prize in Short Fiction. And several more authors acquired agents once their books were signed.

*Saffel:* Del Rey accepts only legitimate agented submissions, with very specific grounds for exceptions. If a member of our editorial staff has met an author at an event such as a writers' conference and has become interested in his proposal, that editor may ask that the author send in the submission even if he isn't represented by an agent. For myself, if another author—whose opinions I respect and whose taste I trust—recommends that I take a look at a submission, then I may ask to see that manuscript.

*Carver:* (pictured at right) Agented and unagented projects receive the same treatment at Iowa, in theory at least. I have a bit less patience when an agent sends me an unsolicited 500-page manuscript or a 2-volume reprint possibility than I do when I receive the same package from a random academic author; it does seem as if agents should know to query first. If a project looks iffy to me in terms of price, I am less likely to take a chance on asking for it if it is agented, since I assume that it comes with higher monetary expectations. Furthermore, it's clear that projects sometimes come to us only after all commercial possibilities have been exhausted, yet the agents for these projects still seem to be operating in the commercial world. So, now that I think about it, all things being equal, an agented project is at a disadvantage with us.

# Agents & Ethics: Getting Published Without Losing Your Shirt

BY JEAN V. NAGGAR

Writing is usually a lonely occupation. When at last, after months, even years of wrestling with words and ideas, the writer types in "THE END," prints up the result of mighty labors, and feels the thrill of hefting a bulky pile of crisp pages, it would seem the Herculean task is over. Now, surely, it is merely a matter of locating the right agent, getting the right publisher interested, and the words and ideas, elegantly bound and jacketed, will appear on the shelves of bookstores everywhere.

Easy, right?

Wrong.

These days, the writer must not only create a fine work of the imagination. The aspiring writer must also learn a good deal about how the publishing business works, who the players are, and how to avoid falling into the clutches of a growing number of disreputable "agencies" and "editorial services" that survive on fees paid up front and not on commissions from a job well done. Throughout the years, hardworking, reputable literary agents have striven to distinguish their ways of doing business from the ways of the less particular.

## A brief history of the Association of Authors' Representatives

Early in the 1970s, a small group of independent literary agents who had recently moved to agenting from editorial and other positions in publishing houses, began getting together informally to network and to exchange gossip, war-stories, and survival tips. The group quickly coalesced into something more formal and named itself the Independent Literary Agents Association (ILAA).

This energetic, proactive group of then relatively new agents operated alongside the venerable and respected Society of Authors Representatives (SAR) for some years, maintaining an independent-minded approach to reading fees as it did to other matters.

The SAR had long held its members to a code of appropriate behavior, and in time, a committee formed in the ILAA to discuss many questions of ethical behavior that came up in conversation and in practice. They discussed appropriate behaviors of member agents with each other, with their authors, and with the publishers and editors with whom they dealt. While not wishing in any way to impinge on the free and independent operation of its members, or to create a policing body, certain red-flag issues came up again and again, and the committee decided to develop a code of appropriate behavior for its members.

In 1990, the two associations joined forces and emerged as the Association of Authors' Representatives (AAR), an energized association of literary agents, committed to following high standards of behavior in their professional dealings, charging no reading fees, and avoiding any

**JEAN V. NAGGAR** *is the president of the Jean V. Naggar Literary Agency in New York, and has been working in publishing for thirty years. She was president of Association of Authors' Representatives from 1998 to 1999. A list of member-agents of the AAR, together with a brochure, can be obtained for $7 and a 99¢ SASE by writing to P.O. Box 237201, Ansonia Station, New York NY 10023. The AAR website is www.aar-online.org.*

situation that might introduce a conflict of interest, although it took time for some differences in philosophy to be resolved to the satisfaction of all.

The AAR currently numbers some 350 member agents nationwide. Member agents subscribe annually to a code of ethics that is fast becoming a standard in the publishing industry, and concern themselves with following the latest developments in contracts, royalties, and the optimal dispensation of all rights.

## Creating an ethical standard

The Canon of Ethics that developed from this joining is signed yearly by every member of the AAR when dues are paid. It has produced high standards within an unregulated, unlicensed industry. It is notable that publishers have not developed a similar set of ethical guidelines for their behavior, nor are they likely to do so!

Briefly, the Canon of Ethics ensures the following:

- That members maintain two separate bank accounts so there is no commingling of clients' monies and the agency's operating expenses.
- That prompt disclosure and payment are made to clients regarding monies received from both domestic and foreign sales.
- That members are forbidden to charge reading fees to clients or potential clients, directly or indirectly, beyond the customary return postage charges. In an attempt to deflect potential abuses, the Ethics Committee recently extended this provision. Now, in addition, agents who belong to the AAR may not charge fees for reading manuscripts and proposals at writers' conferences.
- That members of the AAR may not receive a secret profit or enter into any arrangement regarding a client's work that might create a conflict of interest.

While providing this unique standard of ethical behavior authors can depend upon, the AAR still affirms the total independence of its members' individual operations, adoption or rejection of author-agent agreements, commission structures, and negotiations with publishers.

Sometimes, an author attempts to involve the cooperation of the Ethics Committee of the AAR in connection with a particular agent who is not an AAR member or for reasons outside the scope of the Canon of Ethics. Most of these matters, however, are not the purview of the Ethics Committee, which was never intended to be a policing body regarding general "agenting" complaints. Any complaints addressing a *member's* supposed violation of the Canon of Ethics are taken very seriously indeed, and no decision is made without a thorough exploration of all circumstances surrounding the complaint.

## Cooperating to keep up with a changing industry

The AAR also works to inform and educate its agenting community on developments within the publishing industry. At present, the contractual and conceptual problems arising from new electronic technologies and the shrinking of publishing venues due to recent consolidations are taking much of the organization's attention. AAR members have formed task forces to work with publishers on these issues, and have organized forums for the discussion of cutting-edge technologies and their impact on all of us. The AAR makes sure its members are equipped with the information they need to make the decisions that best benefit their writers.

The association also appoints individual agents to act as liaisons with all the major writers' organizations. [See page 316 for a list of Professional Organizations.] They keep abreast of issues concerning these writers' communities and, in turn, inform them of AAR developments, maintaining a steady flow of information. It is more important than ever that authors and agents share information, insights, and move forward together into the changing world of today's publishing scene.

## Making informed choices

Obviously, in choosing an agent, whether through the AAR list or otherwise, there are vast differences in temperament, sensibility, day-to-day practice, and personal style to take into account. To gain a sense of the personalities of several agents, read John Baker's *Literary Agents: A Writer's Introduction* (Macmillan). Every writer should choose the agent best suited for her own needs and disposition. By choosing an agent who is an AAR member, a writer can be sure the agent cares about ethical standards enough to sign on to them on a yearly basis, and because admission to membership requires several recommendations and sale of a specific number of books, it also ensures that the AAR agent you approach is respected by her peers and not a fly-by-night operation.

Your writing career is worth all the advance power you can find to fuel it, and although the temptations out there are many, be advised that reputable agents rarely if ever advertise—most reputable agents obtain new clients through referrals and word of mouth. Agents also cannot make promises about getting your work published. And if your book is going to be published, a reputable publisher will be paying you an advance, not the other way around.

There is no more precious a thing than the painstaking creation of a work of the imagination. Writers are the lifeblood of the publishing industry, the only indispensable element in a continuum that links writer to reader. But the publishing industry is becoming increasingly bound by corporate politics and policies, forcing writers to seek out other kinds of feedback. Publishers are also at the mercy of the media, whose enormous hyping of superlative advances and celebrity has created its own quicksand—into which many writers founder, lured by the pot of gold at the end of the rainbow.

## Using freelance editors

Just when technology has provided aspiring writers with wonderful tools like "spellcheck" and the ability to restructure a manuscript several times without having to retype the entire work, the publishing industry itself has chosen to batten down the hatches, jettison imprints and editors in droves, and consolidate lists—all of which leave little room for the unpublished writer to slip a toe in the door.

Publishing has undergone seismic change. Mergers and consolidations have led to firings and departures of editors, and have caused a general sense of unease among those who are still employed. Departing editors are often not replaced, placing a greater burden on the shoulders of fewer editors, giving them neither the time nor the energy to take on projects that require a lot of editorial work. Unwilling to take risks that might land them among the unemployed, most people in publishing houses hold back on making decisions and choose the path of least resistance.

Consequently, many reputable and not-so-reputable individuals now offer "book-doctoring" services to evaluate material and pummel it into shape before it even reaches the critical eyes of agents and editors. Offering promises of magical editorial input, some of these self-styled "editorial services" exist solely to tease money from the hopeful and empty pockets of the uninformed. The pitfalls are many along the road to publication, and shape-shifting monsters lurk in the deep to seize the unwary and relieve them of their savings.

However, the happier side of this picture is that there *do* exist groups of seasoned professionals, working as individual freelance editors and exercising editorial skills honed from many years spent making decisions at publishing houses. Finding themselves out of a job because of new corporate groupings, they offer an important entrepreneurial opportunity within the changing landscape of the publishing industry. Some of them are beginning to coalesce into associations of their own. Others work alone. They usually do not advertise, and their services are expensive. But they are true publishing professionals and take genuine pleasure in using hard-won skills to help writers find their voices or to pull a publishable work out of chaos.

## Finding Reputable Freelance Editors and Literary Agents

How can a writer tell which face of Janus is smiling in her direction? How do you sift the reputable from the disreputable when you live far from the centers of publishing activity and feed on hope to keep your dreams alive? When you have been rejected by an entire flotilla of agents, and someone out there offers you (for a "small" fee) the opportunity to have your manuscript read by a self-styled "professional" or better yet, offers you publication if you will come up with an "advance" toward it, could this be opportunity knocking at the door? Use the following guidelines to help you decide:

- ☑ Read *Publishers Weekly* for several months before you will need the services of either a book doctor or a literary agent, focusing on new agents who come out of substantial publishing (not necessarily agenting) experience.
- ☑ Attend writers' conferences, and ask around for names of freelance editors and agents with whom people have had positive experiences.
- ☑ From freelance editors, request an advance breakdown of fees before signing any contract including the cost of a reading and editorial letter and the cost of a subsequent in-depth editorial job. Beware of empty promises. A freelance editor cannot guarantee you publication.
- ☑ Ask freelance editors if they will provide samples of previous editing jobs, and discuss the level of editing you will receive for the fees you pay.
- ☑ Request a list of published writers who have worked with this editor, and try to check it out by looking at Acknowledgment pages, etc., unless you are fortunate enough to have access to one of these writers.
- ☑ Ask your librarian or local bookseller if the name of the editor you are considering is at all familiar. Librarians and booksellers read *Publishers Weekly* and attend book conventions, where they sometimes meet editors. They can also make inquiries for you and steer you toward a reputable editor.
- ☑ Familiarize yourself with what services a good agent can and should be able to provide.

Above all, bear in mind that a reputable publisher *will pay you* for the right to publish your book and will not require you to put up your own money.

The Authors Guild and other writers' organizations can provide information about editors and agents. The AAR has also moved consistently, over the years, to help prevent the abuse of authors within the ethical framework for its members. It has never been more important to be wary of golden promises. It has never been more important to enlist the help of a reputable professional.

Happily, writers are hard to discourage. I would only urge you to put as much energy and research into the "tools" with which you hope to achieve publication as you put into writing the work you hope to publish. In achieving a realistic understanding of the limitations and benefits of the publishing industry, and in gaining a sense of the names and roles of the players in that industry, you can avoid costly mistakes and make choices that lead to publication, rather than insolvency.

## Understanding Fees—What Writers Must Know

Before you start searching for an agent, it is imperative that you have an understanding of the different types of fees some agents may charge. Most agents make their living from the commissions they receive after selling their clients' books, but some agents charge additional fees. This book separates the agency listings into two sections: nonfee-charging agents and fee-charging agents. The following explanations should help you decide which type of agent you want to approach.

**Office expenses** Many agents—both those who do and do not charge additional fees—ask the author to pay for photocopying, postage, long-distance phone calls, marketing, and other expenses. An agent should only ask for office expenses *after* agreeing to represent the writer. These expenses should be discussed upfront, and the writer should receive an accounting for them. This money is sometimes returned upon sale of the manuscript. Although a one-time office expense charge is fairly common, be wary of agents who request yearly, quarterly, or even monthly reimbursements without ever selling your manuscript.

**Reading fees** Agents who do not charge reading fees earn their money from commissions. Agencies that do charge reading fees often do so to cover the cost of additional readers or the time spent reading that could have been spent selling. This practice can save the agent time and open the agency to a larger number of submissions. Paying fees benefits writers because they know at least someone will look at their work. Whether such promises are kept depends upon the honesty of the agency. You may pay a fee and never receive a response from the agent, or you may pay someone who will not submit your manuscript to publishers. *In this book, only fee-charging agents who actively make sales are included.*

Reading fees vary from $25 to $500 or more. The fee is usually nonrefundable, but some agents refund the money if they take a writer on as a client or if they sell the writer's manuscript. Keep in mind, however, that payment of a reading fee does *not* ensure representation.

Officially, the Association of Authors' Representatives (AAR) in their Canon of Ethics prohibits members from directly or indirectly charging a reading fee, and the Writers Guild of America (WGA) does not allow WGA signatory agencies to charge a reading fee to WGA members, as stated in the WGA's Artists' Manager Basic Agreement. A signatory may charge you a fee if you are not a member, but most signatory agencies do not charge a reading fee as an across-the-board policy.

**Critique fees** Sometimes a manuscript will interest an agent, but he will point out areas still needing development. Some agencies offer criticism services for an additional fee. Like reading fees, payment of a critique fee does not ensure representation. When deciding if you will benefit from having someone critique your manuscript, keep in mind that the quality and quantity of comments vary widely. The critique's usefulness will depend on the agent's knowledge of the market. Also be aware that an agent who spends a significant portion of his time commenting on manuscripts will have less time to actively market your book.

Some agents refer writers to freelance editors or "book doctors." Make sure you research any critiquing service before sending your work, and don't be charmed by fancy brochures and compliments about your writing. Also be wary of agents who hurriedly refer you to editorial services. While it is not illegal to make a referral, some agents may abuse this practice.

The WGA has a rule preventing their signatories from making referrals to book doctors, and the AAR frowns on them as well if the agent is receiving financial compensation for making the referral. The WGA believes that, while an agent may have good intentions, differentiating agents trying to help writers from those who benefit financially from referrals is too difficult.

# Internet, E-books, and New Opportunities for Writers

BY PETER RUBIE

Electronic publishing really should be broadly defined as digital publishing. It's a visual way of presenting a book page without using paper. The page is displayed on a computer screen by downloading the text from the Internet or by buying a CD-ROM disk or DVD.

As of this writing, lots of people are scrabbling for digital or e-rights in the forlorn hope that "thar's gold in them thar hills." Yet, despite all the hype of Gemstar, Palm Pilot technology, and other makers of digital readers, there is no electronic reader that remotely comes close to the ability of the plain printed page to reach thousands of people cheaply and swiftly.

E-publishers create and distribute original "books" (even the term "book" begins to become an anachronism here) that are appearing for the first time in an electronic format.

However, at present, the harsh fact is that relatively few people read books on their computer screens. It's awkward, inconvenient, and, even with the new software that Microsoft and Adobe have introduced, it strains the eyes. What's more, none of the so-called electronic books, such as RocketBooks, Palm Pilot, or Psion, make reading on screen a viable or even pleasant option at present for enough readers—and that's if you can find a book "published" in a format that will work on your computer. It's only a matter of time before an electronic reader really rivals the ease and scope of a book, but for the moment sales of electronic books are limited. At present, an e-book "bestseller" is under 1,000 copies, and an e-book is a very poor cousin to the real thing.

## Are there different types of e-publishing?

Electronic publishing can be divided into three basic categories: commercial, subsidy, and self-publishing.

**Commercial e-publishers** work a lot like traditional publishers. Manuscripts are accepted on the basis of quality and marketability and go through a similar process of review, editing, and proofreading before publication. Writers pay no fee for publication, and they receive royalties.

Commercially published e-books are sold primarily through the publisher's website but are also available from online bookstores (including Amazon.com and Barnes&Noble.com). Some are beginning to be available through stores in the form of handheld readers such as Rocket Editions downloadable for the RocketBook e-reader. As all e-books have ISBNs, they can be ordered through any bookstore.

**Subsidy e-publishers** produce and distribute e-books for a fee, usually about $500 per manuscript, but authors receive a royalty comparable to that offered by commercial e-publishers.

**PETER RUBIE** *is currently the president of The Peter Rubie Literary Agency in New York City. Prior to becoming an agent, he was a publishing house editor whose authors won prizes and critical acclaim. He has also been the editor-in-chief of a Manhattan local newspaper, and a freelance editor and book doctor for major publishers. He is currently the director of the New York University Summer Publishing Institute as well a member of the NYU faculty Center for Publishing, where he teaches the only university-level course in the country on how to become a literary agent. He is a published author of two novels and several books of nonfiction.*

Unlike commercial e-publishers, however, subsidy publishers provide little screening (except for offensive content such as pornography or hate material) and usually accept any manuscript, regardless of quality. Most subsidy publishers provide no editorial services or proofreading (though some offer these services for an extra fee), and books are posted exactly as submitted.

Like commercially published e-books, subsidy-published e-books are available through most online bookstores. They are less likely to be available in a downloadable RocketBook edition, however, and are rarely found in traditional bookstores. They also have ISBNs and can be ordered from any bookstore.

**Self-published** e-books are produced entirely by the author and are usually posted and sold through the author's website, rather than that of a publisher. All the expenses of publication and distribution are handled by the author, who also receives all revenues from book sales rather than just royalties.

### Is e-publishing a good idea?

One big problem with e-books is the wide range of formats the text can be created in. This, of course, effects the distribution of the e-book. E-books are available in a wide range of formats, including rich text, HTML or XTML for Windows and Windows CE, AportisDoc for Palm Pilots, RocketBooks, and Librius books, as well as PDF files read by Adobe Acrobat.

Some publishers still offer only Windows-compatible formats. In fact, one of the problems with e-books is that not many people are willing to spend $500 or more to buy a device just to read an electronic handheld version of a novella.

E-book fiction compares in price to paperbacks, i.e., between $7 and $12, though shorter works, such as Diana Gabaldon's novella, *Hellfire*, (Dreams Unlimited), can be purchased for as little as $2. Stephen King sold his novel, *The Plant*, on an honor system at $1 a download. The experiment, for one of the world's bestselling authors whose books usually sell in the millions, was a miserly 40,000 copies. Nonfiction titles, particularly self-published, can range up to $30 or more.

### What is e-text publishing?

E-text is separate from e-publishing. It is a "bare bones" version of a book that is available in ASCII without any bells and whistles such as underlining, fonts, boldface, and so forth. However, it is readable on almost any computer.

A good example of an e-text project is Project Gutenberg, which reproduces public domain and noncopyrighted material for ready access by anyone who has a computer and a modem.

*Project Gutenberg* was born after Michael Hart was given a grant of $1 million for research on a computer project. Developing a kind of proto-Napster philosophy, Hart realized that once a book (or any other item, such as a picture, sound, etc.) is stored on a computer, any number of copies can and will be available.

*Project Gutenberg* e-texts are made available in "Plain Vanilla ASCII," meaning the low set of the American Standard Code for Information Interchange, so that italics, underlines, and bolds are replaced by capitalization. The reason for this is that 99 percent of all hardware and software can read and search these files.

### Should I sell the e-rights to my book first, then get a traditional publisher?

This is a tough question. It's certainly something to consider, but publishers are becoming wise to this ploy. It may seem to take off the table the contentious question of whether or not a traditional book publisher should share in electronic rights, but it may also handicap a book's chances of regular publication. Publishers are heading toward a concept of being repositories for literature, and as a result, they are striving to get as many rights to a book—including digital—as they can. Once they possess these rights, they are loath to give them up easily. The real battle in e-publishing is going to be over such things as print-on-demand books (POD) and out-of-print clauses.

Most e-publishers only ask for electronic rights, leaving the author free to market print rights and subsidiary rights elsewhere. Most reputable e-publishers post their contracts online. Be cautious of any publisher that posts an incomplete contract, such as a contract that omits key details about royalties or rights.

### Do e-publishers pay normal royalties?

E-publishers often pay 30 percent royalties, usually sent on a quarterly basis. Some traditional publishers are offering as much as 50 percent, while others, such as iPublish, are willing to renegotiate royalty rates as the market changes over the next few years. The royalty statements often break down sales by how many titles were sold on disk, by download, etc. Many e-books pay no royalty advance, sell significantly less than traditional books, and sell much slower. It can take years for a book to become a bestseller, and sales of 500 copies are considered good. The lack of a royalty advance can create other problems for authors. Several genre organizations consider a book commercially published only if an advance is paid, so an e-book may not qualify an author for membership or for an industry award.

### What's a good e-book royalty?

Anywhere from 25 to 50 percent is considered good. Royalties are often accounted for every quarter, rather than twice a year as with traditional publishers.

### What genres sell well in e-books?

Offbeat genre fiction, particularly cross-genre and nontraditional romance, science fiction, and fantasy do well in the e-publishing market. The general philosophy of commercial e-publishing is that it fills the "holes" that traditional publishing is leaving open. They're the publishers to go to when everyone tells you your book is great but. . . . Unlike print publishing, length is far less important in e-publishing. Best-selling author Diana Gabaldon offered her story, *Hellfire* (anthologized in Britain) to Dreams Unlimited because there was no traditional market for 11,000-word historical mystery stories.

### What about the impact of the Internet on traditional publishing?

The Internet is the Wild West of the book world at present. It's in its pioneering infancy and is changing almost daily. Sites go up, sites go down, and finding stability and dependability is a challenge.

It's also developing in ways that are starting to leave behind traditional notions of publishing. Perhaps you've seen the adverts for *inside.com,* a digital magazine declaring that print magazines are dinosaurs. Is this the death knell of the book as we know it? Will printer's ink and paper be replaced by electronic ink on a digital screen? Will the book of the future be contained on a wafer-thin piece of plastic that you slide into an electronic reader in the shape of a book?

I don't believe so, but some would have you think otherwise. Despite electronic publishing's ardent supporters, will it ever be more than an intriguing fringe for a literary avant-garde and those who just can't "make it" in traditional publishing?

Currently, what the Internet can do well is help you target an audience for your traditional paper book and then help you reach that audience in order to increase the sales potential of the book. You can also put the complete text of your paper book in a downloadable form on the Web (as long as your publisher doesn't object), though this is not as effective a use of the Web as some would have you believe at present.

### What if I put my book up on the Web and someone steals my idea?

The big author concern of piracy stops many authors from considering e-publishing, and the truth is there's not much to stop someone from making and distributing copies of your book. In a rather strange about-face, however, e-publishers say that the very limited nature of their market and operation means that there's not much reason to pirate copies.

### What's the best way to choose an e-publisher?

Like anything else to do with publishing, do substantial research before committing to anything.

Does the publisher offer books you like to read? Have you read any of them? If not, do so. Visit each publisher to get a feel for what they publish.

Ask yourself, "Does the publisher have a good website?" Have they won awards or praise from worthwhile organizations?

Is the publisher asking for money up front? If so, be wary.

Who have they published, and what do they consider a sales success to be?

Does the publisher use a proprietary format, or do they port the book to different formats (such as Internet download using Acrobat's PDF format, print on demand, RocketBooks, or Palm Pilot)? Do they offer only downloads, or do they sell disks as well? Do they offer the prospect of also publishing a traditional book if the e-book performs well? Does the publisher get reviews for their e-books, and where? Do they advertise and where? What are the marketing plans for your book? Is the publisher a member of the Association of Electronic Publishers (AEP: http://members.tripod.com/~BestBooksCom/AEP/aep.html); The Electronically Published Internet Connection (EPIC: http://www.eclectics.com/epic/); or the Electronic Publishers Coalition (http://www.epccentral.org/)? Will you feel proud of the finished product?

### Should I be concerned about signing a contract with an e-publisher?

Absolutely. Beware of a demanding contract. Most e-publishers use time-limited contracts that enable either party to terminate the agreement easily after a period of one or two years. Reputable subsidy publishers do the same. Be very careful of anything else, and get advice before committing yourself. Watch out for a contract that asks for other rights (such as print, translation, dramatic, etc.). Give these away and you leave yourself open to sharing with a publisher a percentage of any money you earn from selling those rights later on.

### Why is it that when I browse the Web I find almost no print publishers selling directly to the public?

The fact is that nearly all the book sites you'll go to online to download something to read will be run by someone other than a traditional publisher. These new sites are run by authors, bookstores, or hardware-related companies such as gemstar.com, stephenking.com, booksense.com, amazon.com, barnesandnoble.com, etc. The one obvious exception is iPublish, owned by Time Warner.

This brings us to the point of distribution. Publishers are still in the dark ages when it comes to understanding, identifying, and reaching target audiences through the Web. They still think of books as a mass-market medium like "cornflakes" or "toothpaste." Of course, books do best when they are targeted at audiences interested in what they have to say. Look at the proliferation of special interest magazines, and then try translating that audience into the book world. The one thing the Web has proven is that whoever creates an effective database (i.e., list) of customers will win. Perhaps one day publishers will catch on, but for the moment the worlds of electronic books and traditional publishing are still miles apart, though they are slowly coming together. The best thing an author can do is create an effective website, target his audience, and try to grow an effective database of readers.

### What is the best way to go about letting the world know that you have an electronically published book available?

Almost the only two ways to advertise books that are electronically published or published through other nontraditional means is by a Web page and through newspapers, magazines, newsletters, and e-mail. Target your audience, and then do what you can to reach them.

# Writing from the Heart: How to Grab an Agent's Attention

BY KIMBERLEY CAMERON

When reading submissions, an agent must rely on her instincts. I wish I had the talent and the drive (and you need both), to be a writer, but, as an agent, I have developed other talents that enable me to get as close to the process as possible, which culminate in the ability to sell your work. One of my talents is knowing when a manuscript is publishable. When do I know writing is good enough? When my instincts speak to me, and I actually feel something in my chest cavity that makes me stop and savor what I have been reading. That is what I call "writing that touches the heart," and unfortunately it is a rare occurrence.

Perhaps some writers are not going deep enough or are concentrating on too much action, plot, etc. to keep the pages turning. But when I read a passage that resonates, it touches something deep within me. I'm drawn to it and read it three or four times, trying to find some universal truth that I can share with the composer of the phrase. When I find something in the writing that all people can relate to, either in their innermost thoughts or through their experiences, it brings us closer to knowing the truth of what it means to be a human being. That is the best kind of writing—that which haunts our thoughts.

Unfortunately, I'm seeing more and more material in the submission process, with less and less care to the work. So much of the writing I see is lukewarm—it just doesn't have anything special to recommend it. I want something to grab my attention! I am always looking for material that is fresh, with something new—something that hasn't been on a website so long that every agent or editor has already viewed it. The joy and excitement of being an agent is in discovery.

## Picking the cream of the crop

So, what do I do when I find such intelligent and heartfelt writing? Here is the best-case scenario: I read in my submissions (which amount to about 500 per week) a writer's work that gets my pulse racing. This does not happen often. And if the initial writing is good, I wonder if it can be sustained.

I then call the writer and ask for the entire manuscript, if it's available. I want to know how long it is, if the author has worked with an outside editor and details of the author's background. I also try to get a feeling of the personality of the writer. It's better to represent a good author with a great attitude than a fabulous writer with a bad attitude. Your relationship with your agent is a professional one, but it can—and should be—an enjoyable one as well.

Once I receive the manuscript, I read it maybe two or three times to determine if it needs the additional fine tuning of a freelance editor, or if I feel I can work with the author myself. Because

**KIMBERLEY CAMERON** *helped found Knightsbridge Publishing. In 1991 she joined forces with Dorris Halsey of The Reece Halsey Agency which is a small agency specializing in excellent writing. Among its clients have been Aldous Huxley, William Faulkner, and Upton Sinclair. She opened Reece Halsey North in 1995, and specializes in fiction, and "writing from the heart."*

publishing has become more and more demanding, the editors in New York and elsewhere need manuscripts in the absolute best shape they can be. Agents' reputations depend on the quality of our submissions, as does our relationship with the editors who are in the position to purchase our clients' books.

If I still feel the manuscript needs outside editorial assistance, I suggest that the writer work with someone he feels comfortable with; perhaps someone in his area. If he asks for suggestions, I provide three or four legitimate editors—by that I mean professionals who do this for a living—and let him decide who best fits his needs. I then wait for the final draft, and upon approval sign him to a contract that we both discuss and negotiate. I believe agents should always be available to their writers, within reason. Communication means comfort.

## Getting the masterpiece in the hands of editors

After the contract with the writer is signed, then it's my turn to go to work. I call or go to New York, and my enthusiasm must be contagious. For that to happen, I have to believe with all my heart that I am right. There is an agent by the name of Loretta Barret who was vice president and an executive editor of Doubleday Books for 25 years. She once said something so profound about how agents should feel about their clients' works. She said, and I have her permission to quote her, "Editors can tell me no, but they can't tell me I'm wrong."

It's my faith in an author's work that keeps me going despite the rejections. My client Michael Gellert has written a nonfiction book called *The Fate of America*, which will be published in September of 2001 by Brassey's. It is clearly one of the most intelligent books I've ever had the pleasure of representing—and it was turned down by 25 publishers before it was accepted. But nothing would have stopped me from finding a publisher for it, and I finally did.

So even though we receive many, many rejections for our clients, it's part of the job. And we have to keep going and believing in their talent. The only way we can do this is to know it and feel it in our hearts. If you, the writer, succeed in touching that place, you will have our undivided loyalty and attention.

Even with the best energy and intentions, it doesn't always work, and agents are sometimes as perplexed as our clients as to why a project doesn't sell. Sometimes it can take years. My partner and friend, Dorris Halsey started The Reece Halsey Agency with her husband in 1957. She has sold numerous manuscripts on the first try and some, years later, depending on the circumstances. When we started working together, she gave me the following advice: "Agents are not magicians. We cannot sell a mediocre book. At the same time, we are optimists. Every time we read a query we hope to be struck by lightning—to discover a new and wonderful talent. If we didn't have that hope, we would never open another manila envelope. However, our optimism must be based on realism. Editors today can only take on books they would kill to publish—not books they simply like and admire. We agents must do the same thing. We want to find a jewel. The promise of a new voice is what compels our time and energy . . . ." She has taught me to trust my instincts and to follow my heart, and the rewards have been many.

Hopefully, the manuscript sells and then more work begins. An agent is your representative and ally, and can be very helpful in promoting good communication and relations between the publisher and writer. We protect your interests to the best of our ability, listen with our hearts, and counsel and advise you as you navigate the world of publishing. All because somehow, in some way, your writing touched our hearts.

# Polishing Tips: Is Your Book Ready for Representation?

**BY RACHEL VATER**

So you think you've got a book ready for representation. But are you sure it's ready? Many authors say in retrospect they wish they would have waited a little longer before they started investing the time and money it takes to send out a manuscript they could have polished a little more. But how do you know when it's ready?

Well, I was car-shopping last week, listening to a salesman extoling the virtues of any car I pointed to, when it came to me: Selling a manuscript isn't much different than selling a car. So I've constructed a check-list that works for selling anything, whether it's an automobile, a bracelet on the home shopping channel, or a manuscript. Imagine yourself in the role of the seller, but keep your buyer in mind, and you can use the same technique to sell anything.

## Make sure it's complete

If you were selling a car, you'd want to make sure it had all the parts. You wouldn't want to miss a sale just because a hubcap was missing or the rear-view mirror had vanished. Yet a lot of authors will begin querying agents before they've completed their manuscript. They don't have a whole book to sell yet, but they hope someone will take a chance on them anyway—before they finish it. Nobody wants to buy part of a car, and no agent wants to risk representing part of a manuscript. So remember, novels must be complete before you try to find representation. Nonfiction books must have a complete proposal and outline and at least one sample chapter finished.

## Polish until it shines

You've seen the diamond necklaces on the home shopping channel. They sparkle and glitter as if they've never seen a molecule of dust in their life. They have to. Because even if they're the clearest diamonds in the world, if they weren't polished, no one would want to buy them. A dull necklace wouldn't make anyone grab a phone off the hook. Your writing is the same way. Don't send out your first draft without polishing it until it glows. A good idea is not enough to sell a manuscript—it *has* to be polished. Most authors do several drafts, and some of them can do 10, 20 or even 30 drafts before they get every word just right. If this sounds like a lot of work, it is. If you get tired of your story and think you can't possibly look at it one more time, set it aside for a few weeks while you work on another project, and then you can look at it with fresh eyes again later.

## Get a second opinion

After you've got it polished the best you possibly can, it helps to have a friend or two look it over for you. If you have any friends who are car-savvy, you might ask them to look under your hood. You might have stopped noticing the crack on your windshield, but your friends will spot it right away. Likewise, you'll want to have some friends read over your manuscript to make sure you haven't left any gaping holes in your book. Ask them to let you know of any parts they found confusing or too hard to believe. And if you have any friends who are language-savvy, such as editors or English teachers, ask them to double-check your grammar, spelling, and sentence structure. Writers' groups are excellent sources for feedback for your work. Check your local paper under "clubs" to see if you can find writers' groups in your area. Contact a local bookstore to see if they know of any or if they'd be willing to let you start one at their store. Perhaps they'll help you promote it by prominently displaying your fliers.

## Prepare a pitch

After you feel your car is ready to sell, you'll have to craft the perfect pitch to sell it. What are the best features on the car? Does it have low miles? Great gas mileage? A sunroof? Those are the features you'll want to play up to your customers. Similarly, when you're shopping your manuscript around, you'll want to put your best foot forward in your query letter or your verbal pitch if you have the chance to meet an agent at a conference.

First, you'll start with a hook: "Gas prices are going through the roof these days. Thank goodness for the great gas mileage on this Ford Escort." For your query letter, you'll want to begin the same way: "They say you can't know a man until you've walked a mile in his shoes. But what about a woman? The week I traded in my loafers for high heels, I finally got a chance to understand the trials of a woman's world like never before." Only after you've gotten their attention with your pitch can you give them more details.

## Describe with hard facts

Once you've got a potential buyer's attention, it's time to tell them more. Take a paragraph to summarize the book or give the reason it's important. You'd tell a potential buyer the make and model of your car, so don't forget to tell an agent the genre of your manuscript. Is it a romance or a suspence novel? Remember not to use inflated adjectives. Telling someone your car is "thrilling" or "breathtaking" doesn't give them any real information. If you're selling a car, you'd tell them why it's great. When you're selling your manuscript, don't say your manuscript has "bestseller potential." Instead, explain why the topic is of interest to readers or compare it favorably to other books in your genre.

## Offer credentials

Finally, explain why you're qualified for your role. If you're selling a prize poodle, you'll need to present the customer with a certificate of authentication. Tell them how long you've been breeding dogs and mention the pedigree, that the dog's mother won three blue ribbons in her last dog show. As a writer, you'll want to let an agent know where you've been published previously, what qualifies you to write about the subject matter you've chosen, and why the topic is of interest. For nonfiction books, you'll need to establish yourself as an expert in your field. Write a weekly column for a local paper, set up some radio interviews, or do some public speaking at seminars, conferences or conventions to establish your credibility on the topic.

## Use the grapevine

If you're selling make-up, you'd invite all your friends to a make-up party. If you're selling a book, you'll want to meet as many other writers as you can for advice and tips on the publishing industry. Join writing groups in your area and go to book signings at your local bookstore. Ask writers which agents represent their work and ask for advice or referrals. Take a writing class and ask other writers about publishing opportunities they've found. Ask a writing professor to recommend your work to any editors or agents he thinks might be interested. Go to conferences and meet agents and editors personally to see what they're looking for and talk to them face to face. They may have some tips for you that could lead to representation or publication.

## Advertise

If you're selling off toys from your childhood, you'd benefit from placing an ad in the paper or with an online retailer like ebay. If you're a nonfiction writer, you should consider ways to put yourself and your book's topic in the spotlight. Do you have a website? Do you speak at local colleges? Will a local paper give you a weekly column? Have you considered doing a radio show? Can you hold a workshop for people interested in your topic? Anything you can do to get feedback and notoriety will help sell your book. Don't forget to mention any of these opportunities you've created for yourself in your query letter. An agent wants to see what kind of a following you have the potential to create. Once your book sells, you'll need to be willing to help sell your book with author signings and guest appearances on talk shows. If you already have a loyal following, an agent will be impressed with your initiative.

## Explore the market

Read other books in your genre. If you're selling a car, you'll want to check the Internet to see what price other cars are going for, whether any parts on them have been recalled, how satisfied customers are and any other information about the vehicle in question. For your manuscript, you owe it to yourself to see what other writers are doing and what readers are saying. Read trade magazines like *Publisher's Weekly*. Check out some online bookstores and read customer reviews. Do romance readers praise the characters or the quick pace of the book? Do mystery readers love the suspense or appreciate the picturesque settings? Examine what you love about other books in your genre and compare it to yours. Have you left out anything important?

## Target your buyer

If your friend is allergic to pets, all your best sales techniques will be wasted on her if you're trying to sell her a Persian kitten. Agents also have limitations on what they'll agree to represent, so take some time to make a list of only those agents who represent work in your genre.

## Follow the rules

When I was trying to buy a car, I kept telling the salespeople I didn't need a car with a sunroof or a spoiler, and I didn't want a gray colored car for safety reasons, but that didn't stop a lot of them from showing me the wrong kind of car anyway, which wasted my time and theirs. If an agent asks for the first three chapters of your book, don't send him the whole manuscript. If she says not to send any attachments on e-mail queries, don't think she'll make an exception for you if you can talk her into it. This is not only a waste of time, it will make them believe you're difficult to work with. I've heard agents say they'd rather work with a good writer who was kind and professional than with a brilliant writer who was unpleasant or couldn't follow directions.

## Don't be desperate

Keep in mind that begging, bribing, or threatening someone to buy your car will not work. Offering flowers or cookies will not entice a customer to buy a prize Yorkie. Yet this is a common mistake new writers make, begging an agent to take a look at their query letters or sending bottles of wine or other bribes. And some even resort to rude demands or guilt trips. Not only is this unprofessional, it makes you look desperate. If someone begged you to buy their car, wouldn't you suspect something was wrong with it? If you beg an agent to read your book, they'll wonder why you've had to resort to such groveling. Even if it takes a while to sell your commodities, keep believing that you have something worth selling. If an agent doesn't want to represent your work, don't take it personally. If he offers advice, consider taking it, but if he says he doesn't represent anything in your genre, take him at his word, cross him off the list, and move on.

## Don't give up

If you were selling an oil painting, you'd have to develop your craft and make a name for yourself in art shows and illustrated magazines before you'd have buyers knocking your door down to buy your latest painting. Writing is also a craft that takes time to develop. If you don't sell your first book, stick with it. Begin another book as soon as you start marketing the first one. By the time you hear back from all the agents you plan to query, you'll already be absorbed by your new project, and if you receive rejections, you can console yourself with, "Yes, but those are for my first novel. Wait until they see my second book!" Authors don't always sell their books in the order they write them. Sometimes the attention gained from a second book will help sell the first. But many writers will get discouraged after their early rejections and drop out of the game. If you keep believing in yourself and improving your technique, your writing will outdistance the rest.

# How to Find the Right Agent

A writer's job is to write. A literary agent's job is to find publishers for her clients' books. Any writer who has endeavored to attract the attention of a publishing house knows this is no easy task. But beyond selling manuscripts, an agent must keep track of the ever-changing industry, writers' royalty statements, fluctuating reading habits, and the list continues.

Because publishing houses receive more unsolicited manuscripts each year, securing an agent is becoming more of a necessity. Nevertheless, finding an eager *and* reputable agent is a difficult task. Even the most patient of writers can become frustrated, even disillusioned. Therefore, as a writer seeking agent representation, you should prepare yourself before starting your search. By learning effective strategies for approaching agents, as well as what to expect from an author/agent relationship, you will save yourself time—and quite possibly, heartache. This article provides the basic information on literary agents and how to find one who will best benefit your writing career.

## Make sure you are ready for an agent

With an agent's job in mind, you should ask yourself if you and your work are at a stage where you need an agent. Look at the "Ten Step Checklists for Fiction and Nonfiction Writers," and judge how prepared you are for contacting an agent. Have you spent enough time researching or polishing your manuscript? Sending an agent an incomplete project not only wastes your time but may turn him off in the process. Literary agents are not magicians. An agent cannot sell an unsalable property. He cannot solve your personal problems. He will not be your banker, CPA, social secretary, or therapist. Instead, he will endeavor to sell your book because that is how he earns his living.

Moreover, your material may not be appropriate for an agent. Most agents do not represent poetry, magazine articles, short stories, or material suitable for academic or small presses—the agents' commission earned does not justify spending time submitting these type of works. Those agents who do take on such material generally represent authors on larger projects first, and then represent these smaller items only as a favor for their clients.

If you strongly believe your work is ready to be placed with an agent, make sure you are personally ready to be represented. In other words, before you contact an agent, consider the direction in which your writing career is headed. Besides skillful writers, agencies want clients with the ability to produce more than one book. Most agents will say they represent careers, not books. So as you compose your query letter—your initial contact with an agent—briefly mention your potential. Let an agent know if you've already started drafting your second novel. Let him know that for you writing is more than a half-hearted hobby.

## The importance of research

Nobody would buy a used car without at least checking the odometer, and the savvy shopper would consult the blue books, take a test drive, and even ask for a mechanic's opinion. Because you want to obtain the best possible agent for your writing, you should research the business of agents before sending out query letters. Understanding how agents operate will help you find an agent appropriate for your work, as well as alert you about the types of agents to avoid.

We often receive complaints from writers regarding agents *after* they have already lost money or their work is tied into a contract with an ineffective agent. If they'd put the same amount of effort into researching agents as they did writing their manuscript, they would have saved themselves unnecessary grief.

The best way to educate yourself is to read all you can about agents and other authors. The articles in this book will give you insight not only on how to contact an agent but also how the author/agent relationship works. Organizations such as the Association of Authors' Representatives (AAR), the National Writers Union (NWU), American Society of Journalists and Authors (ASJA), and Poets & Writers, Inc. all have informational material on agenting. (These, along with other helpful organizations, are listed in the back of this book.) *Publishers Weekly* covers publishing news affecting agents and others in the publishing industry in general; discusses specific events in the "Hot Deals" and "Behind the Bestsellers" columns; and occasionally lists individual author's agents in the "Forecasts" section. Their website, www.publishersweekly.com, also offers a wealth of informtion about specific agents.

Even the Internet has a wide range of sites devoted to agents. Through the different forums provided on the Web, you can learn basic information about preparing for your initial contact or more specific material about individual agents. Keep in mind, however, that not everything printed on the Web is a solid fact; you may come across the site of a writer who is bitter because an agent rejected his manuscript. Your best bet is to use the Internet to supplement your other research. For particularly useful sites, refer to "Websites of Interest" in the back of this book.

Through your research, you will discover the need to be wary of some agents. Anybody can go to the neighborhood copy center and order business cards which say she is a literary agent. But that title does not mean she can sell your book. She may ask for a large sum of money, then disappear from society. Becoming knowledgeable about the different types of fees agents may charge is a *crucial* step to take before contacting any agent.

An agent also may not have any connections with others in the publishing industry. An agent's reputation with editors can be her major strength or weakness. While it's true that even top agents are not able to sell every book they represent, an inexperienced agent who submits too many inappropriate submissions will quickly lose her standing with any editor. It is acceptable to ask an agent for recent sales before he agrees to represent you, but keep in mind that some agents consider this information confidential. If an agent does give you a list of recent sales, you can call the publishers' contracts department to ensure the sale was actually made by that agent.

## The pros and cons of location

For years, the major editors and agents were located in New York. If a writer wanted to be published with a big-name house, he had to contact a New York agency. But this has changed over time for many reasons. For starters, publishing companies are appearing all over the country—San Francisco, Seattle, Chicago, Minneapolis. And naturally, agents are locating closer to these smaller publishing hubs.

The recent advances in technology have also had an impact on the importance of location. Thanks to fax machines, the Internet, e-mail, express mail, and inexpensive long-distance telephone rates, an agent no longer needs to live in New York to work closely with a New York publisher. Besides, if a manuscript is truly excellent, a smart editor will not care where the agent lives.

Nevertheless, there are simply more opportunities for agents located in New York to network with editors. They are able to meet face-to-face over lunch. The editor can share his specific needs, and the agent can promote her newest talent. As long as New York remains the publishing capital of the world, the majority of agents will be found there, too.

## Contacting agents

Once your manuscript is prepared and you have a solid understanding of how literary agents work, the time is right to contact an agent. Your initial contact is the first impression you make on an agent; therefore, you want to be professional and brief.

Again, research plays an important role in getting an agent's attention. You'll want to show

## Before You Contact an Agent:
## A Ten-step Checklist for Fiction Writers

☑ **Finish your novel** or short story collection. An agent can do nothing for fiction without a finished product.

☑ **Revise your novel.** Have other writers offer criticism to ensure your manuscript is as finished as you believe possible.

☑ **Proofread.** Don't let your hard work go to waste by turning off an agent with typos or poor grammar.

☑ **Publish** short stories or novel excerpts in literary journals, proving to potential agents that editors see quality in your writing.

☑ **Research** to find the agents of writers you admire or whose work is similar to your own.

☑ **Use the indexes** in this book to construct a list of agents open to new writers and looking for your type of fiction (i.e., literary, romance, mystery).

☑ **Rank your list.** Use the listings in this book to determine the agents most suitable for you and your work, and to eliminate inappropriate agencies.

☑ **Write your synopsis.** Completing this step early will help you write your query letter and save you time later when agents contact you.

☑ **Compose your query letter.** As an agent's first impression of you, this brief letter should be polished and to the point.

☑ **Read about the business** of agents so you are knowledgeable and prepared to act on any offer.

---

her you've done your homework. Read the listings in this book to learn her areas of interest, check out her website to learn more details about how she does business, and find out the names of some of her clients. If there is an author whose book is similar to yours, call the author's publisher. Someone in the "contracts" department can tell you the name of the agent who sold the title, provided an agent was used. Contact that agent, and impress her with your knowledge of her client list.

## Evaluate any offer

Once you've received an offer of representation, you must determine if the agent is right for you. As flattering as any offer may be, you need to be confident that you are going to work well with this person and that this person is going to work hard to sell your manuscript.

You need to know what you should expect once you enter into a business relationship. You should know how much editorial input to expect from your agent; how often he gives updates about where your manuscript has been and who has seen it; and what subsidiary rights the agent represents.

More importantly, you should know when you will be paid. The publisher will send your advance and any subsequent royalty checks directly to the agent. After deducting his commission—usually 10 to 15 percent—your agent will send you the remaining balance. Most agents charge a higher commission of 20 to 25 percent when using a co-agent for foreign, dramatic, or other specialized rights. As you enter into a relationship with an agent, have him explain his specific commission rates and payment policy.

As your potential partner, you have the right to ask an agent for information that convinces you she knows what he's doing. Be reasonable about what you ask, however. Asking for recent sales is okay; asking for the average size of clients' advances is not. Remember, agents are very busy. Often asking general questions like, "How do you work?" or requesting a sample contract, can quickly answer your concerns. An agent's answers should help you make your decision. If

## Before You Contact an Agent: A Ten-step Checklist for Nonfiction Writers

☑ **Formulate a concrete idea** for your book. Sketch a brief outline making sure you have enough material for an entire book-length manuscript.

☑ **Research** works on similar topics to understand the competition and determine how yours is unique.

☑ **Compose sample chapters.** This step should indicate how much time you will need to finish and if your writing needs editorial help.

☑ **Publish** completed chapters in journals. This validates your work to agents and provides writing samples for later in the process.

☑ **Polish your outline** to refer to while drafting a query letter and avoid wasting time when agents contact you.

☑ **Brainstorm** three to four subject categories that best describe your material.

☑ **Use the indexes in this book** to find agents interested in at least two of your subject areas and looking for new clients.

☑ **Rank your list.** Narrow your list further by reading the listings of agencies you found in the indexes; organize the list according to your preferences.

☑ **Write your query.** Describe your premise and your experience professionally and succinctly, to give an agent an excellent first impression of you.

☑ **Read about the business** of agents so you are knowledgeable and prepared to act on any offer.

you are polite and he responds with anger or contempt, that tells you something you need to know about what working together would be like.

Evaluate the agent's level of experience. Agents who have been in the business a while have a larger number of contacts, but new agents may be hungrier, as well as more open to previously unpublished writers. Talk to other writers about their interactions with specific agents. Writers' organizations such as the National Writers Association (NWA), the American Society of Journalists and Authors (ASJA), and the National Writers Union (NWU) maintain files on agents their members have dealt with, and can share this information by written request or through their membership newsletters.

## Understand any contract before you sign

Some agents offer written contracts, some do not. If your prospective agent does not, at least ask for a "memorandum of understanding" that details the basic relationship of expenses and commissions. If your agent does offer a contract, be sure to read it carefully, and keep a copy for yourself. Because contracts can be confusing, you may want to have a lawyer or knowledgeable writer friend check it out before you sign anything.

The National Writers Union (NWU) has drafted a Preferred Literary Agent Agreement and a pamphlet, *Understand the Author-Agent Relationship*, which is available to members. (Membership is $74 and open to all writers actively pursuing a writing career. See "Professional Organizations" in the back of the book for their address.) The union suggests clauses that delineate such issues as:

- the scope of representation (One work? One work with the right of refusal on the next? All work completed in the coming year? All work completed until the agreement is terminated?)
- the extension of authority to the agent to negotiate on behalf of the author
- compensation for the agent, and any co-agent, if used

- manner and time frame for forwarding monies received by the agent on behalf of the client
- termination clause, allowing client to give about thirty days to terminate the agreement
- the effect of termination on concluded agreements as well as ongoing negotiations
- arbitration in the event of a dispute between agent and client

## If things don't work out

Because this is a business relationship, a time may come when it is beneficial for you and your agent to part ways. Unlike a marriage, you don't need to go through counseling to keep the relationship together. Instead, you end it professionally on terms upon which you both agree.

First check to see if your written agreement spells out any specific procedures. If not, write a brief, businesslike letter, stating that you no longer think the relationship is advantageous and you wish to terminate it. Instruct the agent not to make any new submissions and give her a thirty- to sixty-day limit to continue as representative on submissions already under consideration. You can ask for a list of all publishers who have rejected your unsold work, as well as a list of those who are currently considering it. If your agent charges for office expenses, you will have to reimburse him upon terminating the contract. For this reason, you may want to ask for a cap on expenses when you originally enter into an agency agreement. If your agent has made sales for you, he will continue to receive those monies from the publisher, deduct his commission, and remit the balance to you. A statement and your share of the money should be sent to you within thirty days. You can also ask that all manuscripts in his possession be returned to you.

## Final thoughts

Finding an agent is a challenge, but one may be necessary if you want a commercially successful book. Selecting an agent is a task which deserves a lot of time and careful consideration. Above all, it is important to find a person whom you trust and who believes in your work. Now that you know the steps to take to find a literary agent, get started on the right foot and select the right agent for you.

# Targeting and Hooking an Agent

## BY B.J. ROBBINS

As I sit here in my office surrounded by piles of mostly unsolicited submissions, I think about the ways in which writers grab my attention and cause me to request their manuscript or proposal. What are they doing right? And what are the common mistakes writers make that land their work immediately in my "reject" pile?

Here are some tips:

## Do your homework

Nothing is more of a turn-off than receiving a letter addressed "Dear Agent." Or better yet, a form letter in which my name has been scribbled in. My personal favorite: letters addressed to Mr. B.J. Robbins. What this says to me is that you are sending your query to every listing in the book with no thought as to whether or not your material is appropriate for me. This scattershot approach is not only lazy—it doesn't work. What I appreciate is a writer who has made the effort to learn about my agency and the kinds of books I represent. Flattery, if it's not too obsequious, works too.

## Follow the agency's submissions rules

For instance, I ask for the first three chapters of a novel. So don't send Chapter 4, Chapter 23 and Chapter 48. Yes, I know, the first three chapters aren't your best writing, the novel doesn't really get going until page 154, I've heard it all. But if your first three chapters are weak, then rewrite them. After all, have you ever known anyone who reads a book starting in the middle?

## Make your presentation professional

This means sending a straightforward, clear, concise cover or query letter. I like to see a brief description of your book. By brief, I mean no more than two short paragraphs, plus any pertinent biographical information. I don't need your photo nor do I care to know your height or weight. Or age. Unless, of course, this information is relevant to the project. I do want to know where and when you've been published, or if you have a personal story that relates in some way to the book you are writing.

Avoid cutesy, gimmicky presentations, such as the query I once received for a golf book that contained a clod of dirt and a broken tee. Let's just say that after spending the good part of an hour vacuuming dirt out of my keyboard and off my desk I was not inclined to pursue the project.

It's often a good idea to compare your work with that of well-known authors, but please make sure your writing does, in fact, legitimately have something in common with the work of those authors. I once received a query for a novel in which the author compared himself to everyone from Leon Uris to Margaret Mitchell to James Michener, except he, of course, was better. He included a photo of himself with his dog, and provided all his vital statistics, including height, weight and age. And guess what? I did not request the novel.

Please don't tell me how many millions of dollars we'll make, or how you're sure your book

---

**B.J. ROBBINS** *opened her Los Angeles-based literary agency in 1992 after spending many years in book publishing in New York, in jobs ranging from publicist at Simon & Schuster to Marketing Director and Senior Editor at Harcourt Brace.*

will be snapped up by Hollywood and made into a blockbuster movie which will make us even more millions of dollars. Let me decide that for myself.

Avoid the phrase "fiction novel." I hope you know why. If not, please don't send your work to me.

Present one book at a time. Nothing is scarier than a writer who comes at you with 20 different projects, especially when they're all completed novels—and none of them have been published. Pick the best one, which is usually the one you just finished. Think of the others as your practice books.

If you use a referral name, make sure the person referring you actually knows me. I can't tell you how often I receive letters that say "so and so recommended I contact you" and I have no idea who "so and so" is.

My final word about queries or cover letters: make sure your letter is grammatically correct. Do not rely on spell check. Remember that you are presenting yourself as a writer; therefore, spelling, grammar and punctuation are crucial. After all, if you can't write a good letter, how can I be sure you can write a whole book?

## Other pet peeves

Submissions that don't include an SASE or email address. SASE's that are too small. SASE's with the wrong amount of postage. Those strange foreign postal slips no Post Office knows how to handle.

I hate getting unsolicited certified mail. Or any certified mail, for that matter. My mail carrier doesn't deliver it, which means I have to stand in line at my Post Office, and if you've ever had the misfortune to go to mine you'll know why this is a fate worse than death. If you really want to make sure your material has arrived safely, include a postcard with your submission or use an express service.

Do not phone or fax or email. If you have been waiting longer than 8 weeks for a response, feel free to send me a note. By mail. Not certified.

## What I love

I love writers who have done the aforementioned homework. I also appreciate it when writers have taken the time to understand the way the business works. I can tell from their letters, I swear, that they know something about how agents and publishers operate. I am drawn to writers who exude professionalism, who present themselves honestly and without self-aggrandizing. As an example, I've included my vision of a solid cover letter.

Now, it isn't the sexiest letter in the world and of course I invented it, but it shows how simple and straightforward these letters should be. And in the end, your work has to speak for itself, which is why I ask for sample chapters.

Something else I love, and this pertains to nonfiction, is a writer who presents a solid proposal and who has the right credentials to author a book on that subject. Publishers want experts, not amateurs, and if you can bring your professional expertise to the project, along with fabulous writing skills and a marketing platform from which to sell your book, you will likely succeed.

## Some final words of advice

Since part of the title of this article is Hooking an Agent, getting her interested in working with you, I would say this: be flexible. Learn about the business. Be realistic. Understand that even if your agent is fortunate enough to sell your first novel, you probably won't be able to quit your day job. Not yet, anyway. Keep in mind that literary agents cannot singlehandedly save you from financial ruin, nor can they turn you into a star.

Be patient. Be persistent. Remember, most literary agents have small lists and if you've done your homework carefully and target your search and you still get rejections, keep at it. Just

Dear Ms. Robbins:

I read about your agency in the 2002 Guide to Literary Agents and was interested to see that you represent THE GREATEST AMERICAN NOVEL by Author X and THE SECOND GREATEST AMERICAN NOVEL by Author Y. I enjoyed both books tremendously (*see, here's the flattery I mentioned earlier*) and feel that my book shares a similar sensibility with the authors you represent. Plus, you seem like the most brilliant agent to ever grace the planet. (*Okay, I made this up and if someone ever actually wrote this, I would steer very, very clear*).

My novel is the story of a blah blah blah who etc., etc. (*no more than one or two short paragraphs here*). I have had stories published in numerous literary magazines and journals (*insert names here*) and I received my MFA in Writing from the University of the Moment, where I studied with writers such as Mr. Pretentious, Ms. Full-of-Herself, and Joe Humble (*here, insert names of three writers, one famous, one semi-famous, and one complete unknown from whom you learned more than the other two combined. For those lacking a degree, feel free to list current and previous jobs, especially if they're unusual and/or dangerous*).

I hope you will consider my novel for representation and I have enclosed the first three chapters and SASE. I look forward to hearing from you soon.

Yours sincerely,

Sensible Writer

because I say no doesn't mean that another agent won't be wildly enthusiastic and end up leading you to a wonderful publisher.

## One more thing

Make sure you like your agent and that your agent likes you and, even more importantly, loves your work. I've found that enthusiasm and mutual respect are the keys to a successful author/agent relationship.

# Assess with Success: Examining What an Agency Offers

BY OSCAR COLLIER

## Should You Go to a Large Agency or a Small One?

Writers often wonder whether they should go with a small or large agency. As an agent who has sometimes operated alone and sometimes with a partner or a couple of associates, I only know the small agency scene from the inside. But as an editor, however, I dealt with the largest agencies as well as small ones. The question of size is deceptive. What you should ask is, "Do I believe my individual agent can do the best possible job for me?"

In reality, the agent can only maximize the profits from the work she handles—there is nothing magical about the agent or the size of the agency. What sells is the property—the biggest agent can't sell a piece of junk any better than a beginner who has just switched from being a rights assistant for a publisher. If you create a great property—your first novel—your agent, large or small, can sell it. And with enough effort, you could, too.

## Should you pay an agent to read your first novel?

Some agencies charge a "reading fee," and these fees can vary from a small payment the agent has imposed to keep too many beginners from making submissions to quite substantial amounts. As I have sometimes charged a fee and sometimes not, I can say that charging fees doesn't seem to deter authors from submitting works.

The attraction fee-charging agents have is that they usually, in exchange for the fee, provide some kind of an appraisal or criticism even if they reject the work, while those agents who don't charge a fee might write across a query letter, as I do when I'm in a hurry, "Sorry, not for me," or, "Sounds okay, but not my kind of thing," and stuff it immediately in the return envelope to go back to the author. I consider this better than the alternative, a form rejection slip.

The question that arises is, Is criticism bought for a fee worth anything? I have to say that I think it is, and if you can't get a reading any other way, and can afford the fee, it might be worth your while.

To an experienced person in publishing, such as an editor or agent, it is not surprising that most readers' reports sound alike, with criticisms such as poor characterization, much irrelevant material, lack of consistency, poor focus, shifting point of view, weak plot line, wordy, filled with clichés, etc. No matter how tactfully and positively the criticisms are made, or at what length, these are such common flaws that a good report is bound to mention them. It would even be possible to prewrite paragraphs in a word processing program and print a report lightly customized from such canned paragraphs.

**OSCAR COLLIER** *In his more than five years as senior editor of the trade book division of Prentise-Hall and twenty-five years as a successful literary agent, the late Oscar Collier edited or agented such first novels as* Fields of Fire, *by James Webb,* Old House of Fear, *by Russell Kirk, and other books that have been bestsellers, book club selections, excerpted or condensed in magazines, made into movies, published in foreign countries, reprinted in paperback and even translated into Greek. This piece is excerpted from his book,* How to Write & Sell Your First Novel, *by Writer's Digest Books.*

### Should you pay an agency a fee for editorial work?

If an agency also offers editorial services for a fee, I really don't have firm advice for you. Certainly editorial work can sometimes turn an unsalable work into a salable one. What you have to ask yourself is, "Can this agent make the difference?"

The question in my mind is whether, in some instances, anybody, no matter how well intentioned or well qualified, can truly help—for love or money. Often it is better to start over on a new novel rather than dwell endlessly on trying to improve an old, much-rejected one.

I am not against a writer paying for various kinds of help or for the privilege of rubbing shoulders with other writers and people of the publishing world—even if it is only the fee for joining a local writers' club. Knowing the isolation many writers face, I believe it is important that they meet creative people as well as editors, publishers and agents who deal with creative people behind the scenes of publishing.

What are the options open to the lone writer? Dozens of writers' conferences are conducted on campuses and other sites around the country. For a reasonable fee, you can even live in a college dormitory. Besides the writers' clubs and agencies, writers schools and extension courses offer editorial assistance. Surely they could not all remain in existence year after year if they did not fill a need.

Naturally, in such a large clutch, there will be a few bad eggs. It is a caveat emptor situation—buyer, beware. So before you send any money, try to check out the organization—maybe with the Better Business Bureau—or at least find out how long it has been in existence. Some writers' conferences have been running successfully for many years, and I and other agents are sometimes paid an honorarium and expenses to speak at them. Though I always resolve to harden my heart and not pick up any beginners to represent at them, in fact, I usually end up with at least one new client, because talent and originality are hard to ignore.

A final word is to be sure you understand what service is being offered. Real help in getting you published? Or just friendly contacts with writers and editors? Or psychological support? If you want the answer to be "all of the above," you'll probably have to join several groups.

The work of a literary agent—selling and licensing literary rights to literary property—is an esoteric occupation. This was brought home to me convincingly when I was visiting a fashionable summer resort and at a cocktail party met a socially prominent dowager. She asked me what I did, and I said I was a literary agent.

"And what, might I ask, is a literary agent?"

"Well, a literary agent sells or licenses rights to literary property, just as a real estate agent sells or licenses rights to real property."

"Hah!" she said. "I don't believe there could be such an occupation," and stalked off.

## TIPS ON NAVIGATING THE PUBLISHING INDUSTRY

- Consider hiring an agent to help you sell your manuscript. Some types of novels have more need of an agent than others.
- Agents can help negotiate your advance, or up-front payment, when a book is sold to a publisher. Most advances for a first novel range from $3,000 to $10,000.
- If you choose to work without an agent, you must identify potential markets for your work yourself. Examine other publications in the same general category as yours for ideas. Writing and publishing industry magazines offer clues about editors and publishers who specialize in your genre.
- Use resources like *Literary Market Place* and *Novel & Short Story Writer's Market* to identify possible publishers for your work.
- Librarians and bookstore buyers can tell you what types of books have succeeded recently for certain publishers.
- Book reviews show what kind of books a publisher is promoting.
- If you do decide to enlist the help of a literary agent, there are several reference sources

and literary organizations to help you find one.

- Referrals from published authors and others in the publishing industry are useful when seeking an agent or publisher.
- A query letter, a short business letter describing your novel, is another way to contact agents or publishers. Sometimes writers also include a two- to three-page outline of the novel, or the first few chapters, in their queries.
- Multiple submissions of unsolicited queries are perfectly acceptable.
- Don't withdraw other copies of a multiple submission unless a publisher makes you a firm offer.
- A telephone query should also be brief, professional and fact filled.
- If you do enlist an agent, keep the initial contract period brief, in case you and the agent prove incompatible or the agent fails to sell your work.
- Understand the terms of your contract with your agent or publisher.
- Study the details of your royalty provisions. It is to your advantage to retain as many rights as you can.
- Investigate an agency or writers' school that offers editorial assistance. There are many helpful organizations out there, but all fulfill distinctly different needs.

# What's the Difference Between an Agent, Manager, and Entertainment Attorney?

BY JANICE M. PIERONI ESQ.

More often than not, writers are mystified as to whether, when, and why they need agents, managers, or entertainment attorneys.

Writers spend years developing their craft, often nearly destroying themselves in the process. While their friends with corporate jobs buy homes and start families, writers often sacrifice and delay (or, even worse, lose homes and families)—all in the service of creation. When the work of writers finally generates income, shouldn't writers be entitled to every hard-earned penny? Who are these agent, manager, and entertainment attorney bloodsuckers that want a piece of them now, and where were they when they needed them?

Ironically, writers are often at once deeply suspicious and resentful of agents, managers, and entertainment attorneys—and simultaneously devastated by the fact that they haven't been able to land any one of them. Writers fantasize a "perfect" world in which agents, managers, and entertainment attorneys collectively vanish in a "poof", yet concoct elaborate campaigns designed to reel them in.

Writers' typical resentment about agents, managers, and entertainment attorneys tends to diminish once they understand more fully why they might be useful, or even necessary, to launch and sustain their careers.

Contrary to popular belief, many writers have strong relationships with their agents, managers, and/or entertainment attorneys. They see these service providers as crucial elements of their success teams and are more effective, fulfilled, and, hopefully, financially rewarded as a result of these relationships. In the best of circumstances, these collaborations are built on strong foundations of mutual admiration, respect, trust, and genuine commitment.

Whether writers could benefit from the services of agents, managers, or entertainment attorneys, or any combination of these service providers, turns in part on the skills of the particular service providers and in part on writers' strengths and weaknesses, career stages, successes or failures, desire or lack of desire for guidance, mentoring, and coaching, and the strengths or absence of writers' own industry contacts.

Agents, managers, and entertainment attorneys sometimes work with writers independently, and sometimes work in conjunction with one another. Each service provider has a distinct role to play. With proper coordination, the services each provides should be complementary, but not duplicative.

---

**JANICE M. PIERONI, ESQ.** *is an entertainment attorney and writing/script consultant. In addition to her private practice, in Boston, she is a member of the adjunct faculty of Emerson College; a frequent lecturer; a judge of the Massachusetts Film Office's Annual Screenwriting Competition; and a published and produced writer.*

## Literary agents

Literary agents are the most common writers' representatives. Literary agents represent writers of literary properties, which can include: nonfiction, novels, biographies, autobiographies, diaries, memoirs, short story collections, novelizations, plays, television pilots, teleplays, and screenplays. Literary properties can also include columns, essays, magazine articles, and short stories—although these types of writing are often sold by writers because they aren't lucrative enough for agents to take on.

Literary agents are subject to state licensing requirements. In California, for example, literary agents are required to fill out a license application, pay an annual fee of $250, post a surety bond of $10,000, and submit an affidavit of character, fingerprint cards, a proposed agency contract, a schedule of fees, etc. Although California law allows higher commissions, the Writers Guild of America requires that agents who wish to be included on their list of agents take no more than 10% (ten percent) of their clients' gross earnings. No special training or education is required of literary agents; consequently, some hold law or M.B.A. degrees, while others never finished college. In spite of the lack of state-required training or education, my experience has been that most reputable agents have earned undergraduate degrees in English, business or some other area of relevance to their jobs, and quite a few hold M.B.A. or law degrees.

The lifeblood of the literary agent is to work the trenches of the studios and production companies and to unearth trends, developments, and hirings, firings, and promotions—preferably before such information is public knowledge and announced in the trades. They use their instincts and insiders' knowledge to submit clients' work, set up meetings for clients, and seek assignments for clients in the most appropriate places. Studios and production executives bond with agents, and often engage in a lot of maneuverings with them, such as leaking information to them and reading a script slipped to them that they agree they will have "never seen" if they decide to pass on it, because they need each other. Agents control writing talent, and the selection process agents use to find clients saves studios and production companies staggering amounts of dollars they would otherwise have to pay to story editors and script readers to review scripts agents weed out.

Literary agents also negotiate clients' entertainment and publishing deals, although many writers also retain entertainment attorneys to work in coordination with agents to negotiate the finer points of deals and to review contracts. The key to successful collaborations between agents and entertainment attorneys is for writers to make sure both are on board at an early stage of negotiations. Otherwise, the studio, production company, or publishing house is likely to be furious at everyone on the other side for forcing them to engage in the whole negotiation process twice. In addition, writers should make sure they hire agents and entertainment attorneys who are willing to work together; avoid "loose cannons" and persons so obsessed with power and control that they refuse to share information or work collaboratively, often to the detriment of their clients. (Entertainment or publishing companies almost always send out their own contracts, but, when a contract must be drafted from scratch, it is generally drafted by an entertainment attorney.)

Most agents would like to take a very hands-on approach to clients, reading and giving notes on projects, having regular check-ins with clients by phone or e-mail, setting up regular lunches with clients, and inviting clients to parties where they will have a chance to build industry contacts. However, because agents work on commission only, they tend to handle substantial numbers of clients. The end result is that the attention they can afford to give to individual clients, particularly newer or under-performing clients, is often limited. At the same time, the number of markets they are required to cover and to stay on top of has exploded, spreading them even thinner.

Good agents have a special skill that enables them to identify talented writers at early stages of their careers. Agents often would like to take on and develop such newer writers. They also know too well the value of landing clients at early stages of their careers, before agents are fighting over them, and are aware that early support often breeds long-term loyalty. They know, too, that often just having agents sign them on gives talented writers the encouragement they need to keep writing.

However, unless agents are independently wealthy, they cannot run a business based on clients' futures; thus, they can only afford to take on a few clients whose work is not yet sufficiently crafted to sell right away.

Consequently, agents necessarily have to focus most of their attention on clients who already have an income stream—or preferably flood—from writing. Clients who are experiencing rough periods or who haven't yet generated money from writing can sometimes feel pushed to the side. Some writers may feel justifiably undervalued. To some extent, those writers may be able to solve these problems by motivating their agents, creating newer, more marketable projects, or even by switching agents. However, to some degree, the decades-old problem of writers wanting more attention from agents than agents can give them is not only here to stay, but is likely to become worse as agents struggle to stay on top of the ever-changing markets and players, and to remain competitive under the constant pressures to package projects and to have in hand the next blockbuster, star-vehicle.

Even today, many writers find that good agents can single-handedly take care of all of their professional needs. Some writers are lucky enough to land agents who are accessible and provide the kind of hands-on, day-to-day oversight typically associated with managers and the kind of attention to detail in negotiating deals more often associated with entertainment attorneys. Other writers prefer that their associations with their agents be limited to professional endeavors. They would rather spend their time writing and living their lives instead of schmoozing. In addition, they would just as soon have their agents out seeking work for them instead of wasting their time chatting with them on the phone or in a restaurant.

However, many writers, including those who are lucky enough to land agents at early stages of their careers, writers who have taken up writing as a mid-career change, and writers whose stock is falling, frequently have a longing to be mentored by their agents that exceeds even the best-intentioned and most generous agents' abilities to guide and nurture them. In addition, contemporary demands on agents and the surge of interest in writing, particularly screenwriting, nationwide, has left tens of thousands of writers, many of whom are quite talented, rejected outright by agents.

If agents could effectively service all the professional needs of writers, there probably would be considerably less need for managers and entertainment attorneys. Managers and entertainment attorneys increasingly fill a void left by harried agents too busy to help them. Moreover, managers and entertainment attorneys typically have much to offer in the way of services that are quite valuable in their own right regardless of whether such clients already have agents and regardless of the degree of effectiveness of their agents.

## Managers

If agents are great at micro-management, then managers excel at macro-management.

Literary managers (not to be confused with business managers, who manage clients' money) help clients shape their careers to achieve their goals. Literary managers tend to work with far fewer clients than agencies. They are very service-oriented. They tend to have more personalized contact with clients than agents, and to take the longer view of clients' careers. Managers counsel clients on their overall career strategy, and help them identify and reach career goals. They steer clients away from decisions that might sabotage their careers, and help them create, identify, and maximize career-building moves. In addition, they frequently set clients up in relationships with agents, lawyers, publicists, and others who can help advance their careers.

Managers are prohibited from directly soliciting work for clients, but this restriction is seldom enforced and, consequently, frequently violated. Managers often take 5 percent, 10 percent , or

15 percent of their clients' gross earnings. In addition, unlike agents, who are prevented from participating in their clients' projects as producers, managers often participate in clients' projects as producers. Many entertainment industry insiders complain that managers have a conflict of interest in representing their clients when they have a personal stake in their projects; others feel that is an outdated view that does not reflect current industry realities. However, in instances where managers' credentials do not merit their participation in projects as producers, their involvement could be seen as excess baggage and work to the detriment of the projects.

In the last few years, managers have become all the rage, and significant numbers of agents have become managers. The most notable example of this is Michael Ovitz, who left Creative Artists Agency to form Artists Management Group. The rising status of managers has angered agents, who feel at a competitive disadvantage; why should managers be able to take on roles as producers of their clients' projects and to reward themselves with producing fees when they can't? At the same time lawmakers are considering taking on the issue of regulation of managers, agents are pushing for deregulation of agents.

Managers, like agents, are not required to have any special training or education. However, many managers are former agents, so often they have similar backgrounds.

## Entertainment attorneys

While agents tend to be great at working in the trenches of the studios and production companies and managers often excel at planning, launching, and sustaining careers, entertainment lawyers are typically the most effective of the three service providers at negotiating, drafting, and revising entertainment law contracts.

Attorneys are state-regulated. Each state administers a bar exam that enables examiners to determine that its practitioners are qualified to practice law. Bar exams are grueling written exams that test would-be lawyers, often over the course of several days. Prior to taking the exam, most practitioners first complete a three year course of study at an accredited law school, study for six or eight weeks to prepare for the exam, study for and often are tested on professional responsibility and ethics as well, and submit character references and other information for review by the state in which they intend to practice.

If you hire an attorney for an entertainment law matter, you should hire one whose practice is concentrated in entertainment law. Lawyers usually work for an hourly fee, which might be anywhere from about $150 per hour to about $600 per hour. Some lawyers are receptive to working on a percentage basis. Writers should not be discouraged from approaching entertainment attorneys because they have limited funds. The most high-priced attorneys can sometimes be more economical than their fees would suggest; because they are more efficient at what they do than less experienced practitioners, they can frequently do it in a shorter period of time. In addition, the most high priced might have the most flexibility in taking on writers on a pro-bono (without charge), reduced fee, or deferred fee basis. Writers should also be aware that most major cities have organizations comprised of volunteer lawyers for the arts who offer free or reduced fee services to writers; contact your local or state bar association for the number of the organizations near you.

Many writers rely on lawyers when they are first breaking in and do not yet have agents. Studios and production companies will generally accept submissions from agents or entertainment attorneys. Attorneys typically don't initiate contracts, but often back up contacts writers' make with submissions or references.

Experienced professional writers increasingly use lawyers instead of agents because they prefer to pay them an hourly fee instead of a percentage of the hundreds of thousands or often millions they earn. Writers who choose to use lawyers to the exclusion of agents often are also attracted to lawyers' typical attention to details, and the sophisticated drafting abilities most lawyers possess.

In the end, how do you determine which service providers you need? After all is said and done, once you step beyond the formalities of licensing requirements, and the thresholds of professional knowledge and competence, the best providers for writers are the ones who believe in them and their work, and who help bring out the best personal and professional characteristics in them. Much can be accomplished in a professional relationship of mutual admiration and trust. In contrast, no matter how legendary the reputations of the service providers, if they have left a trail of "road kill" wherever they have gone, the pent-up anger and resentment they have provoked may eventually catch up with them, potentially toppling their careers and possibly even yours.

Whether writers decide on agents, managers, or entertainment attorneys, or some combination of the three, they should be proactive in their selections. They shouldn't just sign up with anyone willing to take them on, or accept anyone they find through an "old boy" or "old girl" network. As difficult as this might be to believe, writers often find their agents, managers, and entertainment attorneys are still there for them even after their own friends and family have stopped rooting for them, believing in their writing talents, or trusting that they will eventually succeed.

## The Basics of Contacting Literary Agents

Once you and your manuscript are thoroughly prepared, the time is right to contact an agent. Finding an agent can often be as difficult as finding a publisher. Nevertheless, there are four ways to maximize your chances of finding the right agent: obtain a referral from someone who knows the agent; meet the agent in person at a writers' conference; submit a query letter or proposal; or attract the agent's attention with your own published writing.

### Referrals

The best way to get your foot in an agent's door is to be referred by one of his clients, an editor, or another agent he has worked with in the past. Because an agent trusts his clients, he will usually read referred work before over-the-transom submissions. If you are friends with anyone in the publishing business who has connections with agents, ask politely for a referral. However, don't be offended if another writer will not share the name of his agent.

If you don't have a wide network of publishing professionals, use the resources you do have to get an agent's attention.

### Writers' Conferences

Going to a conference is your best bet for meeting an agent in person. Many conferences invite agents to either give a speech or simply be available for meetings with authors. And agents view conferences as a way to find writers. Often agents set aside time for one-to-one discussions with writers, and occasionally they may even look at material writers bring to the conference. If an agent is impressed with you and your work, she may ask for writing samples after the conference. When you send her your query, be sure to mention the specific conference where you met and that she asked to see your work.

Because this is an effective way to connect with agents, we've asked agents to indicate in their listings which conferences they regularly attend. We've also included a section of **Writers' Conferences**, starting on page 330, where you can find out more information about a particular conference, as well as an agent's availability at a specific conference.

### Submissions

The most common way to contact an agent is by a query letter or a proposal package. Most agents will accept unsolicited queries. Some will also look at outlines and sample chapters. Almost none want unsolicited complete manuscripts. Check the **How to Contact** subhead in each listing to learn exactly how an agent prefers to be solicited. Never call—let the writing in your query letter speak for itself.

Because a query letter is your first impression on an agent, it should be professional and to the point. As a brief introduction to your manuscript, a query letter should only be one page in length, or at maximum, two pages.

- The first paragraph should quickly state your purpose—you want representation.
- In the second paragraph, mention why you have specifically chosen to query him. Perhaps he specializes in your areas of interest or represents authors you admire. Show him you have done your homework.
- In the next paragraph or two, describe the project, the proposed audience, why your book will sell, etc. Be sure to mention the approximate length and any special features.

- Then, discuss why you are the perfect person to write this book, listing your professional credentials, speaking experience, or relevant expertise.
- Close your query with an offer to send either an outline, sample chapters, or the complete manuscript—depending on your type of book.

For examples of actual query letters that led authors straight to publication, see "Queries That Made It Happen" on page 47. For helpful hints on outlines and synopses, see "Outline and Synopsis Workshop" on page 55.

Agents agree to be listed in directories such as the *Guide to Literary Agents* to indicate to writers what they want to see and how they wish to receive submissions. As you start to query agents, make sure you follow their individual submission directions. This, too, shows an agent you've done your research. Some agents ask for an outline or sample chapters, but you should send these only if you are requested to do so. Under the **How to Contact** subhead, agents also indicate if they are open to fax or e-mail query letters. Due to the volume of material agents receive, it may take a long time to receive a reply. You may want to query several agents at a time; agents also indicate in their listings if they consider simultaneous queries and submissions. If an agent requests a manuscript, make sure you provide sufficient postage for its return.

Like publishers, agencies have specialties. Some are only interested in novel-length works. Others are open to a wide variety of subjects and may actually have member agents within the agency who specialize in only a handful of the topics covered by the entire agency.

Before querying any agent, first consult the Agent Specialties Indexes in this book for your manuscript's subject, and identify those agents who handle what you write. Then, read the agents' listings to see if they are appropriate for you and for your work. For more information on targeting your submissions see "How to Find the Right Agent" on page 29 and "Targeting and Hooking an Agent" on page 34.

## Publishing credits

Some agents read magazines or journals to find writers to represent. If you have had an outstanding piece published in a periodical, you may be contacted by an agent wishing to represent you. In such cases, *make sure the agent has read your work*. Some agents send form letters to writers, and such agents often make their living entirely from charging reading fees, not from commissions on sales.

However, many reputable and respected agents do contact potential clients in this way. For them, you already posses attributes of a good client: you have publishing credits and an editor has validated your work. To receive a letter from a reputable agent who has read your material and wants to represent you is an honor.

Occasionally, writers who have self-published or who have had their work published electronically, may attract an agent's attention, especially if the self-published book has sold well or received a lot of positive reviews.

Recently, writers have been posting their work on the Internet in hope of attracting an agent's eye. With all the submissions most agents receive, they likely have little time to peruse writers' websites. Nevertheless, there are agents who do consider the Internet a resource for finding fresh voices. Only the future will show how often writers are discovered through this medium.

# Queries That Made It Happen

## BY ROBERT LEE BREWER

As you may know, an agent can be your new best friend when it comes to publication. Good agents not only try to get books published, but also try to get them positioned to sell well when they hit the bookshelves. Keep in mind that reputable agents don't get paid unless you do. So it is to their advantage to get you the best contract for the most money with the most options and anything else they can manage to obtain. Also, good agents are not usually trying to sell just a book; they are selling an author. The beginning of this friendship is traditionally started with a query letter.

An effective query letter should be easy to read. The ideas expressed should be clear and concise. After all, if the query letter doesn't make sense, an agent will most likely assume the manuscript will be just as murky. A good query letter is also free of grammar and spelling mistakes. To increase the effectiveness of a query letter, it makes sense to address the letter to a specific agent, especially when dealing with a large agency that may have several agents. And remember, you only want to write enough to pique the agent's curiosity so that he or she will ask you to send the manuscript.

As the two authors in this article will show, the elements of a query letter can be very different for each very different agent. However, both authors used a precise and simple numeric system to get their respective agents. They used a very common rule of fives. That is, they sent out query letters in bundles of five at a time. If all five queries were rejected, then a new bundle of five queries would be sent out. In both cases, the writers found an interested agent that appealed to them.

Before you start picking among interested agents though, you need to initiate that writer-agent relationship with a well-developed query letter. Here we interviewed authors Carol Plum-Ucci and Brad Barkley to see how they found their agents. They've also supplied their original query letters, which have comments from their agents about why the queries worked. One of the most effective ways to achieve success in anything is by following proven examples. So don't be afraid to put your finished manuscript down for a minute and try applying these authors' words of wisdom to your own queries.

## Carol Plum-Ucci

"I thought the first time I had an agent, that meant I had a sale. Don't be that naïve," cautions Carol Plum-Ucci, author of *The Body of Christopher Creed* which was published by Harcourt. "I went through two agents before I found Mark, and all the while my skills were still growing." In fact, she had written four books before beginning work on *The Body of Christopher Creed*. However, you can't find those books anywhere but in Plum-Ucci's personal files. They are all unpublished.

Plum-Ucci is on her third agent, which makes her somewhat more experienced than most first time authors on how to deal with agents. For her, the trick of piquing an agent's interest is the easy part: You

**ROBERT LEE BREWER** *is the author of several articles for Writer's Digest Books, especially for WritersMark et.com. He is also the production editor for Guide to Literary Agents and Photographer's Market.* Always open to talk about the business of writing, he can be contacted at robertb@fwpubs.com.

Mr. Mark Ryan
New Brand Agency Group
370 Jefferson Drive, #204,
Deerfield Beach, FL 33442

Dear Mr. Ryan:

*I can't say that compliments make a difference, but they sure don't hurt.*

Of all the agents listed in the directory, you seemed the nicest! (Or maybe it's just one of the other entries I saw. "Impatient, illiterate, ignorant writers I do not allow . . . Remember, I'm selective and cranky!" Gee, I think I'll sign right up.)

Several reasons I feel I have a winning YA in *The Body of Christopher Creed*:

*Very few writers convey an understanding of their market. When an author puts that much attention into their query, and their target market, chances are that they have put the same kind of attention into their craft.*

- The Young Adult Market has been shrinking downward in reading level. Initially designed to market to high school students 14-17, the age bracket has dropped to junior high, with probably sophomores at the highest. I feel I have created a work that cuts with that unusual double-edged sword—would appeal to the lost age group of high school students and also has enough social redeeming value to appeal to teachers, librarians, editors.

- While containing marketable mystiques including horror and some romance, its most redeeming qualities are the characters and the voices they yield. It hits on some contemporary issues, but this ms is different from other YA's in that its essential purpose is not to examine issues and moralize (from which older teens shy away). I am simply telling a story—uncovering a mystery—with real life as a steely backdrop.

- My bone of contention with much of young adult fiction is that many stories are all character, and the plot goes nowhere. Not the case here. I went to great lengths to make sure the unfolding drama turned the pages as well as the voice. Teenagers who enjoy King, Straub, and Clark would find this an easy but absorbing read.

My full-time position is Director of Publications for the Miss America Scholarship Foundation. I have sold two plays, and *The Body of Christopher Creed* is my fifth young adult (I've hit VERY close). I have been spokesperson for the smuggling of black market literature into former communist countries. I would love to speak at high schools and have a good background in marketing, but the best thing that qualifies me to write for this age group is that I've never grown up. I can clip Miss America's manager in the #@! with a rubber band from 30 feet, can gargle the entire national anthem and not choke, and would still be winning belching contests against my daughter's compatriots if she weren't threatening constantly to disown me (she's coming of age, so).

Sincerely,

Carol Plum-Ucci

*I think I called her after the second paragraph to request the full manuscript. Most writers don't realize that who they are is just as important (to some agents) as what they write. In Carol's case, it was clear that she was down-to-earth and had a sense of humor.*

just find out what they want. Then, you offer it to them in a tight, well-constructed query letter, making sure to get the agent's attention right away with a hooking first line. It also helps to let the agent know that you know what market you're writing for, as well as explaining how the experience you have in that specific field adds to your book.

"Because I write for young adults," claims Plum-Ucci, "I always go on for a paragraph about how I can clip Miss America's manager in the butt with a rubber band from thirty feet and gargle the entire national anthem with a soda and not choke. Remember, they are tired and like a good jolt as long as you can find the line between making them smile and grossing them out."

Plum-Ucci's sense of humor is what appealed to her agent, Mark Ryan of the New Brand Agency Group, though the manuscript itself deals with some serious subject matter. The protagonist of the book finds himself pulled into the middle of a mystery concerning the disappearance of the town reject, Christopher Creed.

Before Creed disappears, he sends a cryptic e-mail to the school principal. This e-mail message is the only available clue. That Creed mentions the protagonist by name is what starts the story and the narrator into motion. In a page turner, Plum-Ucci presents a privileged town that is not prepared to accept that people can be unhappy within the city limits. The novel presents some interesting insights into the psychology of a town before rushing to a surprising conclusion—all of it done online in the synapses of the corpseless digital world of e-mail.

Definitely a novel of its time, *The Body of Christopher Creed* has earned Plum-Ucci a lot of recognition; chief on that list is that the American Library Association named it a Michael L. Printz Honor Book. The novel has been optioned by DreamWorks, and her agents have also landed Plum-Ucci a five-year deal with Recorded Books to sell the audio version of the novel.

Even with all this success, Plum-Ucci is not quitting her day job. "The whole thing has been a gas," she relates, "but hasn't really affected me much beyond the grins. For one thing, I won't see the money for a few more months. For another thing, I'm not nearly where I want to be skill-wise."

Plum-Ucci feels a writer should never be content with past accomplishments. It's the future that counts. Also, she feels it is important that you see yourself as a writer, whether you're published or not, because eventually most persistent writers will win out against the stiff odds for getting published.

"The biggest difference I see between myself and people who have not been published is that many people tend to think of a story as 'my story,' " says Plum-Ucci. "It isn't the writer's story. It's the reader's story."

This attention to your audience can go a long way, she contends, both with readers and agents. With a successful hardcover under her belt and a paperback edition due out in bookstores in November, she provides a convincing argument.

"If you don't have any credentials to brag about, talk about the agent you are addressing. Remember pieces of his or her bio from the reference book and state how marvelous that is and how you have a couple things in common as pertains to this book. Everyone likes to hear good things about themselves—agents included."

## Brad Barkley

"From writing the query to finding an agent, the whole process didn't take that long, maybe a month or so," says Brad Barkley, the author of *Money, Love* (Norton). "I first tried referrals from friends, but that didn't work out, I think, for much the same reasons that blind dates never work out. Then I used the *Guide to Literary Agents*, found some agencies I liked based on their preferences and clients, and sent out a first batch of five letters. Three agents came back saying they were not taking new clients. Two invited the manuscript within a week, and one of those became my current agent."

Peter Steinberg came out on top, and his relationship with Barkley

30 Braddock Rd.
Frostburg, MD 21532
301-687-0330

January 5, 1999

Neil Olson
Donadio and Ashworth
121 W. 27th St.
Suite 704
New York, NY 10001

Dear Mr. Olson,

I am a fiction writer and have recently completed my first novel, *Money Love*.

My first book, a collection of stories entitled *Circle View*, was published in 1997 by SMY Press in Dallas. The book gained favorable reviews in the *New York Times Book Review*, *Publisher's Weekly*, *Booklist*, *Dallas Morning New*, and others. Some of the stories originally appeared in *Glimmer Train*, the *Virginia Quarterly Review*, the *Georgia Review*, and work is forthcoming in the *Southern Review*. Last year, one of my stories was short-listed in *Best American Short Stories*, and three years ago I won a Creative Writing Fellowship from the National Endowment for the Arts.

This latest book is a comic novel about a salesman and his family in the mid 1970's. The first chapter was recently published as part of the anniversary issue of the *Dickinson Review*.

If you are interested, I would be very happy to send you the manuscript.

Sincerely,

Brady Barkley

A literary agent would be insane to read this cover letter and not ask to read the full manuscript. The writer has already had a collection of stories published, been shortlisted for "Best American Short Stories," and had work published in some prestigious journals.

As you can see, he devotes hardly any space to the plot of the very work he's trying to get me to read. He doesn't need to. He's already spent years building up his credits, making sure they're impressive before ever attempting to seek representation.

In 1999, I was the 'junior' agent and in charge of going through the unsolicited submissions with our interns. So one piece of advice is to contact the junior agent at whatever agency you're interested in—she or he will, in most cases, be more approachable than the seasoned, 'well-known' agent who already has a full plate.

is described as a friendly one. "I think basic to that relationship is that the writer should feel the agent has a genuine belief in the writer's vision and work," explains Barkley, "so that your books are not seen just as shoes to sell to the next paying customer. That agent ought to have your career in mind, thinking ahead, beyond this next book."

Though *Money, Love* is not Barkley's first book, it is his first novel. He previously published a collection of short stories, *Circle View: Stories*, with SMU Press before beginning the novel. Sometimes focusing on such experience in the query letter does not appeal to an agent as much as describing the story itself. In this case, the experience helped Barkley get the agent he wanted.

As Barkley says himself, "I figured this was enough to pique the interest, or at least the curiosity, of an agent or two. So I didn't spend a lot of time talking about the book or describing it. I focused briefly on that, but mostly on track record. It would be different for another writer with different things to emphasize."

As far as getting published, Barkley doesn't fall for all the hocus pocus talk surrounding the publishing industry. "There are no tricks," he says. "There is no substitute for taking your work seriously enough to labor at it every day. Good work will find a publisher eventually. Publishing is fun, but it's the work—the process, the characters, the themes and ideas, the internal journey of writing—that can alter your life, give you whole new ways of knowing."

*In Money, Love*, Gabe, the narrator, finds himself on a much different journey, one which alters his perspective on what his family is and what he wants out of life. The novel begins with the separation of Gabe's parents, Roman and Gladys, as a result of Roman's inability to keep a steady income. Gladys immediately moves in with Dutch, Roman's brother and Gabe's uncle. Suddenly the differences in the two brothers come to the foreground as they fight for Gladys's affection.

In an effort to finally hit it big and be able to offer Gladys everything she's ever wanted, Roman packs Gabe into a truck along with a sleazy investor friend and a former Miss North Carolina to promote "Death Cars." The plot manages to get more and more interesting, not to mention hilarious. While leading the reader through an odyssey of state fairs and cars shows, *Money, Love* explores the different extremes of material wealth and how it is gained while digging into the psychology of what holds a marriage and family together.

Barkley found the time to write this novel with the help of a Creative Writing Fellowship from the National Endowment for the Arts (NEA). He has also been awarded three Individual Artist Awards from the Maryland State Arts Council. "Those kinds of awards help psychologically, I think, as a kind of big rubber stamp validation of your work," claims Barkley. "They also help on a more practical level, giving me time off—usually in the summer—from teaching so that I can write more or less full time."

After publication, the novel also received recognition, being selected for Barnes & Noble's "Discover Great New Writers" series, as well as being dubbed one of the best first novels of 2000 by *Washington Post* and *Library Journal*. This acknowledgement for himself and his book has translated into a bright future for Barkley, who is now in a two-book deal with St. Martin's Press for a novel and collection of stories. "When these things happen, I feel proud of the book the way you would feel proud of one of your children, like it has left the nest, gone out into the world, and made good."

# How to Interest an Agent: Killer Queries and Queries That Kill

BY LORI PERKINS

Think of the process of finding an agent as dating. You are embarking on a matchmaking experience that should pair you up with someone you may have a relationship with for years, if not for your entire writing career.

Finding an agent is therefore serious business. While we all dream of falling in love, most relationships last because the partners are truly well matched. Your relationship with your agent must be based on this same long-lasting glue.

So what you really want in an agent is someone who is not going to tell you that you are brilliant, but someone who truly understands your work and your vision for how you want to grow as a writer.

## IMPRESSING AN AGENT

My suggestions for impressing the right agent are much the same as I would give to someone going out on a first date.

### 1. Put your best foot forward

You want to make an agent want to read more, and the way to do this is to keep your introduction short, with your most impressive information up front.

Agents are very busy and receive a ton of queries (my agency receives at least 1,000 a month). Your letter must be to the point and informative.

*Never* send a query letter that is longer than one page. Two hundred and fifty words should be more than enough for you to introduce yourself and your book. I have sold more than 2,000 books and have sent out as many pitch letters, and I have never sent a letter to an editor that was longer than one page. If I find myself writing a longer letter, I always edit.

### 2. Make a clean and professional first impression

A dirty, tattered, handwritten query letter is not going to get the same attention as a clean, well-presented letter. Some agents won't even read a handwritten letter. It goes straight in the garbage.

Use white or cream-colored $8\frac{1}{2} \times 11$ bond paper. If your paper is old and yellowed, buy new sheets. Don't use greeting cards or writing paper intended for personal letters. This is a professional relationship, not a quick letter to a friend. Never send a letter printed on erasable bond, because it smudges, often obliterating whole words and sentences.

Since I represent a lot of horror writers, I receive weird query letters. I've been sent letters on black stationery with white letters, queries handwritten in red ink that is supposed to look

**LORI PERKINS** *is the founder of L. Perkins Associates, a literary agency in Riverdale, NY. She is an adjunct professor at New York University where she teaches a class in Literary Agenting for N.Y.U.'s Center for Publishing. She has contributed articles to* Writer's Market, *and a chapter on couponing for the frugality anthology, "The Simple Life" (Berkley). This article is reprinted with permission from* Writer's Digest *from her book* The Insider's Guide to Getting an Agent.

like blood, and all sorts of computer-generated homemade stationery with skulls, vampire bats and coffins as decorations. This is the sign of an amateur and does not impress me. (Actually, it makes me that much more skeptical of the writer's ability to take his work seriously.)

*Never* send a handwritten letter, no matter how clear you think your handwriting is. If you can, also type the envelope or label address. It just looks more professional. Type your letter following standard letter-writing format. Double-space everything you send. Use one-inch margins on all four borders of your letter.

Use 10- or 12-point type. Don't use script or fancy typefaces. Don't typeset your letter or sample chapters to make them look more like a book.

Don't send letters with mistakes. Make the change, and print the letter again. A letter with a mistake hand-corrected by the author shows me that he didn't think I was important enough to run the letter out again.

Also, always check the spelling of the agent's name and title. Some agents won't open letters that are misaddressed. While I will take on someone who sends a query letter addressed to Laurie Perkins, letters addressed to Mr. Perkins have an uphill climb.

## 3. Don't be cute or overly clever

Like the blood-dripping letters described previously, many authors try to get my attention with unusual queries. While I remember getting a query with a blood-dripping plastic axe, I don't remember the book—and I didn't take that author on.

Don't try to bribe the agent either. We've been sent wine, booze, Cuban cigars, coffee mugs, and a box of Vidalia onions as enticements to represent writers, but none of those authors have made it that way. The work has to stand on its own.

Two memorably tasteless queries do stand out. A woman tried to "seduce" my business partner in her query letter, offering to "fondle his adjectives." She enclosed a black & white photograph of herself in a negligee.

Another author started his query with the line, "I'm going to grab you and beat you senseless, Lori Perkins." He then went on to describe in detail the tortures his main character would inflict upon me, but I didn't read any further.

Obviously, we declined to represent both writers.

## 4. Don't tell him you love him on the first date

Some authors manage to get my attention in the first line or paragraph of their query letters, and then ruin that goodwill by saying they have completed ten novels in the closet that they want to send me. Or after I've asked to see sample chapters, they overnight me the material and then call every other day to see if I've read it. Or they tell me they plan on quitting their day jobs as soon as I take them on.

Sometimes, an author's enthusiasm and eagerness for success in his writing career can overwhelm an agent. Just as in a dating situation, it's best to be cautious until you know one another well.

## 5. Don't lie to impress

There's a famous story of an author who made up a quote from a best-selling writer, which his agent used to sell the book for a nice six-figure deal. When an article about the sale appeared, the published author called *The New York Times* to announce that he had never read the book. The publisher rescinded his offer quite publicly.

It's just as impressive to say that you *might* be able to get a quote from Mary Higgins Clark as it is to have one, if you indeed know her (or her daughter, or a friend of a friend who has promised to approach her). Don't fudge the facts with your agent, especially on the first date.

## 6. At the beginning of the author/agent relationship, don't talk about other agents you've sent the novel to

I don't need to know that you've tried to sell the book yourself and, now that it's been rejected by every editor listed in this year's *Writer's Market*, you thought you'd try getting an agent. This is another reason why the query letter should be short: It keeps the author out of trouble.

Don't spend your time talking about your ex-spouse. Authors have given me information way too early that I just don't need to know until we're well on the way to a solid author/agent relationship, much like a date who won't shut up about his first wife/ex-girlfriend.

I also don't want to hear about another writer's career (whether good or bad). Each writer's book is unique.

## 7. Know when it's time to go home

By this, I mean give the prospective agent enough time to read requested material without badgering her. If you must call to ask if she's read your material (after six to eight weeks, unless she's said she'll get to it sooner) and you do get her on the phone, don't keep her on it all day. Until an agent has agreed to take on your work, you don't need to know how she plans on marketing the book and who she's going to send it to.

Likewise, the agent doesn't need to know that you'll be running in the New York Marathon or going to your high school reunion this weekend—unless it relates to your book. Too much information early on is just useless and annoying.

## 8. Don't move too fast

Like the woman who imagines what her married name will be after the first date, don't start wondering how much you're going to get for the book or whether Steven Spielberg will be directing the movie himself, just because an agent has said they'll look at three chapters and an outline.

Don't get ahead of yourself. Don't make assumptions about the future until you know there will *be a* future.

## 9. Don't forget to give her your number

You would be surprised at the number of authors who don't include their telephone numbers in their query letters. Always include your phone number, address, and e-mail address, if you have one.

And, of course, always enclose a self-addressed, stamped envelope or postcard if you really want a response. Many agents just throw away a query letter (and the accompanying manuscript) if it doesn't have an SASE.

Just recently I was sent a certified letter from a woman who works with the FBI on high-profile cases. She obviously thought I was important enough to go to the trouble of making sure the Post Office notified her when I received the letter (this is not necessarily a great idea—it just means that someone at the agency signed for the material, not necessarily the agent herself), but she failed to give me a phone number to reach her. Her personal phone number was unlisted, so the only way I had to get in touch with her was to send her a letter via her SASE. She was lucky that I was that interested in her work. I'm sure other agents just threw the whole submission away.

## 10. Be punctual

Just like going on a date, if you say you're going to be somewhere, be there on time. Call if you're going to be late.

What this means in your relationship with an agent is that if you say you're going to send something that the agent has requested, you should send it right away. If there's some kind of delay, let the agent know.

# Outline and Synopsis Workshop

## BY IAN BESSLER

You've written your Great American Novel or your Nonfiction Tome. After mailing out a punchy, carefully composed query letter, you receive word back that an agent is interested in finding out more about your project. Your task now is to put together a full proposal package. These usually include a cover letter, three sample chapters (or the first 100 pages of a fiction manuscript) and an outline or synopsis. Outline or synopsis? What's the difference?

Agents often use the terms interchangeably, but there is indeed a difference. In general, "outline" refers to nonfiction, while "synopsis" refers to fiction.

Nonfiction is defined by logical and meaningful structure. Your goal when selling a nonfiction project is to detail the logical presentation of facts, ideas and arguments; a nonfiction outline is therefore primarily a structural skeleton showing how each part relates to the whole and in what order the reader encounters each element.

On the other hand, fiction is defined by conflict. Your goal when selling a novel manuscript is to show the characters, the flow of events and how these events are propelled forward by the conflict. A novel synopsis, therefore, is a condensed narrative version of your story from beginning to end that, ideally, reads like your novel, conveys a similar style of writing and sells your novel by grabbing the reader's attention much like the full-scale manuscript.

The nonfiction outline and the novel synopsis are useful means for both the writer and the agent to "step back" from the manuscript and look at the larger outlines of structure and plot.

## THE NONFICTION OUTLINE

The nonfiction outline serves as an annotated table of contents and describes the structure of a book that you either have written or intend to write. It is also a tool used to sell that book to an editor or agent, as well as a valuable labor-saving device for you as a writer. It can indicate what you're getting into and guide how you develop the book idea. Creating an outline for your idea can help impose form and point out further avenues of research and development.

If you intend to pitch an idea for a nonfiction book that has not yet been completed, the outline must convince an agent or editor that the proposed idea has been developed in a way that is both wide-ranging and detailed enough to produce a book-length manuscript's worth of material. They need to know your idea will support a book and not just an article. Your outline must also demonstrate you have a clear grasp of the level of research needed to complete the project and deliver the manuscript on time. If you have not thoroughly investigated what is involved in researching the book, you may begin writing only to lose focus when you come across books, people to interview and other areas of research you had not realized were essential to a thorough treatment of your idea.

The following list covers several pointers for generating an outline:

- **DESCRIBE:** Describe what each section of the book does—how it arranges and presents the material you have gathered on the topic—and not the topic itself. For instance, if the topic of the chapter is the Marine Corps boot camp training process, your outline of the chapters should begin with something like this: "The chapter assesses the boot camp process where recruits are stripped of their individual identities, broken down and then

---

**IAN BESSLER** *is the editor of* Songwriter's Market, *a fiction writer and musician.*

# SAMPLE NONFICTION OUTLINE

Psychedelic Rawk: 1965 to Present

Chapter 1
Designed to Blow Your Mind:
the Psychedelic Sound, the Studio and the Road          23 pages, 10 photos.

The first chapter launches a discussion of the term ''psychedelic''; the corresponding aesthetic and musical features generally considered psychedelic; the associated sound studio technologies; and elements of the live psychedelic music experience. It is divided into three sections.

The first section scrutinizes the aesthetics and musical characteristics of psychedelic rock. It argues that psychedelic music is based on an aesthetic of sound fetishizing radically new, sensual or shocking sound textures, including the perception of familiar sounds as ''strange'' or ''weird'' when placed into new contexts. It argues for a wider interpretation of the term ''psychedelic'' to include any sort of music that allows listeners to defamiliarize themselves with common musical and everyday sounds. As an expansion of this argument, it discusses the inherently slippery and imprecise nature of music terminology and notes the numerous crossover points between psychedelic rock and other genres and schools of musical thought, including ''art rock'' artists such as Frank Zappa, Captain Beefheart, the Velvet Underground and Brian Eno. It expands on these points with a discussion of other common features of psychedelic music, including nonstandard song structures, avant-garde influences, collage, ''found'' sounds, studio chatter and soundscapes.

The second section chronicles the development of specific studio techniques/technologies and the part they have historically played in allowing the expression of the psychedelic aesthetic. It discusses the early multi-track and effects experiments of Les Paul; the innovations of tape loops, phasing, automatic double-tracking and sophisticated mixing techniques refined during mid- to late-Sixties Beatles, Pink Floyd and Jimi Hendrix recording sessions; and modern refinements in sampling, digital effects and computer manipulation of sound.

The third section sketches out a brief overview of the rise of new instrumental and sound-system technology that has made it possible to bring the psychedelic music aesthetic into a live performance context, including new synthesizer technology, the widespread use of small portable effects processors and innovations in PA technology made possible by touring psychedelic bands such as the Grateful Dead and Pink Floyd. This section ends the chapter by scrutinizing other elements of the live psychedelic experience, including the crowd experience, audience participation and musical improvisation, as well visual projections and light shows ranging from the early blobs and phantasms of Haight-Ashbury to modern computerized lighting systems.

Photos: Syd Barrett w/early Pink Floyd, Jefferson Airplane, Brian Eno, Frank Zappa, a photo of the inside of Abbey Road studios in the mid-1960s, Jimi Hendrix in the studio w/engineer Eddie Kramer, Roger Waters onstage w/Pink Floyd, the early-1970s Grateful Dead onstage w/the Wall of Sound, a crowd of Deadheads, a blob projection from the mid-1960s Fillmore West.

rebuilt as Marines. It is divided into three sections. The first part discusses . . ." Once again, the focus is on what the chapter does (it "assesses"), how it is constructed ("divided into three sections") and what information goes in what sections ("The first part discusses . . ."), rather than on a detailed explication of the topic itself.

- **STAY PRESENT:** Write the outline in the present tense for clarity.
- **STAY ACTIVE:** Avoid using the passive voice whenever possible. Avoid a sentence form like this: "The issue of combat unit cohesion is explored." Instead, use a form more like this: "The chapter explores combat unit cohesion." Consistent use of the active voice maintains clarity and punch in the outline.
- **HOOK:** Give each chapter a hook title with impact and clarity. For example, if the book on Marine training is titled *Parris Island Blues*, a chapter encapsulating Marine Corp history could be titled "The Leatherneck Chronicles."
- **BE VIVID:** Use vivid and active verbs to tell what the chapter does. The chapter doesn't just "talk about" the topic, it *unearths* information, *confronts* the possibilities, *expands* a viewpoint or *blasts* a commonly held misconception. Action verbs can liven up your outline and serve as an additional tool for maintaining the active interest of the agent or editor, but be sure not to repeat the same verb too many times.
- **PHOTOS AND ILLUSTRATIONS:** In the upper right-hand corner of the first page of each chapter outline, give a page count for the chapter and a tally of the number of photos and illustrations you intend to use. At the end of each chapter outline, include a short paragraph detailing any photographs or illustrations incorporated into the chapter.

The example outline on page 56 models the principles listed above.

## THE NOVEL SYNOPSIS

A well-written synopsis is an important tool when marketing your novel, and many agents and editors will use it to judge your ability to tell a story. The synopsis is a condensed narrative version of the novel. It should hook the editor or agent by showcasing the central conflict of the book and the interlocking chain of events set off by that conflict. It should incorporate every chapter of your book, and distill every main event, character and plot twist. A synopsis should highlight the element of human drama and emotion that explains *why* the characters in a novel took their particular path. When crafting your synopsis, these pointers form a set of guidelines to lead you through the process of condensing your manuscript:

- **FORMAT:** Type a heading in the upper left-hand corner of the first page, featuring the title of your novel, the genre, an estimated word count for the full manuscript and your name. At the end of the synopsis, type out "THE END" to signify the conclusion of the story.
- **STAY PRESENT:** Write the synopsis in the present tense and third-person point of view. Even if your novel is written in first person, use third person for the synopsis. This allows for consistency and ease in summarizing. Such a summary will also help when an agent pitches the work to an editor.
- **DON'T HOLD BACK:** Tell the entire story, including the ending. Do not tease—tell who lives, who dies, who did it and so on. At this stage of the query process, the agent or editor has already been hooked by your brilliant query letter with the clever teaser, and now they want an overview of the entire project, so don't leave anything out.
- **HOOK:** Start with a hook detailing your primary character and the main conflict of the novel. Give any pertinent information about the lead character, such as age, career, marital status, etc., and describe how that character manifests or is drawn into the primary conflict.
- **SPOTLIGHT:** The first time you introduce a character, spotlight that character by capitalizing his name. If possible, weave the character's initial description into the flow of the text, but don't stray from the narrative with a lengthy or overly-detailed character sketch.
- **CONDENSE:** Don't defeat the purpose of the synopsis by letting it run too long. A

## SAMPLE NOVEL SYNOPSIS

*Obelisk*

Science Fiction

75,000 words

by Maxwell Parker

ARCAS KANE, newly minted agent for the Imperial Galactic Security Apparatus, is eager for promotion within the ranks. Security Apparatus Director DELSIN HISTER, leader of an Imperial faction hostile to the current ruler, sees Kane's ambitions and picks the young man for a mission on the fringe of the galaxy, where archaeologists make a startling discovery.

Buried in the sands of a sparsely populated desert world they find artifacts from times beyond the reckoning of even the oldest histories of the Imperium. The artifacts include obsidian obelisks, perfectly preserved and carved with glyphs and signs. Using bits of lore preserved by the desert planet's nonhuman natives, the scientists decipher part of the message and send news of their discovery.

Kane arrives with the crew of a supply ship and finds the archaeologists murdered, the artifacts destroyed. He searches through bits of surviving scientific data. The obelisks describe a planet, the mythical home system of the human race. The obelisks tell of the abandonment of the home world and the wandering of the human race. They also refer to an ancient doomsday weapon, the source of the destruction.

Kane questions the wary natives. He learns that two of the archaeologists escaped in a ship to retrace the ancient wanderers' steps back to the home planet. He reports in to Hister, who orders Kane to follow.

He departs with the reluctant crew of the supply ship. They spend weeks hopping from world to world, following the trail. Beautiful AVA, the supply ship's executive officer, seduces Kane, and jealous hostility flares between Kane and the ship's captain. Crew members die in mysterious accidents. Suspicion falls on Kane. He suspects a mole among the crew and wonders if he is himself a pawn.

He catches the archaeologists. They find the hulking ruins of a colony generation ship floating lifelessly in orbit around an obscure star system. A search of the colony ship's archives reveals detailed descriptions of the home planet's location and the doomsday device. Hister is shadowing the pursuit. He overtakes them in an Imperial warship. Hister congratulates them on their discovery and urges them all on to the home planet.

Nothing is left of the planet but a charred, sterilized cinder. They detect a beacon in the ruins of a city on the surface. In a bunker beneath the city, they find an artificial intelligence unit waiting for the return of its masters. In between senile harangues by the AI, they coax out the complete history of the war and the formula for the doomsday device.

After returning to orbit, Hister announces that Kane and the others have reached the end of their usefulness and must be liquidated. Hister intends to take the doomsday device information for his own use. Hister's minions lead Kane, Ava and the others away to be ejected from the airlocks. The supply ship's engines explode where it sits docked with the warship. Kane, Ava and one of the archaeologists narrowly escape in a life pod as the ship comes apart at the seams. Hister is sucked into the vacuum of space as the bridge ruptures. Ava reveals her identity as the mole, a spy for the Imperial loyalists. They seal themselves into hibernation pods to wait for rescue by loyalist forces.

THE END

workable rule of thumb for calculating the length of the synopsis is to condense every 25 pages of your novel synopsis down to 1 page. If you follow this formula for a 200-page novel manuscript, you should wind up with 8 pages of synopsis. This formula is not set in stone, however, since some agents like to see even more compression and will frequently ask for a two-page synopsis to represent an entire novel. If in doubt, ask the agent what length he prefers, and tailor your synopsis to his requirement, no more, no less.

- **CUT OUT THE FAT:** Be concise. Include only details of the action essential to the story, and excise excessive adjectives and adverbs. Dialogue is rarely used, but at the same time don't be afraid to feature pivotal quotes, descriptive gems or a crucial scene when you know it will enhance the impact of your synopsis at critical points.
- **RETELL:** Work from your manuscript chapter by chapter, and briefly retell the events of each chapter. You should tell one complete account of your book, although you may use paragraphs to represent chapters or sections. Whenever possible, use a style reflecting the tone of the actual novel—if the novel is dark and moody in tone, then a dark and moody tone is called for in the synopsis.
- **BE SEAMLESS:** Do not intrude in the narrative flow with authorial commentary, and do not let the underlying story framework show in your synopsis. Don't use headings such as "Setting" or phrases like "At the climax of the conflict . . ." or "The next chapter begins with . . ." In short, do not let it read like a nonfiction outline. Your goal is to entrance the agent or editor with the story itself and not to break the spell by allowing the supporting scaffolding to show. These elements should already be self-evident and woven into the narrative. You should also avoid reviewing your own story; the agent or the editor will make his own judgment. Your work should hopefully speak for itself.

The example synopsis on page 58 condenses an entire novel in one page. This is an extreme example of compression as noted above but a demonstration of the principles involved.

## A FEW LAST BITS

A few final tips to consider:

- Include two SASEs with your submission, a #10 business-size SASE for reply and a larger SASE big enough to hold your manuscript, along with enough postage for its return.

- Be sure your proposal package is either laser-printed or neatly typed (no dot matrix) on clean paper sufficiently strong to stand up to handling (do not use erasable bond or onionskin). Also, put a blank piece of paper at the end of the manuscript to protect the last page.

- Be sure to use proper manuscript format (one-inch margins on all four sides of the page, double-spaced, one-sided and left-justified only).

- Resist the urge to cover your manuscript with copyright symbols. Under current copyright law, your work is protected as soon as you put it into tangible form. To many agents and editors, a manuscript sporting copyright symbols is the mark of an amateur.

Not all agents or editors have boiled down an explicit set of nuts-and-bolts guidelines, but the methods outlined in this article will provide you with a repeatable set of steps for framing your ideas with clarity and precision. For further treatments of nonfiction outline issues, refer to *How to Write a Book Proposal*, by Michael Larsen (Writer's Digest Books). For further advice on constructing a synopsis, refer to *Your Novel Proposal: From Creation to Contract*, by Blythe Camenson and Marshall J. Cook (Writer's Digest Books) or *The Marshall Plan for Novel Writing*, by Evan Marshall (Writer's Digest Books).

# Subsidiary Rights: Much More Than a Book

## BY DONYA DICKERSON

Most writers who want to be published envision their book in storefronts and on their friends' coffee tables. They imagine book signings and maybe even an interview on *Oprah*. Usually the dream ends there—having a book published seems exciting enough. In actuality, a whole world of opportunities exists for published writers beyond seeing their books in print. These opportunities are called "subsidiary rights."

Subsidiary rights, or sub-rights, are the additional ways that a book—that the novel or nonfiction work you are writing—can be presented. Any time a book is made into a movie or excerpted in a magazine, a subsidiary right has been sold. If these additional rights to your book are properly "exploited," you'll not only see your book in a variety of forms, but you'll also make a lot more money than you would derive from book sales alone.

Unfortunately, the terminology of subsidiary rights can be confusing. Phrases like "secondary rights," "traditional splits," or "advance against royalty" could perplex any writer. And the thought of negotiating the terms of these rights with a publisher is daunting.

Although there are many advantages to working with agents, the ability to negotiate sub-rights is one of their most beneficial attributes. Through her experience, an agent knows which publishing houses have great sub-rights departments. If she knows a house can make money with a right, she will grant that right to the publisher when the contract is negotiated. Otherwise, she'll keep, or "retain," certain rights for her clients, which she will try to exploit by selling them to her own connections. In an interview in the *2000 Guide to Literary Agents*, writer Octavia Butler said that working with an agent "is certainly a good thing if you don't know the business. It's a good way to hang onto your foreign and subsidiary rights, and have somebody actively peddling those rights because there were years when I lived off subsidiary rights."

If you want to work with an agent, you should have a basic understanding of sub-rights for two reasons. First, you'll want to be able to discuss these rights with your agent intelligently (although you should feel comfortable asking your agent any question you have about sub-rights). Secondly, different agents have more expertise in some sub-right areas than others. If you think your book would make a great movie, you should research agents who have strong film connections. A knowledge of sub-rights can help you find the agent best suited to help you achieve your dreams.

An agent negotiates sub-rights with the publishing house at the same time a book is sold. In fact, the sale of certain sub-rights can even determine how much money the publisher offers for the book. But the author doesn't get paid immediately for these rights. Instead, the author is paid an "advance against royalties." An advance is a loan to the author that is paid back when the book starts earning money. Once the advance is paid, the author starts earning royalties, which are a predetermined percentage of the book's profit.

The agent always keeps certain rights, the publisher always buys certain rights, and the others are negotiated. When an agent keeps a right, she is then free to sell it at will. If she does sell it,

---

**DONYA DICKERSON** *is an editor for Writer's Digest Books and the former editor of the* Guide to Literary Agents.

the money she receives from the purchasing company goes immediately to the author, minus the agent's commission. Usually the companies who purchase rights pay royalties instead of a one-time payment.

If the publisher keeps a particular right, any money that is made from it goes toward paying off the advance more quickly. Because the publisher kept the right, they will keep part of the money it makes. For most rights, half the money goes to the publisher and half goes to the writer, although for some rights the percentages are different. This equal separation of payment is called a "traditional split" because it has become standard over the years. And, of course, the agent takes her commission from the author's half.

Most agents have dealt with certain publishers so many times that they have pre-set, or "boilerplate," contracts, which means they've already agreed to the terms of certain rights, leaving only a few rights to negotiate. The following describes the main sub-rights and discusses what factors an agent takes into account when deciding whether or not to keep a right. As you read through this piece, carefully consider the many opportunities for your book, and encourage your agent and publisher to exploit these rights every chance they get.

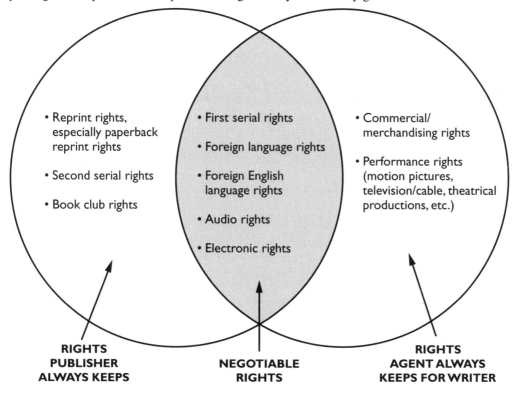

- Reprint rights, especially paperback reprint rights

- Second serial rights

- Book club rights

- First serial rights

- Foreign language rights

- Foreign English language rights

- Audio rights

- Electronic rights

- Commercial/ merchandising rights

- Performance rights (motion pictures, television/cable, theatrical productions, etc.)

**RIGHTS PUBLISHER ALWAYS KEEPS**

**NEGOTIABLE RIGHTS**

**RIGHTS AGENT ALWAYS KEEPS FOR WRITER**

## RIGHTS THE PUBLISHER ALWAYS KEEPS

The following sub-rights are always kept by the publisher and are often called "non-negotiable rights." Money earned from these rights is split between the publisher and the author, and the author's share goes toward paying back the advance. Selling these rights helps the advance earn out faster which hopefully means the writer will receive royalty checks sooner.

### Reprint rights

In publishing, a "reprint right" refers to the paperback edition of the book. When a hardcover book is reprinted in paperback, the reprint right has been used. According to agent Donald

Maass, of the Donald Maass Literary Agency, "In deals with major trade publishers, it's a long-standing practice to grant them control of reprint rights. However, in some cases, a small press deal for instance, we withhold these rights." Traditionally, if a hardcover book sold really well, paperback houses bought the rights to reprint the book in a more affordable version. Any money earned from the paperback was then split fifty/fifty between the publisher and writer. Paperback houses often paid substantial amounts of money for these reprint rights.

But the recent consolidation of publishing houses has changed the value of reprint rights. "In the old days," explains Maass, "most books were hardcover, and paperbacks were cheap versions of the book. Today, so many paperback publishers have either merged with a hardcover publisher or begun their own hardcover publisher, that the business of selling reprint rights has diminished." Now, many publishers make what is called a "hard/soft deal" meaning the house will first print the book in hardcover, and, if the book sells well, they reprint the book in paperback. This type of deal can still benefit writers because they no longer have to split the money earned from reprint with the publisher. Instead, they earn royalties from both the hardcover and paperback versions.

## Book club rights

These days it seems that a book club exists for every possible interest. There are the traditional book clubs, like Book-of-the-Month and its paperback counterpart, the Quality Paperback Book Club. But there are also mystery book clubs, New Age book clubs, book clubs for writers and artists, and even online book clubs. And many major publishers, like Scholastic or Doubleday, have their own book clubs. Most book clubs are very selective, and you should be flattered if your book is chosen for a book club. Like reprint rights, any money made from book club rights is split fifty/fifty between the publisher and the writer. If an agent believes a book will appeal to a certain book club's audience, she will target the manuscript to publishers who have good relationships with—or who own—that book club.

## Serial rights

A serial is an excerpt of the book that appears in a magazine or in another book. To have your book serialized is wonderful because excerpts not only make additional money for you, but they also provide wonderful publicity for your book. There are actually two types of serial rights: first serial and second serial. First serial means the excerpt of the book is available *before* the book is printed. A second serial is an excerpt that appears *after* the book is already in bookstores. First serial rights are actually negotiable—sometimes the right to use them is kept by the agent. Usually an agent's decision is based upon her knowledge of the publications available in the book's subject. If she doesn't know the various magazines that focus on the book's topic, she will let the publisher have this right. Second serial rights, however, are almost always granted to the publisher.

Nonfiction books are more commonly excerpted than fiction. Nonfiction usually stands alone well, and magazines are always eager to use these excerpts because they usually cost less than hiring a freelancer to write original material. Recently, though, serialized fiction has regained popularity. Recently, John Grisham's *A Painted House* made a giant splash by appearing, in six installments, in *The Oxford American*. According to Marc Smirnoff, editor of *The Oxford American*, response to Grisham's story has been "overwhelming. I've heard from several people who think it is the best writing John has done. John wanted to challenge himself and we're always looking for exciting work to publish." Grisham's success will certainly create opportunities for other writers who want to have their novels serialized.

## RIGHTS NEGOTIATED BETWEEN THE AGENT AND PUBLISHER

The owner of these sub-rights is always determined when the book is sold. Often an agent and editor must compromise for these rights. In other words, an agent may agree to sell foreign rights if she can keep electronic rights. Or, an editor will offer more money if he can obtain the audio rights to a book.

## Foreign language rights

If your book might appeal to audiences in a nonEnglish-speaking country, then you'll want an agent who has good connections with foreign co-agents. According to agent James Vines of The Vines Agency, Inc., a "foreign co-agent is someone who specializes in the sales of foreign publishing rights and who has good relationships with the heads of publishing houses throughout the world. These agents work on behalf of a New York agency and approach the foreign publishers with manuscripts and proposals. They will typically have appointments booked at big trade shows like Frankfurt, London Book Fair, and BEA. That's where a lot of the big foreign deals happen." Usually an agent charges a 20 percent commission when a foreign co-agent is used, and the two split the earnings.

"All of my clients have benefited from the sale of foreign rights," continues Vines. For example, "*Kokology*, by Tadahiko Nagao and Isamu Saito started as a big phenomenon in Japan, selling over four million copies in Japan. A game you play about psychology, it's one of those ideas that crosses all languages and cultural boundaries because it's uniquely human—we all want to know more about ourselves." Vines sold the book to Simon & Schuster, then worked with a co-agent to sell it all over the world.

When agents are considering how a book will do abroad, they must be aware of trends in other countries. "Most agents try to stay on top of the foreign markets as much as possible and listen to what foreign co-agents have to say," says Vines. "Trends vary from territory to territory, and I try to keep those trends in mind." Vines also points out that writers can benefit from different sub-rights over a period of time depending on how well a sub-right is selling. "Three or four years ago we were selling more film rights than we are now—studios are not as hungry as they were. Interestingly, as their interest tapered off, the foreign interest increased."

Many publishing houses have foreign counterparts, and often an agent will grant the publisher these rights if she knows the book can be printed by one of these foreign houses. If the publisher has foreign language rights, the author receives an average of 75 percent of any money made when the book is sold to a foreign publisher—minus the agent's commission, of course.

## British rights

Like foreign language rights, the owner of a book's British rights can sell the book to publishers in England. Australia was once included in these rights, but Australian publishers are becoming more independent. If an agent keeps these rights, she will use a co-agent in England and the two will likely split a 20 percent commission. If a publisher has these rights, the traditional split is eighty/twenty with the author receiving the larger share.

## Electronic rights

Stephen King recently caused a big commotion in the publishing world first by using an electronic publisher for his book, *Riding the Bullet*, and then by using the Internet to self-publish his serialized novel, *The Plant*. Many publishing professionals worried that King would start a trend drawing writers away from publishers, while others claimed only high-profile writers like King could ever compete successfully against the vast amounts of information on the Web. Regardless, King's achievement showed that readers are paying attention to the Internet.

Basically, electronic rights refer to the hand-held electronic, Internet, and print-on-demand versions of a book. This right is currently one of the hottest points of contention between agents and publishers because the potential for these rights is unknown. It is quite possible that electronic versions of a book will make a lot of money one day.

This area of publishing is changing so rapidly that both agents and editors struggle with how to handle electronic rights. Many publishers believe any version of a book is the same material as the printed book, and, therefore, they should own the rights. Agents worry, however, that if the publisher lets the book go out of print, the rights to the book will never be returned to the author.

## Audio rights

Before people feared that the Internet would cause the end of traditional book publishing, people worried that audio versions of books would erase the need to have printed books. In actuality, audio books have complimented their printed counterparts and have proven to be a fantastic source of additional income for the person who owns the rights to produce the book in audio form—whether through cassette tape or compact disc.

Many publishers own audio imprints and even audio book clubs, and if they are successful with these ventures, an agent will likely grant the audio rights to the publisher. The traditional split is fifty/fifty. Otherwise, the agent will try to save this right and sell it to a company that can turn it into a profit.

## RIGHTS THE WRITER ALWAYS KEEPS

When a book is sold, an agent always reserves two rights for his authors: performance and merchandising. Some books are naturally more conducive to being made into films or products. And when those sub-rights are exploited, there is usually a lot of money to be made. And a smart agent can quickly identify when a book will be successful in these areas.

## Performance rights

Many writers fantasize about seeing their books on the big screen. And a lot of times, agents share this dream—especially for best-selling titles. If your agent feels your book will work well as a movie, or even as a television show or video game, she will sell these rights to someone in the entertainment industry. This industry works fairly differently than the publishing industry. Usually a producer "options" the right to make your book into a movie. An option means the producer can only make the movie during a specific amount of time, like one year. If the movie isn't made during that time period, the rights revert back to you. You can actually option these rights over and over—making money for every option—without the book ever being made into a movie. Keep in mind, however, that once your book has been optioned, you'll likely lose any say over issues of creative control until the option expires.

As with foreign rights, agents usually work with another agent to sell performance rights. Usually these agents live in Los Angeles and have the connections to producers that agents outside California just don't have. A 20 percent commission is the norm for performance rights, and the money is split between the two agents who partnered to sell these rights.

## Commercial/merchandising rights

Merchandising rights create products—like calendars, cards, action figures, stickers, dolls, and so on—that are based on characters or other elements of your book. Few books transfer well into such products, but they can be successful when they do. Keep in mind that if a producer options the performance rights to your book, the merchandising rights are usually included in the deal.

Agent Steven Malk, of Writers House, made wonderful use of these two rights for his client, Elise Primavera, and her book, *Auntie Claus* (Silver Whistle/Harcourt). According to Malk, "When I first read the manuscript of *Auntie Claus* and saw a couple of Primavera's sample illustrations, I immediately knew the book had a lot of possibilities in the sub-rights realm. First of all, the character of Auntie Claus is extremely memorable and unique, and, from a visual standpoint, she's stunning. Also, the basic concept of the book is completely fresh and original, which is very hard to accomplish with a Christmas book.

"The first thing I did was to approach Saks Fifth Avenue with the idea of featuring *Auntie*

*Claus* in their Christmas windows. In addition to using the book as the theme for their window displays, they created some merchandise that was sold through Saks. It's a perfect project for them; the character of Auntie Claus is so sophisticated and refined, she seemed ideal for their windows.

"Shortly after that, the movie rights were optioned by Nickelodeon with Wendy Finerman attached as a producer—she produced *Forrest Gump* and *Stepmom*. Nickelodeon is currently developing the project, and, when it's released, more merchandise will likely follow."

Like Malk did for Primavera, many agents successfully exploit subsidiary rights every day. If you want the most for your book, look for an agent who has the know-how and connections to take your publishing dream beyond the book and to its fullest potential.

# Scam Alert!

**BY RACHEL VATER**

If you were going into business with another person, you'd make sure you knew him, felt comfortable with him, had the same vision as he did—and that he'd never had trouble with the law or a history of bankruptcy, wouldn't you? As obvious as this sounds, many writers take for granted that any agent who expresses interest in their work is trustworthy. They'll sign a contract before asking any questions, cross their fingers for luck, and simply hope everything will turn out okay.

But don't fall into this trap. Doing a little research ahead of time can save you a lot of frustration later. So how do you check up on an agent? How do you spot a scam before you're already taken in by it?

## BEFORE YOU SUBMIT

First, research the agency itself. What kind of reputation does it have? If it's a well-established literary agency, and all the agents are AAR members, you should be safe from scams. All AAR members are required to abide by a certain code of ethics, and they are not permitted to charge any fees to writers. Even if an agent is not a member of AAR, he should not be charging fees to his clients. His salary should be earned exclusively with commissions. If you feel he may be violating the code of ethics, you can contact the AAR at www.aar-online.org or by writing to: The Association of Authors' Representatives, Inc. P.O. Box 237201, Ansonia Station, New York, NY 10003.

A writer should never pay any fees to an agent, including reading fees, retainers, marketing fees, or submission fees. And rather than paying an agent for a critique service, join a writers group. Invest your time instead of your money. Give feedback to others in exchange for their feedback to you. Then, when you feel your book is in the best possible shape it can be in, ask an English teacher or editor friend to read it over for you.

## BEFORE YOU SIGN

If you have any concerns about the agency's practices, ask the agent about them before you sign. Once an agent is interested in representing you, he should be willing to answer any questions or concerns that you have. If he is rude or unresponsive, or tries to tell you that the information is confidential or classified, the agent is uncommunicative at best and, at worst, is already trying to hide something from you.

An agent should be willing to discuss his recent sales with you: how many, what type of books, and to what publishers. If it's a new agent without a track record, be aware that you're taking more of a risk signing with him than with a more established agent. However, even a new agent should not be new to publishing. Many agents were editors before they were agents, or they worked at an agency as an assistant. This experience in publishing is crucial for making contacts in the publishing industry and learning about rights and contracts. So ask him how long he's been an agent and what he did before becoming an agent. Ask him to name a few editors he thinks may be interested in your work and why they sprang to mind. Has he sold to them before? Do they publish books in your genre?

If an agent has no contacts in the business, he has no more clout than you do yourself. Without publishing prowess, he's just an expensive mailing service. Anyone can make photocopies, slide them into an envelope and address them to "Editor," but without a contact name and a familiar return address on the envelope—or a phone call from a trusted colleague letting an editor know it's on the way and why it's a perfect fit for her publisher—it will land in the slush pile with all the other submissions that don't have representation. And you can do your own mailings with higher priority than such an agent could.

Occasionally, an agent will charge for the cost of photocopies, postage, and long-distance phone calls made on your behalf. This is acceptable as long as he keeps an itemized account of the expenses and you've agreed on a ceiling cost. Be sure to talk over any expenses you don't understand until you have a clear grasp of what you're paying for. Other times, an agent will recognize the value of the content of your work, but will recommend hiring an editor to revise it before he is comfortable submitting it to publishers. In this case, you may find an editor (someone with references you'll check) who understands your subject matter or genre and has some experience getting manuscripts into shape. Occasionally, if your story is exceptional or your ideas and credentials are marketable, but your writing needs help, you will work with a ghostwriter or co-author who will share a percentage of your commission or work with you at an agreed upon cost per hour.

An agent may refer you to editors he knows, but you may instead choose to find an editor in your area you've selected for yourself. Many editors do freelance work and would be happy to help you with your writing project. Of course, before entering into an agreement, make sure you know what you'll be getting for your money. Ask the editor for writing samples, references, or critiques he's done in the past. Make sure you feel comfortable working with him before you give him your business.

An honest agent will not make any money for referring you to an editor.

Some agents claim that charging a reading fee cuts down on the number of submissions they receive, and while that is a very real possibility, I recommend writers work with nonfee-charging agents if at all possible. Nonfee-charging agents have a stronger incentive to sell your work. After all, until they make a sale, they don't make a dime.

Agencies who charge fees don't have the same urgency to sell your work. If you do the math, you can see how much money they're bringing in without selling anything: If an agency has 300 clients, each sending in quarterly marketing fees of $100, the agent is making $400 a year from each client. That's $120,000 a year—and that doesn't include the reading fees or any other fees they collect.

## AFTER YOU'VE SIGNED

Periodically, you should ask your agent for a full report of where your manuscript has been sent including the publishing house and the editor he sent it to. Then, contact a few of the editors/publishers on the list and see if they know your agent and have a strong working relationship with him.

If the agent has ever successfully sold anything to her before (or at least sent her some promising work before), an editor should remember his name. It's a small world in publishing, and news of an agent's reputation spreads very fast.

But this industry is all about contacts, and if you can't find a worthy agent to do this for you, it's entirely possible to do it yourself. Think about it: the agent was once an unknown too. He or she made first contact by knocking on doors or schmoozing it up at conferences. You can do this too. The doors aren't locked to outsiders—they're just harder to find.

It might seem like making toast before baking the bread, but if you can find an interested editor, publisher or producer at a conference or by referral, she can probably recommend an agent to you, or you can choose one yourself based on reputation. If you mention a credible person interested in your work, any agent would be delighted to take over the contract negotiations for you. And letting a legitimate agent haggle over your contract for you instead of going at it yourself will help you keep your rights and negotiate the best advance.

Not everyone has this gift for making contacts, so many writers must rely on agents for the

## If you've been scammed . . .

. . . or if you're trying to prevent a scam, the following resources should be of help:

Contact The Federal Trade Commission, Bureau of Consumer Protection (CRC-240, Washington DC 20580, 1-877-FTC-HELP(382-4357)). While they won't resolve individual consumer problems, the FTC depends on your complaints to help them investigate fraud, and your speaking up may even lead to law enforcement action. Contact them by mail or phone, or visit their website at www.ftc.gov.

Volunteer Lawyers for the Arts (1 E. 53rd St., New York NY 10022) is a group of volunteers from the legal profession who assist with questions of law pertaining to the arts, all fields. You can phone their hotline at (212)319-ARTS (2787), ext. 9 and have your questions answered for the price of the phone call. For further information you can also visit their website at www.vlany.org.

Better Business Bureau (check local listings or visit www.bbb.org)—the folks to contact if you have a complaint or if you want to investigate a publisher, literary agent or other business related to writing and writers.

It's also recommended that you contact your state's attorney general with information about scamming activity. Don't know your attorney general's name? Go to www.attorneygeneral.gov/ags. Here you'll find a wealth of contact information, including a complete list of links to the attorney general's website for each state.

agents' pre-existing contacts. The trouble is, unless you know the agent's track record, you're taking his word for it that he indeed *has* these contacts. If he doesn't, even if he lives right there in California, he's no more able to sell your work for you than you are, even if you're living in Massachusetts. So check out his references and make sure he's made *recent* sales with *legitimate* publishers or production companies.

As a side note, agents *should* return their clients' phone calls or e-mails quickly and keep them informed about prospects. An agent should also consult his clients about any offers before accepting or rejecting them.

## IF YOU'VE BEEN SCAMMED

If you have trouble with your agent, and you've already tried to resolve it yourself to no avail, it may be time to call for help. Please alert the writing community to protect others. If you find agents online, in directories, or in this book who aren't living up to their promises or are charging you money when they're listed as nonfee-charging agents, please let the webmaster or editor of the publication know. Sometimes they can intervene for an author, and if no solution can be found, they can at the very least remove a listing from their directory so that no other authors will be scammed in the future. All efforts are made to keep scam artists out, but in a world where agencies are bought and sold, a reputation can change overnight.

If you have complaints about any business you can call the Better Business Bureau to report them. The BBB will at least file it, and that way, if anyone contacts the BBB before dealing with the business, the BBB will inform them that there are unresolved complaints against the business. Their website is www.bbb.org, or you may send a written complaint to: The Council of Better Business Bureaus, 4200 Wilson Blvd., Suite 800, Arlington, VA 22203-1838. Or call (703)276-0100 or fax them at (703)525-8277.

Finally, legal action may seem like a drastic step, but people do it sometimes. You can file a suit with the Attorney General and try to find some other people who want to sue for fraud with you. The Science Fiction Writers of America website, www.sfwa.org, offers sound advice on recourse you can take in these situations. (See this page for further details: www.sfwa.org/beware/overview.html.)

If you live in the same state as your agent, it may be possible to settle the score in small claims court, a viable option for collecting smaller damages and a way to avoid lawyer fees. The jurisdiction of the small claims court includes cases in which the claim is $5,000 or less (this varies from state to state, but should still cover the amount you're suing for.) Keep in mind suing takes a lot of effort and time. You'll have to research all the necessary legal steps. If you have lawyers in your family, that could be a huge benefit if they'll agree to help you organize your case, but legal assistance is not necessary.

And authors occasionally do fight back and win. For instance, in a case against an agent named Dorothy Deering, many scammed authors came together to testify against her literary agency. After bilking writers out of millions of dollars, she was found guilty of fraud, and she's now in prison.

Some authors have been taken for more money than you can imagine. Promises of publication made them write checks for thousands of dollars. This can be one of the most frustrating roadblocks on the path to publication, leaving authors feeling betrayed and angry.

## MOVING ON AND STARTING AGAIN

Above all, if you've been scammed, don't waste time blaming yourself. It's not your fault if someone lies to you. In cases like this, it's good to believe in karma. People who do good, who are kind, who help you—they will be rewarded. People who scam, cheat, lie and steal—they

---

### Warning signs! Beware of:

- Excessive typos or poor grammar in an agent's correspondence.
- A form letter accepting you as a client, praising generic things about your book that could apply to any book. An agent should call or send a personalized letter. A good agent doesn't take on a new client very often, so when she does, it's a special occasion that warrants a personal note or phone call.
- Unprofessional contracts that ask you for money upfront, contain clauses you haven't discussed, or are covered with amateur clip-art or silly borders.
- Rudeness when you inquire about any points you're unsure of. Don't employ any business partner who doesn't treat you with respect, as an equal.
- Pressure, by way of threats, bullying, or bribes. A good agent is not desperate to represent more clients. He invites worthy authors, but leaves the final decision up to them.
- Promises of publication. No agent can guarantee you a sale. Not even the top agents sell everything they choose to represent. They can only send your work to the most appropriate places, have it read with priority, and negotiate you a better contract if a sale does happen.
- A print-on-demand book contract or any contract offering you no advance. You can sell your own book to an e-publisher any time you wish without an agent's help. An agent should pursue traditional publishing routes with respectable advances. (There are a few exceptions: Some larger publishing houses are developing new lines of e-books, but they also offer fair advances.)

These websites may be of further interest to you:
http://www.sff.net/people/alicia/artscam.htm
http://www.writer.org/scamkit.htm
http://www.sfwa.org/writing/agents.htm

will get what's coming to them. It might take a while for their actions to catch up to them, and you might wonder how they can even look at themselves in the mirror without feeling overwhelming guilt, but they'll get theirs. Money doesn't buy happiness or fulfillment, and at the end of the day, they have to live with what they've done. Meanwhile, you'll keep writing and believing in yourself. You'll be able to face yourself in the mirror. One day, you'll see your work in print and you'll tell everyone what a rough road it was to get there, but how you wouldn't trade it for anything in the world.

Because writing is a part of us. It's what we do, what we love. And sometimes, it's how we make sense of the world and come to understand events in our lives and heal from them. And without our consent, no one can break our spirit or take that away from us.

# What to Ask—and Not Ask—an Agent

If an agent is interested in representing your work, congratulations! Nevertheless, you may have some concerns about whether this agent is the best person for you. The following is a list of appropriate questions to ask an agent who offers you a contract. Because an agent is busy, you'll want to pick only five or six of the questions most important to you to ask.

These are questions you ask only *after* the agent agrees to take you on as a client. In other words, don't take up the agent's time with these questions if you are only considering sending the agent a query letter. Also listed below are questions that you'll want to avoid asking—doing so may cause an agent to doubt your professionalism.

## Do ask:

1) What about my work interests you?
2) What can I do to be a good client?
3) Who are some other authors you represent and what are examples of recent sales you've made for those authors?
4) How much career guidance do you give clients?
5) Are you interested in representing me for this one title or throughout my writing career?
6) What is your commission? Does your commission change if you use a foreign or film co-agent?
7) Do you charge clients for office expenses? If so, what is your policy? Do you have a ceiling amount for such expenses?
8) Do you charge any other fees (i.e., reading fee, critiquing fee)?
9) What are your agency's strengths?
10) How often should I expect to be in contact with you?
11) Will you show me rejections from publishers if I request them?
12) Will you consult with me before accepting any offer?
13) Do you work with independent publicists?
14) What are your policies if, for whatever reason, we decided to part company?
15) Do you offer a written contract? If not, what legal provisions can be made to avoid any misunderstandings between us?

For a list of further questions recommended by the Association of Authors' Representatives, go to www.aar-online.org.

## Don't ask:

1) What are some recent advances you've negotiated for your clients?
2) Can I have the phone numbers for some of your clients to use as references?
3) Can you call me at this specific time?
4) How much money are you going to get for my book?
5) Who do I need to talk to in order to get my book made into a movie?

## Listing Policy and Complaint Procedure

Listings in *Guide to Literary Agents* are compiled from detailed questionnaires, phone interviews, and information provided by agents. The industry is volatile, and agencies change frequently. We rely on our readers for information on their dealings with agents and changes in policies or fees that differ from what has been reported to the editor of this book. Write to us if you have new information, questions, or problems dealing with the agencies listed.

Listings are published free of charge and are not advertisements. Although the information is as accurate as possible, the listings are *not* endorsed or guaranteed by the editor or publisher of *Guide to Literary Agents*. If you feel you have not been treated fairly by an agent or representative listed in *Guide to Literary Agents*, we advise you to take the following steps:

☑ First try to contact the agency. Sometimes one phone call or a letter can clear up the matter.

☑ Document all your correspondence with the agency. When you write to us with a complaint, provide the name of your manuscript, the date of your first contact with the agency and the nature of your subsequent correspondence.

☑ We will enter your letter into our files and attempt to contact the agency.

☑ The number, frequency, and severity of complaints will be considered in our decision whether or not to delete the listing from the next edition.

*Guide to Literary Agents* reserves the right to exclude any agency for any reason.

# Markets

## Literary Agents

Agents listed in this section generate 98 to 100 percent of their income from commission on sales. They do not charge for reading, critiquing, or editing. Sending a query to a nonfee-charging agent means you pay only the cost of postage to have your work considered by an agent with an imperative to find salable manuscripts: Her income depends on finding the best publisher for your manuscript.

Because her time is more profitably spent meeting with editors, she will have little or no time to critique your writing. Agents who don't charge fees must be selective and often prefer to work with established authors, celebrities, or those with professional credentials in a particular field.

Some agents in this section may charge clients for office expenses such as photocopying, foreign postage, long distance phone calls, or express mail services. Make sure you have a clear understanding of what these expenses are before signing any agency agreement. While most agents deduct expenses from the advance or royalties before passing them on to the author, a few agents included in this section charge their clients a one-time "marketing" or "handling" fee up front. These agents have a ( $ ) preceding their listing.

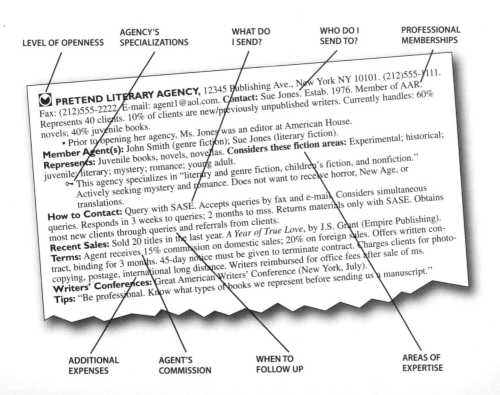

LEVEL OF OPENNESS / AGENCY'S SPECIALIZATIONS / WHAT DO I SEND? / WHO DO I SEND TO? / PROFESSIONAL MEMBERSHIPS

ADDITIONAL EXPENSES / AGENT'S COMMISSION / WHEN TO FOLLOW UP / AREAS OF EXPERTISE

## Quick Reference Icons

At the beginning of each listing, you will find one or more of the following symbols to help you quickly identify features particular to that listing.

**N:** Agency new to this edition.

☑ Change in address, contact information or phone number from last year's edition.

$ Agents who charge fees to previously unpublished writers only.

▣ Agents who make sales to electronic publishers. For more information on this topic, read "The Flight to Quantity: Will the Internet Ruin It for Everybody" on page 51.

⧮ Canadian agency.

⊕ International agency.

## Level of Openness

Each agency has an icon indicating its openness to submissions. Before contacting any agency, check the listing to make sure it is open to new clients.

◻ Newer agency actively seeking clients.

◑ Agency seeking both new and established writers.

◒ Agency prefers to work with established writers, mostly obtains new clients through referrals.

◎ Agency handling only certain types of work or work by writers under certain circumstances.

⊘ Agency not currently seeking new clients. We include these agencies to let you know they are currently not open to new clients. *Unless you have a strong recommendation from someone well respected in the field, our advice is to avoid approaching these agents.*

For quick reference, a chart of these icons and their meanings is printed on the inside covers of this book.

Canadian and International agents are included in this section. Canadian agents have a ( ⧮ ) preceding their listing while International agents have a ( ⊕ ) preceding their listing. Remember to include an International Reply Coupon (IRC) with your self-addressed envelope when contacting Canadian and International agents.

## SUBHEADS

Each listing is broken down into subheads to make locating specific information easier. In the first section, you'll find contact information for each agency. You'll also learn if they belong to any professional organizations which can tell you a lot about an agency. For example, members of the Association of Authors' Representatives (AAR) are prohibited from charging reading or evaluating fees. (An explanation of all organizations' acronyms is available on page 321.) Further information is provided which indicates an agency's size, its willingness to work with a new or previously unpublished writer, and its general areas of interest.

**Member Agents:** Agencies comprised of more than one agent list member agents and their individual specialties to help you determine the most appropriate person for your query letter.

**Represents:** Here agencies specify what nonfiction and fiction subjects they consider. Make sure you query only agents who represent the type of material you write. To help narrow your search, check the **Agents Specialties Index** in the back of the book.

⚬┰ Look for the key icon to quickly learn an agent's areas of specialization or specific strengths (i.e., editorial or marketing experience, sub-rights expertise, etc.). Agents mention here what specific areas they are currently seeking as well as subjects they do *not* wish to receive.

**How to Contact:** Most agents open to submissions prefer initially to receive a query letter briefly describing your work. (See "Queries That Made It Happen" on page 47.) Some agents ask for an outline and a number of sample chapters, but you should send these only if requested to do so. Here agents also mention if they accept queries by fax or e-mail, if they consider simultaneous submissions, and their preferred way of meeting new clients.

**Recent Sales:** To give a sense of the types of material they represent, agents provide specific titles they've sold as well as a sampling of clients' names. Some agents consider their client list confidential and may only share names once they agree to represent you.

**Terms:** Provided here are details of an agent's commission, whether a contract is offered and for how long, and what additional office expenses you might have to pay if the agent agrees to represent you. Standard commissions range from 10 to 15 percent for domestic sales, and 15 to 20 percent for foreign or dramatic sales with the difference going to the co-agent who places the work.

**Writers' Conferences:** A great way to meet an agent is at a writers' conference. Here agents list the ones they attend. For more information about a specific conference, check the **Writers' Conferences** section starting on page 287.

**Reading List:** Learn what magazines and journals agents read to discover potential clients.

**Tips:** Agents offer advice and additional instructions for writers looking for representation.

---

### For More Information

For a detailed explanation of the agency listings and for more information on approaching agents, read "Reading the Listings in the *Guide to Literary Agents*" and "How to Find the Right Agent." Be sure to read the several informative articles at the beginning of this book to fully understand the process a writer should go through when finding a literary agent.

---

## SPECIAL INDEXES TO HELP YOUR SEARCH

**Additional Nonfee-charging Agents:** Many literary agents are also interested in scripts; many script agents will also consider book manuscripts. Nonfee-charging script agents who primarily sell scripts but also handle at least 10 to 15 percent book manuscripts appear among the listings in this section, with the contact information, breakdown of work currently handled, and a note to check the full listing in the script section. Those nonfee-charging script agencies that sell scripts and less than 10 to 15 percent book manuscripts may not appear in this section. Complete listings for these agents appear in the Script Agents section.

**Agents Specialties Index:** In the back of the book on page 325 is an index which organizes agencies according to the subjects they are interested in receiving. This index should help you compose a list of agents specializing in your areas. Cross-referencing categories and concentrating on agents interested in two or more aspects of your manuscript might increase your chances of success. Agencies open to all nonfiction or fiction topics are grouped under the subject heading "open."

**Agencies Indexed by Openness to Submissions:** This index lists agencies according to their receptivity to new clients.

**Geographic Index:** For writers looking for an agent close to home, this index lists agents state-by-state.

**Agents Index:** Often you will read about an agent who is an employee of a larger agency and you may not be able to locate her business phone or address. Starting on page 380 is a list of agents' names in alphabetical order along with the name of the agency they work for. Find the name of the person you would like to contact, then check the agency listing.

**Listing Index:** This index lists all agencies, independent publicists, and writers' conferences listed in the book.

# NONFEE-CHARGING AGENTS

**A.L.P. LITERARY AGENCY, Authors Launching Pad**, P.O. Box 5069, Redwood City CA 94063. (415)326-6918. Fax: (415)326-6918. **Contact:** Devorah B. Harris. Estab. 1997. Represents 8-12 clients. 40% of clients are new/unpublished writers. Currently handles: 55% nonfiction books; 30% novels; 15% scholarly books.

• Prior to becoming an agent, Ms. Harris spent 9 years at Harper & Row, Scott Foresman, Little Brown and was a longtime member of The LOFT, "the place for literature and the arts in the Midwest."

**Represents:** Nonfiction books; novels. **Considers these nonfiction areas:** agriculture/horticulture; americana; animals; anthropology/archaeology; art/architecture/design; biography/autobiography; business/economics; child guidance/parenting; computers/electronic; cooking/foods/nutrition; crafts/hobbies; creative nonfiction; current affairs; education; ethnic/cultural interests; gardening; gay/lesbian issues; government/politics/law; health/medicine; history; how-to; humor/satire; interior design/decorating; juvenile nonfiction; language/literature/criticism; memoirs; military/war; money/finance; multicultural; music/dance; nature/environment; New Age/metaphysics; philosophy; photography; popular culture; psychology; recreation; regional; religious/inspirational; science/technology; self-help/personal improvement; sex; sociology; software; spirituality; sports; theater/film; translation; travel; true crime/investigative; women's issues/studies; young adult. **Considers these fiction areas:** feminist; humor/satire; literary; regional; religious/inspirational; romance.

Oₓ Actively seeking "fresh, juicy new titles from previously published authors. We love books that have regional flavors." Does not want to receive children's books and science fiction.

**How to Contact:** Submit outline, 1-2 sample chapter(s). Responds in 1 month to queries; 1 month to mss. Obtains most new clients through recommendations from others.

**Recent Sales:** New agency with pending sales.

**Terms:** Offers written contract, binding for life of the book or until termination; 1 month notice must be given to terminate contract. Charges clients for photocopying, phone calls and mailing expenses "only if incurred and not to exceed over $300."

**Tips:** "Let your cover letter be brief—that it may be an irresistable invitation to the rest of your writing."

**CAROLE ABEL LITERARY AGENT**, 160 W. 87th St., New York NY 10024. Member of AAR. This agency did not respond to our request for information. Query before submitting.

**ACACIA HOUSE PUBLISHING SERVICES LTD.**, 51 Acacia Road, Toronto, Ontario M4S 2K6, Canada. (416)484-8356. Fax: (416)484-8356. **Contact:** (Ms.) Frances Hanna. Estab. 1985. Represents 50 clients. Works with a small number of new/unpublished writers. Currently handles: 30% nonfiction books; 70% novels. Ms. Hanna has been in the publishing business for 30 years, first in London (UK) as a fiction editor with Barrie & Jenkins and Pan Books, and as a senior editor with a packager of mainly illustrated books. She was condensed books editor for 6 years for *Reader's Digest* in Montreal, senior editor and foreign rights manager for (the then) W.M. Collins & Sons (now HarperCollins) in Toronto. Her husband, Vice President Bill Hanna, has over 40 years experience in the publishing business.

**Member Agents:** Bill Hanna (business, self-help, modern history).

**Represents:** Nonfiction books; novels. **Considers these nonfiction areas:** animals; biography/autobiography; language/literature/criticism; memoirs; military/war; music/dance; nature/environment; theater/film; travel. **Considers these fiction areas:** action/adventure; detective/police/crime; literary; mainstream/contemporary; mystery/suspense; thriller.

Oₓ This agency specializes in contemporary fiction: literary or commercial. Actively seeking "outstanding first novels with literary merit." Does not want to receive horror, occult, science fiction.

**How to Contact:** Query with outline and SASE. *No unsolicited mss.* No e-mail or fax queries. Responds in 6 weeks to queries. Returns materials only with SASE.

**Recent Sales:** Sold 35 titles in the last year. Also made numerous international rights sales. This agency prefers not to share information on specific sales or clients.

**Terms:** Agent receives 15% commission on English language sales, 20% on dramatic sales, 25% commission on foreign sales. Charges clients for photocopying, postage and courier, as necessary.

**Tips:** "I prefer that writers be previously published, with at least a few articles to their credit. Strongest consideration will be given to those with, say, three or more published books. However, I *would* take on an unpublished writer of outstanding talent."

**AGENTS INC. FOR MEDICAL AND MENTAL HEALTH PROFESSIONALS**, P.O. Box 4956, Fresno CA 93744. (559)438-8289. Fax: (559)438-1883. **Contact:** Sydney H. Harriet, Ph.D., Psy. D., director. Estab. 1987. Member of APA. Represents 49 clients. 70% of clients are new/unpublished writers. Currently handles: 80% nonfiction books; 20% novels.

• Prior to opening his agency, Dr. Harriet was a professor of English, psychologist, and radio and television reporter.

**Represents:** Nonfiction books; novels. **Considers these nonfiction areas:** cooking/foods/nutrition; health/medicine (mind-body healing); psychology; science/technology; self-help/personal improvement; sociology; sports (medicine, psychology); law. **Considers these fiction areas:** *Currently representing previously published novelists only.*

> O—┓ This agency specializes in writers who have education and experience in the business, legal and health professions. It is helpful if the writer is licensed but not necessary. Prior nonfiction book publication not necessary. For fiction, previously published fiction is prerequisite for representation. Does not want memoirs, autobiographies, stories about overcoming an illness, science fiction, fantasy, religious materials and children's books.

**How to Contact:** Query with SASE. Considers simultaneous queries. Responds in 1 month to queries; 1 month to mss.

**Recent Sales:** Sold 5 titles in the last year. *Infantry Soldier*, by George Neil (University of Oklahoma Press); *SAMe, The European Arthritis and Depression Breakthrough*, by Sol Grazi, M.D. and Maria Costa (Prima); *What to Eat if You Have Diabetes*, by Danielle Chase M.S. (Contemporary).

**Terms:** Agent receives 15% commission on domestic sales; 20% commission on foreign sales. Offers written contract, binding for 6-12 months (negotiable).

**Writers' Conferences:** Scheduled as a speaker at a number of conferences across the country in 2001-2002. "Contact agency to book authors and agents for conferences."

**Tips:** "Remember, query first. Do not call to pitch an idea. The only way we can judge the quality of your idea is to see how you write. Please, unsolicited manuscripts will not be read if they arrive without a SASE. Currently we are receiving more than 200 query letters and proposals each month. Send complete proposal/manuscript only if requested. Please, please ask yourself why someone would be compelled to buy your book. If you think the idea is unique, spend the time to create a query and then a proposal where every word counts. Fiction writers need to understand that the craft is just as important as the idea. 99% of the fiction is rejected because of sloppy overwritten dialogue, wooden characters, predictable plotting and lifeless narrative. Once you finish your novel, put it away and let it percolate, then take it out and work on fine-tuning it some more. A novel is never finished until you stop working on it. Would love to represent more fiction writers and probably will when we read a manuscript that has gone through a dozen or more drafts. Because of rising costs, we no longer can respond to queries, proposals, and/or complete manuscripts without receiving a return envelope and sufficient postage."

**🛇$ ◐ THE AHEARN AGENCY, INC.**, 2021 Pine St., New Orleans LA 70118-5456. (504)861-8395. Fax: (504)866-6434. E-mail: pahearn@aol.com. **Contact:** Pamela G. Ahearn. Estab. 1992. Member of RWA. Represents 25 clients. 20% of clients are new/unpublished writers. Currently handles: 15% nonfiction books; 85% novels.

> • Prior to opening her agency, Ms. Ahearn was an agent for eight years and an editor with Bantam Books.

**Represents:** Nonfiction books; novels; short story collections (if stories previously published). **Considers these nonfiction areas:** animals; biography/autobiography; business/economics; child guidance/parenting; current affairs; ethnic/cultural interests; gay/lesbian issues; health/medicine; history; juvenile nonfiction; music/dance; popular culture; self-help/personal improvement; theater/film; true crime/investigative; women's issues/studies. **Considers these fiction areas:** action/adventure; contemporary issues; detective/police/crime; ethnic; family saga; fantasy; feminist; gay/lesbian; glitz; historical; horror; humor/satire; juvenile; literary; mainstream/contemporary; mystery/suspense; psychic/supernatural; regional; romance; science fiction; thriller; westerns/frontier.

> O—┓ This agency specializes in historical romance; also very interested in mysteries and suspense fiction. Does not want to receive category romance.

**How to Contact:** Query with SASE. Accepts e-mail queries, but no attachments. Considers simultaneous queries. Responds in 1 month to queries; 10 weeks to mss. Obtains most new clients through recommendations from others, solicitations, conferences.

**Recent Sales:** *Still of the Night*, by Meagan McKinney (Kensington); *A Notorious Love*, by Sabrina Jeffries (Avon); *Black Lotus*, by Laura Joh Rowland (St. Martin's Press).

**Terms:** Agent receives 15% commission on domestic sales; 20% commission on foreign sales. Offers written contract, binding for 1 year; renewable by mutual consent.

**Writers' Conferences:** Midwest Writers Workshop; Moonlight & Magnolias; RWA National Conference (Orlando); Virginia Romance Writers (Williamsburg VA); Florida Romance Writers (Ft. Lauderdale FL); Golden Triangle Writers Conference; Bouchercon (Monterey, November).

**Tips:** "Be professional! Always send in exactly what an agent/editor asks for, no more, no less. Keep query letters brief and to the point, giving your writing credentials and a very brief summary of your book. If one agent rejects you, keep trying—there are a lot of us out there!"

---

**THE PUBLISHING FIELD** is constantly changing! Agents often change addresses, phone numbers, or even companies. If you're still using this book and it is 2003 or later, buy the newest edition of *Guide to Literary Agents* at your favorite bookstore or order directly from Writer's Digest Books at (800)289-0963.

**ALIVE COMMUNICATIONS, INC.**, 7680 Goddard St., Suite 200, Colorado Springs CO 80920. (719)260-7080. Fax: (719)260-8223. Website: www.alivecom.com. **Contact:** Submissions Dept. Estab. 1989. Member of AAR, CBA. Represents 200+ clients. 5% of clients are new/unpublished writers. Currently handles: 50% nonfiction books; 30% novels; 4% story collections; 5% novellas; 10% juvenile books; 1% syndicated material.

**Member Agents:** Rick Christian, president (blockbusters, bestsellers); Greg Johnson (popular/commercial nonfiction and fiction, Christian organizations); Kathryn Helmers (popular/literary nonfiction and fiction, spirituality, memoir); Jerry "Chip" MacGregor (popular/commercial nonfiction and fiction, new authors with breakout potential); Linda Glasford (gift, women's fiction/nonfiction, Christian living); Lee Hough (popular/commercial nonfiction and fiction, thoughtful spirituality, children's).

**Represents:** Nonfiction books; novels; short story collections; novellas; juvenile books. **Considers these nonfiction areas:** biography/autobiography; business/economics; child guidance/parenting; how-to; religious/inspirational; self-help/personal improvement; sports; women's issues/studies. **Considers these fiction areas:** action/adventure; contemporary issues; detective/police/crime; family saga; historical; humor/satire; juvenile; literary; mainstream/contemporary; mystery/suspense; religious/inspirational; thriller; westerns/frontier; young adult.

O→ This agency specializes in fiction, Christian living, how-to, children's and commercial nonfiction. Actively seeking inspirational/literary/mainstream fiction and work from authors with established track record and platforms. Does not want poetry, young adult paperback, scripts, dark themes.

**How to Contact:** Submit outline, 3 sample chapter(s), résumé, publishing history, SASE. No e-mail or fax queries. Considers simultaneous queries. Responds in 2 weeks to queries; 1 month to mss. Returns materials only with SASE. Obtains most new clients through recommendations from clients and publishers.

**Recent Sales:** Sold 300 titles in the last year. *Left Behind series*, Tim LaHaye and Jerry B. Jenkins (Tyndale); *Jerusalem Heart*, Bodie and Brock Thoene (Viking); *Soul Survivor*, Philip Yancey (Doubleday); *Paul*, by Walter Wangesin (Zondervan).

**Terms:** Agent receives 15% commission on domestic sales; 25% commission on foreign sales. Offers written contract; 60-day written notice notice must be given to terminate contract.

**Reading List:** Reads literary, religious, and mainstream journals to find new clients. "Our goal is always the same—. to find writers whose use of language is riveting and powerful."

**Tips:** "Rewrite and polish until the words on the page shine. Provide us with as much personal and publishing history information as possible. Endorsements and great connections may help, provided you can write with power and passion. Alive Communications, Inc. has established itself as a première literary agency. Based in Colorado Springs, we serve an elite group of authors and speakers who are critically acclaimed and commercially successful in both Christian and general markets."

**LINDA ALLEN LITERARY AGENCY**, 1949 Green St., Suite 5, San Francisco CA 94123-4829. (415)921-6437. **Contact:** Linda Allen or Amy Kossow. Estab. 1982. Member of AAR. Represents 35-40 clients.

**Represents:** Nonfiction books; novels (adult). **Considers these nonfiction areas:** anthropology/archaeology; art/architecture/design; biography/autobiography; business/economics; child guidance/parenting; computers/electronic; ethnic/cultural interests; gay/lesbian issues; government/politics/law; history; music/dance; nature/environment; popular culture; psychology; sociology; women's issues/studies. **Considers these fiction areas:** action/adventure; detective/police/crime; ethnic; feminist; gay/lesbian; glitz; horror; literary; mainstream/contemporary; mystery/suspense; psychic/supernatural; regional; thriller.

O→ This agency specializes in "good books and nice people."

**How to Contact:** Query with SASE. Considers simultaneous queries. Responds in 3 weeks to queries. Returns materials only with SASE. Obtains most new clients through recommendations from others.

**Recent Sales:** This agency prefers not to share information on specific sales.

**Terms:** Agent receives 15% commission on domestic sales. Charges for photocopying.

**ALLRED AND ALLRED LITERARY AGENTS**, 7834 Alabama Ave., Canoga Park CA 91304-4905. (818)346-4313. **Contact:** Robert Allred. Estab. 1991. Represents 5 clients. 100% of clients are new/unpublished writers. Currently handles: nonfiction books; novels; movie scripts; TV scripts.

● Prior to opening his agency, Mr. Allred was a writer, assistant producer, associate director and editorial assistant.

**Member Agents:** Robert Allred (all); Kim Allred (all).

**Represents:** Nonfiction books; novels; short story collections; juvenile books; scholarly books; textbooks. **Considers these fiction areas:** action/adventure; confession; detective/police/crime; ethnic; family saga; fantasy; feminist; gay/lesbian; glitz; historical; horror; humor/satire; juvenile; literary; mainstream/contemporary; mystery/suspense; psychic/supernatural; regional; religious/inspirational; romance (contemporary, gothic, historical, regency); science fiction; sports; thriller; westerns/frontier; young adult. **Considers these nonfiction areas:** anthropology/archaeology; art/architecture/design; biography/autobiography; cooking/foods/nutrition; crafts/hobbies; current affairs; education; ethnic/cultural interests; health/medicine; history; how-to; humor/satire; interior design/decorating; juvenile nonfiction; language/literature/criticism; military/war; music/dance; New Age/metaphysics; photography; popular culture; psychology; religious/inspirational; science/technology; self-help/personal improvement; sociology; sports; theater/film; true crime/investigative; women's issues/studies.

**Also Handles:** Feature film; TV movie of the week; episodic drama; sitcom; animation; documentary; soap opera; syndicated material; variety show. **Considers these script subject areas:** action/adventure; biography/autobiography; cartoon/animation; comedy; contemporary issues; detective/police/crime; erotica; ethnic; experimental; family saga;

fantasy; feminist; gay/lesbian; glitz; historical; horror; juvenile; mainstream; multicultural; multimedia; mystery/suspense; psychic/supernatural; regional; religious/inspirational; romantic comedy; romantic drama; science fiction; sports; teen; thriller; western/frontier.

**How to Contact:** Query with SASE. Book: Submit first 25 pages. Script: send entire script. Include 1-2 page synopsis and SASE. No e-mail or fax queries. Considers simultaneous queries. Responds in 3 weeks to queries; 2 months to mss. Returns materials only with SASE. Obtains most new clients through recommendations from others, solicitations.

**Recent Sales:** Sold 5 titles in the last year. *Diamond in the Rough*, by Richard Blacke (Wide Western); *by Red Rose, White Rose*, Betty Stuart (Sunset Publications).

**Terms:** Agent receives 10% commission on domestic sales; 10% commission on foreign sales. Offers written contract, binding for 1 year. 100% of business is derived from commissions on ms sales.

**Tips:** "The synopsis must cover the entire length of the project from beginning to end. A professional appearance in script format, dark and large type, and simple binding go a long way to create good first impressions in this business, as does a professional business manner. We must be able to at least estimate the potential of the whole project before we can expend the time reading it in its entirety. Writers who try to sell us with overblown hyperbole or titillate our curiousity by vaguely hinting at a possible outcome do themselves a disservice; agents don't have time for reading sales copy—just tell us what it's about, and let us make the decision about whether we want to see the entire project."

**ALTAIR LITERARY AGENCY**, 141 Fifth Ave., Suite 8N, New York NY 10010. (212)505-3320. **Contact:** Nicholas Smith, partner. Estab. 1996. Member of AAR. Represents 75 clients. Currently handles: 95% nonfiction books; 3% novels; 2% juvenile books.

**Member Agents:** Andrea Pedolsky, partner; Nicholas Smith, partner.

**Represents:** Nonfiction books; novels. **Considers these nonfiction areas:** anthropology/archaeology; art/architecture/design; biography/autobiography; business/economics; ethnic/cultural interests; gay/lesbian issues; health/medicine; history; how-to; money/finance; music/dance; nature/environment; photography; popular culture; psychology; science/technology; self-help/personal improvement; sports; women's issues/studies; illustrated books; spirituality. **Considers these fiction areas:** historical; literary.

○ᵣ This agency specializes in nonfiction with an emphasis on authors who have a direct connection to their topic, and at least a moderate level of public exposure. Actively seeking solid, well-informed authors who have or are developing a public platform for the subject specialty. Interested in book to museum exhibition. Does not want true crime, memoirs, romance novels.

**How to Contact:** Query with SASE. Considers simultaneous queries. Responds in 3 weeks to queries; 1 month to mss. Obtains most new clients through recommendations from others, solicitations, author queries.

**Recent Sales:** *First You Shave Your Head*, by Geri Larkin (Ten Speed Press/Celestial Arts); *Being an Introvert in an Extrovert World*, by Marti Laney (Workman); *Facing the Fifties*, by Gordon Ehlers, M.D. and Jeffrey Miller (M. Evans & Co.); *Making Her Mark*, by Ernestine Miller (Contemporary Books).

**Terms:** Agent receives 15% commission on domestic sales; 20% commission on foreign sales. Offers written contract, binding for 1 year; 60-day notice must be given to terminate contract. Charges clients for photocopying (edits of the proposal/chapters/ms to author, copies of proposal for submissions), postage (correspondence to author, proposals for submission), and marketing book for translation rights. May refer writers to outside editor but receives no compensation for referral.

**Tips:** "Beyond being able to write a compelling book, have an understanding of the market issues that are driving publishing today."

**MIRIAM ALTSHULER LITERARY AGENCY**, 53 Old Post Rd. N., Red Hook NY 12571. (845)758-9408. Fax: (845)758-3118. E-mail: malalit@ulster.net. **Contact:** Miriam Altshuler. Estab. 1994. Member of AAR. Represents 40 clients. Currently handles: 45% nonfiction books; 45% novels; 5% story collections; 5% juvenile books.

● Ms. Altshuler has been an agent since 1982.

**Represents:** Nonfiction books; novels; short story collections; juvenile books. **Considers these nonfiction areas:** biography/autobiography; ethnic/cultural interests; history; language/literature/criticism; memoirs; multicultural; music/dance; nature/environment; popular culture; psychology; sociology; theater/film; women's issues/studies. **Considers these fiction areas:** literary; mainstream/contemporary; multicultural; thriller.

**How to Contact:** Query with SASE. Prefers to read materials exclusively. No e-mail or fax queries. Considers simultaneous queries. Responds in 2 weeks to queries; 3 weeks to mss. Returns materials only with SASE. Obtains most new clients through recommendations from others.

**Terms:** Agent receives 15% commission on domestic sales; 20% commission on foreign sales. No written contract. Charges clients for overseas mailing, photocopies, overnight mail when requested by author.

**Writers' Conferences:** Bread Loaf Writers' Conference (Middlebury VT, August).

**AMG/RENAISSANCE**, 140 W 57th St., 2nd Floor, New York NY 10019. (212)956-2600. West Coast Office: 9220 Sunset Blvd., Suite 302; Los Angeles CA 90069; (310)858-5365 **Contact:** Joel Gotler. Represents 200 clients and 25 literary estates. 10% of clients are new/unpublished writers. Currently handles: 90% novels; 5% movie scripts; 5% TV scripts; movie and TV rights to books.

**Member Agents:** Judy Fark (LA: film rights, screenwriters); Joel Gotler, partner (LA: film rights); Noah Lukeman (NY: book publishing); Alan Nevins, partner (LA: book publishing); Michael Prevett (LA: film rights); Irv Schwartz, partner (NY: film rights, screenwriters).

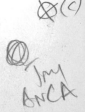

**Represents:** Nonfiction books; novels. **Considers these nonfiction areas:** biography/autobiography; history; theater/film; true crime/investigative. **Considers these fiction areas:** action/adventure; detective/police/crime; family saga; fantasy; historical; humor/satire; literary; mainstream/contemporary; mystery/suspense; science fiction; thriller.
**Also Handles: Considers these script subject areas:** action/adventure; cartoon/animation; comedy; contemporary issues; detective/police/crime; erotica; ethnic; experimental; family saga; fantasy; feminist; gay/lesbian; historical; horror; juvenile; mainstream; mystery/suspense; psychic/supernatural; regional; romantic comedy; romantic drama; science fiction; sports; teen; thriller; western/frontier.
  O─π This management company specializes in selling movies and TV rights from books.
**How to Contact:** Query via recommendations. Obtains most new clients through recommendations from others.
**Recent Sales:** *The Fall of the Soviet Union*, by Anthony Cave-Brown (Harcourt-Brace). *Movie/TV MOW script(s) optioned/sold: Fake Liar Cheat*, by Tod Goldberg (Miramax); *The Discrete Charm of Charlie Monk*, by David Ambrose (StudioCanal); *Sector Seven*, by David Wiesner (Nickelodeon/Good Machine). *Scripting Assignment(s): Without Remorse*, based on a novel by Tom Clancy, adapted by Ross Klavan; *Girl in Hyacinth Blue*, based on a novel by Susan Vreeland, adapted by Richard Russo.
**Terms:** Agent receives 15% commission on domestic sales; 15% commission on dramatic rights sales.

● **BETSY AMSTER LITERARY ENTERPRISES**, P.O. Box 27788, Los Angeles CA 90027-0788. **Contact:** Betsy Amster. Estab. 1992. Member of AAR. Represents over 50 clients. 35% of clients are new/unpublished writers. Currently handles: 65% nonfiction books; 35% novels.
  ● Prior to opening her agency, Ms. Amster was an editor at Pantheon and Vintage for 10 years and served as editorial director for the Globe Pequot Press for 2 years. "This experience gives me a wider perspective on the business and the ability to give focused editorial feedback to my clients."
**Represents:** Nonfiction books; novels. **Considers these nonfiction areas:** biography/autobiography; business/economics; child guidance/parenting; ethnic/cultural interests; gardening; health/medicine; history; money/finance; psychology; sociology; women's issues/studies; cyberculture. **Considers these fiction areas:** ethnic; literary.
  O─π Actively seeking "outstanding fiction (the next Jane Smiley or Wally Lamb) and high profile self-help/psychology." Does not want to receive poetry, children's books, romances, westerns, science fiction.
**How to Contact:** For fiction send query, first 3 pages and SASE. For nonfiction send query or proposal with SASE. For both. No e-mail or fax queries. Considers simultaneous queries. Responds in 1 month to queries; 2 months to mss. Obtains most new clients through recommendations from others, solicitations, conferences.
**Recent Sales:** *You're on Your Own (But I'm Here if You Need Me)*, by Marjorie Savage (Simon & Schuster); *The Memory Room*, by Mary Rakow (Counterpoint); *Driving to Garden City*, by Robin Chotzinoff (Algonquin); *Dogtionary* and *Cationary*, by Sharon Montrose (Viking Studio). Other clients include Wendy Mogel, Susan M. Wilson, E. Barrie Kavasch, Camille Landau & Tiare White.
**Terms:** Agent receives 15% commission on domestic sales. Offers written contract, binding for 1-2 years; 60 days notice must be given to terminate contract. Charges for photocopying, postage, long distance phone calls, messengers and galleys and books used in submissions to foreign and film agents and to magazines for first serial rights.
**Writers' Conferences:** Squaw Valley; Maui Writers Conference; Pacific Northwest Conference; San Diego Writers Conference; UCLA Writers Conference.

● **MARCIA AMSTERDAM AGENCY**, 41 W. 82nd St., New York NY 10024-5613. (212)873-4945. **Contact:** Marcia Amsterdam. Estab. 1970. Signatory of WGA. Currently handles: 15% nonfiction books; 70% novels; 5% movie scripts; 10% TV scripts.
  ● Prior to opening her agency, Ms. Amsterdam was an editor.
**Represents:** Nonfiction books; novels. **Considers these nonfiction areas:** child guidance/parenting; humor/satire; popular culture; self-help/personal improvement. **Considers these fiction areas:** action/adventure; detective/police/crime; horror; humor/satire; mainstream/contemporary; mystery/suspense; romance (contemporary, historical); science fiction; thriller; westerns/frontier; young adult.
**Also Handles:** Feature film; TV movie of the week; sitcom. **Considers these script subject areas:** comedy; mainstream; mystery/suspense; romantic comedy; romantic drama.
**How to Contact:** Submit outline, 3 sample chapter(s), SASE. Responds in 1 month to queries.
**Recent Sales:** *Rosey in the Present Tense*, by Louise Hawes (Walker); *Flash Factor*, by William H. Lovejoy (Kensington). *Movie/TV MOW script(s) optioned/sold: Mad About You*, by Jenna Bruce (Columbia Tristar TV).
**Terms:** Agent receives 15% commission on domestic sales; 20% commission on foreign sales; 10% commission on dramatic rights sales. Offers written contract, binding for 1 year. Charges clients for extra office expenses, foreign postage, copying, legal fees (when agreed upon).
**Tips:** "We are always looking for interesting literary voices."

● ◎ **BART ANDREWS & ASSOCIATES**, 7510 Sunset Blvd., Suite 100, Los Angeles CA 90046. (310)271-9916. **Contact:** Bart Andrews. Estab. 1982. Represents 25 clients. 25% of clients are new/unpublished writers. Currently handles: 100% nonfiction books.
**Represents:** Nonfiction books. **Considers these nonfiction areas:** biography/autobiography; music/dance; theater/film; TV.
  O─π This agency specializes in nonfiction only, and in the general category of entertainment (movies, TV, biographies, autobiographies).

**How to Contact:** Query with SASE. No e-mail or fax queries. Considers simultaneous queries. Responds in 1 week to queries; 1 month to mss.

**Recent Sales:** Sold 50 titles in the last year. *Roseanne*, by J. Randy Taraborrelli (G.P. Putnam's Sons); *Out of the Madness*, by Rose Books packaging firm (HarperCollins).

**Terms:** Agent receives 15% commission on domestic sales; 15% (after subagent takes his 10%) commission on foreign sales. Offers written contract. Charges clients for all photocopying, mailing, phone calls, postage, etc; Writers reimbursed for office fees after the sale of ms.

**Writers' Conferences:** Frequently lectures at UCLA in Los Angeles.

**Tips:** "Recommendations from existing clients or professionals are best, although I find a lot of new clients by seeking them out myself. I rarely find a new client through the mail. Spend time writing a query letter. Sell yourself like a product. The bottom line is writing ability, and then the idea itself. It takes a lot to convince me. I've seen it all! I hear from too many first-time authors who don't do their homework. They're trying to get a book published and they haven't the faintest idea what is required of them. There are plenty of good books on the subject and, in my opinion, it's their responsibility—not mine—to educate themselves before they try to find an agent to represent their work. When I ask an author to see a manuscript or even a partial manuscript, I really must be convinced I want to read it—based on a strong query letter—because of wasting my time reading just for the fun of it."

**ANUBIS LITERARY AGENCY**, 79 Charles Gardner Rd., Leamington Spa, Warwickshire CV313BG Great Britain. Phone: 01926 832644. Fax: 01926 311607. **Contact:** Steve Calcutt. Estab. 1994. Represents 21 clients. 50% of clients are new/unpublished writers. Currently handles: 100% novels.
- Prior to becoming an agent, Mr. Calcutt taught creative writing for Warwick University plus American history—US Civil War.

**Member Agents:** Maggie Heavey (crime); Steve Calcutt (horror/science fiction).

**Represents:** Novels. **Considers these fiction areas:** detective/police/crime; fantasy; historical; horror; science fiction.
- "We are very keen on developing talented new writers. We give support, encouragement and editorial guidance." Actively seeking crime fiction. Does not want to receive children's, nonfiction, journalism or TV/film scripts.

**How to Contact:** Query with SASE, submit proposal package, outline, IRCs. Retunrs materials only with SASE or IRCs. No e-mail or fax queries. Responds in 6 weeks to queries; 3 months to mss. Obtains most new clients through solicitations.

**Recent Sales:** *Salt*, by Adam Roberts (Orion); *Tread Softly*, by Georgie Hale (Hodder & Stoughton); *The Nature of Balance*, by Tim Lebbon (Leisure/Dorchester). Other clients include Richard Irvine, Steve Savile, D.J. Whitbread, Lesley Asquith.

**Terms:** Agent receives 15% commission on domestic sales; 20% commission on foreign sales. No written contract.

**APPLESEEDS MANAGEMENT**, 200 E. 30th St., Suite 302, San Bernardino CA 92404. (909)882-1667. **Contact:** S. James Foiles. Estab. 1988. 40% of clients are new/unpublished writers. Currently handles: 15% nonfiction books; 85% novels.

**Represents:** Nonfiction books; novels. **Considers these nonfiction areas:** true crime/investigative. **Considers these fiction areas:** detective/police/crime; mystery/suspense.

**How to Contact:** Query with SASE. Responds in 2 weeks to queries; 2 months to mss.

**Recent Sales:** This agency prefers not to share information on specific sales.

**Terms:** Agent receives 10-15% commission on domestic sales; 20% commission on foreign sales. Offers written contract, binding for 1-7 years.

**Tips:** "Appleseeds specializes in mysteries with a detective who could be in a continuing series because readership of mysteries is expanding."

**AUTHENTIC CREATIONS LITERARY AGENCY**, 875 Lawrenceville-Suwanee Rd.,, Suite 310-306, Lawrenceville GA 30043. (770)339-3774. Fax: (770)339-7126. E-mail: ron@authenticcreations.com. Website: www.authenticcreations.com. **Contact:** Mary Lee Laitsch. Estab. 1993. Represents 70 clients. 30% of clients are new/unpublished writers. Currently handles: 60% nonfiction books; 40% novels.
- Prior to becoming agents, Ms. Laitsch was a librarian and elementary school teacher; Mr. Laitsch was an attorney and a writer.

**Member Agents:** Mary Lee Laitsch; Ronald E. Laitsch.

**Represents:** Nonfiction books; novels; scholarly books. **Considers these nonfiction areas:** anthropology/archaeology; biography/autobiography; child guidance/parenting; crafts/hobbies; current affairs; history; how-to; science/technology; self-help/personal improvement; sports; true crime/investigative; women's issues/studies. **Considers these fiction areas:** action/adventure; contemporary issues; detective/police/crime; family saga; literary; mainstream/contemporary; mystery/suspense; romance; sports; thriller.

**How to Contact:** Query with SASE. No e-mail or fax queries. Considers simultaneous queries. Responds in 2 weeks to queries; 2 months to mss.

**Recent Sales:** Sold 15 titles in the last year. *Frankenstein—The Legacy* , by Christopher Schildt (Simon & Schuster); *Night of Dracula*, by Christopher Schildt (Simon & Schuster).

**Terms:** Agent receives 15% commission on domestic sales; 15% commission on foreign sales. Charges clients for photocopying.

**Tips:** "Service to our authors is the key to our success. We work with authors to produce a fine product for prospective publishers."

[N] [M] [O] **AUTHORS & ARTISTS GROUP, INC., (Specialized: celebrity autobiographies)**, 19 W. 44th St., New York NY 10036. (212)944-9898. Fax: (212)944-6484. **Contact:** Al Lowman, president. Estab. 1984. Represents 50 clients. 25% of clients are new/unpublished writers. Currently handles: 95% nonfiction books; 5% novels.
  • Prior to becoming an agent, Mr. Lowman was an advertising executive.
**Member Agents:** B.G. Dilworth (nonfiction); Al Lowman (president nonfiction).
**Represents:** Nonfiction books; novels. **Considers these nonfiction areas:** art/architecture/design; biography/autobiography; business/economics; child guidance/parenting; computers/electronic; cooking/foods/nutrition; crafts/hobbies; current affairs; education; ethnic/cultural interests; gay/lesbian issues; health/medicine; history; how-to; humor/satire; interior design/decorating; memoirs; money/finance; music/dance; nature/environment; New Age/metaphysics; photography; popular culture; psychology; religious/inspirational; science/technology; self-help/personal improvement; sociology; sports; true crime/investigative; women's issues/studies. **Considers these fiction areas:** action/adventure; contemporary issues; detective/police/crime; erotica; ethnic; gay/lesbian; horror; humor/satire; mainstream/contemporary; psychic/supernatural; religious/inspirational; thriller.
  ○─ This agency specializes in celebrity-based autobiographies and self-help books; and any books that bring its readers to "higher ground." Actively seeking fresh full-length, adult nonfiction ideas and established novelists. Does not want to receive film and TV scripts, children's stories, poetry or short stories.
**How to Contact:** Fax 1 page query. Considers simultaneous queries. Responds in 3 weeks to queries. Obtains most new clients through recommendations from others.
**Recent Sales:** Sold 20 titles in the last year. *Labelle Cuisine*, by Patti Labelle (Broadway); *Get Skinny on Fabulous Food*, by Suzanne Somers (Crown); *Forgive or Forget*, by Mother Love (HarperCollins). Other clients include Sarah, Duchess of York, Diana Ross, Mary Lou Retton.
**Terms:** Agent receives 15% commission on domestic sales; 20% commission on foreign sales. Charges clients for office expenses, postage, photocopying not to exceed $1,000 without permission of author.

[M] **THE AXELROD AGENCY**, 49 Main St., P.O. Box 357, Chatham NY 12037. (518)392-2100. Fax: (518)392-2944. E-mail: steve@axelrodagency.com. **Contact:** Steven Axelrod. Estab. 1983. Member of AAR. Represents 20-30 clients. 1% of clients are new/unpublished writers. Currently handles: 5% nonfiction books; 95% novels.
  • Prior to becoming an agent, Mr. Axelrod was a book club editor.
**Represents:** Nonfiction books; novels. **Considers these fiction areas:** mystery/suspense; romance; women's.
**How to Contact:** Query with SASE. Considers simultaneous queries. Responds in 3 weeks to queries; 6 weeks to mss. Returns materials only with SASE. Obtains most new clients through recommendations from others.
**Recent Sales:** This agency prefers not to share information on specific sales.
**Terms:** Agent receives 15% commission on domestic sales; 20% commission on foreign sales. No written contract.
**Writers' Conferences:** Romance Writers of America (July).

[O] **JULIAN BACH LITERARY AGENCY**, 22 E. 71st St., New York NY 10021. Member of AAR. This agency did not respond to our request for information. Query before submitting.

[O] **MALAGA BALDI LITERARY AGENCY**, 204 W. 84th St., Suite 3C, New York NY 10024. (212)579-5075. **Contact:** Malaga Baldi. Estab. 1985. Represents 40-50 clients. 80% of clients are new/unpublished writers. Currently handles: 60% nonfiction books; 40% novels.
  • Prior to becoming an agent, Malaga Baldi worked in a bookstore.
**Represents:** Nonfiction books; novels. **Considers these nonfiction areas:** agriculture/horticulture; animals; anthropology/archaeology; art/architecture/design; biography/autobiography; business/economics; cooking/foods/nutrition; current affairs; ethnic/cultural interests; gay/lesbian issues; government/politics/law; health/medicine; history; interior design/decorating; language/literature/criticism; memoirs; money/finance; music/dance; nature/environment; photography; psychology; science/technology; sociology; theater/film; travel; true crime/investigative; women's issues/studies. **Considers these fiction areas:** action/adventure; contemporary issues; detective/police/crime; erotica; ethnic; experimental; feminist; gay/lesbian; historical; literary; mainstream/contemporary; mystery/suspense; regional; thriller.
  ○─ This agency specializes in quality literary fiction and nonfiction. Actively seeking well-written fiction and nonfiction. Does not want to receive child guidance, crafts, juvenile nonfiction, New Age/metaphysics, sports, family saga, fantasy, glitz, juvenile fiction, picture book, psychic/supernatural, religious/inspirational, romance, science fiction, western or young adult.
**How to Contact:** Query with SASE. "Please enclose self-addressed stamped jiffy bag or padded envelope with submission. For acknowledgement of manuscript receipt send via certified mail or UPS." No e-mail or fax queries. Considers simultaneous queries. Responds after a minimum of 10 weeks.

---

**CHECK THE AGENT SPECIALTIES INDEX** to find agents who are interested in your specific nonfiction or fiction subject area.

**Recent Sales:** Sold 20 titles in the last year. This agency prefers not to share information on specific sales.
**Terms:** Agent receives 15% commission on domestic sales; 20% commission on foreign sales. Offers written contract. Charges clients "an initial fee of $50 to cover photocopying expenses. If the manuscript is lengthy, I prefer the author to cover expenses of photocopying."

**● BALKIN AGENCY, INC.**, P.O. Box 222, Amherst MA 01004. (413)548-9835. Fax: (413)548-9836. **Contact:** Rick Balkin, president. Estab. 1972. Member of AAR. Represents 50 clients. 10% of clients are new/unpublished writers. Currently handles: 85% nonfiction books; 5% scholarly books; 5% textbooks; 5% reference books.
• Prior to opening his agency, Mr. Balkin served as executive editor with Bobbs-Merrill Company.
**Represents:** Nonfiction books; scholarly books; textbooks. **Considers these nonfiction areas:** animals; anthropology/archaeology; biography/autobiography; current affairs; health/medicine; history; how-to; language/literature/criticism; music/dance; nature/environment; popular culture; science/technology; sociology; translation; travel; true crime/investigative.
○→ This agency specializes in adult nonfiction. Does not want to receive fiction, poetry, screenplays, computer books.
**How to Contact:** Query with SASE, proposal package, outline. No e-mail or fax queries. Responds in 1 week to queries; 2 weeks to mss. Returns materials only with SASE. Obtains most new clients through recommendations from others.
**Recent Sales:** Sold 30 titles in the last year. *A Natural History of Falsehood*, (W.W. Norton Co.); *Adolescent Depression*, (Henry Holt); *Eliz. Van Lew: A Union Spy in the Heart of the Confederacy*, (biography, Oxford U.P.).
**Terms:** Agent receives 15% commission on domestic sales; 20% commission on foreign sales. Offers written contract, binding for 1 year. Charges clients for photocopying and express or foreign mail.
**Tips:** "I do not take on books described as bestsellers or potential bestsellers. Any nonfiction work that is either unique, paradigmatic, a contribution, truly witty or a labor of love is grist for my mill."

**● LORETTA BARRETT BOOKS INC.**, 101 Fifth Ave., New York NY 10003. (212)242-3420. Fax: (212)807-9579. E-mail: lbarbooks@aol.eom. **Contact:** Loretta A. Barrett or Nick Mullendore. Estab. 1990. Member of AAR. Represents 70 clients. Currently handles: 65% nonfiction books; 35% novels.
• Prior to opening her agency, Ms. Barrett was vice president and executive editor at Doubleday for 25 years.
**Represents:** Nonfiction books; novels. **Considers these nonfiction areas:** agriculture/horticulture; americana; animals; anthropology/archaeology; art/architecture/design; biography/autobiography; business/economics; child guidance/parenting; computers/electronic; cooking/foods/nutrition; crafts/hobbies; creative nonfiction; current affairs; education; ethnic/cultural interests; gardening; gay/lesbian issues; government/politics/law; health/medicine; history; how-to; humor/satire; interior design/decorating; juvenile nonfiction; language/literature/criticism; memoirs; military/war; money/finance; multicultural; music/dance; nature/environment; New Age/metaphysics; philosophy; photography; popular culture; psychology; recreation; regional; religious/inspirational; science/technology; self-help/personal improvement; sex; sociology; software; spirituality; sports; theater/film; translation; travel; true crime/investigative; women's issues/studies; young adult. **Considers these fiction areas:** action/adventure; confession; contemporary issues; detective/police/crime; ethnic; family saga; feminist; gay/lesbian; glitz; historical; humor/satire; literary; mainstream/contemporary; mystery/suspense; psychic/supernatural; religious/inspirational; romance; spiritual; sports; thriller.
○→ This agency specializes in general interest books. No children's or juvenile.
**How to Contact:** Query with SASE. No e-mail or fax queries. Considers simultaneous queries. Responds in 6 weeks to queries. Returns materials only with SASE.
**Recent Sales:** *In Fidelity*, by M.J. Rose; *A Lady First*, by Letitia Baldrige (Viking); *The Age of Spiritual Machines*, by Ray Kurzweil (Viking); *Witness to Hope: The Biography of Pope John Paul II*, by George Weigel (Cliff Street/Harper Collins).
**Terms:** Agent receives 15% commission on domestic sales; 20% commission on foreign sales. Offers written contract. Charges clients for shipping and photocopying.
**Writers' Conferences:** San Diego State University Writer's Conference; Maui Writer's Conference.

**● MARGARET BASCH**, 850 E. Higgins, #125, Schaumburg IL 60173. (847)240-1199. Fax: (847)240-1845. E-mail: lawlady@aol.com. **Contact:** Margaret Basch. Represents 100 clients. 5% of clients are new/unpublished writers. Currently not accepting new clients. Currently handles: 40% nonfiction books; 40% novels; 20% juvenile books.
• Prior to becoming an agent, Ms. Bach was a trial lawyer.
**Recent Sales:** This agency prefers not to share information about specific sales.
**Terms:** Agent receives 10% commission on domestic sales; 10% commission on foreign sales. Offers written contract.
**Tips:** "All of our clients are published and most came from other agents to be with us."

**● JENNY BENT, LITERARY AGENT, HARVEY KLINGER, INC.**, 301 W. 53rd St., New York NY 10019. (212)581-7068. Website: www.jennybent.com. **Contact:** Jenny Bent. Member of AAR. Represents 60 clients. 50% of clients are new/unpublished writers. Currently handles: 70% nonfiction books; 30% novels.
• Prior to joining her agency, Ms. Bent worked as an editor in book publishing and magazines.
**Represents:** Nonfiction books; novels. **Considers these nonfiction areas:** animals; biography/autobiography; child guidance/parenting; ethnic/cultural interests; gay/lesbian issues; health/medicine; history; language/literature/criticism;

popular culture; psychology; religious/inspirational; science/technology; self-help/personal improvement; software; spirituality; women's issues/studies. **Considers these fiction areas:** ethnic; gay/lesbian; literary; mainstream/contemporary; romance.

    **O→** Actively seeking quality fiction from well-credentialed authors. Does not want to receive science fiction, New Age fiction, mysteries, thrillers, children's, self-help from non-credentialed writers.

**How to Contact:** Query with SASE, submit proposal package, outline, résumé, publishing history, author bio. Please always include a bio or résumé with submissions or queries. Accepts e-mail queries, but no attachments. Considers simultaneous queries. Responds in 1 month to queries; 2 months to mss. Returns materials only with SASE. Obtains most new clients through recommendations from others, solicitations, conferences.

**Recent Sales:** Sold 15 titles in the last year. *The Road Home*, by Jone Ha Barras (Ballantine); *The Final Word*, by Craig Wilson (Random House).

**Terms:** Agent receives 15% commission on domestic sales; 25% commission on foreign sales. Offers written contract; 30 days notice must be given to terminate contract. Charges for postage, photocopying.

**Writers' Conferences:** Hurston-Wright (Richmond VA, summer); Washington Independent Writers Spring Writers Conference (Washington DC, May); Washington Romance Writers Spring Retreat; Virginia Romance Writers Conference (Williamsburg VA, March); Austin Writers Conference; Perfect Words (New Orleans).

**N: ⃞** **PAM BERNSTEIN & ASSOCIATES, INC.**, 790 Madison Ave., Suite 310, New York NY 10021. (212)288-1700. Fax: (212)288-3054. **Contact:** Pam Bernstein or Jonette Suitele. Estab. 1992. Member of AAR. Represents 50 clients. 20% of clients are new/unpublished writers. Currently handles: 50% nonfiction books; 50% novels.

    ● Prior to becoming an agent, Ms. Bernstein served as vice president with the William Morris Agency.

**Represents:** Nonfiction books; novels. **Considers these nonfiction areas:** health/medicine; how-to; popular culture; psychology; religious/inspirational; self-help/personal improvement; sociology; true crime/investigative; women's issues/studies. **Considers these fiction areas:** contemporary issues; ethnic; historical; mainstream/contemporary; mystery/suspense; romance (contemporary); thriller.

**How to Contact:** Query with SASE. Responds in 2 weeks to queries.

**Recent Sales:** Sold 25 titles in the last year. *Her Daughter's Eyes*, by Jessica Barksdale Inclen; *Canyon Ranch Guide to Living Younger Longer*, (Simon & Schuster).

**Terms:** Agent receives 15% commission on domestic sales; 20% commission on foreign sales. Offers written contract, binding for 3 years; 30 days notice must be given to terminate contract. 100% of business is derived from commissions on sales. Charges clients for postage and photocopying.

**⃞** **MEREDITH BERNSTEIN LITERARY AGENCY**, 2112 Broadway, Suite 503A, New York NY 10023. (212)799-1007. Fax: (212)799-1145. Estab. 1981. Member of AAR. Represents 100 clients. 20% of clients are new/unpublished writers. Currently handles: 50% nonfiction books; 50% novels.

    ● Prior to opening her agency, Ms. Bernstein served in another agency for 5 years.

**Member Agents:** Meredith Bernstein; Elizabeth Cavanaugh

**Represents:** Nonfiction books; novels. **Considers these nonfiction areas:** animals (pets); business/economics (and e-commerce); child guidance/parenting; creative nonfiction; government/politics/law; health/medicine; psychology; science/technology; spirituality. **Considers these fiction areas:** literary; mystery/suspense; romance; women's fiction.

    **O→** This agency does not specialize, "very eclectic."

**How to Contact:** Query with SASE. No e-mail or fax queries. Considers simultaneous queries. Obtains most new clients through recommendations from others, conferences, also develops and packages own ideas.

**Recent Sales:** *Phatphonics*, by Marion Blanck (Pocher); *7 Steps on the Written Path*, by Nancy Pickard & Lynn Lott (Ballantine).

**Terms:** Agent receives 15% commission on domestic sales; 20% commission on foreign sales. Charges clients $75 disbursement fee/year.

**Writers' Conferences:** Southwest Writers Conference (Albuquereque, August); Rocky Mountain Writers' Conference (Denver, September); Golden Triangle (Beaumont TX, October); Pacific Northwest Writers Conference; Austin League Writers Conference; Willamette Writers Conference (Portland, OR); Lafayette Writers Conference (Lafayette, LA); Surrey Writers Conference (Surrey, BC.); San Diego State University Writers Conference (San Diego, CA).

**☑ ⃞** **DANIEL BIAL AGENCY**, 41 W. 83rd St., Suite 5-C, New York NY 10024-5246. (212)721-1786. Fax: (309)213-0230. E-mail: dbialagency@juno.com. **Contact:** Daniel Bial. Estab. 1992. Represents under 50 clients. 15% of clients are new/unpublished writers. Currently handles: 95% nonfiction books; 5% novels.

    ● Prior to opening his agency, Mr. Bial was an editor for 15 years.

**Represents:** Nonfiction books; novels. **Considers these nonfiction areas:** animals; anthropology/archaeology; biography/autobiography; business/economics; child guidance/parenting; cooking/foods/nutrition; current affairs; ethnic/cultural interests; gay/lesbian issues; government/politics/law; history; how-to; humor/satire; language/literature/criticism; memoirs; military/war; money/finance; music/dance; nature/environment; New Age/metaphysics; popular culture; psychology; religious/inspirational; science/technology; self-help/personal improvement; sociology; spirituality; sports; theater/film; travel; true crime/investigative; women's issues/studies. **Considers these fiction areas:** action/adventure; comic books/cartoon; confession; contemporary issues; detective/police/crime; erotica; ethnic; feminist; gay/lesbian; humor/satire; literary.

**How to Contact:** Submit proposal package, outline. Responds in 2 weeks to queries. Returns materials only with SASE. Obtains most new clients through recommendations from others, solicitations, "good rolodex"

**Recent Sales:** This agency prefers not to share information on specific sales.

**Terms:** Agent receives 15% commission on domestic sales; 20% commission on foreign sales. Offers written contract, binding for 1 year with cancellation clause. Charges clients for overseas calls, overnight mailing, photocopying, messenger expenses.

**Tips:** "Good marketing is a key to success at all stages of publishing—successful authors know how to market themselves as well as their writing."

✓ ◑ **BIGSCORE PRODUCTIONS INC.**, P.O. Box 4575, Lancaster PA 17604. (717)293-0247. Fax: (717)293-1945. E-mail: bigscore@bigscoreproductions.com. Website: www.bigscoreproductions.com. **Contact:** David A. Robie. Estab. 1995. Represents 5-10 clients. 50% of clients are new/unpublished writers.
• Mr. Robie is also the president of Starburst Publishers, an inspirational publisher that publishes books for both the ABA and CBA markets.

**Represents:** Nonfiction books; novels.
O➡ This agency specializes in inspirationl and self-help nonfiction and fiction.

**How to Contact:** Query by e-mail. No fax queries. Considers simultaneous queries. Responds in 1 month to proposals. Queries accepted only by e-mail. No file attachments.

**Recent Sales:** *The Chile Pepper Diet*, by Heidi Allison (HCI); *My Name Isn't Martha, but I can Renovate my Home* series, by Sharon Hanby-Robie (Pocket Books).

**Terms:** Agent receives 15% commission on domestic sales. Offers written contract, binding for 6 months. Charges clients for shipping, ms photocopying, ms photocopying and preparation, and books for subsidiary rights submissions.

**Tips:** "Very open to taking on new clients. Submit a well-prepared proposal that will take minimal fine-tuning for presentation to publishers. Nonfiction writers must be highly marketable and media savvy—the more established in speaking or in your profession, the better."

◑ **VICKY BIJUR**, 333 West End Ave., Apt. 513, New York NY 10023. Member of AAR. This agency did not respond to our request for information. Query before submitting.

◑ **DAVID BLACK LITERARY AGENCY**, 156 Fifth Ave., New York NY 10001. (212)242-5080. Fax: (212)924-6609. **Contact:** David Black, owner. Estab. 1990. Member of AAR. Represents 150 clients. Currently handles: 90% nonfiction books; 10% novels.

**Member Agents:** Susan Raihofer (general nonfiction to literary fiction); Gary Morris (commercial fiction to psychology); Joy E. Tutela (general nonfiction to literary fiction); Laureen Rowland (business, health).

**Represents:** Nonfiction books; novels. **Considers these nonfiction areas:** biography/autobiography; business/economics; government/politics/law; history; memoirs; military/war; money/finance; multicultural; sports. **Considers these fiction areas:** literary; mainstream/contemporary; commercial.
O➡ This agency specializes in business, sports, politics, and novels.

**How to Contact:** Query with SASE, outline. No e-mail or fax queries. Considers simultaneous queries. Responds in 2 months to queries. Returns materials only with SASE.

**Recent Sales:** *Body for Life*, by Bill Phillips with Mike D'Orso (HarperCollins); *Walking with the Wind*, by John Lewis with Micke D'Orso (Simon & Schuster).

**Terms:** Agent receives 15% commission on domestic sales. Charges clients for photocopying and books purchased for sale of foreign rights.

✓ ◑ **BLEECKER STREET ASSOCIATES, INC.**, 532 LaGuardia Place, #617, New York NY 10012. (212)677-4492. Fax: (212)388-0001. **Contact:** Agnes Birnbaum. Estab. 1984. Member of AAR, RWA, MWA. Represents 60 clients. 20% of clients are new/unpublished writers. Currently handles: 65% nonfiction books; 25% novels; 10% syndicated material.
• Prior to becoming an agent, Ms. Birnbaum was a senior editor at Simon & Schuster, Dutton/Signet and other publishing houses.

**Represents:** Nonfiction books; novels; short story collections. **Considers these nonfiction areas:** animals; anthropology/archaeology; biography/autobiography; business/economics; child guidance/parenting; computers/electronic; cooking/foods/nutrition; current affairs; ethnic/cultural interests; gay/lesbian issues; government/politics/law; health/medicine; history; how-to; humor/satire; juvenile nonfiction; memoirs; military/war; money/finance; nature/environment; New Age/metaphysics; popular culture; psychology; religious/inspirational; science/technology; self-help/personal improvement; sociology; sports; true crime/investigative; women's issues/studies. **Considers these fiction areas:** detective/police/crime; erotica; ethnic; family saga; feminist; gay/lesbian; historical; literary; mystery/suspense; psychic/supernatural; romance; thriller.
O➡ "We're very hands-on and accessible. We try to be truly creative in our submission approaches. We've had especially good luck with first-time authors." Does not want to receive science fiction, westerns, poetry, children's books, academic/scholarly/professional books, plays, scripts.

**How to Contact:** Query with SASE. No e-mail or fax queries. Considers simultaneous queries. Responds in 2 weeks to queries; 1 month to mss. Returns materials only with SASE. Obtains most new clients through recommendations from others, solicitations, conferences, "plus, I will approach someone with a letter if his/her work impresses me."

**Recent Sales:** Sold 37 titles in the last year. *African-American Ophelia*, by Christen James and Natasha Tarpley (Doubleday); *Producing Audio with Home PC*, by James Maguire (Que/Pearson); *The Art of War*, by Bevin Alexander.
**Terms:** Agent receives 15% commission on domestic sales; 25% commission on foreign sales. Offers written contract; 30 days notice must be given to terminate contract. Charges for postage, long distance, fax, messengers, photocopies, not to exceed $200.
**Tips:** "Keep query letters short and to the point; include only information pertaining to book or background as writer. Try to avoid superlatives in description. Work needs to stand on its own, so how much editing it may have received has no place in a query letter."

☑ ◑ **REID BOATES LITERARY AGENCY**, 69 Cooks Crossroad, Pittstown NJ 08867. (908)730-8523. Fax: (908)730-8931. E-mail: boatesliterary@att.net. **Contact:** Reid Boates. Estab. 1985. Represents 45 clients. 5% of clients are new/unpublished writers. Currently handles: 85% nonfiction books; 15% novels; very rarely story collections.
**Represents:** Nonfiction books; novels. **Considers these nonfiction areas:** animals; anthropology/archaeology; art/architecture/design; biography/autobiography; business/economics; child guidance/parenting; current affairs; ethnic/cultural interests; government/politics/law; health/medicine; history; language/literature/criticism; nature/environment; psychology; science/technology; self-help/personal improvement; sports; true crime/investigative; women's issues/studies. **Considers these fiction areas:** contemporary issues; family saga; mainstream/contemporary; thriller.
> ⦿ This agency specializes in general fiction and nonfiction, investigative journalism/current affairs; bios and celebrity autobiographies; serious self-help; literary humor; issue-oriented business; popular science. Does not want category fiction.

**How to Contact:** Query with SASE. Responds in 2 weeks to queries; 6 weeks to mss. Obtains most new clients through recommendations from others.
**Recent Sales:** Sold 20 titles in the last year. This agency prefers not to share information on specific sales.
**Terms:** Agent receives 15% commission on domestic sales; 20% commission on foreign sales. Charges clients for photocopying costs above $50.

◑ **BOOK DEALS, INC.**, 417 N. Sangamon St., Chicago IL 60622. (312)491-0300. Fax: (312)491-8091. E-mail: bookdeals@aol.com. Website: www.bookdealsinc.com. **Contact:** Caroline Francis Carney. Estab. 1996. Member of AAR. Represents 40 clients. 30% of clients are new/unpublished writers. Currently handles: 75% nonfiction books; 25% novels.
> • Prior to opening her agency, Ms. Carney was editorial director for a consumer book imprint within Times Mirror and held senior editorial positions in McGraw-Hill and Simon & Schuster.

**Represents:** Nonfiction books; novels (commercial and literary). **Considers these nonfiction areas:** business/economics; child guidance/parenting; cooking/foods/nutrition; ethnic/cultural interests; health/medicine (nutrition); history; how-to; money/finance; multicultural; popular culture; psychology (popular); religious/inspirational; science/technology; self-help/personal improvement; spirituality. **Considers these fiction areas:** ethnic; literary; mainstream/contemporary; women's (contemporary); urban literature.
> ⦿ This agency specializes in highly commercial nonfiction and books for African-American readers. Actively seeking well-crafted fiction and nonfiction from authors with engaging voices and impeccable credentials.

**How to Contact:** For nonfiction, send synopsis, outline/proposal with SASE. For fiction, send query and SASE. Considers simultaneous queries. Responds in 1 month to queries.
**Recent Sales:** Sold 20 titles in the last year. *Stony the Road We Trod*, by Janet Cheatham Bell (Pocket Books); *Sole Sisters*, by Deborah Mathis (Warner Books); *Eat Right for Your Personality Type*, by Dr. Robert Kushner & Nancy Kushner (St. Martin's Press).
**Terms:** Agent receives 15% commission on domestic sales; 20% commission on foreign sales. Offers written contract. Charges clients for photocopying and postage.

◪ **BOOKENDS, LLC**, 136 Long Hill Rd., Gillette NJ 07933. (908)604-2652. E-mail: editor@bookends-inc.com. Website: www.bookends-inc.com. **Contact:** Jessica Faust or Jacky Sach. Estab. 1999. Member of American Book Producers Association. Represents 10 clients. 75% of clients are new/unpublished writers. Currently handles: 50% nonfiction books; 50% novels.
> • Prior to opening their agency, Ms. Faust and Ms. Sach worked at such publishing houses as Berkley, Macmillan and IDG.

**Member Agents:** Jessica Faust (romance, relationships, business, finance, pets, general self-help); Jacky Sach (suspense thrillers, mysteries, literary fiction, spirituality, pets, general self-help)
**Represents:** Nonfiction books; novels. **Considers these nonfiction areas:** animals; biography/autobiography; business/economics; child guidance/parenting; cooking/foods/nutrition; crafts/hobbies; current affairs; ethnic/cultural interests; gay/lesbian issues; health/medicine; how-to; humor/satire; memoirs; money/finance; New Age/metaphysics; psychology; religious/inspirational; self-help/personal improvement; women's issues/studies. **Considers these fiction areas:** contemporary issues; detective/police/crime; ethnic; family saga; feminist; glitz; historical; literary; mainstream/contemporary; mystery/suspense; romance; thriller; young adult.
> ⦿ BookEnds specializes in genre fiction and personality driven nonfiction. Actively seeking romance, mystery, women's fiction, literary fiction and suspense thrillers. For nonfiction, relationships, business, general self-help, women's interest, parenting, pets, spirituality, health and psychology. Does not want to receive children's books, screenplays, science fiction, poetry.

**How to Contact:** Submit outline, 3 sample chapter(s), or submit complete ms. Considers simultaneous queries. Responds in 2 weeks to queries; 6 weeks to mss. Returns materials only with SASE. Obtains most new clients through recommendations from others, solicitations, conferences.

**Recent Sales:** Sold 10 titles in the last year. *The Complete Idiot's Guide to Women's History*, by Sonia Weiss (Macmillan); *Critical Lives: Che Guevara*, by Eric Luther (Macmillan); *Court TV's You Be the Judge*, by Patrick J. Sauer (Warner).

**Terms:** Agent receives 15% commission on domestic sales; 20% commission on foreign sales. Offers written contract. Charges clients for photocopying, messenger, cables, overseas postage, long-distance phone calls, copies of the published book when purchases for subsidiary rights submissions. Expenses will not exceed $150.

**Writers' Conferences:** Harriette Austin Conference (Athens GA, July 2001).

**Tips:** "When submitting material be sure to include any information that might be helpful to the agent. In your query letter you should include the title of the book, your name, your publishing history and a brief 1 or 2 sentence description of the book. Also be sure to let the agent know if you see this book as part of a series and if you've already begun work on other books. Once an agent has expressed interest in representing you it is crucial to let her know who has seen your book and even supply copies of any correspondence you've had with prospective editors."

☑ ☺ ◉ **BOOKS & SUCH, (Specialized: Christian market)**, 4788 Carissa Ave.,, Santa Rosa CA 94505.. (707)538-4184. Fax: (707)538-3937. E-mail: jkgbooks@aol.com. **Contact:** Janet Kobobel Grant. Estab. 1996. Member of CBA (associate). Represents 35 clients. 20% of clients are new/unpublished writers. Currently handles: 36% nonfiction books; 22% novels; 7% juvenile books; 35% children's picture books.

• Before becoming an agent, Ms. Grant was an editor for Zondervan and managing editor for Focus on the Family.

**Represents:** Nonfiction books; novels; juvenile books. **Considers these nonfiction areas:** child guidance/parenting; humor/satire; juvenile nonfiction; religious/inspirational; self-help/personal improvement; women's issues/studies. **Considers these fiction areas:** contemporary issues; family saga; historical; juvenile; mainstream/contemporary; picture books; religious/inspirational; romance; young adult.

○⊸ This agency specializes in "general and inspirational fiction, romance, and in the Christian booksellers market." Actively seeking "material appropriate to the Christian market."

**How to Contact:** Query with SASE. Considers simultaneous queries. Responds in 1 month to queries; 2 months to mss. Returns materials only with SASE. Obtains most new clients through recommendations from others, conferences.

**Recent Sales:** Sold 31 titles in the last year. *In Celebration of Innocence*, by Robin Jones Gunu (Multnomah Publishers); *How to Make a Moose Run and Other Life Lessons My Father Taught Me*, by Gary Stanley (RiverOak). Other clients include Joanna Weaver, Jane Orcutt, B.J. Hoff, Stephanie Grace Whitson.

**Terms:** Agent receives 15% commission on domestic sales; 15% commission on foreign sales. Offers written contract; 2 months notice must be given to terminate contract. Charges clients for postage, photocopying, telephone calls, fax and express mail.

**Writers' Conferences:** Romance Writers of America; Mt. Hermon Writers Conference (Mt. Hermon CA, April 14-18); Sandy Cone Communicators Conference (Sandy Cone MD, September 30-October 4).

**Tips:** "The heart of my motivation is to develop relationships with the authors I serve, to do what I can to shine the light of success on them, and to help be a caretaker of their gifts and time."

☺ **GEORGES BORCHARDT INC.**, 136 E. 57th St., New York NY 10022. (212)753-5785. Fax: (212)838-6518. Estab. 1967. Member of AAR. Represents 200 clients. 10% of clients are new/unpublished writers. Currently handles: 60% nonfiction books; 37% novels; 1% novellas; 1% juvenile books; 1% poetry.

**Member Agents:** Anne Borchardt; Georges Borchardt; DeAnna Heindel; Lourdes Lopez; Valerie Borchardt.

**Represents:** Nonfiction books; novels. **Considers these nonfiction areas:** anthropology/archaeology; biography/autobiography; current affairs; history; memoirs; travel; women's issues/studies. **Considers these fiction areas:** literary.

○⊸ This agency specializes in literary fiction and outstanding nonfiction.

**How to Contact:** Responds in 1 week to queries; 1 month to mss. Obtains most new clients through recommendations from others.

**Recent Sales:** Sold 100 titles in the last year. *An Atonement*, by Ian McEwan (Nan TaHese-Doubleday); *Brown*, by Richard Rodriguez (Viking Penguin).

**Terms:** Agent receives 15% commission on domestic sales; 20% commission on foreign sales. Offers written contract. "We charge clients cost of outside photocopying and shipping manuscripts or books overseas."

☺ **THE BOSTON LITERARY GROUP**, 156 Mount Auburn St., Cambridge MA 02138-4875. (617)547-0800. Fax: (617)876-8474. E-mail: agent@bostonliterary.com. **Contact:** Elizabeth Mack. Estab. 1994. Member of PEN New England. Represents 30 clients. 25% of clients are new/unpublished writers. Currently handles: 95% nonfiction books; 5% novels.

**IF YOU'RE LOOKING** for a particular agent, check the Agents Index to find the specific agency where the agent works. Then check the listing for that agency in the appropriate section.

**Member Agents:** Kirsten Wainwright (psychology, biography, health, current events, memoir, business); Heather Moehn (science, history, fiction).

**Represents:** Nonfiction books. **Considers these nonfiction areas:** animals; anthropology/archaeology; art/architecture/design; biography/autobiography; business/economics; child guidance/parenting; current affairs; ethnic/cultural interests; government/politics/law; health/medicine; history; military/war; money/finance; nature/environment; photography; psychology; science/technology; sociology; true crime/investigative; women's issues/studies.

    O─⚲  Actively seeking "nonfiction manuscripts that have something new and fascinating to say. Good writing skills are essential." Does not want to receive poetry, cookbooks, children's literature.

**How to Contact:** Query with SASE. Prefers to read materials exclusively. Accepts e-mail and fax queries. Responds in 6 weeks to queries. Returns materials only with SASE. Obtains most new clients through recommendations from others, journal articles.

**Recent Sales:** Sold 10 titles in the last year. *Zero: The Biography of a Dangerous Idea*, by Charles Seife (Viking Penguin); *The Skin We're In: Teaching Our Children to be Emotionally Strong*, by Janie Ward (Free Press); *Managing Creativity: The Science of Enterprise-Wide Innovation*, by Jeff Mauzy and Richard Harriman (Harvard Business School Press); *The Resurrection Gene, The Story of the Incredible Race to Clone the Woolly Mammoth*, by Richard Stowe (Perseus).

**Terms:** Agent receives 15% commission on domestic sales; 10% commission on foreign sales. Offers written contract, binding for 1 year; 60-day notice must be given to terminate contract. Charges clients for expenses associated with manuscript submissions (postage, photocopy). Makes referrals to editing service. "We match-make with development editors on promising projects."

⬤ **THE BARBARA BOVA LITERARY AGENCY**, 3951 Gulfshore Blvd., PH1-B, Naples FL 34103. (941)649-7237. Fax: (941)649-0757. E-mail: Bova64@aol.com. **Contact:** Barbara Bova. Estab. 1974. Represents 30 clients. Currently handles: 35% nonfiction books; 65% novels.

**Represents:** Nonfiction books; novels. **Considers these nonfiction areas:** biography/autobiography; science/technology; self-help/personal improvement; true crime/investigative; women's issues/studies; social sciences. **Considers these fiction areas:** action/adventure; detective/police/crime; glitz; mystery/suspense; science fiction; thriller.

    O─⚲  This agency specializes in fiction and nonfiction, hard and soft science.

**How to Contact:** Query with SASE. Obtains most new clients through recommendations from others. "At this time our client list is full and we are accepting no new clients."

**Recent Sales:** Sold 6 titles in the last year. *Ender Hegemon*, by Orson Scott Card (TOR); *Jupiter*, by Ben Bova (TOR); *Chameleon*, by Shirley Kennett (Kensington). Ice Covers the Hole, by Rick Wilber (TOR/Forge) Following Through, by Steve Levinson and Pete C. Greider (Kensington).

**Terms:** Agent receives 15% commission on domestic sales.

**Tips:** This agency also handles foreign rights, movies, television, CDs.

▨ ⬤ **BRADY LITERARY MANAGEMENT**, P.O. Box 164, Hartland Four Corners VT 05049. **Contact:** Upton Brady. Estab. 1986. Represents 100 clients.

**Represents:** Nonfiction books; novels; short story collections; novellas. **Considers these fiction areas:** literary; mainstream/contemporary.

**How to Contact:** Query with SASE, submit for outline, 2 sample chapters for nonfiction; first 50 pages for fiction. Responds in 2 months to queries.

**Recent Sales:** This agency prefers not to share information on specific sales.

**Terms:** Agent receives 15% commission on domestic sales; 20% commission on foreign sales. Charges clients for extensive international postage and photocopying.

✓ ◐ **BRANDT & HOCHMAN LITERARY AGENTS INC.**, (formerly Brandt & Brandt Literary Agents Inc.), 1501 Broadway, New York NY 10036. (212)840-5760. Fax: (212)840-5776. **Contact:** Carl Brandt; Gail Hochman; Marianne Merola; Charles Schlessiger; Meg Giles. Estab. 1913. Member of AAR. Represents 200 clients.

**Represents:** Nonfiction books; novels; short story collections; novellas; juvenile books; journalism. **Considers these nonfiction areas:** animals; anthropology/archaeology; art/architecture/design; biography/autobiography; child guidance/parenting; cooking/foods/nutrition; current affairs; ethnic/cultural interests; gay/lesbian issues; government/politics/law; health/medicine; history; interior design/decorating; language/literature/criticism; music/dance; nature/environment; psychology; science/technology; sports; theater/film; true crime/investigative; women's issues/studies. **Considers these fiction areas:** action/adventure; contemporary issues; detective/police/crime; ethnic; family saga; historical; humor/satire; literary; mainstream/contemporary; mystery/suspense; regional; romance; sports; thriller; young adult.

**How to Contact:** Query with SASE. Considers simultaneous queries. Responds in 1 month to queries. Returns materials only with SASE. Obtains most new clients through recommendations from others.

**Recent Sales:** Sold 50 titles in the last year. This agency prefers not to share information on specific sales. Clients include Scott Turow, Carlos Fuentes, Ursula Hegi, Michael Cunningham, Mary Pope Osborne, Avi.

**Terms:** Agent receives 15% commission on domestic sales; 20% commission on foreign sales. Charges clients for "manuscript duplication or other special expenses agreed to in advance."

**Tips:** "Write a letter which will give the agent a sense of you as a professional writer, your long-term interests as well as a short description of the work at hand."

**THE JOAN BRANDT AGENCY**, 788 Wesley Dr., Atlanta GA 30305-3933. (404)351-8877. **Contact:** Joan Brandt. Estab. 1980. Represents 30 clients. 50% of clients are new/unpublished writers. Currently handles: 45% nonfiction books; 45% novels; 10% juvenile books.
**Represents:** Nonfiction books; novels; short story collections. **Considers these fiction areas:** contemporary issues; detective/police/crime; family saga; literary; mainstream/contemporary; mystery/suspense; thriller.
**How to Contact:** Query with SASE. No e-mail or fax queries. Considers simultaneous queries. Returns materials only with SASE. Obtains most new clients through solicitations.
**Recent Sales:** This agency prefers not to share information on specific sales.
**Terms:** Agent receives 15% commission on domestic sales; 20% commission on foreign sales. No written contract.

**THE HELEN BRANN AGENCY, INC.**, 94 Curtis Rd., Bridgewater CT 06752. Member of AAR. This agency did not respond to our request for information. Query before submitting.

**M. COURTNEY BRIGGS**, 100 N. Broadway Ave., 20th Floor, Oklahoma City OK 73102-8806. **Contact:** M. Courtney Briggs. Estab. 1994. 25% of clients are new/unpublished writers. Currently handles: 5% nonfiction books; 10% novels; 80% juvenile books; 5% multimedia.
• Prior to becoming an agent, Ms. Briggs was in subsidiary rights at Random House for 3 years; an associate agent and film rights associate with Curtis Brown, Ltd.; and an attorney for 9 years.
**Represents:** Nonfiction books; novels; juvenile books. **Considers these nonfiction areas:** animals; biography/autobiography; health/medicine; juvenile nonfiction; self-help/personal improvement; young adult. **Considers these fiction areas:** juvenile; mainstream/contemporary; picture books; young adult.
⊙━ M. Courtney Briggs is an agent and an attorney. "I work primarily, but not exclusively, with children's book authors and illustrators. I will also consult or review a contract on an hourly basis." Actively seeking children's fiction, children's picture books (illustrations and text), young adult novels, fiction, nonfiction.
**How to Contact:** Query with SASE. No e-mail or fax queries. Responds in 2 weeks to queries; 6 weeks to mss. Returns materials only with SASE. Obtains most new clients through recommendations from others.
**Recent Sales:** This agency prefers not to share information on specific sales.
**Terms:** Agent receives 15% commission on domestic sales; 25% commission on foreign sales. Offers written contract, binding for terminated at will; 60—day notice must be given to terminate contract.
**Writers' Conferences:** National Conference on Writing & Illustrating for Children (August).

**BROADWAY PLAY PUBLISHING**, 56 E. 81st St., New York NY 10028-0202. Member of AAR. This agency did not respond to our request for information. Query before submitting.

**MARIE BROWN ASSOCIATES INC.**, 412 W. 154th St., New York NY 10032. (212)939-9725. Fax: (212)939-9728. E-mail: mbrownlit@aol.com. **Contact:** Marie Brown. Estab. 1984. Represents 60 clients. Currently handles: 75% nonfiction books; 10% juvenile books; 15% other.
**Member Agents:** Janell Walden Agyeman; Lisa Davis.
**Represents:** Nonfiction books; juvenile books. **Considers these nonfiction areas:** art/architecture/design; biography/autobiography; business/economics; ethnic/cultural interests; history; juvenile nonfiction; music/dance; religious/inspirational; self-help/personal improvement; theater/film; women's issues/studies. **Considers these fiction areas:** contemporary issues; ethnic; juvenile; literary; mainstream/contemporary.
⊙━ This agency specializes in multicultural and African-American writers.
**How to Contact:** Query with SASE. Prefers to read materials exclusively. No e-mail or fax queries. Responds in 6 weeks to queries. Obtains most new clients through recommendations from others.
**Recent Sales:** *Lookin for Luv*, by Carl Weber (Kensington); *Brown Sugar*, by Carol Taylor (Dutton); *Waiting in Vain*, by Colin Channer (Ballantine/One World); *The Debt*, by Randall Robinson (Dutton); *Gender Talk*, by Johnetta Cole and Beverly Guy Sheftall (Farrar, Straus & Giroux); *Defending the Spirit* , by Randall Robinson (Dutton).
**Terms:** Agent receives 15% commission on domestic sales; 20% commission on foreign sales. Offers written contract.

**ANDREA BROWN LITERARY AGENCY, INC., (Specialized: juvenile)**, P.O. Box 371027, Montara CA 94037-1027. (650)728-1783. Fax: (650)728-1732. E-mail: ablitage@pacbell.net. Website: www.litwest.com. **Contact:** Andrea Brown, president. Estab. 1981. Member of WNBA, SCBWI. 10% of clients are new/unpublished writers. Currently handles: 95% juvenile nonfiction; 5% adult nonfiction nonfiction.
• Prior to opening her agency, Ms. Brown served as an editorial assistant at Random House and Dell Publishing and as an editor with Alfred A. Knopt.
**Member Agents:** Andrea Brown; Laura Rennert.
**Represents:** Nonfiction books (juvenile). **Considers these nonfiction areas:** animals; anthropology/archaeology; art/architecture/design; biography/autobiography; current affairs; ethnic/cultural interests; history; how-to; juvenile nonfiction; nature/environment; photography; popular culture; science/technology; sociology; sports; all nonfiction subjects for juveniles. **Considers these fiction areas:** juvenile; young adult; all fiction genres for juveniles.
⊙━ This agency specializes in "all kinds fo children's books—illustrators and authors." Considers all juvenile fiction areas; all genres of nonfiction.

**How to Contact:** Query with SASE. Accepts e-mail queries. No fax queries. Considers simultaneous queries. Responds in 1 month to queries; 3 months to mss. Obtains most new clients through recommendations from others, referrals from editors, clients and agents.

**Recent Sales:** *Oh Brother*, by Ken Stark (Putnam); *Liberty Street*, by Candice Ransom (Walker).

**Terms:** Agent receives 15% commission on domestic sales; 20% commission on foreign sales. Offers written contract. Charges clients for shipping costs.

**Writers' Conferences:** Austin Writers League; SCBWI, Orange County Conferences; Mills College Childrens Literature Conference (Oakland CA); Asilomar (Pacific Grove CA); Maui Writers Conference; Southwest Writers Conference; San Diego State University Writer's Conference; Big Sur Children's Writing Workshop (Director); William Saroyan Conference; Columbus Writers Conference; Willamette Writers Conference.

**Tips:** "Query first. Taking on very few picture books. Must be unique—no rhyme, no anthropomorphism."

**◯ CURTIS BROWN LTD.**, 10 Astor Place, New York NY 10003-6935. (212)473-5400. Also: 1750 Montgomery St., San Francisco CA 94111. (415)954-8566. **Contact:** Perry Knowlton, chairman; Timothy Knowlton, CEO; Peter L. Ginsberg, president. Member of AAR; signatory of WGA.

**Member Agents:** Laura Blake Peterson; Ellen Geiger; Emilie Jacobson, vice president; Maureen Walters, vice president; Virginia Knowlton ; Timothy Knowlton (film, screenplays, plays); Marilyn Marlow, executive vice president; Ed Wintle (film, screenplays, plays); Mitchell Waters; Elizabeth Harding; Douglas Stewart; Dave Barber (translation rights).

**Represents:** Nonfiction books; novels; short story collections; novellas; juvenile books; poetry books. **Considers these nonfiction areas:** agriculture/horticulture; americana; animals; anthropology/archaeology; art/architecture/design; biography/autobiography; business/economics; child guidance/parenting; computers/electronic; cooking/foods/nutrition; crafts/hobbies; creative nonfiction; current affairs; education; ethnic/cultural interests; gardening; gay/lesbian issues; government/politics/law; health/medicine; history; how-to; humor/satire; interior design/decorating; juvenile nonfiction; language/literature/criticism; memoirs; military/war; money/finance; multicultural; music/dance; nature/environment; New Age/metaphysics; philosophy; photography; popular culture; psychology; recreation; regional; religious/inspirational; science/technology; self-help/personal improvement; sex; sociology; software; spirituality; sports; theater/film; translation; travel; true crime/investigative; women's issues/studies; young adult. **Considers these fiction areas:** action/adventure; comic books/cartoon; confession; contemporary issues; detective/police/crime; erotica; ethnic; experimental; family saga; fantasy; feminist; gay/lesbian; glitz; gothic; hi-lo; historical; horror; humor/satire; juvenile; literary; mainstream/contemporary; military/war; multicultural; multimedia; mystery/suspense; New Age; occult; picture books; plays; poetry; poetry in translation; psychic/supernatural; regional; religious/inspirational; romance; science fiction; short story collections; spiritual; sports; thriller; translation; westerns/frontier; young adult; women's.

**Also Handles:** Movie scripts; feature film; TV scripts; TV movie of the week; stage plays. **Considers these script subject areas:** action/adventure; comedy; detective/police/crime; ethnic; feminist; gay/lesbian; historical; horror; mainstream; mystery/suspense; psychic/supernatural; romantic comedy; romantic drama; thriller; western/frontier.

**How to Contact:** Query with SASE. Prefers to read materials exclusively. No unsolicited mss. No e-mail or fax queries. Responds in 3 weeks to queries; 5 weeks to mss. Obtains most new clients through recommendations from others, solicitations, conferences.

**Recent Sales:** This agency prefers not to share information on specific sales.

**Terms:** Offers written contract. Charges for photocopying, some postage. "There are no office fees until we sell a manuscript."

*22284 AVE. SAN LUIS, WOODLAND HILLS CA 91364-1656*

**✓ ◯ PEMA BROWNE LTD.**, HCR Box 104B, Pine Rd., Neversink NY 12765-9603. (845)985-2936. Website: www.geocities.com/pemabrowneltd. **Contact:** Perry Browne or Pema Browne (. Estab. 1966. Signatory of WGA. Represents 30 clients. Currently handles: 40% nonfiction books; 30% novels & romance novels; 25% juvenile books; 5% movie scripts.

● Prior to opening their agency, Mr. Browne was a radio and TV performer; Ms. Browne was a fine artist and art buyer.

**Member Agents:** Pema Browne (children's fiction and nonfiction, adult nonfiction); Perry Browne (adult fiction, nonfiction).

**Represents:** Nonfiction books; novels; juvenile books; reference books. **Considers these nonfiction areas:** business/economics; child guidance/parenting; cooking/foods/nutrition; ethnic/cultural interests; gay/lesbian issues; health/medicine; how-to; juvenile nonfiction; military/war; money/finance; nature/environment; New Age/metaphysics; popular culture; psychology; religious/inspirational; self-help/personal improvement; spirituality; sports; true crime/investigative; women's issues/studies; reference. **Considers these fiction areas:** action/adventure; contemporary issues; detective/police/crime; erotica; ethnic; feminist; gay/lesbian; glitz; historical; humor/satire; juvenile; literary; mainstream/contemporary (commercial); mystery/suspense; picture books; psychic/supernatural; religious/inspirational; romance (contemporary, gothic, historical, regency); young adult.

**O→** Actively seeking adult nonfiction, juvenile, middle grade, some young adult, picture books, novelty books.

**How to Contact:** Query with SASE. No e-mail or fax queries. Responds in 3 weeks to queries; 6 weeks to mss. Returns materials only with SASE. Obtains most new clients through "editors, authors, *LMP*, *Guide to Literary Agents* and as a result of longevity!"

**Recent Sales:** Sold 10 titles in the last year. *Scared of the Dark*, by Linda Cargill (Cora Verlag); *Sins of the Fathers*, by Susan Scott (Cora Verlag); *A Tender Moment*, by Carol King (Warner iPublish).

**Terms:** Agent receives 15% commission on domestic sales; 20% commission on foreign sales.

**Tips:** "We do not review manuscripts that have been sent out to publishers. If writing romance, be sure to receive guidelines from various romance publishers. In nonfiction, one must have credentials to lend credence to a proposal. Make sure of margins, double-space and use clean, dark type."

**HOWARD BUCK AGENCY**, 80 Eighth Ave., Suite 1107, New York NY 10011. (212)807-7855. **Contact:** Howard Buck or Mark Frisk. Estab. 1981. Represents 75 clients. "We're an all-around agency." Currently handles: 75% nonfiction books; 25% novels.

**Represents:** Nonfiction books; novels. **Considers these nonfiction areas:** agriculture/horticulture; americana; animals; anthropology/archaeology; art/architecture/design; biography/autobiography; business/economics; child guidance/parenting; computers/electronic; cooking/foods/nutrition; crafts/hobbies; creative nonfiction; current affairs; education; ethnic/cultural interests; gardening; gay/lesbian issues; government/politics/law; health/medicine; history; how-to; humor/satire; interior design/decorating; language/literature/criticism; memoirs; military/war; money/finance; multicultural; music/dance; nature/environment; New Age/metaphysics; philosophy; photography; popular culture; psychology; recreation; regional; religious/inspirational; science/technology; sex; sociology; software; spirituality; sports; theater/film; translation; travel; true crime/investigative; women's issues/studies. **Considers these fiction areas:** action/adventure; comic books/cartoon; confession; contemporary issues; detective/police/crime; erotica; ethnic; experimental; family saga; feminist; gay/lesbian; glitz; gothic; hi-lo; historical; humor/satire; literary; mainstream/contemporary; military/war; multicultural; multimedia; mystery/suspense; New Age; occult; plays; poetry; poetry in translation; psychic/supernatural; regional; religious/inspirational; romance; short story collections; spiritual; sports; thriller; translation; westerns/frontier; women's.

○ "We do not read original screenplays."

**How to Contact:** Query with SASE. Responds in 6 weeks to queries. Obtains most new clients through recommendations from others.

**Recent Sales:** This agency prefers not to share information on specific sales.

**Terms:** Agent receives 15% commission on domestic sales. Offers written contract. Charges client for office expenses, postage and photocopying.

**KNOX BURGER ASSOCIATES, LTD.**, 39 ½ Washington Square South, New York NY 10012. Member of AAR. This agency did not respond to our request for information. Query before submitting.

**SHEREE BYKOFSKY ASSOCIATES, INC.**, 16 W. 36th St., 13th Floor, New York NY 10018. Website: www.shereebee.com. **Contact:** Sheree Bykofsky. Estab. 1984, incorporated 1991. Member of AAR, ASJA, WNBA. Currently handles: 80% nonfiction books; 20% novels.

● Prior to opening her agency, Ms. Bykofsky served as executive editor of The Stonesong Press and managing editor of Chiron Press. She is also the author or co-author of more than 10 books. Ms. Bykofsky has a regular column, Ask the Agent, on WritersMarket.com.

**Represents:** Nonfiction books; novels. **Considers these nonfiction areas:** agriculture/horticulture; americana; animals; anthropology/archaeology; art/architecture/design; biography/autobiography; business/economics; child guidance/parenting; computers/electronic; cooking/foods/nutrition; crafts/hobbies; creative nonfiction; current affairs; education; ethnic/cultural interests; gardening; gay/lesbian issues; government/politics/law; health/medicine; history; how-to; humor/satire; interior design/decorating; juvenile nonfiction; language/literature/criticism; memoirs; military/war; money/finance; multicultural; music/dance; nature/environment; New Age/metaphysics; philosophy; photography; popular culture; psychology; recreation; regional; religious/inspirational; science/technology; self-help/personal improvement; sex; sociology; software; spirituality; sports; theater/film; translation; travel; true crime/investigative; women's issues/studies; young adult; **Considers these fiction areas:** literary; mainstream/contemporary.

○ This agency specializes in popular reference nonfiction. "I have wide-ranging interests, but it really depends on quality of writing, originality, and how a particular project appeals to me (or not). I take on very little fiction unless I completely love it—it doesn't matter what area or genre." Does not want to receive poetry, material for children, screenplays.

**How to Contact:** Query with SASE. No unsolicited mss or phone calls. Considers simultaneous queries. Responds in 1 week to queries; 1 month to mss. Returns materials only with SASE. Obtains most new clients through recommendations from others.

**Recent Sales:** Sold 100 titles in the last year. *How to Make Someone Love You in 30 Minutes or Less*, by Nicholas Boothman (Workman); *A Witness Above*, by Kandy Straka (Signet); *Open Your Mind, Open Your Life*, by Tara Gold (Andrews & McMeel).

**Terms:** Agent receives 15% commission on domestic sales; 15% commission on foreign sales. Offers written contract, binding for 1 year. Charges for postage, photocopying and fax.

**Writers' Conferences:** ASJA (New York City); Asilomar (Pacific Grove CA); Kent State; Southwestern Writers; Willamette (Portland); Dorothy Canfield Fisher (San Diego); Writers Union (Maui); Pacific NW; IWWG; and many others.

**Tips:** "Read the agent listing carefully, and comply with guidelines."

**N** **$** **◐** **CAMBRIDGE LITERARY**, 25 Green St., Newburyport MA 01950. (978)499-0374. Fax: (978)499-0374. Website: members.aol.com/mrmv/index.html. **Contact:** Ralph Valentino. Estab. 1994. Member of AAR. Represents 150 clients. 75% of clients are new/unpublished writers. Currently handles: 50% nonfiction books; 35% novels; 15% movie scripts.

● Prior to becoming an agent, Mr. Valentino was a journalist.

**Member Agents:** Michael Valentino (nonfiction); Ralph Valentino (fiction/movie scripts)

**Represents:** Nonfiction books; novels; juvenile books. **Considers these nonfiction areas:** biography/autobiography; cooking/foods/nutrition; current affairs; gay/lesbian issues; health/medicine; history; how-to; memoirs; military/war; sports; travel; true crime/investigative; women's issues/studies; young adult. **Considers these fiction areas:** action/adventure; historical; horror; mainstream/contemporary; romance; science fiction; sports; thriller; westerns/frontier; young adult.

○━ "We like film projects. In the past year we have optioned 4 novels as screenplays. We have also had 2 movies produced." Actively seeking good writing in any area. Does not want to receive new age, poetry.

**Also Handles:** Movie scripts; feature film. **Considers these script subject areas:** action/adventure; horror; mainstream; romantic drama; science fiction; sports; thriller; western/frontier.

**How to Contact:** Query with SASE. Considers simultaneous queries. Responds in 3 weeks to queries; 1 month to mss. Returns materials only with SASE. Obtains most new clients through solicitations.

**Recent Sales:** Sold 8 titles and sold 2 scripts in the last year. *Scream Black Murder*, by Philip McLaren (Intrigue Press); *Cutter's Island*, by Vince Panella (Academy Chicago); *Global Negotiator*, by Jeswald Salacuse (St. Martin's Press). *Movie/TV MOW script(s) optioned/sold: Scream Black Murder*, by Philip McLaren (Smith/Hermion); *Old Cockatoo*, by Craige Cronin (Stewart International Films). Other clients include Dr. Henry Lee, Dr. Anand Khare, Jesse H. Powell.

**Terms:** Agent receives 15% commission on domestic sales; 20% commission on foreign sales. Offers written contract, binding for 6 months; 30 days notice must be given to terminate contract. 10% of business is derived from commissions on ms sales. Charges clients for film projects (when requested by author) at $180 for a 6-month contract. If not requested, there is no fee.

**Tips:** "Do not send unsolicited mss. Query first. Pet peeve is the client who calls every couple of weeks to check on 'what's happening.'"

**N** **CARLISLE & COMPANY**, 24 E. 64th St., New York NY 10021. (212)813-1881. Fax: (212)813-9567. E-mail: mtessler@carlisleco.com. Website: www.carlisleco.com. **Contact:** Michelle Tessler. Estab. 1998. Member of AAR. Represents 100 clients. Currently handles: 60% nonfiction books; 35% novels; 5% story collections.

● Prior to opening his agency, Mr. Carlisle was the Vice President of William Morris for 18 years.

**Member Agents:** Michael Carlisle (narrative nonfiction and literary fiction); Christy Fletcher (literary fiction, biography, narrative nonfiction, pop culture, business, science); Emma Parry (literary fiction, general nonfiction); Lary Chilnick (health, cookbook, psychology, self-help).

**Represents:** Nonfiction books; novels; short story collections. **Considers these nonfiction areas:** biography/autobiography; business/economics; cooking/foods/nutrition; health/medicine; history; memoirs; popular culture; psychology; science/technology; lifestyle. **Considers these fiction areas:** literary; mainstream/contemporary; mystery/suspense; thriller.

○━ This agency has "expertise in nonfiction. We have a strong focus on editorial input on fiction before submission." Does not want to receive science fiction, fantasy, or romance.

**How to Contact:** Query with SASE. Responds in 10 days to queries; 3 weeks to mss. Obtains most new clients through recommendations from others.

**Recent Sales:** Sold 60 titles in the last year. *The World's Measure*, by Ken Adler (Free Press); *Elsie's Story*, by John Casey (Knopf); *The Americans*, by David M. Kennedy (Viking).

**Terms:** Agent receives 15% commission on domestic sales; 20% commission on foreign sales. Offers written contract, binding for 1 book only.

**Writers' Conferences:** Squaw Valley Community Conference (California).

**Tips:** "Be sure to write as original a story as possible. Remember, you're asking the public to pay $25 for your book."

**◐** **MARIA CARVAINIS AGENCY, INC.**, 1350 Avenue of the Americas, Suite 2905, New York NY 10019. (212)245-6365. Fax: (212)245-7196. E-mail: mca@mariacarvainisagency.com. **Contact:** Maria Carvainis, Frances Kuffel. Estab. 1977. Member of AAR, Authors Guild, ABA, MWA, RWA; signatory of WGA. Represents 70 clients. 10% of clients are new/unpublished writers. Currently handles: 34% nonfiction books; 65% novels; 1% poetry.

● Prior to opening her agency, Ms. Carvainis spent more than 10 years in the publishing industry as a senior editor with Macmillan Publishing, Basic Books, Avon Books, where she worked closely with Peter Mayer and Crown Publishers. Ms. Carvainis has served as a member of the AAR Board of Directors and AAR Treasurer, as well as serving as chair of the AAR Contracts Committee. She presently serves on the AAR Royalty Committee.

**Member Agents:** Frances Kuffel (Executive Vice President).

**TO FIND AN AGENT** near you, check the Geographic Index.

**Represents:** Nonfiction books; novels. **Considers these nonfiction areas:** biography/autobiography; business/economics; health/medicine; memoirs; science/technology (pop science); women's issues/studies. **Considers these fiction areas:** fantasy; historical; literary; mainstream/contemporary; mystery/suspense; romance; thriller; young adult.

   O➤ Does not want to receive science fiction or children's.

**How to Contact:** Query with SASE. Responds in 3 weeks to queries; 3 months to mss. Obtains most new clients through recommendations from others, solicitations, conferences, 60% from conferences/referrals; 40% from query letters.

**Recent Sales:** *The Switch and Envy*, by Sandra Brown (Warner Books); *The Guru Guide to the Knowledge Economy*, by Joseph H. Boyett and Jimmie T. Boyett (John Wiley and Sonts); *Trophy Widow*, by Michael Kahn (TOR/Forge); *Paint It Black*, by P.J. Parrish (Kensington); *Heroin*, by Charlie Smith (W.W. Norton); *Last Breath*, by Peter Stark (Ballantine); *The Devil's Hearth*, by Phillip DePoy (St. Martin's Press); *Private Captain*, by Marty Crisp (Philomel). Other clients include Mary Balogh, David Bottoms, Pam Conrad, Cindy Gerard, Sarah Isidore, Samantha James, Kristine Rolofson, William Sessions, Jose Yglesias, Fred Haefele, D. Anna Love, Fred Willard.

**Terms:** Agent receives 15% commission on domestic sales; 20% commission on foreign sales. Offers written contract, binding for 2 years. Charges clients for foreign postage, bulk copying.

**Writers' Conferences:** BEA; Frankfurt Book Fair.

◐ ◎ **MARTHA CASSELMAN LITERARY AGENCY, (Specialized: cookbooks)**, P.O. Box 342, Calistoga CA 94515-0342. (707)942-4341. Fax: (707)942-4358. **Contact:** Martha Casselman. Estab. 1978. Member of IACP. Represents 30 clients. Currently handles: 100% nonfiction books.

**Represents:** Nonfiction books (food-related proposals and cookbooks). **Considers these nonfiction areas:** agriculture/horticulture; anthropology/archaeology; biography/autobiography; cooking/foods/nutrition; health/medicine; women's issues/studies.

   O➤ This agency specializes in "nonfiction, especially food books." Does not want to receive children's book material.

**How to Contact:** Query with SASE, proposal package, outline, 3 sample chapter(s). Do not send any submission without querying first. Responds in 3 weeks to queries. Obtains most new clients through recommendations from others.

**Terms:** Agent receives 15% commission on domestic sales; 20% commission on foreign sales. Charges clients for photocopying, overnight and overseas mailings.

**Writers' Conferences:** IACP; other food-writers' conferences.

**Tips:** "No tricky letters; no gimmicks; always include SASE or mailer, or we can't contact you."

◐ **CASTIGLIA LITERARY AGENCY**, 1155 Camino Del Mar, Suite 510, Del Mar CA 92014. (858)755-8761. Fax: (858)755-7063. **Contact:** Julie Castiglia. Estab. 1993. Member of AAR, PEN. Represents 50 clients. Currently handles: 55% nonfiction books; 45% novels.

**Member Agents:** Winifred Golden; Julie Castiglia

**Represents:** Nonfiction books; novels. **Considers these nonfiction areas:** animals; anthropology/archaeology; biography/autobiography; business/economics; child guidance/parenting; cooking/foods/nutrition; current affairs; ethnic/cultural interests; health/medicine; history; language/literature/criticism; money/finance; nature/environment; New Age/metaphysics; psychology; religious/inspirational; science/technology; self-help/personal improvement; sociology; women's issues/studies. **Considers these fiction areas:** contemporary issues; ethnic; glitz; literary; mainstream/contemporary; mystery/suspense; women's (especially).

   O➤ Does not want to receive horror, science fiction, screenplays or academic nonfiction.

**How to Contact:** Query with SASE. No fax queries. Responds in 2 months to mss. Returns materials only with SASE. Obtains most new clients through recommendations from others, solicitations, conferences.

**Recent Sales:** Sold 23 titles in the last year. *Scent of Orange Blossoms*, by Kitty Morse (Ten Speed); *Power of Attraction*, by Geri Sullivan and Saffi Crawford (Ballantine); *Storybook Style*, by Doug Keister and Arrol Gellner (Penguin).

**Terms:** Agent receives 15% commission on domestic sales; 25% commission on foreign sales. Offers written contract; 6-week notice must be given to terminate contract. Charges clients for excessive postage and copying.

**Writers' Conferences:** Southwestern Writers Conference (Albuquerque NM, August); National Writers Conference; Willamette Writers Conference (Oregon); San Diego State University (California); Writers at Work (Utah).

**Tips:** "Be professional with submissions. Attend workshops and conferences before you approach an agent."

◐ **JAMES CHARLTON ASSOCIATES**, 680 Washington St., #2A, New York NY 10014. (212)691-4951. Fax: (212)691-4952. **Contact:** Lisa Friedman. Estab. 1983. Currently handles: 100% nonfiction books.

**Represents:** Nonfiction books. **Considers these nonfiction areas:** child guidance/parenting; cooking/foods/nutrition; health/medicine; how-to; humor/satire; military/war; popular culture; sports.

   O➤ This agency specializes in military history, sports.

**How to Contact:** Query with SASE. Responds in 2 weeks to queries. Obtains most new clients through recommendations from others.

**Recent Sales:** Sold 24 titles in the last year. *The Violence Handbook*, by Dr. George Gellert (West View); *Wisdom of the Popes*, by Tom Craughwell (St. Martin's Press).

**Terms:** Agent receives 15% commission on domestic sales. Offers written contract; 60-day cancellation clause notice must be given to terminate contract.

**Writers' Conferences:** Oregon Writer's Conference (Portland); Oklahoma Writer's Conference.

**JANE CHELIUS LITERARY AGENCY**, 548 Second St., Brooklyn NY 11215. Member of AAR. This agency did not respond to our request for information. Query before submitting.

**WM CLARK ASSOCIATES**, 325 W. 13th St., New York NY 10014-1219. (212)675-2784. Fax: (212)675-8394. E-mail: wcquery@wmclark.com. Website: www.wmclark.com. **Contact:** William Clark. Estab. 1999. Member of AAR. 4.25% of clients are new/unpublished writers. Currently handles: 50% nonfiction books; 50% novels.
  • Prior to opening WCA, Mr. Clark was an agent at the Virginia Barber Literary Agency and William Morris Agency.
**Represents:** Nonfiction books; novels; short story collections. **Considers these nonfiction areas:** art/architecture/ design; biography/autobiography; current affairs; ethnic/cultural interests; history; memoirs; music/dance; popular culture; religious/inspirational (Eastern religion philosophy only); science/technology; sociology; theater/film; translation. **Considers these fiction areas:** contemporary issues; ethnic; historical; literary; mainstream/contemporary; Southern fiction.
  **O—** "As one of the new breed of media agents recognizing their expanded roles in today's ever-changing media landscape, William Clark represents a diverse range of commercial and literary fiction and quality nonfiction to the book publishing, motion picture, television, and new media fields."
**How to Contact:** Prefers to read materials exclusively. No unsolicited mss. E-mail queries only. Responds in 2 weeks to queries. Obtains most new clients through recommendations from others.
**Recent Sales:** Sold 25 titles in the last year. *The Vogue Photographic Archive*, (Viking Studio); *Boogie Woogie*, by Danny Moynihan (St. Martin's Press); *Housebroken*, by David Eddie (Riverhead); *Stardust Melodies*, by Will Friedwald (Alfred A. Knopf); *Mark Hampton: The Art of Friendship*, by Duane Hampton (HarperCollins). Other clients include Molly Jong-Fast, William Monahan, Cornelia Bailey, Sarah Schulman, James St. James, Jonathan Stone, Dr. Doreen Virtue, Mian Mian.
**Terms:** Agent receives 15% commission on domestic sales; 20% commission on foreign sales. Offers written contract.
**Tips:** "E-mail queries should include a general description of the work, a synopsis/outline if available, biographical information, and publishing history, if any."

**CLAUSEN, MAYS & TAHAN, LLC**, 249 W. 34th St., Suite 605, New York NY 10001-2815. (212)239-4343. Fax: (212)239-5248. E-mail: cmtassist@aol.com. **Contact:** Stedman Mays, Mary M. Tahan. Estab. 1976. 10% of clients are new/unpublished writers. Currently handles: nonfiction books.
**Member Agents:** Stedman Mays; Mary M. Tahan; Rachelle Leon.
**Represents:** Nonfiction books. **Considers these nonfiction areas:** biography/autobiography; cooking/foods/nutrition; health/medicine; history; how-to; humor/satire; memoirs; money/finance; psychology; religious/inspirational; spirituality; women's issues/studies; fashion/beauty/style; relationships; also rights for books optioned for TV movies and feature films.
**How to Contact:** Query with SASE, proposal package, outline. No e-mail or fax queries. Considers simultaneous queries. Responds in 3 weeks to queries; 1 month to mss. Returns materials only with SASE.
**Recent Sales:** *The Okinawa Program*, by Bradley Willcox, M.D., Craig Willcox, Ph.D. and Makoto Suzuki, M.D. (Clarkson Potter); *Loving Him Without Losing Him*, by Beverly Engel (Wiley & Sons); *Does This Make Me Look Fat?*, by Leah Feldon (Villard); *Cosmic Banditos: A Novel*, by Allan C. Weisbecker (NAL); *The Rules and The Rules II*, by Ellen Fein and Sherrie Schneider (Warner Books); *What the IRS Doesn't Want You to Know*, by Martin Kaplan and Naomi Weiss (Villard); *The Official RENT-A-HUSBAND Guide to a Safe, Problem-Free Home*, by Kaile R. Warren, Jr. and Jane Craig (Broadway); *In Search of Captain Zero: A Memoir*, by Allan C. Weisbecker (Tarcher).
**Terms:** Agent receives 15% commission on domestic sales; 20% commission on foreign sales. Charges clients for postage, shipping, and photocopying.
**Tips:** "Research proposal writing and the publishing process. Always study your book's competition. Send a proposal and outline instead of complete manuscript for faster response. Always pitch books in writing, not over the phone."

**CLIENT FIRST—A/K/A LEO P. HAFFEY AGENCY**, P.O. Box 128049, Nashville TN 37212-8049. (615)463-2388. E-mail: c1st@nashville.net. Website: www.c-1st.com or www.nashville/net/~c1. **Contact:** Robin Swensen. Estab. 1990. Signatory of WGA. Represents 21 clients. 25% of clients are new/unpublished writers. Currently handles: 40% novels; 60% movie scripts.
  • See the expanded listing for this agency in Script Agents.

**RUTH COHEN, INC. LITERARY AGENCY**, P.O. Box 2244, La Jolla CA 92038-2244. (858)456-5805. **Contact:** Ruth Cohen. Estab. 1982. Member of AAR, Authors Guild, Sisters in Crime, RWA, SCBWI. Represents 45 clients. 15% of clients are new/unpublished writers. Currently handles: 5% nonfiction books; 60% novels; 35% juvenile books.
  • Prior to becoming an agent, Ms. Cohen served as directing editor at Scott Foresman & Company (now HarperCollins).
**Represents:** Novels (adult); juvenile books. **Considers these nonfiction areas:** ethnic/cultural interests; women's issues/studies. **Considers these fiction areas:** ethnic; historical; juvenile; literary; mainstream/contemporary; mystery/ suspense; picture books; young adult.

☛ This agency specializes in "quality writing in contemporary fiction, women's fiction, mysteries, thrillers and juvenile fiction." Does not want to receive poetry, westerns, film scripts or how-to books.

**How to Contact:** Submit outline, 1 sample chapter(s). Responds in 3 weeks to queries. Returns materials only with SASE. Obtains most new clients through recommendations from others, solicitations.

**Recent Sales:** This agency prefers not to share information on specific sales.

**Terms:** Agent receives 15% commission on domestic sales; 20% commission on foreign sales. Offers written contract, binding for 1 year. Charges for foreign postage, phone calls, photocopying submissions and overnight delivery of mss when appropriate.

**Tips:** "As the publishing world merges and changes, there seem to be fewer opportunities for new writers to succeed in the work that they love. We urge you to develop the patience, persistence and preseverance that have made this agency so successful. Prepare a well-written and well-crafted manuscript, and our combined best efforts can help advance both our careers."

**JOANNA LEWIS COLE, LITERARY AGENT**, 404 Riverside Dr., New York NY 10025. Member of AAR. This agency did not respond to our request for information. Query before submitting.

**FRANCES COLLIN LITERARY AGENT**, P.O. Box 33, Wayne PA 19087-0033. (702)733-1017. Fax: (702)733-1215. E-mail: dwauhob@aol.com. **Contact:** Frances Collin. Estab. 1948. Member of AAR. Represents 90 clients. 1% of clients are new/unpublished writers. Currently handles: 50% nonfiction books; 48% novels; 1% textbooks; 1% poetry.

**Member Agents:** Calvin Maefield (literary).

**Represents:** Nonfiction books; novels. **Considers these nonfiction areas:** anthropology/archaeology; biography/autobiography; health/medicine; history; nature/environment; true crime/investigative. **Considers these fiction areas:** detective/police/crime; ethnic; family saga; fantasy; historical; literary; mainstream/contemporary; mystery/suspense; psychic/supernatural; regional; romance (historical); science fiction.

**How to Contact:** Query with SASE. Responds in 1 week to queries; 2 months to mss. Obtains most new clients through recommendations from others.

**Recent Sales:** This agency prefers not to share information on specific sales.

**Terms:** Agent receives 15% commission on domestic sales; 20% commission on foreign sales. Offers written contract. Charges clients for overseas postage for books mailed to foreign agents; photocopying of mss, books, proposals; copyright registration fees; registered mail fees; passes along cost of any books purchased.

**COLUMBIA LITERARY ASSOCIATES, INC.**, 7902 Nottingham Way, Ellicott City MD 21043-6721. (410)465-1595. Fax: Call for number. **Contact:** Linda Hayes. Estab. 1980. Currently not accepting new clients.

**COMMUNICATIONS AND ENTERTAINMENT, INC.**, 2851 S. Ocean Blvd., #5K, Boca Raton FL 33432-8407. (561)391-9575. Fax: (561)391-7922. E-mail: jlbearde@bellsouth.net. **Contact:** James L. Bearden. Estab. 1989. Represents 10 clients. 50% of clients are new/unpublished writers. Currently handles: 10% novels; 5% juvenile books; 40% movie scripts; 40% TV scripts.

• See the expanded listing for this agency in Script Agents.

**DON CONGDON ASSOCIATES INC.**, 156 Fifth Ave., Suite 625, New York NY 10010. (212)645-1229. Fax: (212)727-2688. E-mail: congdon@veriomail.com. **Contact:** Don Congdon, Michael Congdon, Susan Ramer, Christina Concepcion. Estab. 1983. Member of AAR. Represents 100 clients. Currently handles: 50% nonfiction books; 50% novels.

**Represents:** Nonfiction books; novels. **Considers these nonfiction areas:** agriculture/horticulture; americana; animals; anthropology/archaeology; art/architecture/design; biography/autobiography; business/economics; child guidance/parenting; computers/electronic; cooking/foods/nutrition; crafts/hobbies; creative nonfiction; current affairs; education; ethnic/cultural interests; gardening; gay/lesbian issues; government/politics/law; health/medicine; history; how-to; humor/satire; interior design/decorating; juvenile nonfiction; language/literature/criticism; memoirs; military/war; money/finance; multicultural; music/dance; nature/environment; New Age/metaphysics; philosophy; photography; popular culture; psychology; recreation; regional; religious/inspirational; science/technology; self-help/personal improvement; sex; sociology; software; spirituality; sports; theater/film; translation; travel; true crime/investigative; women's issues/studies; young adult. **Considers these fiction areas:** action/adventure; comic books/cartoon; confession; contemporary issues; detective/police/crime; erotica; ethnic; experimental; family saga; fantasy; feminist; gay/lesbian; glitz; gothic; hi-lo; historical; horror; humor/satire; juvenile; literary (especially); mainstream/contemporary; military/war; multicultural; multimedia; mystery/suspense; New Age; occult; picture books; plays; poetry; poetry in translation; psychic/supernatural; regional; religious/inspirational; romance; science fiction; short story collections; spiritual; sports; thriller; translation; westerns/frontier; young adult; women's.

**How to Contact:** Query with SASE. Responds in 1 week to queries; 1 month to mss. Obtains most new clients through recommendations from others.

**Recent Sales:** *Me Talk Pretty One Day*, by David Sedaris (Little, Brown); *The Gravity of Sunlight*, by Rosa Shand (Soho); *You Only Die Twice*, by Edna Buchanan (HarperCollins).

**Terms:** Agent receives 15% commission on domestic sales. Charges client for extra shipping costs, photocopying, copyright fees and book purchases.

**Tips:** "Writing a query letter with a self-addressed stamped envelope is a must."

**CONNOR LITERARY AGENCY**, 2911 W. 71st St., Minneapolis MN 55423. (612)866-1426. Fax: (612)869-4074. E-mail: coolmkc@aol.com. **Contact:** Marlene Connor Lynch. Estab. 1985. Represents 50 clients. 30% of clients are new/unpublished writers. Currently handles: 50% nonfiction books; 50% novels.
- Prior to opening her agency, Ms. Connor served at the Literary Guild of America, Simon and Schuster and Random House. She is author of *What is Cool: Understanding Black Manhood in America* (Crown).
**Member Agents:** Deborah Coker (children's books); John Lynch (assistant).
**Represents:** Nonfiction books; novels; juvenile books; especially with a minority slant. **Considers these nonfiction areas:** business/economics; child guidance/parenting; cooking/foods/nutrition; crafts/hobbies; current affairs; ethnic/cultural interests; government/politics/law; health/medicine; how-to; humor/satire; interior design/decorating; language/literature/criticism; money/finance; photography; popular culture; self-help/personal improvement; sports; true crime/investigative; women's issues/studies. **Considers these fiction areas:** horror; literary; mainstream/contemporary; multicultural; mystery/suspense; romance (suspense); thriller; women's.
- O━ This agency specializes in popular fiction and nonfiction.
**How to Contact:** Query with SASE, outline. Responds in 1 month to queries; 6 weeks to mss. Obtains most new clients through recommendations from others, solicitations, conferences, grapevine.
**Recent Sales:** *Outrageous Commitments*, by Ronn Elmore (HarperCollins); *Seductions*, by Snow Starborn (Sourcebooks).
**Terms:** Agent receives 15% commission on domestic sales; 25% commission on foreign sales. Offers written contract, binding for 1 year.
**Writers' Conferences:** Howard University Publishing Institute; Mid-West Romance Writer's Conference; BEA; Agents, Agents, Agents; Texas Writer's Conference; Detroit Writer's Conference.
**Tips:** "Seeking previously published writers with good sales records and new writers with real talent."

**THE DOE COOVER AGENCY**, P.O. Box 668, Winchester MA 01890. (781)721-6000. Fax: (781)721-6727. **Contact:** Doe Coover, president. Estab. 1985. Represents 75 clients. Currently handles: 80% nonfiction books; 20% novels.
- Prior to becoming agents, Ms. Coover and Ms. Mohyde were editors for over a decade.
**Member Agents:** Doe Coover (cooking, general nonfiction); Colleen Mohyde (literary and commercial fiction, general nonfiction and journalism).
**Represents:** Nonfiction books; novels. **Considers these nonfiction areas:** anthropology/archaeology; biography/autobiography; business/economics; child guidance/parenting; cooking/foods/nutrition; ethnic/cultural interests; health/medicine; history; language/literature/criticism; memoirs; money/finance; nature/environment; psychology; sociology; travel; true crime/investigative; women's issues/studies. **Considers these fiction areas:** literary; mainstream/contemporary (commercial).
- O━ This agency specializes in cookbooks, serious nonfiction—particularly books on social issues—as well as fiction (literary and commercial), journalism and general nonfiction. Does not want children's books.
**How to Contact:** Query with SASE, outline. No e-mail or fax queries. Considers simultaneous queries. Returns materials only with SASE. Obtains most new clients through recommendations from others, solicitations.
**Recent Sales:** Sold 25-30 titles in the last year. *L'Apprentissage*, by Jacques Pepin (William Morrow Cookbooks); *Consciously Female*, by Tracy W. Gaudet, M.D. and Louisa Kasdon Sidell (Bantam Dell); *The Mind Cure*, by Suzanne Berne (Algonquin Books). **Movie/TV MOW script(s) optioned/sold:** *Mr. White's Confession*, by Robert Clark. Other clients include Peter Lynch, Suzanne Berne, Deborah Madison, Sandra Shea, Rick Bayless, Marion Cunningham.
**Terms:** Agent receives 15% commission on domestic sales; 15% commission on foreign sales.
**Writers' Conferences:** BEA (Chicago).

**CORE CREATIONS, LLC**, 9024 S. Sanderling Way, Littleton CO 80126. (303)683-6792. E-mail: agent@eoncity.com. Website: www.eoncity.com/agent. **Contact:** Calvin Rex. Estab. 1994. Represents 10 clients. 70% of clients are new/unpublished writers. Currently handles: 30% nonfiction books; 60% novels; 5% novellas; 5% games.
- Prior to becoming an agent, Mr. Rex managed a small publishing house.
**Member Agents:** Calvin Rex.
**Represents:** Nonfiction books; novels; novellas. **Considers these nonfiction areas:** gay/lesbian issues; how-to; humor/satire; psychology; true crime/investigative. **Considers these fiction areas:** detective/police/crime; horror; science fiction.
- O━ This agency specializes in "bold, daring literature." Agency has strong "experience with royalty contracts and licensing agreements."
**How to Contact:** Query with SASE, proposal package, outline. Responds in 3 weeks to queries; 3 months to mss. Obtains most new clients through recommendations from others, solicitations, through the Internet.
**Terms:** Agent receives 15% commission on domestic sales; 20% commission on foreign sales. Offers written contract. Charges clients for postage (applicable mailing costs).
**Writers' Conferences:** Steamboat Springs Writers Group (Colorado, July); Rocky Mountain Fiction Writers Colorado Gold Conference.
**Tips:** "Have all material proofread. Visit our webpage before sending anything. We want books that dare to be different. Give us a unique angle, a new style of writing, something that stands out from the crowd!"

**[N]  ROBERT CORNFIELD LITERARY AGENCY**, 145 W. 79th St., New York NY 10024-6468. (212)874-2465. Fax: (212)874-2641. E-mail: rcbccron@aol.com. **Contact:** Robert Cornfield. Estab. 1979. Member of AAR. Represents 60 clients. 20% of clients are new/unpublished writers. Currently handles: 60% nonfiction books; 20% novels; 20% scholarly books.

• Prior to opening his agency, Mr. Cornfield was an editor at Holt and Dial Press.

**Represents:** Nonfiction books; novels. **Considers these nonfiction areas:** animals; anthropology/archaeology; art/architecture/design; cooking/foods/nutrition; language/literature/criticism; music/dance. **Considers these fiction areas:** literary.

O→ This agency specializes in film, art, literary, music criticism, food, fiction.

**How to Contact:** Query with SASE. Responds in 3 weeks to queries. Obtains most new clients through recommendations from others.

**Recent Sales:** Sold 15-20 titles in the last year. *Mixed Signals*, by Richard Barrios (Routledge); *Multiple Personalities*, by Joan Acorella (Jossey-Bass).

**Terms:** Agent receives 10% commission on domestic sales; 20% commission on foreign sales. No written contract. Charges for postage, excessive photocopying.

**[✓]  CRAWFORD LITERARY AGENCY**, 94 Evans Rd., Barnstead NH 03218. (603)269-5851. Fax: (603)269-2533. E-mail: CrawfordLit@att.net. **Contact:** Susan Crawford. Estab. 1988. Represents 40 clients. 10% of clients are new/unpublished writers. Currently handles: 50% nonfiction books; 50% novels.

**Member Agents:** Susan Crawford; Lorne Crawford (commercial fiction); Scott Neister (scientific/techno thrillers); Kristen Hales (parenting, psychology, New Age, self help).

**Represents:** Nonfiction books; novels (commercial fiction). **Considers these nonfiction areas:** religious/inspirational; self-help/personal improvement; women's issues/studies; celebrity/media. **Considers these fiction areas:** action/adventure; mystery/suspense; thriller (medical).

O→ This agency specializes in celebrity and/or media-based books and authors. Actively seeking action/adventure stories, medical thrillers, suspense thrillers, suspense thrillers, celebrity projects, self-help, inspirational, how-to and women's issues. Does not want to receive short stories, poetry.

**How to Contact:** Query with SASE. No e-mail or fax queries. Responds in 3 weeks to queries. Returns materials only with SASE. Obtains most new clients through recommendations from others, solicitations, conferences.

**Recent Sales:** Sold 22 titles in the last year. *Krane on Producing*, by Jonathan D. Krane (Renaissance Books); *The John Lennon Affair*, by Robert S. Levinson (Forge Books); *Housebroken*, by Richard Karn and George Mair (HarperCollins); *With Ossie & Ruby*, by Ruby Dee and Ossie Davis (William Morrow); *PSI/Net*, by Billy Dee Williams and Rob MacGregor (TOR/Forge). Other clients include John Travolta, Billy Dee Williams, Producer Jonathan Krane.

**Terms:** Agent receives 15% commission on domestic sales; 20% commission on foreign sales. Offers written contract, binding for 90 days; 100% of business is derived from commissions on ms sales.

**Writers' Conferences:** International Film & Writers Workshop (Rockport ME); Maui Writers Conference

** RICHARD CURTIS ASSOCIATES, INC.**, 171 E. 74th St., Suite 2, New York NY 10021. (212)772-7363. Fax: (212)772-7393. E-mail: jhacrworth@curtisagency.com. Website: www.curtisagency.com. **Contact:** Pam Valvera. Estab. 1969. Member of RWA, MWA, WWA, SFWA; signatory of WGA. Represents 100 clients. 5% of clients are new/unpublished writers. Currently handles: 50% nonfiction books; 50% novels.

• Prior to opening his agency, Mr. Curtis was an agent with the Scott Meredith Literary Agency for 7 years and has authored over 50 published books.

**Member Agents:** Richard Curtis; Jennifer Hackworth; Amy Victoria Meo.

**Represents:** Nonfiction books; novels; scholarly books. **Considers these nonfiction areas:** agriculture/horticulture; americana; animals; anthropology/archaeology; art/architecture/design; biography/autobiography; business/economics; child guidance/parenting; computers/electronic; cooking/foods/nutrition; crafts/hobbies; creative nonfiction; current affairs; education; ethnic/cultural interests; gardening; gay/lesbian issues; government/politics/law; health/medicine; history; how-to; humor/satire; interior design/decorating; juvenile nonfiction; language/literature/criticism; memoirs; military/war; money/finance; multicultural; music/dance; nature/environment; New Age/metaphysics; philosophy; photography; popular culture; psychology; recreation; regional; religious/inspirational; science/technology; self-help/personal improvement; sex; sociology; software; spirituality; sports; theater/film; translation; travel; true crime/investigative; women's issues/studies; young adult. **Considers these fiction areas:** action/adventure; comic books/cartoon; confession; contemporary issues; detective/police/crime; erotica; ethnic; experimental; family saga; fantasy; feminist; gay/lesbian; glitz; gothic; hi-lo; historical; horror; humor/satire; juvenile; literary; mainstream/contemporary; military/war; multicultural; multimedia; mystery/suspense; New Age; occult; picture books; plays; poetry; poetry in translation; psychic/supernatural; regional; religious/inspirational; romance; science fiction; short story collections; spiritual; sports; thriller; translation; westerns/frontier; young adult; women's.

O→ This agency specializes in general and literary fiction and nonfiction, as well as genre fiction such as science fiction, romance, horror, fantasy, action-adventure.

**How to Contact:** Query with SASE, outline, 3 sample chapter(s). No e-mail or fax queries. Responds in 1 month to queries; 1 month to mss. Obtains most new clients through recommendations from others, solicitations, conferences.

**Recent Sales:** Sold 100 titles in the last year. *Courtney Love: The Real Story*, by Poppy Z. Brite (Simon & Schuster); *Vitals*, by Greg Bear (Del Rey/Random House); *Expendable*, by James Gardner (Avon). Other clients include Jennifer Blake, Leonard Maltin, Earl Mindell and Barbara Parker.

**Terms:** Agent receives 15% commission on domestic sales; 20% commission on foreign sales. Offers written contract, binding for book-by-book basis. Charges for photocopying, express, fax, international postage, book orders.
**Writers' Conferences:** Romance Writers of America; Nebula Science Fiction Conference.

 **JAMES R. CYPHER, THE CYPHER AGENCY,** 816 Wolcott Ave., Beacon NY 12508-4261. Phone/fax: (845)831-5677. E-mail: jimcypher@prodigy.net. Website: pages.prodigy.net/jimcypher/. **Contact:** James R. Cypher. Estab. 1993. Member of Authors Guild. Represents 37 clients. 41% of clients are new/unpublished writers. Currently handles: 100% nonfiction books.
- Prior to opening his agency, Mr. Cypher worked as a corporate public relations manager for a Fortune 500 multi-national computer company for 28 years.

**Represents:** Nonfiction books. **Considers these nonfiction areas:** biography/autobiography; current affairs; ethnic/cultural interests; gay/lesbian issues; government/politics/law; health/medicine; history; how-to; language/literature/criticism; memoirs (travel); money/finance; music/dance; nature/environment; popular culture; psychology; science/technology; self-help/personal improvement; sociology; sports; theater/film; travel (memoirs); true crime/investigative; women's issues/studies.
- ○⊸ Actively seeking a wide variety of topical nonfiction. Does not want to receive humor; pets; gardening; cooking books; crafts; spiritual; religious or New Age topics.

**How to Contact:** Query with SASE, proposal package, outline, 2 sample chapter(s). Accepts e-mail and fax queries. Considers simultaneous queries. Responds in 2 weeks to queries; 6 weeks to mss. Obtains most new clients through recommendations from others, conferences, networking on online computer service.
**Recent Sales:** Sold 6 titles in the last year. *Rebel with a Cause: A Season with NASCAR Star Tony Stewart*, by Monte Dutton (Brassey's, Inc.); *Hoare and the Matter of Treason*, by Wilder Perkins (St. Martin's Press); *Gay Spirituality: The Role of Gay Identity in the Transformation of Human Consciousness*, by Toby Johnson (Alyson Publications); *The Cancer Pain Sourcebook*, by Roger S. Cicala, M.D.(Lowell House); *NASCAR's Most Wanted: The Top 10 Book of Outrageous Drivers, Wild Rides, and Other Oddities*, by James A. McLaurin (Brassey's, Inc.); *Revolution in Zanzibar: An American's Cold War Tale*, by Donald K. Petterson (Westview Press).
**Terms:** Agent receives 15% commission on domestic sales; 20% commission on foreign sales. Offers written contract; 30-day cancellation clause notice must be given to terminate contract. 100% of business is derived from commissions on ms sales. Charges clients for postage, photocopying, overseas phone calls and faxes.

 **DARHANSOFF & VERRILL LITERARY AGENTS,** 236 W. 26th St., Suite 802, New York NY 10001. (917)305-1300. Fax: (917)305-1400. Estab. 1975. Member of AAR. Represents 100 clients. 10% of clients are new/unpublished writers. Currently handles: 25% nonfiction books; 60% novels; 15% story collections.
**Member Agents:** Liz Darhansoff; Charles Verrill; Leigh Feldman; Tal Gregory.
**Represents:** Nonfiction books; novels; short story collections. **Considers these nonfiction areas:** anthropology/archaeology; health/medicine; history; language/literature/criticism; nature/environment; science/technology. **Considers these fiction areas:** literary; mystery/suspense.
- ○⊸ Specializes in literary fiction.

**How to Contact:** Query with SASE. Responds in 2 weeks to queries. Obtains most new clients through recommendations from others.
**Recent Sales:** *At Home in Mitford*, by Jan Karon (Viking); *Cold Mountain*, by Charles Frazier (Atlantic Monthly Press). Other clients include Arthur Golden.

**JOAN DAVES AGENCY,** 21 W. 26th St., New York NY 10010. (212)685-2663. Fax: (212)685-1781. **Contact:** Jennifer Lyons, director. Estab. 1960. Member of AAR. Represents 100 clients. 10% of clients are new/unpublished writers.
**Represents:** Nonfiction books; novels. **Considers these nonfiction areas:** biography/autobiography; gay/lesbian issues; popular culture; translation; women's issues/studies. **Considers these fiction areas:** ethnic; family saga; gay/lesbian; literary; mainstream/contemporary.
- ○⊸ This agency specializes in literary fiction and nonfiction, also commercial fiction.

**How to Contact:** Query with SASE. No e-mail or fax queries. Considers simultaneous queries. Responds in 3 weeks to queries; 6 weeks to mss. Returns materials only with SASE. Obtains most new clients through recommendations from others, solicitations.
**Recent Sales:** Sold 70 titles in the last year. *Fire on the Mountain*, by John N. Maclean (Morrow).
**Terms:** Agent receives 15% commission on domestic sales; 20% commission on foreign sales. Offers written contract, binding for per book basis; 100% of business is derived from commissions on ms sales. Charges for office expenses.
**Tips:** "A few queries translate into representation."

 **LIZA DAWSON ASSOCIATES,** 240 W. 35th St., Suite 500, New York NY 10001. (212)465-9071 or (212)629-9212. **Contact:** Liza Dawson or Rebecca Kurson. Member of AAR, MWA, Women's Media Group. Represents 40 clients. 10% of clients are new/unpublished writers. Currently handles: 60% nonfiction books; 40% novels.
- Prior to becoming an agent, Ms. Dawson was an editor for 20 years, spending 11 years at William Morrow as vice president and 2 at Putnam as executive editor.

**Member Agents:** Liza Dawson; Rebecca Kurson (science, women's issues, narrative nonfiction, literary fiction).

**Represents:** Nonfiction books; novels; scholarly books. **Considers these nonfiction areas:** biography/autobiography; business/economics; health/medicine; history; how-to; memoirs; psychology; self-help/personal improvement; sociology; women's issues/studies. **Considers these fiction areas:** ethnic; family saga; historical; literary; mystery/suspense; regional; thriller.

> This agency specializes in readable literary fiction, thrillers, mainstream historicals and women's fiction, academics, historians, journalists, self-help and psychology. "My specialty is shaping books and ideas so that a publisher will respond quickly." Actively seeking talented professionals. Does not want to receive westerns, science fiction, sports, computers, juvenile.

**How to Contact:** Query with SASE. Responds in 3 weeks to queries; 6 weeks to mss. Obtains most new clients through recommendations from others, conferences.

**Recent Sales:** Sold 35 titles in the last year. *Darjeeling*, by Bharti Kirchner (St. Martin's); *Wild Mothers*, (Algonquin); *Even Dogs Go Home to Die*, by Linda St. John (HarperCollins); *The Neal Pollack Anthology of American Literature*, by Neal Pollack (HarperCollins); *Poker Nation*, by Andy Bellin (HarperCollins).

**Terms:** Agent receives 15% commission on domestic sales; 20% commission on foreign sales. Offers written contract. Charges clients for photocopying and overseas postage.

**Writers' Conferences:** Pacific Northwest Book Conference (Seattle, July).

**Reading List:** Reads *The Sun*, *New York Review of Books*, *The New York Observer*, *Utne Reader*, and *The Wall Street Journal* to find new clients.

**Tips:** "Please include a detailed bio with any query letter, let me know somehow that you've done a little research, that you're not just interested in any agent but someone who is right for you."

**☑ ⊘ DeFIORE AND COMPANY**, 853 Broadway, Suite 1715, New York NY 10003. Phone/fax: (212)505-7979. E-mail: info@defioreandco.com. Website: www.defioreandco.com. **Contact:** Brian DeFiore. Estab. 1999. Represents 25 clients. 50% of clients are new/unpublished writers. Currently handles: 70% nonfiction books; 30% novels.

> • Prior to becoming an agent, Mr. DeFiore was Publisher of Villard Books 1997-1998; Editor-in-Chief of Hyperion 1992-1997; Editorial Director Delacorte Press 1988-1992.

**Member Agents:** Brian DeFiore (popular nonfiction, business, pop culture, parenting, commercial fiction); Mark S. Roy (literary fiction, spirituality, gay & lesbian).

**Represents:** Nonfiction books; novels. **Considers these nonfiction areas:** biography/autobiography; business/economics; child guidance/parenting; cooking/foods/nutrition; gay/lesbian issues; health/medicine; money/finance; multicultural; popular culture; psychology; religious/inspirational; self-help/personal improvement; sports. **Considers these fiction areas:** ethnic; gay/lesbian; literary; mainstream/contemporary; mystery/suspense; thriller.

**How to Contact:** Query with SASE. Considers simultaneous queries. Responds in 2 weeks to queries; 6 weeks to mss. Returns materials only with SASE. Obtains most new clients through recommendations from others.

**Recent Sales:** Sold 15 titles in the last year. *Shooting Doctor Jack*, by Norman Green (HarperCollins); *Mr. Fix-It Introduces You to Your House*, by Lou Manfredini (Ballantine). Other clients include Jeff Arch, Corey Donaldson, Lori Fairweather, Joel Engel, Christopher Keane, Robin McMillan, Jessica Teich, Brian D'Amato, Jimmy Lerner, Ronna Lichtenborg, Fran Sorin, Christine Dimmick.

**Terms:** Agent receives 15% commission on domestic sales; 20% commission on foreign sales. Offers written contract; 10-day notice must be given to terminate contract. Charges clients for photocopying, overnight delivery (deducted only after a sale is made).

**Writers' Conferences:** Maui Writers Conference (Maui HI, September).

**☑ ◯ JOÉLLE DELBOURGO ASSOCIATES, INC.**, 450 Seventy Ave., Suite 3004, New York NY 10123. (212)279-9027. Fax: (212)279-8863. E-mail: infojdelbourgo.com. Website: www.delbourgo.com. **Contact:** Joelle Delbourgo. Estab. 1999. Represents 30 clients; 35% of clients are new/previously unpublished writers. Currently handles: 70% nonfiction books; 25% novels; 5% short story collections.

> • Prior to becoming an agent, Ms. Delbourgo was an editor and publishing executive for over 25 years, most recently as Senior VP and Editor-in-Chief at HarperCollins.

**Member Agents:** Joelle Delbourgo (serious nonfiction, history, psychology, medicine, health, politics, science, self-help, literary fiction); Jessica Lichtenstein (quality fiction, practical nonfiction).

**Represents:** Nonfiction, novels. short story collections. **Considers these nonfiction areas:** animals; anthropology/archaeology; biography/autobiography; business; child guidance/parenting; cooking/food/nutrition; current affairs; education; ethnic/cultural interests; government/politics/law; health/medicine; history; how-to; humor; interior design/decorating; language/literature/criticism; memoirs; military/war; money/finance/economics; multicultural; music/dance/the-

**FOR EXPLANATIONS OF THESE SYMBOLS,**
**SEE THE INSIDE FRONT AND BACK COVERS OF THIS BOOK**

ater/film; nature/environment; New Age/metaphysics; photography; popular culture; psychology; religious/inspirational; science/technology; self-help/personal improvement; sociology; sports; travel; true crime/investigative; women's issues/ women's studies. **Considers these fiction areas:** contemporary issues; detective/police/crime; family saga; historical; literary; mainstream; multicultural; mystery/suspense; thriller/espionage.

> O— "We are a quality agency as opposed to a volume agency. Our long-term editorial and publishing expertise makes us distinct. I have 25 years 'insider' experience. I know what publishers want and I'm also an expert marketer who works with authors to develop their platforms." Actively seeking narrative nonfiction, history, serious works, literary fiction. Does not want to receive genre fiction or light humor.

**How to Contact:** Query with SASE or send outline and 2 sample chapters. Does not accept queries by e-mail and fax. Considers simultaneous queries. Prefers to read mss exclusively. Responds in 3 weeks on queries; 1 month on mss. Returns materials only with SASE. Obtains most new clients through recommendations from others, solicitations of authors.

**Recent Sales:** Sold 10 titles in the last year. *Moon Women*, by Pamela Duncan (Bantam Dell); *The Speed of Light*, by Elizabeth Rosney (Ballantine); *Heal This Dependency*, by Robert Bornstein and Mary Languirand (New Market Press); *Becoming Myself: How the Death of Your Parents Can Transform Your Life*, by Shari Butler, Ph.D.; *Making Peace with God*, by Harold Bloomfield Ph.D. (Tarcher/Penguin Putnam). Other clients include Noah ben Shea, Laura Berman Fortgang, Lou Marinoff.

**Terms:** Agent receives 15% commission on domestic sales; 20% on foreign sales. Offers written contract.

**⬤ DH LITERARY, INC.**, P.O. Box 990, Nyack NY 10960-0990. (212)753-7942. E-mail: dhendin@aol.com. **Contact:** David Hendin. Estab. 1993. Member of AAR. Represents 30 clients. 20% of clients are new/unpublished writers. Currently handles: 60% nonfiction books; 20% novels; 10% scholarly books; 20% syndicated material.

> ● Prior to opening his agency, Mr. Hendin served as president and publisher for Pharos Books/World Almanac as well as senior VP and COO at sister company United Feature Syndicate.

**Represents:** Nonfiction books; novels; syndicated material. **Considers these nonfiction areas:** animals; anthropology/ archaeology; child guidance/parenting; ethnic/cultural interests; government/politics/law; health/medicine; history; language/literature/criticism; money/finance; nature/environment; psychology; science/technology; women's issues/studies. **Considers these fiction areas:** literary; mainstream/contemporary; mystery/suspense; thriller.

> O— This agency specializes in trade nonfiction and newspaper syndication of columns or comic strips.

**How to Contact:** Query with SASE. Considers simultaneous queries. Responds in 6 weeks to queries. Returns materials only with SASE. Obtains most new clients through recommendations from others.

**Recent Sales:** Sold 18-20 titles in the last year. *Pink Flamingo Murders*, by Elaine Viets (Dell); *Age of Anxious Anxiety*, by Tom Tiede (Grove Atlantic); *History of American Etiquette*, by Judith Martin (Norton).

**Terms:** Agent receives 15% commission on domestic sales; 20% commission on foreign sales. Offers written contract, binding for 1 year. Charges for out of pocket expenses for postage, photocopying ms, and overseas phone calls specifically related to a book.

**Tips:** "Have your project in mind and on paper before you submit. Too many writers/cartoonists say 'I'm good...get me a project.' Publishers want writers with their own great ideas and their own unique voice. No faxed submissions."

**☑ ⬤ DHS LITERARY, INC.**, 2528 Elm St., Suite 350, Dallas TX 75226. (214)363-4422. Fax: (214)363-4423. E-mail: submissions@dhsliterary.com. Website: www.dhsliterary.com. **Contact:** David Hale Smith, president. Estab. 1994. Represents 45 clients. 25% of clients are new/unpublished writers. Currently handles: 60% nonfiction books; 40% novels.

> ● Prior to opening his agency, Mr. Smith was an editor at a newswire service.

**Represents:** Nonfiction books; novels. **Considers these nonfiction areas:** biography/autobiography; business/economics; child guidance/parenting; cooking/foods/nutrition; current affairs; ethnic/cultural interests; popular culture; sports; true crime/investigative. **Considers these fiction areas:** detective/police/crime; erotica; ethnic; feminist; historical; literary; mainstream/contemporary; mystery/suspense; sports; thriller.

> O— This agency specializes in commercial fiction and nonfiction for adult trade market. Actively seeking thrillers, mysteries, suspense, etc., and narrative nonfiction. Does not want to receive poetry, short fiction, children's books.

**How to Contact:** One-page queries via e-mail only. No paper queries accepted unless requested by agency. Will request more material if appropriate. Considers simultaneous queries. Responds in 1 month to queries. Obtains most new clients through recommendations from others, solicitations, conferences.

**Recent Sales:** Sold 35 titles in the last year. *Extreme Success*, by Rich Fittke (Simon & Schuster); *Never Count Out the Dead*, by Boston Teran (St. Martin's Press/Minotaur).

**Terms:** Agent receives 15% commission on domestic sales; 25% commission on foreign sales. Offers written contract; 10 days notice must be given to terminate contract. Charges for client expenses, i.e., postage, photocopying.

**Tips:** "Remember to be courteous and professional, and to treat marketing your work and approaching an agent as you would any formal business matter. When in doubt, always query first via e-mail. Visit our website for more information."

**⬤ SANDRA DIJKSTRA LITERARY AGENCY**, 1155 Camino del Mar, Suite 515, Del Mar CA 92014-2605. (619)755-3115. **Contact:** Sandra Zane. Estab. 1981. Member of AAR, Authors Guild, PEN West, Poets and Editors, MWA. Represents 100 clients. 30% of clients are new/unpublished writers. Currently handles: 60% nonfiction books; 35% novels; 5% juvenile books.

**Member Agents:** Sandra Dijkstra.

**Represents:** Nonfiction books; novels. **Considers these nonfiction areas:** anthropology/archaeology; business/economics; child guidance/parenting; cooking/foods/nutrition; ethnic/cultural interests; government/politics/law; health/medicine; history; language/literature/criticism; military/war; money/finance; nature/environment; psychology; science/technology; sociology; sports; women's issues/studies. **Considers these fiction areas:** ethnic; feminist; literary; mainstream/contemporary; mystery/suspense; thriller.

O— "We specialize in a number of fields."

**How to Contact:** Submit proposal package, outline, sample chapter(s). No e-mail queries. Responds in 6 weeks to queries. Obtains most new clients through recommendations from others, solicitations, conferences.

**Recent Sales:** *The Mistress of Spices*, by Chitra Divakaruni (Anchor Books); *The Flower Net*, by Lisa See (HarperCollins); *Outsmarting the Menopausal Fat Cell*, by Debra Waterhouse (Hyperion).

**Terms:** Agent receives 15% commission on domestic sales; 20% commission on foreign sales. Offers written contract, binding for 1 year. Charges clients for expenses "from years we are active on author's behalf to cover domestic costs so that we can spend time selling books instead of accounting expenses. We also charge for the photocopying of the full ms or nonfiction proposal and for foreign postage."

**Writers' Conferences:** "Have attended Squaw Valley, Santa Barbara, Asilomar, Southern California Writers Conference, Rocky Mountain Fiction Writers, to name a few. We also speak regularly for writers groups such as PEN West and the Independent Writers Association."

**Tips:** "Be professional and learn the standard procedures for submitting your work. Give full biographical information on yourself, especially for a nonfiction project. Always include SASE with correct return postage for your own protection of your work. Query with a 1 or 2 page letter first and always include postage. Nine page letters telling us your life story, or your book's, are unprofessional and usually not read. Tell us about your book and write your query well. It's our first introduction to who you are and what you can do! Call if you don't hear within a reasonable period of time. Be a regular patron of bookstores and study what kind of books are being published. READ. Check out your local library and bookstores—you'll find lots of books on writing and the publishing industry that will help you! At conferences, ask published writers about their agents. Don't believe the myth that an agent has to be in New York to be successful—we've already disproved it!"

**THE JONATHAN DOLGER AGENCY**, 49 E. 96th St., Suite 9B, New York NY 10128. (212)427-1853. **Contact:** Herbert Erinmore. President: Jonathan Dolger. Estab. 1980. Member of AAR. Represents 70 clients. 25% of clients are new/unpublished writers. Query before submitting.

**Represents:** Nonfiction books; novels; illustrated books.

O— This agency specializes in adult trade fiction and nonfiction, and illustrated books.

**How to Contact:** Query with SASE. No e-mail queries.

**Recent Sales:** Sold 15-20 titles in the last year. This agency prefers not to share information on specific sales.

**Terms:** Agent receives 15% commission on domestic sales; 25% commission on foreign sales. Charges clients for "standard expenses."

**Tips:** "Writer must have been previously published if submitting fiction. Prefers to work with published/established authors; works with a small number of new/previously unpublished writers."

**JANIS A. DONNAUD & ASSOCIATES, INC.**, 525 Broadway, 2nd Floor, New York NY 10012. (212)431-2664. Fax: (212)431-2667. E-mail: jdonnaud@aol.com. **Contact:** Janis A. Donnaud. Member of AAR; signatory of WGA. Represents 40 clients. 10% of clients are new/unpublished writers. Currently handles: 90% nonfiction books; 10% novels.

● Prior to opening her agency, Ms. Donnaud was Vice President, Associate Publisher, Random House Adult Trade group.

**Represents:** Nonfiction books; novels. **Considers these nonfiction areas:** art/architecture/design; biography/autobiography; child guidance/parenting; cooking/foods/nutrition; creative nonfiction; current affairs; health/medicine; humor/satire; psychology (pop). **Considers these fiction areas:** literary.

O— This agency specializes in health, medical, cooking, humor, pop psychology, narrative nonfiction, photography, art, literary fiction, biography, parenting, current affairs. "We give a lot of service and attention to clients." Actively seeking serious narrative nonfiction; literary fiction; cookbooks; health and medical by authors with an established platform in their area of specialty. Does not want to receive poetry, mysteries, juvenile books, romances, science fiction, young adult, religious fantasy.

**How to Contact:** Query with SASE, description of book and 2-3 pages of sample material. Prefers to read materials exclusively. Accepts e-mail and fax queries. Responds in 1 month to queries; 1 month to mss. Obtains most new clients through recommendations from others.

**Recent Sales:** Sold 25 titles in the last year. *The Flambaya Tree*, by Clara Kelly (Random House); *Nancy Silverton's Sandwiches from the LaBrea Bakery*, by Nancy Silverton (Knopf).

**Terms:** Agent receives 15% commission on domestic sales; 20% commission on foreign sales. Offers written contract; 30-day notice must be given to terminate contract. Charges clients for messengers, photocopying, purchase of books.

**JIM DONOVAN LITERARY**, 4515 Prentice St., Suite 109, Dallas TX 75206. **Contact:** Jim Donovan, president; Kathryn McKay. Estab. 1993. Represents 25 clients. 25% of clients are new/unpublished writers. Currently handles: 75% nonfiction books; 25% novels.

**Member Agents:** Jim Donovan (president); Kathryn McKay.
**Represents:** Nonfiction books; novels. **Considers these nonfiction areas:** biography/autobiography; business/economics; child guidance/parenting; current affairs; health/medicine; history; military/war; money/finance; music/dance; nature/environment; popular culture; sports; true crime/investigative. **Considers these fiction areas:** action/adventure; detective/police/crime; historical; horror; literary; mainstream/contemporary; mystery/suspense; sports; thriller; westerns/frontier.

    O━ This agency specializes in commercial fiction and nonfiction. Does not want to receive poetry, humor, short stories, juvenile, romance or religious work.

**How to Contact:** Query with SASE. For nonfiction, send query letter. For fiction, send 2- to 5-page outline and 3 sample chapters. No e-mail or fax queries. Considers simultaneous queries. Responds in 1 month to queries; 1 month to mss. Obtains most new clients through recommendations from others, solicitations.

**Recent Sales:** Sold 27 titles in the last year. *The Patriot Traitor*, by Michael Kauffman (Random House); *Unitas*, by Dan McGraw (Doubleday); *The Road to Ballybunion*, by Tony Finn (Sleeping Bear).

**Terms:** Agent receives 15% commission on domestic sales; 20% commission on foreign sales. Offers written contract, binding for 1 year; written notice must be given to terminate contract. Charges clients for some postage and photocopying—"author is notified first." Writers reimbursed for office fees after the sale of ms.

**Tips:** "The vast majority of material I receive, particularly fiction, is not ready for publication. Do everything you can to get your fiction work in top shape before you try to find an agent. I've been in the book business since 1981. In retail (as a chain buyer), as an editor, and as a published author. I'm open to working with new writers if they're serious about their writing and are prepared to put in the work necessary—the rewriting—to become publishable."

✅ 🌐 ⊘ **DORIAN LITERARY AGENCY**, Upper Thornehill, 27 Church Rd., St. Mary Church, Torquay Devon TQ1 4Q4, England. Phone/fax: 44 (0) 1803 312095. **Contact:** Dorothy Lumley. Estab. 1986. Represents 48 clients. 10% of clients are new/unpublished writers. Currently handles: 5% nonfiction books; 85% novels; 10% story collections.

    • Prior to becoming an agent, Ms. Lumley was a paperback editor.

**Member Agents:** Dorothy Lumley (popular adult fiction).
**Represents:** Nonfiction books; novels; short story collections. **Considers these nonfiction areas:** popular culture; self-help/personal improvement. **Considers these fiction areas:** detective/police/crime; family saga; fantasy; historical; horror; literary; mainstream/contemporary; mystery/suspense; romance; science fiction; thriller; young adult.

    O━ This agency is a small specialist agency that offers personal service and editorial input. Does not want to receive poetry, nonfiction of specialist type, autobiographies, plays, children's books.

**How to Contact:** Query with SASE, submit proposal package, outline, 1-3 sample chapter(s), IRCs. No e-mail or fax queries. Considers simultaneous queries. Responds in 2 weeks to queries; 6 weeks to mss. Returns materials only with SASE. Obtains most new clients through recommendations from others.

**Recent Sales:** *Avengers/Defilers*, by B. Lumley (TOR); *Sand Reckoner/Wolf Hunt*, by G. Bradshaw (TOR); *Dark Terrors*, by S. Jones.

**Terms:** Agent receives 10% commission on domestic sales; 15% (to USA) commission on foreign sales. No written contract. Charges clients for photocopying of mss, extra copies of book for rights sales.

**Writers' Conferences:** Romantic Novelists Association
**Tips:** "Although my client list really is full, I shall occasionally take on new clients."

🔄 **DOYEN LITERARY SERVICES, INC.**, 1931 660th St., Newell IA 50568-7613. (712)272-3300. **Contact:** (Ms.) B.J. Doyen, president. Estab. 1988. Represents 20 clients. 20% of clients are new/unpublished writers. Currently handles: 90% nonfiction books; 10% novels.

    • Prior to opening her agency, Ms. Doyen worked as a published author, teacher, guest speaker and wrote and appeared in her own weekly TV show airing in 7 states.

**Represents:** Nonfiction books; novels. **Considers these nonfiction areas:** agriculture/horticulture; americana; animals; anthropology/archaeology; art/architecture/design; biography/autobiography; business/economics; child guidance/parenting; computers/electronic; cooking/foods/nutrition; crafts/hobbies; creative nonfiction; current affairs; education; ethnic/cultural interests; gardening; gay/lesbian issues; government/politics/law; health/medicine; history; how-to; humor/satire; interior design/decorating; juvenile nonfiction; language/literature/criticism; memoirs; military/war; money/finance; multicultural; music/dance; nature/environment; New Age/metaphysics; philosophy; photography; popular culture; psychology; recreation; regional; religious/inspirational; science/technology; self-help/personal improvement; sex; sociology; software; spirituality; sports; theater/film; translation; travel; true crime/investigative; women's issues/studies; young adult. **Considers these fiction areas:** contemporary issues; family saga; historical; literary; mainstream/contemporary; occult; psychic/supernatural.

    O━ This agency specializes in nonfiction and occasionally handles genre and mainstream fiction for adults. Actively seeking business, health, how-to, psychology; all kinds of adult nonfiction suitable for the major trade publishers. Prefers fiction from published novelists only. Does not want to receive pornography, children's, poetry.

**How to Contact:** Query with SASE. Considers simultaneous queries. Responds in 2 weeks to mss. Responds immediately to queries. Returns materials only with SASE.

**Terms:** Agent receives 15% commission on domestic sales; 20% commission on foreign sales. Offers written contract, binding for 1 year.

**Tips:** "Our authors receive personalized attention. We market aggressively, undeterred by rejection. We get the best possible publishing contracts. We are very interested in nonfiction book ideas at this time; will consider most topics."

Many writers come to us from referrals, but we also get quite a few who initially approach us with query letters. Do not use phone queries unless you are successfully published or a celebrity. It is best if you do not collect editorial rejections prior to seeking an agent, but if you do, bu up-front and honest about it. Do not submit your manuscript to more than one agent at a time—querying first can save you (and us) much time. We're open to established or beginning writers—just send us a terrific letter with SASE!"

◑ **ROBERT DUCAS**, The Barn House, 244 Westside Rd., Norfolk CT 06058. (860)542-5733. Fax: (860)542-5469. E-mail: robertducas@aol.com. **Contact:** Robert Ducas. Estab. 1981. Represents 55 clients. 15% of clients are new/unpublished writers. Currently handles: 70% nonfiction books; 28% novels; 2% scholarly books.

• Prior to opening his agency, Mr. Ducas ran the *London Times* and the *Sunday Times* in the U.S. from 1966 to 1981.

**Represents:** Nonfiction books; novels; novellas. **Considers these nonfiction areas:** animals; biography/autobiography; business/economics; current affairs; gay/lesbian issues; government/politics/law; health/medicine; history; memoirs; military/war; money/finance; nature/environment; science/technology; sports; travel; true crime/investigative. **Considers these fiction areas:** action/adventure; contemporary issues; detective/police/crime; family saga; literary; mainstream/contemporary; mystery/suspense; sports; thriller.

◛ This agency specializes in nonfiction, journalistic exposé, biography, history. Does not want to receive women's fiction.

**How to Contact:** Query with SASE. Responds in 2 weeks to queries; 2 months to mss. Obtains most new clients through recommendations from others.

**Recent Sales:** Sold 10 titles in the last year. This agency prefers not to share information on specific sales.

**Terms:** Agent receives 15% commission on domestic sales; 20% commission on foreign sales. Charges clients for photocopying, postage, messengers, overseas couriers to subagents.

◑ **DUNHAM LITERARY**, 156 Fifth Avenue, Suite 625, New York NY 10010-7002. (212)929-0994. Fax: (212)929-0904. **Contact:** Jennie Dunham. Estab. 2000. Member of AAR. Represents 50 clients. 15% of clients are new/unpublished writers. Currently handles: 25% nonfiction books; 25% novels; 50% juvenile books.

• Prior to opening her agency, Ms. Dunham worked as a literary agent for Russell & Volkening.

**Represents:** Nonfiction books; novels; short story collections; juvenile books. **Considers these nonfiction areas:** anthropology/archaeology; art/architecture/design; biography/autobiography; business/economics; current affairs; education; ethnic/cultural interests; gay/lesbian issues; government/politics/law; health/medicine; history; juvenile nonfiction; language/literature/criticism; music/dance; nature/environment; photography; popular culture; psychology; science/technology; sociology; sports; women's issues/studies. **Considers these fiction areas:** ethnic; juvenile; literary; mainstream/contemporary; mystery/suspense; picture books; thriller; young adult.

**How to Contact:** Query with SASE. No fax queries. Responds in 1 week to queries; 2 months to mss. Obtains most new clients through recommendations from others, solicitations.

**Recent Sales:** *Fake Liar Cheat*, by Tod Goldberg; *Enemy Glory*, by Karen Michalson; *Molly*, by Nancy Jones; *And Baby Makes Four*, by Hilory Wagner; *A Positive Life*, by River Huston and photographed by Mary Berridge; *Reflexology Socks*, by Michelle Kluck; *Letters of Intent*, by Meg Daly and Anna Bondoc; *The Wonderful Wizard of Oz* (pop-up), by Robert Sabuda; *A Little Princess*, by Barbara McClintock; *Clever Beatrice*, illustrated by Heather Solomon; *The World's Wide Open*, by Bettye M. Stroud; *Who Will Tell My Brother?*, by Marlene Carvell; *Skin Game*, by Caroline Kettlewell; *Goddess In My Pocket*, by Patricia Telesco.

**Terms:** Agent receives 15% commission on domestic sales; 20% commission on foreign sales. Writers reimbursed for office fees after the sale of ms.

◒ **HENRY DUNOW** *＋CARLSON* **LITERARY AGENCY**, 22 W. 23rd St., 5th Floor, New York NY 10010. Member of AAR. This agency did not respond to our request for information. Query before submitting. *FICTION*

◑ **DUPREE/MILLER AND ASSOCIATES INC. LITERARY**, 100 Highland Park Village, Suite 350, Dallas TX 75205. (214)559-BOOK. Fax: (214)559-PAGE. E-mail: dmabook@aol.com. **Contact:** Submissions Department. President: Jan Miller. Estab. 1984. Member of ABA. Represents 200 clients. 20% of clients are new/unpublished writers. Currently handles: 75% nonfiction books; 25% novels.

**Member Agents:** Jan Miller; Michael Broussard; Shannon Miser-Marven (business affairs); Kym Elizondo.

**Represents:** Nonfiction books; novels; scholarly books; syndicated material. **Considers these nonfiction areas:** agriculture/horticulture; americana; animals; anthropology/archaeology; art/architecture/design; biography/autobiography; business/economics; child guidance/parenting; computers/electronic; cooking/foods/nutrition; crafts/hobbies; creative nonfiction; current affairs; education; ethnic/cultural interests; gardening; gay/lesbian issues; government/politics/law; health/medicine; history; how-to; humor/satire; interior design/decorating; juvenile nonfiction; language/literature/criticism; memoirs; military/war; money/finance; multicultural; music/dance; nature/environment; New Age/metaphysics; philosophy; photography; popular culture; psychology; recreation; regional; religious/inspirational; science/technology; self-help/personal improvement; sex; sociology; software; spirituality; sports; theater/film; translation; travel; true crime/investigative; women's issues/studies; young adult. **Considers these fiction areas:** action/adventure; contemporary issues; detective/police/crime; ethnic; experimental; family saga; feminist; gay/lesbian; glitz; historical; humor/satire; literary; mainstream/contemporary; mystery/suspense; picture books; psychic/supernatural; religious/inspirational; sports; thriller.

O—☝ This agency specializes in commercial fiction, nonfiction.

**How to Contact:** Query with SASE, outline. Considers simultaneous queries. Responds in 4 months to mss. Obtains most new clients through recommendations from others, conferences, lectures and "very frequently through publisher's referrals."

**Recent Sales:** Sold 25 titles in the last year. *Life Strategies for Teens*, by Jay McGraw (Simon & Schuster); *Bringing the Family Back to the Table*, by Art Smith (Hyperion).

**Terms:** Agent receives 15% commission on domestic sales. Offers written contract. Charges clients $20 processing fee and express mail charges.

**Writers' Conferences:** Southwest Writers (Albuquerque NM); Brazos Writers (College Station TX).

**Tips:** If interested in agency representation, "it is vital to have the material in the proper working format. As agents' policies differ, it is important to follow their guidelines. The best advice I can give is to work on establishing a strong proposal that provides sample chapters, an overall synopsis (fairly detailed) and some bio information on yourself. Do not send your proposal in pieces; it should be complete upon submission. Remember you are trying to sell your work and it should be in its best condition."

✔ ◎ ⊘ **DWYER & O'GRADY, INC., (Specialized: children's books)**, P.O. Box 239, Lempster NH 03605-0239. (603)863-9347. Fax: (603)863-9346. **Contact:** Elizabeth O'Grady. Estab. 1990. Member of SCBWI. Represents 20 clients. Currently handles: 100% juvenile books.

● Prior to opening their agency, Mr. Dwyer and Ms. Grady were booksellers and publishers.

**Member Agents:** Elizabeth O'Grady (children's books); Jeff Dwyer (children's books).

**Represents:** Juvenile books. **Considers these nonfiction areas:** juvenile nonfiction. **Considers these fiction areas:** juvenile; picture books; young adult.

O—☝ This agency represents only writers and illustrators of children's books. Does not want to receive submissions that are not for juvenile audiences.

**How to Contact:** Not accepting new clients. No unsolicited mss. Obtains most new clients through recommendations from others, direct approach by agent to writer whose work they've read.

**Recent Sales:** Sold 13 titles in the last year. *A Gardener's Alphabet*, by Mary Azarian (Houghton Mifflin); *Many Many Moons*, by Mary Azarian (Little Brown); *Hinkley Fire*, by Ted Rose (Houghton Mifflin); *Talkin' 'Bout Bess*, by Earl B. Lewis (Orchard Books). Other clients include Kim Ablon, Mary Azarian, Tom Bedett, Odds Bodkin, Donna Clair, Leonard Jenkins, E.B. Lewis, Rebecca Rule, Steve Schuch, Virginia Stroud, Natasha Tarpley, Zong-Zhou Wang, Rashida Watson.

**Terms:** Agent receives 15% commission on domestic sales; 20% commission on foreign sales. Offers written contract; 30-day notice must be given to terminate contract. Charges clients for "photocopying of longer manuscripts or mutually agreed upon marketing expenses."

**Writers' Conferences:** Book Expo; American Library Association; Society of Children's Book Writers & Illustrators.

 ◑ **JANE DYSTEL LITERARY MANAGEMENT, INC.**, One Union Square West, Suite 904, New York NY 10003. (212)627-9100. Fax: (212)627-9313. Website: www.dystel.com. **Contact:** Miriam Goderich. Estab. 1994. Member of AAR. Represents 300 clients. 50% of clients are new/unpublished writers. Currently handles: 65% nonfiction books; 25% novels; 10% cookbooks.

● Jane Dystel Literary Management recently acquired the client list of Bedford Book Works.

**Member Agents:** Stacey Glick; Jane Dystel; Miriam Goderich; Jo Fagan; Michael Bourret.

**Represents:** Nonfiction books; novels; cookbooks. **Considers these nonfiction areas:** animals; anthropology/archaeology; biography/autobiography; business/economics; child guidance/parenting; cooking/foods/nutrition; current affairs; education; ethnic/cultural interests; gay/lesbian issues; government/politics/law; health/medicine; history; humor/satire; military/war; money/finance; New Age/metaphysics; popular culture; psychology; religious/inspirational; science/technology; true crime/investigative; women's issues/studies. **Considers these fiction areas:** action/adventure; contemporary issues; detective/police/crime; ethnic; family saga; gay/lesbian; literary; mainstream/contemporary; mystery/suspense; thriller.

O—☝ This agency specializes in commercial and literary fiction and nonfiction plus cookbooks.

**How to Contact:** Query with SASE. Responds in 3 weeks to queries; 6 weeks to mss. Obtains most new clients through recommendations from others, solicitations, conferences.

**Recent Sales:** *The Sparrow and Children of God*, by Mary Russell; *Water Carry Me*, by Thomas Moran; *Today, I Am a Ma'am*, by Valerie Harper; *Dark Waters: The NR-1, America's Secret Submarine*, by Lee Vyborny and Don Davis.

**Terms:** Agent receives 15% commission on domestic sales; 19% commission on foreign sales. Offers written contract, binding for book to book basis. Charges for photocopying. Gallery charges and book charges from the publisher are passed on to the author.

**Writers' Conferences:** West Coast Writers Conference (Whidbey Island WA, Columbus Day weekend); University of Iowa Writer's Conference; Pacific Northwest Writer's Conference; Pike's Peak Writer's Conference; Santa Barbara Writer's Conference; Harriette Austin's Writer's Conference.

**EDUCATIONAL DESIGN SERVICES, INC., (Specialized: education)**, P.O. Box 253, Wantagh NY 11793-0253. (718)539-4107 or (516)221-0995. **Contact:** Bertram L. Linder, president; Edwin Selzer, vice president. Estab. 1979. Represents 17 clients. 70% of clients are new/unpublished writers. Currently handles: 100% textbooks. **Represents:** Scholarly books; textbooks. **Considers these nonfiction areas:** anthropology/archaeology; business/economics; child guidance/parenting; current affairs; education; ethnic/cultural interests; government/politics/law; history; language/literature/criticism; military/war; money/finance; science/technology; sociology; women's issues/studies; all K-12 market.

O— This agency specializes in textual material for educational market.

**How to Contact:** Query with SASE, proposal package, outline, 1-2 sample chapter(s). Considers simultaneous queries. Responds in 1 month to queries; 6 weeks to mss. Returns materials only with SASE. Obtains most new clients through recommendations from others, solicitations, conferences.

**Recent Sales:** Sold 4 titles in the last year. *How to Solve the Word Problems in Arithmetic Grades 6-8*, by P. Pullman (McGraw-Hill/Schaum); *How to Solve Word Problems in Mathematics*, by D. Wayne (McGraw-Hill/Schaum); *First Principles of Cosmology*, by E.V. Linder (Addison-Wesley Longman).

**Terms:** Agent receives 15% commission on domestic sales; 25% commission on foreign sales. Offers written contract. Charges clients for photocopying, actual postage/shipping costs.

**PETER ELEK ASSOCIATES**, (The Content Company, Inc.), 5111 JFK Blvd. E., West New York NJ 07093. (201)558-0323. Fax: (201)558-0307. E-mail: info@theliteraryagency.com. **Contact:** Lauren Mactas. Estab. 1979. Represents 20 clients. Currently handles: 70% nonfiction books; 30% juvenile books.

**Member Agents:** Gerardo Greco (director of project development/multimedia).

**Represents:** Nonfiction books; juvenile books (nonfiction, picture books). **Considers these nonfiction areas:** anthropology/archaeology; child guidance/parenting; juvenile nonfiction; nature/environment; popular culture; science/technology; true crime/investigative.

O— This agency specializes in children's picture books, adult nonfiction.

**How to Contact:** Query with SASE, proposal package, outline. Prefers to read material exclusively. Accepts e-mail and fax queries. Responds in 3 weeks to queries; 5 weeks to mss. Obtains most new clients through recommendations from others, studying bylines in consumer and trade magazines and in regional and local newspapers.

**Recent Sales:** Sold 8 titles in the last year. *Princess*, by Hugh Brewster (HarperCollins); *Pearl Harbor: An Illustrated History*, by Dan van der Vat (Perseus/Basic Books).

**Terms:** Agent receives 15% commission on domestic sales; 20% commission on foreign sales. If required, charges clients for wholesale photocopying, typing, courier charges.

**Writers' Conferences:** Frankfurt Book Fair (Frankfurt Germany, October); LIBF (England); Bologna Children's Book Fair (Italy); APBA, Sidney; Australia

**Tips:** "Do your research thoroughly before submitting proposal. Only fresh and original material considered."

**ELITE ONLINE**, P.O. Box 145, Highspire PA 17034-0145. (717)948-0666. Fax: (717)948-4131. E-mail: DannyBoy_17034@yahoo.com. **Contact:** Daniel M. Kane. Estab. 2000. Represents 10 clients. 40% of clients are new/unpublished writers. Currently handles: 90% novels; 10% story collections.

**Member Agents:** Daniel M. Kane; Alma Maria Garcia (science fiction).

**Represents:** Novels; short story collections. **Considers these fiction areas:** action/adventure; feminist; gay/lesbian; horror; humor/satire; psychic/supernatural; science fiction.

O— This agency no longer specializes in the placement of e-books, but focuses on print publication almost exclusively. "We offer quick response time whenever possible, and the author never pays reading fees or for editorial assistance. We make an investment of time in each of our authors."

**How to Contact:** Submit synopsis, with complete ms; include sufficient postage if return is requested. Prefers to read materials exclusively. Electronic copy may be requested at a later time. Responds in under 2 to mss. Obtains most new clients through solicitations.

**Recent Sales:** This agency prefers not to share information on specific sales.

**Terms:** Agent receives 15% commission on print sales, 18% on direct electronic sales commission on domestic sales. Offers written contract, binding for 14 months.; 90-day notice must be given to terminate contract. Charges clients prior to sale for photocopying, printing, postage.

**Tips:** "To paraphrase Clive Barker, no matter how dark or bizarre your imagination, there's probably a market for your work. When in doubt, submit. Include your e-mail address, where most of our correspondence takes place. Our pet peeve is problems with basic grammar/spelling. We represent no one exclusively (unless requested), but rather on a per project basis. When doing gay characters, no stereotypes. No religious material."

---

**ALWAYS INCLUDE** a self-addressed, stamped envelope (SASE) for reply or return of your query or manuscript.

**ETHAN ELLENBERG LITERARY AGENCY**, 548 Broadway, #5-E, New York NY 10012. (212)431-4554. Fax: (212)941-4652. E-mail: agent@ethanellenberg.com. Website: www.ethanellenberg.com. **Contact:** Ethan Ellenberg, Michael Psaltis. Estab. 1983. Represents 80 clients. 10% of clients are new/unpublished writers. Currently handles: 25% nonfiction books; 75% novels.
- Prior to opening his agency, Mr. Ellenberg was contracts manager of Berkley/Jove and associate contracts manager for Bantam.

**Member Agents:** Michael Psaltis (commercial fiction, literary fiction, mysteries, cookbooks, women's fiction, popular science and other unique nonfiction); Ethan Ellenberg.

**Represents:** Nonfiction books; novels. **Considers these nonfiction areas:** biography/autobiography; business/economics; child guidance/parenting; cooking/foods/nutrition; current affairs; health/medicine; history; humor/satire; juvenile nonfiction; New Age/metaphysics; popular culture; psychology; religious/inspirational; science/technology; self-help/personal improvement; spirituality; true crime/investigative. **Considers these fiction areas:** detective/police/crime; family saga; fantasy; historical; juvenile; literary; mainstream/contemporary; mystery/suspense; picture books; romance; science fiction; thriller; young adult.

   O→ This agency specializes in commercial fiction, especially thrillers and romance/women's fiction. "We also do a lot of children's books." Actively seeking commercial and literary fiction, children's books, break-through nonfiction. Does not want to receive poetry, short stories, westerns, autobiographies.

**How to Contact:** For fiction: Send introductory letter (with credits, if any), outline, first 3 chapters. For nonfiction: Send query letter and/or proposal, 1 sample chapter if written. For children's books: Send introductory letter (with credits, if any), up to 3 picture book mss, outline and first 3 chapters for longer projects, SASE. No fax queries. Accepts e-mail queries, no attachments. Considers simultaneous queries. Responds in 10 days to queries; 1 month to mss. Returns materials only with SASE.

**Recent Sales:** Sold 100 in the last 2 years titles in the last year. *Glory Denied*, by Thomas Philpott (Norton); *No Other Option*, by Marcus Wynne (Tor Books); *Hypercane*, by Ben Miller (NAL/Dutton); *Hunters of the Dark Sea*, by Mel Odom (TOR Books).

**Terms:** Agent receives 15% commission on domestic sales; 10% commission on foreign sales. Offers written contract. Charges clients for "direct expenses only limited to photocopying, postage."

**Writers' Conferences:** RWA National; Novelists, Inc.; and other regional conferences.

**Tips:** "We do consider new material from unsolicited authors. Write a good clear letter with a succinct description of your book. We prefer the first three chapters when we consider fiction. For all submissions you must include SASE for return or the material is discarded. It's always hard to break in, but talent will find a home. We continue to see natural storytellers and nonfiction writers with important books."

**NICHOLAS ELLISON, INC.**, affiliated with Sanford J. Greenburger Associates, 55 Fifth Ave., 15th Floor, New York NY 10003. (212)206-6050. Fax: (212)436-8718. **Contact:** Alicka Pistek. Estab. 1983. Represents 70 clients. Currently handles: 25% nonfiction books; 75% novels.
- Prior to becoming an agent, Mr. Ellison was an editor at Minerva Editions, Harper & Row and editor-in-chief at Delacorte.

**Member Agents:** Alicka Pistek

**Represents:** Nonfiction books; novels. **Considers most nonfiction areas. Considers these fiction areas:** literary; mainstream/contemporary.

   O→ Does not want to receive biography or self-help.

**How to Contact:** Query with SASE. Responds in 6 weeks to queries.

**Recent Sales:** *The Lion's Game*, by Nelson DeMille (Warner); *Equivocal Death*, by Amy Gutman (Little, Brown). Other clients include Olivia Goldsmith, P.T. Deutermann, James Webb, Nancy Geary.

**Terms:** Agent receives 15% commission on domestic sales; 20% commission on foreign sales.

**ANN ELMO AGENCY INC.**, 60 E. 42nd St., New York NY 10165. (212)661-2880, 2881. Fax: (212)661-2883. **Contact:** Lettie Lee. Estab. 1961. Member of AAR, MWA, Authors Guild.

**Member Agents:** Lettie Lee; Mari Cronin (plays); A.L. Abecassis (nonfiction).

**Represents:** Nonfiction books; novels. **Considers these nonfiction areas:** anthropology/archaeology; art/architecture/design; biography/autobiography; business/economics; child guidance/parenting; computers/electronic; cooking/foods/nutrition; current affairs; education; health/medicine; history; how-to; juvenile nonfiction; money/finance; music/dance; photography; popular culture; psychology; self-help/personal improvement; theater/film; true crime/investigative; women's issues/studies. **Considers these fiction areas:** action/adventure; contemporary issues; detective/police/crime; ethnic; family saga; feminist; glitz; historical; juvenile; literary; mainstream/contemporary; mystery/suspense; psychic/supernatural; regional; romance (contemporary, gothic, historical, regency); thriller; young adult.

**How to Contact:** Letter queries *only* with SASE. No fax queries. Responds in 3 months to queries. Obtains most new clients through recommendations from others.

**Recent Sales:** This agency prefers not to share information on specific sales.

**Terms:** Agent receives 15% commission on domestic sales; 20% commission on foreign sales. Offers written standard AAR contract. Charges clients for "special mailings or shipping considerations or multiple international calls. No charge for usual cost of doing business."

**Tips:** "Query first, and when asked only please send properly prepared manuscript. A double-spaced, readable manuscript is the best recommendation. Include SASE, of course."

*insider* **report**

# Payoff for a dream

The pursuit of art sometimes seems to be a hopeless ordeal. Admit it—the thought has crossed your mind more than once that all those hours spent working on your craft aren't going to pay off in the end. You've secretly added up the hours spent on your novel and multiplied them by minimum wage, just to see if any payoff could ever come close to compensating you for all those early mornings and late nights. What could ever make it worth it?

How about a seven figure, three-book deal? And maybe another seven figure deal for your novel's movie rights thrown in?

Sound like a fairy tale? For 31-year old, first-time author Brad Thor, this isn't fiction. His first novel, an international thriller titled *The Lions of Lucerne*, led to outstanding success for the

**Brad Thor**

author: a seven-figure book deal and, within not more than forty-eight hours of this remarkable coup, a movie deal. Despite the novelist's whirlwind success, however, he is no overnight wonder. Thor's achievements are the result of hard work and a sought-out partnership with his agent, Heide Lange of Sanford J. Greenburger Associates.

## Where it all began—and almost ended

Thor's literary career started long before Pocket Books or any movie rights. "I started writing when I was a kid, just for fun. When my parents were going through their divorce I seemed to really pick it up. I became a voracious reader and a writer, writing plays and short stories."

It was in college, however, that Thor was faced with the conscious choice of no longer just writing, but becoming a self-declared writer. "I went to the University of Southern California, which is in Los Angeles. I went in, per my father's desire, as a business administration major, and I couldn't stand it. One day, in the middle of a managerial economics class, I thought, 'I would rather take a bullet between the eyes than be a middle manager for the rest of my life.' So I packed up my books, got out of that class and never went back to another business class. Instead, I took the Strong-Campbell personality test and found that I scored off the board in the artistic arena. I had known for a long time in my soul that what I wanted to do was write, so I changed my major to creative writing."

As a writing major, Thor worked under the tutelage of the head of the USC creative writing department, author T.C. Boyle (*The Road to Wellville, The Tortilla Curtain, Riven Rock*), who acted as a mentor to the young writer. "That was all it really took to make sure that the fire was 100 percent lit as far as writing was concerned," says Thor. It was Boyle who gave Thor his first glimpse at what was to come later. "On the last day of class he pulled me aside and said, 'I want you to know, I really feel that you should be writing. You could be making a living as a successful author. This is what you should be doing.' "

And so Thor, fresh out of school, took the money he had saved while working in school and set off for Paris. He hoped to write his novel in the setting that inspired so many of his favorite writers, such as Hemingway and Henry Miller. Paris, however, held no *Farewell to Arms* or *Tropic of Cancer* for Thor. "I thought it was too solitary. I really felt alone as I spent my days writing in this little apartment all by myself."

Frustrated, Thor turned his attentions away from his novel to other endeavors. Having lived overseas and traveled Europe extensively, he knew that young people were traveling, and it made no sense to him that his travel experience didn't look anything like the travel shows he saw on television. "I realized that the only travel programming was for people my parents' age," Thor recalls. So, he set out to change that. "I talked to public television and said, 'There should be a travel show to show young people how to do it on a budget. I want to write it and host it too.' " Public television liked the idea and told him that, if he could find the money and produce the shows, they might put them on. "I ended up pulling together a travel series called *Traveling Lite* and doing two whole seasons of it, twenty-three episodes. I wrote all the episodes, did all the research, and I enjoyed the writing tremendously."

If it was the writing that kept him interested in producing *Traveling Lite*, it was also the thing that pointed him away from it. "In the back of my mind there was always, okay, this is great, you really enjoy this, and this is going to be a part of your life and your development that you're going to look back on fondly, but when are you going to write that book? I met a kid while I was traveling who was living somewhere and working on his novel, and I asked, Why is that not me? And finally I said, It's not you because you haven't committed to it."

## Unlikely inspiration and shared determination

Thor's decision to sit down and do it wasn't just the result of a nagging desire, however. He needed a bit more prompting, provided by his wife and . . . Arnold Schwarzenegger? "I had been telling my wife that if I died, the one thing on my deathbed that I'd regret having not done was writing a book and being published. We had seen an interview with Maria Shriver, who had written a children's book, and she talked about the process of writing and how she was kind of putting it off. Finally her husband, Arnold Schwarzenegger, started saying (delivered in a heavy Austrian accent), 'Don't talk about it—do it!' " Along with this inspired quote Thor's wife added, "Listen, I know it's a daunting task to write a book. What you need is protected time. That's your time to work on your dream, your book." She also provided the financial stability for him to write *The Lions of Lucerne* by bringing in income while he wrote. "As a man and a husband, it was difficult. I feel that a lot of men do kind of measure themselves by how productive they are as far as bringing money in and taking care of their family. But, by the same token, I wasn't going to let that be an excuse to put off writing any further. So, I was a lucky guy that my wife was willing to support me while I worked on my novel."

Despite the support of his family and friends, Thor still found it difficult to face the daunting task of finally writing a novel. "I think we're all given some special ability that we're supposed to fulfill in life, and I had known it was writing for a long time. One of the things that I tell friends is, once you have discovered what it is, that one special thing that you are out here to do, I think it becomes the most terrifying thing in the world to go after. I mean, I had been running away from this ability for fifteen years, since I was a kid, and once I finally [sat down and] did it, the fear—well, there's a Chinese saying that I once got in a fortune cookie that I carried around in my wallet forever which is, "Small worries will vanish if you tackle them bravely." Thor's worries were all for naught, as he learned when he finally devoted some time to the writing process. "It was as if I was all of a sudden seeing the story materialize around me. My fingers were working on the keys, but I was just an observer. As an author, sometimes people say you're the facilitator, you direct the characters, but I just sat and it all unfolded in front of me."

### A collaborative process

The completion of *The Lions of Lucerne* was just the beginning of Thor's story. He knew that, if he wanted people to read the novel, he was going to have to find somebody to champion his work. "When I first sat down at twenty-one to write my novel, I thought it was a very solitary and lonely process, but sitting down almost ten years later at thirty and actually completing a novel, I realized that it's actually a very collaborative process—there are a lot of people involved from the research stage all the way through the publicity stage." The first thing Thor did was head to the bookstore for books on getting published. There he found *Guide to Literary Agents*, in which he read about author Linda Nichols and the success that her book, *The Handyman*, found when she chose agent Theresa Park to represent her work. Thor, intrigued by the article, decided to check out the agency that Park was with, Sanford J. Greenburger Associates, on the Internet. That's where he was first introduced to his future agent. "There was one agent there in particular who really caught my eye, and her name was Heide Lange. Heide's married to a writer, she has a fine arts background, plus, the website talked about how her negotiations benefited all of the parties. I thought, here's somebody with not only great business sense, but also an artistic and creative background and on-going life."

After mailing Lange a query letter, he sent the manuscript and was impressed with the way it was received. "Heide was the first agent who actually read the whole thing and could quote to me from it and say, 'Here's where I think the book is strong, here's where I think you need to work on it before it's ready to send to publishers.'" Lange turned out to be just what he was looking for in an agent. "I feel that there's no substitute for having that good personal relationship with your agent, because I do believe it is collaborative. Your agent is really a partner in the business with you who wants to help you get the best price and terms for your work."

Thor's instincts about Lange were right to the tune of that seven-figure, three-book deal. "Heide was amazing. That she's a very, very good negotiator is one of the skills evident in her profile on the website. I will never forget when she called me up and said, 'Are you sitting down?'" Thor was, in his own words, "blown away," not only by the financial payoff, but by the three-book deal as well. "To be in a three-book deal is so wonderful because it means that they want to build a long-term relationship with me, and that's what I want, too. Of course, seven-figures is fantastic, but I can actually say that the three-book deal had the stronger effect overall." Somehow, the story of Thor's book deal was leaked to Inside.com, a media industry website, and within 48 hours of getting a contract with Pocket Books, *The Lions of Lucerne's* film rights sold for another seven figure amount.

### Advice for what you want

You're no doubt asking yourself, "How can I experience such success as this? How can I be like Brad Thor?" Thor's advice isn't groundbreaking, but his recent accomplishments prove its importance. "It's been said that if you love what you do, the money will follow. The key is, to quote Shakespeare, 'To thine own self be true.' " You will also need someone to take care of your dream. "The advice that I would give is, when you get your book to a point that you are really proud of it, you start looking for agents," says Thor. "Do your due diligence, do your homework, make a hit list of agents, and then be tough." Being tough involves searching for an agent that's a perfect fit. "I think it's important to have somebody as serious about championing your work as you are. I would say to hold out until you find somebody who really understands what you're doing work-wise and believes in it as much as you do."

Finding the right agent, however, won't be easy work. "Sometimes you will get agents who say, It's not right for me, but if you want to call me, I'll tell you why. Always take that opportunity. You have to have the sensory acuity to be consistently fine-tuning your approach." Thor's final bit of advice is perhaps most important: Never give up. "Every rejection means that you are that much closer to a yes. You need to be unfailing in your devotion to that book."

So, if one too many rejections has got you thinking about hanging it all up and taking a middle-management job, or if you're just having a hard time sitting down every day to give your time to that never-ending tome, take heart. Brad Thor, now doing the edit on *The Lions of Lucerne* and working on his second novel for Pocket Books, stands as proof that there are definitely rewards to sticking it out, no matter what it takes. So finish that piece, find an agent and hang in there for what you know you deserve.

—*Rodney A. Wilson*

**N ○ ELAINE P. ENGLISH, Graybill & English, LLC**, 1920 N. St. NW, Suite 620, Washington DC 20036-1619. (202)861-0106. Fax: (202)457-0662. E-mail: ElaineEngl@aol.com. Website: www.graybillandenglish.com. **Contact:** Elaine English. Member of AAR. Represents 2 clients. 100% of clients are new/unpublished writers. Currently handles: 100% novels.
   ● Ms. English is an attorney specializing in media and publishing law.
**Member Agents:** Elaine English (women's fiction, including romance).
**Represents:** Novels; women's fiction, including single title romance. **Considers these fiction areas:** historical; mainstream/contemporary; multicultural; romance; women's.
   ○➛ "While not as an agent, per se, I have been working in publishing for over fifteen years. Also, I'm affiliated with other agents who represent a broad spectrum of projects." Actively seeking women's fiction, including single title romances. Does not want to receive anything other than above.
**How to Contact:** Submit outline, 3 sample chapter(s), SASE. Accepts e-mail queries. Responds in 3 weeks to queries; 2 months to mss. Returns materials only with SASE. Obtains most new clients through solicitations.
**Terms:** Agent receives 15% commission on domestic sales; 20% commission on foreign sales. Offers written contract; 30 days notice must be given to terminate contract. Charges only for expenses directly related to sales of manuscript (long distance, postage, copying).
**Writers' Conferences:** Washington Romance Writers (Harpers Ferry, April); Novelists Inc. (Philadelphia, September).

**◢ FELICIA ETH LITERARY REPRESENTATION**, 555 Bryant St., Suite 350, Palo Alto CA 94301-1700. (650)375-1276. Fax: (650)375-1277. E-mail: feliciaeth@aol.com. **Contact:** Felicia Eth. Estab. 1988. Member of AAR. Represents 25-35 clients. Works with established and new writers. Currently handles: 85% nonfiction books; 15% adult novels.
**Represents:** Nonfiction books; novels. **Considers these nonfiction areas:** animals; anthropology/archaeology; biography/autobiography; business/economics; child guidance/parenting; current affairs; ethnic/cultural interests; gay/lesbian issues; government/politics/law; health/medicine; history; nature/environment; popular culture; psychology; science/technology; sociology; true crime/investigative; women's issues/studies. **Considers these fiction areas:** ethnic; feminist; gay/lesbian; literary; mainstream/contemporary; thriller.
   ○➛ This agency specializes in "provocative, intelligent, thoughtful nonfiction on a wide array of subjects which are commercial and high-quality fiction; preferably mainstream and contemporary."
**How to Contact:** Query with SASE, outline. Considers simultaneous queries. Responds in 3 weeks to queries; 1 month to mss.
**Recent Sales:** Sold 7-10 titles in the last year. *Recovering the Power of the Ancestral Mind*, by Dr. Gregg Jacobs (Viking); *The Ulster Path*, by Will Ferguson (Grove/Atlantic); *Socrates Cafe*, by Chris Phillips (W.W. Norton); *Imperfect Harmony*, by Joshua Coleman (St. Martin's); *Baby Catcher: Chronicles of a Modern Midwife*, by Peggy Vincent (Charles Scribner's); *The Devil's Cup*, by Stewart Allen (Soho Press).

**Terms:** Agent receives 15% commission on domestic sales; 20% commission on foreign sales; 20% commission on dramatic rights sales. Charges clients for photocopying, express mail service—extraordinary expenses.
**Writers' Conferences:** Independent Writers of LA (Los Angeles); Conference of National Coalition of Independent Scholars (Berkley CA); Writers Guild.
**Tips:** "For nonfiction, established expertise is certainly a plus, as is magazine publication—though not a prerequisite. I am highly dedicated to those projects I represent."

**⊘ FALLON LITERARY AGENCY**, 15 E. 26th St., Suite 1609, New York NY 10010. Member of AAR. This agency did not respond to our request for information. Query before submitting.

**◉ FARBER LITERARY AGENCY INC.**, 14 E. 75th St., #2E, New York NY 10021. (212)861-7075. Fax: (212)861-7076. E-mail: farberlit@aol.com. Website: www.donaldfarber.com. **Contact:** Ann Farber; Dr. Seth Farber. Estab. 1989. Represents 40 clients. 50% of clients are new/unpublished writers. Currently handles: 40% nonfiction books; 15% scholarly books; 45% stage plays.
**Member Agents:** Ann Farber (novels); Seth Farber (plays, scholarly books, novels).
**Represents:** Nonfiction books; novels; juvenile books; textbooks; stage plays. **Considers these nonfiction areas:** child guidance/parenting; cooking/foods/nutrition; music/dance; psychology; theater/film. **Considers these fiction areas:** action/adventure; contemporary issues; humor/satire; juvenile; literary; mainstream/contemporary; mystery/suspense; thriller; young adult.
**How to Contact:** Submit outline, 3 sample chapter(s), SASE. Prefers to read materials exclusively. Accepts e-mail and fax queries. Responds in 1 month to queries; 2 month to mss. Obtains most new clients through recommendations from others.
**Recent Sales:** Sold 5 titles in the last year. *The Capp Street Carnival*, by Sandra Dutton; *The Gardens of Frau Hess*, by Milton Marcus; *Hot Feat*, by Ed Bullins; *Bright Freedom Song*, by Gloria Houston (Harcourt Brace & Co.).
**Terms:** Agent receives 15% commission on domestic sales; 20% commission on foreign sales. Offers written contract, binding for 1 year. Client must furnish copies of ms, treatments and any other items for submission.
**Tips:** "Our attorney, Donald C. Farber, is the author of many books. His services are available to the agency's clients as part of the agency service at no additional charge."

**☑ ⊘ FEIGEN/PARRENT LITERARY MANAGEMENT**, 10158 Hollow Glen Circle, Bel Air CA 90077-2112. (310)271-4722. Fax: (310)274-0503. E-mail: feigenparrentlit@aol.com. **Contact:** Brenda Feigen, Joanne Parrent. Estab. 1995. Member of PEN USA West, Authors Guild, LA County Bar Association. Represents 35-40 clients. 20-30% of clients are new/unpublished writers. Currently handles: 40% nonfiction books; 30% novels; 25% movie scripts; 5% TV scripts.
  ● Ms. Feigen is also an attorney and producer; Ms. Parrent is also a screenwriter and author.
**Member Agents:** Brenda Feigen (books, books-to-film); Joanne Parrent (screenplays).
**Represents:** Nonfiction books; novels. **Considers these nonfiction areas:** biography/autobiography; business/economics; current affairs; gay/lesbian issues; government/politics/law; health/medicine; how-to; memoirs; money/finance; psychology; self-help/personal improvement; theater/film; women's issues/studies. **Considers these fiction areas:** family saga; feminist; gay/lesbian; literary; Must be professionally formatted and under 130 pages.
  O▬ This agency is actively seeking "material about women, including strong, positive individuals. The material can be fiction, memoir or biographical. Does not want to receive horror, science fiction, religion, pornography. "No poetry or short stories unless author has been published by a major house."
**Also Handles:** Feature film; TV movie of the week. **Considers these script subject areas:** action/adventure; comedy; contemporary issues; family saga; feminist; gay/lesbian; thriller.
**How to Contact:** Query only with 2-page synopsis, author bio by regular mail with SASE. Prefers to read materials exclusively. No fax queries. Considers simultaneous queries. Responds in 3 weeks to queries; 6 weeks to mss. Returns materials only with SASE. Obtains most new clients through recommendations from other clients and publishers, through the Internet, and listings in *Literary Market Place*.
**Recent Sales:** Sold 6 titles and sold 1 scripts in the last year. *Defy the Darkness*, by Joe Rosenblum with David Kohn (Praeger); *The Courage to Care*, by Joanne Parrent (Macmillan). *Movie/TV MOW script(s) optioned/sold: Read Easy*, by Jay Milner (Tomorrow Entertainment).
**Terms:** Agent receives 15% commission on domestic sales; 20% commission on foreign sales. Offers written contract, binding for 1 year. Charges clients for postage, long distance calls, photocopying.
**Tips:** "If we like a book or screenplay we will either, at the writer's choice, represent it as agents or offer to produce it ourselves if the material is of real interst to us personally."

**[N] ◉ FEIGENBAUM PUBLISHING CONSULTANTS, INC.**, 61 Bounty Lane, Jericho NY 11753. (516)937-1909. Fax: (516)681-9121. E-mail: readrovers@aol.com. **Contact:** Laurie Feigenbaum. Represents 3 clients. 0% of clients are new/unpublished writers. Currently handles: 50% nonfiction books; 50% novels.
  ● Prior to becoming an agent, Ms. Feigenbaum was a Contracts Director.
**Represents:** **Considers these fiction areas:** romance.
  O▬ This agency specializes in contracts negotiation and permissions clearance. "I handle copyright and trademark registrations and research." Actively seeking romance. Does not want anything else.

**How to Contact:** Send outline/proposal, indicating any prior publishing experience. Accepts e-mail and fax queries. Considers simultaneous queries. Responds in 2 weeks to queries. Returns materials only with SASE. Obtains most new clients through recommendations from others.

**Recent Sales:** Sold 12 titles in the last year.

**Terms:** Agent receives 10% commission on domestic sales. No written contract.

**Writers' Conferences:** RWA.

☑ 🖳 ◎ **JUSTIN E. FERNANDEZ, AGENT/ATTORNEY**, E-mail: lit4@aol.com. **Contact:** Justin E. Fernandez. Estab. 1996. Represents 5-10 clients. 80% of clients are new/previously unpublished writers. Currently handles: 30% nonfiction; 60% fiction; 10% other.

• Prior to opening his agency, Mr. Fernandez, a 1992 graduate of the University of Cincinnati College of Law, served as a law clerk with the Ohio Court of Appeals, Second Appellate District (1992-94), and as a literary agent for Paraview, Inc., New York (1995-96).

**Represents:** Nonfiction, fiction, screen/teleplays and digital "art," (software, multimedia/Internet-related products). **Considers most nonfiction and fiction genres.**

**How to Contact:** Query first. "E-mail queries only." Considers simultaneous queries and submissions. Obtains most new clients through referrals or queries from listings.

**Terms:** Agent receives 10% commission on domestic sales; 15% on foreign sales; 20% with foreign co-agent. Offers written contract.

**Tips:** "Query letters are business letters. The tone should be measured, reasonably formal and matter-of-fact. Include facts such as book length (word count), genre, intended audience, favorable comparisons to other successful books of its type, and information about the book's niche (how much competition is there and what is it?) Ultimately, you should try to explain why your book will succeed in its niche. Keep personal data to a minimum unless it relates to publication credit or notoriety. Manuscripts should be very carefully edited for typos, grammar, sense, word-choice, brevity, clarity, and 'flow' of the narrative. Do not send unsolicited attached files. A query must be in the body of an e-mail message."

◎ ◎ **FLANNERY LITERARY, (Specialized: juvenile books)**, 1140 Wickfield Court, Naperville IL 60563-3300. (630)428-2682. Fax: (630)428-2683. **Contact:** Jennifer Flannery. Estab. 1992. Represents 33 clients. 90% of clients are new/unpublished writers. Currently handles: 100% juvenile books.

• Prior to opening her agency, Ms. Flannery was an editorial assistant.

**Represents:** Juvenile books. **Considers these nonfiction areas:** juvenile nonfiction; young adult; all nonfiction subjects for juveniles and young adults. **Considers these fiction areas:** humor/satire; juvenile; literary; mainstream/contemporary; mystery/suspense; picture books; young adult.

○╍ This agency specializes in children's and young adult, juvenile fiction and nonfiction.

**Also Handles:** Feature film; TV movie of the week; animation; miniseries. **Considers these script subject areas:** action/adventure; cartoon/animation; comedy; contemporary issues; ethnic; family saga; historical; juvenile; mainstream; mystery/suspense; sports; teen; western/frontier.

**How to Contact:** Query with SASE. Responds in 3 weeks to queries; 1 month to mss. Obtains most new clients through recommendations from others, solicitations.

**Recent Sales:** Sold 20 titles in the last year. This agency prefers not to share information on specific sales.

**Terms:** Agent receives 15% commission on domestic sales; 20% commission on foreign sales. Offers written contract, binding for life of book in print; 30 day notice must be given to terminate contract. 100% of business is derived from commissions on ms sales.

**Writers' Conferences:** SCBWI Fall Conference.

**Tips:** "Write an engrossing, succinct query describing your work."

◎ **PETER FLEMING AGENCY**, P.O. Box 458, Pacific Palisades CA 90272. (310)454-1373. **Contact:** Peter Fleming. Estab. 1962. Currently handles: 100% nonfiction books.

**Represents:** Nonfiction books; Considers.

○╍ This agency specializes in "nonfiction books: innovative, helpful, contrarian, individualistic, free market . . . with bestseller potential."

**How to Contact:** Query with SASE. Obtains most new clients through "through a different, one-of-a-kind idea for a book usually backed by the writer's experience in that area of expertise."

**Recent Sales:** *Rulers of Evil*, by F. Tupper Saussy (HarperCollins).

**Terms:** Agent receives 15% commission on domestic sales; 25% commission on foreign sales. Offers written contract, binding for 1 year. Charges clients "only those fees agreed to in writing, i.e., NY-ABA expenses shared. We may ask for a TV contract, too."

**Tips:** "You can begin by self-publishing, test marketing with direct sales, starting your own website."

◎ **B.R. FLEURY AGENCY**, P.O. Box 149352, Orlando FL 32814-9352. (407)895-8494. Fax: (407)898-3923 or (888)310-8142. E-mail: brfleuryagency@juno.com. **Contact:** Blanche or Margaret Fleury. Estab. 1994. Signatory of WGA. Currently handles: 70% nonfiction books; 30% scripts.

**Represents:** Nonfiction books; novels. **Considers these nonfiction areas:** health/medicine; how-to; humor/satire; money/finance; New Age/metaphysics; self-help/personal improvement; spirituality; true crime/investigative. **Considers these fiction areas:** fantasy; horror; humor/satire; literary; psychic/supernatural; science fiction; thriller.

**Also Handles:** Feature film; TV movie of the week. **Considers these script subject areas:** detective/police/crime; fantasy; horror; mystery/suspense; psychic/supernatural; thriller.

**How to Contact:** Query with SASE or call for information. Prefers to read materials exclusively. Accepts 1-page e-mail queries, no attachments. Responds in 3 months to mss. Responds immediately to queries. Obtains most new clients through recommendations from others, listings.

**Recent Sales:** Sold 5 titles in the last year. This agency prefers not to share information on specific sales.

**Terms:** Agent receives 15% commission on domestic sales. Offers written contract, binding for as per contract. Receives commission according to WGA guidelines. Charges clients for business expenses directly related to work represented.

**Tips:** "Read your work aloud with someone who is not in love with you before you send it to us." E-mail queries should be 1 page maximum, no attachments.

**THE FOGELMAN LITERARY AGENCY**, 7515 Greenville, Suite 712, Dallas TX 75231. (214)361-9956. Fax: (214)361-9553. E-mail: foglit@aol.com. Website: www.fogelman.com. Also: 599 Lexington Ave., Suite 2300, New York NY 10022. (212)836-4803 **Contact:** Evan Fogelman. Estab. 1990. Member of AAR. Represents 100 clients. 2% of clients are new/unpublished writers. Currently handles: 40% nonfiction books; 40% novels; 10% scholarly books; 10% TV scripts.

• Prior to opening his agency, Mr. Fogelman was an entertainment lawyer. He is still active in the field and serves as chairman of the Texas Entertainment and Sports Lawyers Association.

**Member Agents:** Evan Fogelman (nonfiction, women's fiction); Linda Kruger (women's fiction, nonfiction).

**Represents:** Nonfiction books; novels. **Considers these nonfiction areas:** biography/autobiography; business/economics; child guidance/parenting; current affairs; education; ethnic/cultural interests; government/politics/law; health/medicine; popular culture; psychology; sports; true crime/investigative; women's issues/studies. **Considers these fiction areas:** historical; literary; mainstream/contemporary; romance (all sub-genres).

○→ This agency specializes in women's fiction and nonfiction. "Zealous advocacy" makes this agency stand apart from others. Actively seeking "nonfiction of all types; romance fiction." Does not want to receive children's/juvenile.

**How to Contact:** Query with SASE. Considers simultaneous queries. Responds in 3 months to mss. Responds "next business day" to queries. Returns materials only with SASE. Obtains most new clients through recommendations from others.

**Recent Sales:** Sold 60 titles in the last year. Clients include Caroline Hunt, Katherine Sutcliffe, Crystal Stovall.

**Terms:** Agent receives 15% commission on domestic sales; 10% commission on foreign sales. Offers written contract, binding for project-to-project.

**Writers' Conferences:** Romance Writers of America; Novelists, Inc.

**Tips:** "Finish your manuscript, and see our website."

**THE FOLEY LITERARY AGENCY**, 34 E. 38th St., New York NY 10016-2508. (212)686-6930. **Contact:** Joan Foley or Joseph Foley. Estab. 1961. Represents 10 clients. Rarely takes on new clients. Currently handles: 75% nonfiction books; 25% novels.

**Represents:** Nonfiction books; novels.

**How to Contact:** Query with letter, brief outline, SASE. Responds promptly to queries. Obtains most new clients through recommendations from others.

**Recent Sales:** This agency prefers not to share information on specific sales.

**Terms:** Agent receives 10% commission on domestic sales; 15% commission on foreign sales. 100% of business is derived from commissions on ms sales.

**Tips:** Desires brevity in querying.

**FORT ROSS INC. RUSSIAN-AMERICAN PUBLISHING PROJECTS**, 26 Arthur Place, Yonkers NY 10701-1703. (914)375-6448. Fax: (914)375-6439. E-mail: ftross@ix.netcom.com. Website: www.fortross.net. **Contact:** Dr. Vladimir P. Karsev. Estab. 1992. Represents 100 clients. 2% of clients are new/unpublished writers. Currently handles: 50% nonfiction books; 40% novels; 10% juvenile books.

**Member Agents:** Ms. Olga Borodyanskaya, St. Petersburg, Russia, phone: 7-812-1738607 (fiction, nonfiction); Mr. Konstantin Paltchikov, Moscow, Russia, phone: 7-095-2035280 (romance, science fiction, fantasy, thriller).

**Represents:** Nonfiction books; novels; juvenile books. **Considers these nonfiction areas:** biography/autobiography; history; memoirs; psychology; self-help/personal improvement; true crime/investigative. **Considers these fiction areas:** action/adventure; detective/police/crime; fantasy; horror; juvenile; mystery/suspense; romance (contemporary, gothic, historical, regency); science fiction; thriller; young adult.

    O☞ This agency specializes in selling rights for Russian books and illustrations (covers) to American publishers and American books and illustrations for Europe; also Russian-English and English-Russian translations. Actively seeking adventure, fiction, mystery, romance, science fiction, thriller from established authors and illustrators for Russian and European markets.

**How to Contact:** Send published book or galleys. Accepts e-mail and fax queries. Considers simultaneous queries. Returns materials only with SASE.

**Recent Sales:** Sold 12 titles in the last year. *Immigrants*, by Howard Fast (Baronet [Czech Republic]); *Max*, by Howard Fast (Baronet [Czech Republic]); *Kiss of Midas*, by George Vainer (Neri [Italy]).

**Terms:** Agent receives 10% commission on domestic sales; 20% commission on foreign sales. Offers written contract, binding for 2 years; 2-month notice must be given to terminate contract.

**Tips:** "Authors and book illustrators (especially cover art) are welcome for the following genres: romance, fantasy, science fiction, mystery and adventure."

✓ Ⓞ **FORTHWRITE LITERARY AGENCY**, 23852 W. Pacific Coast Hwy., Suite 701, Malibu CA 90265. (310)456-5698. Fax: (310)456-6589. E-mail: agent@kellermedia.com. Website: www.Kellermedia.com. **Contact:** Wendy Keller. Estab. 1989. Member of Women's National Association for Female Executives, Society of Speakers, Authors & Consultants. Represents 20 clients. 10% of clients are new/unpublished writers. Currently handles: 80% nonfiction books; 20% foreign and other secondary rights.

    ● Prior to opening her agency, Ms. Keller was the associate publisher of Los Angeles' second largest Spanish-language newpaper.

**Represents: Considers these nonfiction areas:** art/architecture/design; biography/autobiography; business/economics; child guidance/parenting; cooking/foods/nutrition; crafts/hobbies; current affairs; health/medicine (and alternative health); history; how-to; interior design/decorating; nature/environment (ecology); psychology (pop); religious/inspirational; self-help/personal improvement; spirituality (inspirational); theater/film; women's issues/studies; home maintenance and management; writing; consumer reference.

    O☞ This agency specializes in "serving authors who are or plan to also be speakers. Our sister company is a speaker's bureau." Also handles foreign, ancillary, upselling (selling a previously published books to a larger publisher) and other secondary and subsidiary rights. Actively seeking "professional manuscripts by highly qualified authors." Does not want to receive "fiction, get-rich-quick of first person narrative on health topics."

**How to Contact:** No unsolicited mss. Prefers e-mail queries, no attachments. Considers simultaneous queries. Responds in 2 weeks to queries; 6 weeks to mss. Returns materials only with SASE. Obtains most new clients through referrals, recommendations by editors, queries, satisfied authors, conferences.

**Recent Sales:** Sold 11 titles in the last year. *Air Rage: Crisis in the Skies*, by Andrew Thomas (Prometheus); *The Secrets of Word-of-Mouth Marketing*, by George Silverman (AMACom); *Super Smoothies*, by Cherie Calbom (Warner); *The Cult of the Born Again Virgin: How Single Women Are Reclaiming Their Sexual Power*, by Wendy Keller (Health Communications, Inc.).

**Writers' Conferences:** BEA; Frankfurt Booksellers' Convention; Maui Writer's Conference; Attends regional conferences and regularly talks on finding an agent, how to write nonfiction proposals, book marketing, query writing, creativity enhancement, persevering for creatives.

**Tips:** "Write only on a subject you know well, and be prepared to show a need in the market for your book. We prefer to represent authors who are already presenting their material publicly through seminars or other media."

Ⓞ **FOX CHASE AGENCY, INC.**, Public Ledget Bldg. 930, Philadelphia PA 19106. Member of AAR. This agency did not respond to our request for information. Query before submitting.

Ⓞ **LYNN C. FRANKLIN ASSOCIATES, LTD.**, 1350 Broadway, Suite 2015, New York NY 10018. (212)868-6311. Fax: (212)868-6312. E-mail: agency@fsainc.com. **Contact:** Lynn Franklin and Claudia Nys. Estab. 1987. Member of PEN America. Represents 30-35 clients. 50% of clients are new/unpublished writers. Currently handles: 90% nonfiction books; 10% novels.

**Represents:** Nonfiction books; novels. **Considers these nonfiction areas:** biography/autobiography; current affairs; health/medicine; history; memoirs; New Age/metaphysics; psychology; religious/inspirational (inspirational); self-help/personal improvement; spirituality. **Considers these fiction areas:** literary; mainstream/contemporary (commercial).

    O☞ This agency specializes in general nonfiction with a special interest in health, biography, international affairs, and spirituality.

**How to Contact:** Query with SASE. No unsolicited mss. Considers simultaneous queries. Responds in 2 weeks to queries; 6 weeks to mss. Obtains most new clients through recommendations from others, solicitations.

**Recent Sales:** *The Rich Part of Life*, by Jim Kokorus (St. Martin's Press/film rights secured by Columbia Pictures); *Health on Your Own Terms*, by Frank Lipman, M.D. (Tarcher/Putnam); *After Breast Cancer Treatment: A Survivor's Guide to Renewed Health and Happiness*, by Hester Hill Schnipper (Bantam/Dell).

**Terms:** Agent receives 15% commission on domestic sales; 20% commission on foreign sales. Offers written contract; 60-day notice must be given to terminate contract. 100% of business is derived from commissions on ms sales. Charges clients for postage, photocopying, long distance telephone if significant.

**JEANNE FREDERICKS LITERARY AGENCY, INC.**, 221 Benedict Hill Rd., New Canaan CT 06840. (203)972-3011. Fax: (203)972-3011. E-mail: jfredrks@optonline.net. **Contact:** Jeanne Fredericks. Estab. 1997. Member of AAR, Authors Guild. Represents 90 clients. 10% of clients are new/unpublished writers. Currently handles: 98% nonfiction books; 2% novels.
- Prior to opening her agency, Ms. Fredericks was an agent and acting director with the Susan P. Urstadt Inc. Agency.

**Represents:** Nonfiction books. **Considers these nonfiction areas:** animals; anthropology/archaeology; biography/autobiography; business/economics; child guidance/parenting; cooking/foods/nutrition; crafts/hobbies; gardening; health/medicine (and alternative health); history; how-to; interior design/decorating; money/finance; nature/environment; photography; psychology; science/technology; self-help/personal improvement; sports; women's issues/studies.
- This agency specializes in quality adult nonfiction by authorities in their fields.

**How to Contact:** Query first with SASE. Then send outline/proposal, 1-2 sample chapters and SASE. No fax queries. Accepts e-mail queries if short; no attachments. Considers simultaneous queries. Responds in 3 weeks to queries; 2 months to mss. Returns materials only with SASE. Obtains most new clients through recommendations from others, solicitations, conferences.

**Recent Sales:** Sold 20 titles in the last year. *The Gardener's Way*, by Maureen Gilmer (NTC/Contemporary); *The Art of Pounding Flowers*, by Laura Martin (QVC Books); *Getting Ready for Baby*, by Hélène Stelian (Chronicle).

**Terms:** Agent receives 15% commission on domestic sales; 20% commission on foreign sales; 25% commission with foreign co-agent. Offers written contract, binding for 9 months; 2 months notice must be given to terminate contract. Charges client for photocopying of whole proposals and mss, overseas postage, priority mail and express mail services.

**Writers' Conferences:** PEN Women Conference (Williamsburg VA, February); Connecticut Press Club Biennial Writer's Conference (Stamford CT, April); ASJA Annual Writers' Conference East (New York NY, May); BEA (Chicago, June).

**Tips:** "Be sure to research the competition for your work and be able to justify why there's a need for it. I enjoy building an author's career, particularly if s(he) is professional, hardworking, and courteous. Aside from eight years of agenting experience, I've had ten years of editorial experience in adult trade book publishing that enables me to help an author polish a proposal so that it's more appealing to prospective editors. My MBA in marketing also distinguishes me from other agents."

**☑ ◑ JAMES FRENKEL & ASSOCIATES**, 414 S. Randall Ave., Madison WI 53715. (608)255-7977. Fax: (608)255-5852. E-mail: jfrenkel@panit.com. **Contact:** James Frenkel. Estab. 1987. Represents 35 clients. 20% of clients are new/unpublished writers. Currently handles: 5% nonfiction books; 65% novels; 7% story collections; 2% novellas; 7% juvenile books; 1% scholarly books; 2% movie scripts; 4% media tie-ins/ multimedia; 1% syndicated material; 6% anthologies.
- Mr. Frenkel has been involved in the publishing industry for 25 years, in positions ranging from editor to publisher.

**Member Agents:** James Frenkel; Tracy Berg; Jesse Vogel.

**Represents:** Nonfiction books; novels. **Considers these nonfiction areas:** biography/autobiography; self-help/personal improvement; true crime/investigative. **Considers these fiction areas:** contemporary issues; detective/police/crime; ethnic; fantasy; feminist; historical; mainstream/contemporary; mystery/suspense; science fiction; thriller; westerns/frontier; young adult.
- "We welcome and represent a wide variety of material."

**How to Contact:** Query with SASE, outline, 4 sample chapter(s). Prefers to read materials exclusively. No e-mail or fax queries. Responds in 2 months to queries; 6 months to mss. Obtains most new clients through recommendations from others, conferences.

**Recent Sales:** Sold 12 titles in the last year. *Veiled Threats, Died to Match*, by Deborah Donnelly (Delacorte/Dell); *The Crucible Trilogy*, by Sarah Douglass (TOR).

**Terms:** Agent receives 15% commission on domestic sales; 25% commission on foreign sales. Offers written contract, until terminated in writing. Charges clients for office expenses. "Amounts vary from title to title, but photocopying and submission costs are deducted after (and only after) a property sells."

**Tips:** "If there are markets for short fiction or nonfiction in your field, use them to help establish a name that agents will recognize. Too many times we receive poorly written letters and manuscripts rife with simple spelling errors. This is your work—take the time and effort to put together the best presentation you can."

**⊞ ◑ SARAH JANE FREYMANN LITERARY AGENCY**, 59 W. 71st St., Suite 9B, New York NY 10023. (212)362-9277. Fax: (212)501-8240. **Contact:** Sarah Jane Freymann. Represents 100 clients. 20% of clients are new/unpublished writers. Currently handles: 75% nonfiction books; 23% novels; 2% juvenile books.

**Represents:** Nonfiction books; novels; illustrated books. **Considers these nonfiction areas:** animals; anthropology/archaeology; art/architecture/design; biography/autobiography; business/economics; child guidance/parenting; cooking/foods/nutrition; current affairs; ethnic/cultural interests; gay/lesbian issues; health/medicine; history; interior design/

ANCA

decorating; nature/environment; psychology; religious/inspirational; self-help/personal improvement; women's issues/ studies; lifestyle. **Considers these fiction areas:** contemporary issues; ethnic; literary; mainstream/contemporary; mystery/suspense; thriller.

**How to Contact:** Query with SASE. Responds in 2 weeks to queries; 6 weeks to mss. Obtains most new clients through recommendations from others.

**Recent Sales:** *Just Listen*, by Nancy O'Hara (Broadway); *Flavors*, by Pamela Morgan (Viking); *Silent Thunder*, by Katherine Payne (Simon & Schuster).

**Terms:** Agent receives 15% commission on domestic sales; 20% commission on foreign sales. Offers written contract. Charges clients for long distance, overseas postage, photocopying. 100% of business is derived from commissions on ms sales.

**Tips:** "I love fresh new passionate works by authors who love what they are doing and have both natural talent and carefully honed skill."

**☑ ◎ MAX GARTENBERG, LITERARY AGENT,** 521 Fifth Ave., Suite 1700, New York NY 10175-0038. (212)292-4354. Fax: (973)535-5033. E-mail: gartenbook@att.net. **Contact:** Max Gartenberg. Estab. 1954. Represents 30 clients. 5% of clients are new/unpublished writers. Currently handles: 90% nonfiction books; 10% novels.

**Represents:** Nonfiction books; novels. **Considers these nonfiction areas:** agriculture/horticulture; animals; art/architecture/design; biography/autobiography; child guidance/parenting; current affairs; health/medicine; history; military/ war; money/finance; music/dance; nature/environment; psychology; science/technology; self-help/personal improvement; sports; theater/film; true crime/investigative; women's issues/studies.

**How to Contact:** Query with SASE. No e-mail or fax queries. Considers simultaneous queries. Responds in 2 weeks to queries; 6 weeks to mss. Obtains most new clients through recommendations from others, occasionally by "following up on good query letters"

**Recent Sales:** *Stealing Secrets, Telling Lies*, by James Gannon (Brassey's); *Encyclopedia of North American Sports History*, by Ralph Hickok (Facts-On-File).

**Terms:** Agent receives 15% commission on first domestic sales; 10% subsequent commission on domestic sales; 15-20% commission on foreign sales.

**Tips:** "This is a small agency serving established and new writers whose work it is able to handle are few and far between. Nonfiction is more likely to be of interest here than fiction, and category fiction not at all."

**◎ GELFMAN SCHNEIDER LITERARY AGENTS, INC.,** 250 W. 57th St., New York NY 10107. (212)245-1993. Fax: (212)245-8678. **Contact:** Jane Gelfman, Deborah Schneider. Estab. 1981. Member of AAR. Represents 150 clients. 10% of clients are new/unpublished writers.

**Represents:** Nonfiction books; novels; 'We represent adult, general, hardcover fiction and nonfiction, literary and commercial, and some mysteries." **Considers these fiction areas:** literary; mainstream/contemporary; mystery/suspense.

　　**O─** Does not want to receive romances, science fiction, westerns or children's books.

**How to Contact:** Query with SASE. Responds in 1 month to queries; 2 months to mss. Obtains most new clients through recommendations from others.

**Terms:** Agent receives 15% commission on domestic sales; 20% commission on foreign sales. Offers written contract. Charges clients for photocopying, messengers and couriers.

**☑ ◎ GHOSTS & COLLABORATORS INTERNATIONAL, (Specialized: ghost writing),** division of James Peter Associates, Inc., P.O. Box 358, New Canaan CT 06840. (203)972-1070. E-mail: gene_brissie@msn.com. **Contact:** Gene Brissie. Estab. 1971. Member of AAR. Represents 54 clients. Currently handles: 100% nonfiction books.

**Represents:** Nonfiction collaborations and ghost writing assignments.

　　**O─** This agency specializes in representing only published ghost writers and collaborators, nonfiction only.

**How to Contact:** Prefers to read materials exclusively.

**Recent Sales:** Sold 40 titles in the last year. Clients include Clients include Alan Axelrod, Carol Turkington, George Mair, Brandon Toropov, Alvin Moscow, Richard Marek, Susan Shelly.

**Terms:** Agent receives 15% commission on domestic sales; 20% commission on foreign sales. Offers written contract.

**Tips:** "We would like to hear from professional writers who are looking for ghosting and collaboration projects. We invite inquiries from book publishers who are seeking writers to develop house-generated ideas and to work with their authors who need professional assistance."

**☒ ◎ THE GISLASON AGENCY,** 219 Main St. SE, Suite 506, Minneapolis MN 55414-2160. (612)331-8033. Fax: (612)332-8115. E-mail: gislasonbj@aol.com. **Contact:** Barbara J. Gislason. Estab. 1992. Member of Member of Minnesota State Bar Association, Art & Entertainment Law Section (former chair), Internet Committee, Minnesota Intellectual Property Law Association Copyright Committee (former chair).; Also a member of SFWA, MWA, RWA, Sisters in Crime, University Film Society (board member) and Neighborhood Justice (board member). 50% of clients are new/unpublished writers. Currently handles: 25% nonfiction books; 75% novels.

　　● Ms. Gislason became an attorney in 1980, and continues to practice Art & Entertainment Law. She has been nationally recognized as a Leading American Attorney and a Super Lawyer.

**Member Agents:** Deborah Sweeney (fantasy, science fiction); Molly Hennen (partials, nonfiction); Kellie Hultgren (fantasy, science fiction); Adam Kintopf (fantasy, science fiction); Robert E. Ozasky (mystery); Tracy LaChance (romance); Kris Olson (mystery).

**Represents:** Nonfiction books; novels. **Considers these nonfiction areas:** animals (behavior/communications); health/medicine (alternative); New Age/metaphysics; psychology (popular); science/technology; self-help/personal improvement; sociology; spirituality. **Considers these fiction areas:** fantasy; mystery/suspense; romance; science fiction; thriller (legal).

Oⁿ Do not send personal memoirs, poetry or children's books.

**How to Contact:** Fiction: Query with synopsis, first 3 chapters and SASE. Nonfiction: Query with proposal and sample chapters; published authors may submit complete ms. Responds in 1 month to queries; 3 months to mss. Obtains most new clients through recommendations from others, conferences, *Guide to Literary Agents, Literary Market Place* and other reference books.

**Recent Sales:** *Historical Romance # 4*, by Linda Cook (Kensington); *Dancing Dead*, by Deborah Woodworth (Harper-Collins); *Autumn World*, by Joan Verba, et al (Dragon Stone Press).

**Terms:** Agent receives 15 commission on domestic sales; 20 commission on foreign sales. Offers written contract, binding for 1 year with option to renew. Charges clients for photocopying and postage.

**Writers' Conferences:** Romance Writers of America; Midwest Fiction Writers; University of Wisconsin Writer's Institute. Also attend state and regional writers conferences.

**Tips:** "Cover letter should be well written and include a detailed synopsis (if fiction) or proposal (if nonfiction), the first three chapters and author bio. Appropriate SASE required. We are looking for a great writer with a poetic, lyrical or quirky writing style who can create intriguing ambiguities. We expect a well-researched, imaginative and fresh plot that reflects a familiarity with the applicable genre. If submitting nonfiction work, explain how the submission differs from and adds to previously published works in the field. Scenes with sex and violence must be intrinsic to the plot. Remember to proofread, proofread, proofread. If the work was written with a specific publisher in mind, this should be communicated. In addition to owning an agency, Ms. Gislason practices law in the area of Art and Entertainment and has a broad spectrum of entertainment industry contacts."

**GOLDFARB & ASSOCIATES**, 1501 M St. NW, Washington DC, 20005-2902. (202)466-3030. Fax: (202)293-3187. E-mail: rglawlit@aol.com. **Contact:** Ronald Goldfarb. Estab. 1966. "Minority" of clients are new/unpublished writers. Currently handles: 75% nonfiction books; 25% novels; increasing TV and movie deals.

● Ron Goldfarb's book (his ninth), *Perfect Villains, Imperfect Heroes*, was published by Random House. His tenth, *TV or not TV: Courts, Television, and Justice* (NYU Press), 1998.

**Member Agents:** Ronald Goldfarb, Esq. (nonfiction); Robbie Anna Hare; Kristin Auclair; Kimberlee Damen.

**Represents:** Nonfiction books; novels. **Considers these nonfiction areas:** agriculture/horticulture; americana; animals; anthropology/archaeology; art/architecture/design; biography/autobiography; business/economics; child guidance/parenting; computers/electronic; cooking/foods/nutrition; crafts/hobbies; creative nonfiction; current affairs; education; ethnic/cultural interests; gardening; gay/lesbian issues; government/politics/law; health/medicine; history; how-to; humor/satire; interior design/decorating; juvenile nonfiction; language/literature/criticism; memoirs; military/war; money/finance; multicultural; music/dance; nature/environment; New Age/metaphysics; philosophy; photography; popular culture; psychology; recreation; regional; religious/inspirational; science/technology; self-help/personal improvement; sex; sociology; software; spirituality; sports; theater/film; translation; travel; true crime/investigative; women's issues/studies; young adult. **Considers these fiction areas:** action/adventure; contemporary issues; detective/police/crime; ethnic; feminist; glitz; literary; mainstream/contemporary; mystery/suspense; thriller; and "considerable holocaust literature on behalf of museums and individual authors."

Oⁿ This agency specializes primarily in nonfiction but has a growing interest in well-written fiction. "Given our D.C. location, we represent many journalists, politicians and former federal officials. We arrange collaborations. We also represent a broad range of nonfiction writers and novelists." Actively seeking "fiction with literary overtones; strong nonfiction ideas." Does very little children's fiction or poetry.

**How to Contact:** Send outline/synopsis with 1-2 sample chapters (include SASE if return requested). No fax queries. Responds in 1 month to queries; 2 months to mss. Obtains most new clients through recommendations from others.

**Recent Sales:** Sold 35 titles in the last year. *Spin This*, by Stuart Eizenstat (Bill Press). Other clients include Congressman John Kasich, Diane Rehm, Susan Eisenhower, Dan Moldea, Roy Gutman, Leonard Garment, Sargent Shriver, Harlem Jazz Museum.

**Terms:** Charges clients for photocopying, long distance phone calls, postage.

**Writers' Conferences:** Washington Independent Writers Conference ; Medical Writers Conference; VCCA; participates in many ad hoc writers' and publishers' groups and events each year.

**Tips:** "We are a law firm which can help writers with related legal problems, Freedom of Information Act requests, libel, copyright, contracts, contracts, etc. As published authors ourselves, we understand the creative process."

---

**TO HELP YOU UNDERSTAND** and use the information in these listings, see "Reading the Listings in the *Guide to Literary Agents*" in the front of this book.

*Frances Goldin   Sam Stoloff*
*Matt McGowen*

**⊘ FRANCES GOLDIN**, 57 E. 11th St., Suite 5B, New York NY 10003. Member of AAR. This agency did not respond to our request for information. Query with SASE before submitting. *(WP, rep'd by Sydelle Kramer*

**◑ GOODMAN ASSOCIATES**, 500 West End Ave., New York NY 10024-4317. (212)873-4806. **Contact:** Elise Simon Goodman. Estab. 1976. Member of AAR. Represents 100 clients.
   ● Arnold Goodman is current chair of the AAR Ethics Committee.
**Member Agents:** Elise Simon Goodman; Arnold P. Goodman.
**Represents:** Nonfiction books; novels. **Considers most adult nonfiction and fiction areas**.
   ○━ Does not want to receive poetry, articles, individual stories, children's or YA material.
**How to Contact:** Query with SASE. Responds in 10 days to queries; 1 month to mss.
**Terms:** Agent receives 15% commission on domestic sales; 20% commission on foreign sales. Charges clients for certain expenses: faxes, toll calls, overseas postage, photocopying, book purchases.

**Ⓝ ◑ GOODMAN-ANDREW-AGENCY, INC.**, 1275 N. Harper, #7, West Hollywood CA 90046. (323)656-3785. Fax: (323)656-3975. **Contact:** Sasha Goodman. Estab. 1992. Represents 25 clients. 50% of clients are new/unpublished writers. Currently handles: 50% nonfiction books; 50% novels.
**Represents:** Nonfiction books; novels. **Considers these nonfiction areas:** agriculture/horticulture; anthropology/archaeology; art/architecture/design; biography/autobiography; business/economics; child guidance/parenting; cooking/foods/nutrition; current affairs; education; ethnic/cultural interests; gay/lesbian issues; government/politics/law; health/medicine; history; how-to; language/literature/criticism; music/dance; nature/environment; popular culture; psychology; self-help/personal improvement; sociology; sports; theater/film; true crime/investigative; women's issues/studies. **Considers these fiction areas:** contemporary issues; ethnic; gay/lesbian; literary; mainstream/contemporary.
   ○━ "Not big on genre fiction."
**How to Contact:** Submit outline, 2 sample chapter(s). Considers simultaneous queries. Responds in 3 weeks to queries; 3 months to mss. Returns materials only with SASE.
**Recent Sales:** Sold 10 titles in the last year. *Person or Persons Unknown*, by Bruce Alexander (Putnam); *Taking Charge When You're Not in Control*, by Patricia Wiklund, Ph.D. (Ballantine).
**Terms:** Agent receives 15% commission on domestic sales. Offers written contract. Charges clients for postage.
**Writers' Conferences:** Pacific Northwest (Seattle, July).
**Tips:** "Query with 1-page letter, brief synopsis and 2 chapters. Patience, patience, patience. Always enclose return postage/SASE if you want your material returned. Otherwise, say you do not. Remember the agent is receiving dozens of submissions per week so try to understand this, and be patient and courteous."

**◻ CARROLL GRACE LITERARY AGENCY**, P.O. Box 10938, St. Petersburg FL 33733. (727)865-2099. **Contact:** Pat Jozwiakowski, Sunny Mays. Estab. 1999. Represents 50 clients. 95% of clients are new/unpublished writers. Currently handles: 10% nonfiction books; 90% novels.
**Member Agents:** Ms. Sunny Mays (acquisitions director/agent); Ms. Pat Jozwiakowski (agent).
**Represents:** Nonfiction books; novels. **Considers these nonfiction areas:** history; true crime/investigative; women's issues/studies. **Considers these fiction areas:** action/adventure; detective/police/crime; family saga; fantasy; historical; horror; literary; mainstream/contemporary; mystery/suspense (amateur sleuth, cozy, culinary); psychic/supernatural; romance (contemporary, gothic, historical, regency); thriller; westerns/frontier.
   ○━ "We understand how difficult it is for a new writer to obtain an agent or a publisher. We want to guide careers and encourage our clients to their top potential by offering our experience and knowledge." Actively seeking romance, fantasy, mystery/suspense, psychic supernatural, timeswept (romance with time travel).
**How to Contact:** Query with SASE, synopsis, 5 sample chapter(s). No e-mail or fax queries. Considers simultaneous queries. Responds in 6 weeks to queries; 2 months to mss.
**Recent Sales:** Sold 1 titles in the last year. *Tunnel Vision*, by Rob Marshall (Algora).
**Terms:** Agent receives 15% commission on domestic sales; 20% commission on foreign sales. Offers written contract, binding for binding time determined on a book-by-book basis.; 90-day notice must be given to terminate contract. notice must be given to terminate contract. Charges clients for photocopying, international and express postage, faxes, postage.
**Tips:** "Make sure your manuscript is as near to finished as possible—be neat and orderly. Study manuscript formatting, check your manuscript for spelling, grammar and punctuation errors."

**☑ ◑ ASHLEY GRAYSON LITERARY AGENCY**, 1342 18th St., San Pedro CA 90732. Fax: (310)514-1148. Member of AAR.
**Member Agents:** Ashley Grayson (science fiction, fantasy, young adult); Carolyn Grayson (women's fiction, romance, children's, nonfiction); Dan Hooker (contemporary fiction, science fiction, horror, sports).
**How to Contact:** No e-mail or fax queries. Considers simultaneous queries.
**Recent Sales:** Sold 80 titles in the last year. *Tokyo Suckerpunch*, by Isaac Adamson (HarperCollins); *The Return*, by Buzz Aldrin and John Barnes (TOR/Forge).
**Terms:** Charges for "extraordinary expenses such as express mail service costs for overseas submissions."

**◷ SANFORD J. GREENBURGER ASSOCIATES, INC.**, 55 Fifth Ave., New York NY 10003. (212)206-5600. Fax: (212)463-8718. Website: www.greenburger.com. **Contact:** Heide Lange. Estab. 1945. Member of AAR. Represents 500 clients.

**Member Agents:** Heidi Lange; Faith Hamlin; Beth Vesel; Theresa Park; Elyse Cheney; Dan Mandel; Julie Barer.
**Represents:** Nonfiction books; novels. **Considers these nonfiction areas:** agriculture/horticulture; americana; animals; anthropology/archaeology; art/architecture/design; biography/autobiography; business/economics; child guidance/parenting; computers/electronic; cooking/foods/nutrition; crafts/hobbies; creative nonfiction; current affairs; education; ethnic/cultural interests; gardening; gay/lesbian issues; government/politics/law; health/medicine; history; how-to; humor/satire; interior design/decorating; juvenile nonfiction; language/literature/criticism; memoirs; military/war; money/finance; multicultural; music/dance; nature/environment; New Age/metaphysics; philosophy; photography; popular culture; psychology; recreation; regional; religious/inspirational; science/technology; self-help/personal improvement; sex; sociology; software; spirituality; sports; theater/film; translation; travel; true crime/investigative; women's issues/studies; young adult. **Considers these fiction areas:** action/adventure; contemporary issues; detective/police/crime; ethnic; family saga; feminist; gay/lesbian; glitz; historical; humor/satire; literary; mainstream/contemporary; mystery/suspense; psychic/supernatural; regional; sports; thriller.

    ○┭ Does not want to receive romances or westerns.
**How to Contact:** Query with SASE. Considers simultaneous queries. Responds in 3 weeks to queries; 2 months to mss.
**Recent Sales:** Sold 200 titles in the last year. This agency prefers not to share information on specific sales. Clients include Andrew Ross, Margaret Cuthbert, Nicholas Sparks, Mary Kurcinka, Linda Nichols, Edy Clarke and Peggy Claude Pierre, Brad Thor, Dan Brown.
**Terms:** Agent receives 15% commission on domestic sales; 20% commission on foreign sales. Charges for photocopying, books for foreign and subsidiary rights submissions.

**◐ ARTHUR B. GREENE**, 101 Park Ave., 26th Floor, New York NY 10178. (212)661-8200. Fax: (212)370-7884.
**Contact:** Arthur Greene. Estab. 1980. Represents 20 clients. 10% of clients are new/unpublished writers. Currently handles: 25% novels; 10% story collections; 10% novellas; 25% movie scripts; 10% TV scripts; 10% stage plays; 10% other.

    ● See the expanded listing for this agency in Script Agents.

**⊕ ◐ GREGORY AND RADICE AUTHORS' AGENTS**, 3 Barb Mews, London W6 7PA, England. 020-7610-4676. Fax: 020-7610-4686. E-mail: info@gregoryradice.co.uk. Website: www.gregoryradice.co.uk. **Contact:** Jane Gregory, sales; Broo Doherty, editorial; Jane Barlow, rights. Estab. 1987. Member of Association of Authors' Agents. Represents 60 clients. Currently handles: 10% nonfiction books; 90% novels.

    ● Prior to becoming an agent, Ms. Gregory was Rights Director for Chatto & Windus.
**Member Agents:** Jane Gregory (sales); Broo Doherty (editorial); Jane Barlow (rights).
**Represents:** Nonfiction books; novels. **Considers these nonfiction areas:** biography/autobiography; government/politics/law; history. **Considers these fiction areas:** action/adventure; detective/police/crime; historical; humor/satire; literary; mainstream/contemporary; multicultural; romance; thriller.

    ○┭ "Jane Gregory is successful at selling rights all over the world, including film and television rights." Well-written, accessible modern novels. Does not want to receive horror, science fiction, fantasy, children's books, scripts, poetry.
**How to Contact:** Query with SASE, or submit outline, 3 sample chapters, SASE. Accepts e-mail queries. Considers simultaneous queries. Returns materials only with SASE. Obtains most new clients through recommendations from others, conferences.
**Recent Sales:** Sold 100 titles in the last year. *Birdman*, by Mo Hayder (Bantam UK/Doubleday USA); *A Place of Execution*, by Val McDermid (HarperCollins UK); *Shape of Snakes*, by Minette Walters (Fawcett UK/Putnam USA); *Dying Voices*, by Laura Wilson (Orion UK/Bantam USA); *Facing the Light*, by Adele Geras (Orion UK/10 foreign publishers).
**Terms:** Agent receives 15% commission on domestic sales; 20% commission on foreign sales. Offers written contract, binding for book-to-book; 3 months notice must be given to terminate contract. Charges clients for photocopying of whole typescripts and copies of book for submissions.
**Writers' Conferences:** CWA Conference (United Kingdom, Spring); Dead on Deansgate (Manchester, Autumn); Boucheron (location varies, Autumn).

**Ⓝ ◐ BLANCHE C. GREGORY, INC.**, 2 Tudor City Place, New York NY 10017. (212)697-0828. Fax: (212)697-0828. E-mail: gert@bcgliteraryagency.com. Website: www.bcgliteraryagency.com. **Contact:** Gertrude Bregman. Member of AAR.
**Represents:** Nonfiction books; novels; juvenile books (some).

    ○┭ This agency is especially strong in international subrights sales.
**How to Contact:** Query with SASE. No e-mail or fax queries.
**Recent Sales:** This agency prefers not to share information on specific sales. Clients include Lilian Jackson Braun, Peter Miller, Thomas Savage.
**Terms:** Agent receives 15% commission on domestic sales; 20% commission on foreign sales.

**Ⓞ MAXINE GROFFSKY LITERARY AGENCY**, 853 Broadway, Suite 708, New York NY 10003. Member of AAR. This agency did not respond to our request for information. Query before submitting.

**N:** **JILL GROSJEAN LITERARY AGENCY**, 1390 Millstone Rd., Sag Harbor NY 11963-2214. (631)725-7419. Fax: (631)725-8632. E-mail: JILL6981@aol.com. Website: www.hometown.aol.com/JILL6981/myhomepage/index.ht ml. **Contact:** Jill Grosjean. Estab. 1999. Represents 11 clients. 100% of clients are new/unpublished writers. Currently handles: 1% nonfiction books; 99% novels.

- Prior to becoming an agent, Ms. Grosjean was manager of an independent bookstore. She also worked in publishing and advertising.

**Represents:** Nonfiction books (some); novels (mostly). **Considers these nonfiction areas:** art/architecture/design; gardening; humor/satire; interior design/decorating; nature/environment; travel; women's issues/studies. **Considers these fiction areas:** contemporary issues; historical; humor/satire; literary; mainstream/contemporary; mystery/suspense; regional; romance; thriller.

O→ This agency offers some editorial assistance (i.e., line-by-line edits). Actively seeking mysteries, thrillers, suspense novels. Does not want to receive any nonfiction subjects not indicated above.

**How to Contact:** Query with SASE. Considers simultaneous queries. Responds in 1 week to queries; 1 month to mss. Returns materials only with SASE. Obtains most new clients through recommendations from others, solicitations.

**Recent Sales:** Sold 4 titles in the last year. *Free Bird*, by Greg Garrett (Kensington); *Two Turtledoves*, by Tony Broadbent (Thomas Dunne).

**Terms:** Agent receives 15% commission on domestic sales; 20% commission on foreign sales. No written contract. Charges clients for photocopying, mailing expenses; Writers reimbursed for office fees after the sale of ms.

**Writers' Conferences:** Book Passages Mystery Writer's Conference (Corte Madera CA, July).

**THE GROSVENOR LITERARY AGENCY**, 5510 Grosvenor Lane, Bethesda MD 20814. (301)564-6231. Fax: (301)581-9401. E-mail: dcgrosveno@aol.com. **Contact:** Deborah C. Grosvenor. Estab. 1995. Member of National Press Club. Represents 30 clients. 10% of clients are new/unpublished writers. Currently handles: 80% nonfiction books; 20% novels.

- Prior to opening her agency, Ms. Grosvenor was a book editor for 18 years.

**Represents:** Nonfiction books; novels. **Considers these nonfiction areas:** animals; anthropology/archaeology; art/architecture/design; biography/autobiography; business/economics; child guidance/parenting; current affairs; government/politics/law; health/medicine; history; how-to; language/literature/criticism; military/war; money/finance; music/dance; nature/environment; New Age/metaphysics; photography; popular culture; psychology; religious/inspirational; science/technology; self-help/personal improvement; sociology; spirituality; theater/film; translation; true crime/investigative; women's issues/studies. **Considers these fiction areas:** contemporary issues; detective/police/crime; family saga; gay/lesbian; historical; literary; mainstream/contemporary; mystery/suspense; romance (contemporary, gothic, historical); thriller.

**How to Contact:** Send outline/proposal for nonfiction; send outline and 3 sample chapters for fiction. No e-mail or fax queries. Responds in 1 month to queries; 2 months to mss. Returns materials only with SASE. Obtains most new clients through obtains clients almost exclusively through recommendations from others.

**Recent Sales:** *What it Felt Like: Living in the American Century*, by Henry Allen (Pantheon); *Elvis and Nixon (fiction)*, by Jonathan Lowy (Crown Publishing).

**Terms:** Agent receives 15% commission on domestic sales; 20% commission on foreign sales. Offers written contract; 10-day notice must be given to terminate contract.

**THE CHARLOTTE GUSAY LITERARY AGENCY**, 10532 Blythe, Los Angeles CA 90064-3312. (310)559-0831. E-mail: gusay1@aol.com. Website: www.mediastudio.com/gusay. **Contact:** Charlotte Gusay. Estab. 1988. Member of Authors Guild and PEN; signatory of WGA. Represents 30 clients. 50% of clients are new/unpublished writers.

- Prior to becoming an agent, Ms. Gusay was a vice president for an audiocassette producer and also a bookstore owner.

**Represents:** Nonfiction books; novels; juvenile books; scholarly books. **Considers these nonfiction areas:** agriculture/horticulture; americana; animals; anthropology/archaeology; art/architecture/design; biography/autobiography; business/economics; child guidance/parenting; computers/electronic; cooking/foods/nutrition; crafts/hobbies; creative nonfiction; current affairs; education; ethnic/cultural interests; gardening; gay/lesbian issues; government/politics/law; health/medicine; history; how-to; humor/satire; interior design/decorating; juvenile nonfiction; language/literature/criticism; memoirs; military/war; money/finance; multicultural; music/dance; nature/environment; New Age/metaphysics; philosophy; photography; popular culture; psychology; recreation; regional; religious/inspirational; science/technology; self-help/personal improvement; sex; sociology; software; spirituality; sports; theater/film; translation; travel; true crime/investigative; women's issues/studies; young adult. **Considers these fiction areas:** action/adventure; comic books/cartoon; confession; contemporary issues; detective/police/crime; erotica; ethnic; experimental; family saga; fantasy; feminist; gay/lesbian; glitz; gothic; hi-lo; historical; humor/satire; juvenile; literary; mainstream/contemporary; military/war; multicultural; multimedia; mystery/suspense; New Age; occult; picture books; plays; poetry; poetry in translation; psychic/supernatural; regional; religious/inspirational; spiritual; sports; thriller; translation; westerns/frontier; young adult.

O→ This agency specializes in fiction, nonfiction, children's (multicultural, nonsexist), children's illustrators, screenplays, books to film. Actively seeking "the next *English Patient*." Does not want to receive poetry, science fiction, horror.

**Also Handles:** Feature film. **Considers these script subject areas:** action/adventure; comedy; detective/police/crime; ethnic; experimental; family saga; feminist; gay/lesbian; historical; mainstream; mystery/suspense; romantic comedy; romantic drama; sports; thriller; western/frontier.

**How to Contact:** Query with SASE, 1-2 page synopsis. All unsolicited mss returned unopened. Considers simultaneous queries. Responds in 6 weeks to queries; 10 weeks to mss. Obtains most new clients through recommendations from others, solicitations.

**Recent Sales:** *Baby Love: The Private Files of an Adoption Agency*, by Randi G. Barrow, Esq. (Perigee/Penguin Putnam); *Vintage! The Ultimate Guide to Selected Resale and Vintage Shopping in North America and Online*, by Diana Eden and Gloria Lintermans (Really Great Books).

**Terms:** Agent receives 15% commission on domestic sales; 25% commission on foreign sales; 10% commission on dramatic rights sales. Offers written contract. Shares out-of-pocket expenses such as long distance phone calls, fax, express mail, postage, etc. Also, charges a nominal processing fee, especially when considering unsolicited submissions, decided upon as and when queries arrive in the agency office.

**Writers' Conferences:** Writers Connection (San Jose CA); Scriptwriters Connection (Studio City CA); National Women's Book Association (Los Angeles); California Writers Conference (Monterey CA); San Diego Writers Conference; Maui Writers Conference.

**Tips:** "Please be professional."

**H.W.A. TALENT REPRESENTATIVES**, 3500 W. Olive Ave., Suite 1400, Burbank CA 91505. (818)972-4310. Fax: (818)972-4313. **Contact:** Kimber Wheeler. Estab. 1985. Signatory of WGA. 90% of clients are new/unpublished writers. Currently handles: 10% novels; 90% movie scripts.

● See the expanded listing for this agency in Script Agents.

**REECE HALSEY AGENCY**, 8733 Sunset Blvd., Suite 101, Los Angeles CA 90069. (310)652-2409. Fax: (310)652-7595. **Contact:** Dorris Halsey; Kimberly Cameron. Estab. 1957. Member of AAR. Represents 40 clients. 30% of clients are new/unpublished writers. Currently handles: 30% nonfiction books; 60% novels; 10% movie scripts.

● The Reece Halsey Agency has an illustrious client list largely of established writers, including the estate of Aldous Huxley and has represented Upton Sinclair, William Faulkner and Henry Miller. Ms. Cameron has recently opened a Northern California office and all queries should be addressed to her at the Reece Halsey North office.

**Member Agents:** Dorris Halsey; Kimberley Cameron.

**Represents:** Nonfiction books; novels. **Considers these nonfiction areas:** biography/autobiography; current affairs; history; language/literature/criticism; popular culture; true crime/investigative; women's issues/studies. **Considers these fiction areas:** action/adventure; contemporary issues; detective/police/crime; ethnic; family saga; historical; literary; mainstream/contemporary; mystery/suspense; science fiction; thriller; women's.

O─ This agency specializes mostly in books/excellent writing.

**How to Contact:** Query with SASE. Prefers to read materials exclusively. No e-mail or fax queries. Responds in 3 weeks to queries; 3 months to mss. Obtains most new clients through recommendations from others, solicitations.

**Terms:** Agent receives 15% commission on domestic sales; 10% commission on dramatic rights sales. Offers written contract, binding for 1 year. Requests 6 copies of ms if representing an author.

**Writers' Conferences:** Maui Writers Conference; ABA.

**Tips:** "Always send a well-written query and include a SASE with it!"

**REECE HALSEY NORTH**, 8733 Sunset Blvd., Suite 101, Los Angeles CA 90069. Fax: (310)652-7595 or (310)652-2409. E-mail: bookgirl@worldnet.att.net. Website: www.reecehalseynorth.com or kimberlycameron.com. **Contact:** Kimberly Cameron. Estab. 1995. Member of AAR. Represents 40 clients. 30% of clients are new/unpublished writers. Currently handles: 30% nonfiction books; 70% novels.

**Member Agents:** Kimberley Cameron (Reece Halsey North); Dorris Halsey (by referral only, LA office).

**Represents:** Nonfiction books; novels. **Considers these nonfiction areas:** biography/autobiography; current affairs; history; language/literature/criticism; memoirs; popular culture; spirituality; true crime/investigative; women's issues/studies. **Considers these fiction areas:** action/adventure; ethnic; historical; literary; mainstream/contemporary; mystery/suspense; science fiction. **Considers these script subject areas:** thriller.

O─ This agency specializes in mystery, literary and mainstream fiction, excellent writing. The Reece Halsey Agency has an illustrious client list largely of established writers, including the estate of Aldous Huxley and has represented Upton Sinclair, William Faulkner and Henry Miller. Ms. Cameron has a Northern California office and all queries should be addressed to her at the Tiburon office.

**How to Contact:** Query with SASE. No e-mail or fax queries. Considers simultaneous queries. Responds in 6 weeks to queries; 3 months to mss. Obtains most new clients through recommendations from others, solicitations.

**Recent Sales:** *Jinn*, by Matthew Delaney (St. Martin's Press); *Flu Season*, by Earl Merkel (Dutton-NAL).

**Terms:** Agent receives 15% commission on domestic sales. Offers written contract, binding for 1 year. Requests 6 copies of ms if representing an author.

**Writers' Conferences:** BEA; Maui Writers Conference.

**Reading List:** Reads *Glimmer Train*, *The Sun* and *The New Yorker* to find new clients. Looks for "writing that touches the heart."

**Tips:** "Please send a polite, well-written query and include a SASE with it!"

⊘ **THE MITCHELL J. HAMILBURG AGENCY**, 8671 Wilshire Blvd., Suite 500, Beverly Hills CA 90211-2913. (301)657-1501. **Contact:** Michael Hamilburg. Estab. 1937. Signatory of WGA. Represents 70 clients. Currently handles: 70% nonfiction books; 30% novels.

**Represents:** Nonfiction books; novels. **Considers all nonfiction and most fiction areas.**

   O⟲ Does not want to receive romance.

**How to Contact:** Query with SASE, submit outline, 2 sample chapter(s). Responds in 1 month to mss. Obtains most new clients through recommendations from others, conferences, personal search.

**Recent Sales:** *Fatal North*, by Bruce Henderson (Dutton); *Wildlife Wars*, by Richard Leakey and Virginia Morell (St. Martin's Press); *The Siege of Shangri-La*, by Michael Macrae (Broadway Books).

**Terms:** Agent receives 10-15% commission on domestic sales.

**Tips:** "Good luck! Keep writing!"

⊘ **JEANNE K. HANSON LITERARY AGENCY**, 5441 Woodcrest Dr., Edina MN 55424-1649. Member of AAR. This agency did not respond to our request for information. Query before submitting.

⊘ **HARDEN CURTIS ASSOCIATES**, 850 Seventh Ave., Suite 405, New York NY, 10019. Member of AAR. This agency did not respond to our request for information. Query with SASE before submitting.

⊘ **THE JOY HARRIS LITERARY AGENCY, INC.**, 156 Fifth Ave., Suite 617, New York NY 10010. (212)924-6269. Fax: (212)924-6609. E-mail: gen.office@jhlitagent.com. **Contact:** Joy Harris. Member of AAR. Represents 150 clients. Currently handles: 50% nonfiction books; 50% novels.

**Member Agents:** Leslie Daniels; Stéphanie Abou.

**Represents:** Nonfiction books; novels. **Considers these fiction areas:** action/adventure; comic books/cartoon; confession; contemporary issues; detective/police/crime; erotica; ethnic; experimental; family saga; feminist; gay/lesbian; glitz; gothic; hi-lo; historical; horror; humor/satire; literary; mainstream/contemporary; military/war; multicultural; multimedia; mystery/suspense; New Age; occult; picture books; plays; poetry; poetry in translation; psychic/supernatural; regional; religious/inspirational; romance; short story collections; spiritual; sports; thriller; translation; young adult; women's.

   O⟲ Does not want to receive screenplays.

**How to Contact:** Query with outline/proposal, SASE. Considers simultaneous queries. Responds in 2 months to queries. Obtains most new clients through recommendations from clients and editors.

**Recent Sales:** Sold 15 titles in the last year. This agency prefers not to share information on specific sales.

**Terms:** Agent receives 15% commission on domestic sales; 20% commission on foreign sales. Charges clients for some office expenses.

☑ ◖ **HARTLINE LITERARY AGENCY**, 123 Queenston Dr., Pittsburgh PA 15235-5429. (412)829-2495 or 2483. Fax: (412)829-2450. E-mail: jahart@hartlinemarketing.com. Website: www.hartlinemarketing.com. **Contact:** Joyce A. Hart. Estab. 1990. Represents 15 clients. 30% of clients are new/unpublished writers. Currently handles: 40% nonfiction books; 60% novels.

**Member Agents:** Joyce A. Hart (adult/fiction); Jim Hart (adult/fiction).

**Represents:** Nonfiction books; novels. **Considers these nonfiction areas:** business/economics; child guidance/parenting; cooking/foods/nutrition; money/finance; religious/inspirational; self-help/personal improvement; women's issues/studies. **Considers these fiction areas:** action/adventure; contemporary issues; family saga; historical; literary; mystery/suspense (amateur sleuth, cozy); regional; religious/inspirational; romance (contemporary, gothic, historical, regency); thriller.

   O⟲ This agency specializes in the Christian bookseller market. Actively seeking adult fiction, self-help, nutritional books, devotional, business. Does not want to receive science fiction, erotica, gay/lesbian, fantasy, horror, etc.

**How to Contact:** Submit outline, 3 sample chapter(s). Accepts e-mail and fax queries. Considers simultaneous queries. Responds in 1 month to queries; 2 months to mss. Returns materials only with SASE. Obtains most new clients through recommendations from others.

**Recent Sales:** Sold 7 titles in the last year. *A Burden Shared*, by Jane Kirkpatrick (Harvest Queen); *Secondmile*, by Ron and Janet Benrey (Broadman & Holman); *What We Once Saved*, by Jane Kirkpatrick (Waterbrook).

**Terms:** Agent receives 15% commission on domestic sales. Offers written contract.

◖ **JOHN HAWKINS & ASSOCIATES, INC.**, 71 W. 23rd St., Suite 1600, New York NY 10010. (212)807-7040. Fax: (212)807-9555. E-mail: jhawkasc@aol.com. **Contact:** John Hawkins, William Reiss. Estab. 1893. Member of AAR. Represents over 100 clients. 5-10% of clients are new/unpublished writers. Currently handles: 40% nonfiction books; 40% novels; 20% juvenile books.

**Member Agents:** Moses Cardona; Warren Frazier; Anne Hawkins; John Hawkins; William Reiss; Elly Sidel.

**Represents:** Nonfiction books; novels; juvenile books. **Considers these nonfiction areas:** agriculture/horticulture; americana; animals; anthropology/archaeology; art/architecture/design; biography/autobiography; business/economics; child guidance/parenting; cooking/foods/nutrition; crafts/hobbies; creative nonfiction; current affairs; education; ethnic/cultural interests; gardening; gay/lesbian issues; government/politics/law; health/medicine; history; how-to; humor/satire; interior design/decorating; juvenile nonfiction; language/literature/criticism; memoirs; military/war; money/finance; multicultural; music/dance; nature/environment; New Age/metaphysics; philosophy; photography; popular culture; psy-

chology; recreation; regional; science/technology; self-help/personal improvement; sex; sociology; software; spirituality; sports; theater/film; travel; true crime/investigative; women's issues/studies; young adult. **Considers these fiction areas:** action/adventure; comic books/cartoon; contemporary issues; detective/police/crime; ethnic; experimental; family saga; fantasy; feminist; gay/lesbian; glitz; gothic; hi-lo; historical; horror; humor/satire; juvenile; literary; mainstream/contemporary; military/war; multicultural; multimedia; mystery/suspense; New Age; occult; picture books; plays; poetry; poetry in translation; psychic/supernatural; regional; religious/inspirational; science fiction; short story collections; spiritual; sports; thriller; translation; westerns/frontier; young adult; women's.
**How to Contact:** Query with SASE, submit proposal package, outline. Considers simultaneous queries. Responds in 1 month to queries. Returns materials only with SASE. Obtains most new clients through recommendations from others. *Middle Age*, by Joyce Carol Oates (HarperCollins); *The Muse Asylum*, by David Czuchlewski (Putnam).
**Terms:** Agent receives 15% commission on domestic sales; 20% commission on foreign sales. Charges clients for photocopying.

✓ ◯ **HEACOCK LITERARY AGENCY, INC.**, 707 Seventh St., Tularosa NM 88352. E-mail: gracebooks@aol.com. **Contact:** Rosalie Grace Heacock. Estab. 1978. Member of AAR, Author's Guild, SCBWI. Represents 60 clients. 10% of clients are new/unpublished writers. Currently handles: 100% nonfiction books.
**Represents:** Nonfiction books (adult); juvenile books (children's picture books). **Considers these nonfiction areas:** art/architecture/design; biography/autobiography; how-to; music/dance; nature/environment; psychology; recreation (hiking); science/technology; self-help/personal improvement; spirituality; women's issues/studies. **Considers these fiction areas:** Considers limited selection of top children's book authors; no beginners, please.
    ○↦ Does not want to receive scripts.
**How to Contact:** Query with SASE. Prefers to read materials exclusively. No multiple queries. Responds in 3 weeks to queries; 2 months to mss. Returns materials only with SASE.
**Recent Sales:** Sold 22 titles in the last year. This agency prefers not to share information on specific sales.
**Terms:** Agent receives 15% commission on domestic sales; 15-25% commission on foreign sales. Offers written contract, binding for 1 year.; 95% of business is derived from commissions on ms sales. Charges clients for actual expense for telephone, postage, packing, photocopying. "We provide copies of each publisher submission letter and the publisher's response."
**Writers' Conferences:** Maui Writers Conference; Santa Barbara City College Annual Writer's Workshop; Pasadena City College Writer's Forum; UCLA Symposium on Writing Nonfiction Books; Society of Children's Book Writers and Illustrators, Southwest Writers Conference (Albuquerque); SCBWI Los Altos.
**Reading List:** Reads "all trade journals, also literary magazines and environmental periodicals" to find new clients. Looks for "new ways to solve old problems."
**Tips:** "Take time to write an informative query letter expressing your book idea, the market for it, your qualifications to write the book, the 'hook' that would make a potential reader buy the book. Always enclose SASE; we cannot respond to queries without return postage. Our primary focus is upon books which make a contribution."

✓ ◑ **RICHARD HENSHAW GROUP**, 127 W. 24th St., 4th Floor, New York NY 10011. (212)414-1172. Fax: (435)417-5208. E-mail: submissions@henshaw.com. Website: www.rich.henshaw.com. **Contact:** Rich Henshaw. Estab. 1995. Member of AAR, SinC, MWA, HWA, SFWA. Represents 35 clients. 20% of clients are new/unpublished writers. Currently handles: 30% nonfiction books; 70% novels.
    • Prior to opening his agency, Mr. Henshaw served as an agent with Richard Curtis Associates, Inc.
**Represents:** Nonfiction books; novels. **Considers these nonfiction areas:** animals; biography/autobiography; business/economics; child guidance/parenting; computers/electronic; cooking/foods/nutrition; current affairs; gay/lesbian issues; government/politics/law; health/medicine; how-to; humor/satire; military/war; money/finance; music/dance; nature/environment; New Age/metaphysics; popular culture; psychology; science/technology; self-help/personal improvement; sociology; sports; true crime/investigative; women's issues/studies. **Considers these fiction areas:** action/adventure; detective/police/crime; ethnic; family saga; fantasy; glitz; historical; horror; humor/satire; literary; mainstream/contemporary; mystery/suspense; psychic/supernatural; romance; science fiction; sports; thriller.
    ○↦ This agency specializes in thrillers, mysteries, science fiction, fantasy and horror.
**How to Contact:** Query with SASE. Responds in 3 weeks to queries; 6 weeks to mss. Obtains most new clients through recommendations from others, solicitations, conferences.
**Recent Sales:** Sold 17 titles in the last year. *The Singing of the Dead*, by Dana Stabenow (St. Martin's Press); *Training Our Own Minds*, by Susan Wise Bauer (W.W. Norton); *The Shadow Dancer*, by Margaret Coel (Berkley); *Bad Lawyer*, by David Cray (Carroll & Graf). Other clients include Susan Wise Bauer, Jessie Wise.
**Terms:** Agent receives 15% commission on domestic sales; 20% commission on foreign sales. No written contract. 100% of business is derived from commissions on ms sales. Charges clients for photocopying mss and book orders.
**Tips:** "Please visit our website for more information and current interests. Always include SASE with correct return postage."

---

**CONTACT THE EDITOR** of *Guide to Literary Agents* by e-mail at literaryagents @fwpubs.com with your questions and comments.

☑ ◎ **THE JEFF HERMAN AGENCY LLC**, 332 Bleecker St., #531, New York NY 10014. (212)941-0540. Fax: (212)941-0614. E-mail: jeff@jeffherman.com. Website: www.jeffherman.com. **Contact:** Jeffrey H. Herman. Estab. 1985. Represents 100 clients. 10% of clients are new/unpublished writers. Currently handles: 85% nonfiction books; 5% novels; 5% scholarly books; 5% textbooks.

• Prior to opening his agency, Mr. Herman served as a public relations executive.

**Member Agents:** Deborah Levine (vice president, nonfiction book doctor); Jeff Herman; Amanda White.

**Represents:** Nonfiction books. **Considers these nonfiction areas:** business/economics; computers/electronic; government/politics/law; health/medicine (and recovery issues); history; how-to; psychology (pop); self-help/personal improvement; spirituality; popular reference.

O→ This agency specializes in adult nonfiction.

**How to Contact:** Query with SASE. Accepts e-mail and fax queries. Considers simultaneous queries.

**Recent Sales:** Sold 35 titles in the last year. This agency prefers not to share information on specific sales.

**Terms:** Agent receives 15% commission on domestic sales. Offers written contract. Charges clients for copying, postage.

*914-234-2864   PO Box 57, Pound Ridge NY 10576*

◎ **SUSAN HERNER RIGHTS AGENCY**, P.O. Box 303, Scarsdale NY 10583-0303. (914)725-8967. Fax: (914)725-8969. **Contact:** Susan Herner or Sue Yuen. Estab. 1987. Represents 100 clients. 30% of clients are new/unpublished writers. Currently handles: 60% nonfiction books; 40% novels.

**Member Agents:** Susan Herner, president (nonfiction, thriller, mystery, strong women's fiction); Sue Yuen, vice president (adult commercial fiction); Betty Anne Crawford, director of subsidiary rights and special projects.

**Represents:** Nonfiction books (adult); novels (adult). **Considers these nonfiction areas:** anthropology/archaeology; biography/autobiography; business/economics; child guidance/parenting; cooking/foods/nutrition; current affairs; ethnic/cultural interests; gay/lesbian issues; government/politics/law; health/medicine; history; how-to; language/literature/criticism; nature/environment; New Age/metaphysics; popular culture; psychology; religious/inspirational; science/technology; self-help/personal improvement; sociology; spirituality; true crime/investigative; women's issues/studies. **Considers these fiction areas:** action/adventure; contemporary issues; detective/police/crime; ethnic; family saga; fantasy; feminist; glitz; historical; horror; literary; mainstream/contemporary; mystery/suspense; romance (contemporary, gothic, historical, regency); science fiction; thriller.

O→ This agency is eager to work with new/previously unpublished writers. "I'm particularly looking for strong women's fiction." "I'm particularly interested in women's issues, popular science, and feminist spirituality."

**How to Contact:** Query with SASE, outline, sample chapter(s). Considers simultaneous queries. Responds in 1 month to queries. Returns materials only with SASE.

**Recent Sales:** *Feng Shui for Lovers*, by Raphael Simons (Crown); *Catch a Dream*, by Mary Jane Meier (Signet).

**Terms:** Agent receives 15% commission on domestic sales; 20% commission on foreign sales; 20% commission on dramatic rights sales. Charges clients for extraordinary postage and photocopying. "Agency has two divisions: one represents writers on a commission-only basis; the other represents the rights for small publishers and packagers who do not have in-house subsidiary rights representation. Percentage of income derived from each division is currently 80-20."

**Writers' Conferences:** Vermont League of Writers (Burlington VT); Gulf States Authors League (Mobile AL).

☑ ◎ **HILL & BARLOW AGENCY**, (formerly The Palmer & Dodge Agency), One International Place, Boston MA 02110. (617)428-3514. Fax: (617)428-3500. E-mail: doconnell@hillbarlow.com. Website: www.hillbarlow.com. **Contact:** Diane O'Connell. Estab. 1990. Represents 100 clients. 5% of clients are new/unpublished writers. Currently handles: 80% nonfiction books; 20% novels.

**Member Agents:** John Taylor (Ike) Williams, director (books, film, TV); Jill Kneerin, managing director (books); Rob McQuilken, agent (books); Elaine Rogers, director of subsidiary rights (dramatic rights, foreign, audio).

**Represents:** Nonfiction books; novels. **Considers these nonfiction areas:** anthropology/archaeology; biography/autobiography; business/economics; child guidance/parenting; current affairs; education; ethnic/cultural interests; gay/lesbian issues; government/politics/law; health/medicine; history; language/literature/criticism; money/finance; music/dance; nature/environment; New Age/metaphysics; popular culture; psychology; religious/inspirational; science/technology; self-help/personal improvement; sociology; spirituality; women's issues/studies. **Considers these fiction areas:** ethnic; feminist; gay/lesbian; literary; mainstream/contemporary.

O→ This agency specializes in trade nonfiction and quality fiction for adults. Dramatic rights for books and life story rights only. Does not want to receive genre fiction.

**How to Contact:** Query with outline/proposal. Responds in 1 month to queries; 3 months to mss. Obtains most new clients through recommendations from others.

**Recent Sales:** *Will in the World*, by Stephen Greenblatt; *Nightengales*, by Gillian Gill; *The First Counsel*, by Brad Meltzer (Warner).

**Terms:** Agent receives 15% commission on domestic sales; 20% commission on foreign sales. Offers written contract; 4 months notice must be given to terminate contract. 100% of business is derived from commissions on ms sales. Charges clients for direct expenses (postage, phone, photocopying, messenger service).

**Tips:** "We are taking very few new clients for representation."

◎ **FREDERICK HILL BONNIE NADEL, INC.**, 1842 Union St., San Francisco CA 94123. (415)921-2910. Fax: (415)921-2802. **Contact:** Irene Moore. Estab. 1979. Represents 100 clients.

**How to Contact:** Query with SASE. Considers simultaneous queries. Responds in 5 weeks to queries; 5 weeks to mss. Returns materials only with SASE. Obtains most new clients through recommendations from others.
**Recent Sales:** Sold 20 titles in the last year. Clients include Shelby Foote, The Grief Recovery Institute, Don Wade, Don Zimmer, The Knot.com, David Plowder, PGA of America, Danny Peary, Jahnna Beecham & Malcolm Hillgartner.
**Terms:** Agent receives 15% commission on domestic sales; 20% commission on foreign sales. Offers written contract.
**Tips:** "Please check out our website for more details on our agency. No e-mail submissions please."

**B.J. ROBBINS LITERARY AGENCY**, 5130 Bellaire Ave., North Hollywood CA 91607-2908. (818)760-6602. Fax: (818)760-6616. E-mail: robbinsliterary@aol.com. **Contact:** (Ms.) B.J. Robbins. Estab. 1992. Member of Board of Directors, PEN American Center West. Represents 40 clients. 50% of clients are new/unpublished writers. Currently handles: 50% nonfiction books; 50% novels.
**Member Agents:** Rob McAndrews (commercial fiction).
**Represents:** Nonfiction books; novels. **Considers these nonfiction areas:** biography/autobiography; child guidance/ parenting; current affairs; ethnic/cultural interests; health/medicine; how-to; humor/satire; memoirs; music/dance; popular culture; psychology; self-help/personal improvement; sociology; sports; theater/film; true crime/investigative; women's issues/studies. **Considers these fiction areas:** contemporary issues; detective/police/crime; ethnic; literary; mainstream/contemporary; mystery/suspense; sports; thriller.
**How to Contact:** Submit 3 sample chapter(s), outline/proposal, SASE. No e-mail or fax queries. Considers simultaneous queries. Responds in 2 weeks to queries; 6 weeks to mss. Returns materials only with SASE. Obtains most new clients through recommendations from others, conferences.
**Recent Sales:** Sold 15 titles in the last year. *A Matter of Time*, by John Hough, Jr. (Simon & Schuster/NAL); *The Drums of Quallah Battoo*, by Charles Corn (Dutton).
**Terms:** Agent receives 15% commission on domestic sales; 20% commission on foreign sales. Offers written contract; 3 months notice must be given to terminate contract. 100% of business is derived from commissions on ms sales. Charges clients for postage and photocopying only. Writers charged for fees only after the sale of ms.
**Writers' Conferences:** Squaw Valley Fiction Writers Workshop (Squaw Valley CA, August); Maui Writers Conference; SDSU Writers Conference (San Diego CA, January).

**THE ROBBINS OFFICE, INC.**, 405 Park Ave., New York NY 10022. (212)223-0720. Fax: (212)223-2535. **Contact:** Kathy P. Robbins, owner.
**Member Agents:** David Halpern
**Represents:** Nonfiction books; novels. **Considers these nonfiction areas:** biography/autobiography; government/ politics/law (political commentary); language/literature/criticism (criticism); memoirs; investigative journalism. **Considers these fiction areas:** literary; mainstream/contemporary (commercial); poetry.
➔ This agency specializes in selling serious nonfiction, commercial and literary fiction.
**How to Contact:** Accepts submissions by referral only.
**Recent Sales:** *Why the Future Doesn't Need Us*, by Bill Joy (Viking); *Me Times Three*, by Alex Witchel (Knopf); *New Jack*, by Ted Conover (Random); *Dating Big Bird*, by Laura Zigman (The Dial Press); *War Boy*, by Kief Hillsbery (Rob Weisbach Books); *King of the World*, by David Remnick (Random House).
**Terms:** Agent receives 15% commission on domestic sales; 15% commission on foreign sales; 15% commission on dramatic rights sales. Bills back specific expenses incurred in doing business for a client.

**FLORA ROBERTS**, 393 W. 49th St., Suite 5G, New York NY 10019. Member of AAR. This agency did not respond to our request for information. Please query before submitting.

**ROBINSON TALENT AND LITERARY MANAGEMENT**, 1101 S. Robertson Blvd., Suite 210, Los Angeles CA 90035. (310)278-0801. Fax: (310)278-0807. **Contact:** Margaretrose Robinson. Estab. 1992. Member of franchised by DGA/SAG; signatory of WGA. Represents 150 clients. 10% of clients are new/unpublished writers. Currently handles: 15% nonfiction books; 40% movie scripts; 40% TV scripts; 5% stage plays.
● See the expanded listing for this agency in Script Agents.
**Recent Sales:** This agency prefers not to share information on specific sales.

**LINDA ROGHAAR LITERARY AGENCY, INC.**, 133 High Point Dr., Amherst MA 01002. (413)256-1921. Fax: (413)256-2636. E-mail: lroghaar@aol.com. Website: www.lindaroghaar.com. **Contact:** Linda L. Roghaar. Estab. 1996. Represents 50 clients. 50% of clients are new/unpublished writers. Currently handles: 90% nonfiction books; 10% novels.
● Prior to opening her agency, Ms. Roghaar worked in retail bookselling for 5 years and as a publisher's sales rep for 15 years.
**Represents:** Nonfiction books; novels. **Considers these nonfiction areas:** animals; anthropology/archaeology; biography/autobiography; education; history; nature/environment; popular culture; religious/inspirational; self-help/personal improvement; women's issues/studies. **Considers these fiction areas:** mystery/suspense (amateur sleuth, cozy, culinary, malice domestic).
**How to Contact:** Query with SASE. No e-mail queries. Considers simultaneous queries. Responds in 1 month to queries; 3 months to mss.

**Recent Sales:** *Off the Grid*, by Susan & Satya Kunen (Rodale); *Led by the Spirit*, by Debra Farrington (Jossey Bar); *Crooked Heart*, by Christina Sumners (Bantam).
**Terms:** Agent receives 15% commission on domestic sales; negotiable commission on foreign sales. Offers written contract, binding for binding for negotiable time.

**[N] [icon] THE ROSENBERG GROUP**, 2800 Harlanwood Dr., Fort Worth TX 76109. (817)921-5173. Fax: (817)927-0578. E-mail: rosenberggroup@home.com. Website: www.rosenberggroup.com. **Contact:** Michael Rosenberg (college textbooks and nonfiction); Barbara Collins Rosenberg (fiction). Estab. 1998. Member of AAR, Ms. Rosenberg is a recognized agent of the RWA. Represents 56 clients. 50% of clients are new/unpublished writers. Currently handles: 30% nonfiction books; 30% novels; 10% scholarly books; 30% textbooks.
  • Prior to becoming agents, Michael was an executive editor for Harcourt, and Barbara was a senior editor for Harcourt.
**Member Agents:** Michael Rosenberg (college textbooks, nonfiction); Barbara Rosenberg (fiction).
**Represents:** Nonfiction books; novels; textbooks. **Considers these nonfiction areas:** biography/autobiography; business/economics; child guidance/parenting; current affairs; ethnic/cultural interests; government/politics/law; health/medicine; history; how-to; memoirs; money/finance; nature/environment; popular culture; psychology; self-help/personal improvement; sociology; sports; women's issues/studies. **Considers these fiction areas:** contemporary issues; detective/police/crime; glitz; historical; literary; mainstream/contemporary; mystery/suspense; romance; sports.
  O→ "Barbara is well versed in the romance market (both category and single title). She travels to approximately six romance conferences a year. Michael has many years of experience as an editor and book salesman. We are the only agency in the United States with an expertise in college publishing." Actively seeking romance category or single title, emphasis on contemporary stories, college textbooks for first-year courses, and commercial nonfiction, especially narrative nonfiction. Does not want to receive time-travel, inspirational romances.
**How to Contact:** Query with SASE. No e-mail or fax queries. Responds in 2 weeks to queries; 4-6 weeks to mss. Returns materials only with SASE. Obtains most new clients through recommendations from others, solicitations, conferences.
**Recent Sales:** Sold 24 titles in the last year. *After Twilight*, Dee Davis (Ballantine); *My Twice-Lived Life*, Donald Murray (Ballantine); *Our Land Before We Die*, Jeff Guinn (Jeremy Tarcher); *The Rag and Bone Shop*, by Jeff Raelcham (Zoland Books).
**Terms:** Agent receives 15% commission on domestic sales; 15% commission on foreign sales. Offers written contract; 30 days notice must be given to terminate contract. Postage and photocopying limit of $350 per year.
**Writers' Conferences:** Writer's Roundtable Conference (Dallas TX, March); Romance Writers of America (Denver CO, July).
**Tips:** "Please visit our website before submitting material to us."

**[icon] RITA ROSENKRANZ LITERARY AGENCY**, 440 West End Ave., Suite 15D, New York NY 10024. (212)873-6333. **Contact:** Rita Rosenkranz. Estab. 1990. Member of AAR. Represents 30 clients. 20% of clients are new/unpublished writers. Currently handles: 98% nonfiction books; 2% novels.
  • Prior to opening her agency, Rita Rosenkranz worked as an editor in major New York publishing houses.
**Represents:** Nonfiction books. **Considers these nonfiction areas:** animals; anthropology/archaeology; art/architecture/design; biography/autobiography; business/economics; child guidance/parenting; computers/electronic; cooking/foods/nutrition; crafts/hobbies; current affairs; ethnic/cultural interests; gay/lesbian issues; government/politics/law; health/medicine; history; how-to; humor/satire; interior design/decorating; language/literature/criticism; military/war; money/finance; music/dance; nature/environment; New Age/metaphysics; photography; popular culture; psychology; religious/inspirational; science/technology; self-help/personal improvement; sports; theater/film; women's issues/studies.
  O→ "This agency focuses on adult nonfiction. Stresses strong editorial development and refinement before submitting to publishers, and brainstorms ideas with authors." Actively seeking authors "who are well paired with their subject, either for professional or personal reasons."
**How to Contact:** Submit proposal package, outline, SASE. No e-mail or fax queries. Considers simultaneous queries. Responds in 2 weeks to queries. Obtains most new clients through solicitations, conferences, word of mouth.
**Recent Sales:** Sold 35 titles in the last year. *Flowers, White House Style*, by Dottie Temple and Stan Finegold (S & S); *My Mother's Charms: Cherished Women, Treasured Memories*, by Kathleen Oldford (Harper San Francisco).
**Terms:** Agent receives 15% commission on domestic sales; 20% commission on foreign sales. Offers written contract, binding for 3 years; 60-day written notice must be given to terminate contract. 100% of business is derived from commissions on ms sales. Charges clients for photocopying. Makes referrals to editing service.
**Tips:** "Identify the current competition for your project to make sure the project is valid. A strong cover letter is very important."

**[icon] ROSENSTONE/WENDER**, 3 E. 48th St., New York NY 10017. Member of AAR. This agency did not respond to our request for information. Query before submitting.

**[icons] THE GAIL ROSS LITERARY AGENCY**, 1666 Connecticut Ave. NW, #500, Washington DC 20009. (202)328-3282. Fax: (202)328-9162. E-mail: jennifer@gailross.com. Website: www.gailross.com. **Contact:** Jennifer Manguera. Estab. 1988. Member of AAR. Represents 200 clients. 75% of clients are new/unpublished writers. Currently handles: 90% nonfiction books; 10% novels.

**Member Agents:** Gail Ross.
**Represents:** Nonfiction books; novels. **Considers these nonfiction areas:** anthropology/archaeology; biography/auto-biography; business/economics; education; ethnic/cultural interests; gay/lesbian issues; government/politics/law; health/medicine; humor/satire; money/finance; nature/environment; psychology; religious/inspirational; science/technology; self-help/personal improvement; sociology; sports; true crime/investigative. **Considers these fiction areas:** literary.
    O⇥ This agency specializes in adult trade nonfiction.
**How to Contact:** Query with SASE. Considers simultaneous queries. Responds in 1 month to queries. Obtains most new clients through recommendations from others.
**Recent Sales:** Sold 50 titles in the last year. This agency prefers not to share information on specific sales.
**Terms:** Agent receives 15% commission on domestic sales; 25% commission on foreign sales. Charges for office expenses (i.e., postage, copying).

**CAROL SUSAN ROTH, LITERARY REPRESENTATION, (Specialized: self-help)**, 1824 Oak Creek Dr., Palo Alto CA 94304. (650)323-3795. E-mail: carol@authorsbest.com. **Contact:** Carol Susan Roth. Estab. 1995. Represents 40 clients. 20% of clients are new/unpublished writers. Currently handles: 100% nonfiction books.
    ● Prior to becoming and agent, Ms. Roth was trained as a psychotherapist and worked as a motivational coach, conference producer and promoter for bestselling authors (e.g. Scott Peck, Bernie Siegal, John Gray) and the Heart of Business conference.
**Represents:** Nonfiction books. **Considers these nonfiction areas:** business/economics; health/medicine; money/finance (personal finance/investing); New Age/metaphysics; religious/inspirational; self-help/personal improvement; spirituality.
    O⇥ This agency specializes in spirituality, health, personal growth, personal finance, business. Actively seeking previously published authors—experts in health, spirituality, personal growth, business. Does not want to receive fiction.
**How to Contact:** Submit proposal package, SASE. No e-mail or fax queries. Considers simultaneous queries. Responds in 1 week to queries. Returns materials only with SASE. Obtains most new clients through recommendations from others, solicitations.
**Recent Sales:** Sold 18 titles in the last year. *Changing Careers for Dummies*, by Dr. Carol McClellan (Hungry Minds); *Two Questions*, by Michael Ray (Scribner); *The Chiropractic Way*, by Michael Lenaaz (Bantam).
**Terms:** Agent receives 15% commission on domestic sales; 20% commission on foreign sales. Offers written contract, binding for 3 years; 60-day notice must be given to terminate contract. This agency "asks the client to provide postage and do copying." Offers a proposal development and marketing consulting service on request. Charges $150/hour for service. Service is separate from agenting services.
**Writers' Conferences:** Maui Writer's Conference (Maui HI, September).
**Reading List:** Reads *Yoga, New Age, People, Men's Health, Inquiring Mind, Fast Company,* and *Red Herring* to find new clients. Looks for "ability to write and self-promote."
**Tips:** "Have charisma, content, and credentials—solve an old problem in a new way. I prefer clients with extensive seminar and media experience."

**JANE ROTROSEN AGENCY LLC**, 318 E. 51st St., New York NY 10022. (212)593-4330. Fax: (212)935-6985. E-mail: firstinitiallastname@janerotrosen.com. Estab. 1974. Member of AAR, Authors Guild. Represents over 100 clients. Currently handles: 30% nonfiction books; 70% novels.
**Member Agents:** Jane Rotrosen; Andrea Cirillo; Ruth Kagle; Annelise Robey; Margaret Ruley.
**Represents:** Nonfiction books; novels. **Considers these nonfiction areas:** biography/autobiography; business/economics; child guidance/parenting; cooking/foods/nutrition; current affairs; health/medicine; how-to; humor/satire; money/finance; nature/environment; popular culture; psychology; self-help/personal improvement; sports; true crime/investigative; women's issues/studies. **Considers these fiction areas:** action/adventure; detective/police/crime; family saga; historical; horror; mainstream/contemporary; mystery/suspense; romance; thriller; women's.
**How to Contact:** Query with SASE. No e-mail or fax queries. Responds in 2 months to mss. Responds in 2 weeks (to writers who have been referred by a client or colleague). Returns materials only with SASE.
**Recent Sales:** Sold 120 titles in the last year. This agency prefers not to share information on specific sales.
**Terms:** Agent receives 15% commission on domestic sales; 20% commission on foreign sales. Offers written contract, binding for 3-5 years; 60-day notice must be given to terminate contract. Charges clients for photocopying, express mail, overseas postage, book purchase.

**THE DAMARIS ROWLAND AGENCY**, 510 E. 23rd St., #8-G, New York NY 10010-5020. (212)475-8942. Fax: (212)358-9411. **Contact:** Damaris Rowland or Steve Axelrod. Estab. 1994. Member of AAR. Represents 50 clients. 10% of clients are new/unpublished writers. Currently handles: 25% nonfiction books; 75% novels.
**Represents:** Nonfiction books; novels. **Considers these nonfiction areas:** animals; cooking/foods/nutrition; health/medicine; nature/environment; religious/inspirational; women's issues/studies. **Considers these fiction areas:** historical; literary; mainstream/contemporary; romance (contemporary, gothic, historical, regency).
    O⇥ This agency specializes in women's fiction.
**How to Contact:** Submit outline/proposal, SASE. Responds in 6 weeks to queries. Obtains most new clients through recommendations from others, solicitations, conferences.

**Recent Sales:** *The Next Accident*, by Lisa Gardner; *To Trust a Stranger*, by Karen Robard; *Nursing Homes*, by Peter Silin.

**Terms:** Agent receives 15% commission on domestic sales; 20% commission on foreign sales. Offers written contract; 30 days notice must be given to terminate contract. Charges only if extraordinary expenses have been incurred, e.g., photocopying and mailing 15 mss to Europe for a foreign sale.

**Writers' Conferences:** Novelists Inc. (Denver, October); RWA National (Texas, July); Pacific Northwest Writers Conference.

**THE PETER RUBIE LITERARY AGENCY**, 240 W. 35th St., Suite 500, New York NY 10001. (212)279-1776. Fax: (212)279-0927. Website: www.prlit.com. **Contact:** Peter Rubie, June Clark, or Jennifer DeChiarra. Estab. 2000. Member of AAR. Represents 130 clients. 30% of clients are new/unpublished writers.

• Prior to opening his agency, Mr. Rubie was an agent at Perkins, Rubie & Associates.

**Member Agents:** June Clark (New Age, pop culture, gay issues); Jennifer DeChiarra (children's books, parenting, literary fiction); Peter Rubie (crime, science fiction, fantasy, literary fiction, thrillers, narrative nonfiction, history, commercial science, music).

**Represents:** Nonfiction books; novels. **Considers these nonfiction areas:** cooking/foods/nutrition; creative nonfiction; current affairs; ethnic/cultural interests; music/dance; popular culture; science/technology; theater/film; commercial academic material; TV. **Considers these fiction areas:** action/adventure; detective/police/crime; ethnic; fantasy; gay/lesbian; historical; literary; science fiction; thriller.

**How to Contact:** Query with SASE. Responds in 2 months to queries; 3 months to mss. Returns materials only with SASE. Obtains most new clients through recommendations from others.

**Recent Sales:** *The Glass Harmonica*, by Louise Marley (Berkley); *Shooting at Midnight*, by Gregory Rucka (Bantam); *Violence Proof Your Kids*, (Conari Press); *Toward Rational Exuberance* (Farrar, Straus & Giroux); *On Night's Shore*, by Randall Silvis (St. Martin's Press); *Jewboy*, by Allan Kauffman (Fromm); *Einstein's Refrigerator*, by Steve Silverman (Andrews McMeel); *Hope's End*, by Stephen Chambers (TOR).

**Terms:** Agent receives 15% commission on domestic sales; 20% commission on foreign sales. Offers written contract. Charges clients for photocopying.

**Tips:** "We look for writers who are experts and outstanding prose style. Be professional. Read *Publishers Weekly* and genre-related magazines. Join writers' organizations. Go to conferences. Know your market, and learn your craft. Read Rubie's books *The Elements of Storytelling* (Wiley) and *The Writer's Market Advisor* (Writer's Digest Books)."

**RUSSELL & VOLKENING**, 50 W. 29th St., #7E, New York NY 10001. (212)684-6050. Fax: (212)889-3026. **Contact:** Joseph Regal. Estab. 1940. Member of AAR. Represents 140 clients. 10% of clients are new/unpublished writers. Currently handles: 45% nonfiction books; 50% novels; 3% story collections; 2% novellas.

**Member Agents:** Timothy Seldes (nonfiction, literary fiction); Joseph Regal (literary fiction, thrillers, nonfiction).

**Represents:** Nonfiction books; novels; short story collections; novellas. **Considers these nonfiction areas:** anthropology/archaeology; art/architecture/design; biography/autobiography; business/economics; cooking/foods/nutrition; creative nonfiction; current affairs; education; ethnic/cultural interests; gay/lesbian issues; government/politics/law; health/medicine; history; language/literature/criticism; military/war; money/finance; music/dance; nature/environment; photography; popular culture; psychology; science/technology; sociology; sports; theater/film; true crime/investigative; women's issues/studies. **Considers these fiction areas:** action/adventure; detective/police/crime; ethnic; literary; mainstream/contemporary; mystery/suspense; picture books; sports; thriller.

➤ This agency specializes in literary fiction and narrative nonfiction.

**How to Contact:** Query with SASE. Responds in 1 month to queries; 2 months to mss. Obtains most new clients through recommendations from others, occasionally through query letters.

**Recent Sales:** *The Many Aspects of Mobile Living*, by Martin Clark (Knopf); *The Special Prisoner*, by Jim Lehrer (Random); *The Pick-Up*, by Nadine Gordimer (FSG); *The Beatles in Rishikesh*, by Paul Saltzman (Viking Studio); *Lanterns*, by Marian Wright Edelman (Beacon); *Warriors of God*, by James Reston, Jr. (Doubleday); *The Obituary Writer*, by Porter Shreve (Houghton Mifflin); *Back When We Were Grownups*, by Anne Tyler (Knopf); *Interrogation*, by Thomas H. Cook (Bantam).

**Terms:** Agent receives 15% commission on domestic sales; 20% commission on foreign sales. Charges clients for "standard office expenses relating to the submission of materials of an author we represent, e.g., photocopying, postage."

**Tips:** "If the query is cogent, well written, well presented and is the type of book we'd represent, we'll ask to see the manuscript. From there, it depends purely on the quality of the work."

**N** ⚫ **REGINA RYAN PUBLISHING ENTERPRISES, INC.**, 251 Central Park W., 7D, New York NY 10024. (212)787-5589. Fax: (212)787-0243. E-mail: rryanbooks@aol.com. **Contact:** Regina Ryan. Estab. 1976. Currently handles: 90% nonfiction books; 5% novels; 5% juvenile books.

• Prior to becoming an agent, Ms. Ryan was an editor at Alfred A. Knopf, editor-in-chief of Macmillan Adult Trade, and a book producer.

**Represents:** Nonfiction books; novels; short story collections; juvenile books.

**How to Contact:** Query with SASE. Considers simultaneous queries. Responds in 1 month to queries; 6 weeks to mss. Returns materials only with SASE. Obtains most new clients through recommendations from others.

**Recent Sales:** *Dear Mr. President*, by Andrea Warren (Winslow Press); *How to Build Your Child's Emotional Life*, by Paul Holinger, M.D. (Pocket Books); *We Rode the Orphan Trains*, by Andrea Warren (Houghton Mifflin); *The Uncollected Prose of Dorothy West*, by Lionel Bascon (St. Martin's Press).

**Terms:** Agent receives 15% commission on domestic sales; 15% commission on foreign sales. Offers written contract; 1 month, negotiable notice must be given to terminate contract. Charges clients for all out of pocket expenses, such as long distance, messengers, freight, copying, "if it's more than just a nominal amount."

**Tips:** "Please send an analysis of the competition. This is essential on nonfiction projects."

⚫ **THE SAGALYN AGENCY**, 4825 Bethesda Ave., Suite 302, Bethesda MD 20814. (301)718-6440. Fax: (310)718-6444. E-mail: agency@Sagalyn.com. Website: Sagalyn.com. **Contact:** Raphael Sagalyn. Estab. 1980. Member of AAR. Currently handles: 50% nonfiction books; 25% novels; 25% scholarly books.

○━ Does not want to receive stage plays, screenplays, poetry, science fiction, romance, children's books or young adult books.

**How to Contact:** Send a query letter outlining your professional experience, a synopsis of your book, and a SASE. No phone queries. No fax queries. Accepts e-mail queries but no attachments. Responds in 6 weeks to queries.

**Recent Sales:** This agency prefers not to share information on specific sales.

**Tips:** "We receive between 1,000-1,200 queries a year, which in turn lead to two or three new clients."

**VICTORIA SANDERS & ASSOCIATES LITERARY AGENCY**, 241 Avenue of the Americas, New York NY 10014-4822. (212)633-8811. Fax: (212)633-0525. **Contact:** Victoria Sanders or Diane Dickensheid. Estab. 1993. Member of AAR; signatory of WGA. Represents 75 clients. 25% of clients are new/unpublished writers. Currently handles: 50% nonfiction books; 50% novels.

**Member Agents:** Imani Wilson (assistant literary agent).

**Represents:** Nonfiction books; novels. **Considers these nonfiction areas:** biography/autobiography; current affairs; ethnic/cultural interests; gay/lesbian issues; government/politics/law; history; humor/satire; language/literature/criticism; music/dance; popular culture; psychology; theater/film; translation; women's issues/studies. **Considers these fiction areas:** action/adventure; contemporary issues; ethnic; family saga; feminist; gay/lesbian; literary; thriller.

**How to Contact:** Query with SASE. Considers simultaneous queries. Responds in 3 weeks to queries; 1 month to mss. Returns materials only with SASE. Obtains most new clients through recommendations from others, or "I find them through my reading and pursue."

**Recent Sales:** Sold 15 titles in the last year. *Blindsighted*, by Karin Slaughter (Morrow); *Redemption Song*, by Dr. Bertrice Berry (Doubleday).

**Terms:** Agent receives 15% commission on domestic sales; 20% commission on foreign sales. Offers written contract. Charges for photocopying, ms, messenger, express mail and extraordinary fees. If in excess of $100, client approval is required.

**Tips:** "Limit query to letter, no calls, and give it your best shot. A good query is going to get a good response."

⚫ **SANDUM & ASSOCIATES**, 144 E. 84th St., New York NY 10028-2035. (212)737-2011. Fax: (on request). **Contact:** Howard E. Sandum, managing director. Estab. 1987. Represents 35 clients. 20% of clients are new/unpublished writers. Currently handles: 80% nonfiction books; 20% novels.

**Represents:** Nonfiction books; novels (literary). **Considers these fiction areas:** literary.

○━ This agency specializes in general nonfiction.

**How to Contact:** Query with proposal, sample pages and SASE. Do not send full ms unless requested. Responds in 2 weeks to queries.

**Terms:** Agent receives 15% commission on domestic sales; adjustable commission on foreign sales; adjustable commission on dramatic rights sales. Charges clients for photocopying, air express, long-distance telephone/fax.

○ ⚫ **SCHERF, INC. LITERARY MANAGEMENT**, P.O. Box 80180, Las Vegas NV 89180-0180. (702)243-4895. Fax: (702)243-7460. E-mail: ds@scherf.com. Website: www.scherf.com/literarymanagement.htm. **Contact:** Dietmar Scherf. Estab. 1999. Currently handles: 10% nonfiction books; 85% novels; 5% novellas.

• Prior to opening his agency, Mr. Scherf wrote several nonfiction books, and has been a publisher and editor since 1983.

**Member Agents:** Mr. Dietmar Scherf (fiction/nonfiction); Ms. Gail Kirby (fiction/nonfiction).

**Represents:** Nonfiction books; novels; novellas. **Considers these nonfiction areas:** business/economics; how-to; money/finance; popular culture; psychology; religious/inspirational; self-help/personal improvement; true crime/investigative. **Considers these fiction areas:** action/adventure; literary; mainstream/contemporary; mystery/suspense; religious/inspirational; thriller.

⚬ This agency specializes in discovering new authors, especially in the highly competitive fiction market. "As much as possible, we want to give every new author with a fresh voice a chance to find a publisher for their work. We also manage literary properties for established writers." Actively seeking well-written contemporary fiction with broad commercial appeal. Does not want to receive gay, lesbian, erotica, or anything with foul language.

**How to Contact:** Query with SASE. No e-mail or fax queries. Considers simultaneous queries. Responds in 2 months to queries; 3 months to mss. Returns materials only with SASE. Obtains most new clients through recommendations from others, writing contests, unsolicited queries.

**Recent Sales:** Sold 1 title in the last year. *The Consultant*, by Alec Donzi.

**Terms:** Agent receives 10-15% commission on domestic sales; 15-20% (depending if new or established author) commission on foreign sales. Offers written contract, binding for variable term; 30-day notice must be given to terminate contract. Charges clients for postage, photocopying. Writers reimbursed for office fees after the sale of ms. May refer new writers to editing service. 0% of business is derived from referrals.

**Tips:** "Write the best manuscript, and polish it to the max. Write about a story that you love and are enthusiastic about. Learn good writing skills through books, seminars/courses, etc., especially regarding characterization, dialogue, plot, etc. in respect to novels. Know your competition well, and read books from authors that may fall into your category. In nonfiction, do the best research on your subject and be different from your competition with a new approach."

**SCHIAVONE LITERARY AGENCY, INC.**, 236 Trails End, West Palm Beach FL 33413-2135. (561)966-9294. Fax: (561)966-9294. E-mail: profschia@aol.com. Website: www.freeyellow.com/members8/schiavone/index.html. **Contact:** James Schiavone, Ed.D. Estab. 1996. Member of National Education Association. Represents 40 clients. 2% of clients are new/unpublished writers. Currently handles: 50% nonfiction books; 49% novels; 1% textbooks.

● Prior to opening his agency, Dr. Schiavone was a full professor of development skills at the City University of New York and author of 5 trade books and 3 textbooks.

**Member Agents:** Diane V. Jacques (film and TV rights; e-mail: JNJSF@aol.com).

**Represents:** Nonfiction books; novels; juvenile books; scholarly books; textbooks; movie scripts; feature film; TV movie of the week. **Considers these nonfiction areas:** animals; anthropology/archaeology; biography/autobiography; child guidance/parenting; current affairs; education; ethnic/cultural interests; gay/lesbian issues; government/politics/law; health/medicine; history; how-to; humor/satire; juvenile nonfiction; language/literature/criticism; military/war; nature/environment; popular culture; psychology; science/technology; self-help/personal improvement; sociology; true crime/investigative. **Considers these fiction areas:** contemporary issues; ethnic; family saga; historical; horror; humor/satire; juvenile; literary; mainstream/contemporary; science fiction; young adult.

⚬ This agency specializes in celebrity biography and autobiography. "We have a management division that handles motion picture and TV rights." Actively seeking serious nonfiction, literary fiction and celebrity biography. Does not want to receive poetry.

**How to Contact:** Query with SASE. Considers one page e-mail queries with no attachments. Does not accept phone or fax queries. Considers simultaneous queries. Responds in 2 weeks to queries; 6 weeks to mss. Returns materials only with SASE. Obtains most new clients through recommendations from others, solicitations, conferences.

**Terms:** Agent receives 15% commission on domestic sales; 20% commission on foreign sales. Offers written contract, binding for project period; written notice must be given to terminate contract. Charges clients for long distance, photocopying, postage, special handling. Dollar amount varies with each project depending on level of activity.

**Writers' Conferences:** Key West Literary Seminar (Key West FL, January).

**Tips:** "I prefer to work with established authors published by major houses in New York. I will consider marketable proposals from new/previously unpublished writers."

 🔹🔘 **SUSAN SCHULMAN, A LITERARY AGENCY, (Specialized: health, business, self-help, women's issues)**, 454 W. 44th St., New York NY 10036-5205. (212)713-1633/4/5. Fax: (212)586-8830. E-mail: schulman@aol.com. Website: www.susanschulmanagency.com. **Contact:** Susan Schulman, president. Estab. 1979. Member of AAR, Dramatists Guild, Women's Media Group; signatory of WGA. 10-15% of clients are new/unpublished writers. Currently handles: 70% nonfiction books; 20% novels; 10% stage plays.

**Member Agents:** Susan Schulman (self-help, health, business, spirituality); Christine Morin (children's books, ecology, natural sciences and business books); Bryan Leifert (plays and pitches for films).

**Represents:** Nonfiction books; novels. **Considers these nonfiction areas:** anthropology/archaeology; biography/autobiography; child guidance/parenting; current affairs; education; ethnic/cultural interests; gay/lesbian issues; government/politics/law; health/medicine; history; how-to; juvenile nonfiction; money/finance; music/dance; nature/environment; New Age/metaphysics; popular culture; psychology; religious/inspirational; self-help/personal improvement; sociology; theater/film; translation; true crime/investigative; women's issues/studies. **Considers these fiction areas:** contemporary issues; detective/police/crime; gay/lesbian; historical; literary; mainstream/contemporary; mystery/suspense; young adult.

⚬ This agency specializes in books for, by and about women's issues including family, careers, health and spiritual development, business and sociology, history and economics. Emphasizing contemporary women's fiction and nonfiction books of interest to women.

**Also Handles:** Feature film; stage plays. **Considers these script subject areas:** comedy; contemporary issues; detective/police/crime; feminist; historical; mainstream; mystery/suspense; psychic/supernatural; religious/inspirational; teen.

**How to Contact:** Query with SASE, outline/proposal, SASE. Accepts e-mail and fax queries. Considers simultaneous queries. Responds in 1 week to queries; 6 weeks to mss. Returns materials only with SASE.

**Recent Sales:** Sold 30 titles in the last year. *God Is No Laughing Matter*, by Julia Cameron (Putnam); *Corporate Irresponsibility*, (Yale). *Movie/TV MOW script(s) optioned/sold: In the Skin of a Lion*, by Michael Ondaatje (Serendipity Parent Productions); *Holes*, by Louis Sachar (Phoenix Pictures); *Sideways Stories from Wayside School*, by Louis Sachar (Len Oliver Productions).

**Terms:** Agent receives 15% commission on domestic sales; 7½-10% (plus 7½-10% to co-agent) commission on foreign sales; 10-20% commission on dramatic rights sales. Charges client for special messenger or copying services, foreign mail and any other service requested by client.

**LAURENS R. SCHWARTZ AGENCY**, 5 E. 22nd St., Suite 15D, New York NY 10010-5325. (212)228-2614.
**Contact:** Laurens R. Schwartz. Estab. 1984. Represents 100 clients.
**Represents:** Nonfiction books; novels. General mix of nonfiction and fiction.
**Also Handles:** Movie and TV tie-ins, licensing and merchandising.
**How to Contact:** Query with SASE. No unsolicited mss. Considers simultaneous queries. Responds in 1 month to queries. "Have had 18 best-sellers."
**Terms:** Agent receives 15% commission on domestic sales; 25% commission on foreign sales. "No client fees except for photocopying, and that fee is avoided by an author providing necessary copies or, in certain instances, transferring files on diskette or by e-mail attachment." Where necessary to bring a project into publishing form, editorial work and some rewriting provided as part of service. Works with authors on long-term career goals and promotion.
**Tips:** "I do not like receiving mass mailings sent to all agents. Be selective—do your homework. Do not send everything you have ever written. Choose one work and promote that. Always include an SASE. Never send your only copy. Always include a background sheet on yourself and a one-page synopsis of the work (too many summaries end up being as long as the work)."

**SCOVIL CHICHAK GALEN LITERARY AGENCY**, 381 Park Ave. South, Suite 1020, New York NY 10016. (212)679-8686. Fax: (212)679-6710. E-mail: mailroom@scglit.com. **Contact:** Russell Galen. Estab. 1993. Member of AAR. Represents 300 clients. Currently handles: 70% nonfiction books; 30% novels.
**Member Agents:** Russell Galen; Jack Scovil; Anna Ghosh.
**How to Contact:** Accepts e-mail and fax queries. Considers simultaneous queries.
**Recent Sales:** Sold 100 titles in the last year. *The Pillars of Creation*, by Terry Goodkin (TOR); *The Hand of Dante*, by Nick Tosches (Little, Brown); *Mansions of the Moon*, by Benson Bobrick (Simon & Schuster); *Ship Wrecker*, by Paul Garrison (Morrow).
**Terms:** Charges clients for photocopying and postage.

**SEBASTIAN LITERARY AGENCY**, The Towers, 172 E. Sixth St., #2005, St. Paul MN 55101. (651)224-6670. Fax: (651)224-6895. E-mail: harperlb@aol.com (query only—no attachments). **Contact:** Laurie Harper. Estab. 1985. Member of AAR. Represents 50 clients.
- Prior to becoming an agent, Laurie Harper was owner of a small regional publishing company selling mainly to retail bookstores, including B. Dalton and Waldenbooks. She was thus involved in editing, production, distribution, marketing and promotion. She came to publishing with a business and finance background, including eight years in banking.
**Represents:** Trade nonfiction, select literary fiction. **Considers these nonfiction areas:** biography/autobiography; business/economics; child guidance/parenting; creative nonfiction; current affairs; health/medicine; money/finance; psychology; self-help/personal improvement; sociology; women's issues/studies; consumer reference.
- Ms. Harper is known for working closely with her authors to plan and execute individual short-term and long-term goals. "A successful publishing experience is dependent upon closely coordinated efforts between the writer, the agent, the editor, the publisher's marketing group and sales force, and the booksellers. I give my authors as much advance information as possible so they can work most effectively with the publisher. An author needs every advantage he or she can have, and working closely with the agent can be one of those advantages." Does not want to receive scholarly work, children's or young adult work.
**How to Contact:** Taking new clients selectively; mainly by referral. No e-mail or fax queries. Considers simultaneous queries. Responds in 3 weeks to queries; 6 weeks to mss. Obtains most new clients through "referrals from authors and editors, but some at conferences and some from unsolicited queries from around the country."
**Recent Sales:** Sold 25 titles in the last year. *Bald in the Land of Big Hair*, by Joni Rodgers (HarperCollins); *Short Cycle Selling*, by James Kasper (McGraw-Hill); *Two in the Field*, by Darryl Brock (NAL/Dutton); *For All We Know*, by Peter S. Beagle (Simon & Schuster).
**Terms:** Agent receives 15% commission on domestic sales; 20% commission on foreign sales. Offers written contract. Charges clients a one-time $100 administration fee and charges for photocopies of ms for submission to publisher.

> **CHECK THE AGENT SPECIALTIES INDEX** to find agents who are interested in your specific nonfiction or fiction subject area.

**Writers' Conferences:** ASJA; various independent conferences throughout the country.

**SEDGEBAND LITERARY ASSOCIATES**, 7312 Martha Lane, Fort Worth TX 76112. (817)496-3652. Fax: (425)952-9518. E-mail: sedgeband@aol.com. Website: members.home.net/sedgeband. **Contact:** David Duperre or Ginger Norton. Estab. 1997. 60% of clients are new/unpublished writers. Currently handles: 40% nonfiction books; 60% fiction novels.

**Member Agents:** David Duperre (science fiction/fantasy, scripts, mystery, suspense); Ginger Norton (romance, horror, nonfiction, mainstream).

**Represents:** Nonfiction books; novels; novellas. **Considers these nonfiction areas:** biography/autobiography; ethnic/cultural interests; history; true crime/investigative. **Considers these fiction areas:** action/adventure; contemporary issues; ethnic; experimental; fantasy; horror; literary; mainstream/contemporary; mystery/suspense; psychic/supernatural; romance; science fiction.

○→ This agency is looking for new writers who have patience and are willing to work hard. Actively seeking all types of material.

**How to Contact:** Query with SASE or submit synopsis with SASE. No phone queries accepted. Considers simultaneous queries. Responds in 1 month to queries; 3 months to mss. Returns materials only with SASE. Obtains most new clients through queries, the Internet, referrals.

**Recent Sales:** *Deep in the Woods*, by Edmund Plante (Cora Verlag); *Soulscape*, by John Higgins (America House); *A Dark Magical Place*, by Edmund Plante (Cora Verlag).

**Terms:** Agent receives 15% commission on domestic sales; 20% commission on foreign sales. Offers written contract, binding for 1 year; written notice must be given to terminate contract. Charges clients for postage, photocopies, long distance calls, "until we make your first sale."

**Tips:** "Simply put, we care about people and books, not just money. Do not send a rude query—it will get you rejected no matter how good of a writer you might be. And if we ask to review your work, don't wait to send it for several months. Send it as soon as possible. Also, it is better to wait for a contract offer before asking a lot of questions about publication and movie rights."

**LYNN SELIGMAN, LITERARY AGENT**, 400 Highland Ave., Upper Montclair NJ 07043. (973)783-3631. **Contact:** Lynn Seligman. Estab. 1985. Member of Women's Media Group. Represents 32 clients. 15% of clients are new/unpublished writers. Currently handles: 85% nonfiction books; 10% novels; 5% photography books.

● Prior to opening her agency, Ms. Seligman worked in the subsidiary rights department of Doubleday and Simon & Schuster, and served as an agent with Julian Bach Literary Agency (now IMG Literary Agency).

**Represents:** Nonfiction books; novels. **Considers these nonfiction areas:** anthropology/archaeology; art/architecture/design; biography/autobiography; business/economics; child guidance/parenting; cooking/foods/nutrition; current affairs; education; ethnic/cultural interests; government/politics/law; health/medicine; history; how-to; humor/satire; interior design/decorating; language/literature/criticism; money/finance; music/dance; nature/environment; photography; popular culture; psychology; science/technology; self-help/personal improvement; sociology; theater/film; translation; true crime/investigative; women's issues/studies. **Considers these fiction areas:** detective/police/crime; ethnic; fantasy; feminist; gay/lesbian; historical; horror; humor/satire; literary; mainstream/contemporary; mystery/suspense; romance (contemporary, gothic, historical, regency); science fiction.

○→ This agency specializes in "general nonfiction and fiction. I do illustrated and photography books and represent several photographers for books."

**How to Contact:** Query with SASE, 1 sample chapter(s), outline/proposal. Prefers to read materials exclusively. No e-mail or fax queries. Considers simultaneous queries. Responds in 2 weeks to queries; 2 months to mss. Returns materials only with SASE. Obtains most new clients through referrals from other writers or editors.

**Recent Sales:** Sold 10 titles in the last year. *Big Fat Lies*, by Dr. Glen Gaesser (Gurze Books); *Watching Weddings*, by Carol McD. Wallace (Penguin Putnam); *A Gentleman at Heart*, by Barbara Pierre (Kensington).

**Terms:** Agent receives 15% commission on domestic sales; 25% commission on foreign sales. Charges clients for photocopying, unusual postage or telephone expenses (checking first with the author), express mail.

**SERENDIPITY LITERARY AGENCY, LLC**, 732 Fulton St., Suite 3, Brooklyn NY 11238. (718)230-7689. Fax: (718)230-7689. E-mail: rbrooks@serendipityla.com. Website: www.serendipityla.com. **Contact:** Regina Brooks. Estab. 2000. Represents 12 clients. 20% of clients are new/unpublished writers.

● Prior to becoming an agent, Ms. Brooks was an acquisitions editor for John Wiley & Sons, Inc. and McGraw-Hill Companies.

**Represents:** Nonfiction books; novels; juvenile books; scholarly books; textbooks. **Considers these nonfiction areas:** business/economics; computers/electronic; education; ethnic/cultural interests; how-to; juvenile nonfiction; memoirs; money/finance; multicultural; New Age/metaphysics; popular culture; psychology; religious/inspirational; science/technology; self-help/personal improvement; sports; women's issues/studies. **Considers these fiction areas:** action/adventure; confession; ethnic; historical; juvenile; literary; multicultural; picture books; romance; science fiction; thriller.

○→ Serendipity provides developmental editing. "We help build marketing plans for nontraditional outlets." Actively seeking African-American nonfiction, computer books (nonfiction), juvenile books. Does not want to receive poetry.

**Also Handles:** Scripts, multimedia. **Considers these script subject areas:** ethnic; fantasy; juvenile; multimedia; also interested in children's CD/video projects.

**How to Contact:** Submit outline, 3 sample chapter(s), SASE. Prefers to read materials exclusively. Responds in 1 month to queries; 3 months to mss. Obtains most new clients through recommendations from others, conferences.
**Recent Sales:** This agency prefers not to share information on specific sales. Recent sales available upon request by prospective client.
**Terms:** Agent receives 15% commission on domestic sales; 20% commission on foreign sales. Offers written contract; 60-day notice notice must be given to terminate contract. Charges clients $200 upon signing for office fees or office fees will be taken from any advance. "If author requests editing services, I can offer a list of potential services." 0% of business is derived from referral to editing services.
**Tips:** "Looking for African-American children's books. We also represent illustrators."

☑ ◖ **THE SEYMOUR AGENCY**, 475 Miner St., Canton NY 13617. (315)386-1831. Fax: (315)386-1037. E-mail: mseymour@slic.com. Website: www.theseymouragency.com. **Contact:** Mary Sue Seymour. Estab. 1992. Represents 75 clients. 20% of clients are new/unpublished writers. Currently handles: 30% nonfiction books; 50% novels; 10% scholarly books; 10% textbooks.
   • Ms. Seymour is a retired New York State certified teacher.
**Represents:** Nonfiction books; novels. **Considers these nonfiction areas:** agriculture/horticulture; americana; animals; anthropology/archaeology; art/architecture/design; biography/autobiography; business/economics; child guidance/parenting; computers/electronic; cooking/foods/nutrition; crafts/hobbies; creative nonfiction; current affairs; education; ethnic/cultural interests; gardening; gay/lesbian issues; government/politics/law; health/medicine; history; how-to; humor/satire; interior design/decorating; juvenile nonfiction; language/literature/criticism; memoirs; military/war; money/finance; multicultural; music/dance; nature/environment; New Age/metaphysics; philosophy; photography; popular culture; psychology; recreation; regional; religious/inspirational; science/technology; self-help/personal improvement; sex; sociology; software; spirituality; sports; theater/film; translation; travel; true crime/investigative; women's issues/studies; young adult. **Considers these fiction areas:** action/adventure; detective/police/crime; ethnic; glitz; historical; horror; humor/satire; mainstream/contemporary; mystery/suspense; religious/inspirational; romance (contemporary, gothic, historical, medieval, regency); westerns/frontier; vampire.
   ⚷ Actively seeking nonfiction and well-written novels. Does not want to receive screenplays, short stories, poetry.
**How to Contact:** Query with SASE, synopsis, first 50 pages. No fax queries. Considers simultaneous queries. Responds in 1 month to queries; 3 months to mss. Returns materials only with SASE.
**Recent Sales:** Sold 27 titles in the last year. *Black Soldiers, White Wars*, by Betty Alt (Greenwood).
**Terms:** Agent receives 15% commission on domestic sales; 20% commission on foreign sales. Offers written contract, binding for 1 year.
**Tips:** "Send query, synopsis and first 50 pages. If you don't hear from us, you didn't send SASE. We are looking for nonfiction and romance—women in jeopardy, suspense, contemporary, historical, some regency and any well-written fiction and nonfiction."

◖ **CHARLOTTE SHEEDY AGENCY**, 65 Bleecker St., New York NY 10012. This agency did not respond to our request for information. Query before submitting.

☑ ◖ **THE SHEPARD AGENCY**, M&T Bank Bldg., Suite 3; 1525 Rt. 22, Brewster NY 10509. (845)279-2900 or (845)279-3236. Fax: (845)279-3239. E-mail: shepardagency-ldi@mindspring.com. **Contact:** Jean or Lance Shepard. Currently handles: 75% nonfiction books; 20% novels; 5% juvenile books.
**Represents:** Nonfiction books; novels; juvenile books; scholarly books. **Considers these nonfiction areas:** agriculture/horticulture; animals; biography/autobiography; business/economics; child guidance/parenting; computers/electronic; cooking/foods/nutrition; crafts/hobbies; current affairs; government/politics/law; health/medicine; history; interior design/decorating; juvenile nonfiction; language/literature/criticism; money/finance; music/dance; nature/environment; psychology; religious/inspirational; self-help/personal improvement; sociology; sports; theater/film; women's issues/studies. **Considers these fiction areas:** contemporary issues; family saga; historical; humor/satire; literary; regional; sports; thriller.
   ⚷ This agency specializes in "some fiction; nonfiction: business, biography, homemaking, inspirational, self-help."
**How to Contact:** Query with SASE, outline, sample chapter(s). Accepts e-mail and fax queries. Considers simultaneous queries. Responds in 6 weeks to queries; 2 months to mss. Obtains most new clients through referrals and listings in various directories for writers and publishers.
**Recent Sales:** Sold 27 titles in the last year. This agency prefers not to share information on specific sales.
**Terms:** Agent receives 15% commission on domestic sales. Offers written contract. Charges clients for extraordinary postage, photocopying, long-distance and transatlantic phone calls.
**Tips:** "Provide information on those publishers who have already been contacted, seen work, accepted or rejected same. Provide complete bio and marketing information."

☑ ◖ **THE ROBERT E. SHEPARD AGENCY**, 4111 18th St., Suite 3, San Francisco CA 94114-2411. (415)255-1097. E-mail: query@shepardagency.com. Website: www.shepardagency.com. **Contact:** Robert Shepard. Estab. 1994. Member of Authors Guild (associate). Represents 30 clients. 25% of clients are new/unpublished writers. Currently handles: 90% nonfiction books; 10% scholarly books.

• Prior to opening his agency, Mr. Shepard "spent eight and a half years in trade publishing (both editorial and sales/marketing management). I also consulted to a number of major publishers on related subjects."

**Represents:** Nonfiction books; scholarly books. **Considers these nonfiction areas:** business/economics; current affairs; ethnic/cultural interests; gay/lesbian issues; government/politics/law; history; money/finance; popular culture; science/technology; sociology; sports; women's issues/studies.

    **O—** This agency specializes in nonfiction, particularly key issues facing society and culture. Other specialties include personal finance, business, gay/lesbian subjects. Actively seeking "works in current affairs by recognized experts; also business, personal finance, and gay/lesbian subjects." Does not want to receive autobiography, highly visual works, fiction.

**How to Contact:** Query with SASE. E-mail queries encouraged. Fax and phone queries strongly discouraged. Considers simultaneous queries. Responds in 1 month to queries; 6 weeks to mss. Returns materials only with SASE. Obtains most new clients through recommendations from others, solicitations.

**Recent Sales:** Sold 10 titles in the last year. *The Bear-Proof Investor*, by John Wasik (Henry Holt); *Architect and Critic: The Letters of Frank Lloyd Wright and Lewis Mumford*, (Princeton Architectural Press).

**Terms:** Agent receives 15% commission on domestic sales; 20% commission on foreign sales. Offers written contract, binding for term of project or until canceled; 30-day notice must be given to terminate contract. Charges clients "actual expenses for phone/fax, photocopying, and postage only if and when project sells, against advance."

**Reading List:** Reads *Chronicle of Higher Education*, "certain professional publications and a wide range of periodicals" to find new clients. Looks for "a fresh approach to traditional subjects or a top credential in an area that hasn't seen too much trade publishing in the past. And, of course, superb writing."

**Tips:** "We pay attention to detail. We believe in close working relationships between author and agent and between author and editor. Regular communication is key. Please do your homework! There's no substitute for learning all you can about similar or directly competing books and presenting a well-reasoned competitive analysis. Don't work in a vacuum; visit bookstores, and talk to other writers about their own experiences."

**⬤ WENDY SHERMAN ASSOCIATES, INC.,** 450 Seventh Ave., Suite 3004, New York NY 10123. (212)279-9027. Fax: (212)279-8863. E-mail: wendy@wsherman.com. **Contact:** Wendy Sherman. Estab. 1999. Represents 20 clients. 30% of clients are new/unpublished writers. Currently handles: 50% nonfiction books; 50% novels.

• Prior to becoming an agent, Ms. Sherman worked for Aaron Priest agency and was vice president, executive director of Henry Holt, associate publisher, subsidary rights director, sales and marketing director.

**Member Agents:** Jessica Lichtenstein (romantic suspense); Wendy Sherman.

**Represents:** Nonfiction books; novels. **Considers these nonfiction areas:** psychology. **Considers these fiction areas:** literary; mystery/suspense; romance.

    **O—** "We specialize in developing new writers as well as working with more established writers. My experience as a publisher has proven to be a great asset to my clients."

**How to Contact:** Query with SASE, or send outline/proposal, 1 sample chapter. All unsolicited mss returned unopened. Considers simultaneous queries. Responds in 1 month to queries. Returns materials only with SASE. Obtains most new clients through recommendations from others.

**Recent Sales:** Sold 14 titles in the last year. *Massachusetts, California, Timbuktu*, by Stephanie Rosenfeld (Ballantine); *Cliffs of Despair*, by Tom Hunt (Random House); *A Quiet Storm*, by Rachel Hall (Simon & Schuster); *Still With Me*, by Andrea King Collier (Simon & Schuster). Other clients include Alan Eisenstock, Howard Bahr, Lundy Bancroft, Lise Friedman, Tom Schweich.

**Terms:** Agent receives 15% commission on domestic sales; 20% commission on foreign sales. Offers written contract. Charges for photocopying of ms, messengers, express mail services, etc. (reasonable, standard expenses).

**⬤ THE SHUKAT COMPANY LTD.,** 340 W. 55th St., Suite 1A, New York NY 10019-3744. (212)582-7614. Fax: (212)315-3752. **Contact:** Maribel Rivas, Lysna Scriven-Marzani, Scott Shukat. Estab. 1972. Member of AAR. Currently handles: dramatic works.

**How to Contact:** Query with SASE, outline/proposal or 30 pages.

**⬤ ROSALIE SIEGEL, INTERNATIONAL LITERARY AGENCY, INC.,** 1 Abey Dr., Pennington NJ 08534. (609)737-1007. Fax: (609)737-3708. **Contact:** Rosalie Siegel. Estab. 1977. Member of AAR. Represents 35 clients. 10% of clients are new/unpublished writers. Currently handles: 45% nonfiction books; 45% novels; 10% young adult books and short story collections for current clients.

**Represents:** Nonfiction books; novels; short story collections; young adult books.

    **O—** This agency specializes in foreign authors, especially French, though diminishing.

**How to Contact:** Obtains most new clients through referrals from writers and friends.

**Terms:** Agent receives 15% commission on domestic sales; 20% commission on foreign sales. Offers written contract; 60-day notice must be given to terminate contract. Charges clients for photocopying.

**Tips:** "I'm not looking for new authors in an active way."

**🌐 ⬤ JEFFREY SIMMONS LITERARY AGENCY,** 10 Lowndes Square, London SWIX 9HA, England. (020)7235 8852. Fax: (020)7235 9733. **Contact:** Jeffrey Simmons. Estab. 1978. Represents 46 clients. 50% of clients are new/unpublished writers. Currently handles: 60% nonfiction books; 40% novels.

• Prior to becoming an agent, Mr. Simmons was a publisher and he is also an author.

**Represents:** Nonfiction books; novels. **Considers these nonfiction areas:** biography/autobiography; current affairs; government/politics/law; history; language/literature/criticism; memoirs; music/dance; popular culture; sociology; sports; theater/film; translation; true crime/investigative. **Considers these fiction areas:** action/adventure; confession; detective/police/crime; family saga; literary; mainstream/contemporary; mystery/suspense; psychic/supernatural; thriller.

    O➤ This agency seeks to handle good books and promising young writers. "My long experience in publishing and as an author and ghostwriter means I can offer an excellent service all round, especially in terms of editorial experience where appropriate." Actively seeking quality fiction, biography, autobiography, showbiz, personality books, law, crime, politics, world affairs. Does not want to receive science fiction, horror, fantasy, juvenile, academic books, specialist subjects (i.e., cooking, gardening, religious).

**How to Contact:** Submit sample chapter(s), outline/proposal, IRCs if necessary, SASE. Prefers to read materials exclusively. Responds in 1 week to queries; 1 month to mss. Obtains most new clients through recommendations from others, solicitations.

**Recent Sales:** Sold 18 titles in the last year. *The Scapegoat*, by Don Hale (Century); *Only Fools and Horses*, by Richard Webber (Orion).

**Terms:** Agent receives 10-15% commission on domestic sales; 15% commission on foreign sales. Offers written contract, binding for lifetime of book in question or until it becomes out of print.

**Tips:** "When contacting us with an outline/proposal, include a brief biographical note (listing any previous publications, with publishers and dates). Preferably tell us if the book has already been offered elsewhere."

**◑ EVELYN SINGER LITERARY AGENCY INC.**, P.O. Box 594, White Plains NY 10602-0594. (914)948-5565. **Contact:** Evelyn Singer. Estab. 1951. Represents 30 clients. 10% of clients are new/unpublished writers.

    • Prior to opening her agency, Ms. Singer served as an associate in the Jeanne Hale Literary Agency.

**Represents:** Nonfiction books (trade books only); novels; juvenile books (for over 4th grade reading level). **Considers these nonfiction areas:** anthropology/archaeology; biography/autobiography; business/economics; child guidance/parenting; current affairs; ethnic/cultural interests; government/politics/law; health/medicine; how-to; juvenile nonfiction; money/finance; nature/environment; psychology; religious/inspirational; science/technology; self-help/personal improvement; women's issues/studies. **Considers these fiction areas:** contemporary issues; ethnic; feminist; historical; literary; mainstream/contemporary; mystery/suspense; regional; thriller.

    O➤ This agency specializes in nonfiction (adult/juvenile, adult suspense). Does not want to receive textbooks.

**How to Contact:** Query with SASE. Responds in 3 weeks to queries; 2 months to mss. Returns materials only with SASE. Obtains most new clients through recommendations only.

**Recent Sales:** *The $66 Summer*, by John Armistead (Milkweed); *The Black Cowboy*, by Franklin Folsom (Editorial Cruilla).

**Terms:** Agent receives 15% commission on domestic sales; 20% commission on foreign sales. Offers written contract, binding for 3 years. Charges clients for long-distance phone calls, overseas postage ("authorized expenses only").

**Tips:** "I am accepting very few writers. Writers must have earned at least $20,000 from freelance writing. SASE must accompany all queries and material for reply and or return of ms. Enclose biographical material and double-spaced book outline or chapter outline. List publishers queried and publication credits."

**◐ IRENE SKOLNICK LITERARY AGENCY**, 22 W. 23rd St., 5th Floor, New York NY 10010. (212)727-3648. Fax: (212)727-1024. E-mail: sirene35@aol.com. **Contact:** Irene Skolnick. Estab. 1993. Member of AAR. Represents 45 clients. 75% of clients are new/unpublished writers.

**Member Agents:** Irene Skolnick; Laura Friedman Williams.

**Represents:** Nonfiction books (adult); novels (adult). **Considers these nonfiction areas:** biography/autobiography; current affairs. **Considers these fiction areas:** contemporary issues; historical; literary; mainstream/contemporary.

**How to Contact:** Query with SASE, outline, sample chapter(s). Considers simultaneous queries. Responds in 1 month to queries. Returns materials only with SASE.

**Recent Sales:** *An Equal Music*, by Vikram Seth; *Kaaterskill Falls*, by Allegra Goodman; *Taking Lives*, by Michael Pye; *George Sand: A Woman's Life Writ Large*, by Belinda Jack; *The Temple of Optimism*, by James Fleming.

**Terms:** Agent receives 15% commission on domestic sales; 20% commission on foreign sales. Sometimes offers criticism service; Charges for international postage, photocopying over 40 pages.

**◪ ◑ BEVERLEY SLOPEN LITERARY AGENCY**, 131 Bloor St. W., Suite 711, Toronto Ontario M5S 1S3, Canada. (416)964-9598. Fax: (416)921-7726. E-mail: slopen@inforamp.net. Website: www.slopenagency.on.ca. **Contact:** Beverley Slopen. Estab. 1974. Represents 60 clients. 40% of clients are new/unpublished writers. Currently handles: 60% nonfiction books; 40% novels.

    • Prior to opening her agency, Ms. Slopen worked in publishing and as a journalist.

---

**CONTACT THE EDITOR** of *Guide to Literary Agents* by e-mail at literaryagents @fwpubs.com with your questions and comments.

**Represents:** Nonfiction books; novels; scholarly books; textbooks (college). **Considers these nonfiction areas:** anthropology/archaeology; biography/autobiography; business/economics; current affairs; psychology; sociology; true crime/investigative; women's issues/studies. **Considers these fiction areas:** literary; mystery/suspense.

O━━ This agency has a "strong bent towards Canadian writers." Actively seeking "serious nonfiction that is accessible and appealing to the general reader." Does not want to receive fantasy, science fiction or children's.

**How to Contact:** Query with SASE and IRCs. Returns materials with SASE and Canadian postage only. Accepts short e-mail queries. Considers simultaneous queries. Responds in 2 months to queries. Returns materials only with SASE.

**Recent Sales:** Sold 25 titles in the last year. *Baroque-a-nova*, by Kevin Chang (Penguin Putnam); *Crazy Dave*, by Basil Johnston (Minnesota Historical Society Press); *Fatal Passage*, by Ken McGoogan (HarperCollins Canada). Other clients include historians Modris Eksteins, Michael Marrus, Timothy Brook, critic Robert Fulford, novelists Donna Morrissey (*Kit's Law*), Howard Engel, Morley Torgov.

**Terms:** Agent receives 15% commission on domestic sales; 10% commission on foreign sales. Offers written contract, binding for 2 years; 90 days notice must be given to terminate contract.

**Tips:** "Please no unsolicited manuscripts."

**ROBERT SMITH LITERARY AGENCY LTD.**, 12 Bridge Wharf, 156 Caledonian Road, London England NI 9UU. (020) 7278 2444. Fax: (020) 7833 5680. E-mail: robertsmith.literaryagency@virgin.net. **Contact:** Robert Smith. Estab. 1997. Member of Association of Authors' Agents. Represents 25 clients. 10% of clients are new/unpublished writers. Currently handles: 80% nonfiction books; 20% syndicated material.

● Prior to becoming an agent, Mr. Smith was a book publisher.

**Member Agents:** Robert Smith (all nonfiction); Renuka Harrison (mind/body/spirit).

**Represents:** Nonfiction books; syndicated material. **Considers these nonfiction areas:** biography/autobiography; cooking/foods/nutrition; health/medicine; memoirs; music/dance; New Age/metaphysics; popular culture; self-help/personal improvement; theater/film; true crime/investigative.

O━━ This agency offers clients full management service in all media. Clients are not necessarily book authors. "Our special expertise is in placing newspaper series internationally." Actively seeking autobiographies.

**How to Contact:** Submit outline, outline/proposal, IRCs if necessary, SASE. Prefers to read materials exclusively. Accepts e-mail and fax queries. Responds in 1 week to queries. Returns materials only with SASE. Obtains most new clients through recommendations from others, direct approaches to prospective authors.

**Recent Sales:** Sold 25 titles in the last year. *The Truth At Last*, by Christine Keeler (Sidgwick & Jackson/Macmillan); *Princess Margaret*, by Christopher Warwick (Andre Deutsch); *Presenting on Television*, by Joanne Zorian-Lynn (A&C Black); *Ron Kray*, by Laurie O'Leary (Headline); *The Ultimate Jack the Ripper Sourcebook*, by Stewart Evans and Keith Skinner (Constable Robinson). *Movie/TV MOW script(s) optioned/sold:* *The Guv'nor*, by Lenny McLean and Peter Gerrard (Arrival Films). Other clients include Neil L. Christine Hamilton, James Haspiel, Charles Highem, Geoffrey Guiliano, Norman Parker, Mike Reid, Rochelle Morton, Reg Kray, Julie Chrystyn.

**Terms:** Agent receives 15% commission on domestic sales; 20% commission on foreign sales. Offers written contract, binding for 3 months; 3 months notice must be given to terminate contract. Charges clients for couriers, photocopying and postage, overseas mailings of mss, subject to client authorization.

*[handwritten: Tmy CND]*

*[handwritten: 963 Belvedere Ave, Sleepy Hollow, Plainfield NJ 07060]*

**SMITH-SKOLNIK LITERARY**, 303 Walnut St., Westfield NJ 07090. Member of AAR. This agency specializes in literary fiction. Query with SASE before submitting. *[handwritten: 908-822-1870  1871 FAX]*

**MICHAEL SNELL LITERARY AGENCY**, P.O. Box 1206, Turo MA 02666-1206. (508)349-3718. **Contact:** Michael Snell. Estab. 1978. Represents 200 clients. 25% of clients are new/unpublished writers. Currently handles: 90% nonfiction books; 10% novels.

● Prior to opening his agency, Mr. Snell served as an editor at Wadsworth and Addison-Wesley for 13 years.

**Member Agents:** Michael Snell (business, management, computers); Patricia Smith (nonfiction, all categories).

**Represents:** Nonfiction books. **Considers these nonfiction areas:** agriculture/horticulture; americana; animals; anthropology/archaeology; art/architecture/design; biography/autobiography; business/economics; child guidance/parenting; computers/electronic; cooking/foods/nutrition; crafts/hobbies; creative nonfiction; current affairs; education; ethnic/cultural interests; gardening; gay/lesbian issues; government/politics/law; health/medicine; history; how-to; humor/satire; interior design/decorating; juvenile nonfiction; language/literature/criticism; memoirs; military/war; money/finance; multicultural; music/dance; nature/environment; New Age/metaphysics; philosophy; photography; popular culture; psychology; recreation; regional; religious/inspirational; science/technology; self-help/personal improvement; sex; sociology; software; spirituality; sports; theater/film; translation; travel; true crime/investigative; women's issues/studies; young adult.

O━━ This agency specializes in how-to, self-help and all types of business and computer books, from low-level how-to to professional and reference. Especially interested in business, health, law, medicine, psychology, science, women's issues. Actively seeking "strong book proposals in any nonfiction area where a clear need exists for a new book. Especially self-help, how-to books on all subjects, from business to personal well-being." Does not want to receive "complete manuscripts; considers proposals only. No fiction. No children's books."

**How to Contact:** Query with SASE. Prefers to read materials exclusively. Responds in 1 week to queries; 2 weeks to mss. Obtains most new clients through unsolicited mss, word-of-mouth, *LMP* and *Guide to Literary Agents*.

**Recent Sales:** Sold 51 titles in the last year. *Great Party!*, by Ann Stuart Hamilton (Prentice Hall); *Business is a Contact Sport*, by Tom Gorman (Macmillan); *The Innovator's Tale*, by Craig Hickman (Wiley); *How to Say It to the One You Love*, by Paul Coleman (Prentice Hall); *E-Commerce on a Shoestring*, by Carolyn Howard (Entrepreneur).
**Terms:** Agent receives 15% commission on domestic sales; 15% commission on foreign sales.
**Tips:** "Send a half- to full-page query, with SASE. Brochure 'How to Write a Book Proposal' available on request and SASE. We suggest prospective clients read Michael Snell's book, *From Book Idea to Bestseller* (Prima, 1997)."

**☑ ◑ SOBEL WEBER ASSOCIATES**, 146 E. 19th St., New York NY 10003. (212)420-8585. Fax: (212)505-1017. E-mail: info@sobelweber.com. **Contact:** Nat Sobel, Judith Weber. Represents 125 clients. 15% of clients are new/unpublished writers.

> ⤙ "We edit every book before submitting it to publishers even those of books under contract. For fiction, that may mean two or three drafts of the work. We are less interested in previously published authors, than in pursuing new talent wherever we find it."

**◑ SOUTHERN LITERARY GROUP**, division of L. Perkins Associates, 43 Stamford Dr., Lakeview AR 72642. (870)431-7006. Fax: (870)431-8625. E-mail: bmay@mnthorme.com. **Contact:** Beverly Maycunich. Estab. 2000. Represents 30 clients. 30% of clients are new/unpublished writers.

- Prior to becoming an agent, Ms. Maycunich was a real-estate agent. Her agency is affiliated with L. Perkins Associates.

**Represents:** Nonfiction books; novels. **Considers these nonfiction areas:** current affairs; popular culture; women's issues/studies. **Considers these fiction areas:** action/adventure; contemporary issues; detective/police/crime; ethnic; feminist; historical; literary; mainstream/contemporary; multicultural; mystery/suspense; regional; romance; thriller; young adult; women's fiction.

> ⤙ This agency is open to new writers. Does not want to receive material for children's books.

**How to Contact:** Query with SASE. Considers simultaneous queries. Responds in 1 week to queries; 3 months to mss. Returns materials only with SASE. Obtains most new clients through recommendations from others, the Internet.
**Recent Sales:** This is a new agency with no recorded sales.
**Terms:** Agent receives 15% commission on domestic sales; 20% commission on foreign sales. No written contract. Clients must provide 5 copies of ms.
**Writers' Conferences:** BEA.
**Tips:** "Care about your work. Belong to a writers' organization. Know your competition. The more you do your homework, the better your chance is of being sold."

**☑ ◑ SPECTRUM LITERARY AGENCY**, 320 Central Park W., Suite 1-D, New York NY 10025. **Contact:** Eleanor Wood, president. Represents 80 clients. Currently handles: 10% nonfiction books; 90% novels.
**Member Agents:** Lucienne Diver.
**Represents:** Nonfiction books; novels. **Considers these nonfiction areas:** Considers select nonfiction. **Considers these fiction areas:** contemporary issues; fantasy; historical; mainstream/contemporary; mystery/suspense; romance; science fiction.
**How to Contact:** Query with SASE. Responds in 2 months to queries. Obtains most new clients through recommendations from authors and others.
**Recent Sales:** This agency prefers not to share information on specific sales.
**Terms:** Agent receives 15% commission on domestic sales. Deducts for photocopying and book orders.

**◑ THE SPIELER AGENCY**, 154 W. 57th St., 13th Floor, Room 135, New York NY 10019. (212)757-4439. Fax: (212)757-4439. **Contact:** Ada Muellner. Estab. 1981. Represents 160 clients. 2% of clients are new/unpublished writers.
- Prior to opening his agency, Mr. Spieler was a magazine editor.
**Member Agents:** Joe Spieler; John Thornton (nonfiction); Lisa M. Ross (fiction/nonfiction); Deidre Mullane (nonfiction).
**Represents:** Nonfiction books; literary fiction, children's books. **Considers these nonfiction areas:** biography/autobiography; business/economics; child guidance/parenting; cooking/foods/nutrition; current affairs; gay/lesbian issues; government/politics/law; history; memoirs; money/finance; music/dance; nature/environment (environmental issues); sociology; theater/film; travel; women's issues/studies. **Considers these fiction areas:** family saga; feminist; gay/lesbian; humor/satire; literary.
**How to Contact:** Query with SASE. Prefers to read materials exclusively. No e-mail or fax queries. Considers simultaneous queries. Responds in 2 weeks to queries; 5 weeks to mss. Returns materials only with SASE. Obtains most new clients through recommendations and occasionally through listing in *Guide to Literary Agents*.
**Recent Sales:** *One Market Under God*, by Tom Frank (Doubleday); *Achilles*, by Elizabeth Cook (Picador).
**Terms:** Agent receives 15% commission on domestic sales. Charges clients for long distance phone/fax, photocopying, postage.
**Writers' Conferences:** London Bookfair.

**☑ ◑ PHILIP G. SPITZER LITERARY AGENCY**, 50 Talmage Farm Lane, East Hampton NY 11937. (631)329-3650. Fax: (631)329-3651. E-mail: spitzer516@aol.com. **Contact:** Philip Spitzer. Estab. 1969. Member of AAR. Represents 60 clients. 10% of clients are new/unpublished writers. Currently handles: 50% nonfiction books; 50% novels.

• Prior to opening his agency, Mr. Spitzer served at New York University Press, McGraw-Hill and the John Cushman Associates literary agency.

**Represents:** Nonfiction books; novels. **Considers these nonfiction areas:** biography/autobiography; business/economics; current affairs; ethnic/cultural interests; government/politics/law; health/medicine; history; language/literature/criticism; military/war; music/dance; nature/environment; popular culture; psychology; sociology; sports; theater/film; true crime/investigative. **Considers these fiction areas:** contemporary issues; detective/police/crime; literary; mainstream/contemporary; mystery/suspense; sports; thriller.

**O-π** This agency specializes in mystery/suspense, literary fiction, sports, general nonfiction (no how-to).

**How to Contact:** Query with SASE, outline, 1 sample chapter(s). Responds in 1 week to queries; 6 weeks to mss. Obtains most new clients through recommendations from others.

**Recent Sales:** *Angels Flight*, by Michael Connelly (Little, Brown); *Heartwood*, by James Lee Burke (Hyperion); *Eva Le Gallienne*, by Helen Sheehy (Knopf); *House of Sand and Fog*, by Andre Dubus III (Norton).

**Terms:** Agent receives 15% commission on domestic sales; 20% commission on foreign sales. Charges clients for photocopying.

**Writers' Conferences:** BEA (Chicago).

**✓ Ⓞ STARS, THE AGENCY**, 23 Grant Ave., 4th Floor, San Francisco CA 94108. Fax: (707)748-7395. E-mail: edley07@cs.com. **Contact:** Ed Silver. Estab. 1995. Represents 50-75 clients. 70% of clients are new/unpublished writers. Currently handles: 50% nonfiction books; 25% novels; 25% movie scripts.

• See the expanded listing for this agency in Script Agents.

**Ⓜ NANCY STAUFFER ASSOCIATES**, P.O. Box 1203, Darien CT 06820. (203)655-3717. Fax: (203)655-3704. E-mail: nanstauf@earthlink.net. **Contact:** Nancy Stauffer Cahoon. Estab. 1989. Member of the Authors Guild. 10% of clients are new/unpublished writers. Currently handles: 25% nonfiction books; 75% novels.

**Represents:** Nonfiction books; novels (literary fiction). **Considers these nonfiction areas:** biography/autobiography; creative nonfiction; current affairs; ethnic/cultural interests. **Considers these fiction areas:** contemporary issues; literary; mainstream/contemporary; regional.

**How to Contact:** For fiction: Send query letter with first 20 pages. For nonfiction: Send query letter with table of contents, first 20 pages. No e-mail or fax queries. Considers simultaneous queries. Returns materials only with SASE. Obtains most new clients through referrals from existing clients.

**Recent Sales:** *The Toughest Indian in the World*, by Sherman Alexie (Grove/Atlantic); *Delirium of the Brave*, by William C. Harris (St. Martin's Press); *Where Rivers Change Direction*, by Mark Spragg (Riverhead Books). Arroyo, by Summer Wood (Chronicle).

**Terms:** Agent receives 15% commission on domestic sales; 20% commission on foreign sales; 20% commission on dramatic rights sales.

**Writers' Conferences:** Writers At Work and Entrada; Radcliffe Publishing Course.

**Ⓞ STEELE-PERKINS LITERARY AGENCY**, 26 Island Lane, Canandaigua NY 14424. (716)396-9290. Fax: (716)396-3579. E-mail: pattiesp@aol.com. **Contact:** Pattie Steele-Perkins. Member of AAR, RWA. Currently handles: 100% novels.

• Prior to becoming an agent, Ms. Steele-Perkins was a TV producer/writer for 15 years.

**Represents:** Novels. **Considers these nonfiction areas:** sports (specifically sailing). **Considers these fiction areas:** mainstream/contemporary; multicultural; romance.

**O-π** The Steele-Perkins Literary Agency takes an active role in marketing their clients work including preparation for media appearances. They also develop with the author individual career plans. Actively seeking romance, women's fiction and multicultural works.

**How to Contact:** Submit outline, 3 sample chapter(s), SASE. Considers simultaneous queries. Responds in 6 weeks to queries. Returns materials only with SASE. Obtains most new clients through recommendations from others, solicitations.

**Terms:** Agent receives 15% commission on domestic sales. Offers written contract, binding for 1 year; 30-day notice must be given to terminate contract.

**Writers' Conferences:** National Conference of Romance Writer's of America; Book Expo America Writers' Conferences.

**Tips:** "Be patient. E-mail rather than call. Make sure what you are sending is the best it can be."

**Ⓝ STERLING LORD LITERISTIC, INC.**, 65 Bleecker St., New York NY 10012. (212)780-6050. Fax: (212)780-6095. **Contact:** Peter Matson. Estab. 1952. Signatory of WGA. Represents 600 clients. Currently handles: 50% nonfiction books; 50% novels.

**Member Agents:** Peter Matson; Sterling Lord; Jody Hotchkiss (film scripts); Philippa Brophy; Chris Calhoun; Charlotte Sheedy; George Nicholson; Neeti Madan; Jim Rutman.

**Represents:** Nonfiction books; novels; literary value considered first.

**How to Contact:** Query with SASE. Responds in 1 month to mss. Obtains most new clients through recommendations from others.

**Recent Sales:** This agency prefers not to share information on specific sales. Other clients include Kent Haruf, Dick Francis, Mary Gordon, Sen. John McCain, Simon Winchester.

**Terms:** Agent receives 15% commission on domestic sales; 20% commission on foreign sales. Offers written contract. Charges clients for photocopying.

**STERNIG & BYRNE LITERARY AGENCY**, 3209 S. 55, Milwaukee WI 53219-4433. (414)328-8034. Fax: (414)328-8034. E-mail: jackbyrne@aol.com. **Contact:** Jack Byrne. Estab. 1950s. Member of SFWA, MWA. Represents 30 clients. 10% of clients are new/unpublished writers. Accepting few new clients. Currently handles: 5% nonfiction books; 65% novels; 35% juvenile books.
**Member Agents:** Jack Byrne.
**Represents:** Nonfiction books; novels; juvenile books. **Considers these nonfiction areas:** juvenile nonfiction. **Considers these fiction areas:** action/adventure; fantasy; glitz; horror; juvenile; mystery/suspense; psychic/supernatural; science fiction; thriller; young adult.

    ○┐ "We have a small, friendly, personal, hands-on teamwork approach to marketing. Accepting new clients." Actively seeking science fiction/fantasy. Does not want to receive romance, poetry, textbooks, highly specialized nonfiction.

**How to Contact:** Query with SASE. Responds in 3 weeks to queries; 3 months to mss. Returns materials only with SASE.
**Recent Sales:** Sold 12 titles in the last year. *The Road to Well*, by Gerard Daniel Houarner (Leisure); *Untitled New Novel*, by Andre Norton (Meisha Merlin). Other clients include Clients include Betty Ren Wright, Lyn McComchie
**Terms:** Agent receives 15% commission on domestic sales; 20% commission on foreign sales. Offers written contract, binding for open length of time; 60-day notice must be given to terminate contract.
**Reading List:** Reads *Publishers Weekly, Science Fiction Chronicles*, etc. to find new clients. Looks for "whatever catches my eye."
**Tips:** "Don't send first drafts; have a professional presentation...including cover letter; know your field. Read what's been done...good and bad."

**ROBIN STRAUS AGENCY, INC.**, 229 E. 79th St., New York NY 10021. (212)472-3282. Fax: (212)472-3833. E-mail: springbird@aol.com. **Contact:** Ms. Robin Straus. Estab. 1983. Member of AAR. Currently handles: 65% nonfiction books; 35% novels.

    ● Prior to becoming an agent, Robin Straus served as a subsidary rights manager at Random House and Doubleday and worked in editorial at Little, Brown.

**Represents:** Nonfiction books; novels. **Considers these nonfiction areas:** animals; anthropology/archaeology; art/architecture/design; biography/autobiography; child guidance/parenting; cooking/foods/nutrition; current affairs; ethnic/cultural interests; government/politics/law; health/medicine; history; language/literature/criticism; music/dance; nature/environment; popular culture; psychology; science/technology; sociology; theater/film; women's issues/studies. **Considers these fiction areas:** contemporary issues; family saga; historical; literary; mainstream/contemporary.

    ○┐ This agency specializes in high quality fiction and nonfiction for adults. Takes on very few new clients.

**How to Contact:** For nonfiction: Query with proposal and sample pages. For fiction: Query with brief synopsis and opening chapter or 2. Responds in 1 month to queries; 1 month to mss. No e-mail queries. Returns materials only with SASE. Obtains most new clients through recommendations from others.
**Recent Sales:** This agency prefers not to share information on specific sales.
**Terms:** Agent receives 15% commission on domestic sales; 20% commission on foreign sales. Offers written contract. Charges for "photocopying, express mail services, messenger and foreign postage, etc. as incurred."

**N** **GUNTHER STUHLMANN, AUTHOR'S REPRESENTATIVE**, P.O. Box 276, Becket MA 01223-0276. Estab. 1954. "We are taking on few new clients at this time."

**SUITE A MANAGEMENT TALENT & LITERARY AGENCY**, 1101 S. Robertson Blvd., Suite 210, Los Angeles CA 90035. (310)278-0801. Fax: (310)278-0807. E-mail: suite-a@juno.com. Website: www.suite-a-management .com. **Contact:** Lloyd D. Robinson. Estab. 1996. Signatory of WGA; DGA, SAG. Represents 75 clients. 15% of clients are new/unpublished writers. Currently handles: 20% novels; 40% movie scripts; 15% TV scripts; 5% multimedia; 10% stage plays; 10% animation.

    ● See the expanded listing for this agency in Script Agents.

**THE SUSIJN AGENCY**, 820 Harrow Road, London NW10 5JU England. (020) 8968 7435. Fax: (020) 8354 0415. E-mail: info@thesusijnagency.com. Website: www.thesusijnagency.com. **Contact:** Laura Susijn. Estab. 1998. Currently handles: 15% nonfiction books; 85% novels.

    ● Prior to becoming an agent, Ms. Susijn was a rights director at Sheil Land Associates and at Fourth Estate Ltd.

**Member Agents:** Laura Susijn, Janne Moller.
**Represents:** Nonfiction books; novels. **Considers these nonfiction areas:** biography/autobiography; memoirs; multicultural; popular culture; science/technology; travel. **Considers these fiction areas:** literary.

    ○┐ This agency specializes in international works, selling world rights, representing non-English language writing as well as English. Emphasis on cross-cultural subjects. Self-help, romance, sagas, science fiction, screenplays.

**How to Contact:** Submit outline, 2 sample chapter(s). No e-mail or fax queries. Considers simultaneous queries. Responds in 2 months to queries. Returns materials only with SASE. Obtains most new clients through recommendations from others, via publishers in Europe and beyond.

**Recent Sales:** *Ladies Coupe*, by Anita Nair (Chatto & Windus); *Cover to Cover*, by Robert Craig (Weidenfeld & Nicholson); *Prisoner in a Red Rose Chain*, by Jeffrey Moore (Weidenfeld & Nicholson)*Smell*, by Radhika Jha (Quartet Books); *The Formula One Fanatic*, by Koen Vergeer (Bloomsbury); *A Mouthful of Glass*, by Henk Van Woerden (Granta); *Fragile Science*, by Robin Baker (Macmillan); *East of Acre Lane*, by Alex Wheatle (Fourth Estate). Other clients include Vassallucci, Podium, Atlas, De Arbeiderspers, Tiderne Skifter, MB Agency, Van Oorschot

**Terms:** Agent receives 15% commission on domestic sales; 15-20% commission on foreign sales. Offers written contract; 6 weeks notice must be given to terminate contract. Charges clients for photocopying, buying copies only if sale is made.

---

☑ ☑ **THE SWAYNE AGENCY LITERARY MANAGEMENT & CONSULTING, INC.**, 7 Penn Plaza, 16th Floor, New York NY 10001. (212)391-5438. E-mail: mgray@swayneagency.com. Website: www.swayneagency.com. Estab. 1997. Represents 25 clients. Currently handles: 100% nonfiction books.

**Member Agents:** Susan Barry (science, technology-related nonfiction, business, personal finance, memoir and sports); Lisa Swayne (technology-related, narrative and business nonfiction).

**Represents:** Nonfiction books. **Considers these nonfiction areas:** business/economics; computers/electronic; current affairs; ethnic/cultural interests; how-to; popular culture; science/technology; women's issues/studies.

> ⚓ This agency specializes in authors who participate in multimedia: book publishing, radio, movies and television, and information technology. Does not want to receive westerns, romance novels, science fiction, children's books.

**How to Contact:** Query with SASE, proposal package, outline. Accepts e-mail queries. No fax queries. Considers simultaneous queries. Responds in 6 weeks to mss. Obtains most new clients through recommendations from colleagues and clients.

**Recent Sales:** *Trendspotting*, by Richard Laerner (Penguin/Putnam); *Will Code for Food*, by Bill Lessard and Steve Baldwin (Crown Books); *More Healing Mudras*, by Sabrina Mesko (Ballantine Books); *Healing Mudras*, by Sabrina Mesko (Ballantine); *Citizen Greenspan*, by Justin Martin (Perseus Books); *Nurturing the Writer's Self*, by Bonnie Goldberg (Penguin Putnam).

**Terms:** Agent receives 15% commission on domestic sales; 20% commission on foreign sales. Offers written contract, binding for 1 year; 60 days notice must be given to terminate contract.

**Reading List:** Reads *Harpers*, *New York Times*, *Business Week*, *Wall Street Journal*, *New York Observer*, *Forbes*, *Fortune* to find new clients. Looks for cutting edge business, technology topics and trends and up and coming writers.

---

☑ ☑ **CAROLYN SWAYZE LITERARY AGENCY**, W.R.P.O. Box 39588, White Rock, British Columbia V4B 5L6 Canada. (604)538-3478. Fax: (604)531-3022. E-mail: cswayze@direct.ca. **Contact:** Carolyn Swayze. Also: P.O. Box 3976, Blaine WA 98231-3976. Estab. 1994. Represents 40 clients. 50% of clients are new/unpublished writers. Currently handles: 30% nonfiction books; 50% novels; 15% story collections; 5% juvenile books.

> ● Prior to becoming an agent, Ms. Swayze was an intellectual property law lawyer, published biographer, novelist, columnist.

**Member Agents:** D. Barry Jones (military history, action-adventure); Carolyn Swayze (literary fiction and nonfiction).

**Represents:** Nonfiction books; novels. **Considers these nonfiction areas:** biography/autobiography; child guidance/parenting; cooking/foods/nutrition; ethnic/cultural interests; history; humor/satire; memoirs; military/war; nature/environment; popular culture; self-help/personal improvement; sports; travel; true crime/investigative; women's issues/studies. **Considers these fiction areas:** contemporary issues; ethnic; family saga; historical; humor/satire; literary; mainstream/contemporary; multicultural; mystery/suspense.

> ⚓ This agent has a diverse background, having sold advertising, practised law, written a biography, novels, columns and articles. "Our ratio of first novels and collections is very satisfying." Actively seeking solid proposals for accessible books on sciences, social sciences, philosophy, popular culture, psychology, history and ideas. Does not want to receive science fiction, religious, New Age, horror.

**How to Contact:** Query with SASE, submit proposal package, outline, 3 sample chapter(s). Prefers to read materials exclusively. Accepts e-mail and fax queries. Considers simultaneous queries. Responds in 3 weeks to queries; 6 weeks to mss. Returns materials only with SASE. Obtains most new clients through recommendations from others, solicitations.

**Recent Sales:** Sold 25 titles in the last year. *The Bear's Embrace*, by Patricia Van Tighem (Greystone); *High Wire*, by Steven Galloway (Knopf Canada); *Generica*, by Will Ferguson (Penguin Canada). Other clients include W.P. Kinsella, Bill Gatson, Lorainne Brown, Todd Babiak, Mark Zuehlke, Karen Rivers, Barbara Lambert, Teena Spencer, Wilf Cude, M.A.C. Farrant, Richard Van Camp, Marg Meikle, Taras Grescoe, Paul Grescoe, Miriam Toews, and four teams of co-authors.

---

**TO FIND AN AGENT** near you, check the Geographic Index.

**Terms:** Agent receives 15% commission on domestic sales; 20% commission on foreign sales. Offers written contract. Charges clients for copying and courier expenses to a maximum of $200—always invoiced and often waived for new writers.

**Writers' Conferences:** Pacific Northwest Writers' Conference (Tacoma WA, July 13-16); Surrey Writers' Conference (Surrey BC, October); Willamette Writers' Conference (Portland OR, August). "I do numerous talks on copyright and publishing at colleges, universities, writers' workshops and Word on the Street, Vancouver."

**Tips:** "Please don't telephone to ask if I'm 'taking new writers.' Submit written material which will persuade me to call you."

 **SYDRA TECHNIQUES CORP.**, 481 Eighth Ave., E24, New York NY 10001. (212)631-0009. Fax: (212)631-0715. E-mail: andi9@aol.com. **Contact:** Sid Buck. Estab. 1988. Signatory of WGA. Represents 30 clients. 80% of clients are new/unpublished writers. Currently handles: 10% nonfiction books; 10% novels; 30% movie scripts; 30% TV scripts; 10% multimedia; 10% stage plays.
 • See the expanded listing for this agency in Script Agents.

**THE JOHN TALBOT AGENCY**, 540 W. Boston Post Rd., PMB 266, Mamaroneck NY 10543-3437. (914)381-9463. Website: www.johntalbotagency.com. **Contact:** John Talbot. Estab. 1998. Member of Authors Guild. Represents 50 clients. 15% of clients are new/unpublished writers. Currently handles: 35% nonfiction books; 65% novels.
 • Prior to becoming an agent, Mr. Talbot was a book editor at Simon & Schuster and Putnam Berkley.
**Represents:** Nonfiction books; novels. **Considers these nonfiction areas:** creative nonfiction; general and narrative nonfiction. **Considers these fiction areas:** literary; mystery/suspense.
 ○━ This agency specializes in commercial suspense and literary fiction "by writers who are beginning to publish in magazines and literary journals." Also narrative nonfiction, especially outdoor adventure and spirituality. Does not want to receive children's books, science fiction, fantasy, westerns, poetry, screenplays.
**How to Contact:** Query with SASE. No e-mail or fax queries. Considers simultaneous queries. Responds in 1 month to queries; 2 months to mss. Obtains most new clients through referrals.
**Recent Sales:** Sold 30 titles in the last year. *Manhattan South*, by John Mackie (NAL); *Burden*, by Tony Walters (St. Martin's Press); *Lily of the Valley*, by Suzanne Strempek Shea (Pocket Books); *The Fuck-up*, by Arthur Nersesian (Pocket Books/MTV). Other clients include Doris Meredith, Peter Telep, Robert W. Walker
**Terms:** Agent receives 15% commission on domestic sales; 20% commission on foreign sales. Offers written contract; 2-week notice must be given to terminate contract. Charges clients for photocopying, overnight delivery, additional copies of books needed for use in sale of subsidiary rights, and fees incurred for submitting mss or books overseas.

**[N]** **TALESMYTH ENTERTAINMENT, INC.**, 312 St. John St., Suite #69, Portland ME 04102. (207)879-0307. Fax: (207)775-1067. E-mail: talesmyth@hotmail.com. **Contact:** Thomas Burgess. Estab. 2000. Signatory of WGA. Represents 5 clients. 100% of clients are new/unpublished writers. Currently handles: 10% novels; 10% story collections; 80% movie scripts.
 • See the expanded listing for this agency in Script Agents.

**[N]** **ROSLYN TARG LITERARY AGENCY, INC.**, 105 W. 13th St., New York NY 10011. (212)206-9390. Fax: (212)989-6233. E-mail: roslyntarg@aol.com. **Contact:** Roslyn Targ. Estab. 1945. Member of AAR. Represents 100 clients.
**Member Agents:** Roslyn Targ; Booker Jones.
**Represents:** Nonfiction books; novels; juvenile books; Self-help.
**How to Contact:** Query with outline, proposal, curriculum vitae, SASE. Prefers to read materials exclusively. No mss without query first. Obtains most new clients through recommendations from others, solicitations.
**Recent Sales:** *Forever Amber*, Kathleen Winsor.
**Terms:** Agent receives 15% commission on domestic sales; 20% commission on foreign sales. Charges standard agency fees (bank charges, long distance, postage, photocopying, shipping of books, overseas long distance and shipping, etc.).
**Tips:** "This agency reads on an exclusive basis only."

**PATRICIA TEAL LITERARY AGENCY**, 2036 Vista Del Rosa, Fullerton CA 92831-1336. Phone/fax: (714)738-8333. **Contact:** Patricia Teal. Estab. 1978. Member of AAR. Represents 60 clients. Currently handles: 10% nonfiction books; 90% novels.
**Represents:** Nonfiction books; novels. **Considers these nonfiction areas:** animals; biography/autobiography; child guidance/parenting; health/medicine; how-to; psychology; self-help/personal improvement; true crime/investigative; women's issues/studies. **Considers these fiction areas:** glitz; mainstream/contemporary; mystery/suspense; romance (contemporary, historical).
 ○━ This agency specializes in women's fiction and commercial how-to and self-help nonfiction. Does not want to receive poetry, short stories, articles, science fiction, fantasy, regency romance.
**How to Contact:** *Published authors only.* Query with SASE. No e-mail or fax queries. Considers simultaneous queries. Responds in 10 days to queries; 6 weeks to mss. Returns materials only with SASE. Obtains most new clients through conferences, recommendations from authors and editors.
**Recent Sales:** Sold 30 titles in the last year. *Billionaire Cinderella School*, by Myrna McKenzie (Silhouette); *Working Overtime*, by Helen Conrad (Silhouette).

**Terms:** Agent receives 10-15% commission on domestic sales; 20% commission on foreign sales. Offers written contract, binding for 1 year. Charges clients for photocopying.

**Writers' Conferences:** Romance Writers of America conferences; California State University (San Diego, January); Asilomar (California Writers Club); BEA (Chicago June); Bouchercon; Hawaii Writers Conference (Maui).

**Reading List:** Reads *Publishers Weekly*, *Romance Report* and *Romantic Times* to find new clients. "I read the reviews of books and excerpts from authors' books."

**Tips:** "Include SASE with all correspondence."

**IRENE TIERSTEN LITERARY AGENCY**, 540 Ridgewood Rd., Maplewood NJ 07040. (973)762-4024. Fax: (973)762-0349. E-mail: tiersten@ix.netcom.com. **Contact:** Irene Tiersten. Prefers to work with published/established authors.

**Represents:** Nonfiction books; novels; adult and young adult books.

○➤ Does not want to receive poetry, horror, sadism, science fiction.

**How to Contact:** Prefers to read materials exclusively. Accepts e-mail and fax queries. Responds in 2 weeks to queries; 1 month to mss.

**Recent Sales:** Sold 6 titles in the last year. *The Princesses of Atlantis*, by Lisa Williams Kline (Cricket/Carus).

**Terms:** Agent receives 15% commission on domestic sales; 25% (spit with co-agents abroad) commission on foreign sales; 15% commission on dramatic rights sales. Charges clients for international phone and postage expenses.

**TOAD HALL, INC.**, RR 2, Box 2090, Laceyville PA 18623. (570)869-2942. Fax: (570)869-1031. E-mail: toadhall co@aol.com. Website: www.laceyville.com/Toad-Hall. **Contact:** Sharon Jarvis, Anne Pinzow. Estab. 1982. Represents 35 clients. 10% of clients are new/unpublished writers. Currently handles: 50% nonfiction books; 40% novels; 5% movie scripts; 5% ancillary projects.

● Prior to becoming an agent, Ms. Jarvis was an acquisitions editor.

**Member Agents:** Sharon Jarvis (fiction, nonfiction); Anne Pinzow (TV, movies).

**Represents:** Nonfiction books; novels. **Considers these nonfiction areas:** animals; anthropology/archaeology; business/economics; child guidance/parenting; cooking/foods/nutrition; crafts/hobbies; health/medicine; how-to; nature/environment; New Age/metaphysics; popular culture; religious/inspirational; self-help/personal improvement; spirituality. **Considers these fiction areas:** historical; mystery/suspense; romance (contemporary, historical, regency); science fiction.

○➤ This agency specializes in popular nonfiction, some category fiction. Actively seeking New Age, paranormal—unusual but popular approaches. "We only handle scripts written by our clients who have published material agented by us." Does not want to receive poetry, short stories, essays, collections, children's books.

**How to Contact:** Query with SASE. Prefers to read materials exclusively. For scripts, send outline/proposal with query. No e-mail or fax queries. Responds in 3 weeks to queries; 3 months to mss. Obtains most new clients through recommendations from others, solicitations, conferences.

**Recent Sales:** Sold 6 titles in the last year. *An Improper Bride*, by Sarah Blayne (Kensington); *A Fire in the Sky*, by Vernor Vinge (TOR).

**Terms:** Agent receives 15% commission on domestic sales; 10% commission on foreign sales. Offers written contract, binding for 1 year; 100% of business is derived from commissions on ms sales. Charges clients for photocopying, bank fees and special postage (i.e., express mail).

**Tips:** "Pay attention to what is getting published. Show the agent you've done your homework!"

**ANN TOBIAS—A LITERARY AGENCY FOR CHILDREN'S BOOKS, (Specialized: children's books)**, 520 E. 84th St., Apt. 4L, New York NY 10028. **Contact:** Ann Tobias. Estab. 1988. Represents 25 clients. 50% of clients are new/unpublished writers. Currently handles: 100% juvenile books.

● Prior to opening her agency, Ms. Tobias worked as a children's book editor at Harper, William Morrow, Scholastic.

**Represents:** Juvenile books. **Considers these nonfiction areas:** juvenile nonfiction; young adult. **Considers these fiction areas:** picture books; poetry (for children); young adult; illustrated mss.

○➤ This agency specializes in books for children. Actively seeking material for children.

**How to Contact:** Send entire ms for picture books; 30 pages and synopsis for longer work, both fiction and nonfiction. No phone queries. All queries must be in writing and accompanied by a SASE. Considers simultaneous queries. Responds in 2 months to mss. Returns materials only with SASE. Obtains most new clients through recommendations from editors.

**Recent Sales:** Sold 15 titles in the last year. This agency prefers not to share information on specific sales.

**Terms:** Agent receives 15% commission on domestic sales; 20% commission on foreign sales. No written contract. Charges clients for photocopying, overnight mail, foreign postage, foreign telephone.

**Reading List:** Reads *Horn Book, Bulletin for the Center of the Book* and *School Library Journal*. "These are review media and they keep me up to date on who is being published and by what company."

**Tips:** "Read at least 200 children's books in the age group and genre in which you hope to be published. Follow this by reading another 100 children's books in other age groups and genres so you will have a feel for the field as a whole."

**SUSAN TRAVIS LITERARY AGENCY**, 1317 N. San Fernando Blvd., Suite 175, Burbank CA 91504. (818)557-6538. Fax: (818)557-6549. **Contact:** Susan Travis. Estab. 1995. Represents 10 clients. 60% of clients are new/unpublished writers. Currently handles: 70% nonfiction books; 30% novels.

• Prior to opening her agency, Ms. Travis served as an agent with the McBride Agency and prior to that worked in the Managing Editors Department of Ballantine Books.

**Represents:** Nonfiction books; novels. **Considers these nonfiction areas:** business/economics; child guidance/parenting; cooking/foods/nutrition; ethnic/cultural interests; health/medicine; how-to; popular culture; psychology; self-help/personal improvement; women's issues/studies. **Considers these fiction areas:** contemporary issues; ethnic; historical; literary; mainstream/contemporary; romance (historical).

O→ This agency specializes in mainstream fiction and nonfiction. Actively seeking mainstream nonfiction. Does not want to receive science fiction, poetry or children's books.

**How to Contact:** Query with SASE. Responds in 3 weeks to queries; 6 weeks to mss. Obtains most new clients through recommendations from existing clients, and mss requested from query letters.

**Recent Sales:** This agency prefers not to share information on specific sales.

**Terms:** Agent receives 15% commission on domestic sales; 20% commission on foreign sales. Offers written contract, binding for 1 year; 60-day notice must be given to terminate contract. 100% of business is derived from commissions on ms sales. Charges clients for photocopying of mss and proposals if copies not provided by author.

**SCOTT TREIMEL NY, (Specialized: children's books)**, 434 Lafayette St., New York NY 10003. (212)505-8353. Fax: (212)505-0664. E-mail: mescottyt@earthlink.net. **Contact:** Scott Treimel, Annie Golub. Estab. 1995. Member of AAR. Represents 19 clients. 15% of clients are new/unpublished writers. Currently handles: 100% juvenile books.

• Prior to becoming an agent, Mr. Treimel was an assistant at Curtis Brown, Ltd. (for Marilyn E. Marlow); a rights agent for Scholastic, Inc.; a book packager and rights agent for United Feature Syndicate; a freelance editor and a rights consultant for HarperCollins Children's Books; and the founding director of Warner Bros. Worldwide Publishing.

**Represents:** Children's book authors and illustrators. **Considers these nonfiction areas:** agriculture/horticulture; americana; animals; anthropology/archaeology; art/architecture/design; biography/autobiography; business/economics; child guidance/parenting; computers/electronic; cooking/foods/nutrition; crafts/hobbies; creative nonfiction; current affairs; education; ethnic/cultural interests; gardening; gay/lesbian issues; government/politics/law; health/medicine; history; how-to; humor/satire; interior design/decorating; juvenile nonfiction; language/literature/criticism; memoirs; military/war; money/finance; multicultural; music/dance; nature/environment; New Age/metaphysics; philosophy; photography; popular culture; psychology; recreation; regional; religious/inspirational; science/technology; self-help/personal improvement; sex; sociology; software; spirituality; sports; theater/film; translation; travel; true crime/investigative; women's issues/studies; young adult. **Considers these fiction areas:** action/adventure; comic books/cartoon; confession; contemporary issues; detective/police/crime; erotica; ethnic; experimental; family saga; fantasy; feminist; gay/lesbian; glitz; gothic; hi-lo; historical; horror; humor/satire; juvenile; literary; mainstream/contemporary; military/war; multicultural; multimedia; mystery/suspense; New Age; occult; picture books; plays; poetry; poetry in translation; psychic/supernatural; regional; religious/inspirational; romance; science fiction; short story collections; spiritual; sports; thriller; translation; westerns/frontier; young adult; women's.

O→ This agency specializes in children's books: tightly focused segments of the trade and educational markets. Interested in seeing author-illustrators, first chapter books, middle-grade fiction and young adult fiction.

**How to Contact:** Query with SASE. For longer work, send synopsis and first two chapters. Replies only to materials sent with SASE. No fax queries. Obtains most new clients through recommendations from others, solicitations.

**Recent Sales:** Sold 21 titles in the last year. Sold books to Harper, Dutton, Clarion, Random House, Roaring Brook Press, etc.

**Terms:** Agent receives 15-20% commission on domestic sales; 20-25% commission on foreign sales. Offers verbal or written contract, "binding on a book contract by contract basis." Charges clients for photocopying, overnight/express postage, messengers, and books ordered to sell foreign, film, etc. rights.

**Writers' Conferences:** Can You Make a Living from Children's Books, Society of Children's Book Writers & Illustrators (Los Angeles, August); Society of Children's Book Writers & Illustrators (Los Angeles, August); "Understanding Book Contracts," SCBWI (Watertown NY); "Creating Believable Teen Characters," SCBWI; Picture Book Judge for Tassie Walden Award; New Voices in Children's Literature.

**2M COMMUNICATIONS LTD.**, 121 W. 27 St., #601, New York NY 10001. (212)741-1509. Fax: (212)691-4460. E-mail: morel@bookhaven.com. **Contact:** Madeleine Morel. Estab. 1982. Represents 50 clients. 20% of clients are new/unpublished writers. Currently handles: 100% nonfiction books.

• Prior to becoming an agent, Madeleine Morel worked at a publishing company.

**Represents:** Nonfiction books. **Considers these nonfiction areas:** biography/autobiography; child guidance/parenting; ethnic/cultural interests; gay/lesbian issues; health/medicine; memoirs; music/dance; self-help/personal improvement; theater/film; travel; women's issues/studies.

O→ This agency specializes in adult nonfiction.

**How to Contact:** Query with SASE, submit outline, 3 sample chapter(s). Accepts e-mail and fax queries. Considers simultaneous queries. Responds in 1 week to queries; 1 month to mss. Obtains most new clients through recommendations from others, solicitations.

**Recent Sales:** Sold 20 titles in the last year. *Feng Shui*, by Carole Meltzer (Simon & Schuster); *A Taste of Eire*, by Margaret Johnson (Chronicle).

**Terms:** Agent receives 15% commission on domestic sales; 20% commission on foreign sales. Offers written contract, binding for 2 years. Charges clients for postage, photocopying, long distance calls, faxes.

⬛ **UNITED TRIBES**, 240 W. 35th St., #500, New York NY 10001. (212)534-7646. E-mail: janguerth@aol.com. Website: www.unitedtribes.com. **Contact:** Jan-Erik Guerth. Estab. 1998. Currently handles: 100% nonfiction books.
   • Prior to becoming an agent, Mr. Guerth was a comedian, journalist, radio producer and film distributor.
**Represents:** Nonfiction books; novels. **Considers these nonfiction areas:** anthropology/archaeology; art/architecture/design; biography/autobiography; business/economics; child guidance/parenting; cooking/foods/nutrition; current affairs; education; ethnic/cultural interests; gay/lesbian issues; government/politics/law; health/medicine; history; how-to; language/literature/criticism; memoirs; money/finance; music/dance; nature/environment; popular culture; psychology; religious/inspirational; science/technology (popular); self-help/personal improvement; sociology; theater/film; translation; women's issues/studies.
   ⚬━ This agency represents secular spirituality and serious nonfiction; and ethnic, social, gender and cultural issues, comparative religions, self-help and wellness, science and arts, history and politics, nature and travel, and any fascinating future trends.
**How to Contact:** Submit outline, résumé, SASE. Considers simultaneous queries. Responds in 1 month to queries. Returns materials only with SASE. Obtains most new clients through recommendations from others, solicitations, conferences.
**Recent Sales:** *The World's Squatters*, by Robert Nenwirth (Routledge); *The Green Desert*, by Rita Winters (Wildcat Canyon Press).
**Terms:** Agent receives 15% commission on domestic sales; 20% commission on foreign sales.

◎ **THE RICHARD R. VALCOURT AGENCY, INC., (Specialized: government issues)**, 177 E. 77th St., PHC, New York NY 10021-1934. Phone/fax: (212)570-2340. **Contact:** Richard R. Valcourt, president. Estab. 1995. Represents 25 clients. 20% of clients are new/unpublished writers. Currently handles: 100% nonfiction books.
   • Prior to opening his agency, Mr. Valcourt was a journalist, editor and college political science instructor. He is also editor-in-chief of the International Journal of Intelligence and faculty member at American Military University in Virginia.
**Represents:** Scholarly books.
   ⚬━ This agency specializes in intelligence and other national security affairs. Represents exclusively academics, journalists and professionals in the categories listed.
**How to Contact:** Query with SASE. Prefers to read materials exclusively. No e-mail or fax queries. Responds in 1 week to queries; 1 month to mss. Returns materials only with SASE. Obtains most new clients through recommendations from others, active recruitment.
**Recent Sales:** *China Rising: Den Xiaoping's Legacy*, by Michael E. Marti (Brassey's); *Shadow Warriors of Japan & the Nakano Intelligence School*, by Stephen C. Mercado (Brassey's).
**Terms:** Agent receives 15% commission on domestic sales; 20% commission on foreign sales. Offers written contract. Charges clients for excessive photocopying, express mail, overseas telephone expenses.

ℕ⬛ **VAN DER LEUN & ASSOCIATES**, 32 Grammercy Park South, Suite 11 L, New York NY 10003. (212)982-6165. Fax: (212)477-7082. E-mail: pvanderleun@aol.com. **Contact:** Patricia Van der Leun, president. Estab. 1984. Represents 30 clients. Currently handles: 75% nonfiction books; 25% novels.
   • Prior to becoming an agent, Ms. Van der Leun was a professor of Art History.
**Represents:** Nonfiction books; novels; illustrated books. **Considers these nonfiction areas:** art/architecture/design (art history); biography/autobiography; cooking/foods/nutrition (food and wine, cookbooks); creative nonfiction; current affairs; ethnic/cultural interests; gardening; history; memoirs; travel. **Considers these fiction areas:** action/adventure; comic books/cartoon; confession; contemporary issues; detective/police/crime; erotica; ethnic; experimental; family saga; fantasy; feminist; gay/lesbian; glitz; gothic; hi-lo; historical; humor/satire; juvenile; literary; mainstream/contemporary; military/war; multicultural; multimedia; mystery/suspense; New Age; occult; picture books; plays; poetry; poetry in translation; psychic/supernatural; regional; religious/inspirational; romance; short story collections; spiritual; sports; thriller; translation; westerns/frontier; young adult; women's.
   ⚬━ This agency specializes in fiction, art history, food and wine, gardening, biography.
**How to Contact:** Query with letter only, include SASE. Accepts e-mail and fax queries. Considers simultaneous queries. Responds in 2 weeks to queries.
**Recent Sales:** Sold 6 titles in the last year. *Life Everywhere*, by David Darling (Basic Books); *Rules for the Unruly*, by Marion Wink (Fireside Books/Simon & Schuster); *Sea of Memory*, by Erri de Luca (Ecco Press).
**Terms:** Agent receives 15% commission on domestic sales; 25% commission on foreign sales. Offers written contract. Charges clients for postage and photocopying fo mss.

◎ **ANNETTE VAN DUREN AGENCY**, 11684 Ventura Blvd., #235, Studio City CA 91604. (818)752-6000. Fax: (818)752-6985. **Contact:** Annette Van Duren or Teena Portier. Estab. 1985. Signatory of WGA. Represents 12 clients. 0% of clients are new/unpublished writers. Currently handles: 10% nonfiction books; 50% movie scripts; 40% TV scripts.
   • See the expanded listing for this agency in Script Agents.

**N** ◯ **VENTURE LITERARY**, 3950 Mahaila Ave., D-31, San Diego CA 92122. (619)807-1887. E-mail: venturelite rary@yahoo.com. Website: www.ventureliterary.com. **Contact:** Frank R. Scatoni. Estab. 1999. Represents 15 clients. 60% of clients are new/unpublished writers. Currently handles: 75% nonfiction books; 25% novels.

 • Prior to becoming an agent, Mr. Scatoni worked an a former editor at Simon & Schuster before moving to a small press, Lebhar-Friedman Books.

**Member Agents:** Frank R. Scatoni (general nonficion/mainstream fiction); Greg Dinkin (general nonfiction/business, self-help).

**Represents:** Nonfiction books; novels. **Considers these nonfiction areas:** animals; anthropology/archaeology; biography/autobiography; business/economics; computers/electronic; current affairs; ethnic/cultural interests; government/politics/law; health/medicine; history; language/literature/criticism; memoirs; military/war; money/finance; multicultural; music/dance; nature/environment; popular culture; psychology; religious/inspirational; science/technology; self-help/personal improvement; sports; true crime/investigative; women's issues/studies. **Considers these fiction areas:** action/adventure; contemporary issues; detective/police/crime; ethnic; feminist; historical; horror; humor/satire; literary; mainstream/contemporary; multicultural; mystery/suspense; sports; thriller.

 ⊶ "With more than ten years of editorial experience at major publishers, the partners at Venture Literary know how to shape a proposal or manuscript into a salable piece of work. Scatoni and Dinkin are also published authors and they know what it takes to make a project work and who to send it to. Actively seeking narrative nonfiction.

**How to Contact:** Nonfiction: proposal with 3 sample chapters; fiction: query letter and finished ms. Considers simultaneous queries. Responds in 1 month to queries; 1-3 months to mss. Returns materials only with SASE. Obtains most new clients through recommendations from others.

**Recent Sales:** *Everything I Know about Business I Learned at the Poker Table*, by Jeffrey Sitdmer and Greg Dinkin (Crown).

**Terms:** Agent receives 15% commission on domestic sales; 20% commission on foreign sales. Offers written contract. Photocopying and postage only.

**Writers' Conferences:** San Diego Writers Conference (San Diego, CA).

303 W, 18 ST,    :10001

⊘ **RALPH VICIANANZA, LTD.**, ~~111 Eighth Ave., Suite 1501~~, New York NY 10011. (212)924-7090. Fax: (212)691-9644. Member of AAR. Represents 120 clients. 5% of clients are new/unpublished writers.

**Member Agents:** Ralph M. Viciananza; Chris Lotts; ~~Chris Schelling~~.

**Represents:** Nonfiction books; novels. **Considers these nonfiction areas:** biography/autobiography; business/economics; history; popular culture; religious/inspirational; science/technology. **Considers these fiction areas:** fantasy; literary; mainstream/contemporary (popular fiction); multicultural; science fiction; thriller; women's fiction.

 ⊶ This agency specializes in foreign rights.

**How to Contact:** Query with SASE. No unsolicited mss.

**Recent Sales:** This agency prefers not to share information on specific sales.

**Terms:** Agent receives 15% commission on domestic sales; 20% commission on foreign sales.

⊘ **DAVID VIGLIANO LITERARY AGENCY**, 584 Broadway, Suite 809, New York NY 10012. Member of AAR. This agency did not respond to our request for information. Query before submitting.

⊘ **THE VINES AGENCY, INC.**, 648 Broadway, Suite 901, New York NY 10012. (212)777-5522. Fax: (212)777-5978. E-mail: jv@vinesagency.com. Website: www.vinesagency.com. **Contact:** James C. Vines, Paul Surdi, Ali Ryan, Gary Neuwirth. Estab. 1995. Member of AAR; signatory of WGA. Represents 52 clients. 20% of clients are new/unpublished writers. Currently handles: 50% nonfiction books; 50% novels.

 • Prior to opening his agency, Mr. Vines served as an agent with the Virginia Barber Literary Agency.

**Member Agents:** James C. Vines (quality and commercial fiction and nonfiction); Gary Neuwirth; Paul Surdi (women's fiction, ethnic fiction, quality nonfiction); Ali Ryan (women's fiction and nonfiction, mainstream).

**Represents:** Nonfiction books; novels. **Considers these nonfiction areas:** biography/autobiography; business/economics; current affairs; ethnic/cultural interests; history; how-to; humor/satire; memoirs; military/war; money/finance; nature/environment; New Age/metaphysics; photography; popular culture; psychology; religious/inspirational; science/technology; self-help/personal improvement; sociology; spirituality; sports; translation; travel; true crime/investigative; women's issues/studies. **Considers these fiction areas:** action/adventure; contemporary issues; detective/police/crime; ethnic; experimental; family saga; feminist; gay/lesbian; historical; horror; humor/satire; literary; mainstream/contemporary; mystery/suspense; occult; psychic/supernatural; regional; romance (contemporary, historical); science fiction; sports; thriller; westerns/frontier; women's.

 ⊶ This agency specializes in mystery, suspense, science fiction, women's fiction, ethnic fiction, mainstream novels, screenplays, teleplays.

---

**ALWAYS INCLUDE** a self-addressed, stamped envelope (SASE) for reply or return of your query or manuscript.

**Also Handles:** Feature film; TV scripts. **Considers these script subject areas:** action/adventure; comedy; detective/police/crime; ethnic; experimental; feminist; gay/lesbian; historical; horror; mainstream; mystery/suspense; romantic comedy; romantic drama; science fiction; teen; thriller; western/frontier.

**How to Contact:** Submit outline, 3 sample chapter(s), SASE. Accepts e-mail and fax queries. Considers simultaneous queries. Responds in 2 weeks to queries; 1 month to mss. Returns materials only with SASE. Obtains most new clients through query letters, recommendations from others, reading short stories in magazines, soliciting conferences.

**Recent Sales:** Sold 48 titles and sold 5 scripts in the last year. *America the Beautiful*, by Moon Unit Zappa (Scribner); *The Warmest December*, by Bernice McFadden (Dutton-Plume).

**Terms:** Agent receives 15% commission on domestic sales; 25% commission on foreign sales. Offers written contract, binding for 1 year; 30 days notice must be given to terminate contract. 100% of business is derived from commissions on ms sales. Charges clients for foreign postage, messenger services, photocopying.

**Writers' Conferences:** Maui Writer's Conference.

**Tips:** "Do not follow up on submissions with phone calls to the agency. The agency will read and respond by mail only. Do not pack your manuscript in plastic 'peanuts' that will make us have to vacuum the office after opening the package containing your manuscript. Always enclose return postage."

**MARY JACK WALD ASSOCIATES, INC.**, 111 E. 14th St., New York NY 10003. (212)254-7842. **Contact:** Danis Sher. Estab. 1985. Member of AAR, Authors Guild, SCBWI. Represents 35 clients. 5% of clients are new/unpublished writers. Currently handles: nonfiction books; novels; story collections; novellas; juvenile books; movie scripts; TV scripts.

• This agency is not accepting mss at this time.

**Member Agents:** Danis Sher; Lynne Rabinoff.

**Represents:** Nonfiction books; novels; short story collections; novellas; juvenile books. **Considers these nonfiction areas:** biography/autobiography; current affairs; ethnic/cultural interests; history; juvenile nonfiction; language/literature/criticism; music/dance; nature/environment; photography; sociology; theater/film; translation; true crime/investigative. **Considers these fiction areas:** action/adventure; contemporary issues; detective/police/crime; ethnic; experimental; family saga; feminist; gay/lesbian; glitz; historical; juvenile; literary; mainstream/contemporary; mystery/suspense; picture books; thriller; young adult; satire.

0–¬ This agency specializes in literary works, juvenile.

**Also Handles:** Movie scripts; TV scripts.

**How to Contact:** Query with SASE; will request more if interested. Prefers to read materials exclusively. Responds in 2 months to queries. Obtains most new clients through recommendations from others.

**Recent Sales:** Sold 14 titles in the last year. *National Geographic Photography Guide for Kids*, by Neil Johnson.

**Terms:** Agent receives 15% commission on domestic sales; 15-30% commission on foreign sales. Offers written contract, binding for 1 year.

**WALES, LITERARY AGENCY, INC.**, P.O. Box 9428, Seattle WA 98109-0428. Phone/fax: (206)284-7114. E-mail: waleslit@aol.com. **Contact:** Elizabeth Wales or Adrienne Reed. Estab. 1988. Member of AAR, Book Publishers' Northwest. Represents 65 clients. 10% of clients are new/unpublished writers. Currently handles: 60% nonfiction books; 35% novels; 5% story collections.

• Prior to becoming an agent, Ms. Wales worked at Oxford University Press and Viking Penguin.

**Member Agents:** Elizabeth Wales; Adrienne Reed.

**Represents:** Nonfiction books; novels; short story collections; novellas. **Considers these nonfiction areas:** animals; biography/autobiography; current affairs; ethnic/cultural interests; gay/lesbian issues; history; memoirs; multicultural; nature/environment; popular culture; science/technology; travel; women's issues/studies; open to creative or serious treatments of almost any nonfiction subject. **Considers these fiction areas:** contemporary issues; ethnic; feminist; gay/lesbian; literary; mainstream/contemporary; multicultural; regional.

0–¬ This agency specializes in mainstream nonfiction and fiction, as well as narrative and literary fiction.

**How to Contact:** Query with cover letter, writing sample (no more than 30 pages) and SASE. Accepts e-mail queries. Considers simultaneous queries. Responds in 3 weeks to queries; 6 weeks to mss. Returns materials only with SASE.

**Recent Sales:** Sold 15 titles in the last year. *Fateful Harvest*, by Duff Wilson (HarperCollins); *Midnight to the North*, by Sheila Nickerson (Torch Penguin Putnam); *Sightings*, by Brenda Peterson and Linda Hogan (National Geographic); *Rides: An Auto Biography*, by K. Lake (Algonquin).

**Terms:** Agent receives 15% commission on domestic sales; 20% commission on foreign sales. Offers written contract, binding for book-by-book basis. "We make all our income from commissions. We offer editorial help for some of our clients and help some clients with the development of a proposal, but we do not charge for these services. We do charge clients, after a sale, for express mail, manuscript photocopying costs, foreign postage."

**Writers' Conferences:** Pacific NW Writers Conference (Seattle, July); Writers at Work (Salt Lake City); Writing Rendezvous (Anchorage).

**Tips:** "We are interested in published and non-yet-published writers. Especially encourages writers living in the Pacific Northwest, West Coast, Alaska and Pacific Rim countries to submit work."

**JOHN A. WARE LITERARY AGENCY**, 392 Central Park West, New York NY 10025-5801. (212)866-4733. Fax: (212)866-4734. **Contact:** John Ware. Estab. 1978. Represents 60 clients. 40% of clients are new/unpublished writers. Currently handles: 75% nonfiction books; 25% novels.

● Prior to opening his agency, Mr. Ware served as a literary agency with James Brown Associates/Curtis Brown, Ltd. and as an editor for Doubleday & Company.

**Represents:** Nonfiction books; novels. **Considers these nonfiction areas:** animals; anthropology/archaeology; biography/autobiography; current affairs; health/medicine (academic credentials reqired); history (including oral history, Americana and folklore); language/literature/criticism; music/dance; nature/environment; popular culture; psychology (academic credentials reqired); science/technology; sports; travel; true crime/investigative; women's issues/studies; social commentary; investigative journalism; 'bird's eye' views of phenomena. **Considers these fiction areas:** detective/police/crime; mystery/suspense; thriller; accessible literate noncategory fiction.

**How to Contact:** Query by letter only first, including SASE. No e-mail or fax queries. Considers simultaneous queries Responds in 2 weeks to queries.

**Recent Sales:** *Every Drop for Sale*, by Jeffrey Rothfeder (Putnam); *Ada Blackjack*, by Jennifer Niven (Hyperion); *The Warbler's Call*, by Kenneth A. Brown (Holt); *The Water and the Blood*, by Nancy E. Turner (Regan/HarperCollins). Other clients include Jon Krakauer, Jack Womack, David Robertson.

**Terms:** Agent receives 15% commission on domestic sales; 20% commission on foreign sales; 15% commission on dramatic rights sales. Charges clients for messenger service, photocopying.

**Tips:** "Writers must have appropriate credentials for authorship of proposal (nonfiction) or manuscript (fiction); no publishing track record required. Open to good writing and interesting ideas by new or veteran writers."

**◎ HARRIET WASSERMAN LITERARY AGENCY**, 137 E. 36th St., New York NY 10016. Member of AAR. This agency did not respond to our request for information. Query before submitting.

**◎ WATERSIDE PRODUCTIONS, INC.**, 2191 San Elijo Ave., Cardiff-by-the-Sea CA 92007-1839. (619)632-9190. Fax: (760)632-9295. E-mail: admin@waterside.com. Website: www.waterside.com. **Contact:** Matt Wagner, Margot Maley, David Fugate. President: Bill Gladstone. Estab. 1982. Represents 300 clients. 20% of clients are new/unpublished writers. Currently handles: 100% nonfiction books.

**Member Agents:** Bill Gladstone (trade computer titles, business); Margot Maley (trade computer titles, nonfiction); Matthew Wagner (trade computer titles, nonfiction); Carole McClendon (trade computer titles); David Fugate (trade computer titles, business, general nonfiction, sports books(; Chris Van Buren (trade computer titles, spirituality, self-help); Christian Crumlish (trade computer titles).

**Represents:** Nonfiction books. **Considers these nonfiction areas:** art/architecture/design; biography/autobiography; business/economics; child guidance/parenting; computers/electronic; ethnic/cultural interests; health/medicine; humor/satire; money/finance; nature/environment; popular culture; psychology; sociology; sports.

**How to Contact:** Prefers to read materials exclusively. Query with outline/proposal and SASE. Accepts e-mail queries. Considers simultaneous queries. Responds in 2 weeks to queries; 2 months to mss. Obtains most new clients through recommendations from others.

**Recent Sales:** Sold 300 titles in the last year. *Just for the Fun of It*, by Linus Torvalds (Harper Business); *Windows XP for Dummies*, by Andy Rathbone (Hungry Minds); *The JavaScript Bible*, by Danny Goodman (Hungry Minds); *Dreamweaver Magic*, by Al Sparber (New Ricers).

**Terms:** Agent receives 15% commission on domestic sales; 25% commission on foreign sales. Offers written contract. Charges clients for photocopying and other unusual expenses.

**Writers' Conferences:** "We host the Waterside Publishing Conference each spring in San Diego. Please check our website at www.waterside.com for details."

**Tips:** "For new writers, a quality proposal and a strong knowledge of the market you're writing for goes a long way towards helping us turn you into a published author."

**◎ WATKINS LOOMIS AGENCY, INC.**, 133 E. 35th St., Suite 1, New York NY 10016. (212)532-0080. Fax: (212)889-0506. **Contact:** Katherine Fausset. Estab. 1908. Represents 150 clients.

**Member Agents:** Nicole Aragi (associate); Gloria Loomis (president); Katherine Fausset (agent).

**Represents:** Nonfiction books; novels; short story collections. **Considers these nonfiction areas:** art/architecture/design; biography/autobiography; current affairs; ethnic/cultural interests; history; nature/environment; popular culture; science/technology; true crime/investigative; journalism. **Considers these fiction areas:** literary.

**O─** This agency specializes in literary fiction, nonfiction.

**How to Contact:** Query with SASE by mail only. Prefers to read materials exclusively. Responds in 1 month to queries.

**Recent Sales:** This agency prefers not to share information on specific sales. Clients include Walter Mosley, Edwidge Danticat, Junot Diaz, Cornel West.

**Terms:** Agent receives 15% commission on domestic sales; 20% commission on foreign sales.

**◎ SANDRA WATT & ASSOCIATES**, 1750 N. Sierra Bonita, Hollywood CA 90045-2423. (323)851-1021. Fax: (323)851-1046. E-mail: rondvart@aol.com. Estab. 1977. Represents 55 clients. 15% of clients are new/unpublished writers. Currently handles: 40% nonfiction books; 60% novels.

● Prior to opening her agency, Ms. Watt was vice president of an educational publishing company.

**Member Agents:** Sandra Watt (scripts, nonfiction, novels).

**Represents:** Nonfiction books; novels. **Considers these nonfiction areas:** agriculture/horticulture; animals; anthropology/archaeology; art/architecture/design; crafts/hobbies; current affairs; how-to; humor/satire; language/literature/criticism; memoirs; nature/environment; New Age/metaphysics; popular culture; psychology; religious/inspirational; self-help/personal improvement; sports; travel; true crime/investigative; women's issues/studies; reference. **Considers these fiction areas:** contemporary issues; detective/police/crime; family saga; mainstream/contemporary; mystery/suspense; regional; religious/inspirational; thriller; young adult; women's mainstream novels.

    **O—** This agency specializes in "books to film" and scripts: film noir; family; romantic comedies; books: women's fiction, young adult, mystery, commercial nonfiction. Does not want to receive "first 'ideas' for finished work."

**How to Contact:** Query with SASE. Accepts e-mail and fax queries. Considers simultaneous queries. Responds in 2 weeks to queries; 2 months to mss. Returns materials only with SASE. Obtains most new clients through recommendations from others, referrals and "from wonderful query letters. Don't forget the SASE!"

**Recent Sales:** Sold 6 titles in the last year. *Risk Factor*, by Charles Atkins (St. Martin's Press); *Love is the Only Answer* (Putnam).

**Terms:** Agent receives 15% commission on domestic sales; 25% commission on foreign sales. Offers written contract, binding for 1 year. Charges clients one-time nonrefundable marketing fee of $100 for unpublished authors.

**☑ ◖ SCOTT WAXMAN AGENCY, INC.**, 1650 Broadway, Suite 1011, New York NY 10019. (212)262-2388. Fax: (212)262-0119. Estab. 1997. Member of AAR. Represents 60 clients. 50% of clients are new/unpublished writers. Currently handles: 60% nonfiction books; 40% novels.

    • Prior to opening his agency, Mr. Waxman was editor for five years at HarperCollins.

**Member Agents:** Scott Waxman (all categories of nonfiction, commercial fiction); Wendy Silbert (literary fiction, commercial fiction, narrative nonfiction).

**Represents:** Nonfiction books; novels. **Considers these nonfiction areas:** business/economics; ethnic/cultural interests; health/medicine; history; money/finance; religious/inspirational; sports. **Considers these fiction areas:** action/adventure; historical; literary; mystery/suspense; religious/inspirational; romance (contemporary); sports.

    **O—** "We are always very interested in looking at and expanding our list to include commercial and literary fiction (particularly by recent MFA graduates—Iowa, Johns Hopkins, etc.), as well as many categories of nonfiction."

**How to Contact:** Query with SASE. All unsolicited mss returned unopened. Considers simultaneous queries. Responds in 2 weeks to queries; 6 weeks to mss. Returns materials only with SASE. Obtains most new clients through recommendations from others, solicitations, conferences.

**Terms:** Agent receives 15% commission on domestic sales; 25% commission on foreign sales. Offers written contract; 60 days notice must be given to terminate contract. Charges for photocopying, express mail, fax, international postage, book orders; Refers to editing services for clients only. 0% of business is derived from editing services.

**◖ WECKSLER-INCOMCO**, 170 West End Ave., New York NY 10023. (212)787-2239. Fax: (212)496-7035. **Contact:** Sally Wecksler. Estab. 1971. Represents 25 clients. 50% of clients are new/unpublished writers. Currently handles: 60% nonfiction books; 15% novels; 25% juvenile books.

    • Prior to becoming an agent, Ms. Wecksler was an editor at *Publishers Weekly*; publisher with the international department of R.R. Bowker; and international director at Baker & Taylor.

**Member Agents:** Joann Amparan (general, children's books); Sally Wecksler (general, foreign rights/co-editions, fiction, illustrated books, children's books, business).

**Represents:** Nonfiction books; novels; juvenile books. **Considers these nonfiction areas:** art/architecture/design; biography/autobiography; business/economics; creative nonfiction; current affairs; history; juvenile nonfiction; music/dance; nature/environment; photography; theater/film. **Considers these fiction areas:** contemporary issues; historical; juvenile; literary; mainstream/contemporary; picture books.

    **O—** This agency specializes in nonfiction with illustrations (photos and art). Actively seeking "illustrated books for adults or children with beautiful photos or artwork." Does not want to receive "science fiction or books with violence."

**How to Contact:** Query with SASE, outline, author bio. Responds in 1 month to queries; 2 months to mss. Obtains most new clients through recommendations from others, solicitations.

**Recent Sales:** Sold 11 titles in the last year. *What Every Successful Woman Knows*, by William J. Morin (McGraw-Hill); *Total Career Fitness* (Jossey-Bass).

**Terms:** Agent receives 15% commission on domestic sales; 20% commission on foreign sales. Offers written contract, binding for 3 years.

**Tips:** "Make sure a SASE is enclosed. Send three chapters and outline, clearly typed or word processed, double-spaced, written with punctuation and grammar in approved style. No presentations by fax. Prefers writers who have had something in print."

**◎ THE WENDY WEIL AGENCY, INC.**, 232 Madison Ave., Suite 1300, New York NY 10016. Member of AAR. This agency did not respond to our request for information. Query before submitting.

**◎ CHERRY WEINER LITERARY AGENCY**, 28 Kipling Way, Manalapan NJ 07726-3711. (732)446-2096. Fax: (732)792-0506. E-mail: cherry8486@aol.com. **Contact:** Cherry Weiner. Estab. 1977. Represents 40 clients. 10% of clients are new/unpublished writers. Currently handles: 10-20% nonfiction books; 80-90% novels.

    • This agency is currently not looking for new clients except by referral or by personal contact at writers' conferences.

**Represents:** Nonfiction books; novels. **Considers these nonfiction areas:** self-help/personal improvement; sociology. **Considers these fiction areas:** action/adventure; contemporary issues; detective/police/crime; family saga; fantasy; glitz; historical; mainstream/contemporary; mystery/suspense; psychic/supernatural; romance; science fiction; thriller; westerns/frontier.

    O— This agency specializes in science fiction, fantasy, westerns, mysteries (both contemporary and historical), historical novels, Native American works, mainstream, all the genre romances.

**How to Contact:** Query with SASE. Prefers to read materials exclusively. No e-mail or fax queries. Responds in 1 week to queries; 2 months to mss. Returns materials only with SASE.

**Recent Sales:** Sold 40 titles in the last year. *Earthborn*, by Paul Collins (TOR).

**Terms:** Agent receives 15% commission on domestic sales; 15% commission on foreign sales. Offers written contract. Charges clients for extra copies of mss "but would prefer author do it"; 1st class postage for author's copies of books; Express Mail for important document/manuscripts.

**Writers' Conferences:** Western writers convention; science fiction conventions; fantasy conventions.

**Tips:** "Meet agents and publishers at conferences. Establish a relationship, then get in touch with them reminding them of meetings and conference."

 **THE WEINGEL-FIDEL AGENCY**, 310 E. 46th St., 21E, New York NY 10017. (212)599-2959. **Contact:** Loretta Weingel-Fidel. Estab. 1989. Currently handles: 75% nonfiction books; 25% novels.

    • Prior to opening her agency, Ms. Weingel-Fidel was a psychoeducational diagnostician.

**Represents:** Nonfiction books; novels. **Considers these nonfiction areas:** art/architecture/design; biography/autobiography; memoirs; music/dance; psychology; science/technology; sociology; women's issues/studies; investigative. **Considers these fiction areas:** literary; mainstream/contemporary.

    O— This agency specializes in commercial, literary fiction and nonfiction. Actively seeking investigative journalism. Does not want to receive genre fiction, self-help, science fiction, fantasy.

**How to Contact:** Referred writers only. No unsolicited mss. Obtains most new clients through referrals.

**Recent Sales:** *The New Rabbi*, by Stephen Fried (Bantam); *The Brand New House Book*, by Katherine Salant (Random/Three Rivers); *The V Book*, by Elizabeth G. Stewart, M.D. and Paula Spencer (Bantam).

**Terms:** Agent receives 15% commission on domestic sales; 20% commission on foreign sales. Offers written contract, binding for 1 year; automatic renewal. Bills sent back to clients all reasonable expenses such as UPS, express mail, photocopying, etc.

**Tips:** "A very small, selective list enables me to work very closely with my clients to develop and nurture talent. I only take on projects and writers about which I am extremely enthusiastic."

 **RHODA WEYR AGENCY**, 151 Bergen St., Brooklyn NY 11217. (718)522-0480. **Contact:** Rhoda A. Weyr, president. Estab. 1983. Member of AAR.

**Represents:** Nonfiction books; novels.

    O— This agency is taking on new clients at this time.

**How to Contact:** Obtains most new clients through prefers to work with published/established authors.

**Recent Sales:** Sold over 21 titles in the last year. This agency prefers not to share infomation on specific sales.

**Terms:** Agent receives 15% commission on domestic sales; 20% commission on foreign sales. Charges clients for "heavy duty copying or special mailings (e.g. FedEx etc.)."

**LYNN WHITTAKER, LITERARY AGENT**, Graybill & English, LLC, 1920 N St. NW, Suite 620, Washington DC 20036-1619. (202)861-0106, ext. 37. Fax: (202)457-0662. E-mail: lynnwhittaker@aol.com. Website: www.graybillandenglish.com. Estab. 1998. Member of AAR. Represents 22 clients. 25% of clients are new/unpublished writers. Currently handles: 85% nonfiction books; 15% novels.

    • Prior to becoming an agent, Ms. Whittaker was an editor, owner of a small press, and taught at the college level.

**Represents:** Nonfiction books; novels; short story collections; novellas. **Considers these nonfiction areas:** animals; biography/autobiography; business/economics; current affairs; ethnic/cultural interests; gay/lesbian issues; government/politics/law; history; language/literature/criticism; memoirs; money/finance; multicultural; nature/environment; popular culture; science/technology; sports; travel; women's issues/studies. **Considers these fiction areas:** detective/police/crime; ethnic; experimental; feminist; historical; literary; multicultural; mystery/suspense; sports.

    O— "As a former editor, I especially enjoy working closely with writers to develop and polish their proposal and

**FOR EXPLANATIONS OF THESE SYMBOLS,**
**SEE THE INSIDE FRONT AND BACK COVERS OF THIS BOOK**

manuscripts." Actively seeking literary fiction, sports, history, creative nonfiction of all kinds, nature and science, ethnic/multicultural, women's stories & issues. Does not want to receive romance/women's commercial fiction, children's/young adult, religious, fantasy/horror.

**How to Contact:** Query with SASE, submit proposal package, outline, 2 sample chapter(s). Responds in 2 weeks to queries; 1 month to mss. Returns materials only with SASE. Obtains most new clients through recommendations from others.

**Recent Sales:** *River Woman*, Donna Hemans (Simon & Schuster/Washington Square); *Eleanor Roosevelt's Leadership Advice for Women*, Robin Gerber (Prentice Hall); *A Whole New Ballgame: Michael Jordan Comes to Washington*, Michael Wilbon (Random House); *Stirring the Mud*, by Barbra Herod (Beacon Press). Other clients include Leonard Shapiro, John Tallmadge, Dorothy Sucher, James McGregor Burns, American Women in Radio and Television(AWRT), Phyllis George, Maniza Naqui, Chris Palmer.

**Terms:** Agent receives 15% commission on domestic sales; 20% commission on foreign sales. Offers written contract; 30 days notice must be given to terminate contract. Direct expenses for photocopying of proposals and mss, UPS/FedEx.

**Writers' Conferences:** Creative Nonfiction Conference, (Goucher College MD, August); Washington Independent Writers, (Washington DC, May); Hariette Austin Writers Conference, (Athens GA, July).

**WIESER & WIESER, INC.**, 25 E. 21 St., 6th Floor, New York NY 10010. (212)260-0860. **Contact:** Olga Wieser. Estab. 1975. 30% of clients are new/unpublished writers. Currently handles: 50% nonfiction books; 50% novels.

**Member Agents:** Jake Elwell (history, military, mysteries, romance, sports, thrillers); Olga Wieser (psychology, fiction, pop medical, literary fiction).

**Represents:** Nonfiction books; novels. **Considers these nonfiction areas:** business/economics; cooking/foods/nutrition; current affairs; health/medicine; history; money/finance; nature/environment; psychology; sports; true crime/investigative. **Considers these fiction areas:** contemporary issues; detective/police/crime; historical; literary; mainstream/contemporary; mystery/suspense; romance; thriller.

This agency specializes in mainstream fiction and nonfiction.

**How to Contact:** Query with outline/proposal and SASE. Responds in 2 weeks to queries. Obtains most new clients through queries, authors' recommendations and industry professionals.

**Recent Sales:** *Anatomy of Anorexia*, by Steven Levenkron (Norton); *Tragic Wand*, by James N. Tucker, M.D. (Dutton/Signet); *Napoleon of New York*, by H. Paul Jeffers (Wiley); *The Voyage of the Hunley*, by Edwin P. Hoyt (Burford Books); *Deception Point*, by Dan Brown (Pocket); *Headwind*, by John Nance (Putnam).

**Terms:** Agent receives 15% commission on domestic sales; 20% commission on foreign sales. Offers written contract. Charges clients for photocopying and overseas mailing.

**Writers' Conferences:** BEA; Frankfurt Book Fair.

N **WITHERSPOON & ASSOCIATES, INC.**, 235 E. 31st St., New York NY 10016. (212)889-8626. **Contact:** David Forrer. Estab. 1990. Represents 150 clients. 20% of clients are new/unpublished writers. Currently handles: 50% nonfiction books; 45% novels; 5% story collections.

- Prior to becoming an agent, Ms. Witherspoon was a writer and magazine consultant.

**Member Agents:** Maria Massie; Kimberly Witherspoon; David Forrer; Alexis Hurley.

**Represents:** Nonfiction books; novels. **Considers these nonfiction areas:** anthropology/archaeology; biography/autobiography; business/economics; current affairs; ethnic/cultural interests; gay/lesbian issues; government/politics/law; health/medicine; history; memoirs; money/finance; music/dance; science/technology; self-help/personal improvement; theater/film; travel; true crime/investigative; women's issues/studies. **Considers these fiction areas:** contemporary issues; detective/police/crime; ethnic; family saga; feminist; gay/lesbian; historical; literary; mainstream/contemporary; mystery/suspense; thriller.

**How to Contact:** Query with SASE. Prefers to read materials exclusively. No unsolicited mss. Responds in 1 month to queries. Obtains most new clients through recommendations from others, solicitations, conferences.

**Recent Sales:** This agency prefers not to share information on specific sales.

**Terms:** Agent receives 15% commission on domestic sales; 20% commission on foreign sales. Offers written contract. Office fees are deducted from author's earnings.

**Writers' Conferences:** BEA (Chicago, June); Frankfurt (Germany, October).

**AUDREY A. WOLF LITERARY AGENCY**, 1001 Connecticut Ave. NW, Washington DC 20036. Member of AAR. This agency did not respond to our request for information. Query before submitting.

**THE WONDERLAND PRESS, INC.**, 160 Fifth Ave., Suite 625, New York NY 10010-7003. (212)989-2550. E-mail: litraryagt@aol.com. **Contact:** John Campbell. Estab. 1985. Member of the American Book Producers Association. Represents 32 clients. Currently handles: 90% nonfiction books; 10% novels.

- The Wonderland Press is also a book packager and "in a position to nurture strong proposals all the way from concept through bound books."

**Represents:** Nonfiction books; novels. **Considers these nonfiction areas:** art/architecture/design; biography/autobiography; ethnic/cultural interests; health/medicine; history; how-to; interior design/decorating; language/literature/criticism; photography; popular culture; psychology; self-help/personal improvement. **Considers these fiction areas:** action/adventure; literary; thriller.

☞ This agency specializes in high-quality nonfiction, illustrated, reference, how-to and entertainment books. Does not want to receive poetry, memoir, children's fiction or category fiction.

**How to Contact:** Submit proposal package, outline, SASE. Prefers to read materials exclusively. Accepts e-mail and fax queries. Responds in 5 days to queries; 2 weeks to mss. Obtains most new clients through recommendations from others, solicitations.

**Recent Sales:** Sold 38 titles in the last year. *Nude Body Nude*, by Howard Schatz (HarperCollins); *The Essential Dale Chihuly*, (Abrams).

**Terms:** Agent receives 15% commission on domestic sales. Offers written contract; 30-90 days notice must be given to terminate contract. Offers criticism service, included in 15% commission; Charges clients for photocopying, long-distance telephone, overnight express-mail, messengering.

**Tips:** "We welcome submissions from new authors, but proposals must be unique, of high commercial interest and well written. Follow your talent. Write with passion. Know your market. Submit polished work instead of apologizing for its mistakes, typos, incompleteness, etc. We want to see your best work."

◖ **PAMELA D. WRAY LITERARY AGENCY,** 1304 Dogwood Dr., Oxford AL 36203. (256)835-8008. E-mail: pxchange@hiwaay.net. Website: www.wrayagency.com. **Contact:** Pamela D. Wray. Estab. 1999. Represents 42 clients. 45% of clients are new/unpublished writers. Currently handles: 80% nonfiction books; 20% children's books.

● Prior to becoming an agent, Ms. Wray was CEO and president of her own marketing/design firm for 13 years.

**Member Agents:** Thomas R. Ray (technical, automotive, scientific); David Wray (sports, mechanical); Pamela Wray.

**Represents:** Nonfiction books; children's books. **Considers these nonfiction areas:** art/architecture/design; biography/autobiography; business/economics; child guidance/parenting; computers/electronic; cooking/foods/nutrition; current affairs; education; government/politics/law; health/medicine; how-to; memoirs; military/war; money/finance; religious/inspirational; science/technology; self-help/personal improvement; sociology; sports; travel.

☞ "My specialties are nonfiction (business, technical, medical and memoirs) and in children's books. I have 25 years of personal experience and expertise in marketing, public relations, media consulting, advertising, contract negotiating, publishing and editorial services: freelance, contract and author. I am also a graphic designer and commercial artist. When an author signs with my agency, I personally read, edit and critique his/her manuscript and work with them as a development editor to get the manuscript in the best form for submission. I also develop a detailed marketing and publicity plan, author website, chat room and devise Internet marketing strategies for my clients. The best feature of my services, according to my clients, is that I answer telephone calls, return their calls, and stay in touch with them by e-mail and actively seek author participation in managing their careers by working as a team." Actively seeking children's picture books, nonfiction: business, technical, medical, New Age, government. Does not want to receive hobbies or crafts, design or architecture, nature, photography, or any fiction.

**How to Contact:** Submit synopsis, first 3 chapters and last 3 sample chapter(s), author bio, SASE. Prefers to read materials exclusively. Accepts e-mail and fax queries. Responds in 3 days to queries; 1 month to mss. Returns materials only with SASE. Obtains most new clients through recommendations from others, solicitations, conferences.

**Recent Sales:** Sold 25 titles in the last year.

**Terms:** Agent receives 15% commission on domestic sales; 25% commission on foreign sales; 20% on performance rights commission on dramatic rights sales. Offers written contract, binding for book-to-book basis.; 30-day notice must be given to terminate contract.

**Writers' Conferences:** Southeastern Booksellers Trade Show (Memphis TN); Book Expo America (Chicago IL); Boucheron World Mystery Convention (Washington, DC).

**Tips:** "Please do not e-mail complete manuscripts because I do not have time to read them, just e-mail synopsis first, and I will respond with further information on what I would like to see concerning your manuscripts. When you send a manuscript, please make sure that you have proofread and edited for spelling and major grammatical errors before you submit to an agent. It is disheartening to know that the author has not taken the time to get their manuscripts in form and this lets me know that the author does not pay close attention to the smaller details and is not serious about their work or getting it published. Please send self-addressed, stamped envelopes if you want your work returned; otherwise it is discarded. Please don't submit mansucripts for subjects that I don't represent because I will return these unopened."

☑ ◖ **ANN WRIGHT REPRESENTATIVES,** 165 W. 46th St., Suite 1105, New York NY 10036-2501. (212)764-6770. Fax: (212)764-5125. E-mail: annwrightlit@aol.com. **Contact:** Dan Wright. Estab. 1961. Signatory of WGA. Represents 23 clients. 30% of clients are new/unpublished writers. Currently handles: 50% novels; 40% movie scripts; 10% TV scripts.

● See the expanded listing for this agency in Script Agents.

◖ **WRITERS HOUSE,** 21 W. 26th St., New York NY 10010. (212)685-2400. Fax: (212)685-1781. Estab. 1974. Member of AAR. Represents 440 clients. 50% of clients are new/unpublished writers. Currently handles: 25% nonfiction books; 40% novels; 35% juvenile books.

**Member Agents:** Albert Zuckerman (major novels, thrillers, women's fiction, important nonfiction); Amy Berkower (major juvenile authors, women's fiction, art and decorating, psychology); Merrilee Heifetz (quality children's fiction, science fiction and fantasy, popular culture, literary fiction); Susan Cohen (juvenile and young adult fiction and nonfiction, Judaism, women's issues); Susan Ginsburg (serious and popular fiction, true crime, narrative nonfiction, personality books, cookbooks); Fran Lebowitz (juvenile and young adult, popular culture); Michele Rubin (serious nonfiction); Karen Solem (contemporary and historical romance, women's fiction, narrative nonfiction, horse and animal books); Robin Rue (commercial fiction and nonfiction, YA fiction); Jennifer Lyons (literary, commercial fiction, international fiction, nonfiction and illustrated); Jodi Reamer (juvenile and young adult fiction and nonfiction, adult commercial fiction, popular culture).

**Represents:** Nonfiction books; novels; juvenile books. **Considers these nonfiction areas:** animals; art/architecture/design; biography/autobiography; business/economics; child guidance/parenting; cooking/foods/nutrition; health/medicine; history; interior design/decorating; juvenile nonfiction; military/war; money/finance; music/dance; nature/environment; psychology; science/technology; self-help/personal improvement; theater/film; true crime/investigative; women's issues/studies. **Considers these fiction areas:** action/adventure; comic books/cartoon; confession; contemporary issues; detective/police/crime; erotica; ethnic; experimental; family saga; fantasy; feminist; gay/lesbian; glitz; gothic; hi-lo; historical; horror; humor/satire; juvenile; literary; mainstream/contemporary; military/war; multicultural; multimedia; mystery/suspense; New Age; occult; picture books; plays; poetry; poetry in translation; psychic/supernatural; regional; religious/inspirational; romance; science fiction; short story collections; spiritual; sports; thriller; translation; westerns/frontier; young adult; women's.

    O↖ This agency specializes in all types of popular fiction and nonfiction. Does not want to receive scholarly, professional, poetry or screenplays.

**How to Contact:** Query with SASE. Responds in 1 month to queries. Obtains most new clients through recommendations from others.

**Recent Sales:** *The New New Thing*, by Michael Lewis (Norton); *The First Victim*, by Ridley Pearson (Hyperion); *Into the Garden*, by V.C. Andrews (Pocket); *Midnight Bayou*, by Nora Roberts (Penguin/Putnam); *Love That Dog*, by Sharon Creech (HarperCollins). Other clients include Francine Pascal.

**Terms:** Agent receives 15% commission on domestic sales; 20% commission on foreign sales. Offers written contract, binding for 1 year.

**Tips:** "Do not send mss. Write a compelling letter. If you do, we'll ask to see your work."

✔ Ø **WRITERS' PRODUCTIONS**, P.O. Box 630, Westport CT 06881-0630. (203)227-8199. Fax: (203)227-6349. E-mail: dlm67@worldnet.att.net. **Contact:** David L. Meth. Estab. 1982. Represents 25 clients. Currently handles: 40% nonfiction books; 60% novels.

**Represents:** Nonfiction books; novels; literary quality fiction.

    O↖ This agency specializes in literary-quality fiction and nonfiction, and children's books. "I am not taking on new clients at this time."

**How to Contact:** No new clients accepted at this time. No e-mail or fax queries. Obtains most new clients through recommendations from others.

**Recent Sales:** This agency prefers not to share information on specific sales.

**Terms:** Agent receives 15% commission on domestic sales; 25% commission on foreign sales. Offers written contract. Charges clients for electronic transmissions, long-distance phone calls, express or overnight mail, courier service, etc.

**Tips:** "Send only your best, most professionally prepared work. Do not send it before it is ready. We must have SASE for all correspondence and return of manuscripts."

 ◉ **WRITERS' REPRESENTATIVES, INC.**, 116 W. 14th St., 11th Floor, New York NY 10011-7305. (212)620-0023. E-mail: transom@writersreps.com. Website: www.writersreps.com. **Contact:** Glen Hartley or Lynn Chu. Estab. 1985. Represents 130 clients. 5% of clients are new/unpublished writers. Currently handles: 90% nonfiction books; 10% novels.

    ● Prior to becoming agents, Ms. Chu was a lawyer, and Mr. Hartley worked at Simon & Schuster, Harper & Row and Cornell University Press.

**Member Agents:** Lynn Chu; Glen Hartley; Catharine Sprinkel.

**Represents:** Nonfiction books; novels. **Considers these fiction areas:** literary.

    O↖ This agency specializes in serious nonfiction. Actively seeking serious nonfiction and quality fiction. Does not want to receive motion picture/television screenplays.

**How to Contact:** "Nonfiction submissions should include book proposal, detailed table of contents and sample chapter. For fiction submissions, send sample chapters—not synopses. All submissions should include author biography and publication list. SASE required." Prefers to read materials exclusively. Obtains most new clients through "recommendations from our clients."

**Recent Sales:** Sold 30 titles in the last year. *From Dawn to Decadence*, by Jacques Barun; *Bobos in Paradise*, by David Brooks; *The Mysteries Within*, by Sherwin B. Nuland, M.D.; *Genius and Genius*, by Harold Bloom (Warner Books); *Why There Are No Good Men Left*, by Barbara Dafoe Whitehead (Broadway Books).

**Terms:** Agent receives 15% commission on domestic sales; 20% commission on foreign sales. "We charge clients for out-of-house photocopying as well as messengers, courier services (e.g., Federal Express), etc."

**Tips:** "Always include a SASE that will ensure a response from the agent and the return of material submitted."

✔ ◉ **WYLIE-MERRICK LITERARY AGENCY**, 1138 S. Webster St., Kokomo IN 46902-6357. (765)459-8258 or (765)457-3783. **Contact:** S.A. Martin, Robert Brown. Estab. 1999. Member of SCBWI. Currently handles: 25% nonfiction books; 25% novels; 50% juvenile books.

● Ms. Martin holds a Master's degree in Language Education and is a writing and technology curriculum specialist.

**Member Agents:** S.A. Martin (juvenile/middle grade/young adult); Robert Brown (adult fiction/nonfiction).

**Represents:** Nonfiction books; novels; juvenile books. **Considers these nonfiction areas:** computers/electronic; how-to; juvenile nonfiction; self-help/personal improvement; young adult. **Considers these fiction areas:** historical; juvenile; mainstream/contemporary; picture books; young adult.

O→ This agency specializes in children's and young adult literary as well as mainstream adult fiction. Actively seeking middle-grade/young adult fiction and nonfiction; picturebooks; adult fiction and nonfiction. Does not want to receive any subject not listed above—no erotica, religion, etc.

**How to Contact:** Query with SASE. No e-mail or fax queries. Considers simultaneous queries. Responds in 1 month to queries; 3 months to mss. Returns materials only with SASE. Obtains most new clients through recommendations from others, queries.

**Recent Sales:** This is a new agency with no recorded sales.

**Terms:** Agent receives 15% commission on domestic sales; 20% commission on foreign sales. Offers written contract. Charges clients for postage, photocopying, handling.

**Tips:** "Potential clients should understand their subjects thoroughly and submit only error-free queries and manuscripts. It is critical that writers include the word count and genre of their project in their queries. They should not expect an agent to guess where a project fits into the market place. We only work with writers who show professionalism by understanding the publishing industry, knowing where their projects may fit in the literary market, and having their work polished and ready for publication."

**Ø MARY YOST ASSOCIATES, INC.**, 59 E. 54th St. 72, New York NY 10022. Member of AAR. This agency did not respond to our request for information. Query before submitting.

**✓ Ø ZACHARY SHUSTER HARMSWORTH**, (formerly Zachary Shuster Agency), 729 Boylston St., 5th Floor, Boston MA 02116. (617)262-2400 CA; (212)765-6900 NY. Fax: (617)262-2468 CA ; (212)765-6490 NY. Also: New York Office: 1776 Broadway, Suite 1405, New York, NY 10016. **Contact:** Esmond Harmsworth (CA); Scott Gold (NY). Estab. 1996. Represents 125 clients. 20% of clients are new/unpublished writers. Currently handles: 45% nonfiction books; 45% novels; 5% story collections; 5% scholarly books.

● "Our pricipals include two former publishing and entertainment lawyers, a journalist and an editor/agent."
Lane Zachary was an editor at Random House before becoming an agent.

**Member Agents:** Esmond Harmsworth (commercial and literary fiction, history, science, adventure); Todd Shuster (narrative and prescriptive nonfiction, biography, memoirs); Lane Zachary (biography, memoirs, literary fiction); Jennifer Gates (literary fiction, nonfiction).

**Represents:** Nonfiction books; novels. **Considers these nonfiction areas:** animals; biography/autobiography; business/economics; current affairs; gay/lesbian issues; government/politics/law; health/medicine; history; how-to; language/literature/criticism; memoirs; money/finance; music/dance; psychology; science/technology; self-help/personal improvement; sports; true crime/investigative; women's issues/studies. **Considers these fiction areas:** contemporary issues; detective/police/crime; ethnic; feminist; gay/lesbian; historical; literary; mainstream/contemporary; mystery/suspense; thriller.

O→ This agency specializes in journalist-driven narrative nonfiction, literary and commercial fiction. Actively seeking narrative nonfiction, mystery, commercial and literary fiction, memoirs, history, biographies. Does not want to receive poetry.

**How to Contact:** Query with SASE, submit 50 page sample of ms. Accepts e-mail and fax queries. Considers simultaneous queries. Responds in 3 months to mss. Obtains most new clients through recommendations from others, solicitations, conferences.

**Recent Sales:** Sold 15 titles in the last year. *The Last River*, by Todd Balf (Crown); *Lay That Trumpet in Our Hands*, by Susan McCarthy (Bantam); *Waiting*, by Ha Jin (Alfred A. Knopf—National Book Award winner); *Le Probleme avec Jane*, by Catherine Jenkins (Simon & Schuster). Other clients include Leslie Epstein, David Mixner.

**Terms:** Agent receives 15% commission on domestic sales; 20% commission on foreign sales. Offers written contract, binding for 1 work only.; 30 days notice must be given to terminate contract. Charges clients for postage, copying, courier, telephone. "We only charge expenses if the manuscript is sold."

**Tips:** "We work closely with all our clients on all editorial and promotional aspects of their works."

**Ⓝ Ø SUSAN ZECKENDORF ASSOC. INC.**, 171 W. 57th St., New York NY 10019. (212)245-2928. **Contact:** Susan Zeckendorf. Estab. 1979. Member of AAR. Represents 15 clients. 25% of clients are new/unpublished writers. Currently handles: 50% nonfiction books; 50% novels.

● Prior to opening her agency, Ms. Zeckendorf was a counseling psychologist.

**Represents:** Nonfiction books; novels. **Considers these nonfiction areas:** biography/autobiography; child guidance/parenting; health/medicine; history; music/dance; psychology; science/technology; sociology; women's issues/studies. **Considers these fiction areas:** detective/police/crime; ethnic; historical; literary; mainstream/contemporary; mystery/suspense; thriller.

O→ Actively seeking mysteries, literary fiction, mainstream fiction, thrillers, social history, parenting, classical music, biography. Does not want to receive science fiction, romance. "No children's books."

# insider report

# From lawyer to literary agent: A new partner explains the game

**Esmond Harmsworth**

The grooming years that shaped Esmond Harmsworth's recent career as a literary agent came very early and in unexpected ways.

He can trace most of that grooming to his undergraduate years at Brown University, where his dual majors of history and art history created an anticipated path to Harvard Law School. Life as a literary agent simply hadn't entered the picture yet.

Those years, too, were fraught with much reluctance toward the practice of law. Although law school was "interesting," he says that he clearly felt the weight of past generations of Harmsworth attorneys bearing down on his future.

Yet Harmsworth now recognizes that studying law ultimately influenced his decision, in 1996, to pursue a career as literary agent—one year after graduating from Harvard and clerking in the Supreme Court of Massachussetts. "I didn't expect to move in that direction so soon, but it happened," he says. His early and long-lasting love of reading also swayed him.

In 1996 he joined the literary agency of Zachary & Shuster and has not regretted the transition for one moment. To his benefit, Harmsworth first knew Todd Shuster, also a licensed attorney, from their law school days at Harvard. "I call agenting 'the accidental profession' for good reason," he says. "All my prior school experiences paved the way, surprising even me."

Since that fledgling year, when one of the agency's initial clients was the estate of Louisa May Alcott, it has grown substantially, representing fiction and nonfiction. With locations in New York and Boston, Zachary & Shuster added Harmsworth as a "name partner" in 2000, which means all three partners now share equal responsibilities.

Harmsworth believes this is the ideal profession for him, although he cautions that it's very tough to start a literary agency. "Trying to keep an agency going takes unbelievable patience and perseverance, but that's what it takes to be a writer, too," he says.

The eclectic mix of studying history, art, and law provides Harmsworth with a broad base of subjects about which he's knowledgeable. Even in spite of that base, he knows the chief resource of an agent: he or she must understand the writer's work. "More than just liking or admiring it, I have to understand it completely," he says. "It's the same approach an editor has—that of understanding, of grasping."

Harmsworth adds that while he may make suggestions to a client or prospective client, he never interferes with an author's right to write what he or she desires. "I give advice only," he says. "I share my knowledge of the subject and business. I'll always tell writers if it's publishable, what the market might be, and what interest there is commercially from my point of view." And, he notes, the topic doesn't have to be targeted to his tastes for him to recognize its potential. For instance, books dealing with motherhood may not be relevant for his lifestyle, but he can still judge the commercial value for such titles based on his insider knowledge.

Harmsworth is concerned about the quality of manuscripts and proposals he receives these days. Often they're marred with typos, grammar problems, overt flashiness in appearance, lack of focus, and even lack of clarity. He says that most agents will not tolerate such problems, himself included. He wants to see either a query or manuscript as unflashy as possible. "My pet peeve is this: if you submit a manuscript with glaring errors, it will turn me off quickly." To that end, roughly 30 percent of the manuscripts he receives are returned because of these problems.

He cites a recent manuscript submission as an example. The author included a simple and unadorned three-line cover letter. Yet it hooked Harmsworth; he knew from those three lines that the manuscript was significant and worth reading. The letter was terse and to the point. "A long synopsis is not really helpful, honestly," he says.

Harmsworth believes sloppy queries, manuscripts or proposals justify a rejection, but he stresses that he does open every submission he gets. He subsequently puts a submission into one of three piles: one pile consists of notes for an immediate request of the material described; the second pile is labeled "think about later"; and the third signifies rejection with a remark that the writer might consider another agent for such material.

These days, Harmsworth takes on an equal "50/50" amount of fiction and nonfiction. "I'm looking for fresh, new work, regardless of the genre," he says. "I'm very open to new voices, and I don't restrict myself to looking for a new voice in only fiction or only nonfiction." Nonfiction is easier for him to judge, since it usually appears in the form of a query or book proposal. For nonfiction he prefers reading a query before receiving a proposal. Fiction tends to be more trying; here he prefers receiving 20 to 30 pages of fiction with a brief cover letter.

For Harmsworth, there is no end of being on the lookout for new voices. He reads major magazines and literary journals alike in the quest for potential work, for a potential writer. In fact, the agency recently "discovered" a writer. Upon perusing an issue of the literary magazine *New Letters*, an essay in the issue prompted the agency to contact the writer. In due time the writer signed on with Zachary Shuster Harmsworth, and the writer was contracted to write a full-length memoir based on that one essay.

When an agent-client relationship is established, Harmsworth maintains that a writer should expect a lot from the agent. One of the primary expectations should be returned phone calls— "that may not sound like a big deal, but it is," he says. "Especially if there's an agreement that's been established." Also extremely crucial, and arguably most important of all, is that if a book does *not* sell, the writer should ask the agent for letters from publishers that detail correspondence with the agent.

"A writer should know what happened to a manuscript or proposal, why an editor didn't take it, if there was a glaring problem somehow overlooked in the work. There are many things an editor or publisher might see that could be of invaluable benefit to that piece or work or to that writer," Harmsworth says. It could be a repetitive concern in the manuscript that the author and agent overlooked. In a manner of professionalism, the agent should be able to produce letters from publishers. It's always an advantage for the writer to know what a publisher expresses. Then, too, he wants to look out for the writer's best interests: "Some writers don't want to know what a publisher thinks," he says. "That's perfectly fine, too. I respect that. I wouldn't push it."

Although he hasn't had a stretch of decades in the agent business like some agents he knows, Harmsworth senses he knows the writing and publishing world extremely well. He knows the fundamental questions writers ask, and he knows the truthful answers. The most "Frequently Asked Question" he's asked at conferences, it seems, is "Why hasn't my work had any luck? Why haven't I had any luck as a writer?"

And Harmsworth has an answer: Harmsworth likes to remind writers that many agents he knows are optimistic about receiving manuscripts by writers with interesting projects. However, his experience is that writers send their material to an agent at "too early a stage," he says. It needs re-working, fine-tuning, more editing, more shaping. "If only the writer had spent another six months on the project, working on it, and I mean for both fiction and nonfiction - then it would probably have made a difference." That may be his ultimate advice, he says. Do not hurry the work to an agency; even though a writer is making strides toward getting representation, don't jeopardize a possible relationship by submitting a hastily created manuscript or proposal.

—*Jeffrey Hillard*

**How to Contact:** Query with SASE. Considers simultaneous queries. Responds in 10 days to queries; 3 weeks to mss. Returns materials only with SASE.

**Recent Sales:** *The Key*, by James N. Frey (St. Martin's); *The Hard Scrabble Chronicles*, by Laurie Morrow (Berkley); *The Biography of Bill W.*, by Francis Hartigan (St. Martin's Press).

**Terms:** Agent receives 15% commission on domestic sales; 20% commission on foreign sales. Charges for photocopying, messenger services.

**Writers' Conferences:** Central Valley Writers Conference; The Tucson Publishers Association Conference; Writer's Connection; Frontiers in Writing Conference (Amarillo TX); Golden Triangle Writers Conference (Beaumont TX); Oklahoma Festival of Books (Claremont OK); Mary Mount Writers Conference.

**Tips:** "We are a small agency giving lots of individual attention. We respond quickly to submissions."

# Script Agents

Making it as a screenwriter takes time. For starters, a good script takes time. It takes time to write. It takes time to rewrite. It takes time to write the four or five scripts that precede the really great one. The learning curve from one script to the next is tremendous, and you'll probably have a drawer full of work before you're ready to approach an agent. Your talent has to show on the page, and the page has to excite people.

You'll need both confidence and insecurity at the same time. Confidence to enter the business at all. For a twenty-two-week season, a half-hour sitcom buys two freelance scripts. There are less than 300 network television movies and less than 100 big screen feature films produced each year. Nevertheless, in recent years the number of cable channels buying original movies has grown, independent film houses have sprouted up all over the country, and more studios are buying direct to video scripts—all of which offer a wide range of opportunities for emerging scriptwriters. If you're good and you persevere, you will find work.

Use your insecurity to spur you and your work on to become better. Accept that, at the beginning, you know little. Then go out and learn. Read all the books you can find on scriptwriting, from format to dramatic structure. Learn the formulas, but don't become formulaic. Observe the rules, but don't be predictable. Absorb what you learn, and make it your own.

And finally, you'll need a good agent. In this book we call agents handling screenplays or teleplays script agents, but in true West Coast parlance they are literary agents, since they represent writers as opposed to actors or musicians. Most studios, networks, and production companies will return unsolicited manuscripts unopened for legal protection. An agent has the entree to get your script on the desk of a story analyst or development executive.

The ideal agent understands what a writer writes, is able to explain it to others, and has credibility with individuals who are in a position to make decisions. An agent sends out material, advises what direction a career should take, and makes the financial arrangements. And how do you get a good agent? By going back to the beginning—great scripts.

## THE SPEC SCRIPT

There are two sides to an agent's representation of a scriptwriter: finding work on an existing project and selling original scripts. Most writers break in with scripts written on "spec," that is, on speculation without a specific sale in mind. A spec script is a calling card that demonstrates skills, and gets your name and abilities before influential people. Movie spec scripts are always original, not for a sequel. Spec scripts for TV are always based on existing TV shows, not for an original concept.

More often than not, a spec script will not be made. An original movie spec can either be "optioned" or "bought" outright, with the intention of making a movie, or it can attract rewrite work on a script for an existing project. For TV, on the basis of the spec script, a writer can be invited in to pitch five or six ideas to the producers. If an idea is bought, the writer is paid to flesh out the story to an outline. If that is acceptable, the writer can be commissioned to write the script. At that point the in-house writing staff comes in, and in a lot of cases, rewrites the script. But it's a sale, and the writer receives the residuals every time that episode is shown anywhere in the world. The goal is to sell enough scripts so you are invited to join the writing staff.

What makes a good spec script? Good writing for a start. Write every single day. Talk to as many people you can find who are different from you. Take an acting class to help you really hear dialogue. Take a directing class to see how movies are put together. If you are just getting started, working as an assistant to an established screenwriter can be beneficial. You get excellent experience, and as your name becomes attached to scripts, you'll have more assets to bring with you as you start to approach agents.

Learn the correct dramatic structure, and internalize those rules. Then throw them away and write intuitively. The three-act structure is basic and crucial to any dramatic presentation. Act 1—get your hero up a tree. Act 2—throw a rock at him. Act 3—get him down. Some books will tell you that certain events have to happen by a certain page. What they're describing is not a template but a rhythm. Good scriptwriting is good storytelling.

## Spec scripts for movies

If you're writing for movies, explore the different genres until you find one you feel comfortable writing. Read and study scripts for movies you admire to find out what makes them work. Choose a premise for yourself, not "the market." What is it you care most about? What is it you know the most about? Write it. Know your characters and what they want. Know what the movie is about, and build a rising level of tension that draws the reader in and makes her care about what happens.

For feature films, you'll need two or three spec scripts, and perhaps a few long-form scripts (miniseries, movies of the week or episodics) as well. Your scripts should depict a layered story with characters who feel real, each interaction presenting another facet of their personalities.

Although you should write from your heart, keep in mind that Hollywood follows trends like no other industry. A script on a hot topic means more money for the studio. Current big genres are teen movies with edge, *Sixth Sense*-type thrillers, family-oriented stories, and real-life dramas. Instead of trying to write to a trend, use your stellar script to start one of your own.

## Spec scripts for TV

If you want to write for TV, watch a lot of it. Tape several episodes of a show, and analyze them. Where do the jokes fall? Where do the plot points come? How is the story laid out? Read scripts of a show to find out what professional writers do that works. (Script City, (800)676-2522, and Book City, (800)4-CINEMA, have thousands of movie and TV scripts for sale.)

Your spec script will demonstrate your knowledge of the format and ability to create believable dialogue. Choosing a show you like with characters you're drawn to is important. Current hot shows for writers include *3rd Rock From the Sun*, *Everybody Loves Raymond*, *Law and Order*, *Will & Grace*, and *Felicity*. Newer shows may also be good bets, such as *Popular* and *The Hughleys*. If a show has been on three or more years, a lot of story lines have already been done, either on camera or in spec scripts. Your spec should be for today's hits, not yesterday's.

Television shows where the cast is predominantly composed of teenagers continue to be extremely popular. Shows like *Buffy the Vampire Slayer* and *Dawson's Creek* appealed so strongly to both adult and teen audiences that almost every network raced to add similar shows to their fall lineup. Animated sitcoms like *The Simpsons*, which are aimed at adult audiences, also remain favorites. Most networks now have animated shows in prime-time slots.

You probably already want to write for a specific program. Paradoxically, to be considered for that show your agent will submit a spec script for a different show, because—to protect themselves from lawsuits—producers do not read scripts written for their characters. So pick a show similar in tone and theme to the show you really want to write for. If you want to write for *Dharma & Greg*, submit a spec script for *Two Guys and a Girl*. The hour-long dramatic shows are more individual in nature. You practically would have had to attend med school to write for *ER*, but *Law and Order* and *NYPD Blue* have a number of things in common that would make them good specs for one another. Half-hour shows generally have a writing staff and only occasionally buy freelance scripts. Hour-long shows are more likely to pick up scripts written by freelancers.

In writing a spec script, you're not just writing an episode. You're writing an *Emmy-winning* episode. You are not on staff yet; you have plenty of time. Make this the episode the staff writers wish they had written. But at the same time, certain conventions must be observed. The regular characters always have the most interesting story line. Involve all the characters in the episode. Don't introduce important new characters.

## SELLING YOURSELF TO THE SALESPEOPLE

Scriptwriting is an art and craft. Marketing your work is salesmanship, and it's a very competitive world. Read the trades, attend seminars, stay on top of the news. Make opportunities for yourself.

But at the same time, your writing side always has to be working, producing pages for the selling side to hawk. First you sell yourself to an agent. Then the agent sells herself to you. If you both feel the relationship is mutually beneficial, the agent starts selling you to others.

All agents are open to third-party recommendations, referrals from a person whose opinion is trusted. To that end, you can pursue development people, producers' assistants, anyone who will read your script. Mail room employees at the bigger agencies are agents in training. They're looking for the next great script that will earn them a raise and a promotion to the next rung.

The most common path, however, is through a query letter. In one page you identify yourself, what your script is about and why you're contacting this particular agent. Show that you've done some research, and make the agent inclined to read your script. Find a connection to the agent like "we both attended the same college," or mention recent sales you know through your reading the agent has made. Give a three- or four-line synopsis of your screenplay, with some specific plot elements, not just a generic premise. You can use comparisons as shorthand. *Men in Black* could be described as "*Ghostbusters* meets *Alien*" and lets the reader into the story quickly, through something she's familiar with already. Be sure to include your name, return address, and telephone number in your letter, as well as a SASE. If the response is positive, the agent probably will want to contact you by phone to let you know of her interest, but she will need the SASE to send you a release form that must accompany your script.

Your query might not be read by the agent but by an assistant. That's okay. There are few professional secretaries in Hollywood, and assistants are looking for material that will earn them the step up they've been working for.

To be taken seriously, your script must be presented professionally. You must follow predetermined script formats. Few agents have time to develop talent. A less than professional script will be read only once. If it's not ready to be seen, you may have burned that bridge. Putting the cart before the horse, or the agent before the script, will not get you to where you want to go.

Read everything you can about scripting and the industry. As in all business ventures, you must educate yourself about the market to succeed. There are a vast number of books to read. Samuel French Bookstores [(323)876-0570] offers an extensive catalog of books for scriptwriters. *From Script to Screen*, by Linda Seger and Edward Jay Whetmore, J. Michael Straczynski's *The Complete Book of Scriptwriting* and Richard Walter's *Screenwriting* are highly recommended books on the art of scriptwriting. Study the correct format for your type of script. Cole and Haag's *Complete Guide to Standard Script Formats* is a good source for the various formats. Newsletters such as *Hollywood Scriptwriter* are good sources of information. Trade publications such as *The Hollywood Reporter*, *Premiere*, *Variety* and *Written By* are invaluable as well. A number of smaller magazines have sprung up in the last few years, including *Script Magazine* and *New York Screenwriter*. See the "Books & Publications of Interest" section for more information.

# In the Eyes of the Professor: Secrets to Getting Your Script Read

## BY RICHARD WALTER

Why do so many writers perpetuate the myth that agents will not read material by new writers?

Two accomplished writers whom I first came to know through our program at UCLA recently told me aspiring writers actually become angry with them when they insist they won their first jobs as staff writers on a long running television comedy not through some fancy political ploy, but simply by writing speculative episodes and penning quick, smart letters to agents.

**Richard Walter**

## MAIL MANNERS

One screenwriting educator, however, complains it is absurd for me to suggest writers can win an agent's consideration by simply writing a smart query letter. He argues that what really counts are elaborate, sophisticated alliances, interlocking matrices of relationships developed by schmoozing it up at seminars and panels and in chic, trendy showbiz restaurants, and getting to know the right people. He asserts the reason I tell this dreadful lie is because it's what writers want to hear. Ironically, the last thing writers want to hear is that it is easy to get an agent to consider a screenplay. This is because it is far more soothing to contemplate there is something wrong with the agent than to confront the sorry reality that there's something wrong with the query letter or, worse, the script.

Instead of worrying about clever schemes for winning an agent's agreement to represent a screenplay, writers should worry about writing a screenplay that is genuinely worthy of a good agent's representation. In fact, agents eagerly and urgently seek scripts. My office at UCLA receives dozens of requests every week for new material from new writers. Callers and correspondents actually get mad at me if I fail to supply them. If agents are hard to read, if they are reluctant to consider new writers, how can one explain all of the telephone traffic, letters, faxes, e-mail and even messengers showing up in the flesh, refusing to leave until they are handed a screenplay for delivery to their bosses?

On one occasion no fewer than six agents from what is arguably the most prestigious agency in town showed up in person at my office to stage a full-fledged commando raid (I could have sworn I saw hand grenades strapped to their belts) in demand of screenplays by new writers. I have seen agents appear uninvited at screenwriting award ceremonies, clipboards at the ready, signing new writers as they strut through the door.

### Writing the query

What counts, again, is the writing. To reach an agent a writer need merely write a sharp, short, smart, savvy query letter. If the query letter is properly written it will lead to an invitation

---

**RICHARD WALTER**, *professor and chairman of the UCLA Film and Television Writing Program, lectures on screenwriting throughout the world, and is the author of* Screenwriting: The Art, Craft and Business of Film and Television Writing *and* The Whole Picture: Strategies for Screenwriting Success in the New Hollywood.

to submit the screenplay. In this way it is possible to turn an unsolicited script into one an agent will truly plead to read.

From time to time writers complain they have tried this technique and failed. They assert they wrote to any number of agents and received no solicitations to submit their script; their requests were either outright refused or, more typically, ignored.

When I hear such stories I invariably ask the writers to read me their query letter. In virtually every instance the problem becomes plain as day: the letter is a train wreck. More than likely it contains too much information about the writer and, even more often, about the script.

One of these writers, however, read me his letter, and frankly, it struck me as perfect. I could not for the life of me imagine how any agent—much less dozens upon dozens of agents—could have refused the opportunity to consider the script. After a long silence during which we collectively pondered his dilemma, the writer muttered under his breath, "Maybe it's the synopsis."

"The what?" I asked.

"The synopsis," he said again.

"You sent a synopsis along with your letter?" If a writer encloses a synopsis in his letter, that is what the agent will read.

But don't some agents and agencies insist upon seeing a synopsis?

If they do, keep it short. Treat the synopsis as a tease, a mini-Previews of Coming Attractions dedicated to seducing the agent into wanting to know more about the project. In this regard, the more information you provide, the less likely the agent will want to read the script.

If an agent insists on a synopsis, double-space it and limit it to a single page. Don't try to cram each and every tidbit of story and character into the synopsis. The purpose is to coax the agent into making those discoveries in the script itself.

This query-letter "system" was recently tested and confirmed to work quite well. A screenwriting instructor in a major cosmopolitan center—thousands of miles from Hollywood—conducted a survey at two different university film departments. Students in four screenwriting classes wrote query letters and sent them to a cold sampling of agents gleaned form the Writers Guild Franchised Agencies list.

Before the letters were mailed, however, they had to be approved both by the instructor and all the students in the class. The letters were painstakingly studied, with an eye toward economy and seduction. They went out to agents only after winning approval.

The reported "take" rate (the proportion of favorable responses—that is, invitation to submit the scripts): 96 percent! When the query letters were adjudged to be properly, effectively written, 96 of 100 agents agreed to consider the scripts.

Remember, they did not agree to represent the scripts but merely to consider them. Once an agent agrees to consider a script, it is the script's merit—or lack thereof—that will persuade him to represent it or, conversely, to pass.

If writers are reluctant to believe that agents want to consider their scripts, they find it even more improbable that agents actually want to like those scripts. Should that come as a surprise? Does not anybody reading material prefer to like it than not? And would not any agent covet the prestige of launching a new writer, to say nothing of garnering a hefty commission on the sale of his script?

This is one of those truths that is so obvious it is difficult to see. It obliterates the myth that agents are generally cynics whose greatest pleasure is to dash writers' dreams, break their hearts, bust their chops. On the contrary, agents want to respect what they read. Writers need to recognize the relationship between artist and representative—like that among all members of the creative film family—is not adversarial but collaborative. Writers and agents are not at odds with one another. Both need the same thing: a script that is marketable.

## Sending the query or script

Once again, the simplest, most effective, most straightforward way to win an agent's consideration is simply to write him a standard query letter. I stand behind that proposition today more firmly than ever.

Do not send the letter, or the script, return-receipt requested. Sometimes these parcels result in a notice being left by the carrier instructing the addressee to report to the post office. It's damned frustrating for an agent to schlepp there and stand in line only to discover that what awaits her is a letter from a writer seeking permission to submit a script, or the script itself. It creates an impression, all right, but not the kind any smart writer seeks.

It is a wise idea, also, to avoid any fancy tricks or stunts when submitting scripts. Within days of the birth of my son, for example, I received a package, brightly gift-wrapped, with the inscription "It's a Boy!!!" emblazoned upon it. I figured it was a present for the baby. But it was a screenplay. To the writers who had collaborated on its creation it represented their metaphorical "child." Their hope was to attract special attention.

They attracted special attention, to be sure, but not of the kind they had sought.

More recently I received a huge box. Inside was nothing but packing foam. Amidst all the foam I finally found a single fortune cookie. The "fortune" was the news (presumably lucky for me) that a new script by a new writer was on its way.

I admit it: I was annoyed at having squandered even a little bit of time searching through the packing material to see if there was anything in there, wondering whether or not something had been lost. And I was doubly disturbed having to trek down the hall to the waste bin in order to ditch all that trash. Did this take up a great deal of time? No. But all of the time it did take up—every split second of it—was wasted; it achieved absolutely no other purpose than to create an unfavorable impression upon a potential reader.

The single most preposterous script-submission stunt I ever heard of involved a huge package arriving by special messenger at an agent's office. Inside was a birdcage containing a screenplay and a live bird.

The hapless creature turned out to be a homing pigeon. Attached to its leg was a small leather pouch. A note contained instructions: upon reading the script, the agent was to check "yes" or "no" on a scrap of paper, insert it in the pouch and release the bird at the window. Presumably, the bird would carry the notice to its sender.

But alas, as the script lay at the bottom of the cage, it already contained commentary from the bird; commentary that was at once fowl and foul.

So write a simple, professional query for your script submission, one that lures the agent into wanting to see more. And don't include the script with the letter unless it's requested!

Here follows a reconstruction of a letter written to agents by a film student some years ago.

Note that the first paragraph—one whole sentence long—introduces the writer in a brief but enticing way.

The next paragraph, also a single sentence, hardly describes the screenplay at all. It sets the

---

Dear Mr. Lastfogel:

I am a student at UCLA in the Master of Fine Arts program in Screenwriting.

I have written a screenplay, SHADOW CLAN, an action/adventure story set in contemporary New York City and ninth-century Scotland.

I eagerly seek representation. May I send you the script for your consideration?

Cordially,

genre, time, place and nothing else. Who could refuse to read an action/adventure screenplay set in contemporary New York and ninth-century Scotland?

The letter jumps right to the point, asking: Will you read this and consider representing it/me? That's all a script query must contain. Don't tell too much, just make the agent interested in your script idea. Then you'll get to send the script.

## A FOOLPROOF, SHOCKPROOF, WATERPROOF, TAMPER-RESISTANT METHOD FOR REACHING AND ACQUIRING AN AGENT

While query letters may work for writers seeking representation for feature-length film scripts, it is somewhat trickier in television, particularly for writers seeking to write episodes of existing series.

Too many writers—like too many civilians—are snobs about television. In certain corners of institutions of higher learning, television is referred to only in whispers and even then often as "the T word."

But television is like all other creative expression—film, theater, dance, music, painting, sculpture, literature—in that most of it fails and some small portion of it is truly excellent. Still, even experienced television writers who ought to know better will tell you the real glamour is in film, and they're merely biding their time in TV until they make their breakthrough into theatrical features.

When the Writers Guild went on strike some years ago, I was assigned picket duty at a studio gate, where I ran into an old film school classmate from the University of Southern California, action/adventure meister John Milius (Apocalypse Now, etc.). Wielding bright neon STRIKE! signs, we tramped up and back before the entrance to NBC's massive facility in Burbank.

Spotting our signs, several tourists approached us. "You guys writers?"

We nodded.

"How do you get into TV?" one asked.

"What you really should ask," John quipped, "is how do you get out of TV?"

### TV and money: what's in it for you?

But the truth is that television is the arena where writers are treated and paid most generously. If a top screenplay price is, say, 4 million dollars, consider that for creating and writing the TV series Family Ties, Gary David Goldberg earned more than 40 million dollars.

The greatest show business fortunes consist of trillions of nickels and dimes: record and publishing royalties and, especially, television residuals. In a typical season, for example, an episode of a TV series will rerun in prime time at least once and almost certainly twice. Each rerun under such circumstances pays the writer 100 percent in residuals; that is to say, each time the show is rerun he is paid all over again the whole amount he was paid for writing the piece in the first place. If he got $25,000 for a half-hour sitcom script, in that first season alone he will likely take home three times that much for that one episode.

If that were the end of it, it would still be generous compensation by any standard. But it is not the end; it is merely the beginning. In subsequent seasons the writer will continue to earn residuals, albeit on a declining scale. If, however, the show goes to syndication, even as the individual airings pay less and less, there are more and more of them, so the overall amount of money that accrues actually soars.

And perhaps best of all, to earn all of these payments the writer has to do exactly this: nothing! The residuals that flow to him during his lifetime—and thereafter to his heirs—are payments for work he has already done.

Generally speaking, therefore, financial compensation in television is far greater than in film. The various collaborators in a television series that produces a sufficient number of episodes to qualify for syndication may well share more than a billion dollars among them.

A hit television series is like Star Wars, E.T., and Jurassic Park all rolled up in one. And you can probably toss in Batman, Home Alone and Independence Day, too.

As dizzying as such remuneration may be, writers in television are also treated better than feature film writers, in a host of ways. This ought to come as no surprise, as it is television writers who make up the majority of working Writers Guild members and it is natural to assume, therefore, that the rules and regulations would be designed to favor them.

Note, for example, that a writer at a pitch meeting for a film may be asked to return for further discussions regarding a particular proposal. Indeed, he can be invited back again and again without limit.

And without compensation.

Some writers may consider the many meetings to be encouraging and flattering, but the experience quickly comes to resemble free brain-picking.

In television, on the other hand, after an initial pitch meeting, if a producer wants to discuss the matter further, he must pay at least Writers Guild scale for a story. These days that's something like $4,000-6,000 minimum—and that for only a 2- or 3-page double-spaced outline.

No wonder the television market is tight; no wonder it's uniquely difficult to reach agents handling writers in that arena. Exacerbating this situation is the fact that over the past decade the freelance market in television has largely evaporated. Writers who break through and enjoy sustained success almost invariably are those who, after selling a handful of episodes, end up on staff at a particular show. This causes the availability of freelance work to shrink still further as staff writers consume more and more of the assignments.

## Breaking in

Good news: there is a solution.

Upon encountering resistance from television agents, writers can take another tack altogether: write to the writers. Which writers? The writers of the shows they hope to crack.

How can one find out the names of these writers? Copy them from the tube. Watch the credits as they flit past; if they move too quickly, record the show on your VCR and exploit your freeze-frame capability so there's ample time to read the name (and to spell it correctly).

Once one has the name of the writer, how can one find out the address?

All film and television writers have the same address.

Here it is: c/o The Writers Guild of America, West, Inc., 7000 W. Third Street, Los Angeles, CA 90048.

What should these letters say? First of all, they should praise the writer. You'll never go wrong praising talent. You need to invent some breezy, respectful, affirmative opening gambit. For example:

I offer two promises. One: the sun will set in the west. Two: the writer will answer your letter.

There are two reasons you can count on a reply.

1. Every single successful professional writer—without exception—was once totally un-known.

Lingering in the memory of even the hardest-bitten steel-tempered veteran is the recollection of his scuffling days; he'll be eager to provide support to a fledgling scribe who approaches him in a clever and sincere and, most important of all, respectful manner.

But before all else, you can count on this:

2. Every writer will do anything, will seek any excuse, to avoid working upon the particular assignment in front of him at any given moment.

What could be more odious, more flat-out frightening, than to confront the endless task of filling blank paper—or glowing phosphor—with language worthy of an audience's time and attention?

This is why any writer will seize upon the opportunity to reply. It is the perfect outlet for

Dear [writer's name],

Likely I watch more television than anyone ought to, but every once in a while a show comes along that makes it all worthwhile. Your episode [episode title] of [series title] changed my life forever.

**Next, praise some specific aspect of the writer's work:**

I recall in particular the way [character] confronted [character] over the question of [issue]. When she tells him [line of dialogue] and he responds [line of dialogue], I just about fell out of my La-Z-Boy™ recliner.

I even dropped the channel zapper (which my schnauzer promptly ate).

In what might otherwise have been but a mildly diverting half-hour you were able to keenly and precisely articulate extraordinary insights into the human condition. I'll never view the question of [issue] in quite the same way again.

**Do not state that you are yourself a writer, and that you are willing to commit unnatural acts upon him if he'll only read your work and recommend it to his own agent. Instead, self-effacingly wonder aloud about some arbitrary and mundane aspect of the writer's work habits.**

I've always wondered about the day-to-day methods of talented, disciplined artists such as yourself. I am curious to know, for example, whether you write with pencil and ruled yellow legal pad or utilize a word processor.

Of course, I have no right to presume you will respond to such questions; I recognize that they're none of my business and, moreover, that you are undoubtedly too busy creating still more dazzling fare.

Therefore, I won't squander another moment of your time. Please know that I am forever grateful for your having touched my life. I offer you congratulations and thanks for sharing your considerable gift with me and millions of viewers all around the nation and the world.

Sincerely,

[your name]

---

him to avoid his own work. It offers him a double whammy: he gets to put off his own work and he also wins the chance (not without justification) to feel like a good guy, a caring, generous soul.

Ask yourself: If you were a successful writer and received such an inquiry, would you not reply?

Of course you would.

A friend of mine who is now an enormously successful writer tells me that when he was completely unknown, fresh out of college and working a grim day job, he wrote a letter of appreciation—really nothing more than fan mail—to none other than the renowned novelist, essayist, poet and critic John Updike, complimenting him on his latest book.

He mailed the letter on Monday. Thursday of that same week, there was a handwritten nine-page reply from Updike. No doubt there is solid testimony here to Updike's generosity. But you can also be certain that even John Updike wants to avoid whatever it is that's in front of him on his desk at any given moment.

In the proposed sample letter I suggest that after praising the writer you ask not about profound literary issues but, instead, about the writer's personal work habits. Are writers willing to discuss this subject with perfect strangers?

Just try to stop them!

Just try to get them to shut up!

Writers crave the opportunity to wax prolific, to rant and rave about their particular and peculiar quirks: what level of rag content they seek in their writing bond, how soft the lead in their pencil, which blend of coffee roast they favor in order to stay awake while slogging through their tedium.

In the movie *The Front* (Walter Bernstein), Woody Allen portrays a bartender who fronts for blacklisted writers, writers who cannot sell under their own names because they are politically out of favor. Woody thus receives screen credit for stories he did not write, then secretly passes the remuneration to the actual writers.

His girlfriend quizzes him about his writing but he is always reticent. He asserts that he simply does not like to discuss it. "I don't get it," the girlfriend complains. "Generally you can't get writers to cease prattling on and on about their writing."

Amen to that!

Once the writer has replied to your letter, write back to him, thank him and perhaps ask yet another innocuous question or two. Eventually you will have established enough of a relationship gingerly and delicately to presume to ask the guy to read your script. Perhaps you'll write something like this:

> . . .and finally, I want to let you know that you have so inspired me that I've myself actually written an episode. I do not tell you this in order to solicit your consideration of my wretchedly amateurish effort with an eye toward a recommendation to an agent (yours, for example) but merely to share with you how affirmatively your creativity has affected one particular member of your vast, adoring audience.

I promise two things. One: the sun will rise in the east. Two: the writer will volunteer to show your script to his agent or, at the very least, to recommend it to another agent or even a producer.

He may well do this even if he thinks the script stinks. Perhaps he wants to demonstrate to you—and to himself—that he has the power to get a script deal. But whatever his motivation, it will finally all come down to one and only one thing: the script.

Let it, therefore, be worthy.

# From Submission to Production

BY JOHN MORGAN WILSON

Each year in Hollywood, thousands of scripts are submitted to producers, mostly by agents. Into each production office come hundreds, sometimes thousands of these submissions.

Those sent by the more respected or successful agents generally get read first, but producers try to respond to all agented submissions, since their relationships with agents are crucial to their receiving a continual flow of material. Few producers accept submissions directly from writers for two reasons: taking submissions only through agents enables producers to screen out the weaker material, and it protects them from possible later charges of idea theft or plagiarism. Even those producers who say they will read unsolicited submissions tend to put them aside in a slush pile where they remain unread for weeks, months—sometimes forever. (Many agents do the same with scripts that come in without a referral from a top client.) Most producers who accept unsolicited submissions will require the writer to sign a release form or waiver, which absolves the company from any obligation to read or return the material and limits their liability in any possible future legal actions regarding a similar project they might produce.

How these scripts are physically handled varies from office to office. Some offices are well-organized, with efficient database systems for logging and filing incoming material and moving it through the reading process, from readers to development executives to producers at the top, if the script should get that far. Other offices, particularly the smaller, financially marginal operations, are often sloppy and inconsiderate in dealing with submissions, sometimes literally stacking them up willy nilly on side tables, or tossing them into cardboard boxes in corners, where they get read in no particular order, if they get read at all.

The more professional and efficient production companies prioritize incoming material for reading and try to respond within two weeks. With the majority of these companies, a script or other property will pass through a number of steps.

## Coverage

A "reader" reads the script and prepares a "reader's report," or "coverage." The coverage customarily identifies the script by genre; compresses the story line to a logline description; provides a plot synopsis and thumbnail descriptions of the main characters; offers a fairly detailed evaluation of the material (usually a page); and may include a final set of evaluation boxes to check such as recommend, maybe and pass, or even a place to recommend the writer for an availability file or assignment on another project if the material shows strength in a particular area (structure or dialogue, for example). The exact nature and format of the reader's report will vary from company to company, as will the individual reader's influence in how a script is received higher up, but most readers' reports serve only as the first stopping off point for a script.

---

**JOHN MORGAN WILSON** *has been a freelance reader for* Showtime, *acquisitions coordinator for Viacom Enterprises, news editor and segment producer for Fox Entertainment News, and writer or writer-producer of more than 60 documentary and reality-based TV episodes, including the Discovery Channel's "Hollywood's Greatest Stunts." Wilson is also an award-winning reporter and author of the Benjamin Justice mystery series. This piece is excerpted from his book* Inside Hollywood, *published by Writer's Digest Books.*

This may seem to diminish the purpose and importance of the reader's work, but in a busy production office, studio or agency, it is vital for both legal and administrative reasons. It provides development executives with a concise, efficient way to track and deal with the constant flow of written material, and well-organized records of when it was received, who read it and responded to it, and when it was returned, should that ever become an issue down the road. (Plagiarism and copyright infringement lawsuits are common in the movie industry. Most of these lawsuits are dismissed, and most of the rest are settled for relatively small sums out of court. Now and then, however, writers who feel their story lines have been unfairly ripped off bring strong, well-documented cases, prove them in court, and win sizable settlements, sometimes in the millions of dollars in the cases of very successful films. These are generally paid, at least in part, by special studio insurance policies.)

## The next reading

Readers come in all types, from envious and mean-spirited to intelligent and fair; some will never amount to much career-wise, while others will go on to be top development executives, producers, agents, or even screenwriters. Development executives are aware of this disparity in the quality of reader coverage and read it accordingly, rarely accepting a reader's evaluation at face value. The development executive is primarily looking for a type of story the company might be interested in that looks reasonably well-written in the reader's eyes. If the reader's report indicates a script is not remotely something that would interest the company—a dark, erotic thriller submitted to a company that produces lighthearted family films, for example—the development person may not bother to read the script. Good production companies try to have every submission read beyond the entry-level reader stage, although some busy executives sometimes rely on coverage or a development person's evaluation in lieu of actually reading the script, even when negotiating for it. (I once saw this happen right before my eyes with coverage I had written, as my boss paraphrased my evaluation over the phone as if the words were his own.)

## The story meeting

The better readers are both literate and understand the movie marketplace, and are thrilled when they find that gem of a script among the hundreds of mediocre or inferior screenplays they must read. They know that writing good coverage on a script that eventually is purchased and becomes a hit movie can be important to their careers. (Many others, of course, are timid and weak-willed, fearful of recommending a script the boss might not like.) In some companies, a reader will be in a position to champion a script he or she particularly likes in a "story meeting." In turn, a development executive will take up the cause for a particular script he or she favors, supporting and "selling" it to the upper executives, both for the desire to develop a good movie and the career advancement that is built on such successful choices.

## The pass stage

The fate of many scripts is decided in the story meeting, where scripts are either retained for further reading, discussion and possible deal-making (the lucky few), or rejected outright (the great majority). Scripts are turned down either by phone (the "telephone pass") or mail (the "pass letter"). As a rule, producers try to pass on projects gently, out of kindness using euphemisms and vague excuses rather than the truth, but also to avoid alienating agents or writers they may want to work with again. (Rarely will a copy of a reader's report reach the hands of the agent or writer, unless through close inside contacts.) It is then up to the agent or writer to try to get another reading for the script from another producer (or the agent of a star who might be interested, if that's warranted). These meetings tend to be held in a room convenient for all, and move along at a fairly brisk pace, since everyone in Hollywood is always behind schedule (especially in their reading), late for the next appointment, or coming in late from the last one.

Worth nothing: In Hollywood, meetings are cancelled or postponed by overscheduled executives almost as often as they are announced.

## The deal memo

If a company decides it wants to become involved with a particular property—treatment, original screenplay, published novel—negotiations take place between the production company and, ideally, the agent and/or lawyer representing the writer. These meetings range from easy and cordial to tense and filled with a certain amount of gamesmanship and tough talk. Frequently, there is a lot of give and take regarding money, guaranteed rewrite fees, net point participation and the like, as producers try to hammer out the best deal they can for themselves and agents try to do the same for their clients. (For an inexperienced writer to negotiate with a producer is like a minnow sitting down for lunch with a great white shark. Ideally, writers will focus on the creative aspects of a writer-producer relationship and leave the dirtier business of deal-making to agents and lawyers, which is what they get paid to handle. As a rule, writers try to never talk money with their producers.)

If negotiations are successfully concluded, the producers will either "option" the property for a specific period (usually six months or a year, with clauses for option renewal) or purchase it outright. The producer's lawyers will then issue a "deal memo." a shortened version of the proposed contract, which serves as a legal contract until the more detailed contract can be worked out and drawn up, something that may take months. In some cases, with a less-established writer, the producer will seek a "free option," working with the writer on a handshake basis, with no money changing hands, to see if a viable script comes out of it that mutually benefits both parties. (For an excellent highly detailed breakdown of this entire process, see *The Hollywood Job-Hunter's Survival Guide*).

With a "done deal," the property now goes into development.

## In development

Depending on the terms of the deal, the writer can either be dismissed and replaced by another writer at this point, or, more likely, be retained for at least one rewrite of the script (every script will be rewritten to some extent) that often begins with an "outline" or "treatment" for the proposed new draft. Typically, this process will not proceed easily, with the script moving quickly and smoothly toward production. More likely, the property will enter into what is known in Hollywood as "development hell," a period of many months or even years that involves creative meetings with the producer on changes or new directions for the screenplay, notes (comments and suggestions on the script) from the producer or development executives, input from stars who may become attached and then unattached to the project, and so on. It is common during this period for the writer to work with an assigned development executive, who serves as a creative guide and liaison for the above-the-line talent involved on the project. It is also quite common for the producer to drop the original writer along the way, replacing him or her with a writer the producer feels might handle revisions more productively, or bring in a specialty "script doctor" to work on specific areas of the script, such as dialogue or action scenes. (For a deeper and more detailed look at this process, see John Gregory Dunne's nonfiction account, *Monster*.)

For many writers, development hell is an exasperating, even humiliating process, as they attempt to give the producers what they want, while trying to salvage their own creative vision and personal integrity. Writers frequently blame insensitive or semiliterate producers and studio executives ("suits") for much of their misery. Some years ago, for example, a well-known novelist who also worked in films found himself in a high-level meeting with a production executive at a major studio, listening to the exec complain about his adaptation of a famous novel the studio had purchased. As the "suit" railed on about all of the problems in the script and how it failed to reflect the quality of the book, the writer began to suspect the executive had read neither his novel nor the screenplay, but was relying solely on a reader's coverage. He tested the executive by asking if he felt such-and-such a character in the script needed more work, naming a character that did not actually exist. When the executive replied enthusiastically in the affirmative, the frustrated writer stood up and screamed, "You have the cranial development of an eggplant!" He was escorted off the lot and told never to return; the movie has yet to be made.

Some development situations proceed more productively, however, and result in a screenplay the studio green lights for production.

## Preproduction

It is during this stage that most of the hiring is done, from the director and cast (the above-the-line talent) to the key members of the production crew (the below-the-line talent). Just because a project goes into preproduction is no guarantee it will ever reach its projected start date. Signing the right cast members is particularly crucial and may hinge on yet more script revisions, and countless other vagaries of the marketplace. While development hell is a drawn-out, agonizing process that tests patience, preproduction is a tense period in which the studio can suddenly pull the plug, shutting the project down. Countless screenwriters have seen their projects on the brink of production, only to have a star pull out of the project (or even die), a new studio chief take over and cancel the movie at the last minute, and so on. Since the most successful screenwriting careers are built on a succession of produced movies with a hit now and then along the way, getting that first script into production can literally make or break a career, especially if it goes on to become a critical or box-office hit.

## In production

If everything falls into place, the movie goes into production. The original writer may or may not still be involved at that point. Depending on the deal, if the writer is due production bonus money—significant payments hinging on the start of production—that money becomes due the first day cameras roll. Some writers are welcome on the set and may be involved with revisions all the way through production. Others may be less welcome or even banished from the set and any involvement, depending on their relationship with the producer and other above-the-line talent at that point. Many directors are uncomfortable having the original writer around, particularly if other writers have been brought in for revisions, which is so often the case.

If a writer is lucky enough (or wants) to be invited on the set, he or she is likely to be treated with an indifference bordering on disrespect (though this varies from production to production). At this point, the director is in charge of an enormous, mutating, nearly unmanageable enterprise, and writers are often looked upon as nuisances and distractions. Screenwriters lucky enough to still be involved at the production stage learn to stay out of the way and to speak only when it's necessary—at least until they become big shots, at which point they will probably be producers themselves.

# Agents and Marketing

## BY PAMELA WALLACE

Whew! You did it! You finished a screenplay. You worked hard on it, rewriting and polishing until it was as good as you could possibly make it. If possible, you've even gotten a professional critique. Now you're ready to try to sell it.

That's the hard part.

As difficult as it is to write a good script, it's even harder to sell it. But despite the obstacles, I truly believe that if a script is good enough (or at least commercial enough for the demands of the current market), and the writer is persistent enough in marketing it, the script will sell. That is no guarantee that it will get produced. The vast majority of screenplays that sell never get produced. That is one of the harshest realities of the film business. Nora Ephron, a tremendously talented and successful writer/director (You've Got Mail) said once that only about one out of every four screenplays she writes actually gets produced. She felt that was a good batting average—after all, she was batting .250.

The most important thing I want you to understand is that even if your screenplay doesn't sell, that doesn't mean it isn't good. In fact, the better the script, the harder it seems to be to sell. When you look at the scripts that win Academy Awards, most of them took years to sell. For instance, *Platoon* took more than ten years to sell. My screenplay for *Witness* took over three years to sell. It received more than its fair share of criticism along the way.

How does a screenplay get to the person who's in a position to buy it? Almost always through an agent or entertainment attorney. Unless you have a personal connection to someone in the film business, the only way to get your script read is by having an agent or attorney submit it. Most actors, studios, networks and production companies will return, unopened and unread, any script that is submitted to them "over the transom."

Stories about a waitress handing a script to an actor who was dining in the restaurant where she worked, and shortly thereafter making a six-figure sale, are rare to the point of being nonexistent. The reality is that you must market your screenplay in a professional manner. Approaching someone personally is unprofessional. They will rarely respond to that.

Screenplays get to actors by first going through their agents. Part of the agent's job is screening material submitted to the actor.

There is a significant exception to this rule: screenwriting fellowships and competitions. They are a great way to get around that high wall that surrounds Hollywood. When you apply for a fellowship or submit a script to a competition, your work is viewed by professionals in the industry. Often this leads to a sale, or at least getting an agent.

## Getting an agent

Other than competitions, how do you go about getting an agent? Unfortunately, it tends to be a vicious circle. You can't get an agent without having made your first sale, and you can't

**PAM WALLACE** *began writing screenplays in the mid-1980s and in 1985 she won an academy award for co-writing the movie* Witness. *She has written or co-written several other films, including the award-winning HBO film* If These Walls Could Talk *and movies of the week for CBS and ABC. She has published over 25 novels, several of which have been optioned or produced as movies of the week, miniseries or made-for-cable movies. She lives in Fresno, California. This piece is excerpted from her book* You Can Write a Movie, *published by Writer's Digest Books.*

make your first sale without an agent. However, there is hope. Every year agents take on new writers, usually through personal recommendations, occasionally through reading a spec script that's submitted to them.

Based on my experience with agents, here are the answers to some of the questions most commonly asked of agents.

### Is it better for a new writer to write a feature film spec script or an episode of a TV series?

It's better to write a movie script. Don't differentiate between feature film or TV movie. And don't put act breaks in it, even if you think it would be best as a TV movie, it will be easy to insert act breaks.

### Should you ever pay an agent to read your script?

No.

### Is one script enough to show an agent who's interested?

No. You should always have more than one, to prove that you're productive and not a "one-shot wonder."

### When an agent agrees to look at your script, should you send a treatment along with it?

There is disagreement about this. Some agents feel you should, and some feel you shouldn't. Personally, I feel it's best not to send a treatment, unless it's been specifically requested. It's too easy for an agent to read the treatment and dismiss the story.

### What do most agents look for in a script?

The same thing buyers look for: great dialogue, interesting characters, sound structure and a marketable premise.

### What are big turnoffs for agents?

The same things that turn off buyers—an unprofessional-looking script, one that's very dense and doesn't have a lot of "white space," lots of camera directions.

### How are agents paid?

They receive a percentage (usually 10 percent, sometimes 15) of the saleprice of your screenplay.

### What is a franchised agent?

One who subscribes to the Writers Guild of America's Basic Agreement between Artists and Managers. These agents deal with studios and producers who are signatories to the guild. (All writers must belong to the guild, once they've sold their first script.) Only look for a franchised agent.

### How can you find a list of franchised agents?

The Writers Guild will provide it. Attending screenwriting conferences is also a good way to meet agents.

### Do agents critique your work?

Rarely. There are professionals who will do this for a fee, but shop around to find a reputable one who won't charge an exorbitant fee. The Writer's Guild magazine, *Written By*, usually carries ads for people who do script analysis and critique.

**Should you include a cover letter when you submit a script to an agent?**

Yes, but keep it brief. Don't talk about how brilliant the script is and how much the agent will love it. He'll want to make up his own mind about that. Only include information about yourself that is relevant to the script. For instance, if you've written a medical thriller and you're a physician, mention that.

**Can any attorney serve as an entertainment attorney?**

Technically, yes. But in actuality it's best to hire an experienced entertainment attorney. This kind of attorney basically only negotiates a contract for a writer. He doesn't usually market a script or become involved in a writer's career in any other way. There are two kinds of writers who use attorneys alone, without agents: First, a writer who's so successful that he is offered all the writing-for-hire work he could possibly want and doesn't need an agent to look for work for him. Second, a new writer who hasn't been able to get an agent but has gotten the interest of a reputable entertainment attorney.

## What they're looking for

Everyone in the film business—whether it's an agent considering a new client, an actor, or a buyer at a studio, network or production company—is looking for the same thing: A screenplay that is either so "high concept" that it will make a tremendously commercial movie even if it isn't especially well executed, or a screenplay that is so brilliantly written, so deeply touching and marvelously entertaining, that they fall in love with it, whether it's particularly commercial or not.

There are writers who manage to write and sell scripts they don't love. They're calculated efforts at marketing. But very few writers succeed this way. It's important to be aware of the market overall, what kind of movies are being made and why. But instead of focusing on what "they're" looking for and trying to write accordingly, the best marketing advice I can give to an aspiring writer is to write a screenplay you love, work hard on it and do the best job you possibly can, then be persistent in getting it to agents. With a little bit of luck, an agent will recognize that your script is just what someone is looking for. And the rest will be history. . . .

# You Gotta Love It!
# Madeline DiMaggio: Screenwriter, Writing Teacher, Script Doctor

**BY GEOFF FULLER**

In the screenwriting workshops Madeline DiMaggio conducts throughout the United States and Europe, she has found that writers who "love it most" are ultimately the most successful. She remembers one of her students telling her about a specific turning point in his career.

**Madeline DiMaggio**

"Somebody asked Kevin how many screenplays he wrote before he sold," DiMaggio recounts, "and he said, 'Seven.' And that person asked, 'What kept you going?' And he said, 'You know what? I know the moment I asked myself that question. I was driving on the freeway. I was entering the on-ramp, and an inner voice asked me, "What if I never sell a script?" And then I heard the answer. I'm going to keep writing anyway, because I love it.' "

DiMaggio's student was Kevin Falls, who is now an Emmy winner as the co-executive producer on the popular and critically acclaimed NBC television show, *The West Wing*.

Throughout the interview, DiMaggio framed the points she was making as little scenes. No matter what she was trying to explain, she created a scene in which she played all the parts. It was as if her mind automatically translated everything into the form that films require. The fact is, DiMaggio loves to write; she has been a story editor and creative consultant for Paramount Studios, but writing is her first love. She enjoys the whole process, from idea through development through execution, and if she didn't love it so, she probably wouldn't have achieved the success that she has had to date.

DiMaggio began her career working on "a lot of cop shows," among them the 1970s police drama *Starsky and Hutch*. From there she moved to situation comedies like *Bob Newhart* and *Three's Company*. Later, she wrote movie-length screenplays, or "long form," as she calls it, which are "not necessarily more difficult. It's just that they require different talents."

Most recently, she finished a special for Showtime, *Murder With Privilege*, and the first draft of a movie script for Commotion Films entitled *Catherine Called Birdy*. Both scripts were co-written with Pamela Wallace, a frequent collaborator and the author of *Witness*, a 1985 movie that starred Harrison Ford and garnered an Academy Award for Wallace. DiMaggio characterized *Catherine Called Birdy* as "*Clueless* meets *Shakespeare in Love*. We're on a good roll with that one. It's a fun script. It was like a dream project from the get-go."

**GEOFF FULLER** *is a book editor in Morgantown, West Virginia, and will be a guest editor for* Writer's Digest *magazine in 2002. He has won numerous awards for his writing, and his work will appear this fall in* Mindprints.

## Is there a particular strength to your work? Something you do especially well?

Dialogue. Without any question. I come from an acting background, and I have an ear for dialogue, and pacing and tempo. I highly recommend that writers take an acting class. Some writers are tone deaf, and either you have a good sense or not. It can be taught, but I think with actors it becomes automatic. After all the years of acting that I put in, I'm in tune with the flow and the pacing and the tempo and the fun of dialogue. It's just my favorite thing.

## I understand that a lot of actors will tone up the dialogue, give it more impact.

Yes, that happens a lot. It depends on the power of the actor, but when you look at Aaron Sorkin's work on *West Wing*, I hear the actors don't even stray from an "ahh" in the script. But Sorkin's dialogue is utterly brilliant. It really depends on who the writer is, who the actors are, and what the medium is. And the personality of the director.

## How did you get into script doctoring?

I got into script doctoring through teaching. I was reading writers' material—I go down to Hollywood, I pitch to Hollywood, I write for Hollywood—and I just knew the material wasn't ready. It needed that professional edge.

What I try to provide for writers who are trying to get into the marketplace is the benefit of all my years of rejection. I try to show them how to get into the story later, give the story more edge, have characters we root for, that we're riveted by, and make the story as visual as possible— How to give it all that polish that says "professional."

I'll tell you, there are a lot of good script doctors out there, and I highly recommend that everybody get the critique before they go out because writers are just too close to their material. You've only got one shot. Once a particular company rejects you, you don't have another shot with that company. You want your presentation to be the best it can be.

## What are the most common weaknesses you see in screenplays?

The biggest fatal flaw is structure. Also, the characters need to drive the story forward rather than the plot. Many, many, many times, I'll read a screenplay that's plot-driven and the characters are stuck in there like automatons to take the story from point A to B to C. The next move should be created by the characters and not by the plot.

Give a character a compelling need, and then it's the writer's job to create obstacles to that need, and it's those obstacles that create conflict, that create all the action. We are who we are by what we *don't* get, not what we get. We're made by what we don't get. Character-Need-Obstacle-Action. All good stories are based in conflict. And that's another fatal flaw in screenplays: not enough conflict. The stakes are not high enough. You hear that in Hollywood all the time.

## Do you believe, as Jeffrey Katzenberg and others have maintained, that "the idea is king"?

Yes. You can say, well, doesn't that conflict with the fact that you have to write from your passion, you have to write from your heart? But yes, story is king. Concept is crucial. However, it has to be executed well, and a lot of writers don't have a bent for that high-commercial edge. I mean, if you are Shane Black, and your passion is an action type of *Lethal Weapon* movie, then you are a very lucky individual.

However, what if you are not that kind of writer? When you fabricate that, it shows. To put yourself into a pigeon-hole and attempt to write for the sale, it shows. So I tell writers to be very careful. It's a two-edged sword. Yes, you need an idea that is extremely marketable and strong, but, yes, you also have to have something that's well written, honest. Before you commit to writing, make sure you love your idea. Make sure it makes the hairs on your arm stand up, because you're going to be living with it for a very long time. It takes a long time to write a screenplay, it takes a long time to rewrite it, and it takes a long time to market it. You better love what you're doing, because it's a commitment.

### Do you think there's a difference between the way males and females approach story and idea in a script?

That's an excellent question, and I think there is. Writers need to watch that. They talk about ageism in Hollywood, they talk about genderism, they talk about all those things that to some extent exist, but what often happens is that you can see those things in a script. You can read a writer's age in a script and you can read the gender, and that's not good. Because that's the writer taking a point of view. So you want to be careful of that. I think women can write action, and I think men can go into the heart of a woman. They can go into a woman's soul. *Unmarried Woman*, a very old film, is a brilliant insight into being a female, and it was written by a man. But try to detach yourself from who you are and just write a good story, so that it's not identifiable. Hollywood tries to pigeonhole you, and you can avoid that to some degree if you keep your own point of view out of the story.

### What, exactly, is a "coverage?"

It's unavoidable and it's a roulette table. When you turn in a screenplay, it does not get to the producer, it does not get to the story editor—almost always it goes to the reader. And the reader writes coverage on the material. The reader might be somebody's kid who's home for summer vacation or the reader can be a member of the Writers Guild who's been doing it for 25 years. It's the luck of the draw. Unless you get with some very small production company or you get read by somebody you can get to directly, it always happens through coverage.

The reader essentially writes a synopsis of what the story is about, who the characters are, what's wrong with the story, if it works, if it doesn't, if the writer is recommended for other projects. That way someone can look at the coverage and decide if the screenplay should be passed on to someone up the ladder. And it's not only "Is it well written?" but whether the story fits the company's agenda.

### Discuss the difference between a treatment and a full screenplay.

A treatment is in prose, and it's basically a synopsis of the storyline done in present tense, just like all movies are made in present tense. You don't put in the treatment what couldn't be shown on the screen. I don't have the luxury of going into interior monologue like I do in a book. Essentially, it's a synopsis of the storyline of the movie.

### I've heard it recommended that an aspiring screenwriter work on a treatment before writing a full screenplay.

I absolutely agree with that, but the treatment is for the writer, it's not to market. It's to get the story down with a strong beginning, middle, and end. It's to create a structure that works, and from that, the writer can create the screenplay. Everything in the screenplay should matter. A treatment should be like an artist's work table where you can cut and paste and make sure the story works before you commit to a first draft.

In fact, when Pam [Wallace] and I work together, we start with one page. Then we expand it to three or four pages. Then we expand it to maybe ten pages. Before we absolutely agree on storyline, we know where we're going, we deal with issues before it's written—what we want to accomplish, what we want to say, the tone, the stakes. Then we go to first draft.

### What about pitches? Does every writer need to frame their story in two or three sentences?

I highly recommend that all writers do that. It doesn't necessarily mean that they market it like that, but it clarifies things for the writer. In my classes, I ask writers, 'What movie is it most like?' Not because they're copying the film or plagarizing it, but because it roots the writer in knowing tone. It roots the writer in knowing what they want to accomplish. I tell writers, "If you can't define it, you can't write it." I ask writers to define their story in four or five lines.

### What kinds of objections to that do you hear?

Objections?

### Like, "My story's much too complex to . . . "

Ah! You know, I was teaching an advanced screenwriting course in Hawaii, and I don't believe there's such a thing as an advanced screenwriter. I mean, a writer can be experienced, but every story has a new set of challenges. But these people were considered advanced because they were all in the process of writing screenplays. So I said to them, "Your first assignment is to go home and come back tomorrow with three lines of what your story is about." Out of about twelve writers, six could do it. If you can't define the main line of action in your story, you've got a problem.

So here's a story about a lost alien who gets befriended by boys who help him find his way back home. Well, that's *ET*. There's a lot that's not in there—the government finding him, dying on the operating table, Eliot bringing him home. Fine, fine, but that's not the kernel of what the story is about. That's not what it hinges on.

### And once the writer defines that, the writer can pitch it?

Writers are terrified of pitching. Absolutely terrified. So I try to tell writers not to worry about pitching because they won't be doing it. I mean, the bottom line is that until you can write a screenplay and can prove that you can write, you won't be invited in by companies who want to hear your idea. The most important marketing tool you will ever have is your screenplay. That's number one. The most important thing a writer can do is write a good screenplay.

### A couple of last things: What do you see as the hottest trends in Hollywood today?

Don't ever go by trends. By the time you write and market, the trend has passed. It takes too long to write the stories, too long to market them. Never try to create on a trend. People may say, "The teen market is flooded" or "The public is tired of Vietnam stories," but there will always be a teen market, there will always be another Vietnam story. The point is that if you try to create on a trend, you will always be behind the wave. You want to get out front. That means that you should always save everything you do, because the trend will come back around.

I'm marketing something now that's twelve years old. The screenplay that Pam [Wallace] and I did recently was from a book that the producer couldn't set up for four years. These things are not overnight! Whatever you get rejected on, keep it in your portfolio, because you never know when you can pull it up, when you can rewrite it, when it'll be timely. None of it's a waste.

### In her book, *You Can Write a Movie*, Pamela Wallace said that the two most important things are to believe in yourself and to write from the heart. You've mentioned a lot of useful things today, a lot of good advice, but what would be your two primary pieces of advice?

That's a very good question. I definitely agree with writing from your heart because I think writers must feel passionately about what they write about. That comes across in the read. I think many times writers try to be too commercial, and they aren't writing from the truth of who they are. The most important thing that happens in a script is its emotional honesty. I was with a very well-known agent once and he said he read a screenplay that he knew wouldn't be commercial, but it was so emotionally honest, he took on that writer as a client because he could feel it in the read—that passion, that truth.

And the love of what you're doing is absolutely key, because I'll tell you what, I've been in workshops with incredible writers and good writers, and it's not the incredible writers who necessarily make it. It's not even all the time the good writers. It's the writers that love it the most and hang in there the longest. Those are the ones who make it.

---

### DiMaggio Highly Recommends . . .

- Never turn in a treatment unless it's asked for, because it encourages readers not to read.
- Take an acting class. That's why so many actors are good writers, because they have a good ear.
- Get a critique before you send your script out, because you're just too close to your material to be objective.
- Enter as many contests as you can. You get read by professionals, and you get noticed. The word gets out on the grapevine.

---

# Making The Leap to Feature Film: James Kearns Applauds the Group Effort

BY RACHEL VATER

James Kearns is no novice at script writing. Having written every-thing from plays, to sitcoms, to dramas, to TV movies, Kearns contin-ues to prove his dedication to writing classy work with *John Q.*, his upcoming feature film. With powerful advocates at Evolution Management and Writers and Artists agency on his side, Kearns has had the chance to see his script produced by New Line Cinema, starring Denzel Washington. Anticipating the appearance of *John Q.* in cinemas February 2002, Kearns shares his thoughts on writing.

**James Kearns**

### Can you tell us a little about the basic premise for *John Q.*?

The idea for *John Q.* is actually very simple. What do you do when your child is faced with a life-threatening disease and needs an opera-tion you can't afford, and no one will help—not the hospital, not the various governmental, health and social agencies—no one. John Quincy Archibald, played by Denzel Washington in the movie, would do anything to save his son's life, even if that means taking over the emergency room of a major metropolitan hospital, which—in an act of desperation—he does.

### Where did you first get the idea for *John Q.*?

The idea came from an article I read in the newspaper, about a wealthy man who had heart problems and needed a transplant. He got one fairly quickly, and he said if he wasn't rich he'd be dead now. And that was how the idea was born. Basically, if you didn't have the money, you really couldn't get a $300,000 operation. I did a lot of research and found out that hospitals wouldn't cover the cost of the operation for people with limited health care, which is the case of the Denzel Washington character in *John Q.* Hospitals aren't in the business of being charita-ble. When I asked people in the transplant surgery departments at Cedars Sinai and Columbia Presbyterian hospital in New York if hospital administrators would deny care to someone who couldn't afford it, they had to say yes. One of them even said, "Yes, we're faced with that all the time, people who fall through the cracks."

### Once you began work on this script, how many drafts did it go through?

I wrote a lot of them. I rewrote it several times, and then upon selling it, New Line had ideas they wanted addressed.

### Was it difficult for you to incorporate those ideas into your script?

For the most part it was a very positive experience. New Line people genuinely liked the movie and were moved by the story. They felt the next stage was to get a director involved, which was Nick Cassavetes. Once Nick came aboard, he wanted some changes made within the script that answered questions he or the studio had. It is a collaborative medium. In this case, I was fortunate, because their questions, if anything, were just to make the script better, deepen the characters' lives.

The script did stay very much intact, mainly because Nick Cassavetes is a very talented, supportive and insightful director. If it's different in any way, I would be hard pressed to tell what the differences are. They were just ideas that he had suggested to me to see if they could work, and when I tried them out, they did.

### Once you have an idea, how do you proceed from there?

From the idea, one could spend a long time jotting things down. The research doesn't come until I make a decision there's something there, a commanding idea. Often I will query a couple of people and see if they agree. In the case of *John Q.*, my agent at the time said, "What? Are you crazy to write something like that?" But other people were very receptive to it, and that helped me. Then I do an outline, a beat sheet. When you're writing your own spec scripts, you make the rules up yourself, but when you're working for hire—and I do a lot of that with all the different things I've done for television and for film—a story outline is one of the steps you're hired to do by a studio or network. You get paid for it. And in that story outline, they can see where it's going. So I'm used to doing anywhere from 20- to 30-page story outlines.

### Did you write the script with Denzel Washington in mind for the lead role?

No. It was not written for a white man or a black man. There was a point where I met with [director] Ron Howard, who said, "The great thing here is that this man could be anybody." Some extremely gifted actors were interested in this role at one point, including Dustin Hoffman, Samuel Jackson, Liam Neeson, and Al Pacino. But I honestly believe that Denzel Washington, with the integrity and dignity he brings to a role and where he is in his career right now, he sounds and feels like the guy that I wrote. I don't know what that means except he's terrific in this movie. He'll break your heart.

### It sounds like Denzel really connected to the role.

Yes. He brought his heart and soul every day to the part. And Nick Cassavetes, the director, is very good with actors. They want to work with him. He brings a lot out of them, helps their performance. That's important to an actor.

### What about the other actors?

Of course, when Denzel signed on, a lot of other people became interested, not just because they wanted to do this piece; they wanted to work with him because he brings the level of performance up. Kimberley Elise is in this, and James Woods, and Robert Duvall and Ray Liotta. There are a lot of big names in *John Q.* and a lot of younger actors who are not household names, but are really distinguishing themselves in this.

### You sound as if you know a lot about the inner-workings of this project. How involved were you in the actual making of the movie? Were you kept apprised throughout the production process?

Yes, I was. But that's unusual for a writer. I wish more writers could work with directors as closely as I worked with Nick Cassavetes. There was a lot of respect for the material. I sat down with Nick before and we agreed to go forward. When I asked to be involved, he said, "I *want* you involved." That stayed true through the rewrite process until the point where pre-production started, and then I really wasn't needed. There's not much a writer can do at that point. I did go to the set in Toronto, where the movie was filmed, and I took my family up there. We spent some time on the set and saw the movie being made, and I was invited to be a part of that.

### And you've had a chance to see some screenings of it?

I've seen two screenings. The first one I saw had no temporary score, and all the bells and whistles weren't there. The second was a research screening for an invited audience, and it scored very high. The audience gave it a "very high recommend" rating. They laughed in all the right places. Believe it or not there are some funny things in there. You could feel the emotion. They were very vocal. I don't think you're going to find that in every screening. They were actually saying things out loud: "Oh, my God! No! I can't believe it!" When John Q. takes over the emergency room, I was hopeful people would empathize with him, not feel that he was a villain. And it was like Rocky. They were like, "*Yeah*!"

### More enthusiasm than you were expecting then?

Yeah, to my mind it's a controversial decision by the main character to go that far. But I think Denzel plays it so beautifully, you just love this guy the moment you meet him. He has a lot of integrity. He loves his kid, he loves his family, you know that his back is against the wall and he's run out of options. He goes from being an accepting, generous man to being a very desperate man, and I believe the audience will really connect to his plight.

### With *John Q.* completed and due to hit the cinemas at the end of 2001, what are you looking to do next?

I've got a television movie I wrote now being filmed in Australia. I wrote it four years ago. That's the nature of this business: hurry up and wait. Luckily, writers get paid when they're a member of the WGA and work with studios, but you like to see your work get done once in a while. So that's happening now, and meanwhile I'm looking at new feature projects. Some of the stuff I get sent to either rewrite or adapt from books just isn't the kind of material I'm interested in, and I'm taking my time to find the right next project.

### Do you prefer to do your own original material, or is adapting something also of interest to you?

I've only done adaptations two times, but I'm definitely interested in doing more. It can be gratifying to find a story that really interests you, that you want to write. There are a lot of book rights bought by the studios that need adaptations and you need to remain open to that. A good idea is a good idea, and I can't come up with every one of them. I've sold a lot of original stuff, but part of what I've done over the years is work on assignment. Sometimes they come to you and say, "We have this project. Would you like to do it?" But even then, you have to come up with ideas and a particular take on things. But I would say 60 percent of it comes to me; 40 percent I have to generate.

### Do certain genres interest you more than others, or are you careful not to pigeon-hole yourself too much?

Well, that's a problem out here, because you know they see you in a certain way. *John Q.* is a social drama with some suspenseful elements. So perhaps the town looks at such a writer as being more right for a thriller or drama than for a comedy. I happen to like romantic comedy. But then you're coming up against the studios who say, "Well, gee, he's not known for that and we don't know if he can deliver." But I guess if you put it on a page and write it yourself, then it's either there or it isn't. I intend to focus on dramatic material, and hopefully, it's got some funny stuff in it.

### Now that you're an accomplished screenwriter, it sounds like you have a clear direction of where you're going and have your pick of projects, but how did you first get started in the script writing business?

I started as a playwright in New York writing for the theater and had plays done in workshops and in larger venues. Then I had a play called *Days in the Dark Light* staged in California. It attracted some attention from Hollywood, but I wasn't interested in doing movies at that time, and my wife didn't want to move out here. So I went back to New York, where the realities of the theater started to drag me down—just how difficult it was, and how, while maybe creatively enriching, was not financially rewarding. Then my wife got pregnant, and I decided I'd better start looking elsewhere. I had another play produced in New York, but then I started writing for television.

That was about 14 years ago. I wrote for shows like *Dynasty*, *Highway to Heaven*, *Tour of Duty*, and a show called *A Year in the Life*. I wrote some sit-coms, and I was on the staff of *Wiseguy*. Then the strike of 1988 came and changed the face of the business. Hour-long dramas started to suffer because sit-coms were king, and there were fewer jobs available for writers in the hour-long format. But I could see the shifts coming in the business, and I was trying to prepare for them. I wrote a screenplay called *Dead of Summer* that sold to Universal. It didn't get produced, but I continued to work and write for movies and long-form television and dramatic series. A lot of that work got made, but *John Q.* is my first feature film to be produced.

### When and how did you first work with an agent?

When I first started to write plays, I didn't have an agent. And then I got a theater agent. If you don't have an agent, there are ways to try to get somebody to pay attention to your work. But at the end of the day, I think you need an agent to introduce your work to all the potential buyers and producers. As a playwright, I don't think it was ever a problem finding an agent. Sometimes the problem is finding a *good* agent.

### How did you come to work with Writers & Artists agency?

I have a management company called Evolution Management, which also happened to be the producers of *John Q.* My manager, Marc Burg, is head of Evolution Management, and I also work with Oren Koulis and Steven Gates.

The screenwriting business has changed over the years, and there is this feeling that the more people you have in your corner, the better. Actors have always had personal managers, but now a lot of writers and directors also have taken that route. Evolution Management took me over to Writers & Artists. They first gave them the script, and Marti Blumenthal and Rich Freeman were over there, and they were very excited about it. So that's how I became a Writers & Artists client.

### A lot of scripts, even once they're negotiated, never make it to film. What are some of the things you feel *John Q.* had in its favor to see it all the way through production?

Your guess is as good as mine as to what makes a movie go. In the case of *John Q.*, they truly liked this script, and to New Line's credit, Mike De Luca [then-president] and Richard Saperstein [senior executive vice president] fell in love with the central premise. They really wanted to make it.

When studios find something that excites them, they develop it. They try to get interest from directors and get actors involved. Actors drive the business. Getting an actor attached is often what makes or breaks the movie, but it's tremendously difficult. Sometimes it works and sometimes it doesn't. There are no rules. This is a $45 million movie, and that's a lot of money to spend on anything. So it's extremely difficult to get a movie made, and studios pick and choose carefully. Having a star attached puts everyone more at ease.

### Do you think it's necessary for a scriptwriter to live in or near Hollywood?

I think it's difficult for a beginner not to live here. If you have a way to get your script read and seen, I don't think you absolutely *have* to live here, but the industry is here.

### What advice would you give to an aspiring screenwriter?

I would recommend that they get their hands on as many different screenplays as they can so they're familiar with the form. There are books of the best screenplays out there. There are collected works of certain writers, like Woody Allen or Quentin Tarantino. There are books on screenwriting and the three-act structure, which I think is critical to learn. I wouldn't necessarily get married to it, but it can be a guide, and it's very helpful.

Assuming they want to be screenwriters and they like movies, they should get as familiar with the form, see as many movies, read as many scripts as they can. At that point, I would suggest they write some idea they can't *not* write. They've *got* to write this thing, whether it's a comedy or a thriller or a drama. They should just get something on paper. Because part of writing is rewriting, and once you've written a good first draft, you've got a blueprint from which to continue. And then the real work begins.

Another thing that a writer could benefit from is screenwriting or playwriting workshops. It's good experience to get in there and hear what other people are doing, to fight for your ideas and listen to what other people have to say about your work. That's part of the process for the rest of your life. You're going to hear criticism during your entire career as a writer, and at first it *can* be difficult to take, but as time goes on you get to realize how valuable it can be.

# Script Agents:
# Nonfee-charging and Fee-charging

This section contains agents who sell feature film scripts, television scripts, and theatrical stage plays. The listings in this section differ slightly from those in the literary agent sections. Nonfee-charging and fee-charging script agencies are listed together. Fee-charging script agents are indicated by a clapper ( 🎬 ) symbol. A breakdown of the types of scripts each agency handles is included in the listing.

Many of the script agents listed here are signatories to the Writers Guild of America Artists' Manager Basic Agreement. They have paid a membership fee and agreed to abide by the WGA's standard code of behavior. Agents who are WGA signatories are not permitted to charge a reading fee to WGA members, but are allowed to do so to nonmembers. They are permitted to charge for critiques and other services, but they may not refer you to a particular script doctor. Enforcement is uneven, however. Although a signatory can, theoretically, be stripped of its signatory status, this rarely happens.

A few of the listings in this section are actually management companies. The role of managers is quickly changing in Hollywood—they were once only used by actors, or "tallent," and the occasional writer. Now many managers are actually selling scripts to producers.

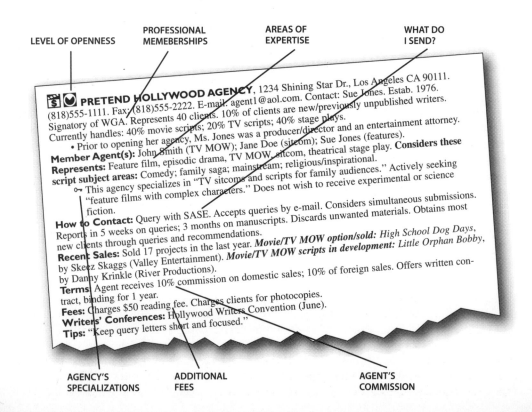

LEVEL OF OPENNESS    PROFESSIONAL MEMEBERSHIPS    AREAS OF EXPERTISE    WHAT DO I SEND?

**PRETEND HOLLYWOOD AGENCY**, 1234 Shining Star Dr., Los Angeles CA 90111. (818)555-1111. Fax: (818)555-2222. E-mail: agent1@aol.com. Contact: Sue Jones. Estab. 1976. Signatory of WGA. Represents 40 clients. 10% of clients are new/previously unpublished writers. Currently handles: 40% movie scripts; 20% TV scripts; 40% stage plays.

• Prior to opening her agency, Ms. Jones was a producer/director and an entertainment attorney.

**Member Agent(s):** John Smith (TV MOW); Jane Doe (sitcom); Sue Jones (features).

**Represents:** Feature film, episodic drama, TV MOW, sitcom, theatrical stage play. **Considers these script subject areas:** Comedy; family saga; mainstream; religious/inspirational.

➤ This agency specializes in "TV sitcoms and scripts for family audiences." Actively seeking "feature films with complex characters." Does not wish to receive experimental or science fiction.

**How to Contact:** Query with SASE. Accepts queries by e-mail. Considers simultaneous submissions. Reports in 5 weeks on queries; 3 months on manuscripts. Discards unwanted materials. Obtains most new clients through queries and recommendations.

**Recent Sales:** Sold 17 projects in the last year. *Movie/TV MOW option/sold: High School Dog Days*, by Skeez Skaggs (Valley Entertainment). *Movie/TV MOW scripts in development: Little Orphan Bobby*, by Danny Krinkle (River Productions).

**Terms:** Agent receives 10% commission on domestic sales; 10% of foreign sales. Offers written contract, binding for 1 year.

**Fees:** Charges $50 reading fee. Charges clients for photocopies.

**Writers' Conferences:** Hollywood Writers Convention (June).

**Tips:** "Keep query letters short and focused."

AGENCY'S SPECIALIZATIONS    ADDITIONAL FEES    AGENT'S COMMISSION

## Quick Reference Icons

At the beginning of some listings, you will find one or more of the following symbols for quick identification of features particular to that listing.

**N** Agency new to this edition.

**✓** Change in address, contact information or phone number from last year's edition.

**$** Fee-charging script agent.

**□** Agents who make sales to electronic publishers.

**✪** Canadian agency.

**⊕** International agency.

## Level of Openness

Each agency has an icon indicating its openness to submissions. Before contacting any agency, check the listing to make sure it is open to new clients.

**□** Newer agency actively seeking clients.

**◑** Agency seeking both new and established writers.

**◐** Agency prefers to work with established writers, mostly obtains new clients through referrals.

**◎** Agency handling only certain types of work or work by writers under certain circumstances.

**⊘** Agency not currently seeking new clients. We include these agencies to let you know they are currently not open to new clients. *Unless you have a strong recommendation from someone well respected in the field, our advice is to avoid approaching these agents.*

It's a good idea to register your script before sending it out, and the WGA offers a registration service to memebers and nonmembers alike. Membership in the WGA is earned through the accumulation of professional credits and carries a number of significant benefits. Write the Guild for more information on specific agencies, script registration, and membership requirements.

Like the literary agents listed in the nonfee-charging and fee-charging sections of this book, some script agencies ask that clients pay for some or all of the office fees accrued when sending out scripts. Some agents ask for a one-time "handling" fee up front, while others deduct office expenses after a script has been sold. Always have a clear understanding of any fee an agent asks you to pay.

Canadian and International agents are included in this section. Canadian agents have a ( ✪ ) preceding their listing, while International agents have a ( ⊕ ) preceding their listing. Remember to include an International Reply Coupon (IRC) with your self-addressed envelope when contacting Canadian and International agents.

When reading through this section, keep in mind the following information specific to the script agent listings:

## SUBHEADS

Each listing is broken down into subheads to make locating specific information easier. In the first section, you'll find contact information for each agency. You'll also learn if the agent is a WGA signatory or a member of any other professional organizations. (An explanation of all organizations' acronyms is available on page 321.) Further information is provided which indicates an agency's size, its willingness to work with a new or previously unpublished writer, and a percentage breakdown of the general types of scripts the agency will consider.

**Member Agents:** Agencies comprised of more than one agent list member agents and their

individual specialties to help you determine the most appropriate person for your query letter.
**Represents:** Make sure you query only agents who represent the type of material you write. To help you narrow your search, we've included an **Agents Specialties Index** and the **Script Agents Format Index** in the back of the book.
Look for the key icon to quickly learn an agent's areas of specializations and individual strengths. Agents also mention here what specific areas they are currently seeking as well as subjects they do *not* wish to receive.
**How to Contact:** Most agents open to submissions prefer initially to receive a query letter briefly describing your work. Script agents usually discard material sent without a SASE. Here agents also indicate if they accept queries by fax or e-mail, if they consider simultaneous submissions, and their preferred way of meeting new clients.
**Recent Sales:** Reflecting the different ways scriptwriters work, agents list scripts optioned or sold, and scripting assignments procured for clients. The film industry is very secretive about sales, but you may be able to get a list of clients or other references upon request—especially if the agency is interested in representing your work.
**Terms:** Most agents' commissions range from 10 to 15 percent, and WGA signatories may not earn over 10 percent from WGA members.
**Fees:** Agencies who charge some type of fee (for reading, critiques, consultations, promotion, marketing, etc.) are indicated with a clapper ( ) symbol by their name. Also listed here are any additional office fees the agent asks the client to pay.
**Writers' Conferences:** For screenwriters unable to move to Los Angeles, writers' conferences provide another venue for meeting agents. For more information about a specific conference, check the **Writers' Conferences** section starting on page 287.
**Tips:** Agents offer advice and additional instructions for writers looking for representation.

## SPECIAL INDEXES

**Additional Script Agents:** Many script agents are also interested in book manuscripts; many literary agents will also consider scripts. Agents who primarily sell books but also handle at least 10 to 15 percent scripts appear among the listings in this section, with the contact information, breakdown of work currently handled and a note to check the full listing in either the Nonfee-charging or Fee-charging sections. Those literary agents who sell mostly books and less than 10 to 15 percent scripts do not appear in this section. Complete listings for these agents appear in the Nonfee-charging section.
**Agents Specialties Index:** In the back of the book on page 325 is an index divided into various subject areas specific to scripts, such as mystery, romantic comedy, and teen. This index should help you compose a list of agents specializing in your areas. Cross-referencing categories and concentrating on agents interested in two or more aspects of your manuscript might increase your chances of success. Agencies open to all categories are grouped under the subject heading "open."
**Script Agents Format Index:** Following the **Agents Specialties Index** is an index organizing agents according to the script types they consider: such as TV movie of the week (MOW), sitcom, or episodic drama.
**Agencies Indexed by Openness to Submissions:** This index lists agencies according to their receptivity to new clients.
**Geographic Index:** For writers looking for an agent close to home, this index lists agents state-by-state.
**Agents Index:** Often you will read about an agent who is an employee of a larger agency and you may not be able to locate her business phone or address. Starting on page 380, is a list of agents' names in alphabetical order along with the name of the agency they work for. Find the

name of the person you would like to contact and then check the agency listing.

**Listing Index:** This index lists all agencies, independent publicists, and writers' conferences listed in the book.

---

### For More Information

For a detailed explanation of the agency listings and for more information on approaching agents, read "Using Your *Guide to Literary Agents* to Find an Agent and Choosing" and "Using a Literary Agent" starting on page 2. Also, take note of the articles dealing specifically with contacting—and working with—script agents that start on page 204.

---

## SCRIPT AGENTS

**⊛ ABOVE THE LINE AGENCY**, 9200 Sunset Blvd., #804, Los Angeles CA 90069. (310)859-6115. Fax: (310)859-6119. **Contact:** Bruce Bartlett. Owner: Rima Bauer Greer. Estab. 1994. Signatory of WGA. Represents 35 clients. 10% of clients are new/unpublished writers. Currently handles: 95% movie scripts; 5% TV scripts.
  • Prior to opening her agency, Ms. Greer served as president with Writers & Artists Agency.
**Represents:** Feature film; TV movie of the week. **Considers these script subject areas:** cartoon/animation; writers and directors.
**How to Contact:** Query with SASE. Responds in 1 month to queries.
**Recent Sales:** *3 Stooges*, Matheson (Columbia), *Charlie's Angels*, Ryan Rowe (Columbia), *Constantine*, Frank Cappello (Warner Brothers). *Scripting Assignment(s): Mephisto in Onyx*, by Greg Widen (Miramax), *Prometheus Project*, by Engelbach and Wolff (Fox).
**Terms:** Agent receives 10% commission on domestic sales; 10% commission on foreign sales.

**⊛ ABRAMS ARTISTS AGENCY**, 275 Seventh Ave., 26th Floor, New York NY 10001. (646)486-4600. Fax: (646)486-2358. **Contact:** Jack Tantleff. Estab. 1986. Member of AAR; signatory of WGA.
**Member Agents:** Jack Tantleff (theater, TV, film); Charmaine Ferenczi (theater); John Santoianni (TV, film, theater).
**Represents:** Feature film; episodic drama; sitcom; animation (TV); soap opera; Musical. **Considers these script subject areas:** comedy; contemporary issues; mainstream; mystery/suspense; romantic comedy; romantic drama.
  ○☞ This agency specializes in theater, film, TV.
**How to Contact:** Query with SASE, outline. Returns material only with SASE.
**Recent Sales:** This agency prefers not to share information on specific sales.
**Terms:** Agent receives 10% commission on domestic sales; 10% commission on foreign sales; 10% commission on dramatic rights sales.

**▣ ⊛ ACME TALENT & LITERARY**, 6310 San Vicente Blvd., #520, Los Angeles CA 90048. (323)954-2263 (CA); (212)328-0388(NY). Fax: (323)954-2262 (CA); (212)328-0391(NY). Also: 875 Ave. of the Americas, Suite 2108, New York NY 10001. **Contact:** Lisa Lindo Lieblein. Estab. 1993. Signatory of WGA. Represents 12 clients. Currently handles: movie scripts; TV scripts; Internet rights.
**Member Agents:** Lisa Lindo Lieblein (feature film specs); "also 11 additional agents handling talent in Los Angeles, and 3 agents in New York."
**Represents:** Feature film. **Considers these script subject areas:** action/adventure; biography/autobiography; cartoon/animation; comedy; contemporary issues; detective/police/crime; erotica; ethnic; experimental; family saga; fantasy; feminist; gay/lesbian; glitz; historical; horror; juvenile; mainstream; multicultural; multimedia; mystery/suspense; psychic/supernatural; regional; religious/inspirational; romantic comedy; romantic drama; science fiction; sports; teen; thriller; western/frontier.
  ○☞ This agency specializes in "feature films, completed specs or pitches by established produced writers and new writers." Actively seeking great feature scripts. No unsolicited material.
**How to Contact:** Query with SASE. Considers simultaneous queries. Responds in 2 weeks to queries. Returns materials only with SASE. Obtains most new clients through recommendations from established industry contacts, production companies of note, and reputable entertainment attorneys.
**Recent Sales:** "Since the beginning of this year, Acme has become a major player in the Internet/original content world of dot coms with websodes on several sites. Gaming division, Acme Interactive, is the newest division of the company handling videogames and game developers. Paramount's *Save the Last Dance* was sold by Acme."
**Terms:** Agent receives 10% commission on domestic sales; 10% commission on foreign sales. Offers written contract, binding for 2 years.
**Tips:** "We are very hands on, work developmentally with specs in progress. Individual attention due to low number of clients. All sales have been major 6-7 figures. Call, e-mail with any questions."

**N** ☑ **THE AGENCY**, 1800 Avenue of the Stars, Suite 1114, Los Angeles CA 90067-4206. (310)551-3000. **Contact:** Jerry Zeitman. Estab. 1984. Signatory of WGA. Represents 300 clients. No new/previously unpublished writers. Currently handles: 45% movie scripts; 45% TV scripts; 10% syndicated material.

**Represents:** Feature film; TV movie of the week; episodic drama; sitcom; animation; miniseries. **Considers these script subject areas:** action/adventure; cartoon/animation; comedy; contemporary issues; detective/police/crime; ethnic; family saga; fantasy; historical; horror; juvenile; mainstream; mystery/suspense; psychic/supernatural; romantic comedy; romantic drama; science fiction; teen; thriller; western/frontier; women's issues; military/war.

○━ This agency specializes in TV and motion pictures.

**How to Contact:** Query with SASE. Responds in 2 weeks to queries. Obtains most new clients through recommendations from others.

**Recent Sales:** This agency prefers not to share information on specific sales.

**Terms:** Agent receives 10% commission on domestic sales; 10% commission on foreign sales. Offers written contract, binding for 2 years.

☑ **ALLRED AND ALLRED, LITERARY AGENTS**, 7834 Alabama Ave., Canoga Park CA 91304-4905. (818)346-4313. **Contact:** Robert Allred. Estab. 1991. Represents 5 clients. 100% of clients are new/unpublished writers.

• See the expanded listing for this agency in Literary Agents: Nonfee-charging.

☑ **THE ALPERN GROUP**, 15645 Royal Oak Rd., Encino CA 91436. (818)528-1111. Fax: (818)528-1110. **Contact:** Jeff Alpern. Estab. 1994. Represents 50 clients. 10% of clients are new/unpublished writers. Currently handles: 30% movie scripts; 60% TV scripts; 10% stage plays.

• Prior to opening his agency, Mr. Alpern was an agent with William Morris.

**Member Agents:** Jeff Alpern (president), Liz Wise, Jeff Aghassi.

**Represents:** Movie scripts; feature film; TV scripts; TV movie of the week; episodic drama; miniseries. **Considers these script subject areas:** action/adventure; biography/autobiography; cartoon/animation; comedy; contemporary issues; detective/police/crime; erotica; ethnic; experimental; family saga; fantasy; feminist; gay/lesbian; glitz; historical; horror; juvenile; mainstream; multicultural; multimedia; mystery/suspense; psychic/supernatural; regional; religious/inspirational; romantic comedy; romantic drama; science fiction; sports; teen; thriller; western/frontier.

**How to Contact:** Query with SASE. Responds in 1 month to queries.

**Terms:** Agent receives 10% commission on domestic sales. Offers written contract.

**N** ☑ **MICHAEL AMATO AGENCY**, 1650 Broadway, Suite 307, New York NY 10019. (212)247-4456 or (212)247-4457. **Contact:** Michael Amato. Estab. 1970.; Member of SAG, AFTRA. Represents 6 clients. 2% of clients are new/unpublished writers.

**Represents:** Feature film; TV movie of the week; episodic drama; animation; documentary; miniseries. **Considers these script subject areas:** action/adventure.

○━ This agency specializes in action/adventure scripts.

**How to Contact:** Query. Responds in 1 month to queries. Obtains most new clients through recommendations from others.

**Recent Sales:** This agency prefers not to share information on specific sales.

☑ ☑ **AMG/RENAISSANCE LITERARY AGENCY**, 140 W. 57th St., 2nd Floor, New York NY 10019. NY(212)956-2600, LA(310)858-5365. West Coast Office: 9220 Sunset Blvd., Suite 302, Los Angeles CA 90069. **Contact:** Joel Gotler. Member of SAG, AFTRA, DGA. Represents 200 clients and 25 literary estates clients. 10% of clients are new/unpublished writers. Currently handles: 90% novels; 10% movie and TV scripts.

• See the expanded listing for this agency in Literary Agents: Nonfee-charging.

☑ **MARCIA AMSTERDAM AGENCY**, 41 W. 82nd St., New York NY 10024-5613. (212)873-4945. **Contact:** Marcia Amsterdam. Estab. 1970. Signatory of WGA. Currently handles: 15% nonfiction books; 70% novels; 5% movie scripts; 10% TV scripts.

• See the expanded listing for this agency in Literary Agents: Nonfee-charging.

**N** **THE ARTISTS AGENCY**, 10000 Santa Monica Blvd., Suite 305, Los Angeles CA 90035. (310)277-7779. Fax: (310)785-9338. **Contact:** Mike Wise. Estab. 1974. Signatory of WGA. Represents 80 clients. 20% of clients are new/unpublished writers. Currently handles: 50% movie scripts; 50% TV scripts.

---

**THE PUBLISHING FIELD** is constantly changing! Agents often change addresses, phone numbers, or even companies. If you're still using this book and it is 2003 or later, buy the newest edition of *Guide to Literary Agents* at your favorite bookstore or order directly from Writer's Digest Books at (800)289-0963.

**Represents:** Movie scripts (feature film); TV movie of the week. **Considers these script subject areas:** action/adventure; comedy; contemporary issues; detective/police/crime; mystery/suspense; romantic comedy; romantic drama; thriller.

**How to Contact:** Query with SASE. Responds in 2 weeks to queries. Obtains most new clients through recommendations from others.

**Recent Sales:** This agency prefers not to share information on specific sales.

**Terms:** Agent receives 10% commission on dramatic rights sales. Offers written contract, binding for 1-2 years, per WGA.

**◎ BASKOW AGENCY**, 2948 E. Russell Rd., Las Vegas NV 89120. (702)733-7818. Fax: (702)733-2052. E-mail: jaki@baskow.com. **Contact:** Jaki Baskow. Estab. 1976. Represents 8 clients. 40% of clients are new/unpublished writers. Currently handles: 5% nonfiction books; 5% novels; 20% movie scripts; 70% TV scripts.

**Member Agents:** Crivolus Sarulus (scripts), Jaki Baskow.

**Represents:** Feature film; TV movie of the week; episodic drama; sitcom; documentary; miniseries; variety show. **Considers these script subject areas:** action/adventure; biography/autobiography; comedy; contemporary issues; family saga; glitz; mystery/suspense; religious/inspirational; romantic comedy; romantic drama; science fiction (juvenile only); thriller.

    **0—** Actively seeking unique scripts/all-American true stories, kids projects and movies of the week. Does not want to receive heavy violence.

**How to Contact:** Submit outline, proposal and treatments. Accepts e-mail and fax queries. Responds in 1 month to queries. Obtains most new clients through recommendations from others.

**Recent Sales:** Sold 3 movie/TV MOW scripts in the last year. *Malpractice*, by Larry Leirketen (Blakely), *Angel of Death*, (CBS). Other clients include Cheryl Anderson, Camisole Prods, Michael Store.

**Terms:** Agent receives 10% commission on domestic sales; 10% commission on foreign sales. Offers written contract.

**✓ ◎ THE BENNETT AGENCY**, 1129 State St., Suite 9, Santa Barbara CA 93101. (805)963-7600. Fax: (805)963-7603. **Contact:** Carole Bennett. Estab. 1984. Member of DGA; signatory of WGA. Represents 15 clients. 2% of clients are new/unpublished writers. Currently handles: 5% movie scripts; 95% TV scripts.

**Member Agents:** Carole Bennett (owner), Kristin Stiff (assistant).

**Represents:** Feature film; sitcom. **Considers these script subject areas:** comedy; family saga; mainstream.

    **0—** This agency specializes in TV sitcoms.

**How to Contact:** Query with SASE. Considers simultaneous queries. Responds in 2 months to queries. Returns materials only with SASE. Obtains most new clients through recommendations from others.

**Recent Sales:** "Most of our clients are on the writing staff of such half-hour sitcoms as *Friends* and *Dharma & Greg*."

**Terms:** Agent receives 10% commission on domestic sales. Offers written contract.

**◎ BERMAN BOALS AND FLYNN INC.**, 208 W. 30th St., #401, New York NY 10001. (212)868-1068. **Contact:** Judy Boals or Jim Flynn. Estab. 1995. Member of AAR; signatory of WGA. Represents 35 clients.

**Represents:** Feature film; TV scripts; stage plays.

    **0—** This agency specializes in dramatic writing for stage, film, TV.

**How to Contact:** Query with SASE. Obtains most new clients through recommendations from others.

**Recent Sales:** This agency prefers not to share information on specific sales.

**Terms:** Agent receives 10% commission on domestic sales.

**✓ ◎ THE BOHRMAN AGENCY**, 8899 Beverly Blvd., Suite 811, Los Angeles CA 90048. (310)550-5444. Fax: (310)550-5445. **Contact:** Michael Hruska, Caren Bohrman, Rob Seltzner. Signatory of WGA.

**Represents:** Novels; feature film; TV scripts. **Considers these script subject areas:** action/adventure; biography/autobiography; cartoon/animation; comedy; contemporary issues; detective/police/crime; erotica; ethnic; experimental; family saga; fantasy; feminist; gay/lesbian; glitz; historical; horror; juvenile; mainstream; multicultural; multimedia; mystery/suspense; psychic/supernatural; regional; religious/inspirational; romantic comedy; romantic drama; science fiction; sports; teen; thriller; western/frontier.

**How to Contact:** Query with SASE. No unsolicited mss. Obtains most new clients through recommendations from others.

**Recent Sales:** This agency prefers not to share information on specific sales.

**◎◎◎ ALAN BRODIE REPRESENTATION**, 211 Piccadilly, London W1J 9WF, England. 0207-917-2871. Fax: 0207-917-2872. E-mail: alanbrodie@aol.com. **Contact:** Alan Brodie or Sarah McNair. Member of PMA. 10% of clients are new/unpublished writers.

    **0—** This agency specializes in stage, film and television.

**How to Contact:** All unsolicited mss returned unopened. North American writers should send SAE with IRCs for response, available at most post offices.

**Recent Sales:** This agency prefers not to share information on specific sales.

**Terms:** Agent receives 10-15% commission on domestic sales. Charges clients for photocopying.

**Tips:** "Biographical details can be helpful. Generally only playwrights whose work has been performed will be considered."

**[N] [●] BRUCE BROWN AGENCY**, 1033 Gayley Ave., Suite 207, Los Angeles CA 90024-3417. (310)208-1835. Fax: (310)208-2485. **Contact:** Bruce Brown. Estab. 1993. Signatory of WGA. Represents 40 clients. 5% of clients are new/unpublished writers.
**Member Agents:** Jennifer Good, Dave Brown.
**Represents:** Feature film; TV movie of the week; episodic drama; sitcom; animation; soap opera. **Considers these script subject areas:** action/adventure; biography/autobiography; cartoon/animation; comedy; contemporary issues; detective/police/crime; erotica; ethnic; experimental; family saga; fantasy; feminist; gay/lesbian; glitz; historical; horror; juvenile; mainstream; multicultural; multimedia; mystery/suspense; psychic/supernatural; regional; religious/inspirational; romantic comedy; romantic drama; science fiction; sports; teen; thriller; western/frontier.
　　O→ This agency specializes in situation comedy and drama (television series); writers and directors; TV longform, features, cable, soap operas, animation.
**How to Contact:** Query with SASE. Obtains most new clients through recommendations from others.
**Recent Sales:** This agency prefers not to share information on specific sales.
**Terms:** Agent receives 10% commission on domestic sales. Offers written contract, binding for 2 years.

**[●] CURTIS BROWN LTD.**, 10 Astor Place, New York NY 10003-6935. (212)473-5400. Fax: (212)473-5400. **Contact:** Perry Knowlton, chairman emeritas, Timothy Knowlton, CEO. Also: 1750 Montgomery St., San Francisco CA 94111. (415)954-8566. **Contact**: Peter L. Ginsberg, president. Queries to Blake Peterson.
　　● See the expanded listing for this agency in Literary Agents: Nonfee-charging.

**[✓] [●] DON BUCHWALD & ASSOCIATES, INC.**, 6500 Wilshire Blvd., Suite 2200, Los Angeles CA 90048. (323)655-7400. Fax: (323)655-7470. Website: www.donbuchwald.com. Estab. 1977. Signatory of WGA. Represents 50 clients.
**Represents:** Movie scripts; feature film; TV scripts; TV movie of the week; episodic drama; sitcom; documentary; miniseries.
　　O→ This agency represents talent and literary clients.
**How to Contact:** Query with SASE. Accepts fax queries. Considers simultaneous queries. Obtains most new clients through recommendations from others.

**[✓] [●] KELVIN C. BULGER AND ASSOCIATES**, 11 E. Adams St., Suite 604, Chicago IL 60603. Phone/fax: (312)692-1002. E-mail: kcbwoi@aol.com. **Contact:** Kelvin C. Bulger. Estab. 1992. Signatory of WGA. Represents 25 clients. 90% of clients are new/unpublished writers. Currently handles: 75% movie scripts; 25% TV scripts.
**Member Agents:** Kevin C. Bulger, Melanie Barnes Zeleke, Baku Talbert.
**Represents:** Feature film; TV movie of the week; documentary; syndicated material. **Considers these script subject areas:** action/adventure; cartoon/animation; comedy; contemporary issues; ethnic; family saga; religious/inspirational.
**How to Contact:** Query with SASE. Accepts e-mail and fax queries. Considers simultaneous queries. Responds in 3 weeks to queries; 2 months to mss. Returns materials only with SASE. Obtains most new clients through recommendations from others, solicitations.
**Recent Sales:** This agency prefers not to share information on specific sales.
**Terms:** Agent receives 10% commission on domestic sales; 10% commission on foreign sales. Offers written contract, binding for 6-12 months.
**Tips:** "Proofread before submitting to agent. We only reply to letters of inquiry if SASE is enclosed."

**[$] [◎] SUZANNA CAMEJO & ASSOC.**, 3000 W. Olympic Blvd., Santa Monica CA 90404. (310)449-4054. Fax: (310)449-4026. E-mail: scamejo@earthlink.net. **Contact:** Elizabeth Harris. Estab. 1992. Represents 10 clients. 30% of clients are new/unpublished writers. Currently handles: 5% novels; 80% movie scripts; 10% TV scripts; 5% life stories.
**Member Agents:** Suzanna Camejo (issue oriented), Elizabeth Harris (creative associate).
**Represents:** Nonfiction books; novels; feature film; TV scripts; life stories. **Considers these nonfiction areas:** animals; nature/environment; women's issues/studies. **Considers these fiction areas:** ethnic; family saga; romance; environmental; animal. **Considers these script subject areas:** contemporary issues; ethnic; family saga; feminist; historical; romantic comedy; romantic drama; science fiction; thriller; environmental.
　　O→ This agency specializes in environmental issues, animal rights, women's stories, art-oriented, children/family. Does not want to receive action/adventure, violence.
**How to Contact:** Submit outline/proposal. Considers simultaneous queries. Responds in 1 month to mss. Returns materials only with SASE. Obtains most new clients through recommendations from others, solicitations.
**Recent Sales:** *Movie/TV MOW script(s) optioned/sold: Primal Scream*, by John Shirley (Showtime);.*The Christmas Project*, by Joe Hindy (Ganesha Partners).
**Terms:** Agent receives 10% commission on domestic sales; 10% commission on foreign sales. Offers written contract, binding for 1 year; 3 weeks notice must be given to terminate contract.
**Fees:** Charges $20 reading fee (per script or ms). Critiques of storyline, subplot, backstory, pace, characterization, dialogue, marketability, commerciality by professional readers; Charges postage for returned scripts.
**Tips:** "If the feature script is well written (three acts, backstory, subplot), with good characters and dialogue, the material is moving, funny or deals with important issues and is nonviolent (no war stories, please), we will read it and consider it for representation." Attends Cannes Film Festival (France, May); Telluride Film Festival (Colorado, September); Sundance Film Festival (Utah, January); AFM (Los Angeles, February).

✓ ◎ **THE MARSHALL CAMERON AGENCY**, 19667 NE 20th Lane, Lawtey FL 32058. (904)964-7013. E-mail: marshall_cameron_agency@onebox.com. **Contact:** Margo Prescott. Estab. 1986. Signatory of WGA. Currently handles: 100% movie scripts.
**Member Agents:** Margo Prescott, John Pizzo (New York co-agent).
**Represents:** Feature film. **Considers these script subject areas:** action/adventure; comedy; contemporary issues (drama); detective/police/crime; mainstream; thriller.
　　○━ This agency specializes in feature films.
**How to Contact:** Query with SASE. Accepts e-mail queries. No fax queries. Considers simultaneous queries. Responds in 1 week to queries; 2 months to mss. Returns materials only with SASE. Obtains most new clients through recommendations from others, solicitations.
**Recent Sales:** This agency prefers not to share information on specific sales.
**Terms:** Agent receives 10% commission on domestic sales; 20% commission on foreign sales. Offers written contract, binding for 1 year.
**Tips:** "Often professionals in film will recommend us to clients. We also actively solicit material. Always enclose a SASE with your query."

◎ **CEDAR GROVE AGENCY ENTERTAINMENT**, P.O. Box 1692, Issaquah WA 98027-0068. (425)837-1687. E-mail: cedargroveagency@juno.com. Website: freeyellow.com/members/cedargrove/index.html. **Contact:** Renee MacKenzie, Samantha Powers. Estab. 1995. Member of Cinema Seattle. Represents 7 clients. 100% of clients are new/unpublished writers. Currently handles: 90% movie scripts; 10% TV scripts.
　　● Prior to becoming agents, Ms. Taylor worked for the stock brokerage firm, Morgan Stanley Dean Witter; Ms. Powers was a customer service/office manager; Ms. MacKenzie was an office manager and recently a Production Manager.
**Member Agents:** Amy Taylor (Senior Vice President-Motion Picture Division), Samantha Powers (Executive Vice President-Motion Picture Division), Renee MacKenzie (Story Editor).
**Represents:** Feature film; TV movie of the week; sitcom. **Considers these script subject areas:** action/adventure; biography/autobiography; comedy; detective/police/crime; family saga; juvenile; mystery/suspense; romantic comedy; science fiction; sports; thriller; western/frontier.
　　○━ Cedar Grove Agency Entertainment was formed in the Pacific Northwest to take advantage of the rich and diverse culture as well as the many writers who reside there. Does not want period pieces, horror genres, children scripts dealing with illness, or scripts with excessive substance abuse.
**How to Contact:** Query with SASE, 1-page synopsis. Responds in 10 days to queries; 2 months to mss. Obtains most new clients through referrals and website.
**Recent Sales:** This agency prefers not to share information on specific sales.
**Terms:** Agent receives 10% commission on domestic sales. Offers written contract, binding for 6-12 months; 30-day notice must be given to terminate contract.
**Tips:** "We focus on finding that rare gem, the undiscovered, multi-talented writer, no matter where they live. Write, write, write! Find time everyday to write. Network with other writers when possible, and write what you know. Learn the craft through books. Read scripts of your favorite movies. Enjoy what you write!"

✓ ○ **CHADWICK & GROS LITERARY AGENCY**, Garden District Branch, POD 65163, Baton Rouge LA 70896-5163. (225)338-9861. Fax: (775)206-1180. E-mail: agentAP@Ocfilm.com or C.G.UK@Worldfilm.com. Website: colorpro.com/chadwick-gros/. **Contact:** Tony Seigan, associate director/overseas officer; Anna Piazza, director. Estab. 1998. Represents 30 clients. 95% of clients are new/unpublished writers. Currently handles: 90% movie scripts; 10% TV scripts.
　　● Prior to becoming an agent, Ms. Piazza was a talent scout for Rinehart & Associates.
**Member Agents:** Tony Seigan (associate director/overseas officer), David J. Carubba (business manager), C.J. Myerson (president of Institute of Baton Rouge Qford Writers [I-BROWS] Colony), Theron T. Jacks (business advisor).
**Represents:** Feature film; TV movie of the week; sitcom. **Considers these script subject areas:** action/adventure; biography/autobiography; comedy; detective/police/crime; family saga; juvenile; mystery/suspense; romantic comedy; science fiction; sports; thriller; western/frontier.
　　○━ Actively seeking "good attitudes; tough-minded, sure-footed, potential pros." Does not want to receive period pieces, horror genres, children scripts dealing with illness, or scripts with excessive substance abuse.
**How to Contact:** Query with SASE, 1-page synopsis. Accepts queries during February, July and October. Accepts e-mail and fax queries. Considers simultaneous queries. Responds in 10 days to queries; 2 months to mss. Returns materials only with SASE. Obtains most new clients through recommendations from others, website.
**Recent Sales:** Sold 16 scripts in the last year. *Carrot Tips*, by J. Seivers (Generation X), *The Author, The Ouida Link, Whorehouse Roux.*
**Terms:** Agent receives 10% commission on domestic sales; 15% commission on foreign sales. Offers written contract, binding for 1-2 years; 6-month notice required notice must be given to terminate contract. Charges clients for all communications with C&G—phone, fax, postage and handling—fees fall to queries/clients; that is, office expenses, postage, photocopying, but NO MARKETING FEE.
**Tips:** "Be most businesslike when you tap on an agency's door. Agencies are business offices, and every exchange costs money, time, effort, grief or joy."

✓ ◙ **CLIENT FIRST-A/K/A LEO P. HAFFEY AGENCY**, P.O.Box 128049, Nashville TN 37212-8049. (615)463-2388. E-mail: c1st@nashville.net. Website: www.c-1st.com or www.nashville.net/~cl. **Contact:** Robin Swensen. Estab. 1990. Signatory of WGA. Represents 21 clients. 25% of clients are new/unpublished writers. Currently handles: 40% novels; 60% movie scripts.
**Member Agents:** Leo Haffey (attorney/agent in the motion picture industry).
**Represents:** Feature film; animation. **Considers these script subject areas:** action/adventure; cartoon/animation; comedy; contemporary issues; detective/police/crime; family saga; historical; mystery/suspense; romantic drama (contemporary, historical); science fiction; sports; thriller; western/frontier.
    O— This agency specializes in movie scripts and novels for sale to motion picture industry.
**Also Handles:** Nonfiction books (self-help); novels; short story collections; novellas.
**How to Contact:** Query with SASE. Considers simultaneous queries. Responds in 1 week to queries; 2 months to mss. Returns materials only with SASE. Obtains most new clients through recommendations from others.
**Recent Sales:** This agency prefers not to share information on specific sales.
**Terms:** Offers written contract, binding for negotiable length of time.
**Tips:** "The motion picture business is a numbers game like any other. The more you write the better your chances are of success. Please send a SASE along with your query letter."

◙ **COMMUNICATIONS AND ENTERTAINMENT, INC.**, 2851 South Ocean Blvd., #5K, Boca Raton FL 33432-8407. (561)391-9575. Fax: (561)391-7922. E-mail: jlbearde@bellsouth.net. **Contact:** James L. Bearden. Estab. 1989. Represents 10 clients. 50% of clients are new/unpublished writers. Currently handles: 10% novels; 5% juvenile books; 40% movie scripts; 40% TV scripts.
    ● Prior to opening his agency, Mr. Bearden worked as a producer/director and an entertainment attorney.
**Member Agents:** James Bearden (TV/film), Roslyn Ray (literary).
**Represents:** Movie scripts; TV scripts; syndicated material.
    O— This agency specializes in TV, film and print media. Actively seeking "synopsis, treatment or summary." Does not want to receive "scripts/screenplays unless requested."
**Also Handles:** Novels; juvenile books. **Considers these nonfiction areas:** history; music/dance; theater/film. **Considers these fiction areas:** action/adventure; comic books/cartoon; fantasy; historical; mainstream/contemporary; science fiction; thriller.
**How to Contact:** For scripts, query with SASE. For books, query with outline/proposal or send entire ms., Responds in 1 month to queries; 3 months to mss. Obtains most new clients through recommendations from others.
**Recent Sales:** This agency prefers not to share information on specific sales.
**Terms:** Agent receives 10% commission on domestic sales; 5% commission on foreign sales. Offers written contract, binding for varies with project.
**Tips:** "Be patient."

◙ **COMMUNICATIONS MANAGEMENT ASSOCIATES**, 1129 Sixth Ave., #1, Rockford IL 61104-3147. (815)964-1335. Fax: (815)964-3061. **Contact:** Thomas R. Lee. Estab. 1989. Represents 30 clients. 50% of clients are new/unpublished writers. Currently handles: 5% nonfiction books; 10% novels; 80% movie scripts; 5% TV scripts.
**Member Agents:** Jack Young.
**Represents:** Feature film; TV movie of the week; animation; documentary; miniseries. **Considers these script subject areas:** action/adventure; biography/autobiography; cartoon/animation; comedy; contemporary issues; detective/police/crime; erotica; fantasy; historical; horror; juvenile; mainstream; psychic/supernatural; religious/inspirational; romantic comedy; romantic drama; science fiction; teen; thriller; western/frontier.
    O— This agency specializes in research, editing and financing.
**Also Handles:** Novels; short story collections; novellas; juvenile books; scholarly books; poetry books. **Considers these fiction areas:** action/adventure (adventure); detective/police/crime; erotica; fantasy; historical; horror; juvenile; mainstream/contemporary; mystery/suspense; picture books; romance (historical, regency); science fiction; thriller; westerns/frontier; young adult.
**How to Contact:** Query with SASE, outline/proposal, 3 sample chapter(s). Discards unwanted material., Accepts e-mail and fax queries. Considers simultaneous queries. Obtains most new clients through recommendations from others.
**Recent Sales:** This agency prefers not to share information on specific sales. Send query for list of credits.
**Terms:** Agent receives 10% commission on domestic sales; 15% commission on foreign sales. Offers written contract, binding for 2-4 months; 60 days notice must be given to terminate contract. Charges clients for postage, photocopying and office expenses.
**Writers' Conferences:** BEA.
**Tips:** "Don't let greed or fame-seeking, or anything but a sincere love of writing push you into this business."

◙ **THE COPPAGE COMPANY, (III)**, 5411 Carmellia Ave., North Hollywood CA 91601. (818)980-8806. Fax: (818)980-8824. **Contact:** Judy Coppage. Estab. 1985. Signatory of WGA; Member of DGA, SAG, AFTRA.
**Represents:** Feature film; TV scripts (original).
    O— This agency specializes in "writers who also produce, direct and act."
**How to Contact:** Obtains most new clients through recommendation only.
**Recent Sales:** This agency prefers not to share information on specific sales.

**Terms:** Agent receives 10% commission on domestic sales; 10% commission on foreign sales. Offers written contract, binding for 2 years.

**⦾ DOUROUX & CO.**, 445 S. Beverly Dr., Suite 310, Beverly Hills CA 90212-4401. (310)552-0900. Fax: (310)552-0920. E-mail: douroux@relaypoint.net. Website: www.relaypoint.net/~douroux. **Contact:** Michael E. Douroux. Estab. 1985. Member of DGA; signatory of WGA. 20% of clients are new/unpublished writers. Currently handles: 50% movie scripts; 50% TV scripts.
**Member Agents:** Michael E. Douroux (chairman/CEO).
**Represents:** Movie scripts; feature film; TV scripts; TV movie of the week; episodic drama; sitcom; animation. **Considers these script subject areas:** action/adventure; comedy; detective/police/crime; family saga; fantasy; historical; mainstream; mystery/suspense; romantic comedy; romantic drama; science fiction; thriller; western/frontier.
**How to Contact:** Query with SASE. Accepts e-mail queries. Considers simultaneous queries.
**Recent Sales:** This agency prefers not to share information on specific sales.
**Terms:** Agent receives 10% commission on domestic sales. Offers written contract, binding for 2 years. Charges for photocopying only.

**◎ DRAMATIC PUBLISHING, (Specialized: theatrical works)**, 311 Washington St., Woodstock IL 60098. (815)338-7170. Fax: (815)338-8981. E-mail: plays@dramaticpublishing.com. Website: www.dramaticpublishing.com. **Contact:** Linda Habjan. Estab. 1885. Currently handles: 2% textbooks; 98% stage plays.
**Represents:** Stage plays.
   **O⇨** This agency specializes in a full range of stage plays, musicals, adaptations, and instructional books about theater.
**How to Contact:** Submit complete ms, SASE. Responds in 6 months to queries.
**Recent Sales:** This agency prefers not to share information on specific sales.

**⦾ EPSTEIN-WYCKOFF AND ASSOCIATES**, 280 S. Beverly Dr., #400, Beverly Hills CA 90212-3904. (310)278-7222. Fax: (310)278-4640. **Contact:** Karin Wakefield. Estab. 1993. Signatory of WGA. Represents 15 clients. Currently handles: 1% nonfiction books; 1% novels; 60% movie scripts; 30% TV scripts; 2% stage plays.
**Member Agents:** Karin Wakefield (literary), Craig Wyckoff (talent);. Gary Epstein (talent).
**Represents:** Feature film; TV movie of the week; episodic drama; sitcom; animation; miniseries; soap opera; stage plays. **Considers these script subject areas:** action/adventure; comedy; contemporary issues; detective/police/crime; erotica; family saga; feminist; gay/lesbian; historical; juvenile; mainstream; mystery/suspense; romantic comedy; romantic drama; teen; thriller.
   **O⇨** This agency specializes in features, TV, books and stage plays.
**Also Handles:** Nonfiction books; novels.
**How to Contact:** Responds in 1 month to solicited mss. Obtains most new clients through recommendations from others.
**Recent Sales:** This agency prefers not to share information on specific sales.
**Terms:** Agent receives 15% commission on domestic sales; 20% commission on foreign sales; 10% commission on dramatic rights sales. Offers written contract, binding for 1 year. Charges clients for photocopying.

**⟦$⟧ ⦿ ESQ. MANAGEMENT**, P.O. Box 16194, Beverly Hills CA 90209-2194. (310)252-9879. **Contact:** Patricia E. Lee, Esq. Estab. 1996. Member of Motion Picture Editors Guild. Represents 2 clients. 0% of clients are new/unpublished writers. Currently handles: 100% movie scripts.
   ● Prior to opening her agency, Ms. Lee was a film editor.
**Represents:** Feature film; TV movie of the week; sitcom; animation; miniseries. **Considers these script subject areas:** action/adventure; biography/autobiography; cartoon/animation; comedy; contemporary issues; detective/police/crime; erotica; ethnic; fantasy; feminist; gay/lesbian; historical; horror; juvenile; mystery/suspense; psychic/supernatural; religious/inspirational; romantic comedy; romantic drama; science fiction; teen; thriller; western/frontier.
   **O⇨** This management company specializes in representing people who are working professionals in more than one area. Actively seeking writers who have been optioned and/or have made at least one sale previously.
**How to Contact:** Query with SASE, synopsis. Discards unwanted queries; returns mss. No e-mail or fax queries. Considers simultaneous queries. Obtains most new clients through listings in agents/managers directories; print ads; referrals.
**Recent Sales:** This agency prefers not to share information on specific sales.
**Terms:** Agent receives 9% commission on domestic sales; 9% commission on foreign sales. Offers written contract, binding for 2 years, during which contract can only be terminated under certain specified circumstances. "During the 2-year period, contract can only be terminated under certain specified circumstances."

---

**IF YOU'RE LOOKING** for a particular agent, check the Agents Index to find the specific agency where the agent works. Then check the listing for that agency in the appropriate section.

**Fees:** "No reading fee unless material submitted for our critiquing/proofreading service. Rates vary from $150-450 depending on length of report." 10% of business is derived from criticism fees. Payment of criticism fee does not ensure representation. Charges clients $30/month for postage, photocopying, etc.
**Tips:** "Make sure you've got a good query letter. Enclose a résumé or a bio."

☑ ⃝ **FEIGEN/PARRENT LITERARY MANAGEMENT**, 10158 Hollow Glen Circle, Bel Air CA 90077-2112. (310)271-4722. Fax: (310)274-0503. E-mail: feigenparrentlit@aol.com. **Contact:** Brenda Feigen, Joanne Parrent. Estab. 1995. Member of PEN USA West, Authors Guild, LA County Bar Association. Represents 35-40 clients. 20-30% of clients are new/unpublished writers. Currently handles: 40% nonfiction books; 30% novels; 25% movie scripts; 5% TV scripts.
- See the expanded listing for this agency in Literary Agents: Nonfee-charging.

⃝ **FILM ARTISTS ASSOCIATES**, 13563 Ventura Blvd., 2nd Floor, Sherman Oaks CA 91423. (818)386-9669. Fax: (818)386-9363. **Contact:** Penrod Dennis. Signatory of WGA.
**How to Contact:** Considers simultaneous queries.
**Terms:** Agent receives 10% commission on domestic sales; 10% commission on foreign sales. Offers written contract, binding for 1 year; After 6 months, 1-month notice must be given to terminate contract.
**Tips:** "Know your craft, know your market, submit accordingly and professionally. Be receptive to criticism and feedback."

⃝ **FILMWRITERS LITERARY AGENCY**, 4932 Long Shadow Dr., Midlothian VA 23112. (804)744-1718. **Contact:** Helene Wagner. Signatory of WGA.
- Prior to opening her agency, Ms. Wagner was director of the Virginia Screenwriter's Forum for 7 years and taught college level screenwriting classes. "As a writer myself, I have won or been a finalist in most major screenwriting competitions throughout the country and have a number of my screenplays optioned. Through the years I have enjoyed helping and working with other writers. Some have gone on to have their movies made, their work optioned, and won national contests."
**Represents:** Feature film; TV movie of the week; miniseries. **Considers these script subject areas:** action/adventure; comedy; contemporary issues; detective/police/crime; historical; juvenile; mystery/suspense; psychic/supernatural; romantic comedy; romantic drama; teen; thriller.
- ⊶ This agency is actively seeking "original and intelligent writing; professional in caliber, correctly formatted and crafted with strong characters and storytelling." Does not want "clones of last year's big movies, somebody's first screenplay that's filled with "talking heads", camera directions, real life "chit-chat" that doesn't belong in a movie, or a story wiht no conflict or drama in it."
**How to Contact:** "I'm not taking new clients now." Obtains most new clients through recommendations from others.
**Recent Sales:** *Movie/TV MOW script(s) optioned/sold: Woman of His Dreams*, by Jeff Rubin (Ellenfreyer Productions).
**Terms:** Agent receives 10% commission on domestic sales; 10% commission on foreign sales. Offers written contract. Clients supply photocopying and postage. Writers reimbursed for office fees after the sale of ms.
**Tips:** "Professional writers should wait until they have at least four drafts done before they send out their work because they know it takes that much hard work to make a story and characters work. Show me something I haven't seen before with characters that I care about, that jump off the page. I not only look at writer's work, I look at the writer's talent. If I believe in a writer, even though a piece may not sell, I'll stay with the writer and help nurture that talent which a lot of the big agencies won't do."

⃝ **B.R. FLEURY AGENCY**, P.O. Box 149352, Orlando FL 32814-9352. (407)895-8494. Fax: (407)898-3923. E-mail: brfleuryagency@juno.com. **Contact:** Blanche or Margaret. Estab. 1994. Signatory of WGA. Currently handles: 70% nonfiction books; 30% movie scripts.
- See expanded listing for this agency in Literary Agents: Nonfee-charging.

Ⓜ **THE BARRY FREED CO.**, 2040 Ave. of the Stars, #400, Los Angeles CA 90067. (310)277-1260. Fax: (310)277-3865. E-mail: blfreed@aol.com. **Contact:** Barry Freed. Signatory of WGA. Represents 15 clients. 95% of clients are new/unpublished writers. Currently handles: 100% movie scripts.
- Prior to opening his agency, Mr. Freed worked for ICM.
**Represents:** Feature film; TV movie of the week. **Considers these script subject areas:** action/adventure; comedy; contemporary issues; detective/police/crime; ethnic; family saga.
- ⊶ Actively seeking adult drama, comedy, romantic comedy. Does not want to receive period, science fiction.
**How to Contact:** Query with SASE. Prefers to read materials exclusively. Accepts e-mail and fax queries. Responds in 3 months to mss. Responds immediately to queries. Obtains most new clients through recommendations from others.
**Recent Sales:** This agency prefers not to share information on specific sales.
**Terms:** Offers written contract, binding for 2 years.
**Tips:** "Our clients are a high qualified small roster of writers who write comedy, action adventure/thrillers, adult drama, romantic comedy."

**ROBERT A. FREEDMAN DRAMATIC AGENCY, INC.**, 1501 Broadway, Suite 2310, New York NY 10036. (212)840-5760. **Contact:** Robert A. Freedman, president; Selma Luttinger, vice president; Marta Praeger and Robin Kaver, associates. Estab. 1928. Member of AAR; signatory of WGA.

● Prior to opening his agency, Mr. Freedman has served as vice president of the dramatic division of AAR.

**Represents:** Movie scripts; TV scripts; stage plays.

☞ This agency prefers to work with established authors; works with new authors. Specializes in plays, movie scripts and TV scripts.

**How to Contact:** Query with SASE. All unsolicited mss returned unopened. Responds in 2 weeks to queries; 3 months to mss.

**Recent Sales:** "We will speak directly with any prospective client concerning sales that are relevant to his/her specific script."

**Terms:** Agent receives 10% commission on domestic sales. Charges clients for photocopying.

**SAMUEL FRENCH, INC.**, 45 W. 25th St., New York NY 10010-2751. (212)206-8990. Fax: (212)206-1429. E-mail: samuelfrench@earthlink.net. Website: www.samuelfrench.com. **Contact:** Lawrence Harbison, editor. Estab. 1830. Member of AAR.

**Member Agents:** Brad Lorenz, Alleen Hussung, Linda Kirkland, Charles R. Van Nostrand.

**Represents:** Theatrical stage play; musicals. **Considers these script subject areas:** comedy; contemporary issues; detective/police/crime; ethnic; fantasy; horror; mystery/suspense; thriller.

☞ This agency specializes in publishing plays which they also license for production.

**How to Contact:** Query with SASE or submit complete ms. Accepts e-mail and fax queries. Considers simultaneous queries. Responds in 2-8 months to mss. Responds immediately to queries.

**Recent Sales:** This agency prefers not to share information on specific sales.

**Terms:** Agent receives variable commission on domestic sales.

**THE GAGE GROUP**, 9255 Sunset Blvd, Suite 515, Los Angeles CA 90069. (310)859-8777. Fax: (310)859-8166. Estab. 1976. Member of DGA; signatory of WGA. Represents 34 clients.

**Represents:** Movie scripts; feature film; TV scripts; theatrical stage play. **Considers these script subject areas:** action/adventure; biography/autobiography; cartoon/animation; comedy; contemporary issues; detective/police/crime; erotica; ethnic; experimental; family saga; fantasy; feminist; gay/lesbian; glitz; historical; horror; juvenile; mainstream; multicultural; multimedia; mystery/suspense; psychic/supernatural; regional; religious/inspirational; romantic comedy; romantic drama; science fiction; sports; teen; thriller; western/frontier; considers all script subject areas.

**How to Contact:** Query with SASE. Responds in 1 month to queries; 1 month to mss.

**Recent Sales:** This agency prefers not to share information on specific sales.

**Terms:** Agent receives 10% commission on domestic sales; 10% commission on foreign sales.

**GEDDES AGENCY**, 8430 Santa Monica Blvd., #200, West Hollywood CA 90069. **Contact:** Literary Department. Estab. 1983 in L.A., 1967 in Chicago. Member of SAG, AFTRA; signatory of WGA. Represents 15 clients.

**Member Agents:** Ann Geddes, Ron Singer

**Represents:** Feature film; TV movie of the week; episodic drama; sitcom; miniseries; variety show. **Considers these script subject areas:** action/adventure; comedy; contemporary issues; detective/police/crime; ethnic; experimental; fantasy; horror; mainstream; mystery/suspense; psychic/supernatural; romantic comedy; romantic drama; science fiction; teen; thriller.

**How to Contact:** Query with SASE, synopsis. Responds in 2 months only if interested to mss. Obtains most new clients through recommendations from others, mailed-in synopses.

**Recent Sales:** This agency prefers not to share information on specific sales.

**Terms:** Agent receives 10% commission on domestic sales. Offers written contract, binding for 1 year. Charges for "handling and postage for a script to be returned-otherwise it is recycled."

**Tips:** "Send in query—say how many scripts you have available for representation. Send synopsis of each one. Mention something about yourself."

**THE LAYA GELFF LITERARY AND TALENT AGENCY**, (formerly The Laya Gelff Agency), 16133 Ventura Blvd., Suite 700, Encino CA 91436. (818)996-3100. Estab. 1985. Signatory of WGA. Represents many clients. Currently handles: 50% movie scripts; 40% TV scripts; 10% book mss.

**Represents:** Feature film, TV scripts.

☞ This agency specializes in TV and film scripts; WGA members preferred. "Also represents writers to publishers."

**How to Contact:** Query with SASE. Responds in 3 weeks to queries; 6 weeks to mss. "Must have SASE for reply." Does not accept queries by e-mail or fax. Considers simultaneous queries and submissions. Obtains new clients through recommendations from others.

**Recent Sales:** This agency prefers not to share information on specific sales.

**Terms:** Agent receives 10% commission on domestic sales; 10% on foreign sales. Offers standard WGA contract.

**Fees:** Charges reading fee for book representation only.

**N MICHELLE GORDON & ASSOCIATES**, 260 S. Beverly Dr., Suite 308, Beverly Hills CA 90212. (310)246-9930. **Contact:** Michelle Gordon. Estab. 1993. Signatory of WGA. Represents 4 clients. None of clients are new/previously unpublished writers. Currently handles: 100% movie scripts.
**Represents:** Movie scripts. **Considers these script subject areas:** biography/autobiography; contemporary issues; detective/police/crime; feminist; government/politics/law, psychology, true crime/investigative, women's studies.
**How to Contact:** Query with SASE. Responds in 3 weeks to queries if interested. Obtains most new clients through recommendations from others, solicitations.
**Recent Sales:** This agency prefers not to share information on specific sales.
**Terms:** Agent receives 10% commission on domestic sales; 10% commission on foreign sales. Offers written contract, binding for 1 year.

**GRAHAM AGENCY**, 311 W. 43rd St., New York NY 10036. (212)489-7730. **Contact:** Earl Graham. Estab. 1971. Represents 40 clients. 30% of clients are new/unpublished writers. Currently handles: movie scripts; stage plays.
**Represents:** Feature film; theatrical stage play.
  ○━ This agency specializes in playwrights and screenwriters only. "We're interested in commercial material of quality." Does not want to receive one-acts or material for children.
**How to Contact:** Query with SASE. No e-mail or fax queries. Responds in 3 months to queries; 6 weeks to mss. Obtains most new clients through recommendations from others, solicitations.
**Recent Sales:** This agency prefers not to share information on specific sales.
**Terms:** Agent receives 10% commission on dramatic rights sales.
**Tips:** "Write a concise, intelligent letter giving the gist of what you are offering."

**ARTHUR B. GREENE**, 101 Park Ave., 26th Floor, New York NY 10178. (212)661-8200. Fax: (212)370-7884. **Contact:** Arthur Greene. Estab. 1980. Represents 20 clients. 10% of clients are new/unpublished writers. Currently handles: 25% novels; 10% story collections; 10% novellas; 25% movie scripts; 10% TV scripts; 10% stage plays; 10% other.
**Represents:** Feature film; TV movie of the week; stage plays. **Considers these script subject areas:** action/adventure; detective/police/crime; horror; mystery/suspense.
  ○━ This agency specializes in movies, TV, fiction.
**Also Handles:** Novels. **Considers these nonfiction areas:** animals; music/dance; sports; theater/film. **Considers these fiction areas:** action/adventure; detective/police/crime; horror; mystery/suspense; sports; thriller.
**How to Contact:** Query with SASE. Responds in 2 weeks to queries. Obtains most new clients through recommendations from others.
**Recent Sales:** This agency prefers not to share information on specific sales.
**Terms:** Agent receives 10% commission on domestic sales; 20% commission on foreign sales. No written contract. 100% of business is derived from commissions on ms sales.

**THE SUSAN GURMAN AGENCY**, 865 West End Ave., #15A, New York NY 10025-8403. (212)749-4618. Fax: (212)864-5055. **Contact:** Susan Gurman. Estab. 1993. Signatory of WGA. 28% of clients are new/unpublished writers. Currently handles: 70% movie scripts; 30% stage plays.
**Member Agents:** Gail Eisenberg (associate agent), Susan Gurman.
**Represents:** Feature film; TV movie of the week; theatrical stage play. **Considers these script subject areas:** comedy; detective/police/crime; family saga; horror; mainstream; mystery/suspense; romantic comedy; romantic drama; thriller; true stories.
  ○━ This agency specializes in referred screenwriters and playwrights.
**Also Handles: Considers these nonfiction areas:** biography/autobiography; true crime/investigative. **Considers these fiction areas:** action/adventure (adventure); detective/police/crime; family saga; fantasy; horror; literary; mainstream/contemporary; mystery/suspense; picture books; thriller.
**How to Contact:** Responds in 2 weeks to queries; 2 months to mss. Obtains most new clients through recommendations from others.
**Recent Sales:** This agency prefers not to share information on specific sales.
**Terms:** Agent receives 10% commission on domestic sales; 10% commission on foreign sales.

**H.W.A. TALENT REPRESENTATIVES**, 3500 W. Olive Ave., Suite 1400, Burbank CA 91505. (818)972-4310. Fax: (818)972-4313. **Contact:** Kimber Wheeler. Estab. 1985. Signatory of WGA. 60% of clients are new/unpublished writers. Currently handles: 10% novels; 90% movie scripts.
**Represents:** Movie scripts; TV scripts. **Considers these script subject areas:** action/adventure; biography/autobiography; cartoon/animation; comedy; contemporary issues; detective/police/crime; ethnic; family saga; fantasy; feminist; gay/lesbian; horror; mystery/suspense; psychic/supernatural; romantic comedy; romantic drama; science fiction; sports; thriller.
**Also Handles:** Novels.
**How to Contact:** Query with SASE, outline/proposal.
**Recent Sales:** This agency prefers not to share information on specific sales.
**Terms:** Agent receives 10% commission on domestic sales. Offers written contract, binding for 1 year; WGA rules on termination apply.

**Tips:** "A good query letter is important. Use any relationship you have in the business to get your material read."

☑ ◖ **HART LITERARY MANAGEMENT**, 3541 Olive St., Santa Ynez CA 93460. (805)686-7912. Fax: (805)686-7912. E-mail: hartliteraryagency@hotmail.com. Website: hartliterary.com. **Contact:** Susan Hart. Estab. 1997. Signatory of WGA. Represents 35 clients. 95% of clients are new/unpublished writers. Currently handles: 2% nonfiction books; 98% movie scripts.

&bull; Prior to opening the agency, Ms. Hart was a screenwriter.

**Represents:** Movie scripts; feature film; TV movie of the week. **Considers these script subject areas:** biography/autobiography; family saga; horror; juvenile; mainstream; science fiction; teen.

**How to Contact:** Query with SASE. Accepts e-mail and fax queries. Considers simultaneous queries. Responds in 2 weeks to queries. Returns materials only with SASE. Obtains most new clients through solicitations.

**Recent Sales:** *Annus Horribilis (My Horrible Year)*, by J. McIluaine (Millbrook Farm Productions/Showtime).

**Terms:** Agent receives 10% domestic or worldwide sales on gross income written any source from the screenplays. Offers written contract, binding for 1 year. Charges clients for photocopies and postage; $6.50 domestic, $10 Canadian and $12 International.

**Tips:** "I want a great story spell-checked, formatted, and "typed" in industry standard 12 point Courier or Courier New only, between 95-120 pages maximum. No overt gore, sex, violence."

☑ 🖫 ◖ **GIL HAYES & ASSOCIATES**, 5125 Barry Rd., Memphis TN 38117. (901)650-1888. **Contact:** Gil Hayes. Estab. 1992. Represents 10 clients. 40% of clients are new/unpublished writers. Currently handles: 100% movie scripts.

**Member Agents:** Gil Hayes.

**Represents:** Movie scripts. **Considers these script subject areas:** biography/autobiography; comedy; contemporary issues; family saga; mainstream; mystery/suspense.

ᴏ➥ This agency specializes in serious scripts.

**How to Contact:** Query with outline/proposal., No e-mail or fax queries. Responds in 3 months to queries; 6 months to mss. Obtains most new clients through recommendations from others.

**Recent Sales:** This agency prefers not to share information on specific sales.

**Terms:** Agent receives 10% commission on dramatic rights sales. Offers written contract, binding for usually 2 years.

**Fees:** Criticism service: $50 for script, $100 if requesting written notes in advance. Published writers write and review all critiques. Some major input from writers I already represent if area is appropriate. Writers must provide bound copies, usually 5-10 at a time if I represent them. Payment of criticism fee does not ensure representation.

**Tips:** "Always register with WGA or copyright material before sending to anyone."

◖ **CAROLYN HODGES AGENCY**, 1980 Glenwood Dr., Boulder CO 80304-2329. (303)443-4636. Fax: (303)443-4636. E-mail: hodgesc@earthlink.net. **Contact:** Carolyn Hodges. Estab. 1989. Signatory of WGA. Represents 15 clients. 75% of clients are new/unpublished writers. Currently handles: 15% movie scripts; 45% TV scripts.

&bull; Prior to opening her agency, Ms. Hodges was a freelance writer and founded the Writers in the Rockies Screenwriting Conference.

**Represents:** Feature film; TV movie of the week. **Considers these script subject areas:** comedy (light, black); romantic comedy; thriller (suspense, psychological).

ᴏ➥ This agency represents screenwriters for film and TV MOW. Does not want TV sitcom, drama or episodics.

**How to Contact:** Query with SASE. Accepts e-mail and fax queries. Considers simultaneous queries. Responds in 1 week to queries; 10 weeks to mss. Returns materials only with SASE. Obtains most new clients through recommendations from others.

**Recent Sales:** Available upon request.

**Terms:** Agent receives 10% commission on domestic sales; 10% commission on foreign sales. Offers written contract. No charge for criticism. "I always try to offer concrete feedback, even when rejecting a piece of material."

**Tips:** "Become proficient at your craft. Attend all workshops accessible to you. READ all the books applicable to your area of interest. READ as many 'produced' screenplays as possible. Live a full, vital and rewarding life so your writing will have something to say. Get involved in a writer's support group. Network with other writers. Receive 'critiques' from your peers and consider merit of suggestions. Don't be afraid to re-examine your perspective. Do yourself a favor and don't submit the 'first draft' of 'first script' to agents. Immature writing is obvious and will hurt your chance of later submissions."

◖ **BARBARA HOGENSON AGENCY**, 165 West End Ave., Suite 19-C, New York NY 10023. (212)874-8084. Fax: (212)362-3011. **Contact:** Barbara Hogenson. Estab. 1994. Member of AAR; signatory of WGA. Represents 60 clients. 5% of clients are new/unpublished writers. Currently handles: 35% nonfiction books; 15% novels; 15% movie scripts; 35% stage plays.

&bull; Prior to opening her agency, Ms. Hogenson was with the prestigious Lucy Kroll Agency for 10 years.

**Represents:** Feature film; TV movie of the week; sitcom; soap opera; theatrical stage play.

**Also Handles:** Nonfiction books; novels. **Considers these nonfiction areas:** biography/autobiography; history; interior design/decorating; music/dance; popular culture; theater/film. **Considers these fiction areas:** action/adventure; detective/police/crime; ethnic; historical; humor/satire; literary; mainstream/contemporary; mystery/suspense; romance (contemporary); thriller.

**How to Contact:** Query with SASE, outline. No unsolicited mss. Responds in 1 month to queries. Obtains most new clients through recommendations from others.
**Recent Sales:** *The Eighth Day*, by Tornton Wilder (Hallmark). **Book Sales:** *Daniel Plainway*, by Van Reid; *Life Lessons*, by Elizabeth Kubler-Ross, *South Mountain Road*, by Hesper Anderson (Simon & Schuster).
**Terms:** Agent receives 10% commission on domestic sales; 20% commission on foreign sales; 10% commission on dramatic rights sales. Offers written contract.

**HUDSON AGENCY**, 3 Travis Lane, Montrose NY 10548. (914)737-1475. Fax: (914)736-3064. E-mail: hudagency@juno.com. Website: www.hudsonagency.net. **Contact:** Susan Giordano. Estab. 1994. Signatory of WGA. Represents 30 clients. 50% of clients are new/unpublished writers. Currently handles: 50% movie scripts; 50% TV scripts.
**Member Agents:** Sue Giordano (features, live action), Cheri Santone (features and animation), Sunny Bik (Canada contact).
**Represents:** Feature film; TV movie of the week; sitcom; animation; documentary; miniseries. **Considers these script subject areas:** action/adventure; cartoon/animation; comedy; contemporary issues; detective/police/crime; family saga; fantasy; juvenile; mystery/suspense; romantic comedy; romantic drama; teen; western/frontier.
> This agency specializes in feature film and TV. Also specializes in animation writers. Actively seeking "writers with television and screenwriting education or workshops under their belts." Does not want to receive "R-rated material, no occult, no one that hasn't taken at least one screenwriting workshop."
**How to Contact:** Query with SASE, outline, sample pages. Accepts e-mail and fax queries. Considers simultaneous queries. Responds in 1 week to queries; 3 weeks to mss. Returns materials only with SASE. Obtains most new clients through recommendations from others.
**Recent Sales:** Sold 1 script in the last year. *Becoming Dick*, by Rick Gitelson (E! TV).
**Terms:** Agent receives 10% commission on domestic sales; 10% commission on foreign sales.
**Tips:** "Yes, we may be small, but we work very hard for our clients. Any script we are representing gets excellent exposure to producers. Our network has over 1,000 contacts in the business and growing rapidly. We are GOOD salespeople. Ultimately it all depends on the quality of the writing and the market for the subject matter. Do not query unless you have taken at least one screenwriting course and read all of Syd Field's books."

**INTERNATIONAL CREATIVE MANAGEMENT**, 8942 Wilshire Blvd., Beverly Hills CA 90211. (310)550-4000. Fax: (310)550-4100. East Coast Office: 40 W. 57th St., New York NY 10019. (212)556-5600. Fax: (212)556-5665. Member of AAR; signatory of WGA.
● See expanded listing for this agency in Literary Agents: Nonfee-charging.

**INTERNATIONAL LEONARDS CORP.**, 3612 N. Washington Blvd., Indianapolis IN 46205-3534. (317)926-7566. **Contact:** David Leonards. Estab. 1972. Signatory of WGA. Currently handles: 50% movie scripts; 50% TV scripts.
**Represents:** Feature film; TV movie of the week; sitcom; animation; variety show. **Considers these script subject areas:** action/adventure; cartoon/animation; comedy; contemporary issues; detective/police/crime; horror; mystery/suspense; romantic comedy; science fiction; sports; thriller.
**How to Contact:** Query with SASE. Prefers to read materials exclusively. Responds in 1 month to queries; 6 months to mss. Returns materials only with SASE. Obtains most new clients through recommendations from others, solicitations.
**Recent Sales:** This agency prefers not to share information on specific sales.
**Terms:** Agent receives 10% commission on domestic sales; 10% commission on foreign sales. Offers written contract, following WGA standards, which vary.

**JARET ENTERTAINMENT**, 2017 Pacific Ave., Suite 2, Venice CA 90291. (310)883-8807. Fax: (310)822-0916. E-mail: jaretentertainment@yahoo.com. Website: www.Jaretentertainment.com. **Contact:** Susan Sullivan. Represents 20 clients. 70% of clients are new/unpublished writers. Currently handles: 75% movie scripts; 25% TV scripts.
**Member Agents:** Seth Jaret (manager/producer), Susan Sullivan (creative executive), Nathan Santell (senior assistant/junior manager), Carrie Weiner (story editor), Liz Miller (development assistant).
**Represents:** Movie scripts; TV scripts; TV movie of the week; animation. **Considers these script subject areas:** action/adventure; biography/autobiography; cartoon/animation; comedy; mystery/suspense; psychic/supernatural; romantic comedy; romantic drama; science fiction; sports; thriller.
> This management company specializes in creative, out-of-the-box thinking. "We're willing to take a chance on well-written materials." Actively seeking science fiction, smart romantic comedy. Does not want "any projects with unnecessary violence, westerns, or antyhing you've seen before-studio programmers, black comedy or period pieces that drag out and are boring."
**How to Contact:** Query with SASE. Discards unwanted material., Accepts e-mail and fax queries. Considers simultaneous queries. Obtains most new clients through recommendations from others.
**Recent Sales:** Sold 5 scripts in the last year. *Bumper to Bumper*, (Fox); *The Fraud Prince*, (Warner Brothers). **Scripting Assignment(s):** *Girl in the Curl*, (Paramount).
**Terms:** Agent receives 10% commission on domestic sales. Offers written contract, binding for 10-24 months.

**LESLIE KALLEN AGENCY**, 15760 Ventura Blvd., Suite #700, Encino CA 91436. (818)906-2785. Fax: (818)906-8931. Website: www.lesliekallen.com. **Contact:** J.R. Gowan. Estab. 1988.
**Represents:** Feature film; TV movie of the week.
 ⊶ This agency specializes in feature film, gamers, animators and MOWs.
**How to Contact:** Query with SASE.
**Recent Sales:** This agency prefers not to share information on specific sales.
**Terms:** Agent receives 10% commission on domestic sales.
**Tips:** "Write a 1- to 2- paragraph query that makes an agent excited to read the material."

**CHARLENE KAY AGENCY**, 901 Beaudry St., Suite 6, St.Jean/Richelieu Quebec J3A 1C6 Canada. (450)348-5296. **Contact:** Louise Meyers, director of development. Estab. 1992. Member of BMI; signatory of WGA. 100% of clients are new/unpublished writers. Currently handles: 50% movie scripts; 50% TV scripts.
 • Prior to opening her agency, Ms. Kay was a screenwriter.
**Member Agents:** Louise Meyers, Karen Forsyth.
**Represents:** Feature film; TV scripts; TV movie of the week; episodic drama; sitcom; animation. **Considers these script subject areas:** action/adventure; biography/autobiography; family saga; fantasy; psychic/supernatural; romantic comedy; romantic drama; science fiction.
 ⊶ This agency specializes in teleplays and screenplays. "We seek stories that are out of the ordinary, something we don't see too often. A well-written and well-constructed script is important." Does not want to receive "thrillers or barbaric and erotic films. No novels, books, or manuscripts."
**How to Contact:** Query with SASE, outline/proposal, IRCs for submissions outside of Canada. No e-mail or fax queries. Considers simultaneous queries. Responds in 1 month to queries; 10 weeks to mss. Returns materials only with SASE.
**Recent Sales:** This agency prefers not to share information on specific sales.
**Terms:** Agent receives 10% commission on domestic sales; 10% commission on foreign sales. Offers written contract, binding for 1 year.
**Tips:** "This agency is listed on the WGA lists and query letters arrive by the dozens every week. As our present clients understand, success comes with patience. A sale rarely happens overnight, especially when you are dealing with totally unknown writers. We are not impressed by the credentials of a writer, amateur or professional or by his or her pitching techniques, but by his or her story ideas and ability to build a well-crafted script."

**KERIN-GOLDBERG ASSOCIATES**, 155 E. 55th St., #5D, New York NY 10022. (212)838-7373. Fax: (212)838-0774. **Contact:** Charles Kerin. Estab. 1984. Signatory of WGA. Represents 29 clients. Currently handles: 30% movie scripts; 30% TV scripts; 40% stage plays.
**Represents:** Movie scripts; feature film; TV scripts; TV movie of the week; episodic drama; sitcom; miniseries; syndicated material; variety show; stage plays. **Considers these script subject areas:** action/adventure; biography/autobiography; cartoon/animation; comedy; contemporary issues; detective/police/crime; erotica; ethnic; experimental; family saga; fantasy; feminist; gay/lesbian; glitz; historical; horror; juvenile; mainstream; multicultural; multimedia; mystery/suspense; psychic/supernatural; regional; religious/inspirational; romantic comedy; romantic drama; science fiction; sports; teen; thriller; western/frontier.
 ⊶ This agency specializes in theater plays, screenplays, teleplays.
**How to Contact:** Query with SASE. Responds in 1 month to queries; 2 months to mss. Obtains most new clients through recommendations from others.
**Recent Sales:** This agency prefers to not share information on specific sales.
**Terms:** Agent receives 10% commission on domestic sales; 10% commission on foreign sales. Offers written contract.

**WILLIAM KERWIN AGENCY**, 1605 N. Cahuenga, Suite 202, Hollywood CA 90028. (323)469-5155. **Contact:** Al Wood and Bill Kerwin. Estab. 1979. Signatory of WGA. Represents 5 clients. Currently handles: 100% movie scripts.
**Represents:** Movie scripts. **Considers these script subject areas:** mystery/suspense; romantic comedy; romantic drama; science fiction; thriller.
**How to Contact:** Query with SASE. Responds in 1 day to queries; 1 month to mss. Obtains most new clients through recommendations from others, solicitations.
**Recent Sales:** *Steel death*, featuring Jack Scalia (HBO or TMC film).
**Terms:** Agent receives 10% commission on domestic sales; 10% commission on foreign sales. Offers written contract, binding for 1-2 years; 30 days notice must be given to terminate contract. Offers free criticism service.
**Tips:** "Listen. Be nice."

**THE JOYCE KETAY AGENCY**, 1501 Broadway, Suite 1908, New York NY 10036. (212)354-6825. Fax: (212)354-6732. **Contact:** Joyce Ketay, Carl Mulert, Wendy Streeter. Signatory of WGA.
**Member Agents:** Joyce Ketay, Carl Mulert, Wendy Streeter.
**Represents:** Feature film; TV movie of the week; episodic drama; sitcom; theatrical stage play. **Considers these script subject areas:** action/adventure; comedy; contemporary issues; detective/police/crime; ethnic; experimental; family saga; fantasy; feminist; gay/lesbian; glitz; historical; juvenile; mainstream; mystery/suspense; psychic/supernatural; romantic comedy; romantic drama; thriller; western/frontier.
 ⊶ This agency specializes in playwrights and screenwriters only. Does not want to receive novels.

**Recent Sales:** This agency prefers not to share information on specific sales.

**PAUL KOHNER, INC., (Specialized: film rights)**, 9300 Wilshire Blvd., Suite 555, Beverly Hills CA, 90212-3211. (310)550-1060. **Contact:** Stephen Moore. Estab. 1938. Member of ATA; signatory of WGA. Represents 150 clients. 10% of clients are new/unpublished writers.
**Represents:** Feature film; TV movie of the week; episodic drama; sitcom; animation; documentary; miniseries; soap opera; variety show; stage plays; Film/TV rights to published books. **Considers these script subject areas:** action/adventure; comedy; family saga; historical; mainstream; mystery/suspense; romantic comedy; romantic drama.
  O— This agency specializes in film and TV rights sales and representation of film and TV writers.
**How to Contact:** "All unsolicited material is automatically discarded unread."
**Recent Sales:** This agency prefers not to share information on specific sales.
**Terms:** Agent receives 10% commission on domestic sales; 10% commission on foreign sales. Offers written contract, binding for 1-3 years. "We charge clients for copying manuscripts or scripts for submission unless a sufficient quantity is supplied by the author."

**EDDIE KRITZER PRODUCTIONS**, 8484 Wilshire Blvd., Suite 205, Beverly Hills CA 90211. (323)655-5696. Fax: (323)655-5173. E-mail: producedby@aol.com. Website: www.eddiekritzer.com. **Contact:** Clair Weer, executive story editor. Estab. 1995. Represents 20 clients. 50% of clients are new/unpublished writers. Currently handles: 25% nonfiction books; 5% novels; 10% movie scripts; 15% TV scripts; 1% stage plays; 1% syndicated material.
  • See the expanded listing for this agency in Literary Agents: Nonfee-charging.

**THE CANDACE LAKE AGENCY**, 9200 Sunset Blvd., Suite 820, Los Angeles CA 90069. (310)247-2115. Fax: (310)247-2116. E-mail: clagency@bwkliterary.com. **Contact:** Candace Lake. Estab. 1977. Member of DGA; signatory of WGA. 50% of clients are new/unpublished writers. Currently handles: 20% novels; 40% movie scripts; 40% TV scripts.
**Member Agents:** Candace Lake (president/agent), Richard Ryba (agent), Elaine Valencia (assistant).
**Represents:** Feature film; TV movie of the week; episodic drama; sitcom. **Considers these script subject areas:** action/adventure; biography/autobiography; cartoon/animation; comedy; contemporary issues; detective/police/crime; erotica; ethnic; experimental; family saga; fantasy; feminist; gay/lesbian; glitz; historical; horror; juvenile; mainstream; multicultural; multimedia; mystery/suspense; psychic/supernatural; regional; religious/inspirational; romantic comedy; romantic drama; science fiction; sports; teen; thriller; western/frontier.
  O— This agency specializes in screenplay and teleplay writers.
**Also Handles:** Novels. **Considers these fiction areas:** action/adventure; comic books/cartoon; confession; contemporary issues; detective/police/crime; erotica; ethnic; experimental; family saga; fantasy; feminist; gay/lesbian; glitz; gothic; hi-lo; historical; horror; humor/satire; juvenile; literary; mainstream/contemporary; military/war; multicultural; multimedia; mystery/suspense; New Age; occult; picture books; plays; poetry; poetry in translation; psychic/supernatural; regional; religious/inspirational; romance; science fiction; short story collections; spiritual; sports; thriller; translation; westerns/frontier; young adult.
**How to Contact:** Query with SASE. No unsolicited material. Accepts e-mail and fax queries. Considers simultaneous queries. Responds in 1 month to queries; 3 months to mss. Returns materials only with SASE. Obtains most new clients through recommendations from others.
**Recent Sales:** This agency prefers not to share information on specific sales.
**Terms:** Agent receives 10% commission on domestic sales; 10% commission on foreign sales. Offers written contract, binding for 2 years.

**LARCHMONT LITERARY AGENCY**, 444 N. Larchmont Blvd., Suite 200, Los Angeles CA 90004. (323)856-3070. E-mail: agency@larchmontlit.com. **Contact:** Joel Millner or Tony Zequeira. Estab. 1998. Member of DGA; signatory of WGA. Currently handles: 5% novels; 90% movie scripts; 5% TV scripts.
  • Prior to becoming an agent, Mr. Millner attended NYU Film School and participated in The William Morris agent training program.
**Represents:** Movie scripts; feature film. **Considers these script subject areas:** action/adventure; biography/autobiography; cartoon/animation; comedy; contemporary issues; detective/police/crime; fantasy; historical; horror; mainstream; mystery/suspense; psychic/supernatural; romantic comedy; romantic drama; science fiction; sports; thriller.
  O— This agency specializes in feature writers and feature writer/directors. "We maintain a small, highly selective client list and offer a long-term career management style of agenting that larger agencies can't provide." Actively seeking spec feature scripts or established feature writers.
**Also Handles:** Novels. **Considers these fiction areas:** action/adventure; fantasy; historical; horror; humor/satire; juvenile; literary; mainstream/contemporary; mystery/suspense; romance; science fiction; sports; thriller.
**How to Contact:** Query with SASE. Accepts e-mail queries. Prefers to read materials exclusively. Responds in 2 weeks to queries. Obtains most new clients through recommendations from others.
**Recent Sales:** This agency prefers not to share information on specific sales.
**Terms:** Agent receives 10% commission on domestic sales. No written contract.
**Writer's Conferences:** NYU Film School (Los Angeles, June).
**Tips:** "Please do not send a script until it is in its best possible draft."

☑ ◐ **LEGACIES**, 501 Woodstork Circle, Bradenton FL 34209-7393. (941)792-9159. Fax: (941)795-0552. **Contact:** Marcy Ann Amato, executive director. Estab. 1993. Member of Florida Motion Picture & Television Association, Board of Talent Agents, Dept. of Professional Regulations License No. TA 0000404; signatory of WGA. 50% of clients are new/unpublished writers. Currently handles: 10% novels; 80% movie scripts; 10% stage plays.
**Represents:** Feature film. **Considers these script subject areas:** comedy; contemporary issues; family saga; feminist; historical.
   O⌐ This agency specializes in screenplays.
**How to Contact:** Query with SASE. Considers simultaneous queries. Responds in 2 weeks to queries; 6 weeks to mss.
**Recent Sales:** *Death's Parallel*, by Dr. Oakley Jordan (Rainbow Books). *Movie/TV MOW script(s) optioned/sold:* *Aurora Leigh*, by Raleigh Marcell; *Elsie Venner*, by Raleigh Marcell.
**Terms:** Agent receives 15% commission on domestic sales; 20% commission on foreign sales. Offers written contract.
**Tips:** "New writers should purchase script writing computer programs, or read and apply screenplay format before submitting."

◐ **PAUL S. LEVINE LITERARY AGENCY**, 1054 Superbra Ave., Venice CA 90291-3940. (310)450-6711. Fax: (310)450-0181. E-mail: pslevine@ix.netcom.com. Website: www.netcom.com/~pslevine/lawliterary.html. **Contact:** Paul S. Levine. Estab. 1996. Member of Attorney-State Bar of California. Represents 100 clients. 75% of clients are new/unpublished writers. Currently handles: 30% nonfiction books; 30% novels; 10% movie scripts; 30% TV scripts.
   • See the expanded listing for this agency in Literary Agents: Nonfee-charging.

✂ ◐ **LIVINGSTON COOKE**, 457A Danforth Ave., Suite 201, Toronto Ontario M4K 1P1 Canada. (416)406-3390. Fax: (416)406-3389. E-mail: livcooke@idirect.ca. **Contact:** Elizabeth Griffen. Estab. 1992. Represents 200 clients. 30% of clients are new/unpublished writers. Currently handles: 50% nonfiction books; 30% novels; 10% movie scripts; 10% TV scripts.
   • See the expanded listing for this agency in Literary Agents: Nonfee-charging.

◐ **THE LUEDTKE AGENCY**, 1674 Broadway, Suite 7A, New York NY 10019. (212)765-9564. Fax: (212)765-9582. **Contact:** Elaine Devlin. Estab. 1997. Signatory of WGA. Represents 35 clients. 20% of clients are new/unpublished writers. Currently handles: 70% movie scripts; 10% TV scripts; 20% stage plays.
   • Prior to becoming an agent, Penny Luedtke was in classical music management; Elain Devlin was in film development, story editing; Marcia Weiss was an attorney, owner of a music agency.
**Member Agents:** Penny Luedtke (primarily represents talent-some special project writers), Elaine Devlin (screenwriters, playwrights), Marcia Weiss (screenwriters, television writers).
**Represents:** Movie scripts; feature film; TV scripts; TV movie of the week; sitcom; miniseries; soap opera; theatrical stage play; stage plays. **Considers these script subject areas:** action/adventure; biography/autobiography; cartoon/animation; comedy; contemporary issues; detective/police/crime; ethnic; family saga; fantasy; feminist; gay/lesbian; historical; horror; juvenile; mainstream; multicultural; multimedia; mystery/suspense; psychic/supernatural; regional; religious/inspirational; romantic comedy; romantic drama; science fiction; sports; teen; thriller; western/frontier.
   O⌐ "We are a small shop and like it that way. We work closely with our writers developing projets and offer extensive editorial assistance." Actively seeking well-written material. Does not want any project with graphic or explicit violence against women or children.
**How to Contact:** Query with SASE. No e-mail or fax queries. Considers simultaneous queries. Responds in 1 month to queries; 3 months to mss. Returns materials only with SASE. Obtains most new clients through recommendations from others.
**Recent Sales:** This agency prefers not to share information on specific sales.
**Terms:** Agent receives 10% commission on domestic sales; 15% commission on foreign sales. Offers written contract, binding per WGA standards. Charges clients for reimbursement of expenses for couriers, messengers, international telephone and photocopying.

◐ **ROBERT MADSEN AGENCY**, 1331 E. 34th St., Suite #1, Oakland CA 94602-1032. (510)223-2090. Website: communities.msn.com/therobertmadsenliterary/agency. **Contact:** Agent: Robert Madsen. Senior Editor: Liz Madsen. Estab. 1992. Represents 5 clients. 100% of clients are new/unpublished writers. Currently handles: 25% nonfiction books; 25% fiction books novels; 25% movie scripts; 25% TV scripts.
   • See the expanded listing for this agency in Literary Agents: Nonfee-charging.

◐ **MAJOR CLIENTS AGENCY**, 345 N. Maple Dr., #395, Beverly Hills CA 90210. (310)205-5000. Fax: (310)205-5099. **Contact:** Donna Williams Fontno. Estab. 1985. Signatory of WGA. Represents 200 clients. 0% of clients are new/unpublished writers. Currently handles: 30% movie scripts; 70% TV scripts.
**Represents:** Movie scripts; feature film; TV scripts; TV movie of the week; sitcom. **Considers these script subject areas:** detective/police/crime; erotica; family saga; horror; mainstream; mystery/suspense; sports; thriller.
   O⌐ This agency specializes in TV writers, creators, directors, film writers/directors.
**How to Contact:** Submit outline/proposal, SASE. Responds in 2 weeks to queries; 1 month to mss.
**Recent Sales:** This agency prefers not to share information on specific sales.
**Terms:** Agent receives 10% commission on domestic sales; 10% commission on foreign sales. Offers written contract.

☑ ☑ **THE MANAGEMENT COMPANY**, 1337 Ocean Ave., Suite F, Santa Monica CA 90401. (310)990-5602. **Contact:** Tom Klassen. Represents 15 clients.
- Prior to starting his agency Mr. Klassen was an agent with International Creative Management (ICM).

**Member Agents:** Tom Klasen, F. Miguel Valenti, Jacob Vonk, Helene Taber, Paul Davis.

**Represents:** movie scripts; feature film; TV scripts; episodic drama; sitcom; miniseries.
- ○━ Actively seeking "really good comedies." Does not want horror scripts.

**Also Handles:** Juvenile books.

**How to Contact:** Query with SASE. No e-mail or fax queries. Responds in 2 weeks to queries. Returns materials only with SASE. Obtains most new clients through recommendations from others, conferences.

**Recent Sales:** Sold 7 scripts in the last year.

**Terms:** Agent receives 10% commission on domestic sales; 10% commission on foreign sales. Offers written contract, binding for 2 years.

**Writer's Conferences:** Sundance Film Festival, New York Film Festival, Telluride, Atlanta, Chicago, Minnesota.

**Tips:** "We only accept query letters with a short, one-page synopsis. We will request full manuscript with a SASE if interested. We rarely take on nonreferred material, but do review query letters and occasionally take on new writers. We have done very well with those we have taken on."

*see Lit. Ag.*

☑ ☑ **MANUS & ASSOCIATES LITERARY AGENCY, INC.**, 145 Park Ave., New York NY 10022. NY (212)644-8020, CA (650)470-5151. Fax: NY (212)644-3374, CA (650)470-5159. Also: ~~375 Forest Ave., Palo Alto CA 94301~~ **Contact:** Janet Manus (New York); Jillian Manus (California). Estab. 1985. Member of AAR. Represents 75 clients. 15% of clients are new/unpublished writers. Currently handles: 60% nonfiction books; 30% novels; 10% juvenile books.
- See the expanded listing for this agency in Literary Agents: Nonfee-charging.

☑ **THE STUART M. MILLER CO.**, 11684 Ventura Blvd., #225, Studio City CA 91604-2699. (818)506-6067. Fax: (818)506-4079. E-mail: smmco@aol.com. **Contact:** Stuart Miller. Estab. 1977. Member of DGA; signatory of WGA. Currently handles: 10% novels; 50% movie scripts; 40% multimedia.

**Represents:** Movie scripts. **Considers these script subject areas:** action/adventure; biography/autobiography; cartoon/animation; comedy; contemporary issues; detective/police/crime; family saga; historical; mainstream; multimedia; mystery/suspense; romantic comedy; romantic drama; science fiction; sports; teen; thriller.

**Also Handles:** Nonfiction books; novels. **Considers these nonfiction areas:** biography/autobiography; computers/electronic; current affairs; government/politics/law; health/medicine; history; how-to; memoirs; military/war; self-help/personal improvement; true crime/investigative. **Considers these fiction areas:** action/adventure; detective/police/crime; historical; literary; mainstream/contemporary; mystery/suspense; science fiction; sports; thriller.

**How to Contact:** Query with SASE, outline/proposal. Accepts e-mail and fax queries. Considers simultaneous queries. Responds in 3 days to queries; 6 weeks to mss. Returns materials only with SASE.

**Recent Sales:** This agency prefers not to share information on specific sales.

**Terms:** Agent receives 10% commission on domestic sales; 15-20% commission on foreign sales. Offers written contract, binding for 2 years; WGA standard notice must be given to terminate contract.

**Tips:** "Always include SASE, e-mail address, or fax number with query letters. Make it easy to respond."

☑ ◎ ☑ **MOMENTUM MARKETING, (Specialized: Arizona writers)**, P.O. Box 24861, Tempe AZ 85285-4861. (480)777-0365. E-mail: klepage@qwest.net. **Contact:** Kerry LePage. Estab. 1995. Signatory of WGA.
- Prior to opening her agency, Ms. LePage was a marketing consultant and actress.

**Represents:** Feature film; TV movie of the week; episodic drama; sitcom. **Considers these script subject areas:** action/adventure; cartoon/animation; comedy; contemporary issues; detective/police/crime; ethnic; experimental; family saga; fantasy; feminist; gay/lesbian; historical; horror; juvenile; mainstream; mystery/suspense; psychic/supernatural; religious/inspirational; romantic comedy; romantic drama; science fiction; sports; teen; thriller; western/frontier.
- ○━ Represents Arizona-based writers only. Actively seeking Arizona-based writers; projects that could be produced in Arizona; excellent writing.

**How to Contact:** All unsolicited mss returned unopened. Personal referrals only. Obtains most new clients through recommendations from others.

**Recent Sales:** This agency prefers not to share information on specific sales.

**Terms:** Agent receives 10% commission on domestic sales; 10% commission on foreign sales. Offers written contract, binding for 1 year; 10 days notice must be given to terminate contract. Charges for postage, long distance—no more than $50/writer will be charged without their prior approval.

**Tips:** "We are currently looking at Internet-based projects and doing what we can for film in Arizona."

---

**ALWAYS INCLUDE** a self-addressed, stamped envelope (SASE) for reply or return of your query or manuscript.

**MONTEIRO ROSE AGENCY**, 17514 Ventura Blvd., #205, Encino CA 91316. (818)501-1177. Fax: (818)501-1194. E-mail: monrose@ix.netcom.com. Website: www.monteiro-rose.com. **Contact:** Milissa Brockish. Estab. 1987. Signatory of WGA. Represents 50 clients. Currently handles: 40% movie scripts; 20% TV scripts; 40% animation.
**Member Agents:** Candace Monteiro (literary), Fredda Rose (literary), Milissa Brockish (literary), Jason Davis (literary).
**Represents:** Feature film; TV movie of the week; episodic drama; animation. **Considers these script subject areas:** action/adventure; cartoon/animation; comedy; contemporary issues; detective/police/crime; ethnic; family saga; historical; juvenile; mainstream; mystery/suspense; psychic/supernatural; romantic comedy; romantic drama; science fiction; teen; thriller.
  ○⇥ This agency specializes in scripts for animation, TV and film.
**How to Contact:** Query with SASE. Responds in 1 week to queries; 2 months to mss. Returns materials only with SASE. Obtains most new clients through recommendations from others, solicitations.
**Recent Sales:** This agency prefers not to share information on specific sales.
**Terms:** Agent receives 10% commission on domestic sales. Offers written contract, binding for 2 years; 90 days notice must be given to terminate contract. Charges for photocopying.
**Tips:** "It does no good to call and try to speak to an agent before they have read your material, unless referred by someone we know. The best and only way, if you're a new writer, is to send a query letter with a SASE. If agents are interested, they will request to read it. Also enclose a SASE with the script if you want it back."

**DEE MURA ENTERPRISES, INC.**, 269 W. Shore Dr., Massapequa NY 11758-8225. (516)795-1616. Fax: (516)795-8757. E-mail: samurai5@ix.netcom.com. **Contact:** Dee Mura, Ken Nyquist. Estab. 1987. Signatory of WGA. 50% of clients are new/unpublished writers.
  • See the expanded listing for this agency in Literary Agents: Nonfee-charging.

**NIAD MANAGEMENT**, 3465 Coy Dr., Sherman Oaks CA 91423. (818)981-2505. Fax: (818)386-2082. E-mail: wendi@niadmanagement.com. Website: www.niadmanagement.com. **Contact:** Wendi Niad. Estab. 1997. Represents 15 clients. 2% of clients are new/unpublished writers. Currently handles: 1% novels; 95% movie scripts; 2% TV scripts; 1% multimedia; 1% stage plays.
**Represents:** Movie scripts; feature film; TV scripts; TV movie of the week; miniseries; stage plays. **Considers these script subject areas:** action/adventure; biography/autobiography; comedy; contemporary issues; detective/police/crime; ethnic; family saga; historical; horror; mainstream; multicultural; mystery/suspense; psychic/supernatural; romantic comedy; romantic drama; sports; teen; thriller.
**Also Handles: Considers these nonfiction areas:** biography/autobiography. **Considers these fiction areas:** action/adventure; detective/police/crime; family saga; literary; mainstream/contemporary; multicultural; mystery/suspense; psychic/supernatural; romance; thriller.
**How to Contact:** Query with SASE. Accepts e-mail and fax queries. Considers simultaneous queries. Responds in 1 week to queries; 3 months to mss. Returns materials only with SASE. Obtains most new clients through recommendations from others.
**Recent Sales:** Sold 5 scripts in the last year. *The Dan Gable Story*, by Lee Zlotoff (Charles Hirschorn/Disney), *Insider Trading*, by Claudia Salter (USA Network); *Killing the People Upstairs*, by Bruce Griffiths (Max Media). Other clients include Steve Copling, Peter Egan, Karen Kelly, Jim McGlynn, Debra Mooradian, Don Most, Brian Rousso, Fernando Fragata.
**Terms:** Agent receives 10-15% commission on domestic sales. Offers written contract, binding for 1 year; 30-day notice must be given to terminate contract.

**OMNIQUEST ENTERTAINMENT**, 843 Berkeley St., Santa Monica CA 90403-2503. (310)453-6549. Fax: (310)453-2523. E-mail: info@omniquestmedia.com. Website: www.omniquestmedia.com. **Contact:** Michael Kaliski. Estab. 1997. Currently handles: 5% novels; 5% juvenile books; 40% movie scripts; 10% TV scripts; 20% multimedia; 15% stage plays.
**Member Agents:** Michael Kaliski, Traci Belushi.
**Represents:** Movie scripts; feature film; TV scripts; TV movie of the week; episodic drama; sitcom; miniseries; syndicated material; stage plays. **Considers these script subject areas:** action/adventure; biography/autobiography; comedy; contemporary issues; detective/police/crime; experimental; family saga; fantasy; historical; mainstream; multimedia; mystery/suspense; psychic/supernatural; romantic comedy; romantic drama; science fiction; thriller; dv shorts for internet.
  ○⇥ Actively seeking books that can be adapted for film and scripts. Does not want to receive erotic material. Novels; short story collections; novellas. **Considers these fiction areas:** action/adventure; detective/police/crime; experimental; family saga; fantasy; literary; psychic/supernatural; romance; science fiction; thriller.
**Also Handles:** Novels; short story collections; novellas. **Considers these fiction areas:** action/adventure; detective/police/crime; experimental; family saga; fantasy; literary; psychic/supernatural; romance; science fiction; thriller.
**How to Contact:** Query with SASE, or send outline and 2-3 sample chapters. Accepts e-mail and fax queries. Considers simultaneous queries. Returns materials only with SASE. Obtains most new clients through recommendations from others.
**Recent Sales:** This agency prefers not to share information on specific sales.
**Terms:** Agent receives 15% commission on domestic sales; 15% commission on foreign sales. Offers written contract.

**FIFI OSCARD AGENCY, INC.**, 24 W. 40th St., New York NY 10018. **Contact:** Ivy Fischer Stone. Estab. 1956. Member of AAR; signatory of WGA. Represents 108 clients. 5% of clients are new/unpublished writers. Currently handles: 60% nonfiction books; 10% novels; 30% stage plays.
- See the expanded listing for this agency in Literary Agents: Nonfee-charging.

**DOROTHY PALMER**, 235 W. 56 St., New York NY 10019. Phone/fax: (212)765-4280. (press *51 for fax). Estab. 1990. Signatory of WGA. Represents 12 clients. 0% of clients are new/unpublished writers. Currently handles: 70% movie scripts; 30% TV scripts.
- In addition to being a literary agent, Ms. Palmer has worked as a talent agent for 30 years.

**Represents:** Feature film; TV movie of the week; episodic drama; sitcom; miniseries. **Considers these script subject areas:** action/adventure; comedy; contemporary issues; detective/police/crime; family saga; feminist; mainstream; mystery/suspense; romantic comedy; romantic drama; thriller.

> O— This agency specializes in screenplays, TV. Actively seeking successful, published writers (screenplays only). Does not want to receive work from new or unpublished writers.

**How to Contact:** Query with SASE. Prefers to read materials exclusively. Published writers *only*. Returns materials only with SASE. Obtains most new clients through recommendations from others.
**Recent Sales:** This agency prefers not to share information on specific sales.
**Terms:** Agent receives 10% commission on domestic sales; 10% commission on foreign sales. Offers written contract, binding for 1 year. Charges clients for postage, photocopies.
**Tips:** "Do *not* telephone. When I find a script that interests me, I call the writer. Calls to me are a turn-off because they cut into my reading time."

**PANDA TALENT**, 3721 Hoen Ave., Santa Rosa CA 95405. (707)576-0711. Fax: (707)544-2765. **Contact:** Audrey Grace. Estab. 1977. Member of SAG, AFTRA, Equity; signatory of WGA. Represents 10 clients. 80% of clients are new/unpublished writers. Currently handles: 5% novels; 50% movie scripts; 40% TV scripts; 5% stage plays.
**Member Agents:** Steven Grace (science fiction/war/action), Vicki Lima (mysteries/romance), Cleo West (western/true stories).
**Represents:** Feature film; TV movie of the week; episodic drama; sitcom. **Considers these script subject areas:** action/adventure; comedy; detective/police/crime; ethnic; family saga; mystery/suspense; romantic comedy; romantic drama; science fiction; thriller; western/frontier.
**How to Contact:** Not accepting anything at this time.
**Recent Sales:** This agency prefers not to share information on specific sales.
**Terms:** Agent receives 10% commission on domestic sales; 10% commission on foreign sales.

**THE PARTOS COMPANY**, 6363 Wilshire Blvd., Suite 227, Los Angeles CA 90048. (323)951-1320. Fax: (323)951-1324. **Contact:** Jim Barquette. Estab. 1991. Signatory of WGA. Represents 20 clients. 50% of clients are new/unpublished writers. Currently handles: 90% movie scripts; 10% TV scripts (features only).
**Member Agents:** Walter Partos (below the line and literary), Jim Barquette (literary), Cynthia Guber (actors).
**Represents:** Movie scripts; feature film; TV scripts; TV movie of the week.
> O— This agency specializes in independent features.

**How to Contact:** Query with SASE. Responds in 1 month to queries; 3 months to mss. Currently not considering new clients.
**Recent Sales:** This agency prefers not to share information on specific sales.
**Terms:** Agent receives 10% commission on domestic sales; 10% commission on foreign sales. Offers written contract, binding for 1 year plus WGA rider W.

**BARRY PERELMAN AGENCY**, 1155 N. Laceniga, #508, W. Hollywood CA 90069. Phone/fax: (310)659-1122. Estab. 1982. Member of DGA; signatory of WGA. Represents 40 clients. 15% of clients are new/unpublished writers. Currently handles: 100% movie scripts.
**Member Agents:** Barry Perelman (motion picture/packaging).
**Represents:** Movie scripts. **Considers these script subject areas:** action/adventure; biography/autobiography; contemporary issues; detective/police/crime; historical; horror; mystery/suspense; romantic comedy; romantic drama; science fiction; thriller.
> O— This agency specializes in motion pictures/packaging.

**How to Contact:** Query with SASE, outline/proposal. Responds in 1 month to queries. Obtains most new clients through recommendations from others, solicitations.
**Recent Sales:** This agency prefers not to share information on specific sales.
**Terms:** Agent receives 10% commission on domestic sales; 10% commission on foreign sales. Offers written contract, binding for 1-2 years. Charges clients for postage and photocopying.

**STEPHEN PEVNER, INC.**, 248 W. 73rd St., 2nd Floor, New York NY 10023. (212)496-0474. 100 N. Crescent Dr., Beverly Hills CA 90210. (310)385-4160. Fax: (310)385-6633. E-mail: spevner@aol.com. **Contact:** Stephen Pevner. Estab. 1991. Member of AAR. Represents 50 clients. 50% of clients are new/unpublished writers. Currently handles: 25% nonfiction books; 25% novels; TV scripts; stage plays.
- See the expanded listing for this agency in Literary Agents: Nonfee-charging.

◐ **A PICTURE OF YOU**, 1176 Elizabeth Dr., Hamilton OH 45013-3507. (513)863-1108. Fax: (513)863-1108. E-mail: apoy1@aol.com. **Contact:** Lenny Minelli. Estab. 1993. Signatory of WGA. Represents 45 clients. 50% of clients are new/unpublished writers. Currently handles: 80% movie scripts; 10% TV scripts; 10% syndicated material.

  • Prior to opening his agency, Mr. Minelli was an actor/producer for 10 years. Also owned and directed a talent agency and represented actors and actresses from around the world.

**Member Agents:** Michelle Chang (fiction/nonfiction books).

**Represents:** Feature film; TV movie of the week; episodic drama; sitcom; animation; documentary; miniseries; syndicated material. **Considers these script subject areas:** action/adventure; biography/autobiography; cartoon/animation; comedy; contemporary issues; detective/police/crime; erotica; ethnic; experimental; family saga; fantasy; feminist; gay/lesbian; glitz; historical; horror; juvenile; mainstream; multicultural; multimedia; mystery/suspense; psychic/supernatural; regional; religious/inspirational; romantic comedy; romantic drama; science fiction; sports; teen; thriller; western/frontier.

  ⚏ This agency specializes in screenplays and TV scripts.

**Also Handles:** Nonfiction books; novels; short story collections; novellas. **Considers these nonfiction areas:** gay/lesbian issues; history; juvenile nonfiction; music/dance; religious/inspirational; self-help/personal improvement; theater/film. **Considers these fiction areas:** action/adventure; detective/police/crime; erotica; ethnic; family saga; fantasy; gay/lesbian; glitz; historical; horror; literary; mainstream/contemporary; mystery/suspense; religious/inspirational; romance (contemporary, gothic, historical); thriller; westerns/frontier; young adult.

**How to Contact:** Query with SASE. Accepts e-mail and fax queries. Considers simultaneous queries. Responds in 3 weeks to queries; 1 month to mss. Obtains most new clients through recommendations from others, solicitations.

**Recent Sales:** *Lost and Found*, by J.P. Brice; *So Long*, by Patrick Cappella. *Scripting Assignment(s): The Governor*, by Gary M. Cappetta.

**Terms:** Agent receives 10% commission on domestic sales; 15% commission on foreign sales. Offers written contract, binding for 1 year; 90-day notice must be given to terminate contract. Charges clients for postage/express mail and long distance calls.

**Tips:** "Make sure that the script is the best it can be before seeking an agent."

■ ◐ **JIM PREMINGER AGENCY**, 450 N. Roxbury, PH 1050, Beverly Hills CA 90210. (310)860-1116. Fax: (310)860-1117. E-mail: general@premingeragency.com. Estab. 1980. Member of DGA; signatory of WGA. Represents 75 clients. 20% of clients are new/unpublished writers. Currently handles: 1% nonfiction books; 1% novels; 47% movie scripts; 50% TV scripts; 1% stage plays.

**Member Agents:** Jim Preminger (television and features), Dean Schramm (features and television), Ryan L. Saul (features and television), Melissa Read (television and features).

**Represents:** Feature film; TV movie of the week; episodic drama; sitcom; miniseries; Internet.

  ⚏ This agency specializes in representing showrunners for television series, writers for television movies, as well as directors and writers for features.

**How to Contact:** "No unsolicited material." Obtains most new clients through recommendations from others.

**Recent Sales:** This agency prefers not to share information on specific sales.

**Terms:** Agent receives 10% commission on domestic sales; 10% commission on foreign sales.

◐ **THE QUILLCO AGENCY**, 3104 W. Cumberland Court, Westlake Village CA 91362. (805)495-8436. Fax: (805)373-9868. E-mail: quillco2@aol.com. **Contact:** Sandy Mackey (owner). Estab. 1993. Signatory of WGA. Represents 30 clients.

**Represents:** Feature film; TV movie of the week; animation; documentary.

**How to Contact:** Prefers to read materials exclusively. Not accepting query letters at this time. Returns materials only with SASE.

**Recent Sales:** This agency prefers not to share information on specific sales.

**Terms:** Agent receives 10% commission on domestic sales; 10% commission on foreign sales.

✓ ◐ **DAN REDLER ENTERTAINMENT**, 18930 Ringling St., Tarzana CA 91356. (818)776-0938. **Contact:** Dan Redler. Represents 10 clients. Currently handles: 100% movie scripts.

**Represents:** Movie scripts; feature film. **Considers these script subject areas:** action/adventure; biography/autobiography; comedy; contemporary issues; detective/police/crime; ethnic; family saga; fantasy; feminist; historical; horror; juvenile; mainstream; mystery/suspense; psychic/supernatural; romantic comedy; romantic drama; science fiction; sports; teen; thriller.

  ⚏ Actively seeking mainstream and contemporary scripts. Does not want to receive small noncommercial stories.

**How to Contact:** Query with SASE. Prefers to read materials exclusively. Responds in 2 weeks to queries; 1 month to mss. Returns materials only with SASE.

**Recent Sales:** This agency prefers not to share information on specific sales.

**Terms:** Agent receives 10% commission on domestic sales; 10% commission on foreign sales. Offers written contract, binding for 2 years. Client must supply all copies of scripts.

**Tips:** "We offer personal service, indepth career guidance, and aggressive sales efforts."

⊘ **REDWOOD EMPIRE AGENCY**, P.O. Box 1946, Guerneville CA 95446-1146. (707)869-1146. E-mail: redemp @sonic.net. **Contact:** Jim Sorrells or Rodney Shull. Estab. 1992. Represents 10 clients. 90% of clients are new/unpublished writers. Currently handles: 100% movie scripts.

**Represents:** Feature film; TV movie of the week; animation (movie). **Considers these script subject areas:** comedy; contemporary issues; erotica; family saga; feminist; gay/lesbian; mainstream; mystery/suspense; romantic comedy; romantic drama; thriller.

    O— This agency specializes in screenplays, big screen or TV.

**How to Contact:** Query with SASE, 1-page synopsis. Responds in 1 week to queries; 1 month to mss. Obtains most new clients through word of mouth, letter in *Hollywood Scriptwriter.*

**Recent Sales:** This agency prefers not to share information on specific sales.

**Terms:** Agent receives 10% commission on domestic sales; 10% commission on foreign sales. Offers criticism service: structure, characterization, dialogue, format syles. No fee for criticism service.

**Tips:** "Most interested in ordinary people confronting real-life situations."

◐ **MICHAEL D. ROBINS & ASSOCIATES**, 23241 Ventura Blvd., #300, Woodland Hills CA 91364. (818)343-1755. Fax: (818)343-7355. E-mail: mdr2@msn.com. **Contact:** Michael D. Robins. Estab. 1991. Member of DGA; signatory of WGA. 10% of clients are new/unpublished writers. Currently handles: 5% nonfiction books; 5% novels; 20% movie scripts; 60% TV scripts; 10% syndicated material.

    ● Prior to opening his agency, Mr. Robins was a literary agent at a mid-sized agency.

**Represents:** Movie scripts; feature film; TV scripts; TV movie of the week; episodic drama; animation; miniseries; syndicated material; stage plays. **Considers these script subject areas:** action/adventure; biography/autobiography; cartoon/animation; comedy; contemporary issues; detective/police/crime; erotica; ethnic; experimental; family saga; fantasy; feminist; gay/lesbian; glitz; historical; horror; juvenile; mainstream; multicultural; multimedia; mystery/suspense; psychic/supernatural; regional; religious/inspirational; romantic comedy; romantic drama; science fiction; sports; teen; thriller; western/frontier.

**Also Handles:** Nonfiction books; novels. **Considers these nonfiction areas:** history; humor/satire; memoirs; military/war; popular culture; science/technology; true crime/investigative; urban lifestyle. **Considers these fiction areas:** action/adventure; comic books/cartoon; detective/police/crime; family saga; fantasy; gay/lesbian; mainstream/contemporary; westerns/frontier (frontier); young adult.

**How to Contact:** Query with SASE. Accepts e-mail and fax queries. Considers simultaneous queries. Responds in 1 week to queries; 1 month to mss. Obtains most new clients through recommendations from others.

**Recent Sales:** This agency prefers not to share information on specific sales.

**Terms:** Agent receives 10% commission on domestic sales; 10% commission on foreign sales. Offers written contract, binding for 2 years; 4 months notice must be given to terminate contract.

◐ **ROBINSON TALENT AND LITERARY MANAGEMENT**, 1101 S. Robertson Blvd., Suite 210, Los Angeles CA 90035. (310)278-0801. Fax: (310)278-0807. **Contact:** Margaretrose Robinson. Estab. 1992. Member of DGA/SAG. Represents 150 clients. 10% of clients are new/unpublished writers. Currently handles: 15% novels; 40% movie scripts; 40% TV scripts; 5% stage plays.

    ● Prior to becoming an agent, Ms. Robinson worked as a designer.

**Member Agents:** Margaretrose Robinson (adaptation of books and plays for development as features or TV MOW), Kevin Douglas (scripts for film and TV).

**Represents:** Feature film; TV movie of the week; episodic drama; documentary; miniseries; variety show; stage plays; CD-ROM. **Considers these script subject areas:** action/adventure; cartoon/animation; comedy; contemporary issues; detective/police/crime; erotica; ethnic; experimental; family saga; fantasy; mainstream; mystery/suspense; psychic/supernatural; religious/inspirational; romantic comedy; romantic drama; science fiction; sports; teen; thriller; western/frontier.

    O— "We represent screenwriters, playwrights, novelists and producers, directors."

**How to Contact:** Submit outline/proposal, synopsis, log line. Obtains most new clients through recommendations from others.

**Recent Sales:** This agency prefers not to share information on specific sales. Clients include Steve Edelman, Merryln Hammond, Michael Hennessey.

**Terms:** Agent receives 10% commission on domestic sales; 10% commission on foreign sales. Offers written contract, binding for 2 years minimum. Charges clients for photocopying, messenger, FedEx, and postage when required.

**Tips:** "We are a talent agency specializing in the copyright business. Fifty percent of our clients generate copyright-screenwriters, playrights and novelists. Fifty percent of our clients service copyright—producers, directors and cinematographers. We represent only produced, published and/or WGA writers who are eligible for staff TV positions as well as novelists and playwrights whose works may be adapted for film on television."

---

**FOR INFORMATION ON THE CONFERENCES** agents attend, refer to the **Writers' Conferences** section in this book.

☑ 🏷 Ⓜ **JACK SCAGNETTI TALENT & LITERARY AGENCY,** 5118 Vineland Ave., #102, North Hollywood CA 91601. (818)762-3871. Fax: (818)761-6629. **Contact:** Jack Scagnetti. Estab. 1974. Member of Academy of Television Arts and Sciences; signatory of WGA. Represents 50 clients. 50% of clients are new/unpublished writers. Currently handles: 20% nonfiction books; 70% movie scripts; 10% TV scripts.

• Prior to becoming an agent, Mr. Scagnetti wrote nonfiction books and magazine articles on movie stars, sports and health subjects and was a magazine and newspaper editor.

**Member Agents:** Janet Brown (books), David Goldman (script analyst).

**Represents:** Feature film; TV movie of the week; episodic drama; sitcom; animation (movie); miniseries. **Considers these script subject areas:** action/adventure; comedy; detective/police/crime; family saga; historical; horror; mainstream; mystery/suspense; romantic comedy; romantic drama; sports; thriller.

O–ᴙ This agency specializes in film books with many photographers. Actively seeking books and screenplays. Does not want to receive TV scripts for existing shows.

**Also Handles:** Nonfiction books; novels. **Considers these nonfiction areas:** biography/autobiography; cooking/foods/nutrition; current affairs; health/medicine; how-to; military/war; music/dance; self-help/personal improvement; sports; true crime/investigative; women's issues/studies. **Considers these fiction areas:** action/adventure; contemporary issues; detective/police/crime; family saga; historical; mainstream/contemporary; mystery/suspense; picture books; romance (contemporary); sports; thriller; westerns/frontier.

**How to Contact:** Query with outline/proposal and SASE. No fax queries. Responds in 1 month to queries; 2 months to mss. Returns materials only with SASE. Obtains most new clients through recommendations from others, solicitations.

**Recent Sales:** *Kastner's Cutthroats*, (44 Blue Prod.). *Movie/TV MOW scripts in development*: Pain, by Charles Pickett (Concorde-New Horizons).

**Terms:** Agent receives 15% commission on domestic sales; 15% commission on foreign sales; 10% commission on dramatic rights sales. Offers written contract, binding for 6 months-1 year.

**Fees:** Offers criticism service (books only). "Fee depends upon condition of original copy and number of pages." Charges clients for postage and photocopies.

**Tips:** "Write a good synopsis, short and to the point and include marketing data for the book."

🅽 Ⓜ ◎ **SUSAN SCHULMAN, A LITERARY AGENCY, (Specialized: health, business, self-help/women's issues)**, 454 W. 44th St., New York NY 10036-5205. (212)713-1633/4/5. Fax: (212)586-8830. E-mail: schulman@aol.com. **Contact:** Susan Schulman, president. Estab. 1979. Member of AAR, Dramatists Guild, Women's Media Group; signatory of WGA. 10-15% of clients are new/unpublished writers. Currently handles: 70% nonfiction books; 20% novels; 10% stage plays.

• See the expanded listing for this agency in Literary Agents: Nonfee-charging.

Ⓜ **SHAPIRO-LICHTMAN,** Shapiro-Lichtman Building, 8827 Beverly Blvd., Los Angeles CA 90048. Fax: (310)859-7153. **Contact:** Maritn Shapiro. Estab. 1969. Signatory of WGA. 10% of clients are new/unpublished writers. **Represents:** Feature film; TV movie of the week; episodic drama; sitcom; animation (movie, TV); miniseries; soap opera; variety show. **Considers these script subject areas:** action/adventure; cartoon/animation; comedy; contemporary issues; detective/police/crime; ethnic; family saga; historical; horror; mainstream; mystery/suspense; romantic comedy; romantic drama; science fiction; teen; thriller; western/frontier.

**Also Handles:** Nonfiction books; novels; novellas. **Considers these nonfiction areas:** agriculture/horticulture; americana; animals; anthropology/archaeology; art/architecture/design; biography/autobiography; business/economics; child guidance/parenting; computers/electronic; cooking/foods/nutrition; crafts/hobbies; creative nonfiction; current affairs; education; ethnic/cultural interests; gardening; gay/lesbian issues; government/politics/law; health/medicine; history; how-to; humor/satire; interior design/decorating; juvenile nonfiction; language/literature/criticism; memoirs; military/war; money/finance; multicultural; music/dance; nature/environment; New Age/metaphysics; philosophy; photography; popular culture; psychology; recreation; regional; religious/inspirational; science/technology; self-help/personal improvement; sex; sociology; software; spirituality; sports; theater/film; translation; travel; true crime/investigative; women's issues/studies; young adult. **Considers these fiction areas:** action/adventure; comic books/cartoon; confession; contemporary issues; detective/police/crime; erotica; ethnic; experimental; family saga; fantasy; feminist; gay/lesbian; glitz; gothic; hi-lo; historical; horror; humor/satire; juvenile; literary; mainstream/contemporary; military/war; multicultural; multimedia; mystery/suspense; New Age; occult; picture books; plays; poetry; poetry in translation; psychic/supernatural; regional; religious/inspirational; romance; science fiction; short story collections; spiritual; sports; thriller; translation; westerns/frontier; young adult.

**How to Contact:** Query with SASE. Responds in 10 days to queries. Returns materials only with SASE. Obtains most new clients through recommendations from others.

**Recent Sales:** This agency prefers not to share information on specific sales.

**Terms:** Agent receives 10% commission on domestic sales; 20% commission on foreign sales. Offers written contract, binding for 2 years.

Ⓜ **KEN SHERMAN & ASSOCIATES,** 9507 Santa Monica Blvd., Beverly Hills CA 90210. (310)273-3840. Fax: (310)271-2875. **Contact:** Ken Sherman. Estab. 1989. Member of DGA, BAFTA, PEN Int'l; signatory of WGA. Represents 50 clients. 10% of clients are new/unpublished writers. Currently handles: nonfiction books; juvenile books; movie scripts; TV scripts; fiction.

• Prior to opening his agency, Mr. Sherman was with the William Morris Agency, The Lantz Office, and Paul Kohner, Inc.

**Represents:** Movie scripts; TV scripts; film and television rights to books. **Considers these script subject areas:** action/adventure; biography/autobiography; cartoon/animation; comedy; contemporary issues; detective/police/crime; erotica; ethnic; experimental; family saga; fantasy; feminist; gay/lesbian; glitz; historical; horror; juvenile; mainstream; multicultural; multimedia; mystery/suspense; psychic/supernatural; regional; religious/inspirational; romantic comedy; romantic drama; science fiction; sports; teen; thriller; western/frontier.

O━ This agency specializes in solid writers for film TV, books and rights to books for film and TV.

**Also Handles:** Nonfiction books; novels. **Considers these nonfiction areas:** agriculture/horticulture; americana; animals; anthropology/archaeology; art/architecture/design; biography/autobiography; business/economics; child guidance/parenting; computers/electronic; cooking/foods/nutrition; crafts/hobbies; creative nonfiction; current affairs; education; ethnic/cultural interests; gardening; gay/lesbian issues; government/politics/law; health/medicine; history; how-to; humor/satire; interior design/decorating; juvenile nonfiction; language/literature/criticism; memoirs; military/war; money/finance; multicultural; music/dance; nature/environment; New Age/metaphysics; philosophy; photography; popular culture; psychology; recreation; regional; religious/inspirational; science/technology; self-help/personal improvement; sex; sociology; software; spirituality; sports; theater/film; translation; travel; true crime/investigative; women's issues/studies; young adult. **Considers these fiction areas:** action/adventure; comic books/cartoon; confession; contemporary issues; detective/police/crime; erotica; ethnic; experimental; family saga; fantasy; feminist; gay/lesbian; glitz; gothic; hi-lo; historical; horror; humor/satire; juvenile; literary; mainstream/contemporary; military/war; multicultural; multimedia; mystery/suspense; New Age; occult; picture books; plays; poetry; poetry in translation; psychic/supernatural; regional; religious/inspirational; romance; science fiction; short story collections; spiritual; sports; thriller; translation; westerns/frontier; young adult.

**How to Contact:** Contact by referral only please. Responds in 1 month to mss.

**Recent Sales:** Sold 25 scripts in the last year. *Priscilla Salyers Story*, by Andrea Baynes (ABC);.*Toys of Glass*, by Martin Booth (ABC/Saban Ent.), *Brazil*, by John Updike (film rights to Glaucia Carmagos), *Fifth Sacred Thing*, by Starhawk (Bantam), *Questions From Dad*, by Dwight Twilly (Tuttle), *Snow Falling on Cedars*, by David Guterson (Universal Pictures), *The Witches of Eastwick-The Musical*, by John Updike (Cameron Macintosh, Ltd.).

**Terms:** Agent receives 15% commission on domestic sales; 10% commission on dramatic rights sales. Offers written contract. Charges clients for reasonable office expenses, postage, photocopying, and other negotiable expenses.

**Writer's Conferences:** Maui, Squaw Valley, Santa Barbara, Santa Fe, Aspen Institute, Aspen Writers Foundation, etc.

◖ **SILVER SCREEN PLACEMENTS**, 602 65th St., Downers Grove IL 60516-3020. (630)963-2124. Fax: (630)963-1998. E-mail: silverscreen@mediaone.net. **Contact:** William Levin. Estab. 1989. Signatory of WGA. Represents 11 clients. 100% of clients are new/unpublished writers. Currently handles: 10% novels; 10% juvenile books; 80% movie scripts.

• Prior to opening his agency, Mr. Levin did product placement for motion pictures/TV

**Represents:** Movie scripts; feature film. **Considers these script subject areas:** action/adventure; comedy; contemporary issues; detective/police/crime; family saga; fantasy; historical; juvenile; mainstream; mystery/suspense; science fiction; thriller; young adult.

O━ Actively seeking screenplays for young adults, 17-30. Does not want to receive horror, religious, X-rated.

**Also Handles:** Novels; juvenile books. **Considers these nonfiction areas:** education; juvenile nonfiction; language/literature/criticism. **Considers these fiction areas:** action/adventure; contemporary issues; detective/police/crime; family saga; fantasy; historical; humor/satire; juvenile; mainstream/contemporary; mystery/suspense; science fiction; thriller; young adult.

**How to Contact:** Brief query with outline/proposal and SASE. No e-mail or fax queries. No fax queries. Responds in 1 week to queries; 2 months to mss. Obtains most new clients through recommendations from others, listings with WGA and *Guide to Literary Agents*.

**Recent Sales:** Sold 4 options and 2 scripts in the last year. This agency prefers not to share information on specific sales. Clients include Jean Hurley, Charles Geier, Robert Smola, August Tonne, Michael Jeffries and Robert Helley.

**Terms:** Agent receives 15% commission on foreign sales; 10% (screenplay/teleplay sales) commission on dramatic rights sales. Offers written contract, binding for 2 years. May make referrals to freelance editors. Use of editors does not ensure representation. 0% of business is derived from referrals to editing service.

**Tips:** "Advise against 'cutsie' inquiry letters."

▨ ◖ **SOLOWAY GRANT KOPALOFF & ASSOCIATES**, 414 Wilshire Blvd., Los Angeles CA 90048. (323)782-1854. Fax: (323)782-1877. E-mail: sgkassoc@pacbell.net. **Contact:** Don Kopaloff. Estab. 1976. Signatory of WGA; AFF, DGA.

**Member Agents:** Arnold Soloway, Susan Grant, Don Kopaloff, Michelle Wallerstein.

**Represents:** Movie scripts; TV scripts. **Considers these script subject areas:** action/adventure; biography/autobiography; cartoon/animation; comedy; contemporary issues; detective/police/crime; erotica; ethnic; experimental; family saga; fantasy; feminist; gay/lesbian; glitz; historical; horror; juvenile; mainstream; multicultural; multimedia; mystery/suspense; psychic/supernatural; regional; religious/inspirational; romantic comedy; romantic drama; science fiction; sports; teen; thriller; western/frontier.

**How to Contact:** Query with SASE. After query letter is accepted, writer must sign release. Not accepting unsolicited mss. Responds in 1 month to queries.
**Recent Sales:** This agency prefers not to share information on specific sales.
**Terms:** Agent receives 10% commission on domestic sales; 10% commission on foreign sales. May make referrals to freelance editors. Use of editors does not ensure representation. 0% of business is derived from referrals to editing service.
**Tips:** "Advise against 'cutsie' inquiry letters."

◐ **CAMILLE SORICE AGENCY**, 13412 Moorpark St., #C, Sherman Oaks CA 91423. (818)995-1775. **Contact:** Camille Sorice. Estab. 1988. Signatory of WGA.
**Represents:** Novels; feature film. **Considers these script subject areas:** action/adventure; comedy; detective/police/crime; family saga; historical; mystery/suspense; romantic comedy; romantic drama; western/frontier.
**How to Contact:** Query with synopsis, SASE. No e-mail or fax queries. Prefers to read materials exclusively. No e-mail or fax queries. Responds in 6 weeks to mss.
**Recent Sales:** This agency prefers not to share information on specific sales.
**Tips:** "No calls. Query letters accepted."

▣ ◐ **STANTON & ASSOCIATES LITERARY AGENCY**, 4413 Clemson Dr., Garland TX 75042-5246. (972)276-5427. Fax: (972)276-5426. E-mail: preston8@onramp.net. Website: www.grahamcomputers.com/stanton.html and writerscape.com. **Contact:** Henry Stanton, Harry Preston. Estab. 1990. Signatory of WGA. Represents 36 clients. 90% of clients are new/unpublished writers. Currently handles: 50% nonfiction books; 50% movie scripts.
   ● Prior to joining the agency, Mr. Preston was with the MGM script department and an author and screenwriter for 40 years.
**Represents:** Feature film; TV movie of the week. **Considers these script subject areas:** action/adventure; comedy; romantic comedy; romantic drama; thriller.
   ⊶ Does not want to see science fiction, fantasy or horror.
**How to Contact:** Query with SASE. Accepts e-mail and fax queries. Considers simultaneous queries. Responds in 1 week to queries; 1 month to mss. Returns materials only with SASE. Obtains most new clients through recommendations from others.
**Recent Sales:** *Thelma Who?*, (Scarecrow Press), *Dream of Desire*, (Denlinger's Press), *Faces of Angels*, (Publishamerica); *Love on Lesbos* (Creative Works Publishing)
**Terms:** Agent receives 15% commission on domestic sales. Offers written contract, binding for 2 years. Returns scripts with reader's comments.
**Tips:** "We have writers available to edit or ghostwrite screenplays and books. Fees vary dependent on the writer."

☑ ◐ **STARS, THE AGENCY**, 23 Grant Ave., 4th Floor, San Francisco CA 94108. Fax: (707)748-7395. E-mail: edley07@cs.com. **Contact:** Ed Silver. Estab. 1995. Represents 50-75 clients. 70% of clients are new/unpublished writers. Currently handles: 50% nonfiction books; 25% novels; 25% movie scripts.
   ● Prior to becoming an agent, Mr. Silver was an entertainment business manager.
**Member Agents:** Ed Silver.
**Represents:** Movie scripts; feature film; TV movie of the week. **Considers these script subject areas:** action/adventure; comedy; contemporary issues; detective/police/crime; erotica; ethnic; experimental; family saga; mainstream; mystery/suspense; romantic comedy; romantic drama; sports; thriller.
   ⊶ This agency specializes in theatrical screenplays, MOW and miniseries. Actively seeking "anything good and distinctive."
**Also Handles:** Nonfiction books; novels. **Considers these nonfiction areas:** Considers general nonfiction areas.
**Considers these fiction areas:** action/adventure; detective/police/crime; erotica; experimental; historical; humor/satire; literary; mainstream/contemporary; mystery/suspense; thriller; young adult.
**How to Contact:** Query with SASE. Considers simultaneous queries. Responds in 1 month to queries. Returns materials only with SASE. Obtains most new clients through recommendations from others, queries from WGA agency list.
**Recent Sales:** Sold 8 titles and optioned 3 scripts in the last year. *Cannabible*, (Ten Speed), *Big Book of Training Games*, (McGraw Hill), *Mayan Phrase Book*, (Hippocrene).
**Terms:** Agent receives 15% commission on domestic sales; 20% commission on foreign sales; 10% commission on dramatic rights sales. Offers written contract; 30 days notice must be given to terminate contract.

◐ **STEIN AGENCY**, 5125 Oakdale Ave., Woodland Hills CA 91364. (818)594-8990. Fax: (818)594-8998. E-mail: mail@thesteinagency.com. **Contact:** Mitchel Stein. Estab. 2000. Signatory of WGA. Represents 60 clients. Currently handles: 20% movie scripts; 80% TV scripts.
**Member Agents:** Mitchel Stein (TV/motion picture), Jim Ford (TV/motion picture).
**Represents:** Movie scripts; TV scripts; episodic drama; sitcom. **Considers these script subject areas:** action/adventure; detective/police/crime; family saga; fantasy; mainstream; mystery/suspense; psychic/supernatural; romantic comedy; romantic drama; science fiction; teen; thriller.

**How to Contact:** Query with SASE. Discards material without SASE. Accepts e-mail and fax queries. Considers simultaneous queries. Responds in 1 week to queries. Returns materials only with SASE. Obtains most new clients through recommendations from others.
**Recent Sales:** Sold 10 scripts in the last year. This agency prefers not to share information on specific sales.
**Terms:** Agent receives 10% commission on domestic sales; 10% commission on foreign sales. Offers written contract.

**Ⓞ STONE MANNERS AGENCY**, 8436 W. Third St., Suite 740, Los Angeles CA 90048. (323)655-1313. **Contact:** Tim Stone. Estab. 1982. Signatory of WGA. Represents 25 clients.
**Represents:** Movie scripts; TV scripts. **Considers these script subject areas:** action/adventure; biography/autobiography; cartoon/animation; comedy; contemporary issues; detective/police/crime; erotica; ethnic; experimental; family saga; fantasy; feminist; gay/lesbian; glitz; historical; horror; juvenile; mainstream; multicultural; multimedia; mystery/suspense; psychic/supernatural; regional; religious/inspirational; romantic comedy; romantic drama; science fiction; sports; teen; thriller; western/frontier.
**How to Contact:** Not considering scripts at this time.
**Recent Sales:** This agency prefers not to share information on specific sales.
**Terms:** Agent receives 10% commission on domestic sales; 10% commission on foreign sales.

**Ⓞ SUITE A MANAGEMENT TALENT & LITERARY AGENCY**, (formerly Suite A Management), 1101 S. Robertson Blvd., Suite 210, Los Angeles CA 90035. (310)278-0801. Fax: (310)278-0807. E-mail: suite-A@juno.com. Website: www.suite-a-management.com. **Contact:** Lloyd D. Robinson. Estab. 1996. Member of DGA; SAG; signatory of WGA. Represents 75 clients. 15% of clients are new/unpublished writers. Currently handles: 20% novels; 40% movie scripts; 15% TV scripts; 5% multimedia; 10% stage plays; 10% animation.
   ● Prior to opening this agency, Mr. Robinson owned Lenhoff/Robinson Talent & Literary Agency, Inc. for over 5 years.
**Represents:** Feature film; TV movie of the week; animation. **Considers these script subject areas:** action/adventure; biography/autobiography; cartoon/animation; comedy; contemporary issues; detective/police/crime; erotica; ethnic; experimental; family saga; fantasy; feminist; gay/lesbian; glitz; historical; horror; juvenile; mainstream; multicultural; multimedia; mystery/suspense; psychic/supernatural; regional; religious/inspirational; romantic comedy; romantic drama; science fiction; sports; teen; thriller; western/frontier.
   ⊶ This agency represents writers, producers and diretors of Movies of the Week for Network and cable, features with budgets under 10 million and pilots/series. Included among clients are a large percentage of novelists whose work is available for adaptation to screen and television. Actively seeking writers with produced credits.
**How to Contact:** Fax 1-page bio (educational/credits), including title, WGA registration number, 2 sentence log line and 1 paragraph synopsis., Accepts e-mail and fax queries. Considers simultaneous queries. Responds in 10 days to fax queries. Returns materials only with SASE. Obtains most new clients through recommendations from others, new writers from various conferences.
**Recent Sales:** Sold 1 title and 2 scripts in the last year. *The Dangerous World of Harry Austin*; *Cold Harvest*, starring Gary Daniels. **Book Sales:***Contessa*, by Jack Fitzgerald (Excel).
**Terms:** Agent receives 10% commission on domestic sales; 10% commission on foreign sales. Offers written contract, binding for 1 year; 3 months notice must be given to terminate contract. Charges for overnight mail, printing and duplication charges. All charges require "prior approval" by writer.
**Writer's Conferences:** Sherwood Oaks College (Hollywood), Infotainment Annual, Black Talent News (Los Angeles, April), Writers Connection (Los Angeles, August).

**☑ Ⓞ SYDRA TECHNIQUES CORP.**, 481 Eighth Ave., E 24, New York NY 10001. (212)631-0009. Fax: (212)631-0715. E-mail: andi9@aol.com. **Contact:** Sid Buck. Estab. 1988. Signatory of WGA. Represents 30 clients. 80% of clients are new/unpublished writers. Currently handles: 10% nonfiction books; 10% novels; 30% movie scripts; 30% TV scripts; 10% multimedia; 10% stage plays.
   ● Prior to opening his agency, Mr. Buck was an artist's agent.
**Represents:** Feature film; TV movie of the week; episodic drama; sitcom. **Considers these script subject areas:** action/adventure; cartoon/animation; comedy; contemporary issues; detective/police/crime; family saga; mainstream; mystery/suspense; science fiction; sports.
   ⊶ "We are open."
**How to Contact:** Query with SASE, outline/proposal. Accepts e-mail and fax queries. Responds in 1 month to queries. Obtains most new clients through recommendations from others.
**Recent Sales:** This agency prefers not to share information on specific sales.
**Terms:** Agent receives 10% commission on domestic sales; 15% commission on foreign sales. Offers written contract, binding for 2 years; 120 days notice must be given to terminate contract.

**Ⓞ TALENT SOURCE**, 107 E. Hall St., P.O. Box 14120, Savannah GA 31416-1120. (912)232-9390. Fax: (912)232-8213. E-mail: mshortt@ix.netcom.com. Website: www.talentsource.com. **Contact:** Michael L. Shortt. Estab. 1991. Signatory of WGA. 35% of clients are new/unpublished writers. Currently handles: 85% movie scripts; 15% TV scripts.
   ● Prior to becoming an agent, Mr. Shortt was a television program producer/director.

**Represents:** Feature film; TV movie of the week; episodic drama; sitcom. **Considers these script subject areas:** comedy; contemporary issues; detective/police/crime; erotica; family saga; juvenile; mainstream; mystery/suspense; romantic comedy; romantic drama; teen.

> O→ Actively seeking "character-driven stories (e.g., *Sling Blade*, *Sex Lies & Videotape*)." Does not want to receive "big budget special effects science fiction."

**How to Contact:** Query with SASE, outline. Responds in 10 weeks to queries. Obtains most new clients through recommendations from others.

**Recent Sales:** This agency prefers not to share information on specific sales.

**Terms:** Agent receives 10% commission on domestic sales; 15% commission on foreign sales. Offers written contract.

**[N] [◐] TALESMYTH ENTERTAINMENT, INC.,** 312 St. John St., Suite #69, Portland ME 04102. (207)879-0307. Fax: (207)775-1067. E-mail: talesmyth@hotmail.com. **Contact:** Thomas Burgess. Estab. 2000. Signatory of WGA. Represents 5 clients. 100% of clients are new/unpublished writers. Currently handles: 10% novels; 10% story collections; 80% movie scripts.

> • Prior to becoming an agent, Mr. Burgess produced short films and managed a restaurant.

**Member Agents:** Thomas "TJ" Burgess (screenplays/book-length fiction).

**Represents:** Movie scripts; feature film. **Considers these script subject areas:** action/adventure; comedy; detective/police/crime; fantasy; historical; horror; mystery/suspense; psychic/supernatural; romantic comedy; romantic drama; science fiction; thriller; western/frontier.

> O→ "As a writer and producer myself I have a keen eye for industry trends and an amazing way to have the write ear hear the right pitch. I work to develop writers to marketable levels as well as represent authors that are ready for publication." Actively seeking mainstream and genre novels with strong character and thematic development throughout. Screenplays with a strong driving plot and meaningful character/plot development. Does not want romance, juvenile, children or young adult-oriented stories.

**Also Handles:** Novels; short story collections; **Considers these fiction areas:** action/adventure; detective/police/crime; fantasy; historical; horror; humor/satire; mainstream/contemporary; mystery/suspense; New Age; psychic/supernatural; thriller; westerns/frontier.

**How to Contact:** Query with SASE. "Talesmyth Entertainment accepts new submissions from July 1 to December 31 only each calendar year to ensure each project is reviewed with due attention. Submissions received between January 1 and July 30 will be returned." Responds in 10 days to queries; 1 month to mss. Obtains most new clients through recommendations from others.

**Recent Sales:** Clients include Gary Hauger, Kevin Brown, F. Allen Farnham, Christopher Cairnduff, Michael Lewin.

**Terms:** Agent receives 10% commission on domestic sales; 15% commission on foreign sales. Offers written contract, binding for 1 year; 60 days notice must be given to terminate contract. "All submissions, whether accepted or rejected, will receive at minimum a one-page critique penned by the agent that reviewed the material. At this time all reviews are completed by T.J. Burgess, president of Talesmyth Entertainment. No fee is charged for this critique."

**Tips:** "Be sure to submit only your best work for consideration. I don't want to see something you just want to get rid of, because I will probably respond in kind. Be certain that your query does a good job of selling me the story and characters and is not just a playful enticement with a "quirky twist." A solid query should summarize the plot and character development in an interesting fashion in one page or less as well as briefly address your expertise in the area or other relevant facts about the market for the story presented, anything else is a waste of your and my time."

**[◐] ANNETTE VAN DUREN AGENCY,** 11684 Ventura Blvd., #235, Studio City CA 91604. (818)752-6000. Fax: (818)752-6985. **Contact:** Annette Van Duren or Teena Portier. Estab. 1985. Signatory of WGA. Represents 12 clients. 0% of clients are new/unpublished writers. Currently handles: 10% novels; 50% movie scripts; 40% TV scripts.

**Represents:** Feature film; TV movie of the week; episodic drama; sitcom; animation.

**How to Contact:** Not accepting new clients., Obtains most new clients through recommendations from others.

**Recent Sales:** This agency prefers not to share information about specific sales.

**Terms:** Agent receives 10% commission on domestic sales. Offers written contract, binding for 2 years.

**[N] [◐] VISIONARY ENTERTAINMENT,** 8265 Sunset Blvd., #104, Hollywood CA 90046. (323)848-9538. Fax: (323)848-8614. E-mail: tparz@aol.com. **Contact:** Tom Parziale. Represents 50 clients. 20% of clients are new/unpublished writers. Currently handles: 75% movie scripts; 25% TV scripts.

> • Prior to becoming an agent, Ms. Hopkins was a studio executive. Visionary Entertainment formerly focused representing talent and has recently started representing writers as well.

**Member Agents:** Tom Parziale (actors and writers).

**Represents:** Movie scripts; feature film; TV scripts; episodic drama; sitcom. **Considers these script subject areas:** action/adventure; biography/autobiography; cartoon/animation; comedy; contemporary issues; detective/police/crime; erotica; ethnic; experimental; family saga; fantasy; feminist; gay/lesbian; glitz; historical; horror; juvenile; mainstream; multicultural; multimedia; mystery/suspense; psychic/supernatural; regional; religious/inspirational; romantic comedy; romantic drama; science fiction; sports; teen; thriller; western/frontier.

> O→ Actively seeking fresh ideas and good writers. Does not want to receive cliched ideas.

**Also Handles:** Novels. **Considers these fiction areas:** action/adventure; comic books/cartoon; confession; contemporary issues; detective/police/crime; erotica; ethnic; experimental; family saga; fantasy; feminist; gay/lesbian; glitz; gothic; hi-lo; historical; horror; humor/satire; juvenile; literary; mainstream/contemporary; military/war; multicultural; multimedia; mystery/suspense; New Age; occult; picture books; plays; poetry; poetry in translation; psychic/supernatural; regional; religious/inspirational; romance; science fiction; short story collections; spiritual; sports; thriller; translation; westerns/frontier; young adult; women's.

**How to Contact:** Send outline/proposal. Discards unwanted queries and mss., Accepts e-mail and fax queries. Considers simultaneous queries. Responds in 1 month to queries. Obtains most new clients through recommendations from others.

**Recent Sales:** Sold 4 scripts in the last year. *The Fighting Temptations*, by Elizabeth Hunter (MTV Films Paramount); *Never Been Kissed*, by Scott Murphy (Kushner-Locke); *Ship of Ghouls*, by Jeff Walch (Bandeira/Dreamworks); *How to Lose a Man in Ten Days*, by Michelle Alexander (Paramount).

**Terms:** Agent receives 15% commission on domestic sales. Offers written contract, binding for 2 years; 60 days notice must be given to terminate contract.

**Tips:** "Write well, and don't use cliche themes or characters."

**WARDLOW AND ASSOCIATES**, 1501 Main St., Suite 204, Venice CA 90291. (310)452-1292. Fax: (310)452-9002. E-mail: wardlowaso@aol.com. **Contact:** Jeff Ordway. Estab. 1980. Signatory of WGA. Represents 30 clients. 5% of clients are new/unpublished writers. Currently handles: 50% movie scripts; 50% TV scripts.

**Member Agents:** David Wardlow (literary, packaging), Jeff Ordway (literary).

**Represents:** Feature film; TV movie of the week; episodic drama; sitcom; miniseries. **Considers these script subject areas:** action/adventure; biography/autobiography; cartoon/animation; comedy; contemporary issues; detective/police/crime; erotica; ethnic; experimental; family saga; fantasy; feminist; gay/lesbian; glitz; historical; horror; juvenile; mainstream; multicultural; multimedia; mystery/suspense; psychic/supernatural; regional; religious/inspirational; romantic comedy; romantic drama; science fiction; sports; teen; thriller; western/frontier.

O→ Does not want to receive "new sitcom/drama series ideas from beginning writers."

**How to Contact:** Query with SASE. Will not read unsolicited screenplays/mss., Accepts e-mail and fax queries. Considers simultaneous queries. Returns materials only with SASE. Obtains most new clients through recommendations from others, solicitations.

**Recent Sales:** This agency prefers not to share information on specific sales.

**Terms:** Agent receives 10% commission on domestic sales; 10% commission on foreign sales. Offers written contract, binding for 1 year.

**DONNA WAUHOB AGENCY**, 3135 Industrial Rd., #204, Las Vegas NV 89109-1122. (702)733-1017. Fax: (702)733-1215. E-mail: dwauhob@aol.com. **Contact:** Donna Wauhob. Represents 7 clients. Currently handles: 60% movie scripts; 40% TV scripts.

● Prior to opening her agency, Ms. Wauhob was a model, secretary, and an AF of M agent since 1968.

**Represents:** Movie scripts; feature film; TV scripts; TV movie of the week; episodic drama; sitcom; animation; miniseries; soap opera; variety show. **Considers these script subject areas:** action/adventure; cartoon/animation; comedy; detective/police/crime; family saga; juvenile; romantic comedy; romantic drama; teen; thriller; western/frontier.

O→ Actively seeking film and TV scripts, juvenile, teen action, cartoon, comedy, family.

**Also Handles:** Nonfiction books; novels; short story collections; juvenile books; poetry books. **Considers these nonfiction areas:** animals; child guidance/parenting; cooking/foods/nutrition.

**How to Contact:** Accepts e-mail and fax queries. Considers simultaneous queries. Responds in 2 months to queries.

**Recent Sales:** This agency prefers not to share information on specific sales.

**Terms:** Agent receives 10% commission on domestic sales; 10% commission on foreign sales. Offers written contract; 6 months notice must be given to terminate contract.

**PEREGRINE WHITTLESEY AGENCY**, 345 E. 80 St., New York NY 10021. (212)737-0153. Fax: (212)734-5176. E-mail: pwwag4@aol.com. **Contact:** Peregrine Whittlesey. Estab. 1986. Signatory of WGA. Represents 30 clients. 50% of clients are new/unpublished writers. Currently handles: 10% movie scripts; 90% stage plays.

**Represents:** Feature film; stage plays.

O→ This agency specializes in playwrights who also write for screen and TV.

**How to Contact:** Query with SASE. Prefers to read materials exclusively. Accepts e-mail and fax queries. Responds in 1 week to queries; 1 month to mss. Obtains most new clients through recommendations from others.

**Recent Sales:** Sold 20 scripts in the last year. *Christmas Movie*, by Daroh Cloud (CBS). Productions at Coconut Grove, Oregon Shakespeare Festival, South Coast Rep.

## FOR EXPLANATIONS OF THESE SYMBOLS,
## SEE THE INSIDE FRONT AND BACK COVERS OF THIS BOOK

**Terms:** Agent receives 10% commission on domestic sales; 15% commission on foreign sales. Offers written contract, binding for 2 years.

**📠 ♥ WINDFALL MANAGEMENT**, 4084 Mandeville Canyon Rd., Los Angeles CA 90049-1032. (310)471-6317. Fax: (310)471-4577. E-mail: windfall@deltanet.com. **Contact:** Jeanne Field. Represents 20 clients. Currently handles: 20% novels; 50% movie scripts; 25% TV scripts; 5% stage plays.
- Prior to becoming a manager, Ms. Field was a producer in the film and television business.

**Represents:** Movie scripts; TV scripts; TV movie of the week; documentary; miniseries; books to the film industry. **Considers these script subject areas:** action/adventure; biography/autobiography; comedy; contemporary issues; detective/police/crime; experimental; family saga; fantasy; feminist; gay/lesbian; historical; juvenile; mainstream; multimedia; mystery/suspense; romantic comedy; romantic drama; science fiction; sports; teen; thriller; western/frontier.

> Windfall is a management company representing writers and books to the film and television industry. "We are especially interested in mainstream and independent film writers or playwrights." Actively seeking well-written material that can be attractive to the entertainment industry.

**How to Contact:** All unsolicited mss returned unopened.
**Recent Sales:** This agency prefers not to share information on specific sales.

**THE WRIGHT CONCEPT**, 1612 W. Olive Ave., Suite 205, Burbank CA 91506. (818)954-8943. Fax: (818)954-9370. E-mail: mrwright@wrightconcept.com. Website: www.wrightconcept.com. **Contact:** Marcie Wright, Steven Dowd. Estab. 1985. Signatory of WGA; DGA. Currently handles: 50% movie scripts; 50% TV scripts.
**Member Agents:** Marcie Wright (TV/movie), Steven Dowd.
**Represents:** Movie scripts; feature film; TV scripts; TV movie of the week; episodic drama; sitcom; animation; syndicated material; variety show. **Considers these script subject areas:** action/adventure; teen; thriller.

> This agency specializes in TV comedy writers and feature comedy writers.

**How to Contact:** Query with SASE. Accepts e-mail and fax queries. Responds in 2 weeks to queries. Obtains most new clients through recommendations from others, solicitations.
**Recent Sales:** Sold 10-15 scripts in the last year. *Rule Number Three*, by Robert Kuhn (Fox 2000); *Dead Celebrities*, by Tomas Romero (Top Cow).
**Terms:** Agent receives 10% commission on domestic sales. Offers written contract, binding for 1 year; 90 days notice must be given to terminate contract.
**Writer's Conferences:** Southwest Writers Workshop (Albuquerque, August), Fade-In Magazine Oscar Conference (Los Angeles, May), Fade-In Magazine Top 100 People in Hollywood (Los Angeles, August), University of Georgia's Harriett Austin Writers Conference, Houston Film Festival, Dallas Screenwriters Association, San Francisco Writers Conference, The American Film Institute.

**♥ ANN WRIGHT REPRESENTATIVES**, 165 W. 46th St., Suite 1105, New York NY 10036-2501. (212)764-6770. Fax: (212)764-5125. E-mail: annwrightlit@aol.com. **Contact:** Dan Wright. Estab. 1961. Signatory of WGA. Represents 23 clients. 30% of clients are new/unpublished writers. Currently handles: 50% novels; 40% movie scripts; 10% TV scripts.
- Prior to becoming an agent, Mr. Wright was a writer, producer and production manager for film and television (alumni of CBS Television).

**Represents:** Feature film; TV movie of the week; episodic drama; sitcom. **Considers these script subject areas:** action/adventure; comedy; detective/police/crime; gay/lesbian; historical; horror; mainstream; mystery/suspense; psychic/supernatural; romantic comedy; romantic drama; sports; thriller; western/frontier.

> This agency specializes in "books or screenplays with strong motion picture potential." Prefers to work with published/established authors; works with a small number of new/previously unpublished authors. "Eager to work with any author with material that we can effectively market in the motion picture business worldwide." Actively seeking "strong competitive novelists and screen writers." Does not want to receive fantasy or science fiction projects at this time.

**Also Handles:** Novels. **Considers these fiction areas:** action/adventure; detective/police/crime; feminist; gay/lesbian; humor/satire; literary; mainstream/contemporary; mystery/suspense (suspense); romance (contemporary, historical, regency); sports; thriller; westerns/frontier.
**How to Contact:** Query with SASE, outline. Prefers to read materials exclusively. Does not read unsolicited mss., Responds in 3 weeks to queries; 4 months to mss. Returns materials only with SASE.
**Recent Sales:** Sold 6 scripts in the last year. This agency prefers not to share information on specific sales.
**Terms:** Agent receives 10% commission on domestic sales; 15-20% commission on foreign sales; 10% on dramatic sales; 20% on packaging. Offers written contract, binding for 2 years. Critiques only works of signed clients; Charges clients for photocopying expenses.
**Tips:** "Send a letter with SASE. Something about the work, something about the writer."

**♥ WRITER STORE**, 2004 Rockledge Rd., Atlanta GA 30324. (404)874-6260. Fax: (404)874-6330. E-mail: writerstore@mindspring.com. **Contact:** Rebecca Shrager or Brenda Eanes. Signatory of WGA. Represents 16 clients. 80% of clients are new/unpublished writers. Currently handles: 10% novels; 90% movie scripts.
**Member Agents:** Rebecca Shrager, Brenda Eanes.

**Represents:** Movie scripts; feature film; TV scripts; TV movie of the week; animation; miniseries. **Considers these script subject areas:** action/adventure; biography/autobiography; cartoon/animation; comedy; contemporary issues; detective/police/crime; ethnic; family saga; fantasy; glitz; historical; mainstream; multicultural; mystery/suspense; psychic/supernatural; regional; romantic comedy; romantic drama; science fiction; sports; teen; thriller.

    O⌐ This agency makes frequent trips to Los Angeles to meet with producers and development directors. "We make it a priority to know what the buyers are looking for. People Store, the sister company of Writer store, has been in business since 1983 and is one of the oldest, largest, and most well respected SAG talent agencies in the southeast. Writer Store reaps the benefits of a wide variety of contacts in the industry developed over a number of years by People Store." Actively seeking action-adventure, urban (dramas and comedies), thrillers, GOOD comedies of all types, GOOD science fiction, Native American, MOWs, sports, music related, based on a true story pieces, big budget. Does not want disgusting horror, toilet humor, short stories (unless it'a an anthology), children's books.

**Also Handles:** Novels. **Considers these fiction areas:** action/adventure; comic books/cartoon; detective/police/crime; family saga; fantasy; glitz; historical; humor/satire; literary; mainstream/contemporary; multicultural; mystery/suspense; New Age; psychic/supernatural; regional; romance; science fiction; sports; thriller; young adult.

**How to Contact:** Query with SASE, synopsis. Accepts e-mail and fax queries. Considers simultaneous queries. Responds in a few to queries; 2 months to mss. Returns materials only with SASE. Obtains most new clients through solicitations.

**Recent Sales:** This agency prefers not to share information on specific sales.

**Terms:** Agent receives 10% commission on domestic sales; 10% commission on foreign sales. Offers written contract, binding for generally 2 years.

**Writer's Conferences:** Words Into Pictures (Los Angeles, June).

**Tips:** "Do not send unsolicited manuscripts. They will not be read. Send brief, concise query letter and synopses. No pictures please. Be sure you understand the craft of screenwriting and are using the proper format."

◉ **WRITERS & ARTISTS AGENCY**, 19 W. 44th St., Suite 1000, New York NY 10036. (212)391-1112. Fax: (212)575-6397. West Coast location: 8383 Wilshire Blvd., Suite 550, Beverly Hills CA 90211. (323)866-0900. Fax: (323)659-1985 **Contact:** William Craver, Nicole Graham, Jeff Berger. Estab. 1970. Member of AAR; signatory of WGA. Represents 100 clients.

**Represents:** Movie scripts; feature film; TV scripts; TV movie of the week; episodic drama; miniseries; stage plays; stage musicals. **Considers these script subject areas:** action/adventure; biography/autobiography; cartoon/animation; comedy; contemporary issues; detective/police/crime; erotica; ethnic; experimental; family saga; fantasy; feminist; gay/lesbian; glitz; historical; horror; juvenile; mainstream; multicultural; multimedia; mystery/suspense; psychic/supernatural; regional; religious/inspirational; romantic comedy; romantic drama; science fiction; sports; teen; thriller; western/frontier.

**How to Contact:** Query with SASE, author bio, brief description of the project. No unsolicited mss., Responds in 1 month to queries only when accompanied by SASE. Obtains most new clients through professional recommendation.

**Recent Sales:** This agency prefers not to share information on specific sales.

# Independent Publicists

You spent years writing your book, then several more months sending queries to agents. You finally find an agent who loves your work, but then you have to wait even more time as she submits your manuscript to editors. After a few months, your agent closes a great deal for your work with a publishing house you really admire. Now you can sit back and wait for the money to start rolling in, right?

If you've learned anything about publishing so far, you've learned that getting a book published takes a lot of work. And once you find a publisher, your work doesn't stop. You have to focus now on selling your book to make money and to ensure that publishing companies will work with you again. Industry experts estimate that 50,000 books are published each year in the U.S. This number is only going to increase with the ease of Internet publishing. What can you do to ensure that your book succeeds with this amount of competition?

While most publishing houses do have in-house publicists, their time is often limited and priority is usually given to big-name authors who have already proved they will make money for the publisher. Often writers feel their books aren't getting the amount of publicity they had hoped for. Because of this, many authors have decided to work with an independent publicist.

To help you market your book after publication, we've included a section of independent publicists, or speakers' agents, in this book. Like agents, publicists view publishing as a business. And their business goal is to see that your book succeeds. And usually publicists are more than happy to work in conjunction with your editor, your publisher, and your agent. Together they can form a strong team that will help make you a publishing sensation.

## What to look for in a publicist

When choosing an independent publicist, you'll want someone who has business savvy and experience in sales. And, of course, you'll want someone who is enthusiastic about you and your writing. When looking through the listings in this section, look at each person's experience both prior to and after becoming a publicist. The radio and television shows on which their clients have appeared can indicate the caliber of their contacts, and the recent promotions they have done for their clients' books can reveal their level of creativity.

You'll also want to look for a publicist who is interested in your subject area. Like agents and publishing houses, most independent publicists specialize. By focusing on specific areas, publicists can actually do more for their clients. For example, if a publicist is interested in cookbooks, she can send her clients to contacts she has on Cooking Network shows, editors at gourmet cooking magazines, bookstores which have cafés, and culinary conferences. The more knowledge a publicist has about your subject, the more opportunities she will find to publicize your work.

## How to make the initial contact

Contacting independent publicists should be much less stressful than the query process you've gone through to find an agent. Most publicists are open to a phone call, though some still prefer to receive a letter or an e-mail as the initial contact. Often you can receive a referral to a publicist through an agent, an editor, or even another writer. Because publicists do cost more out-of-pocket money than an agent, there isn't the same competition for their time. Of course, not every publicist you call will be the best fit for you. Be prepared to hear that the publicist already has a full client load, or even that she doesn't have the level of interest in your work that you want a publicist to have.

## How much money should I spend?

As you read over the listings of independent publicists, you'll quickly notice that many charge a substantial amount of money for their services. The cost of a publicist can be quite daunting, especially to a new writer. *You should only pay what you feel comfortable paying and what you can reasonably afford.* Keep in mind, however, that any money you spend on publicity will come back to you in the form of more sold books. A general rule of thumb is to budget one dollar for every copy of your book that is printed. For a print run of 10,000, you should expect to spend $10,000.

There are ways you can make working with a publicist less of a strain on your purse strings. If you received an advance for your book, you can use part of it to help with your marketing expenses. Some publishers will agree to match the amount of money an author pays on outside publicity. If your publicist's bill is $2,000, you would pay half and your publisher would pay the other half. Be sure to ask your publishing house if this option is available to you. And most publicists are very willing to work with their clients on a marketing budget.

# Authors: Your Publisher Needs Your Help

BY JOHN KREMER

Don't think that you can write a book and then sit back and let the publisher do the rest. While that works for a few authors, it doesn't work for most. Not if you want to sell books. Not if you want to have a bestseller. Listen to publishers. Hear the kinds of authors they like working with. Become one of those authors.

## How to get reviews

Send out review copies. Send out lots of them. Send out more than you think you should. Hit every major newspaper and magazine which you think might be at all interested in the subject of your book. In most cases this means sending out between 300 and 500 review copies.

Don't be stingy about sending out review copies. For every hundred copies you send out, you'll get perhaps ten reviews. And those ten reviews will bring you anywhere from ten to one hundred direct sales and many more indirect sales. Even at a conservative estimate, you'll receive 200 orders for every 100 copies you send out. That's cheap advertising.

If your list of media is selective and your book appeals to a wide potential audience, that rate of return will be even higher. Note that the above estimate is based on sending your review copies to media which regularly review or feature similar books.

For other possibilities on your media list (that is, those media which are not prime prospects for reviewing your books), send a news release, brochure, and reply card offering a review copy upon request. Then send them a review copy if they request one.

Here's one example of the impact of giving away sufficient (even abundant) review copies:

- When Epson came out with their first dot matrix printer they sent 500 printers to the major opinion makers in the computer industry. They did not say, "Use this printer for ninety days and then send it back." No, instead they said, "It's yours. Keep it. Use it any way you want. Enjoy." As a result, by the time other dot matrix printers got their promotional campaigns underway, Epson had already established itself as the standard among the movers and shakers in the industry. So, of course, when these people wrote about computer printers, they naturally talked about Epson—simply because that was the printer they used. Note, however, that this giveaway policy would not have worked if Epson had not produced a solid, reliable printer. Similarly, sending out review copies will not help you unless your book is actually worthy of review.
- A major literary agent for some of the best-known cookbook authors says that one of the most effective ways to promote cookbooks is to send out plenty of review copies to anyone

**JOHN KREMER** *is the owner of Open Horizons as well as editor of the* Book Marketing Update *newsletter. He is the author of* 1001 Ways to Market Your Books, The Complete Direct Marketing Sourcebook, High-Impact Marketing on a Low-Impact Budget, Do-It-Yourself Book Publicity Kit, *and* Celebrate Today. *As a consultant, his clients include a self-published author who has sold over a million books, a new age publisher with 60 titles, and a $100,000,000 publisher with a rapidly growing list of 1,000 titles. This piece is excerpted from* 1001 Ways to Market Your Books *(Open Horizons), reprinted with permission of the author. For more information, see Kremer's website www.bookmarket.com.*

involved with food—from newspaper and magazine food editors to teachers at cooking schools and owners of gourmet cooking shops. The word-of-mouth these people create is worth any amount of regular advertising.

Budget 5 to 10 percent of your first printing as giveaways—for reviewers, booksellers, and key opinion makers. The majority of these review copies should be given away in the first four months or, better yet, months before your book's publication date.

## The importance of author interviews

Author interviews are useful in propelling a book to bestseller status. Few radio and television shows actually review books, but many of them do interview authors. And despite what you may think, radio and television shows are not incompatible with either selling or reading books. Research shows that book sales are helped by television exposure (via talk shows and interviews), and that people who watch a lot of TV also read a lot of books. Indeed, key television shows sell more books than reviews in major print media such as the *New York Times Book Review*.

Interviews, of course, can appear in print as well. Both print and audio or video interviews have certain advantages over book reviews. Here are a few of those advantages:

1. They tend to be more personal and intimate. They give the reader a better feeling for the author's intent in writing the book as well as the author's qualifications.
2. More people watch talk shows and read newspaper/magazine features than read book review sections of newspapers.
3. The author has greater control over what will be covered in the interview; hence, the author can be sure to include more promotional comments about the book.
4. Most interviews are longer than reviews and, in general, the greater the length, the greater the impact.
5. Interviews are more involving, lively, and interesting than book reviews.

## Organizing effective author tours

Author tours can be expensive, a hassle to put together, and very wearing on the author, but for some books they can make a major difference for sales. In general, author tours are not productive unless the author is a celebrity and/or the subject of the book has a wide appeal or is connected to a current issue of interest to many people.

Author tours are not easy to arrange. Not only do you have the additional expense of long-distance phone calls, but you must also fit interviews into a tighter schedule since you cannot afford to stay more than a day or two in one city. Note that if you hire an outside publicity service, it will cost you about $3,000 per city to book and coordinate an author tour.

My *Do-It-Yourself Publicity Kit* includes a number of worksheets and procedures to help you organize an author tour with a minimum amount of effort. Here are a few suggestions to make the tour more effective:

- Consider doing several short tours rather than one long one. Not only would this be easier on you, but it could also save you money (especially if you can organize the mini-tours around your normal business or vacation travel).
- Here are the major cities that publishers regularly schedule for author tours: Atlanta, Boston, Chicago, Dallas, Houston, Los Angeles, Miami, New York, Philadelphia, San Diego, San Francisco, Seattle, and Washington, D.C. Second tier cities include: Cleveland, Denver, Kansas City, Milwaukee, New Orleans, Palm Beach, Pittsburgh, Portland, and St. Louis.
- Arrange for a local contact in each city, someone who can pick you up at the airport and take care of any other driving during your stay in the city. This local contact could be one of your publisher's sales representatives, a local relative, or a professional media escort service.
- When booking interviews, don't forget other possible appearances that could boost sales

for your book. Check to see if any bookstores would be willing to host an autograph session. Try to schedule a speaking engagement with a local club, association, or business. Visit any key wholesalers, distributors, or other sales outlets. Look into any local celebrations or other events.

Warner Book's authors have been found in many places on their tours besides bookstore signings and media interviews. Richard Simmons worked out on center stage in many malls. Alice Medrich whipped up chocolate truffles in local gourmet shops. Robert Ballard recreated the last night on the *Titanic* for students. Kirk Douglas signed his latest novel in the lobbies of movie theaters.

- Call the regional bureaus of Associated Press and United Press International and ask that your appearance be listed in their Day Book. The Day Book is a calendar of events which is checked every day by media sources which subscribe to the AP or UPI services. This could, again, result in additional interviews or other coverage.

- Be sure the local newspaper calendars also list your appearances.

- Do a road show. To promote their books (including *Pirate Utopias* and *Chaosophy*), Autonomedia/Semiotexte sent the six-member Bindlestiff Family Circus on a cross country tour where they performed sideshow acts and comedy at colleges, rock clubs, and theaters. The fire-eaters and blockheads took turns pitching the publisher's 100+ titles. The performers toured the country in a bookmobile.

- Hold a launch party. To kick off the publication of *Final Curtain* by Margaret Burk and Gary Hudson, Seven Locks Press hosted a luncheon on the *Wild Goose* yacht, formerly owned by John Wayne. Pfeifer-Hamilton, another small publisher, had launched books in museums, art stores, and sports bars.

- Do something unusual. To promote his book, *Bad As I Wanna Be*, NBS star Dennis Rodman showed up at a Barnes & Noble signing in New York wearing a complete wedding ensemble, including dress, veil, gloves, and bouquet. This appearance not only gained him plenty of notice in the press, it also resulted in a 35 percent increase in sales of the book throughout the Barnes & Noble chain.

- Do a virtual tour. In 1996, W.W. Norton and Pacific Bell used videoconferencing to promote Walter Mosely's mystery, *A Little Yellow Dog*. While Mosely read selections from the book and answered questions from the audience at the Pasadena Public Library, his presentation was videocasted live to three other libraries in California. Attendees at the other sites were able to participate in the question-and-answer session.

# Working with a Publicist—A Consumer's Guide

## BY GAIL LEONDAR

Your book is finished. Your book is published. Hurrah. Now your work can begin. Publicity—the public activity that takes place between a book, its author, and its potential readers—is an enormously important part of the process of becoming an author that people read, remember, and discuss. Since media attention rarely happens on its own, someone must generate book reviews, magazine and newspaper features, and radio and television interviews on behalf of you and your book. That someone will most likely be either you or the publicist you hire.

Many authors are surprised and dismayed to learn that their publishers are ill equipped to generate the kind of media attention their books deserve. Large publishing houses employ a staff of publicists, who do their best to call media attention to the many books to which they are assigned. Neither negligence nor incompetence prohibits these generally capable, generally intelligent people from devoting appropriate time and attention to every book they promote. A publicist at one of the large houses can publicize dozens, or even hundreds, of books per year. If your book is on your publisher's "A" list (of books perceived as potential blockbusters) your publisher's publicist will be able to give your book a good deal of attention for a few months. If it is on the "B" list, he or she will probably not be able to devote much time to it. The situation is often no better at small presses, which only infrequently employ a publicist who is not burdened with editing, proofreading, clerical or other duties. In-house publicists sincerely want to publicize books. They sincerely try. And many sincerely succeed for at least a portion of the books on their list. But they can not exploit every media opportunity for every one of their books.

So, an author of a new book has three options: bemoan the lost opportunities to inform her reading public about her new book, self-promote, or hire a publicist. Publicizing your own book can be an enormously empowering experience. If you have the time and the self-esteem to call up book review editors and television producers and talk them into giving you media coverage, you will likely emerge a more confident and better writer. If however, you lack the resources to promote your own book properly, find someone to help you. And do it quickly.

The media are primarily interested in forthcoming and new books. Do not wait until your book is pulled from bookstores without having gotten the publicity it needs. Hire a publicist before your book hits the stores. A book with an April publication date is old news by August. Even the best publicist will be unable to generate much media attention once you have waited for your publisher to conclude its publicity campaign before engaging her. Start looking for a publicist three to six months before your book's publication date. A good publicist has significant relationships with newspaper editors and reporters, television hosts and producers, and freelance journalists of all types. Experienced publicists will know which media outlets will most likely be interested in your subject matter, and who at these outlets might admire your book. He or she has earned journalists' trust by having repeatedly introduced them to articulate, appropriate

**GAIL LEONDAR-WRIGHT** *is the founder of gail leondar public relations, which promotes books on progressive social issues.*

interview guests. Those relationships will benefit you as your publicist contacts these journalists on your behalf.

As when hiring any professional, ask your friends for recommendations of good publicists. There are a lot of us out there, and most (but not all of us I'm sorry to report) are capable and honest. When you find someone who seems to understand and appreciate your book and who seems to know how to publicize books similar to yours, ask for references. I've entered into contracts with over a hundred authors and have rarely been asked for phone numbers of satisfied clients. Ask for a list of the books your potential publicist has promoted, copies of television producers and hosts with whom the publicist has ongoing, beneficial relationships.

Do not allow yourself to be impressed by the fact that your potential publicist charges large fees. A large fee does not necessarily indicate a better publicist. If money is tight, tell this to the publicists you are interviewing. I work on a sliding scale. So do others.

Understand that you are not paying your publicist for results. You are paying for effort. No amount of money can buy a review in *The New York Times* or an interview on "Fresh Air." Be realistic in terms of what you can expect to see in the way of results.

Once you have engaged a publicist, stay involved. Call if you learn of media outlets that might be interested in your book. Let your publicist know if an event in the news relates to the subject of your book. Results of your publicist's effort should start appearing within several weeks after the contract begins. Realize that, unless you are already famous, most of your publicists' requests for reviews and interviews will be turned down. This is neither an indication of the quality of your publicist nor a criticism of your writing. It is simply the way publicity campaigns work.

A good publicist will not take on a book she does not think she can publicize. But, even the best publicist occasionally overestimates the extent to which she will be able to produce results. If your publicist is producing no media interviews, however, ask why. A client once hired me after his original publicist told him she had been unable to get him any interviews because the media was out covering a story of national urgency on the day that she phoned. Obviously, a competent publicist phones more than once, and never on a day as unlikely to generate results as the day this publicist chose.

Most book publicists are honorable people with enviable rolodexes. Good publicists can open up amazing opportunities for you to talk about your work on television, radio and in print. If you work with one, your career will never look the same.

# 10 Commandments for Becoming a Best-Selling Author

## BY LEANN PHENIX

### I. The Book is Published on the First Day, Not the Last

The publishing of the book is the beginning of the process, not the end. Approach marketing your book with the same zeal it took to write it. Marketing a book is at least as hard as writing one. There are more than 260 million people residing in this country. For your book to be a success, you must find those 1,000 or 1 million Americans who need or want the information contained in your book.

### II. Thou Shalt Learn the Path of Book Distribution

Book distribution is chaotic, archaic, demanding, disturbing, and anything but easy. Most authors want to be able to go to their local

**Leann Phenix**

bookstore and find copies of their work. In order for that to happen, you must learn the nonsensical world of book distribution. If you land a national media interview, what good does it do you if consumers rush to the bookstore and they cannot find your book? Consumers are too busy and distracted to give you a second chance.

Think in thirds. One third of your breathing/sleeping/eating time went to writing your masterpiece. Another third of that time must be devoted to marketing. Just as important, the final third goes to distribution.

### III. Thou Shalt Believe in Thyself

It's hard to fake passion. If you, the author, don't care about and believe in your book and yourself, no one else will. The public is smarter than most people think, and so are journalists. They can hear insincerity.

### IV. Know Thy Media as Thyself

Every form of media has its own cherished traditions, rigid requirements, and keys to success. Understanding what your hosts and their audiences need from you is essential for getting the most out of media exposure. Know what hooks a journalist's audience, and be ready to deliver.

Know that there are 16,000 daily newspapers, nearly 6,000 weeklies and monthlies, more

**LEANN PHENIX** *is CEO of Phenix & Phenix Literary Publicists, Inc, a marketing firm devoted to authors and publishers. The firm creates national media attention on quality books and has been the force behind numerous best-sellers, including* Kiss of God *by Marshall Ball. Ball, a 15-year old poet, was first introduced to the public on* Oprah, *and his best-selling book sold more than 500,000 copies. Phenix began her career as a journalist and has held positions with Texas newspapers that include columnist, managing editor and editor. In May 2001, she was awarded the "Communicator of the Year" from the Austin Chapter of Women in Communication. This article is reprinted by permission from Phenix's website: www.bookpros.com.*

than 350 general interest magazines, 650 television station outlets, and over 3,000 radio talk shows in North America.

You must learn about: trade press, general business media, minority media, daily newspapers, weekly newspapers, wire services, syndicated columns, Sunday supplements, consumer magazines, regional magazines, city magazines, biweeklies, radio stations, television stations, syndicated radio and television programs, and online media.

Learn the exact function of each of these roles in the media: trafficker, researcher, booker, assignment editor, talent coordinator, segment producer, producer, executive producer, publisher, editor, managing editor, special sections editor, reporter, stringer, and freelancer.

## V. Thou Shalt Not Spurn Small Opportunities

Don't turn your nose up at smaller media outlets. Demanding to start with *Oprah* will get you nowhere, fast. You never know who will read an article or hear an interview. Laughing the local paper out of your office could be dismissing the chance of a lifetime.

P.T. Barnum said it best. "Without publicity a terrible thing happens: Nothing." Notice he didn't qualify where the publicity happened. The essential element is that you make it happen.

## VI. Thou Shalt Not Endeavor to Build Rome in a Day

You didn't write your book overnight. Don't expect fame to come any faster. Marketing a book is a long, sometimes tedious process that, like any other good thing in life, takes time. Give it a chance to succeed!

Jay Conrad Levinson, the author of *Guerrilla Marketing*, says: "Create a sensible marketing plan, then stick with it until it proves itself to you. How long might that take? Maybe three months. Probably six months. And maybe even as long as a year. But you will never, never, never know whether the plan is working within the first 60 days."

## VII. Thou Shalt Not Quit Before the Race Is Run

If you had stopped writing before getting to "The End," you wouldn't have a book at all. Virtually every author depends on perseverance to see them through to the final chapter. This is just as true for marketing the book as it is for writing it.

Mark Victor Hansen, one of the two authors of *Chicken Soup for the Soul*, says, "The bottom line is that 90 percent of what it takes to succeed is publicity, marketing, and promoting. A great book that no one knows about is absolutely useless."

## VIII. Thou Shalt Surround Thyself with Professionals

You don't hesitate to get a professional lawyer, accountant, publisher. Why hesitate to hire a professional publicist? Check our references. Check our results. When you are satisfied that we are partnership material, trust our judgement and abilities. Second guessing us is akin to second guessing your lawyer or accoutant.You chose them because they are experts. So are we.

## IX. Thou Shalt Take Risks

Success often comes only at the cost of taking a chance. Do things differently; be creative in marketing your book. No one else has written the book you wrote. Use the same originality and innovation in marketing it.

## X. Make a Commitment to the Commandments

Read the 10 Commandments often. Commit to following them daily. Commit yourself to persevere and you will succeed.

# Hire the Publicist to Get the Publishing Deal

## BY R. SCOTT PENZA

If you've written a hot manuscript, your publishing deal is probably less than one phone call away. The determining factor is who places the call. You or your publicist. Many of our clients come to us with really sellable material. They also carry the emotional burden and measurable weight of hundreds of rejection letters. Frustrated by sweating hours at their keyboards crafting query letters that, through some writers guide's magical formula, might defy the laws of physics and capture the critical essence and impact of their novels in three paragraphs what it took 400 pages to create, these authors are frequently sobered by the quantum stream of endless declines— "Thank you for considering our agency but we're not reviewing new material at this time . . ." "Due to the highly competitive nature of the publishing industry we must be highly selective in the titles and writers whom we sign . . ." "We know you have spent a great deal of time on your project and put your passion into every page but our client roster is currently full . . ."

**Scott Penza**

© Ayn Moldave

You don't need one more "Dear John, my harem is full letter" to establish that you're full of disappointment. What you may need is one more call. Not to an agent or publisher or published writer who may be willing to introduce you to his or her agent. No, if your material is really good, really really good, you probably need to phone in a literary publicist.

Now wait a minute, you may be thinking, aren't publicists those behind-the-scenes hacks who turn magazine editors' faces red as they turn down high profile client feature interviews for anything less than a cover story? The smooth operators who know how to spin an angle out of thin air so quick, you could dry your laundry in their mouths? The insiders who don't need a membership at Bally's Health Club because they can just as easily bench press their 50 pound Rolodexes?

Well, who better equipped to run your manuscript to a prospective agent or publisher?

Too often, too many authors think that the role of a publicist is to get great press after the book has crossed the border from *sign on the dotted line* to on the shelf at Borders. Not so. In fact, at this literary public relations firm and certainly others, publicists are frequently hired by marketing savvy authors to pitch the project to an agent or to a prospective publisher. Why is this a highly effective approach to landing a deal? Well, here's the theory. One theory, anyway. Because of the explosion in publishing due in large part to online outlets like *amazon.com* and the swallowing up of smaller houses by mainstream houses, themselves adopted by entertainment behemoths, not to forget the skyrocketing expense for advertising a book's release in mainstream media, the traditional houses have placed greater emphasis on shelf-ready manuscripts escorted

**R. SCOTT PENZA** *has served in the entertainment, high tech and literary public relations industry for more than 15 years. He is president of Great Press Public Relations/Los Angeles, which is a Division of Creative Hive Integrated Marketing. Penza's firm is always on the lookout for the next best-seller. To contact him, write:* gr8press@aol.com *or visit his site at* www.creativehivegroup.com.

through their doors with a well-written and carefully strategized marketing plan. Many of these houses have severely cut back on their editorial departments. The day of the assigned editor who sticks with the unknown author from query to rewrite to galley is vaporizing like yesterday's dot.com. So when an agent gets the call from the PR guy or PR gal, she is more likely to take a look at your book because, after all, there's a PR firm behind it. *There must be something here worth looking at.*

Publishers, we have found, often echo that reaction. Only they're more likely to consider the economic opportunities created by having a publicist attached to the project as well. If an author has been signed by a PR firm—in advance of the deal—then the author is thinking ahead. And if the author has established a working relationship with a publicist, chances are strong that that publicist will be around the day the galleys are prepped for release to reviewers and thereafter. The point: a publishing house less inclined to invest heavily into the marketing of an untried, new author (you know first hand, or you've heard the story: you work a lifetime to get a deal, you get lucky and get the deal, the house ignores your book save for a mention on their list) will be more inclined to sign and work with the new author's marketing strategy if the author is footing the publicist's bill to push the work in the press. Of course, many times, a house will contribute to, even split the publicist's fee. It's in their best interest. PR will always be a less expensive buy than advertising. It makes sense to have someone on board the project who can decisively lock those radio and television talk show bookings in a timely fashion, who can potentially influence the outcome of a major metropolitan daily literary review, and who can make the author a household name just in time for the second or third book.

Professionals in the literary public relations industry recognize the value of a call. Rarely do they waste a call. When our agency signs an unsigned author who walks through our doors with a page turner, the first step in the representation process is to research who the most appropriate agents or publishers are for the specific manuscript in question. Tapping in-house databases, personal contacts, and online research, our staff will identify anywhere from 10-15 agents who are, in our opinion, best suited and probably most interested in representing the property. Considerations include the numbers of titles similar to our client's manuscript the agent has signed in the past 2 years, disclaimers in agency guides and market intelligence garnered at the trade shows and through personal contact.

After identifying a preliminary target list, we typically conduct an *agency audit*. This approach, which involves pre-pitching the author's project without revealing title or author, is borrowed from the proven media audit conducted by most PR firms prior to pitching a story. The goal is to secure an approximate read on the media's reaction to a particular story by randomly testing the story on a handful of print and electronic journalists. Some in our profession dub this the "dangle the carrot" approach because the publicist is literally enticing the reporter's reaction by holding back, giving up a little, and amassing data. If the pre-pitch shows that the story has legs, i.e. the majority of randomly (or purposefully) selected journalists reacted favorably, many of those same journalists will be included on the media target list when the full pitch is underway. Having expressed interest *before* all the details were disclosed, those same journalists are more likely to take a look at the story when it's ready for release later on.

The same holds true for agents. Or so we have found. During the agency audit phase of our client representation, our research in advance of the phone calls will provide us with 10, maybe 15 reasonable targets who are ideal for presentation of a new property. Phoning these agents one by one, our staff quickly determines if there is interest in the particular subject area. If so, what would the agent be looking for to consider taking the property from read to representation? What about the markets in general? Does the agent see a need for this type of property now? Has the window passed? Should we wait? What about the news climate? For example, while the market is flooded with self-help books, could this be the best time for another entry about the Freudian psychoanalytic psychotherapeutic approach to weight loss since the Federal government recently released new obesity guidelines suggesting that more than half the nation is over-weight?

With a new belt-tightening Bush administration in place and the resurgence in dialogue about a national missile defense shield lighting up the respective radars of evening newscasts coast-to-coast, is there room in the children's market for a book and CD written and recorded by two aerospace engineers who, by day, build weapons of mass destruction like the Stealth Fighter, but, by night, found time to produce a project designed to steer hurting kids away from suicide as the only answer to their emotional problems? These are the types of considerations the seasoned literary publicist brings to the 30 second phone call, which, if she is on the job, usually develops into a five to ten minute phone call followed by a *"So, when can I see the book?"*

Like with any marketing endeavor, getting the agent to look at the book by tapping the resources and instincts of a professional lit pub takes personal financial investment. While there are private PR "hacks" who will take on an author for $750-1,800, usually for anywhere from one to three months, the motto *You get what you pay for* more often applies to an industry like PR. The high-end firms typically charge anywhere from $2,000 to $3,000 per month plus expenses. Some firms insist on a minimum three-month contract, others represent their author clients on a month-to-month arrangement. While a three-month contract totaling a potential $9,000 to $10,000 may seem steep, consider the time and hours and personal cost of a writing career that produces great material but, because you couldn't get your manuscript before the right people, goes nowhere. Reciprocally, consider the $10,000 against a potential $50,000-150,000 advance if your book is signed. Suddenly, the value of hiring a literary publicist seems to make a great deal of sense . . . and dollars.

When you've sweated over and finally finished that Great American novel, or breakthrough self-help book, or creative children's illustrated story, submitted it to hundreds of agents and received hundreds of rejections, we suggest you put down your manuscript and pick up the phone. Don't call 911. Not yet. Call your local literary publicist. We'll take care of setting your work on fire.

# Independent Publicists

When reading through the listings of independent publicists, use the following key to help you fully understand the information provided:

## SUBHEADS FOR QUICK ACCESS TO INFORMATION

Each listing is broken down into subheads to make locating specific information easier. In this first paragraph, you'll find contact information for each independent publicist. Further information is provided which indicates the company's size and experience in the publishing industry. **Members:** To help you find a publicist with a firm understanding of your book's subject and audience, we include the names of all publicists and their specialties. The year the member joined the company is also provided, indicating an individual's familiarity with book publicity. **Specializations:** Similar to the agents listed in this book, most publicists have specific areas

LEVEL OF OPENNESS    AREAS OF INTEREST    EXPERIENCE WITH BOOK PUBLICITY

**[N] [symbol] PRETEND PUBLICIST**, 149 Big Money Ave., New York NY 10012. (212)555-1590. Fax: (212)555-2258. E-mail: publicize@sellbooks.com. **Contact:** Sue Smith. Estab. 1989; specifically with books since 1992. Currently works with 30 clients. 20% of clients are new/first-time writers.
 • Prior to becoming an independent publicist, Ms. Smith worked in the sales department of Specialty House Publishers.
**Members:** Sue Smith (health, parenting, at firm since 1989); Mark Anderson (business, fiction, at firm since 1994).
**Specializations:** Nonfiction, fiction. **Interested in these nonfiction areas:** business; child guidance/parenting; computers/electronics; cooking/food/nutrition; education; health/medicine; popular culture; self-help; personal improvement. **Interested in these fiction areas:** literary; mainstream; sports. Other types of clients include publishers.
**Services:** Provides detailed outline of services provided, media training, brochures; website assistance; sends material to magazines/newspapers for reviews. Book tours include bookstores, specialty stores, radio interviews, TV interviews, speaking engagements. Assists in coordinating travel plans. Clients have appeared on *Oprah*, *Good Morning America*. Media kit includes author's biography, testimonials, articles about author, sample interview questions, book request information. Helps writer obtain endorsements. Recent promotions included "creating a display for bookstores in the shape of a stage for a book on famous actors and actresses."
  ☞ This independent publicist specializes in "topic of health and personal improvement. We are looking for unique subjects that lend themselves to creative marketing plans."
**How to Contact:** Call or e-mail. Responds in 2 weeks. Returns materials only with SASE. Obtains most new clients through recommendations from publishers, agents. Contact four months prior to book's publication.
**Clients:** *Exercise Creatively*, by Bob Brown (Fit Publishing); *A Mother's Guide to Free Time*, by Jane Johnson (Parent's Press). References and contact numbers available for potential clients.
**Costs:** Clients charged flat fee ($500-1,000); monthly retainer ($1,000-2,500). Works with clients on marketing budget. Offers written contract, binding for 1 year.
**Writers' Conferences:** Write For Money (New York, June).
**Tips:** "Have a passion for your subject and your audience."

COMPANY'S SPECIALIZATIONS    COST    SERVICES PROVIDED

## Quick Reference Icons

- **N:** Independent publicist new to this edition.
- Ⓞ New independent publicist actively seeking clients.
- Ⓐ Independent publicist interested in working with both new and established writers.
- Ⓜ Independent publicist open only to established writers.
- Ⓞ Independent publicist who specializes in specific types of work.
- Ⓞ Independent publicist not currently open to new clients.

of interest. A publicist with a knowledge of your book's subject will have contacts in your field and a solid sense of your audience.

**Services:** This subhead provides important details about what the publicist can do for you, including a list of services available for clients, book tour information, television shows on which clients have appeared, contents of media kits, and examples of recent promotions done by the publicist.

⚷ Look for the key icon to quickly learn the publicist's areas of specialization and specific marketing strengths.

**How to Contact:** Unlike literary agents, most independent publicists are open to phone calls, letters, and e-mail—check this subhead to see the individual publicist's preference. Also pay close attention to the time frame the publicist needs between your initial contact and your book's publication date.

**Clients:** To give a better sense of their areas of interest, independent publicists list authors they have helped to promote. Publicists also indicate here if they are willing to provide potential clients with references.

**Costs:** Specific details are provided on how publicists charge their clients. Although the costs seem high, the payback in terms of books sold is usually worth the additional expense. Publicists indicate if they work with clients on a marketing budget and if they offer a written contract.

**Writers' Conferences:** A great way to meet and learn more about publicists is at writers' conferences. Here publicists list the ones they attend. For more information about a specific conference, check the **Writers' Conferences** section starting on page 287.

**Tips:** Advice and additional instructions are given for writers interested in working with an independent publicist.

## SPECIAL INDEXES

**Independent Publicists Indexed by Openness to Submissions:** This index lists publicists according to their receptivity to new clients.

**Geographic Index:** For writers looking for an agent close to home, this index lists independent publicists state-by-state.

**Listing Index:** This index lists all agencies, independent publicists, and writers' conferences listed in the book.

### For More Information

For more information on working with independent publicists, read the informative articles on pages 261 to 270.

**N** ⊘ **ACHESON-GREUB, INC.**, P.O. Box 735, Friday Harbor WA 98250-0735. (360)378-2815. Fax: (360)378-2841. **Contact:** Alice B. Acheson. Estab. 1981; specifically with books for 31 years. Currently works with 9 clients. 20% of clients are new/first-time writers.

● Prior to becoming a freelance publicist, Ms. Acheson was a trade book editor preceded by high school Spanish teacher.

**Specializations:** Nonfiction, fiction, children's books. **Interested in these nonfiction areas:** art/architecture/design, biography/autobiography, juvenile nonfiction, language/literature/criticism, memoirs, multicultural, music/dance/theater/film, nature/environment, photography. **Interested in these fiction areas:** contemporary issues, historical, juvenile, literary, mainstream, multicultural, mystery/suspense, picture book.

**Services:** Provides detailed outline of services provided, media training, market research, send material to magazines/newspapers for reviews, brochures. Book tours include bookstores, radio interviews, TV interviews, newspaper interviews, magazine interviews. Assists in coordinating travel plans. Clients have appeared on CBS-TV, *Early Show*, CNN, and innumerable radio, TV shows nationwide. Media kit includes author's biography, testimonials, articles about author, basic information on book, professional photos, sample interview questions. Clients responsible for writing promotional material. Helps writer obtain endorsements.

○━ "We mentor so writers can do the work on their own for their next projects."

**How to Contact:** Call or e-mail. Send letter with SASE. Responds in 2 weeks unless on teaching trip. Returns materials only with SASE. Obtains most new clients through recommendations from others and conferences. Contact 8 months prior to book's publication.

**Clients:** *Africa*, by Art Wolfe (Wildlands Press); *Divorce Hangover*, by Anne Newton Walther, M.S. (Tapestries Publishing); *Great Lodges of the National Parks*, by Christine Barnes (W.W. West, Inc.). References and contact numbers available for potential clients.

**Costs:** Clients charged hourly fee. Works with clients on marketing budget. Offers written contract. Contract can be terminated upon written notification.

**Writers' Conferences:** Publishers Marketing Association University (New York NY, May 1-2, 2002).

**N** ⊘ **BRICKMAN MARKETING**, 395 Del Monte Center, #250, Monterey CA 93940. (831)633-4444. E-mail: brickman@brickmanmarketing.com. Website: www.brickmanmarketing.com. **Contact:** Wendy Brickman. Estab. 1990; specifically with books for 11 years. Currently works with 30 clients. 10% of clients are new/first-time writers.

● Prior to becoming a freelance publicist, Ms. Brickman worked in public relations in the home video industries.

**Specializations:** Nonfiction, children's book, academic. **Interested in these nonfiction areas:** biography/autobiography; business; education; ethnic/cultural interests; health/medicine; history; how-to; interior design/decorating; music/dance/theater/film; nature/environment; New Age/metaphysics; popular culture; self-help/personal improvement; travel; women's issues/women's studies. **Interested in these fiction areas:** children's. Other types of clients include home video producers and a wide variety of businesses.

**Services:** Provides media training, market research, fax news releases, send material to magazines/newspapers for reviews. Book tours include bookstores, specialty stores, radio interviews, TV interviews, newspaper interviews, magazine interviews, speaking engagements, conferences, schools, universities. Clients have appeared on Howie Mandel, CNN, more local TV and syndicated radio. Media kit includes author's biography, testimonials, articles about author, basic information on book, professional photos, sample interview questions, book request information. Helps writer obtain endorsements.

○━ "My wide variety of clients and contacts makes me a valuable publicist."

**How to Contact:** E-mail. Responds in 1 week. Discards unwanted queries and mss. Obtains most new clients through recommendations from others. Contact 4 months prior to book's publication.

**Clients:** *What Do They Say When You Leave the Room*, by Brigid McGrath (Eudemonia); *Diet for Allergies*, by Raphael Rethner. Other clients include Carol Teten, Robert Abel.

**Costs:** Clients charged hourly retainer fee or monthly retainer. No written contract.

**N** ◒ ◎ **BRODY PUBLIC RELATIONS**, 145 Route 519, Stockton NJ 08559-1711. (609)397-3737. Fax: (609)397-3666. E-mail: bebrody@aol.com. Website: http://members.aol.com/bethbrodyPR. **Contact:** Beth Brody. Estab. 1988; specifically with books for 13 years. Currently works with 8-10 clients. 10% of clients are new/first-time writers. **Members:** Beth Brody (nonfiction, at firm for 13 years).

## FOR EXPLANATIONS OF THESE SYMBOLS,
## SEE THE INSIDE FRONT AND BACK COVERS OF THIS BOOK

**Specializations:** Nonfiction. **Interested in these nonfiction areas:** business; child guidance/parenting; education; health/medicine; how-to; military/war; money/finance/economics; music/dance/theater/film; popular culture; psychology; self-help/personal improvement; travel. **Interested in these fiction areas:** cartoons/comic. Other types of clients include musicians, artists, dotcoms, healthcare.

**Services:** Provides detailed outline of services provided, fax news releases, electronic news release, send material to magazines/newspapers for reviews, brochures, websites assistance, website publicity. Book tours include bookstores, specialty stores, radio interviews, TV interviews, newspaper interviews, magazine interviews, speaking engagements, conferences, libraries, schools, universities. Assists in coordinating travel plans. Clients have appeared on *Oprah Winfrey Show*, *Sally Jessy Raphael*, *Good Morning America*. Media kit includes author's biography, testimonials, articles about author, basic information on book, sample interview questions, book request information. Helps writer obtain endorsements.

**How to Contact:** Call or e-mail. Responds in 48 hours. Obtains most new clients through recommendations from others. Contact 6 months prior to book's publication.

**Clients:** Music Sales Corporation, Crown Business, Random House, Berkeley Publishing. Other clients include Dow Jones, Don & Bradstreet, Foundations Behaviorial Health, JVC Music, Magweb.com. References and contact numbers available for potential clients.

**Costs:** Clients charged hourly retainer fee; monthly retainer. Offers written contract.

**Writers' Conferences:** Book Expo (New York NY, May 2002).

**Tips:** "Contact a publicist after you have secured a publisher and distributor."

**[N] [◎] EVENT MANAGEMENT SERVICES, INC.**, 519 Cleveland St., Suite 205, Clearwater FL 33757. (727)443-7115, ext. 201. E-mail: mfriedman@event-management.com. Website: www.event-management.com. **Contact:** Marsha Friedman. Estab. 1990; specifically with books for 11 years. Currently works with 15 clients. 0% of clients are new/first-time writers.

• Prior to becoming a freelance publicist, Ms. Friedman worked in PR and event management.

**Members:** Martha Conway (senior campaign manager, partner); Amy Summers (account manager, at firm for 3 years); Rich Ghazzarian (account manager, at firm for 3 years); Ben Ice (business development, at firm for 2 years).

**Specializations:** Nonfiction. **Interested in these nonfiction areas:** animals; cooking/food/nutrition; current affairs; ethnic/cultural interests; government/politics/law; health/medicine; how-to; interior design/decorating; money/finance/ economics; nature/environment; science/technology; sports; travel. Other types of clients include medical doctors, corporations in natural health industry, entertainment industry.

**Services:** Provides detailed outline of services provided. Book tours include bookstores, radio interviews, TV interviews, newspaper interviews, magazine interviews. Clients have appeared on *GMA*, *Today*, *60 Minutes*, *CBS This Morning*, *Maury Povich*, *Montel*. Media kit includes author's biography, press release that gives the actual show idea or story.

    **O─**  "We are paid on performance and our specialty is radio and TV. We book anywhere from 30 to 80 interviews per week!"

**How to Contact:** Call, e-mail or fax. Send letter with SASE. Responds in 2 weeks. Discards unwanted queries and mss. Obtains most new clients through recommendations from others or an initial contact on our part. Contact 6 months prior to book's publication or after book's publication.

**Clients:** *Anti Aging Bible*, by Dr. Earl Mindell (Simon & Schuster); *Slimdown For Life*, by Larry North (Kensington); *Special Trust*, by Robert McFarlane (Multi Media); *Selling Online*, by Jim Carrol and Rick Broadhead (Dearborn). Other clients include Jimmy Hoffa, Jr., Harry Browne, The Temptations. References and contact numbers available for potential clients.

**Costs:** Clients charged on per placement basis $165 (radio)-$5,000 (national TV). Works with clients on marketing budget. Offers written contract.

**Tips:** "Check references to see how much media they book every week/month. Find out if they have knowledge of your area of expertise."

**[N] [○] FIRSTWORD AGENCY**, P.O. Box 521534, Salt Lake City UT 84152-1534. (801)463-0976. Fax: (801)463-1650. E-mail: info@firstwordagency.com. Website: www.firstwordagency.com. **Contact:** Stephanie Kallbacka, president. Estab. 2000; specifically with books for 2 years. Currently works with 10 clients. 75% of clients are new/first-time writers.

• Prior to becoming a freelance publicist, Ms. Kallbacka worked in public relations.

**Members:** Stephanie Kallbacka (media relations, at firm for one year).

**Specializations:** Nonfiction, fiction, children's book, academic. **Interested in these nonfiction areas:** art/architecture/ design; biography/autobiography; business; child guidance/parenting; computers/electronics; cooking/food/nutrition; history; how-to; humor; language/literature/criticism; memoirs; military/war; music/dance/theater/film; New Age/metaphysics; popular culture; self-help/personal improvement; sports; travel; women's issues/women's studies; young adult. **Interested in these fiction areas:** action/adventure; detective/police/crime; experimental; historical; horror; humor/ satire; juvenile; literary; mainstream; mystery/suspense; New Age/metaphysical; thriller/espionage; westerns/frontier; young adult. Other types of clients include music labels, film directories.

**Services:** Provides detailed outline of services provided, media training, international publicity, if applicable, fax news releases, electronic news release, send material to magazines/newspapers for reviews, brochures, website assistance, website publicity. Book tours include bookstores, specialty stores, radio interviews, TV interviews, newspaper interviews, magazine interviews, speaking engagements, conferences, libraries, schools, universities. Assists in coordinating travel plans. Media kit includes, résumé, author's biography, testimonials, articles about author, basic information on book, suggested story topics, professional photos, sample interview questions, book request information. Helps writer obtain endorsements.

> O→ FirstWord Agency offers personal interaction with the author. "We help first time authors gain media exposure through creative and unique publicity campaigns."

**How to Contact:** E-mail, fax, send letter with 3 sample chapters with SASE. Responds in 2 weeks. Returns materials only with SASE. Obtains most new clients through recommendations from others, queries/solicitations. Contact 1-6 months prior to book's publication.

**Clients:** *Hairdresser to the Stars*, by Ginger Blymyer (Xlibris); *The Sandscrapers*, by Griffin T. Garnett (Infinity Publishing); *Baseball's Greatest Players: The Saga Continues*, by David Skiner (Superior Books); *Hearing Footsteps*, by Edward Kallbacka (Infinity Publishing). Other clients include Talking Cloud Records. References and contact numbers available for potential clients.

**Costs:** Clients charged flat fee $100-1,000/project; hourly retainer fee $20-60; monthly retainer $1,000-2,500. Works with clients on marketing budget. Offers written contract, usually binding for 3-12 months; negotiable. 1 month notice must be given to terminate contract.

**Writers' Conferences:** Book Expo America (Chicago IL, 2002); Infinity Publishing (Philadelphia PA, several throughout 2002).

**Tips:** "At FirstWord Agency, it is important for both us and the author to be dedicated to the subject of our authors' work. We value close relationships with each of our clients and work together to achieve success on their behalf."

◉ **THE FORD GROUP**, 1250 Prospect St., Suite Ocean-5, La Jolla CA 92037. (858)454-3314. Fax: (858)454-3319. E-mail: fordgroup@aol.com. Website: www.fordsisters.com. **Contact:** Arielle Ford. Estab. 1987; specifically with books since 1990. Currently works with 10 clients. 50% of clients are new/first-time writers.

> • Ms. Ford has been a publicist since 1976.

**Members:** Katherine Kellmeyer (self-help, health, spirituality, relationships, at firm since 1997).

**Specializations:** Nonfiction. **Interested in these nonfiction areas:** health/medicine; how-to; New Age/metaphysics; psychology; religious/inspirational; self-help/personal improvement.

**Services:** Provides detailed outline of services provided, audio/video tapes, media training, fax news releases, electronic news release, material to magazines/newspapers for reviews. Book tours include bookstores, radio interviews, TV interviews, newspaper interviews, magazine interviews, speaking engagements (limited amount). Clients have appeared on *Oprah, Larry King Live, Good Morning America, AP Radio, The Today Show, CNN, Fox News, Art Bell Show.* Media kit includes author's biography, testimonials, articles about author, basic information on book, professional photos, sample interview questions. Helps writer obtain endorsements. "We created the 'World's Largest Pot of Chicken Soup' to serve 7,000 homeless on Thanksgiving 5 years ago to launch one of the *Chicken Soup for the Soul* books. We ended up on NBC-TV network news and a photo in *USA Today*."

> O→ "We live and breathe our niche: self-help, alternative medicine and spirituality—we completely understand the category and love promoting it."

**How to Contact:** Call, e-mail or fax. Responds within 3 days. Returns unwanted material. Obtains most new clients through recommendations from others. Contact 6 months prior to book's publication.

**Clients:** *How to Know God*, by Deepak Chopra (Harmony); *Spiritual Divorce*, by Debbie Ford; *Send Me Someone*, Diana Wentworth; *When Your Moment Comes*, by Dan Pallotta; *The Reconnection*, by Eric Pearl.

**Costs:** Charges clients flat fee ($6,000-26,000); monthly retainer ($4,000-7,000). Works with clients on marketing budget. Offers written contract, binding on a book-by-book basis. 30-day notice must be given to terminate contract.

**Tips:** "Make sure your publicist (the person who actually will be making the calls on your behalf) is passionate about your book and is experienced in pitching your subject matter."

☑ ◉ **GARIS AGENCY—NATIONAL PUBLICISTS**, 6965 El Camino Real, #105-110, La Costa CA 92009-4195. (760)471-4807. Fax: (253)390-4262. E-mail: publicists@aol.com. Website: http://members.aol.com/publicists. **Contact:** R.J. Garis. Estab. 1989; specifically with books since 1989. Currently works with 50 clients. 20% of clients are new/first-time writers.

> • Prior to becoming a publicist, Mr Garis was a promoter and producer.

**Members:** Taryn Roberts (associate national publicist, at firm since 1997); R.J. Garis.

**Specializations:** Nonfiction, fiction, script. **Interested in these nonfiction areas:** animals; biography/autobiography; business; child guidance/parenting; current affairs; gay/lesbian issues; government/politics/law; health/medicine; how-to; humor; interior design/decorating; juvenile nonfiction; memoirs; military/war; money/finance/economics; multicultural; music/dance/theater/film; nature/environment; New Age/metaphysics; photography; popular culture; psychology; science/technology; self-help/personal improvement; sociology; sports; travel; true crime/investigative; women's issues/women's studies; young adult. **Interested in these fiction areas:** action/adventure; cartoon/comic; contemporary issues; detective/police/crime; erotica; ethnic; family saga; fantasy; feminist; gay/lesbian; glitz; horror; humor/satire; juvenile; literary; mainstream; multicultural; mystery/suspense; New Age/metaphysical; picture book; psychic/supernatural; romance; science fiction; sports; thriller/espionage; westerns/frontier; young adult.

**Services:** Provides media training, international publicity, if applicable, fax news releases, electronic news release, material to magazines/newspapers for reviews, website assistance, website publicity. Book tours include bookstores, specialty stores, radio interviews, TV interviews, newspaper interviews, magazine interviews, speaking engagements, conferences. Assists in coordinating travel plans. Clients have appeared on *Oprah, Dateline, Leeza, CNN, Sally, Extra,*

*48 Hours, Good Morning America, Montel, Inside Edition, 20/20, Today.* Media kits include résumé, author's biography, testimonials, articles about author, basic infomation on book, professional photos, sample interview questions, book request information. Helps writer obtain endorsements. "We designed media information for author Missy Cummings (*Hornet's Nest*)—which resulted in TV interviews on *Extra, Inside Edition* and a print feature in *The Star.*"

    **O—** This company specializes in "quality media that works! Morning radio, national TV, regional TV, major newspapers and national magazines. We currently book over 2,000 media interviews a year."

**How to Contact:** Call or e-mail. Responds in 2 weeks. Discards unwanted materials. Obtains most new clients through recommendations from others. Contact 4-6 months prior to book's publication.

**Clients:** *Hornet's Nest*, by Missy Cummings (iUniverse); *Little Kids Big Questions*, by Dr. Judi Craig (Hearst Books); *There Are No Accidents*, by Robert Hopcke (Penguin Putnam); *Anger Work*, by Dr. Robert Puff (Vantage Press). References and contact numbers available for potential clients.

**Costs:** Charges clients flat fee ($1,500-5,000); monthly retainer ($1,000-3,000). Works with clients on marketing budget. Offers written contract, binding for a minimum of 3 months. 30-day notice must be given to terminate contract.

**Tips:** "Check references. Look for a publicist based in California or New York (that is where the media is)."

**⬤ CAMERON GRAY COMMUNICATIONS**, 12101 Greenway Ct., Suite 101, Fairfax VA 22033. (703)725-9300. Fax: (703)832-0711. E-mail: cameron@camerongray.com. **Contact:** Cameron Gray. Estab. 2000; specifically with books since 2000.

    ● Prior to becoming a publicist, Mr. Gray was an assistant producer and guest coordinator with the *G. Gordon Liddy Show* for eight years.

**Members:** Cameron Gray (nonfiction, lifestyle, pop culture, political works).

**Specializations:** Nonfiction. **Interested in these nonfiction areas:** biography/autobiography; business; child guidance/parenting; computers/electronics; current affairs; education; government/politics/law; health/medicine; military/war; money/finance/economics; popular culture; psychology; science/technology; self-help/personal improvement; sociology; sports; true crime/investigative; women's issues/women's studies. Other types of clients include "anyone looking for affordable, broad radio exposure."

**Services:** Provides international publicity, if applicable, fax news releases, electronic news releases. Book tours include radio interviews, selected chat room events. Clients have appeared on *The G. Gordon Liddy Show, The Roger Hedgecock Show, Daybreak USA, Online Tonight,* and countless other radio shows. Media kit includes author's biography, testimonials, articles about author, basic information on book, sample interview questions.

    **O—** Cameron Gray Communications is "one of the nation's only publicity firms that specifically targets radio outlets, and radio sells the most books of any media."

**How to Contact:** Call, e-mail, or fax, or send letter with entire ms, outline/proposal. Responds in 1 week. Discards unwanted material. Obtains most new clients through recommendations from others. Contact after book's publication.

**Clients:** *Avoiding Mr. Wrong*, by Stephen Arterburn (Thomas Nelson Publishers); *Get Anyone To Do Anything*, by David Lieberman (St. Martin's Press); *Beyond Valor*, by Patrick O'Donnell (Free Press); *Dr. Atkins Age Defying Diet*, by Dr. Robert Atkins (St. Martin's Press). References and contact numbers available for potential clients.

**Costs:** Client charged monthly retainer ($2,000-3,000). Offers written contract.

**🅽 ⬤ GREATER TALENT NETWORK, INC.,** 437 Fifth Ave., New York NY 10016-2205. (212)645-4200. Fax: (212)627-1471. E-mail: gtn@greatertalent.com. Website: www.gtnspeakers.com. **Contact:** Don Epstein. Estab. 1980; specifically with books for 20 years. Currently works with 100 clients.

**Members:** Don Epstein (corporate/literary, at firm over 20 years); Debra Greene (corporate/literary, at firm 20 years); Kenny Rahtz (corporate/associations, at firm 20 years); Barbara Solomon (health/hospitals/public relations, at firm 15 years); David Evenchick (Fortune 1000, at firm for 7 years); Josh Yablon (technology/corporate management, at firm for 8 years); Lisa Bransdorf (college/university, at firm for 6 years).

**Specializations:** Nonfiction, fiction, academic. **Interested in these nonfiction areas:** business, computers/electronics, current affairs, education, government/politics/law, humor, money/finance/economics, multicultural, popular culture, science/technology, sports, women's issues/women's studies. Other types of clients include government officials, athletes, CEO's, technology, media.

**Services:** Provides detailed outline of services provided, international publicity, if applicable, fax news releases, brochures, website publicity. Book tours include radio interviews, TV interviews, newspaper interviews, speaking engagements. Assists in coordinating travel plans. Clients have appeared on all major networks. Media kit includes author's biography, testimonials, articles about author, professional photos, book request information.

    **O—** "We understand authors' needs and publishers' wants."

**How to Contact:** Call, e-mail, fax. Discards unwanted queries and mss. Obtains most new clients through recommendations from others. Contact once a platform is started.

---

**CONTACT THE EDITOR** of *Guide to Literary Agents* by e-mail at literaryagents @fwpubs.com with your questions and comments.

**Clients:** *A Man in Full*, by Tom Wolfe (Farrar Straus & Giroux); *The New New Thing*, by Michael Lewis (W.W. Norton); *Potus Speaks*, by Michael Waldman (Simon & Schuster); *Little Green Men*, by Christopher Buckley (Random House); *October Sky*, by Homer Hickam (Delacorte). Other clients include John Douglas, Richard Preston, Andy Borowitz. References and contact numbers available for potential clients.

**Costs:** Clients charged variable commission. Offers written contract.

**[N] THE IDEA NETWORK**, P.O. Box 38, Whippany NJ 07981. (973)560-0333. Fax: (973)560-0960. E-mail: esaxton @bellatlantic.net. Website: www.televisionexposure.com. **Contact:** Erin Saxton, founder. Estab. 2000, specifically with books for 4 years. Currently works with 10-15 clients. 2% of clients are new/first-time writers.

• Prior to becoming a freelance publicist, Ms. Saxton was a TV producer.

**Members:** Jen Urezzio (vice president, media relations, at firm for 1 year).

**Specializations:** Nonfiction. **Interested in these nonfiction areas:** child guidance/parenting, cooking/food/nutrition, crafts/hobbies, current affairs, health/medicine, how-to, interior design/decorating, money/finance/economics, psychology, women's issues/women's studies. "We don't work with many fiction writers and take them on a case by case system."

**Services:** Provides detailed outline of services, provided, audio/video tapes, media training, fax news releases, electronic news release, send material to magazines/newspapers for reviews, website publicity. Book tours include radio interviews, TV interviews, newspaper interviews, magazine interviews. Clients have appeared on *The View*, *The Today Show*, Fox News Channel. Media kit includes author's biography, basic information on book, professional photos. Helps writer obtain endorsements.

○➤ "This company is founded by a TV Producer and therefore knows what a producer is looking for in a 'pitch.' Because of our background, our clients have an advantage."

**How to Contact:** Call, e-mail, fax. Responds in 1 week. Discards unwanted queries and mss. Obtains most new clients through recommendations from others, queries/solicitations, responses from press we've received. Contact 6 months prior to book's publication.

**Clients:** *Chicken Soup for the Soul*, by Mark Victor Hansen and Jack Canfield (HCI Enterprises).

**Costs:** Clients charged monthly retainer $3,500-10,000 and by project. Offers written contract. "We usually put dates within the contract." 1 month notice must be given to terminate contract.

**✓ ◐ ◎ KSB PROMOTIONS, (Specializes: general lifestyle books)**, 55 Honey Creek NE, Ada MI 49301-9768. (616)676-0758. Fax: (616)676-0759. E-mail: pr@ksbpromotions.com. Website: www.ksbpromotions.com. **Contact:** Kate Bandos. Estab. 1988; specifically with books since 1988. Currently works with 20-40 clients; 25% of clients are new/first-time writers.

• Prior to becoming a publicist, Ms. Bandos was a PR director for several publishers.

**Members:** Kate Bandos (travel, cookbooks, at firm since 1988); Doug Bandos (radio/TV, at firm since 1989).

**Specializations:** Nonfiction, children's books. **Interested in these nonfiction areas:** child guidance/parenting; cooking/food/nutrition; health/medicine; travel; gardening; home/how-to; general lifestyle.

**Services:** Provides detailed outline of services provided, sends material to magazines/newspapers for reviews. Book tours include radio interviews, TV interviews, newspaper interviews, magazine interviews. Clients have appeared on *Good Morning America, CNN, Business News Network, Parent's Journal, New Attitudes* and others. Media kit includes author's biography, testimonials, articles about author, basic information on book, sample interview questions, book request information, recipes for cookbooks, other excerpts as appropriate. Helps writers obtain endorsements.

○➤ This company specializes in cookbooks, travel guides, parenting books, and other general lifestyle books. "Our specialty has allowed us to build relationships with key media in these areas. We limit ourselves to those clients we can personally help."

**How to Contact:** Call or e-mail. Responds in 2 weeks. Returns unwanted material only with SASE. Obtains most new clients through recommendations from others, conferences, listings in books on publishing. Contact 6-8 months prior to book's publication.

**Clients:** *The Home Depot 1-2-3 Series*, (Meredith Books); *Along Interstate 75*, by Dave Hunter (Mile Oak Publishing). Other clients include AAA Publishing, PassPorter, World Leisure Corp. References and contact numbers available for potential clients.

**Costs:** Client charged per service fee ($500 minimum). "Total of contracted services is divided into monthly payments." Offers written contract. 30-day notice must be given to terminate contract.

**Writers' Conferences:** PMA University; BookExpo America.

**Tips:** "Find a publicist who has done a lot with books in the same area of interest since they will know the key media, etc."

**[N] ◐ KT PUBLIC RELATIONS**, 1905 Cricklewood Cove, Fogelsville PA 18051-1509. (610)395-6298. Fax: (610)395-6299. E-mail: KT4PR@aol.com. Website: www.webbookstars.com. **Contact:** Kae Tienstra. Estab. 1993; specifically with books for 22 years. Currently works with 8 clients. 20% of clients are new/first-time writers.

• Prior to becoming a freelance publicist, Ms. Tienstra was a freelance writer.

**Members:** Kae Tienstra (writing, client contact, media relations, at firm 8 years); Jon Tienstra (editing, administration, at firm 5 years); Jan Hooker-Haring (writing, booking, at firm 3 years).

**Specializations:** Nonfiction, fiction. **Interested in these nonfiction areas:** agriculture/horticulture, animals, child guidance/parenting, cooking/food/nutrition, crafts/hobbies, health/medicine, how-to, interior design/decorating, nature/ environment, New Age/metaphysics, psychology, religious/inspirational, self-help/personal improvement, travel. **Interested in these fiction areas:** mainstream. Other types of clients include nonprofit institution, publishers.

**Services:** Provides detailed outline of services provided, media training, send material to magazines/newspapers for reviews, brochures. Book tours include bookstores, radio interviews, TV interviews, newspaper interviews, magazine interviews, speaking engagements, universities. Assists in coordinating travel plans. Clients have appeared on *Today*, CNN, CBS Radio, *Sally Jesse Raphael*, *Today Weekend Edition*, *Home Matters*, *Christopher Lowell*. Media kit includes author's biography, testimonials, articles about author, basic information on book, professional photos, sample interview questions, book request information, segment suggestions for TV, radio, pitch letter. Helps writer obtain endorsements.

&#9758; "Our personal, hands-on approach assures authors the one-on-one guidance they need. Our subsidiary service, WEBbookSTARS.com provides special, low-cost, self-paced author publicity service."

**How to Contact:** Call, e-mail or fax. Send letter with sample chapters and SASE. Responds in 1 week. Returns materials only with SASE. Obtains most new clients through recommendations from others and conferences. Contact 6 months prior to book's publication or after book's publication once a platform is started.

**Clients:** *The New American Backyard*, by Kris Medic (Rodale); *Flea Market Decorating*, by Vickie Ingham (Meredith); *The Black Man's Guide to Good Health*, by James Reed, M.D. (Hilton Publishing). Other clients include Prentice Hall, Better Homes & Gardens Books, Himalayan Institute, *Yoga International Magazine*. References and contact numbers available for potential clients.

**Costs:** Clients charged per service fee $1,500; monthly retainer $1,500. Works with clients on marketing budget. Offers written contract, binding for 6 months minimum. 1 month notice must be given to terminate contract.

**Writers' Conferences:** Book Expo America (New York NY, May 2002).

**Tips:** "We are a small, focused organization, designed to provide personal service. Authors who sign on with us work with us, not with junior staffers."

**N &#9635; GAIL LEONDAR PUBLIC RELATIONS**, 21 Belknap St., Arlington MA 02474-6605. (781)648-1658. E-mail: glpr@aol.com. **Contact:** Gail Leondar-Wright. Estab. 1992; specifically with books for 9 years. Currently works with 16 clients. 50% of clients are new/first-time writers.

&#8226; Prior to becoming a freelance publicist, Ms. Leondar-Wright directed theater.

**Specializations:** Nonfiction, fiction, academic, any books on progressive social issues. **Interested in these nonfiction areas:** biography/autobiography, current affairs, education, ethnic/cultural interests, gay/lesbian issues, government/ politics/law, history, multicultural, music/dance/theater/film, sociology, women's issues/women's studies. **Interested in these fiction areas:** feminist, gay/lesbian.

**Services:** Provides detailed outline of services provided. Book tours include bookstores, radio interviews, TV interviews, newspaper interviews. Clients have appeared on *Fresh Air Morning Edition*, *Weekend Edition*, CNN, C-SPAN. Media kit includes author's biography, testimonials, articles about author, basic information on book, professional photos, sample interview questions. Clients responsible for writing promotional material.

&#9758; glpr promotes only books on progressive social interviews. Our contacts give excellent interviews, primarily on noncommercial radio, including NPR.

**How to Contact:** Call or e-mail. Responds in less than 1 week. Return only with SASE. Obtains most new clients through recommendations from others. Contact 6 months prior to book's publication.

**Clients:** *A Desperate Passion*, by Dr. Helen Caldicott (Norton); *The Good Heart*, by The Dalai Lama (Wisdom); *Love Canal*, by Lois Gibbs (New Society Publishers); *Gender Outlaw*, by Kate Bornstein (Routledge). Other clients include The Lambda Literary Awards. References and contact numbers available for potential clients.

**Costs:** Clients charged flat fee $2,000-15,000. Works with clients on marketing budget. Offers written contract, binding for typically 3 months.

**&#9673; MEDIA MASTERS PUBLICITY**, 1957 Trafalger Dr., Romeoville IL 60446. (815)254-7383. Fax: (815)254-7357. E-mail: tracey@mmpublicity.com. Website: www.mmpublicity.com. **Contact:** Tracey Daniels. Estab. 1998. Currently works with 10 clients. 10% of clients are new/first-time writers.

&#8226; Prior to becoming an independent publicist, Ms. Daniels worked in English Education—middle school and high school.

**Members:** Tracy Defina (new authors, education, at firm since 1999); Marie Garcarm (marketing, at firm since 2001).

**Specializations:** Children's books, nonfiction. **Interested in these nonfiction areas:** biography/autobiography; child guidance/parenting; cooking/food/nutrition; education; how-to; juvenile nonfiction; self-help/personal improvement; young adult. **Interested in these fiction areas:** juvenile; picture book; young adult. Other types of clients include publishers.

**Services:** Provides detailed outline of services provided, fax news releases, electronic news release, material to magazines/newspapers for reviews, brochures, website assistance, website publicity. Book tours include bookstores, specialty stores, radio interviews, TV interviews, newspaper interviews, magazine interviews, schools. Clients have appeared on CNN, *Talk America*, CBS, ABC, VOA, *USA Radio Network*, *AP Radio Network*, *20/20*. "Each media kit varies depending on focus, client needs and budget." Helps writer obtain endorsements. "For a picture book called *Bee Keepers*, we promoted a Pennsylvania author and Pennsylvania publisher to Pennsylvania bookstores (as well as national outlets) by sending 'Made-in-Pennsylvania' honey along with the book."

# *insider* report

# Self-help Author Teaches Self-promotion

For someone who detested English class and couldn't wait to unlock the mysteries of algebraic equations in high school, Dr. Grace Cornish has a solid command of the written word and two best-selling books to prove it. Resisting the universal popularity of escape fiction, Cornish has built her success exploring an entirely different genre—self-help. "I speak about real issues that will empower someone to take another direction or create change," says the world renowned writer and speaker. "Fictitious characters offer vacation; I offer what's pragmatic."

**Dr. Grace Cornish**

From her debut self-published book, *A Fortune of Being Yourself*, to the most recent self-improvement guide, *Ten Good Choices That Empower Black Women's Lives*, Cornish has inspired audiences since 1991 with her motivational discourses. Cornish's growing popularity may have to do with the authenticity of her candid autobiographical approach to writing. She has no reservations about sharing her personal experiences and connecting to readers directly with a "been there-done that" attitude. During a time when hardly any self-help books for black women were available, Cornish's third novel, *Radiant Women of Color*, brought enormous success. A short time later, *Ten Bad Choices that Ruin Black Women's Lives* stormed best-seller lists just three weeks off the press. All of her books represent genuine people, recognizable situations and candid resolutions. Fancy psychological lexicon is abandoned for simple narrative, and humor replaces the serious tone emanated in many other self-help guides. More than anything else, these books are about empowerment, delivering the unflinching range of emotions that shape our daily existence.

A self-proclaimed "positive esteem queen," Cornish began her professional journey as an image consultant for holistic firms. Utilizing a background in business and a Ph.D. in social psychology, she promoted alternative choices in finance, fitness and spirituality at seminars in universities, churches and non-profit events across the country. While Cornish landed speaking engagements on radio and television programs such as *Good Day New York* and the *Queen Latifah Show*, the demand for her instructional advice soared. She has spoken at packed forums in England, Switzerland, Jamaica, and France, among hundreds of venues in the United States.

As Cornish always concluded her sessions with a beneficial affirmation, fans requested something written that they could take home as a keepsake. "I was a bit out of my element at first since I spoke from the heart—sometimes for nearly three hours or more-without rehearsing or writing anything down," says Cornish. "I had talked so much, I didn't even know what would be most important to record on paper!"

Consequently, Cornish was encouraged to write *A Fortune of Being Yourself*. Determined to offer the book to her audiences as soon as possible, she published and marketed it herself. As the publishing process was an entirely new dimension for Cornish, she claims the self-publishing aisle of Barnes & Noble in Manhattan became her personal library. Upon learning all she could, Cornish asked the general manager if she could display the book in the front window for a short time. Additionally, she sent out promotional mailings and traveled extensively for book signings. Within months, the book gained notoriety, and the international publisher Panorama Editorial purchased and translated *A Fortune of Being Yourself* into Spanish.

"I have a passion for inspiring people, and during a time in which self perception was finally being reviewed in books like *Chicken Soup for the Soul*, I saw a need for my book," asserts Cornish. "I was just too impatient for a direction from an agent or publisher at the time."

In contrast today, Cornish has established herself with publishing giants, Crown and Three Rivers Press, and pronounces no complaints. Cornish now works alongside agent Barbara Lowenstein of acclaimed New York team, Lowenstein & Associates, and contends they have had a favorable alliance from the start.

Whether or not getting published was on her original agenda, "Dr. Grace" (as noted by popular magazines including *Essence, Black Men, Heart & Soul*, and *Atlanta Daily World*) is accredited as being the no-nonsense self-help queen for all races and genders. Coinciding with the success of her books, Cornish has appeared as keynote speaker at women's summits, governors' conferences, university commemorations, and even sporting events. While her books are targeted to women, she says the response by men has been just as immense. She receives several hundred inquiries per week as a request for a speaking engagement, private consultation or benefit party, but she claims she's yet to be drained of energy. After all, with three assistants to answer phone calls, faxes and letters, Cornish does actually allow herself breaks in between writing, attending functions and promoting her books.

Although many writers discard self-promotion once they've established a relationship with a top-notch publisher, Cornish does not recommend it. She insists that because a book is most alive during its first three months on store shelves, it's imperative to "stretch out its existence" by sending out mailings, introducing yourself to book buyers and initiating discussions about your work at schools and non-profit events, for instance. "If you sit around and wait for promotional opportunities to come to you, you are certainly not living up to your full potential as a writer. Show your face and make people remember who you are," suggests Cornish.

Influenced early in life by the writings of Napoleon Hill and passages from *The Bible*, Cornish aspires to help people with their personal development. If her books seem all too direct or autobiographical, it's because she characterizes hundreds of clients who have trusted her to share their personal stories. Cornish also reveals her *own* pain and loss, quest for identity and self-contentment. The stories she's told over the years haven't always extended to happy endings. When she was ten years old, she witnessed the death of her mother by an obsessive and controlling lover. Twenty years later, her aunt was killed in the same fashion.

"At that young age, I knew I would someday dedicate my life to helping people rid themselves of anxiety, despondency, and frustration, and replace those feelings with hope, joy and peace of mind," says Cornish.

As specific as the self-help genre happens to be, Dr. Grace commands that the same tools for success apply to *all* writers: good intentions, persistence, talent, and a trustworthy agent. And . . . "if you have something dynamic to offer, do your research and make it happen. People are eager to hear what you have to say."

—*Candi Cross*

○ "I have over eight years of book publicity experience. My company delivers 'publicity with personality'—we go beyond just covering the basics."

**How to Contact:** E-mail or send letter with outline/proposal and sample chapters. Responds in 2 weeks. Returns materials only with SASE. Obtains most new clients through recommendations from others. Contact 3 months prior to book's publication.

**Clients:** Clients include Fitzhenry & Whiteside Children's Books, HarperCollins Children's Books, Choutte, NorthSouth Books, NorthWord Books for Young Readers, Boyds Mills Press, plus individual authors. Reference and contact numbers available for potential clients.

**Costs:** Charges for services depend on client's needs and budget. Offers written contract. 30-day notice must be given to terminate contract.

**Writers' Conferences:** BEA, ALA.

**PHENIX & PHENIX LITERARY PUBLICISTS, INC.**, 4412 Spicewood Springs, Suite 102, Austin TX 78759. (512)478-2028. Fax: (512)478-2117. E-mail: info@bookpros.com. Website: www.bookpros.com. **Contact:** Champ Covington. Estab. 1994; specifically with books since 1994. Currently works with 20 clients. 50% of clients are new/first-time writers.

**Members:** Marika Flatt (director of media relations, at firm since 1997); Andrew Berzanskis (publicist, at firm since 1999); Leann Phenix (CEO/marketing, at firm since 1994); Elaine Froelich (publicist).

**Specializations:** Nonfiction, fiction, children's books, academic, coffee table books, biographies. **Interested in these nonfiction areas:** animals; biography/autobiography; business; child guidance/parenting; computers/electronics; current affairs; health/medicine; money/finance/economics; multicultural; religious/inspirational; self-help/personal improvement; sports; travel; true crime/investigative; women's issues/women's studies; young adult. **Interested in these fiction areas:** action/adventure; confessional; contemporary issues; detective/police/crime; family saga; historical; humor/satire; multicultural; mystery/suspense; regional; religious/inspirational; sports; young adult. Other types of clients include publishers.

**Services:** Provides detailed outline of services provided, media training, fax news releases, electronic news release, material to magazines/newspapers for reviews, brochures, website publicity. Book tours include bookstores, specialty stores, radio interviews, TV interviews, newspaper interviews, magazine interviews. Clients have appeared on *Oprah*, CNN, CNBC, *Fox News Network*, *Leeza*, *Montel*, *Good Morning America*, *Talk America Radio Network*, *Business News Network*, *Westwood One Radio Network*, *UPI Radio Network*. Media kit includes author's biography, testimonials, articles about author, basic information on book, professional photos, sample interview questions, book request information, press releases, excerpts. Recent promotions included video press releases, mystery contest, online publicity campaigns, creative angles for fiction positioning.

○ This company has a first 30-day strategy (develop strategy, positioning, press materials), and created 4 bestsellers in 1999.

**How to Contact:** Call, e-mail, fax or send letter with entire ms. Responds in 5 days. Discards unwanted material. Obtains most new clients through recommendations from others, conferences, website. Contact 2-4 months prior to book's publication or after book's publication.

**Clients:** *Kiss of God*, by Marshall Ball (Health Communications); *True Women/Hill Country*, by Janice Woods Windle (Longstreet Press); *Wizard of Ads*, by Roy Williams (Bard Press); *Faith on Trial*, by Pamela Ewen (Broadman & Holman). Other clients include Dr. Ivan Misner, Lisa Shaw-Brawley, Michele O'Donnell, Patrick Seaman (Timberwolf Press), Continuum Press. References and contact number available for potential clients.

**Costs:** Charges clients per placement basis ($100-5,000); per service fee ($500-3,000); monthly retainer ($2,500-6,500). Works with clients on a marketing budget. Offers written contract binding for 4-6 months.

**Writers' Conferences:** Craft of Writing (Denton, TX).

**Tips:** "Find a publicist that will offer a guarantee. Educate yourself on the book/publicity process."

**RAAB ASSOCIATES**, 345 Millwood Rd., Chappaqua NY 10514. (914)241-2117. Fax: (914)241-0050. E-mail: info@raabassociates.com. Website: www.raabassociates.com. **Contact:** Susan Salzman Raab. Estab. 1986; specifically with books since 1986. Currently works with 10 clients. 10% of clients are new/first-time writers.

● Prior to becoming an independent publicist, Ms. Salzman Raab worked on staff at major publishing houses in the children's book industry.

**Members:** Susanna Reich (associate, at firm since 2000); Susan Salzman Raab (partner, at firm since 1986).

**Specializations:** Children's books, parenting books. **Interested in these nonfiction areas:** juvenile nonfiction, young adult, parenting. **Interested in these fiction areas:** juvenile, picture book, young adult, parenting. Other types of clients include publishers, toy companies, audio companies.

**Services:** Provides detailed outline of services provided; market research; material to magazines/newspapers for review; website assistance; website development and extensive online publicity. Book tours include bookstores, specialty stores, radio interviews, TV interviews, newspaper interviews, magazine interviews, schools and libraries. Can also assist in coordinating travel plans. Clients have appeared on NPR, CNN, C-Span, Radio-Disney, PRI. Media kit includes author's biography, testimonials, articles about author, basic information on book, sample interview questions, book request information. Helps writer obtain endorsements.

O⇥ "We are the only PR agency to specialize in children's and parenting books."

**How to Contact:** Call or e-mail. Responds in 2 weeks. Returns materials only with SASE. Obtains most new clients through recommendations from others, conferences. Contact 4 months prior to book's publication.

**Clients:** Sometimes references and contact numbers available to potential clients (most often to publishers, rather than authors).

**Costs:** Clients charged per service fee. Offers written contract. 90-day notice must be given to terminate contract.

**Writers' Conferences:** Society of Children's Book Writers & Illustrators (New York National); Society of Children's Book Writers & Illustrators (Regional Meeting); Book Expo America (Chicago, May/June); American Library Association (Chicago, July); Bologna Bookfair (April).

☑ Ⓞ **ROCKS-DEHART PUBLIC RELATIONS (BOOK PUBLICITY)**, 811 Boyd Ave., Suite 201, Pittsburgh PA 15238. (412)820-3004. Fax: (412)820-3007. E-mail: celiarocks@aol.com. Website: www.Rocks-DeHartPublicRelations.com. **Contact:** Celia Rocks. Estab. 1993; specifically with books since 1993. Currently works with 10 clients; 20% of clients are new/first-time writers.

• Prior to becoming a publicist, Ms. Rocks was a publicity specialist at Burson Marsteller.

**Members:** Dottie DeHart (principal, at firm since 1993); Leslie Ogle (copywriter, at firm since 1996); Megan Johnson (account executive, at firm since 1999).

**Specializations:** Nonfiction, business, lifestyle. **Interested in these nonfiction areas:** biography/autobiography; business; cooking/food/nutrition; current affairs; health/medicine; how-to; humor; popular culture; psychology; religious/inspirational; self-help/personal improvement; sociology; travel; women's issues/women's studies. Other types of clients include major publishing houses.

**Services:** Provides detailed outline of services provided. Book tours include bookstores, specialty stores, radio interviews, TV interviews, newspaper interviews, magazine interviews, speaking engagements, conferences, libraries, schools, universities. Clients have appeared on *ABC World News, Oprah* and others. Media kit includes author's biography, testimonials, articles about author, basic information on book, professional photos, sample interview questions, book request information, breakthrough plan materials, and "any other pieces that are helpful." Helps writers obtain endorsements. Recent promotions included "taking a book like *Fishing for Dummies* and sending gummy worms with packages."

O⇥ This company specializes in IDG "Dummies" Books, business, management, and lifestyle titles. "We are a highly creative firm that understands the best way to obtain maximum publicity."

**How to Contact:** Call or e-mail. Responds in 1 week. Obtains most new clients through recommendations from others. Contact 4-6 months prior to book's publication.

**Clients:** *Teenvester.Com* by Modu and Walker (Putnam/Perigree); *Getting Your Foot in the Door When You Don't Have a Leg to Stand On* by Rob Sullivan (McGraw-Hill). Other clients include Prima Press, IDG, Dearborn, Jossey-Bass.

**Costs:** Client charged monthly retainer ($3,000-5,000). Works with clients on marketing budget. Offers written contract. 30-day notice must be given to terminate contract.

**Tips:** "We have a solid reputation for excellence and results."

Ⓝ Ⓞ **SHERRI ROSEN PUBLICITY**, 80 S. Main St., Suite 2A, Milltown NJ 08850. Phone/fax: (732)448-9441. E-mail: sherri@sherrirosen.com. Website: www.sherrirosen.com. **Contact:** Sherri Rosen. Estab. 1997, specifically with books for 11 years. Currently works with 4 clients. 50% of clients are new/first-time writers.

• Prior to becoming a freelance publicist, Ms. Rosen was an actress.

**Specializations:** Nonfiction, fiction, children's book, events, healers. **Interested in these nonfiction areas:** child guidance/parenting, cooking/food/nutrition, current affairs, education, ethnic/cultural interests, gay/lesbian issues, health/medicine, how-to, humor, juvenile nonfiction, memoirs, music/dance/theater/film, New Age/metaphysics, popular culture, psychology, religious/inspirational, self-help/personal improvement, travel, women's issues/women's studies, young adult. **Interested in these fiction areas:** action/adventure, confessional, erotica, ethnic, experimental, family saga, fantasy, feminist, humor/satire, literary, mainstream, multicultural, New Age/metaphysical, psychic/supernatural, religious/inspirational, romance, young adult. Other types of clients include healers, business people, spiritual teachers.

**Services:** Provides detailed outline of services provided, audio/video tapes, international publicity, if applicable, send material to magazines/newspapers for reviews, brochures. Book tours include bookstores, radio interviews, TV interviews, newspaper interviews, magazine interviews, speaking engagements, conferences, libraries, schools, universities. Assists in coordinating travel plans. Clients have appeared on *Oprah, Montel, Politically Incorrect, Leeza, Men are from Mars*. Media kit includes author's biography, testimonials, articles about author, basic information on book, professional photos, sample interview questions, book request information. Clients responsible for writing promotional material. Helps writer obtain endorsements.

☞ "I work with eclectic clientele—sex books, spiritual books, personal inspirational, self-help books. What is distinct is I will only work with people I like, and I have to like and respect what they are doing."

**How to Contact:** E-mail. Responds immediately. Discards unwanted queries or returns materials only with SASE. Obtains most new clients through recommendations from others, listings with other services in our industry. Contact 3 months prior to book's publication if possible; after book's publication once a platform is started.

**Clients:** *How to Satisfy a Woman*, by Maura Hayden (self-published); *Men Who Can't Love*, by Steven Carten (Harper-Collins); *Rebirth of the Goddess*, by Carol Christ (Addison-Wesley); *Buddhism Without Belief*, by Stephen Batchelor (Riberhead). Other clients include Eli Jaxon-Bear, Sandra Rothenberger, Elizabeth Ayres. References and contact numbers available for potential clients.

**Costs:** Clients charged hourly retainer fee $125; monthly retainer $4,000. Offers written contract. One month notice must be given to terminate contract.

**Tips:** "Make sure you like who you will be working with most important, because you work so closely."

◐ **ROYCE CARLTON, INC.**, 866 United Nations Plaza, Suite 587, New York, NY 10017. (212)335-7700. Fax: (212)888-8659. E-mail: info@roycecarlton.com. Website: www.roycecarlton.com. **Contact:** Carlton Sedgeley. Estab. 1968. Currently works with 50 clients.

• Royce Carlton, Inc. is a lecture agency and management firm for some 50 speakers who are available for lectures and special engagements.

**Members:** Carlton S. Sedgeley, president (at firm since 1968); Lucy Lepage, executive vice president (at firm since 1968); Helen Churko, vice president (at firm since 1984).

**Specializations:** Royce Carlton works with many different types of speakers. Other clients include celebrities, writers, journalists, scientists, etc.

**Services:** Provides "full service for all our clients to lecture."

☞ "We are the only lecture agency representing all our clients exclusively."

**How to Contact:** Call, e-mail, or fax. Discards unwanted material. Obtains most new clients through recommendations from others, or initiates contact directly.

**Clients:** *Tuesdays with Morrie*, by Mitch Albom; *House Made of Dawn*, by N. Scott Momaday. Other clients include Joan Rivers, Elaine Pagels, Walter Mosley. References and contact numbers available for potential clients.

**Costs:** Client charged per placement; commission. Offers written contract. 30-day notice must be given to terminate contract.

**N** ◐ **SMITH PUBLICITY**, P.O. Box 67, Fairless Hills PA 19030. (215)946-5775. Fax: (215)943-6025. E-mail: info@smithpublicity.com. Website: www.smithpublicity.com. **Contact:** Dan Smith. Estab. 1997; specifically with books for 4 years. Currently works with 10 clients. 70% of clients are new/first-time writers.

• Prior to becoming a freelance publicist, Mr. Smith was a freelance public relations specialist and promotional writer.

**Members:** Dan Smith (writing, marketing analysis, campaign management, at firm 4 years); Melissa Gill (media research/media relations, at firm 2 years); Catherine Vella (media contact development, at firm 1 year); Fran Rubin (marketing, business development, at firm 3 years).

**Specializations:** Nonfiction, fiction. **Interested in these nonfiction areas:** government/politics/law, how-to, humor, multicultural, New Age/metaphysics, popular culture, self-help/personal improvement, true crime/investigative. **Interested in these fiction areas:** confessional, experimental, family saga, humor/satire, mainstream, New Age/metaphysical, psychic/supernatural. Other types of clients include entrepreneurs, business specialties.

**Services:** Provides detailed outline of services provided, media training, international publicity, if applicable, market research, fax news releases, electronic news release, send material to magazines/newspapers for reviews, website assistance, website publicity. Book tours include bookstores, radio interviews, TV interviews, newspaper interviews, magazine interviews, speaking engagements. Assists in coordinating travel plans. Clients have appeared on *Montel, Sally Jesse Raphael, Extra, Good Morning America, Howard Stern, O'Reilly Factor, Ken Hamblin, Mike Gallagher, Daybreak USA*. Media kit includes author's biography, testimonials, articles about author, basic information on book, sample interview questions. Developed "Mob Lingo and Trivia Quiz" for fictional organized crime novel, which resulted in more than 40 interviews for the author.

☞ "We find angles which interest the media, while offering affordable rates with unparalled customer service."

**How to Contact:** Call, e-mail or fax. Responds in 1 week. Returns materials only with SASE. Obtains most new clients through recommendations from others, queries/solicitations, conferences. Contact 4 months prior to book's publication or after book's publication.

**Clients:** *Conversations with Tom*, by Walda Woods (White Rose Publishing); *Emotionally Intelligent Parenting*, by Dr. Steven Tobias (Random House). Other clients include John Paul Christ, Jack Nadel, Peter DeVice, Lester O'Shea, Dead End Street, Dr. Arnold Nesenberg, Carol DeCuffa. References and contact numbers available for potential clients.

**Costs:** Clients charged flat fee $500-1,200; monthly retainer $500-1,600. Offers written contract. 3 months notice must be given to terminate contract.

**Writers' Conferences:** Book Expo America (New York City).

**Tips:** "Don't be afraid to ask questions. Speak with at least three different publicists before deciding. Have fun with your project and enjoy the ride!"

**N** ◑ **THE SPIZMAN AGENCY**, Atlanta GA 30327. E-mail: spizagency@aol.com. www.spizmanagency.com. **Contact:** Robyn or Willy Spizman. Estab. 1981; specifically with books for 20 years. 50% of clients are new/first-time writers.

• Prior to becoming a freelance publicist, co-owner Robyn Spizman was the author of 68 published books and a consumer reporter on TV.

**Specializations:** Nonfiction, fiction, children's book, academic. **Interested in these nonfiction areas:** business, child guidance/parenting, computers/electronics, cooking/food/nutrition, crafts/hobbies, current affairs, education, ethnic/cultural interests, health/medicine, history, how-to, humor, interior design/decorating, juvenile nonfiction, language/literature/criticism, memoirs, military/war, money/finance/economics, multicultural, music/dance/theater/film, nature/environment, New Age/metaphysics, photography, popular culture, psychology, religious/inspirational, science/technology, self-help/personal improvement, sociology, sports, travel,true crime/investigative, women's issues/women's studies, young adult. **Interested in these fiction areas:** business, contemporary issues, internet, mainstream, inspirational, young adult.

**Services:** Provides detailed outline of services provided, media training, international publicity, if applicable, market research, fax news releases, electronic news release, send material to magazines/newspapers for reviews, brochures, websites assistance, website publicity. Book tours include bookstores, specialty stores, radio interviews, TV interviews, newspaper interviews, magazine interviews, satellite media tours, speaking engagements, conferences, libraries, schools, universities. Assists in coordinating travel plans. Clients have appeared on *Oprah*, CNN, *NBC Today*, HGTV. Media kit includes résumé, author's biography, testimonials, articles about author, basic information on book, professional photos, sample interview questions, book request information. Helps writer obtain endorsements. Recent promotions included a one hour show on a client's book on CNN—the author starred in the entire show.

**How to Contact:** E-mail. Responds in 1 week. Returns materials only with SASE. Obtains most new clients through recommendations from others. Contact 6 months prior to book's publication, once a platform is started.

**Clients:** *II Immutable Laws of the Internet*, by Al and Laura Ries (harperCollins); *Live, Learn & Pass It On*, by H. Jackson Brown, Jr. (Rutledge Hill). Other clients include Turner Broadcasting, Glaxo Welcome, Reproductive Biology Associates. References and contact numbers available for potential clients.

**Costs:** Monthly retainer. Works with clients to help create a marketing budget. Offers written contract. 1 month notice must be given to terminate contract.

**Writers' Conferences:** Book Expo (Chicago).

**Tips:** "It gets down to one thing—who they know and what they know, plus years of successful clients. We score high on all counts."

**N** ◑ **TALION.COM**, 330 SW 43rd St. PMB K-547, Renton WA 98055. (425)228-7131. Fax: (425)228-3965. E-mail: Feedback@Talion.com. Website: www.Talion.com. **Contact:** Bev Harris. Estab. 1996; specifically with books for 15 years. Currently works with 200 clients. 60% of clients are new/first-time writers.

• Prior to becoming a freelance publicist, Ms. Harris spent 20 years marketing for books, newsletters and corporate marketing and publicity.

**Members:** Bev Harris (literary and corporate publicity, at firm for 15 years); Terrayel Cartmill (literary and music publicity); Ian Gantt (literary publicity and computer work).

**Specializations:** Nonfiction, fiction, children's book, personalities, events, political activists. **Interested in these nonfiction areas:** animals, anthropology/archaeology, biography/autobiography, business, child guidance/parenting, computers/electronics, cooking/food/nutrition, current affairs, ethnic/cultural interests, government/politics/law, health/medicine, how-to, humor, interior design/decorating, juvenile nonfiction, military/war, money/finance/economics, multicultural, music/dance/theater/film, nature/environment, New Age/metaphysics, popular culture, psychology, religious/inspirational, science/technology, self-help/personal improvement, sports, travel, true crime/investigative, women's issues/women's studies, young adult. **Interested in these fiction areas:** action/adventure, contemporary issues, detective/police/crime, ethnic, fantasy, feminist, historical, horror, humor/satire, juvenile, literary, mainstream, multicultural, mystery/suspense, New Age/metaphysical, psychic/supernatural, religious/inspirational, romance, science fiction, sports, thriller/espionage, westerns/frontier, young adult. Other types of clients include musicians, political and social activists, performing artists, corporate.

**Services:** Provides detailed outline of services provided, audio/video tapes, fax news releases, electronic news release, send material to magazines/newspapers for reviews, websites assistance, website publicity. Book tours include radio interviews, TV interviews, newspaper interviews, magazine interviews. Clients have appeared on *Montel Williams*, *Oprah*, *20/20*, *Howard Stern*, *Dr. Laura*, *Good Morning America*, CNN, *Geraldo Rivera*. Media kit includes author's biography, basic information on book, sample interview questions, online press kits, story angles, backgrounders, news releases. "We created media personas like 'The Ultimate Hollywood Storyteller' (over 500 radio talk shows to promote his audio books) and 'The Headhunter' (wears grass skirt, carries spear, shows up at corporate downsizing to promote book on job headhunting with his 'pink slip attack')."

○━ Talion.com is the only PR firm specializing in inexpensive publicity. Free online do-it-yourself info, packages start at $349, many affordable a la carte offerings.

**How to Contact:** Call or e-mail. Responds in 1 week. Discards unwanted queries and mss. Obtains most new clients through recommendations from others and on website. Contact anytime—PR is matched to current needs.

**Clients:** *Dollars, Diamonds, Destiny & Death: My Life with the Richest Girl in the World*, by James E. Higgins III (VCA publishing); *Elusive Innocence*, by Dean Tong (Huntington House); *St. Jude's Secret*, by Daniel Jones (X-LIBRIS);

*Game Plan*, by Charles Wilson (St. Martin's Press). Other clients include handling many assignments for presidential election 2000 (publicizing Afro-American voter disenfranchisement); Gene Autry Museum; Alpha 200. References and contact numbers available for potential clients.

**Costs:** Clients charged per service fee $199-1,500. Works with clients on marketing budget. No written contract. Provide written confirmation of assignments. No requirement for contract obligations.

**Writers' Conferences:** BEA (June 2002).

**Tips:** "Visit 'Top Ten Publicity Blunders'—a comprehensive free online tutorial containing real-life wisdom on every aspect of publicity—www.Talion.com/TopTen.htm."

**WARWICK ASSOCIATES**, 18340 Sonoma Hwy., Sonoma CA 95476. (707)939-9212. Fax: (707)938-3515. E-mail: sws@vom.com. Website: www.warwickassociates.net. **Contact:** Simon Warwick-Smith, president. Estab. 1983; specifically with books for 18 years. Currently works with 24 clients. 12% of clients are new/first-time writers.
- Prior to becoming a freelance publicist, Mr. Warwick-Smith was Senior Vice President Marketing, Associated Publishers Group (books).

**Members:** Patty Vadinsky (celebrity, sports, at firm 6 years); Simon Warwick-Smith (metaphysics, business, at firm 18 years); Warren Misuraca (travel, writing, at firm 8 years).

**Specializations:** Nonfiction, children's books, spirituality. **Interested in these nonfiction areas:** biography/autobiography, business, child guidance/parenting, computers/electronics, cooking/food/nutrition, government/politics/law, health/medicine, how-to, New Age/metaphysics, psychology, religious/inspirational, self-help/personal improvement, sports, travel. Other types of clients include celebrity authors.

**Services:** Provides media training, market research, fax news releases, electronic news release, send material to magazines/newspapers for reviews, brochures, websites assistance, website publicity. Book tours include bookstores, specialty stores, radio interviews, TV interviews, newspaper interviews, magazine interviews, speaking engagements, online interviews. Assists in coordinating travel plans. Clients have appeared on *Larry King*, *Donahue*, *Oprah*, *Good Morning America*. Media kit includes résumé, author's biography, testimonials, articles about author, basic information on book, professional photos, sample interview questions, book request information. Helps writer obtain endorsements.

**How to Contact:** See website. Responds in 2 weeks. Return only with SASE. Obtains most new clients through recommendations from others and on website. Contact 6 months prior to book's publication.

**Clients:** References and contact numbers available for potential clients.

**Costs:** Works with clients on marketing budget. Offers written contract binding for specific project.

**WORLD CLASS SPEAKERS & ENTERTAINERS**, 28025 Dorothy Dr., Suite 202, Aqoura Hills CA 91301. (818)991-5400. Fax: (818)991-2226. E-mail: info@speak.com. Website: www.speak.com. **Contact:** Joseph I. Kessler. Estab. 1965.

**Specializations:** Nonfiction, academic. **Interested in these nonfiction areas:** business; humor; money/finance/economics; psychology; science/technology; self-help/personal improvement; sociology; sports; women's issues/women's studies; high profile/famous writers. Other types of clients include experts in all fields.

**Services:** Provides market research, send material to magazines/newspapers for reviews, brochures, website publicity. Book tours include radio interviews, TV interviews, newspaper interviews, magazine interviews, speaking engagements, conferences, universities. Assists in coordinating travel plans. Media kits include author's biography, testimonials, articles about author, professional photos. Helps writer obtain endorsements.

**How to Contact:** Call, e-mail or fax. Responds in 1 week. Discards unwanted materials. Obtains most new clients through recommendations from others. Contact prior to book's publication.

**Costs:** Charges clients per placement basis ($1,500 minimum); 30% commission. Works with clients on marketing budget. Offers written contract. 60-90 day notice must be given to terminate contract.

**THE WRITE PUBLICIST & CO.**, 120 Adair Circle, Fayetteville GA 30215-8234. (770)716-3323. E-mail: thewritepublicist@earthlink.net. Website: www.thewritepublicist.com. **Contact:** Regina Lynch-Hudson. Estab. 1990; specifically with books for 10 years. Currently works with 5 clients. 50% of clients are new/first-time writers.
- Prior to becoming a publicist Ms. Lynch-Hudson was Public Relations director for a 4-star resort.

**Specializations:** Nonfiction, fiction, children's book, multicultural, ethnic and minority market books. **Interested in these nonfiction areas:** biography/autobiography, business, education, ethnic/cultural interests, health/medicine, how-to, juvenile nonfiction, multicultural, religious/inspirational, women's issues/women's studies. **Interested in these fiction areas:** confessional, contemporary issues, erotica, ethnic, family saga, humor/satire, mainstream, multicultural, religious/inspirational, romance, science fiction, sports. Other types of clients include physicians, lawyers, entertainers, artists.

**Services:** Provides international publicity, if applicable, electronic news release, send material to magazines/newspapers for reviews, website publicity. Book tours include bookstores, radio interviews, TV interviews, newspaper interviews, magazine interviews, schools, universities. Assists in coordinating travel plans. Clients have appeared on *Oprah*, all national TV networks. Media kit includes author's biography, basic information on book, professional photos, book request information, propriety innovative enclosures that insure and increase the opportunity for publication. Helps writer obtain endorsements. "We paired Dr. Marcus Wells, Bariatrics specialist, with obese readers in various cities. He flew in and became consultant to many readers."

> O━ Twelve years experience publicizing people, places, products, performances. Owner of company was syndicated columnist to 215 newspapers, which solidified media contacts.

**How to Contact:** E-mail. Send book or ms. Responds in 1 week. Returns materials only with SASE. Obtains most new clients through recommendations from others. "90% of our clients are referred nationally." Contact 1 month prior to book's publication or after book's publication.

**Clients:** *Lifestyles for the 21st Century*, by Dr. Marcus Wells (Humanics Publishing); *Preconceived Notions*, by Robyn Williams (Noble Press); *Fed Up With the Fanny*, by Franklin White (Simon & Schuster). Other clients include Vernon Jones, CEO of DeKalb County; Atlanta Perinatal Associates; Tonda Smith, news anchor. "Our clients' contracts state that they will not be solicited by prospective clients. Our website shows photos of clients who give their recommendation by consenting to be placed on our website."

**Costs:** Clients charged flat fee $9,500-15,000. Works with clients on marketing budget. Offers written contract. Three day notice before our company has invested time interviewing the client and writing their release must be given to terminate a contract.

**Tips:** "Does the publicist have a website that actually pictures clients? Our site ranks No. 1 with Yahoo!—as one of few PR sites that actually depicts clients."

**⊞N ◑ MERYL ZEGAREK PUBLIC RELATIONS, INC.**, 255 W. 108th St., Suite 9D1, New York NY 10025. (917)493-3601. Fax: (917)493-3598. E-mail: mz@mzpr.com. Website: www.mzpr.com. **Contact:** Meryl Zegarek. Worked specifically with books for 25 years.

> ● Prior to becoming a freelance publicist, Ms. Zegarek was a publicity director of two divisions of Knopf Books, Random House.

**Specializations:** Nonfiction, fiction. "I do a large number of Jewish subjects and nonreligious spiritual books and authors." **Interested in these nonfiction areas:** animals, anthropology/archaeology, art/architecture/design, current affairs, ethnic/cultural interests, government/politics/law, health/medicine, history, how-to, humor, interior design/decorating, language/literature/criticism, multicultural, music/dance/theater/film, nature/environment, New Age/metaphysics, photography, popular culture, psychology, religious/inspirational, science/technology, self-help/personal improvement, sociology, travel, true crime/investigative, women's issues/women's studies. **Interested in these fiction areas:** action/adventure, contemporary issues, detective/police/crime, ethnic, historical, literary, multicultural, mystery/suspense, New Age/metaphysical, psychic/supernatural, religious/inspirational, science fiction, thriller/espionage. Other types of clients include organizations, nonprofits, business, human rights organizations.

**Services:** Provides detailed outline of services provided, media training, international publicity, if applicable, send material to magazines/newspapers for reviews, website publicity. Book tours include bookstores, radio interviews, TV interviews, newspaper interviews, magazine interviews, speaking engagements, universities. Assists in coordinating travel plans. Clients have appeared on *Oprah*, *Good Morning America*, *Fresh Air* (NPR), *Morning Edition* (NPR). Media kit includes résumé, author's biography, testimonials, articles about author, basic information on book, professional photos, sample interview questions, book request information. Helps writer obtain endorsements. Nationwide print and radio campaigns with give-aways—with National Television and radio producing a *New York Times* bestseller.

> O━ "I have been a publicity director for three major publishing houses during a twenty-five year career in book publicity. I have experience in every genre of book with established contacts in TV, radio and print—as well as bookstores and speaking venues."

**How to Contact:** Call, e-mail or fax. Send letter with entire ms, outline/proposal, sample chapters with SASE. Responds in 2 weeks. Returns material only with SASE. Obtains most new clients through recommendations from others. Contact 6 months prior to book's publication, if possible.

**Clients:** *In My Brothers Image*, by Eugene Pogany (Viking/Penguin); *You Can't Do That on Broadway*, by Amy Homes (HarperCollins); *Hitler's Niece*, by Ron Hanson (HarperCollins); *Lit From Within*, by Victoria Mocon (Harper SF). Other clients include Bright Sky Press, Hidden Spring Books, Jewish Publication Society. References and contact numbers available for potential clients.

**Costs:** Clients charged flat fee, hourly retainer fee for consultations, monthly retainer (divide up flat fee payable by month). Offers written contract. One month notice must be given to terminate contract.

**Tips:** "Call early, months in advance of publication!"

# Writer's Conferences

Attending a writers' conference that includes agents gives you the opportunity to listen and learn more about what agents do, as well as the chance to show an agent your work. Ideally, a conference should include a panel or two with a number of agents to give writers a sense of the variety of personalities and tastes of different agents.

Not all agents are alike: some are more personable and sometimes you simply click better with one agent over another. When only one agent attends a conference there is tendency for every writer at that conference to think, "Ah, this is the agent I've been looking for!" When the number of agents attending is larger, you have a wider group from which to choose and you may have less competition for the agent's time.

Besides including panels of agents discussing what representation means and how to go about securing it, many of these gatherings also include time, either scheduled or impromptu, to meet briefly with an agent to discuss your work.

You may interest agents by meeting them in person and discussing your work. If they're impressed, they will invite you to submit a query, a proposal, a few sample chapters, or possibly your entire manuscript. Some conferences even arrange for agents to review manuscripts in advance and schedule one-on-one sessions where you can receive specific feedback or advice on your work. Such meetings often cost a small fee, but the input you receive is usually worth the price. For helpful hints on how to make the most of meetings with agents, see "Make an Agent Fall in Love with You," by Mark Ryan on page 288.

Ask writers who attend conferences and they'll tell you that at the very least you'll walk away with more knowledge than you came with. At the very best, you'll receive an invitation to send an agent your material!

# Make an Agent Fall in Love With You

BY MARK RYAN

Professional writer seeks available agent. Should be confident, experienced, and fun at parties. Must have a big heart but also be a tough negotiator. Should be creative but grounded and consistent. Must be honest, emotionally available, and not afraid of long-term commitment. Should not be overextended. Must be of good character, as well as liked and respected in his community. Age and looks not important but passion and charisma are a must. Long-distance relationships okay as long as you spend some time in New York.

**Mark Ryan**

You know there is a Prince (or Princess) Charming out there just for you. In fact, you could have written this ad yourself. But if he (let's stick with "he" for simplicity's sake) is out there—the agent of your dreams—and he is available, how can you find him and make him yours? Well, you could access any writers' resource (print or electronic), and query listed agents by snail mail or e-mail. This approach, however, is like looking for a mate through Brides-by-mail. It might work, but the risk factor is high. And if you have ever responded to a personal ad, you know how difficult it is to get a sense of someone in 50 words or less.

Attending a writers' conference is the best way for you to initiate contact with an agent. Most conferences schedule author/agent appointments (10-20 minutes each). And if formal appointments aren't available, you can still approach an agent and make your pitch. Remember, good agents don't represent books—they represent *authors*. "Who you are" is just as important as "what you write." And nothing communicates who you are more than a face to face meeting. Attending a conference also communicates your willingness to grow as a writer, and your willingness to network.

Okay, let's assume you have written a terrific book. And let's pretend you arrived two days ago at a writers' conference (visit www.shawguides.com for a complete directory of conferences). During the opening night reception you spotted him—your dreamboat agent—from across the room. You liked his energy and the way he treated other writers in the buffet line. Plus he had nice eyes and smelled good. The next day you sat in on his workshop and asked an editor about his reputation. "Five stars," she said with a nod and a smile. Now you've decided he is the one for you, and today you're going to make a move. How best to get his attention, without losing your dignity?

## Be yourself

One of the biggest turnoffs for an agent is when a potential partner tries to be someone or something that she is not. If you want to pick up an agent, be yourself. If you are funny, be funny. If you are serious, be serious. And have faith that you will meet someone who understands and appreciates your style. As an agent, I have to be myself as well. My approach is more open, down-to-earth, and nurturing than some agents. As a result, some writers might wonder if I am a strong negotiator. Others understand that a sensitive man isn't necessarily weak.

You aren't going to click with everyone. If you are a Supermodel on the prowl, but you are also a brunette (and I prefer blondes), well . . . you get the picture. And don't go out and dye your hair—find someone who prefers brunettes. Publishing, like dating, is highly subjective and personal. There are elements of logic, but there are also elements of emotion. Our firm passes on many publishable projects simply because we aren't in love with the concept, execution, and author. Falling in "like" isn't enough. We have to fall in love. That's the only way we can pitch each project to editors and publishers with enthusiasm.

If you're nervous about your meeting, do something to relax. Yoga. Tae Kwon Do. Ice cream. Whatever. If you shake uncontrollably or apologize repeatedly for being nervous, you aren't going to score points. Agents smell fear and fear is rarely associated with success. Granted, if your burning hunk of an agent is indeed the one for you, he will look past your neuroses, accept you as you are, and put you at ease. If he doesn't, move on. The world of publishing is a pond, not an ocean, but there are still plenty of fish to choose from. Remember, you have something worthwhile to offer your prospective partner. You've spent years developing your communication skills, you know what makes a relationship work, and you are not going to be high-maintenance.

Once, during a visit to New York, a well-known author suggested I do something to make myself more memorable. He didn't make this suggestion because I made a bad impression. He made it because he is a first-impression guru, and that's what his books are about. "I wear red shoes," he said. I tried not to laugh. "I think some people go too far to be remembered," I said. "The last thing I need is to be on a panel at some writers' conference and have someone ask me why I'm wearing red shoes. I'd have to say, 'So people remember me.' Yuck."

If there is something about you—externally—that makes you memorable, fine. Just don't dwell on it. Beauty will get a man's attention, but it won't keep it there for long. Don't go out and buy red shoes (or lingerie) to try and impress an agent. If you want to make a great first impression, be genuine. Let people remember you for something that really matters—not the way you look, but the way you make people *feel*. Relax, and be yourself.

## Flirt

Whatever you can do to make your dream agent feel good, do it. He's been "on" for the last two days, aware that he's constantly being watched. He's been patient, attentive, entertaining. He's tired from a long flight and an even longer delay. And he was up late last night editing a manuscript when he wanted to be in the Jacuzzi. In the last twelve hours he's delivered a keynote presentation and two workshops. He's sat through twenty pitch sessions and been approached by countless other authors—in the hallways, over meals, even in the bathroom (please, do *not* pass an agent your manuscript underneath a bathroom stall). If you are mindful of your prospective partner's wants and needs, it's an edge. The astute agent will notice, appreciate, and remember your kindness. And he will give your project closer attention. Less savvy agents may not recognize your gifts but they, too, will experience their effect.

Approach your agent with a confident walk (strut?) and a smile. And thank the agent for his time. It might sound simple, but many authors fail to express their gratitude. Some feel entitled to the meeting because they paid to attend the conference. Some think their project is so good that agents should fawn over them. Some are insecure. Whatever the reason, it's a faux pas. Saying, "Thank you for meeting with me" is good manners, and it sets a nice tone for your meeting.

Make your prospective agent blush by complimenting his presentation, eyes, or red shoes (if he's wearing red shoes and you *really* think they look nice). Just compliment something, and make sure your compliment is genuine. Agents aren't just editors, they are salespeople. And salespeople, especially good ones, detect insincerity. Ask a question or two about your agent's background. How did he get started? Does he have a dream project? Is he a writer as well as an agent? Does he attend many conferences? Expressing interest in him will make him purr.

If you really want to go for it, ask him if he has any down time during the conference and invite him out for a drink or a meal. You can do this solo or invite him to join some of your friends. I've never turned down such an offer unless I already had other plans. Even then, I usually invite the author to join my party. You have nothing to lose by making such an offer. It's gracious of you to extend the invitation and the worst he can say is no. Remember, the fastest way to a man's heart is indeed his stomach. And if your dream agent connects with you on a personal level, he's even more likely to say yes. In fact, you might be rescuing him from a dozen other writers he might not connect with as well as he does with you. Don't be shy, take a chance.

## Listen

Although you may want to impress an agent with your knowledge, don't jump the gun. Be a good dance partner and let him lead. No worthwhile agent is going to talk during your entire meeting and keep you from making your pitch—although he might tease you a bit. Wait until he opens the door for you, then glide through it.

Listening closely will help you catch valuable clues about what your potential partner deems important. Maybe you will adjust your pitch slightly, based on a comment he makes. Every second of conversation is an opportunity for you to learn about that agent and the business of publishing. Absorb every word, every intonation, every bit of body language, every silence, and every bit of sub-text.

If the agent you're trying to seduce isn't melting after you've used your most alluring lines (be brutally honest with yourself), do *not* cut and run. Play it cool and ask questions about the agenting or publishing process. You've got him on your arm for the duration of the date—make it count.

## Cut to the chase

Successful agents sit through more than 10,000 pitches each year. Write down what you want to say, before you say it. Practice your pitch with other experienced writers. And get to the point. Small talk is nice, but the one thing you and your dream agent want to know (above all else), is how he can help you make money and develop your career. You only have 10-20 minutes to sell yourself. Don't be demure—there are other love interests in line behind you.

Whose writing makes your heart race? Available agents want to know. This information will give the inquiring agent a sense of how well read you are. Be a voyeur and get to know your competition, intimately. Getting in bed with the works of other writers will increase the uniqueness of your work, and it will give you the confidence and means to explain why your work is special.

Position yourself as an expert on the topic you are writing about. What are the subjects and themes that keep you up late at night? What do you talk to friends, loved ones, and strangers about? Books that begin in this private place are the ones that endure. They come from a spot deep within you, a place that no one can take away or imitate. This is your gift—your story.

If you are pitching fiction, gain an agent's trust by speaking not only of plot and characters, but themes. The movie *Titanic* is not about a sinking ship. It is a love story that takes place on a sinking ship. *The Godfather* isn't about crime. It's about family. Let your tentative agent know who your main character is. What does she want? What are the obstacles in her way? What is she going to do to circumvent them? Good writing, like good love, is in the details. And depth, is an agent's greatest aphrodisiac.

When you meet an agent, don't just communicate ideas. Let him feel what you feel. That is, after all, what your writing is supposed to do. If the chemistry is right, it won't take much to get him excited—you won't have to force it. You will have similar backgrounds, similar interests, and similar goals. Don't forget to watch his body language, and listen. Is that a gong? Or wedding bells?

Express your desire and ability to aggressively market your works. Again, don't be passive.

And remember, it's all in the details. Read books on marketing and find creative ways to apply the ideas therein to your project. Join organizations and associations related to your field. Such affiliations will give you extra knowledge and credibility, as well as invaluable contacts and support. In this case, bigger is always better. And more is always better.

Another thing you can do to win an agent over is provide rave reviews about you and/or your work, written by successful authors (use these tactics to win *them* over). This strategy will require a great deal of legwork, but it's worth it. Last year I met a woman at a conference who told me she had a stellar recommendation from Clive Cussler (in writing). End of meeting. "Please send us the complete manuscript," I said. "Let's get together later for a cup of coffee."

Okay, the pitch is over. You've expressed interest and made yourself vulnerable. Is he going to say "I love you"? If he doesn't, you're ready to thank him and begin looking for your next prospect as you exit the room. He remains silent. You watch his chest rise as he takes a deep breath and leans back in his black vinyl chair. "I'd like to get to know you better," he says. "Send us three chapters and a complete proposal after the conference, along with an SASE. And thanks for letting us take a look. We'll get back to you promptly."

Congratulations. Your first date has been a success and he's asked you for another. But don't go out and buy a wedding dress yet. He hasn't proposed, and you still have a lot of work to do. Do *not* attempt to hand him your manuscript during or after your meeting—regardless of his interest. The last thing he wants to do, unless he specifically states otherwise, is jam one more thing into his suitcase.

Your dream agent is out there, preparing himself for you with the same care with which you are preparing yourself for him. But you have to make yourself available. Securing an agent (especially one you love, who loves you back with equal measure) takes time and effort. Get out there, and be yourself. Flirt. Listen. Cut to the chase. Keep working your charms and, before you know it, you might be the next one at the altar [wink].

Available agent seeks professional author. Should be confident, ambitious, and fun at parties. Must view the author/agent relationship as a partnership. Should be creative but grounded and consistent. Must be honest, emotionally available, and not afraid of long-term commitment. Should not be overextended. Must be of good character, as well as liked and respected in her community. Age and looks not important but passion and charisma are a must. Long-distance relationships okay, as long as you send chocolates on Valentine's Day.

# Writers' Conferences

Many writers try to make it to at least one conference a year, but cost and location can count as much as subject matter when determining which conference to attend. There are conferences in almost every state and province that can provide answers to our questions about writing and the publishing industry. Conferences also connect you with a community of other writers. Such connections help you learn about the pros and cons of different agents writers have worked with, and give you a renewed sense of purpose and direction in your own writing.

When reading through this section, keep in mind the following information to help you pick the best conference for your needs:

## REGIONS
To make it easier for you to find a conference close to home—or to find one in an exotic locale to fit into your vacation plans—we've separated this section into geographical regions. The regions are as follows:

**Northeast (pages 293-297):** Connecticut, Maine, Massachusetts, New Hampshire, New York, Rhode Island, Vermont.

**Midatlantic (pages 297-298):** Washington DC, Delaware, Maryland, New Jersey, Pennsylvania.

**Midsouth (pages 298-299):** North Carolina, South Carolina, Tennessee, Virginia, West Virginia.

**Southeast (pages 300-301):** Alabama, Arkansas, Florida, Georgia, Louisiana, Mississippi, Puerto Rico.

**Midwest (pages 301-303):** Illinois, Indiana, Kentucky, Michigan, Ohio.

**North Central (pages 303-304):** Iowa, Minnesota, Nebraska, North Dakota, South Dakota, Wisconsin.

**South Central (pages 304-308):** Colorado, Kansas, Missouri, New Mexico, Oklahoma, Texas.

**West (pages 308-314):** Arizona, California, Hawaii, Nevada, Utah.

**Northwest (page 314):** Alaska, Idaho, Montana, Oregon, Washington, Wyoming.

**Canada (pages 314-316).**

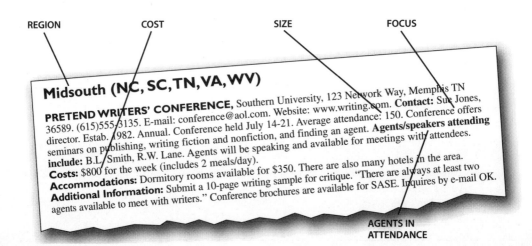

REGION       COST       SIZE       FOCUS

**Midsouth (NC, SC, TN, VA, WV)**

**PRETEND WRITERS' CONFERENCE,** Southern University, 123 New York Way, Memphis TN 36589. (615)555-3135. E-mail: conference@aol.com. Website: www.writing.com. **Contact:** Sue Jones, director. Estab. 1982. Annual. Conference held July 14-21. Average attendance: 150. Conference offers seminars on publishing, writing fiction and nonfiction, and finding an agent. **Agents/speakers attending** include: B.L. Smith, R.W. Lane. Agents will be speaking and available for meetings with attendees. **Costs:** $800 for the week (includes 2 meals/day). **Accommodations:** Dormitory rooms available for $350. There are also many hotels in the area. **Additional Information:** Submit a 10-page writing sample for critique. "There are always at least two agents available to meet with writers." Conference brochures are available for SASE. Inquires by e-mail OK.

AGENTS IN ATTENDANCE

## SUBHEADS

Each listing is divided into subheads to make locating specific information easier. In the first section, you'll find contact information for each conference. Also given are conference dates, specific focus, and size. If a conference is small, you may receive more individual attention from speakers. If it is large, there may be a greater number and variety of agents in attendance. Finally, names of agents who will be speaking or have spoken in the past are listed along with details about their availability during the conference. Calling a conference director to verify the names of agents in attendance is always a good idea.

**Costs:** Looking at the price of seminars, plus room and board, may help writers on a tight budget narrow their choices.

**Accommodations:** Here conferences list overnight accommodation and travel information. Often conferences held in hotels will reserve rooms at a discount price and may provide a shuttle bus to and from the local airport.

**Additional Information:** A range of features are given here, including information on contests, individual meetings, and the availability of brochures.

## Northeast (CT, MA, ME, NH, NY, RI, VT)

**BREAD LOAF WRITERS' CONFERENCE**, Middlebury College, Middlebury VT 05753. (802)443-5286. Fax: (802)443-2087. E-mail: blwc@middlebury.edu. Website: www.middlebury.edu/~blwc. **Contact:** Noreen Cargill, administrative coordinator. Estab. 1926. Annual. Conference held in late August. Conference duration: 11 days. Average attendance: 230. For fiction, nonfiction and poetry. Held at the summer campus in Ripton, Vermont (belongs to Middlebury College).
**Costs:** $1,798 (includes room/board) (2001).
**Accommodations:** Accommodations are at Ripton.

**HOFSTRA UNIVERSITY SUMMER WRITERS' CONFERENCE**, 250 Hofstra University, UCCE, Hempstead NY 11549-1090. (516)463-5016. Fax: (516)463-4833. E-mail: uccelibarts@hofstra.edu. Website: www.hofstra.edu (under "Academics/Continuing Education," there are details on dates, faculty, general description, tuition). **Contact:** Kenneth Henwood, director, Liberal Arts Studies. Estab. 1972. Annual (every summer, starting week after July 4). Conference held July 8 to July 19, 2002. Average attendance: 65. Conference offers workshops in short fiction, nonfiction, poetry, juvenile fiction, stage/screenwriting and, on occasion, one other genre such as detective fiction or science fiction. Workshops in prose and poetry for high school student writers are also offered. Site is the university campus, a suburban setting, 25 miles from NYC. **Previous agent/speakers have incuded:** Oscar Hijuelos, Robert Olen Butler, Hilma and Meg Wolitzer, Budd Schulberg and Cynthia Ozick. Agents will be speaking and available for meetings with attendees.
**Costs:** Non-credit (2 meals, no room): approximately $410 per workshop or $630 for two workshops. Credit: Approximately $1,100/workshop (2 credits) and $2,100/workshop (4 credits), graduate and undergraduate. Continental breakfast and lunch are provided daily; tuition also includes cost of banquet.
**Accommodations:** Free bus operates between Hempstead Train Station and campus for those commuting from NYC. Dormitory rooms are available for approximately $350 for the 2 week conference.
**Additional Information:** "All workshops include critiquing. Each participant is given one-on-one time for a half hour with workshop leader. We submit work to the Shaw Guides Contest and other writers' conferences and retreats contests when appropriate."

---

## Quick Reference Icons

At the beginning of some listings, you will find one or more of the following symbols for quick identification of features particular to that listing.

**N:** Conference new to this edition.

**✓** Change in address, contact information, phone number or e-mail address from last year's edition.

**✶** Canadian conference.

**🌐** International conference.

## Get the Most from a Conference

Squeeze the most out of a conference by getting organized and staying involved. Follow these steps to ensure a worthwhile event.

**Before you go:**
- **Become familiar with all the pre-conference literature,** particularly the agenda. Study the maps of the area, especially the locations of the rooms in which your meetings/ events are scheduled.
- **Make a list of three to five objectives you'd like to obtain,** e.g., whom you want to meet, what you want to learn more about, what you want to improve on, how many new markets you want to find.

**At the conference:**
- **Budget your time.** Label a map so you know ahead of time where, when and how to get to each session. Note what you want to do most. Then, schedule time with agents and editors for critique sessions.
- **Don't be afraid to explore new areas.** You are there to learn. Pick one or two sessions you wouldn't typically attend. This is an education; keep your mind open to new ideas and advice.
- **Allow time for mingling.** Some of the best information is given after the session. Find out "frank truths" and inside scoops. Asking people what they've learned at the conference will trigger a conversation that may branch into areas you want to know more about but won't hear from the speakers.
- **Learn about agents, editors and new markets.** Which are more open to new writers? Find a new contact in your area for future support.
- **Collect everything:** guidelines, sample issues, promotional fliers, and especially business cards. Make notes about the personalities of the people you meet to remind you later who to contact and who to avoid.
- **Find inspiration for future projects.** While you're away from home, people-watch, take a walk, a bike ride, or drive. You may even want to take pictures to enhance your memory.

**After the conference:**
- **Evaluate.** Write down the answers to these questions: Would I attend again? What were the pluses and minuses, e.g., speakers, location, food, topics, cost, lodging? What do I want to remember for next year? What should I try to do next time? Who would I like to meet?
- **Write a thank-you letter** to an agent or editor who has been particularly helpful. They'll remember you when you later submit.

**IWWG MEET THE AUTHORS, AGENTS AND EDITORS: THE BIG APPLE WORKSHOPS**, % International Women's Writing Guild, P.O. Box 810, Gracie Station, New York NY 10028-0082. (212)737-7536. Fax: (212)737-9469. E-mail: iwwg@iwwg.com. Website: www.iwwg.com. **Contact:** Hannelore Hahn, executive director. Estab. 1980. Conferences held generally the third weekend in April and the second weekend in October. Average attendance: 200. Workshops to promote creative writing and professional success. Held at the City Athletic Club of New York, midtown New York City. **Previous agents/speakers have included:** Meredith Bernstein and Rita Rosenkranz. Sunday afternoon openhouse with agents and editors. Agents will be speaking and available for meetings with attendees. **Costs:** $130 for members for the weekend; $150 for nonmembers for the weekend.
**Accommodations:** Information on transportation arrangements and overnight accommodations made available.
**Additional Information:** Workshop brochures/guidelines are available for SASE. Inquires by fax and e-mail OK. "Many contacts have been made between agents and authors over the years."

**IWWG SUMMER CONFERENCE**, % International Women's Writing Guild, P.O. Box 810, Gracie Station, New York NY 10028-0082. (212)737-7536. Fax: (212)737-9469. E-mail: hirhahn@aol.com. Website: www.iwwg.com. **Contact:** Hannelore Hahn, executive director. Estab. 1977. 24th Annual. Conference generally held from 2nd Friday to 3rd Friday in August. Average attendance: 500, including international attendees. Conference to promote writing in all genres, personal growth and professional success. Conference is held "on the tranquil campus of Skidmore College in Saratoga Springs, NY, where the serene Hudson Valley meets the North Country of the Adirondacks." Seventy-five different workshops are offered everyday. Theme: "Writing Towards Personal and Professional Growth."
**Costs:** $850 for week-long program with room and board. $400 for week-long program for commuters.
**Accommodations:** Transportation by air to Albany, New York, or Amtrak train available from New York City. Conference attendees stay on campus.
**Additional Information:** Features "lots of critiquing sessions and networking." Conference brochures/guidelines available for SASE. Inquires by fax and e mail OK.

☑ **NEW ENGLAND WRITERS CONFERENCE**, Box 483, Windsor VT 05089-0483. (802)674-2315. E-mail: newvtpoet@aol.com. Website: www.hometown.aol.com/newvtpoet/myhomepage/profile/html. **Contact:** Dr. Frank and Susan Anthony, co-directors. Estab. 1986. Annually. Conference held third Saturday in July. Conference duration: 1 day. Average attendance: 150. Held at the Grace-Outreach building 1 mile from Dartmouth campus. Panel on agents, children's publishing, fiction, nonfiction, and poetry. **Previous agents/speakers have included:** John Talbot Agency, Dana Gioia, Wesley McNair, Michael C. White.
**Costs:** $15 (includes seminar sessions, open readings, light lunch, writers' panel and ticket drawings).
**Accommodations:** "Hotel list can be made available. There are many hotels in the area."
**Additional Information:** "This annual conference continues our attempt to have a truly affordable writers conference that has as much as most 3-4 day events." Brochures available for SASE or on website. Inquiries by e-mail.

☑ **THE PERIPATETIC WRITING WORKSHOP, INC.**, P.O. Box 299, Mount Tremper NY 12457. (845)688-9730. E-mail: peripatetic@prodigy.net. Website: http://pages.prodigy.net/peripatetic. Estab. 1991. Annual and ongoing through the year. Summer conference held in June; two ongoing conferences held throughout the year. Summer conference duration: 1-2 weeks. Average attendance: 14. Fiction, nonfiction, short story collections. Conference held often at Byrdcliffe Artist Colony in Woodstock, NY. In 2001, conference held in Ireland. "In 2000, the publishing panel centered on changes in publishing brought about by the Internet." **Previous agents/speakers have included:** Ann Rittenberg (agent, Ann Rittenberg Literary Agency, Inc.); John Baker (editorial director, *Publishers Weekly*). Agents will be speaking and available for meetings with attendees.
**Costs:** In 2000, $1500 for 2 weeks, live in; $850 for 1 week, live in; $550 for 2 weeks, local; $300 for 1 week, local.
**Accommodations:** Accommodations are available and include bedroom/study and breakfast and lunch. "We rent a large house either in Woodstock or from the Byrdcliffe Artist Colony."
**Additional Information:** "We offer a free 50-page private tutorial with a published writer. We specialize in full-length nonfiction and fiction manuscripts, short story collections, and developing book proposals." Brochures available for SASE or on website. Inquiries by e-mail OK.

**SOCIETY OF CHILDREN'S BOOK WRITERS & ILLUSTRATORS CONFERENCE/HOFSTRA CHILDREN'S LITERATURE CONFERENCE**, University College for Continuing Education, 250 Hofstra University, Hempstead NY 11549-1090. (516)463-5016. Fax: (516)463-4833. E-mail: uccelibarts@hofstra.edu. **Contact:** Kenneth Henwood. Estab. 1985. Annual. Conference to be held April 20, 2002. Average attendance: 200. Conference to encourage good writing for children. "The conference brings together writers, illustrators, librarians, agents, publishers, teachers and other professionals who are interested in writing for children. Each year we organize the program around a theme. Last year it was 'Finding Your Voice.' "The conference takes place at the Student Center Building of Hofstra University, located in Hempstead, Long Island. "We have two general sessions, five break-out groups." **Previous agents/speakers have included:** Paula Danziger and Ann M. Martin, and a panel of children's book editors who critique randomly selected first-manuscript pages submitted by registrants. Agents will be speaking and available for meetings with attendees.
**Costs:** $70 (previous year) for SCBWI members; $78 for nonmembers. Continental breakfast and full luncheon included.
**Additional Information:** Special interest groups are offered in submission procedures, fiction, nonfiction, writing picture books, illustrating picture books, poetry and scriptwriting.

**STATE OF MAINE WRITERS' CONFERENCE**, 18 Hill Rd., Belmont MA 02478-4303. **Contact:** June A. Knowles, Mary E. Pitts, co-chairs. Estab. 1941. Annual. Conference held in August. Conference duration: 4 days. Average attendance: 50. "We try to present a balanced as well as eclectic conference. In addition to time and attention given to poetry, we also have children's literature, mystery writing, travel, novels/fiction, nonfiction, and other issues of interest to writers. Our speakers are publishers, editors, writers and other professionals. Our concentration is, by intention, a general view of writing to publish. We are located in Ocean Park, a small seashore village 14 miles south of Portland. Ours is a summer assembly center with many buildings from the Victorian Age. The conference meets in Porter Hall, one of the assembly buildings which is listed on the National Register of Historic Places." **Previous agents/ speakers have included:** Carolyn Barstow (author/teacher/librarian); Roy Fairfield (author/teacher); Oscar Greene (author); Del Jakeman (author); Carl Little (author/artist/lecturer); Elizabeth Morse (researcher/teacher); Wesley McNair (poet, Maine faculty); and others. "We usually have about 10 guest presenters a year." Agents will be speaking, leading workshops and available for meetings with attendees.
**Costs:** $90 (includes the conference supper; if registering after August 10, $100). There is a reduced fee, $45, for students ages 21 and under. The fee does not include housing or meals which must be arranged separately by the conferees.
**Accommodations:** An accommodations list is available. "We are in a summer resort area and motels, guest houses and restaurants abound."
**Additional Information:** "We have about nine contests on various genres. An announcement is available in the spring. The prizes, all modest, are awarded at the end of the conference and only to those who are registered." Program available in June for SASE.

**TEA WITH ELEANOR ROOSEVELT**, International Women's Writing Guild, P.O. Box 810, Gracie Station, New York NY 10028-0082. (212)737-7536. Fax: (212)737-9469. E-mail: iwwg@iwwg.com. Website: www.IWWG.com. **Contact:** Hannelore Hahn, executive director. Estab. 1980. Annual conference held March 31, 2001. Conference duration: 1 day of writing. Average attendance: 50. Held at the Eleanor Roosevelt Center at Val-Kill in Hyde Park, NY. Two hours from New York City in the Hudson Valley.
**Costs:** $75 (includes lunch).
**Additional Information:** Brochure/guidelines available for SASE. Inquiries by e-mail and fax OK.

**☑ WESLEYAN WRITERS CONFERENCE**, Wesleyan University, Middletown CT 06459. (860)685-3604. Fax: (860)685-2441. E-mail: agreene@wesleyan.edu. Website: www.wesleyan.edu/writing/conferen.html. **Contact:** Anne Greene, director. Estab. 1956. Annual. Conference held the last week in June. Average attendance: 100. Fiction techniques, novel, short story, poetry, screenwriting, nonfiction, literary journalism, memoir. The conference is held on the campus of Wesleyan University, in the hills overlooking the Connecticut River. Features readings of new fiction, guest lectures on a range of topics including publishing and daily seminars. "Both new and experienced writers are welcome." **Agents/speakers attending include:** Edmond Harmsworth (Zachary Schuster Agency); Daniel Mandel (Sanford J. Greenburger Associates); Dorian Karchmar. Agents will be speaking and available for meetings with attendees.
**Costs:** In 2001, day rate $725 (includes meals); boarding students' rate $845 (includes meals and room for 5 nights).
**Accommodations:** "Participants can fly to Hartford or take Amtrak to Meriden, CT. We are happy to help participants make travel arrangements." Meals and lodging are provided on campus. Overnight participants stay on campus.
**Additional Information:** Manuscript critiques are available as part of the program but are not required. Participants may attend seminars in several different genres. Scholarships and teaching fellowships are available, including the Jakobson awards for fiction writers and poets and the Jon Davidoff Scholarships for journalists. Inquiries by e-mail and fax OK.

**WRITERS CONFERENCE 2002**, (formerly Publish & Prosper in 2001), ASJA 1501 Broadway, Suite 302, New York NY 10036. (212)997-0947. Fax: (212)768-7414. E-mail: staff@asja.org. Website: www.asja.org. **Contact:** Brett Harvey, executive director. Estab. 1971. Annual. Conference held April 12-14, 2002. Conference duration: 2 days. Average attendance: 500. Nonfiction. Held at Grand Hyatt in New York. For 2002, panels to include "Packaging and Re-selling Your Work," "Writing for the Web," "Networking Secrets from Pro Writers." **Previous agents/speakers have included:** Dominick Dunne, James Brady, Dana Sobel. Agents will be speaking.
**Costs:** $195 (includes lunch).
**Accommodations:** "The hotel holding our conference always blocks out discounted rooms for attendees."
**Additional Information:** Brochures available in February. Registration form on website. Inquiries by e-mail and fax OK.

# Midatlantic (DC, DE, MD, NJ, PA)

**☑ BALTIMORE WRITERS' ALLIANCE CONFERENCE**, P.O. Box 410, Riderwood MD 21139. (410)377-5265. E-mail: bdiehl@jhsph.edu. Website: www.baltimorewriters.org. **Contact:** Barbara Diehl, coordinator. Estab. 1994. Annual. Conference held November. Conference duration: 1 day. Average attendance: 150-200. Writing and getting

published—all areas. Held at Towson University. Topics have included: mystery, science fiction, poetry, children's writing, legal issues, grant funding, working with an agent, book and magazine panels. **Previous agents/speakers have included:** Nat Sobel (Sobel/Weber Associates); Nina Graybill (Graybill and English). Agents will be speaking.
**Costs:** $70-80 (includes all-day conference, lunch and snacks). Manuscript critiques for additional fee.
**Accommodations:** Hotels close by, if required.
**Additional Information:** Inquiries by e-mail OK. May register through BWA website.

**THE COLLEGE OF NEW JERSEY WRITERS' CONFERENCE**, English Dept., The College of New Jersey, P.O. Box 7718, Ewing NJ 08628-0718. (609)771-3254. Fax: (609)637-5112. E-mail: write@tcnj.edu. **Contact:** Jean Hollander, director. Estab. 1980. Annual. Conference held April 18, 2002. Conference duration: 9 a.m. to 10 p.m. Average attendance: 600-1,000. "Conference concentrates on fiction (the largest number of participants), poetry, children's literature, play and screenwriting, magazine and newspaper journalism, overcoming writer's block, nonfiction and memoir writing. Conference is held at the student center at the college in two auditoriums and workshop rooms; also Kendall Theatre on campus. We focus on various genres: romance, detective, mystery, TV writing, etc." Topics have included "How to Get Happily Published," "How to Get an Agent" and "Earning a Living as a Writer." The conference usually presents twenty or so authors, editors and agents, plus two featured speakers. **Previous agents/speakers have included:** Arthur Miller, Saul Bellow, Toni Morrison, Joyce Carol Oates, Erica Jong, Alice Walker and John Updike. Last year's evening presentation featured keynote speaker Spike Lee. Agents will be speaking and available for meetings with attendees.
**Costs:** General registration $40 for entire day, plus $10 for evening presentation. Lower rates for students.
**Additional Information:** Brochures/guidelines available.

**MID-ATLANTIC MYSTERY BOOK FAIR & CONVENTION**, Detecto Mysterioso Books at Society Hill Playhouse, 507 S. Eighth St., Philadelphia PA 19147-1325. (215)923-0211. Fax: (215)923-1789. E-mail: shp@erols.com. Website: www.erols.com/shp. **Contact:** Deen Kogan, chairperson. Estab. 1991. Annual. Convention held October. Average attendance: 450-500. Focus is on mystery, suspense, thriller, true crime novels, "an examination of the genre from many points of view." **Previous agents/speakers have included:** Lawrence Block, Jeremiah Healy, Neil Albert, Michael Connelly, Paul Levine, Eileen Dreyer, Earl Emerson, Wendy Hornsby. Agents will be speaking and available for informal meetings with attendees.
**Costs:** $135 registration fee.
**Accommodations:** Attendees must make their own transportation arrangements. Special room rate available at convention hotel.
**Additional Information:** "The Bookroom is a focal point of the convention. Twenty-five specialty dealers are expected to exhibit and collectables range from hot-off-the-press bestsellers to 1930's pulp; from fine editions to reading copies." Conference brochures/guidelines are available for SASE or by telephone. Inquiries by e-mail and fax OK.

☑ **NEW JERSEY ROMANCE WRITERS PUT YOUR HEART IN A BOOK CONFERENCE**, P.O. Box 513, Plainsboro NJ 08536. (732)946-4044. E-mail: awalradt@aol.com or kathyeq@aol.com. Website: www.geocities.com/SoHo/Gallery/7019. **Contact:** Anne Walradt or Kathy Quick. Estab. 1984. Annual. Conference held October 11-12, 2002. Average attendance: 500. Conference concentrating on romance fiction. "Workshops offered on various topics for all writers of romance, from beginner to multi-published." Held at the Doubletree Hotel in Somerset NJ. **Previous agents/speakers have included:** Nora Roberts, Kathleen Woodiwiss, Patricia Gaffney, Jill Barnett, Debbie Macomber, Kay Hooper.
**Costs:** $135 (New Jersey Romance Writers members) and $165 (nonmembers).
**Accommodations:** Special hotel rate available for conference attendees.
**Additional Information:** Sponsors Put Your Heart in a Book Contest for unpublished writers and the Golden Leaf Contest for published members of RWA. Conference brochures, guidelines and membership information are available for SASE. "Appointments offered for conference attendees, both published and unpublished, with editors and/or agents in the genre." Massive bookfair open to public with authors signing copies of their books; proceeds donated to literacy charities.

☑ **PENNWRITERS ANNUAL CONFERENCE**, R.R. #2, Box 241, Middlebury Center PA 16935-9776. (570) 368-2144. Fax: (570)376-2674. E-mail: pmatter@csrlink.net. Website: www.pennwriters.org. **Contact:** Paula Matter, conference co-ordinator 2002. Estab. 1987. Annually. Conference held third weekend of May. Conference duration: 3 days. Average attendance: 120. "We try to cover as many genres each year as we can." Held at the Holiday Inn Grantville—spacious facility with most workshop rooms on one level. **Previous agents/speakers have included:** Rita Rosenkrantz, Cherry Weiner, Fran Collin. Agents will be speaking and available for meetings with attendees.
**Costs:** $130 for members in 2002 (includes all workshops and panels, as well as any editor or agent appointments). There is an additional charge for Friday's keynote dinner and Saturday night's dinner activity.
**Accommodations:** "We have arranged a special rate with the hotel, and details will be in our brochure. Our rate for conference attendees is $82 plus tax/night. The hotel has a shuttle to and from the airport."
**Additional Information:** "We are a multi-genre group encompassing the state of PA and beyond." Brochures available February for SASE. Inquiries by e-mail and fax OK.

**SANDY COVE CHRISTIAN COMMUNICATORS CONFERENCE**, Sandy Cove Bible Conference, 60 Sandy Cove Rd., North East MD 21901. (800)287-4843 or (800)234-2683. Website: www.sandycove.org. **Contact:** Jim Watkins, director. Estab. 1991. Annual. Conference begins first Sunday in October. Conference duration: 4 days (Sunday dinner through Thursday). Average attendance: 200. "There are major, continuing workshops in fiction, article writing, nonfiction books, and beginner's and advanced workshops. Twenty-eight one-hour classes touch many topics. While Sandy Cove has a strong emphasis on available markets in Christian publishing, all writers are more than welcome. Sandy Cove is a full-service conference center located on the Chesapeake Bay. All the facilities are first class with suites, single or double rooms available." **Previous agents/speakers have included:** Francine Rivers (bestselling novelist); Lisa Bergen, Waterbrook Press; Ken Petersen (editor, Tyndale House); Linda Tomblin (editor, *Guideposts*); and Andrew Scheer (*Moody Magazine*).
**Costs:** Call for rates.
**Accommodations:** "Accommodations are available at Sandy Cove. Information available upon request." Cost is $250 double occupancy room and board, $325 single occupancy room and board for 4 nights and meals.
**Additional Information:** Conference brochures/guidelines are available. "For exact dates, please visit our website."

■ **WASHINGTON INDEPENDENT WRITERS (WIW) SPRING WRITERS CONFERENCE**, 733 15th St. NW, Suite 220, Washington DC 20005. (202)347-4973. Fax: (202)628-0298. E-mail: info@washwriter.org. Website: www.washwriter.org. **Contact:** Melissa Herman, executive director. Estab. 1975. Annual. Conference held May 10-11. Conference duration: Friday and Saturday. Average attendance: 250. "Gives participants a chance to hear from and talk with dozens of experts on book and magazine publishing as well as on the craft, tools and business of writing." **Previous agents/speakers have included:** Erica Jong, John Barth, Kitty Kelley, Diane Rehm and Lawrence Block. New York and local agents at every conference.
**Costs:** $125 members; $175 nonmembers; $210 membership and conference.
**Additional Information:** Brochures/guidelines available for SASE in mid-February.

# Midsouth (NC, SC, TN, VA, WV)

■ **AMERICAN CHRISTIAN WRITERS CONFERENCES**, P.O. Box 110390, Nashville TN 37222-0390. (800)21-WRITE. Fax: (615)834-7736. E-mail: regaforder@aol.com. Website: www.ACWriters.com (includes schedule of cities). **Contact:** Reg Forder, director. Estab. 1981. Annual. Conference duration: 2 days. Average attendance: 60. Fiction, nonfiction, scriptwriting. To promote all forms of Christian writing. Conferences held throughout the year in 36 US cities.
**Costs:** Approximately $169 plus meals and accommodation.
**Accommodations:** Special rates available at host hotel. Usually located at a major hotel chain like Holiday Inn.
**Additional Information:** Conference brochures/guidelines are available for SASE.

**N: BLUE RIDGE WRITERS CONFERENCE**, 911 Allendale Court, Blacksburg VA 24060. (540)961-3115. E-mail: Bevturner@vt.edu. Estab. 1984. Annual. Conference held in February. Conference duration: 1 day. Average attendance: 70-90. Novels, children's literature, poetry, adult fiction, creative nonfiction, journalism and the memoir. Held on the Virginia Tech campus, Blacksburg. **Previous speakers/agents have included:** Fred Chappell, Pinkney Bennett, Lee Smith, Ellen Gilchrist, John Casey and Katharine Soniat.
**Costs:** $65 general, $30 students. "No other costs included."
**Accommodations:** Information is available in brochure.

■ **HIGHLAND SUMMER CONFERENCE**, Box 7014, Radford University, Radford VA 24142-7014. (540)831-5366. Fax: (540)831-5004. E-mail: gedwards@radford.edu or jasbury@radford.edu. Website: www.radford.edu/~arsc. **Contact:** JoAnn Asbury, assistant to director. Chair, Appalachian Studies Program: Dr. Grace Toney Edwards. Estab. 1978. Annual. Conference held first 2 weeks of June in 2002. Conference duration: 12 days. Average attendance: 25. Fiction, nonfiction, screenwriting. **Previous speakers/agents have included:** Bill Brown, Chris Holbrook, Rita Quillen, Kevin Stewart. Agents will be speaking and available for meetings with attendees.
**Costs:** "The cost is based on current Radford tuition for 3 credit hours plus an additional conference fee. On-campus meals and housing are available at additional cost. In 2001, conference tuition was $369 for in-state undergraduates, $1,100 for out-of-state undergraduates, $477 for in-state graduates, $930 for out-of-state graduates."
**Accommodations:** "We do not have special rate arrangements with local hotels. We do offer accommodations on the Radford University Campus in a recently refurbished residence hall. (In 2001 cost was $17-26 per night.)"
**Additional Information:** "Conference leaders typically critique work done during the two-week conference, but do not ask to have any writing submitted prior to the conference beginning." Conference brochures/guidelines are available after February for SASE. Inquiries by e-mail and fax OK.

**NORTH CAROLINA WRITERS' NETWORK FALL CONFERENCE**, P.O. Box 954, Carrboro NC 27510-0954. (919)967-9540. Fax: (919)929-0535. E-mail: mail@ncwriters.org. Website: www.ncwriters.org (includes "history and information about the NC Writers' Network and our programs. Also has a links page to other writing-related websites"). **Contact:** Shannon Woolfe, program & services director. Estab. 1985. Annual. "2001 Conference will be held in Char-

lotte, NC, November 16-18." Average attendance: 450. Fiction, nonfiction, screenwriting. "The conference is a weekend full of workshops, panels, readings and discussion groups. We try to have a variety of genres represented. In the past we have had fiction writers, poets, journalists, editors, children's writers, young adult writers, storytellers, playwrights, screenwriters, technical writing, web-based writing, etc. We take the conference to a different location in North Carolina each year in order to best serve our entire state. We hold the conference at a conference center with hotel rooms available." Agents will be speaking and available for meetings with attendees. **Previous agents/speakers have included:** Christy Fletcher and Neal Bascomb (Carlisle & Co.); Delin Cormeny (PMA Literary & Film Agency); Joe Regal (Viking Press). Agents will be speaking and available for meetings with attendees.
**Costs:** "Conference cost is approximately $175-200 and includes two meals."
**Accommodations:** "Special conference hotel rates are available, but the individual makes his/her own reservations."
**Additional Information:** Conference brochures/guidelines are available for SAE with 2 first-class stamps or on website. Inquiries by fax or e-mail OK.

☑ **POLICE WRITERS CONFERENCE,** Police Writers Association, P.O. Box 738, Ashburn VA 20146. Phone/fax: (703)723-4743. E-mail: leslye@policewriter.com. Website: www.policewriter.com. **Contact:** Leslyeann Rolik. Estab. 1996. Annually. Conference held October 2002. Conference duration: 2 days. Average attendance: 50. Related writing—both fiction and nonfiction. Focuses on police. Held in various hotels in various regions, determined annually. "Each year the conference focuses on helping club members get their work polished and published." **Previous agents/speakers have included:** Paul Bishop (novelist), Ed Dee (novelist), Roger Fulton (editor). Agents will be speaking and available for meetings with attendees.
**Costs:** $225 in 2001 (includes all classes and seminars, writing contest entries and awards luncheons).
**Accommodations:** Hotel arrangements, at special conference rates, are available.
**Additional Information:** "Unpublished police writers are welcome at the conference and as Police Writers Club Members." Brochures available on website. Inquiries by fax OK.

**SEWANEE WRITERS' CONFERENCE,** 310 St. Luke's Hall, Sewanee TN 37383-1000. (931)598-1141. E-mail: cpeters@sewanee.edu. Website: www.sewanee.writers.org (includes general conference information including schedule of events). **Contact:** Wyatt Prunty, conference director. Creative Writing Programs Manager: Cheri B. Peters. Estab. 1990. Annual. Conference held July 16-28, 2002. Conference duration: 12 days. Average attendance: 110. "We offer genre-based workshops (in fiction, poetry and playwriting), not theme-based workshops. The Sewanee Writers' Conference uses the facilities of the University of the South. Physically, the University is a collection of ivy-covered Gothic-style buildings, located on the Cumberland Plateau in mid-Tennessee. We allow invited editors, publishers and agents to structure their own presentations, but there is always opportunity for questions from the audience." **Previous agents/speakers have included:** Tony Earley, Barry Hannah, Romulus Linney, Alice McDermott, Erin McGraw, Padgett Powell, Daisy Foote, Debora Greger, Robert Hass, John Hollander, Margot Livesey, William Logan, Alison Lurie, Tim O'Brien.
**Costs:** Full conference fee was $1,205 in 2001 (includes tuition, board, and basic room).
**Accommodations:** Complimentary chartered bus service is available, on a limited basis, on the first and last days of the conference. Participants are housed in University dormitory rooms. Motel or B&B housing is available but not abundantly so. Dormitory housing costs are included in the full conference fee.
**Additional Information:** "We offer each participant (excluding auditors) the opportunity for a private manuscript conference with a member of the faculty. These manuscripts are due one month before the conference begins." Conference brochures/guidelines are available, "but no SASE is necessary. The conference has available a limited number of fellowships and scholarships; these are awarded on a competitive basis."

☑ **VIRGINIA ROMANCE WRITERS,** (formerly Virginia Romance Writers Conference), P.O. Box 35, Midlothian VA 23113. E-mail: gypsy3@erols.com. Website: www.Geocities.com/SoHo/museum/2164 (includes information about Virginia Romance Writers, authors, monthly meetings, workshops, conferences, contests). **Contact:** Sandra Hughes, president. Fiction, nonfiction, scriptwriting.

# Southeast (AL, AR, FL, GA, LA, MS, Puerto Rico)

☒ **ALL-DAY WORKSHOP,** P.O. Box 8604, Jacksonville FL 32239-8604. (352)687-4661. Fax: (352)687-8097. E-mail: lbarone21@aol.com. Website: www.angelfire.com/fl/RomanceWriting/. **Contact:** Laura Barone, presidential advisor. Estab. 1994. Annually. Conference held spring. Conference duration: 2 days. May expand to include Friday night "night owl sessions." Average attendance: 75-100. Conference focuses on romance novel writing, but is open to the general public and covers all aspects of writing a fictional novel. Held at the Holiday Inn hotel, Bay Meadows, May 3-5, 2002. 2001 theme was Romantic Suspense & Intrigue. **Agents/speakers attending include:** Editor, to be announced. See website for updates.
**Costs:** $65 (includes workshops, welcome packets, 1 raffle ticket, continental breakfast, full buffet lunch).
**Accommodations:** On-site accommodations with special rates available.
**Additional Information:** "We raffle critiques by published authors." Brochures available 1 month before conference date for SASE. Inquiries by e-mail and fax OK.

**ARKANSAS WRITERS' CONFERENCE**, #17 Red Maple Ct., Little Rock AR 72211. (501)312-1747. **Contact:** Barbara Longstreth Mulkey, director. Estab. 1944. Annual. Conference held first weekend in June 2002 (June 7-8). Average attendance: 225. Fiction, nonfiction, scriptwriting and poetry. "We have a variety of subjects related to writing— we have some general sessions, some more specific, but try to vary each year's subjects."
**Costs:** Registration: ($10 one day, $15 for 2), contest entry $5.
**Accommodations:** "We meet at a Holiday Inn Select in Little Rock." Holiday Inn has a bus to and from airport. Rooms average $65-70.
**Additional Information:** "We have 32 contest categories. Some are open only to Arkansans, most are open to all writers. Our judges are not announced before conference but are qualified, many from out of state." Conference brochures are available for SASE after February 1. "We have had 226 attending from 12 states—over 3,000 contest entries from 43 states and New Zealand, Mexico and Canada."

**N. FLORIDA CHRISTIAN WRITERS CONFERENCE**, 2344 Armour Court, Titusville FL 32780. (321)269-5831. **Conference Director:** Billie Wilson. Estab. 1988. Annual. Conference is held February 7-10, 2002. Conference duration: 5 days. Average attendance: 200. To promote "all areas of writing." Conference held at Christian Retreat Center in Bradenton FL. Editors will represent over 45 publications and publishing houses.
**Costs:** $400, includes tuition, food; $500 (double occupancy); $600 (single occupancy).
**Accommodations:** "We provide shuttle from the Tampa airport."
**Additional Information:** Critiques available. "Each writer may submit two works for critique. We have specialists in every area of writing to critique." Conference brochures/guidelines are available for SASE and on website.

**✓ FLORIDA FIRST COAST WRITERS' FESTIVAL**, 9911 Baymeadows Rd., Room 1166, FCCJ, Deerwood Center, Jacksonville FL 32256. (904)997-2669. Fax: (904)997-2727. E-mail: kclower@fccj.org. Website: ww.fccj.org/wf/ (includes festival workshop speakers, contest information). **Contacts:** Kathy Clower and Howard Denson. Estab. 1985. Annual. Conference held May 16-18, 2002. Held at Sea Turtle Inn, Atlantic Beach, FL. Average attendance: 300. All areas: mainstream plus genre. Fiction, nonfiction, scriptwriting, poetry, freelancing, etc. Offers seminars on narrative structure and plotting character development. **Agents/speakers attending include:** Randy Wayne White, Nancy Slonim Aronie, Sandra Kitt, Paul Adams, Sheree Bykofsky (agent), Elizabeth Lund, David Poyer, Lenoe Hart and more to be announced. Agents will be speaking and available for meetings with attendees.
**Costs:** Maximum of $150 for 2 days, with 2 meals.
**Accommodations:** Sea Turtle Inn, (904)249-7402 or 1(800)874-6000, has a special festival rate.
**Additional Information:** Conference brochures/guidelines are available for SASE. Sponsors a contest for short fiction, poetry and novels. Novel judges are David Poyer and Lenore Hart. Entry fees: $30, novels; $10, short fiction; $5, poetry. Deadline: November 1 in each year. "We offer one-on-one sessions at no additional costs for attendees to speak to selected writers, editors, agents on first-come, first served basis."

**N. FLORIDA SUNCOAST WRITERS' CONFERENCE**, University of South Florida, Division of Lifelong Learning, 4202 E. Fowler Ave., MHH-116, Tampa FL 33620-6610. (813)974-2403. Fax: (813)974-5421. E-mail: mglakis @admin.usf.edu. Directors: Steve Rubin, Ed Hirshberg, Betty Moss and Lagretta Lenkar. Estab. 1970. Annual. Held February 7-9, 2002. Conference duration: 3 days. Average attendance: 400. Conference covers poetry, short story, novel and nonfiction, including science fiction, detective, travel writing, drama, TV scripts, photojournalism and juvenile. "We do not focus on any one particular aspect of the writing profession but instead offer a variety of writing related topics. The conference is held on the picturesque university campus fronting the bay in St. Petersburg, Florida." Features panels with agents and editors. **Previous speakers/agents have included:** Lady P.D. James, William Styron, John Updike, Joyce Carol Oates, Francine Prose, Frank McCourt and David Guterson.
**Costs:** Call for information.
**Accommodations:** Special rates available at area motels. "All information is contained in our brochure."
**Additional Information:** Participants may submit work for critiquing. Extra fee charged for this service. Conference brochures/guidelines are available November 2001. Inquiries by e-mail and fax OK.

**OZARK CREATIVE WRITERS INC.**, 75 Robinwood Dr., Little Rock, AR 72227. (501)225-8619. **Contact:** Marsha Camp, conference business manager. Estab. 1975. Annual. Conference held second weekend in October. Conference duration: Thursday through Saturday. Average attendance: 150. Includes programs for all types of writing, about one half of attendees are already published. Conference held at conference center and inn in the Arkansas Ozark mountains. **Previous agents/speakers have included:** Dan Slater (editor, Penguin Putnam); Stephan Harrigan (novelist, screenwriter).
**Costs:** $60, before August 25, $70, after August 25 (includes cocktail party, continental breakfast for 2 days). Friday and Saturday night banquet are optional for an additional fee.
**Accommodations:** Special conference rates available at the Inn of the Ozarks.
**Additional Information:** "The conference has a friendly atmosphere and conference speakers are available. Many speakers return to the conference for the companionship of writers and speakers." Brochures available for SASE.

**WORDS & MUSIC: A LITERARY FEAST IN NEW ORLEANS**, 632 Pirates Alley, New Orleans LA 70116. (504)586-1609. Fax: (504)522-9725. E-mail: faulkhouse@aol.com. Website: www.Wordsandmusic.org. Conference Director: Rosemary James DeSalvo. Estab. 1997. Annual. Conference held September. Conference duration: 5 days.

Average attendance: 350-400. Presenters include authors, agents, editors and publishers. **Previous agents/speakers have included:** Deborah Grosvenor (Deborah Grosvenor Literary Agency); Jenny Bent (Harvey Klinger Agency); M.T. Caen. Agents will be speaking and available for meetings with attendees.
**Additional Information:** Write for additional information.

**WRITING TODAY—BIRMINGHAM-SOUTHERN COLLEGE**, Box 549003, Birmingham AL 35254. (205)226-4921. Fax: (205)226-3072. E-mail: dcwilson@bsc.edu. Website: www.bsc.edu. **Contact:** Annie Green, director of special events. Estab. 1978. Annual. Conference scheduled April 12-13, 2002. Average attendance: 400-500. "This is a two-day conference with approximately 18 workshops, lectures and readings. We try to offer workshops in short fiction, novels, poetry, children's literature, magazine writing, and general information of concern to aspiring writers such as publishing, agents, markets and research. The conference is sponsored by Birmingham-Southern College and is held on the campus in classrooms and lecture halls." **Previous agents/speakers included:** Eudora Welty, Pat Conroy, Ernest Gaines, Ray Bradbury, Erskine Caldwell, John Barth, Galway Kinnoll, Edward Albee. Agents will be speaking and available for meetings with attendees.
**Costs:** $120 for both days (includes lunches, reception, and morning coffee and rolls).
**Accommodations:** Attendees must arrange own transporation. Local hotels and motels offer special rates, but participants must make their own reservations.
**Additional Information:** "We usually offer a critique for interested writers. We have had poetry and short story critiques. There is an additional charge for these critiques." Sponsors the Hackney Literary Competition Awards for poetry, short story and novels. Brochures available for SASE.

# Midwest (IL, IN, KY, MI, OH)

**THE COLUMBUS WRITERS CONFERENCE**, P.O. Box 20548, Columbus OH 43220. (614)451-3075. Fax: (614)451-0174. E-mail: AngelaPL28@aol.com. Website: creativevista.com. Director: Angela Palazzolo. Estab. 1993. Annual. Conference held in September. Average attendance: 200. "The conference covers a wide variety of fiction and nonfiction topics presented by writers, editors and agents. Writing topics have included novel, short story, children's, young adult, science fiction, fantasy, humor, mystery, playwriting, screenwriting, personal essay, travel, humor, cookbook, technical, magazine writing, query letter, corporate, educational and greeting cards. Other topics for writers: finding and working with an agent, targeting markets, research, time management, obtaining grants and writers' colonies." Previous agents/speakers have included: Lee K. Abbott, Lore Segal, Jeff Herman, Doris S. Michaels, Sheree Bykofsky, Mike Harden, Oscar Collier, Maureen F. McHugh, Ralph Keyes, Stephanie S. Tolan, Bonnie Pryor, Dennis L. McKiernan, Karen Harper, Rita Rosenkranz, Mark D. Ryan, Melvin Helitzer, Susan Porter, Les Roberts, Tracey E. Dils, J. Patrick Lewis and many other professionals in the writing field.
**Costs:** Early registration fee is $169 for full conference (includes Friday and Saturday sessions, Friday dinner program, Friday open mic sessions, and Saturday continental breakfast, lunch, and afternoon refreshments); otherwise, fee is $189. Early registration fee for Saturday only is $134; otherwise, fee is $154. Friday dinner program is $38.
**Additional Information:** Call, write, e-mail or send fax to obtain a conference brochure, available mid-summer.

**[N] CHARLENE FARIS SEMINARS FOR BEGINNERS**, 610 W. Poplar St., #4, Zionsville IN 46077-1220. Phone/fax: (317)873-0738. E-mail: photobee@qserve.net. Website: www.freeagent/photobeetle. Director: Charlene Faris. Estab. 1985. Held 2 times/year in the spring and summer near Indianapolis. Conference duration: 2 days. Average attendence: 10. Fiction, nonfiction and photography. Concentration on all areas of publishing and writing, particularly marketing and working with editors.
**Costs:** $200, tuition only; may attend only 1 day for $100.
**Accommodations:** Information on overnight accommodations available.
**Additional Information:** Guidelines available for SASE.

**[N] GREEN RIVER WRITERS NOVELS-IN-PROGRESS WORKSHOP**, 703 Easlbridge Court, Louisville KY 40223. (502)245-4902. E-mail: mary_odell@ntr.net. Directors: Tim Dowe/Tomi Danaher. Estab. 1991. Annual. Conference held in March. Conference duration: 1 week. Average attendance: 55. Open to persons, college age and above, who have approximately 3 chapters (60 pages) or more of a novel. Mainstream and genre novels handled by individual instructors. Short fiction collections welcome. "Each novelist instructor works with a small group (5-7 people) for five days; then agents/editors are there for panels and appointments on the weekend." Site is The University of Louisville's Shelby Campus, suburban setting, graduate dorm housing (private rooms available with shared bath for each 2 rooms). "Meetings and classes held in nearby classroom building. Grounds available for walking, etc. Lovely setting, restaurants and shopping available nearby. Participants carpool to restaurants, etc. This year we are covering mystery, fantasy, mainstream/literary, suspense, historical."
**Costs:** Tuition—$375, housing $25/night private, $22 shared. Does not include meals.
**Accommodations:** "We see that participants without cars have transportation to meals, etc. If participants would rather stay in hotel, we will make that information available."
**Additional Information:** Participants send 60 pages/3 chapters with synopsis and $25 reading fee which applies to tuition. Deadline will be in late January. Conference brochures/guidelines are available for SASE.

☑ **KENTUCKY WOMEN WRITERS CONFERENCE**, The Carnegie Center for Literacy and Learning, 251 W. Second St., Lexington KY 40507. (859)254-4175. Fax: (859)281-1151. E-mail: kywwc@hotmail.com. Website: www.carnegieliteracy.org. **Contact:** Jan Isenhour. Annual. Conference held spring 2002. Fiction, nonfiction, poetry. "Gathering of women writers and scholars—novelists, poets, playwrights, essayists, biographers, journalists—and readers and students of literature. For the past twenty years, several days of reading, lectures, workshops, musical and theater performances and panel discussions about women writers and women's writing have been held both on campus and out in the community." Future sites will be in various venues in the community. Also traditional activities will involve creative writing of all kinds. **Previous agents/speakers have included:** Alice Walker, Barabar Kingsolver, Margaret Atwood, Sena Jeter Naslund, Judith Ortiz Cofer.
**Costs:** To be announced for 2002.
**Accommodations:** A list of area hotels will be provided by the Lexington Convention & Tourist Bureau upon request. Call (859)233-1221.
**Additional Information:** "Manuscript critiques of pre-submitted fiction, poetry, playwriting and nonfiction by registered conference participants will be provided by regional writers." Scholarships are available for those who would otherwise be unable to attend. "For details, contact us at kywwc@hotmail.com."

**THE MID AMERICA MYSTERY CONFERENCE**, Magna cum Murder, The E.B. Ball Center, Ball State University, Muncie IN 47306. (765)285-8975. Fax: (765)747-9566. E-mail: kennisonk@aol.com. Website: www.magnacummurder. com. **Contact:** Kathryn Kennison. Estab. 1994. Annual. Conference held from October 25-27, 2002. Average attendance: 400. Fiction, nonfiction. Held in the Horizon Convention Center and Historic Radisson Hotel Roberts. Conference for crime and detective fiction. **Previous agents/speakers have included:** Val McDermid, Lev Raphael, forensic experts Jim Ebert and Clark Davenport.
**Costs:** For 2001 cost was $175 (includes continental breakfasts, boxed lunches, a reception and a banquet).
**Additional Information:** Sponsors a radio mystery script contest. Send SASE for brochure/guidelines or request via fax or e-mail.

☑ **MIDLAND WRITERS CONFERENCE**, Grace A. Dow Memorial Library, 1710 W. St. Andrews, Midland MI 48640-2698. (989)837-3430. Fax: (989)837-3468. E-mail: ajarvis@midland-mi.org. Website: www.midland-mi.org/gracedowlibrary. Conference Chair: Katherine Redwine. **Contact:** Ann Jarvis, librarian. Estab. 1980. Annual. Conference held June 8, 2002. Average attendance: 100. Fiction, nonfiction, children's and poetry. "The Conference is composed of a well-known keynote speaker and six workshops on a variety of subjects including poetry, children's writing, nonfiction, freelancing, agents, etc. The attendees are both published and unpublished authors. The Conference is held at the Grace A. Dow Memorial Library in the auditorium and conference rooms." **Previous speakers/agents have included:** James W. Armstrong, Ruth Dukelow, Steve Griffin, Tom Powers, Brenda Shannon Yee, Sarah Zettle. Agents will be speaking.
**Costs:** Adult - $50; students, senior citizens and handicapped. A box lunch is available. Costs are approximate until plans for upcoming conference are finalized.
**Accommodations:** A list of area hotels is available.
**Additional Information:** Conference brochures/guidelines are mailed mid-April. Call or write to be put on mailing list. Inquiries by e-mail and fax OK.

☒ **NATIONAL MUSEUM PUBLISHING SEMINAR**, University of Chicago, 5835 S. Kimbark Ave., Chicago IL 60637. (773)702-1682. Fax: (773)702-6814. E-mail: s-medlock@uchicago.edu. **Contact:** Stephanie Medlock, director. Estab. 1988. Biennially. Conference held September 26-29, 2002 at the Chicago Hilton and Towers Hotel. It will be co-sponsored by the Art Institute of Chicago and the Publishing Program. Themes include: the concept of branding, the conflict between popular and academic catalogs, how to conduct photo research, and much more. Conference duration: 2½ days. Average attendance: 250. Primarily nonfiction, writing and editing in museums. "Conference moves to a new city every time and is co-sponsored by the University and different museums." Agents will be attending.
**Costs:** $425, includes a dinner sponsored by the Shedd Aquarium, a lunch, and materials.
**Accomodations:** Accomodations at the Chicago Hilton will be $185/night.
**Additional Information:** Brochures available for SASE after January 1, 2000. Inquiries by fax and e-mail OK.

**OAKLAND UNIVERSITY WRITERS' CONFERENCE**, 231 Varner Hall, Rochester MI 48309-4401. (248)370-3125. Fax: (248)370-4280. E-mail: gjboddy@oakland.edu. Website: www.oakland.edu/contin-ed/writersconf/. **Contact:** Gloria J. Boddy, program director. Estab. 1961. Annual. Conference held October 18-19, 2002. Average attendance: 400. Held at Oakland University: Oakland Center. Conference covers all aspects and types of writing in 36 concurrent workshops on Saturday. "It is a conference for beginning and established writers. It provides an opportunity to exchange ideas and perfect writing skills by meeting with agents, editors and successful writers." Major writers from various genres are speakers for the Saturday conference and luncheon program. Individual critiques and hands-on writing workshops are conducted Friday. Areas: nonfiction, young adult fiction, poetry, short fiction, chapbooks, magazine fiction, essay, script writing. **Previous agents/speakers have included:** Delen Cormeny, agent; Arthur Evans, university press editor; Karen Renaud, small presses. Agents will be speaking and available for meetings with attendees.
**Costs:** 2000: Conference registration: $85; lunch, $15; individual ms, $58; writing workshop, $48.
**Accommodations:** Hotel list is available.

**Additional Information:** Conference brochure/guidelines available after August 2001 for SASE. Inquiries by e-mail and fax OK.

**OF DARK & STORMY NIGHTS, Mystery Writers of America—Midwest Chapter**, P.O. Box 1944, Muncie IN 47308-1944. (765)288-7402. E-mail: spurgeonmwa@juno.com. **Contact:** W.W. Spurgeon, workshop director. Estab. 1982. Annual. Workshop held June 8, 2002. Workshop duration: 1 day. Average attendance: 200. Fiction, nonfiction, scriptwriting, children, young adult. Dedicated to "writing *mystery* fiction and crime-related nonfiction. Workshops and panels presented on plotting, dialogue, promotion, writers' groups, dealing with agents, synopsis and manuscript presentation, plus various technical aspects of crime and mystery." Held at the Holiday Inn, Rolling Meadows IL (suburban Chicago). **Previous agents/speakers have included:** Kimberley Cameron (Reese Halsey North), Javan Kienzle, Victoria Houston, William X. Kienzele, Jay Bonansinga, Brandon DuBois, S.J. Rozan, Barbara D'Amato, Joe Hensley, Hariette Gillem Robinet, Michael Raleigh, James Brewer, Jeremiah Healy. "Our agents speak, do critiques and schmooze with those attending." Agents will be speaking and available for meetings with attendees.
**Costs:** $130 for MWA members; $160 for nonmembers; $50 extra for ms critique.
**Accommodations:** Easily accessible by car or train (from Chicago) Holiday Inn, Rolling Meadows $96/night plus tax; free airport bus (Chicago O'Hare) and previously arranged rides from train.
**Additional Information:** "We accept manuscripts for critique (first 30 pages maximum); $50 cost. Writers meet with critics during workshop for one-on-one discussions." Brochures available for SASE after January 1.

☑ **WRITERS' RETREAT WORKSHOP**, Write It/Sell It, 2507 S. Boston Place, Tulsa OK 74114. (800)642-2494. Fax: (918)583-7625. E-mail: wrwwisi@aol.com. Website: www.writersretreatworkshop.com. **Contact:** Gail Provost Stockwell, director. Estab. 1987. Annual. Conference held May 24-June 2, 2002. Conference duration: 10 days. Average attendance: 30. Novels-in-progress, all genres, narrative nonfiction. Held at Marydale Retreat Center in northern KY. "Teaches a proven step-by-step process for developing and completing a novel for publication, developed originally by the late Gary Provost. The practical application of lessons learned in classes, combined with continual private consultations with staff members, guarantees dramatic improvement in craft, writing technique and self-editing skills." **Agents/Speakers attending include:** Elizabeth Lyon, editor; Simon Lipskar, agent; Jennifer Jackson, agent; T.J. MacGregor, author; Nancy Pickard, author.
**Costs:** $1,695, new students; $1,525 returning students (includes lodging, meals, consultations and course materials.)
**Accommodations:** Marydale Retreat Center provides complimentary shuttle services between Cincinnati airport and the center.

# North Central (IA, MN, NE, ND, SD, WI)

☑ **IOWA SUMMER WRITING FESTIVAL**, 100 Oakdale Campus, Suite W310, University of Iowa, Iowa City IA 52242-1802. (319)335-4160. E-mail: amy-margolis@uiowa.edu. Website: www.uiowa.edu/~iswfest. **Contact:** Amy Margolis, assistant director. Estab. 1987. Annual. Festival held in June and July. Workshops are one week or a weekend. Average attendance: limited to 12/class—over 1,500 participants throughout the summer. Held at University of Iowa campus. "We offer courses in most areas of writing: novel, short story, essay, poetry, playwriting, screenwriting, humor, travel, writing for children, memoir, women's writing, romance and mystery." **Previous agents/speakers have included:** Lee K. Abbott, Susan Power, Joy Harjo, Gish Jen, Abraham Verghese, Robert Olen Butler, Ethan Canin, Clark Blaise, Gerald Stern, Donald Justice, Michael Dennis Browne, Marvin Bell, Hope Edelman. Guest speakers are undetermined at this time.
**Costs:** $400-425/week; $175, weekend workshop (2001 rates). Housing and meals are separate.
**Accommodations:** "We offer participants a choice of accommodations: dormitory, $40/night; Iowa House, $75/night; Sheraton, $75/night (rates subject to changes)."
**Additional Information:** Brochure/guidelines are available in February. Inquiries by fax and e-mail OK.

☑ **SINIPEE WRITERS' WORKSHOP**, Loras College, 1450 Alta Vista, Dubuque IA 52004-0178. (563)588-7139. Fax: (563)588-4962. E-mail: lcrosset@loras.edu. Website: www.loras.edu. **Contact:** Linda Crossett, director of continuing education. Director Emeritus: John Tigges. Estab. 1985. Annual. Conference held April 27, 2002. Average attendance: 50-75. To promote "primarily fiction although we do include poetry, nonfiction, and scriptwriting each program. The mentioned areas are treated in such a way that fiction writers can learn new ways to expand their abilities and writing techniques." The workshop is held on the campus of Loras College in Dubuque. "This campus holds a unique atmosphere and everyone seems to love the relaxed and restful mood it inspires. This in turn carries over to the workshop, and friendships are made that last in addition to learning and experiencing what other writers have gone through to attain success in their chosen field." **Agents/speakers attending include:** Catherine Struck, Jim Schaeffer, Bill Goldberg, Connie Meester. Agents will be speaking and available for meetings with attendees.
**Costs:** $60 early registration; $65 at the door (includes all handouts, necessary materials for the workshop, coffee/snack break, lunch, drinks and snacks at autograph party following workshop).
**Accommodations:** Information is available for out-of-town participants, concerning motels, etc., even though the workshop is 1-day long.

**Additional Information:** Offers The John Tigges Writing Contest for Short Fiction, Nonfiction and Poetry. Limit 1,500 words (fiction or nonfiction), 40 lines (poetry). 1st prize in all 3 categories: $100 plus publication in an area newspaper or magazine; 2nd prize all categories: $50; 3rd prize in all categories: $25. Written critique service available for contest entries, $15 extra. Conference brochures/guidelines are available February for SASE.

**UNIVERSITY OF WISCONSIN AT MADISON WRITERS INSTITUTE**, 610 Langdon St., Madison WI 53703. (608)262-3447. Fax: (608)265-2475. Website: www.dcs.wisc.edu/lsa. **Contact:** Christine DeSmet, director. Estab. 1990. Annual. Conference held July 11-12, 2002. Average attendance: 175. Conference held at University of Wisconsin at Madison. Themes: fiction and nonfiction. Guest speakers are published authors, editors and agents.
**Costs:** Approximately $195 for 2 days; critique fees additional.
**Accommodations:** Info on accommodations sent with registration confirmation. Critiques available. Conference brochures/guidelines are available for SASE.

**WISCONSIN REGIONAL WRITERS' ASSOCIATION INC. CONFERENCES**, Wisconsin Regional Writers' Assn., 510 W. Sunset Ave., Appleton WI 54911-1139. (920)734-3724. E-mail: wrwa@lakefield.net. Website: www.inkwells.net/wrwa. **Contact:** Patricia Dunson Boverhuis, president. Estab. 1948. Conferences held in May and September. Conference duration: 1-2 days. Provides workshops for fiction, nonfiction, scriptwriting, poetry. Presenters include authors, agents, editors and publishers. **Previous agents/speakers have included:** Marcia Preston (editor *Byline Magazine*). Agents will be speaking.
**Additional Information:** Brochure available for SASE or on website. Inquiries by e-mail and fax OK.

# South Central (CO, KS, MO, NM, OK, TX)

✅ **A DAY FOR WRITERS**, P.O. Box 774284, Steamboat Springs CO 80477. (970)879-8079. E-mail: mshfreiberger @cs.com. **Contact:** Harriet Freiberger, director. Estab. 1981. Annual. Conference held July 20, 2002. Conference duration: 1 day. Average attendance: 35. Featured areas of instruction change each year. Held at the restored train depot—home of the Steamboat Springs Arts Council. **Previous agents/speakers have included:** Jim Fergus, Avi, Robert Greer, Renate Wood. Agents will be speaking and available for meetings with attendees.
**Costs:** $35 prior to June 1; $45 after June 1 (includes seminars, catered luncheon). Pre-conference dinner also available at $18/person. Limited enrollment.
**Additional Information:** Brochures available in April for SASE. Inquiries by e-mail OK.

**ASPEN SUMMER WORDS**, Aspen Writers' Foundation, Box 7726, Aspen CO 81612. (800)925-2526. Fax (970)920-5700. E-mail: aspenwrite@aol.com. Website: www.aspenwriters.org. **Contact:** Julie Comins, executive director. Estab. 1975. Annual. Conference held June 2002. Conference duration: 1 week. Average attendance: 100. Retreat for fiction, poetry, nonfiction. Festival includes readings, networking opportunities, private meetings with agents, editors and publishers. **Previous agents/speakers have included:** Pam Houston (fiction writer); Christopher Merrill (poet); Fenton Johnson (memoir writer); Kent Haruf (fiction writer); Adrianne Miller (*Esquire* fiction editor); writers Ursula Hegi; Ted Conover; Dawn Davis (fiction editor) and many more.
**Costs:** $475/full tuition; $150/festival pass (2001).
**Accommodations** Free shuttle to/from airport and around town. Information on overnight accommodations available. Call (800) number for reservations. Rates for 2000: $60/night double; $120/night single suggested off-campus housing.
**Additional Information:** Manuscripts to be submitted for review by faculty prior to conference. Conference brochures are available for SASE or on website.

**THE BAY AREA WRITERS LEAGUE ANNUAL CONFERENCE**, P.O. Box 728, Seabrook TX 77586. (281)268-7500. Fax: (409)762-4787. E-mail: seamus@compuserve.com. Website: www.angelfire.com/tx2/bawl. **Contact:** Jim Casey, webmaster. Estab. 1988. Annually. Conference held May 10-11, 2002. Conference duration: 2 days. Average attendance: 100. "We present a comprehensive range of topics." Conference held at the University of Houston-Clear Lake. **Previous agents/speakers have included:** Michelle Brummer (Donald Maass Agency), Angela Adair-Hoy. Agents will be speaking and available for meetings with attendees.
**Costs:** $85, plus $15 for annual membership (includes all sessions, lunch on both days, Friday evening reception). One-day price is $50.
**Accommodations:** Information is available. "We attempt to assist out-of-town attendees individually."
**Additional Information:** "We have a contest for novice writers in conjunction with the conference." Brochures available March for SASE or on website. Inquiries by fax or e-mail OK.

✅ **FRONTIERS IN WRITING**, P.O. Box 19303, Amarillo TX 79114. (806)354-2305. Fax: (806)354-2536. E-mail: pcs@arn.net. Website: www.users.arn.net/~ppw/. Estab. 1980. Annual. Conference held in June. Duration: 1½ days. Average attendance: 200. Nonfiction, poetry, scriptwriting and fiction (including mystery, romance, mainstream, science fiction and fantasy). **Previous agents/speakers have included:** Don Maass (agent), Cherise Grant (Simon & Schuster editor), Melanie Rigney (*Writer's Digest* editor), Bestseller Nancy Taylor Rosenberg and 1999 Pulitzer Prize winner Michael Cunningham.

**Costs:** 2001 conference: $125 Members; $145 Non-members ($20 for membership). (Includes Friday night dinner, Saturday breakfast, lunch and beverages—lodging and transportation separate.)
**Accommodations:** Special conference room rate.
**Additional information:** Sponsors a contest. Deadline: April. Guidelines available for SASE or on website. Writers may request information via fax. Brochures and guidelines available in December for SASE or on website.

☑ **GLORIETA CHRISTIAN WRITERS' CONFERENCE**, P.O. Box 8, Glorieta NM 87535-0008. (800)797-4222. Fax: (505)757-6149. E-mail: brian.daniel@lifeway.com. **Contact:** Brian Daniel, Glorieta events director. Estab. 1997. Annually. Conference held October 15-19, 2002. Conference duration: Tuesday afternoon through Saturday lunch. Average attendance: 350. Include programs for all types of writing. Conference held in the Lifeway Glorieta Conference Center. **Speakers attending include:** Agents, editors, and professional writers. Agents will be speaking and available for meetings with attendees.
**Costs:** $537, for private rooms, $477, for double-occupancy rooms (includes seminars, meals, lodging). Critiques are available for an additional $35; writing contest held, $5/entry.
**Accommodations:** Hotel rooms are available at the Lifeway Glorieta Conference Center. Sante Fe Shuttle offers service from the Albuquerque or Sante Fe airports to the conference center.
**Additional Information:** Brochures available April 1 for SASE. Inquiries by fax or e-mail OK.

🇳 **HEARTLAND WRITERS CONFERENCE**, P.O. Box 652. Kennett MO 63857. (573)297-3325. Fax: (573)297-3352. E-mail: hwg@heartlandwriters.org. Website: www.heartlandwriters.org. **Contact:** Judy Stamms, attendee liaison. Estab. 1990. Biennial (even years). Conference held June 6-8, 2002. Conference duration: 3 days. Average attendance: 160. Popular fiction (all genres), nonfiction, children's, screenwriting, poetry. Held at the Best Western Coach House Inn in Sikeston MO. Panels for 1998 included "Finding the Time and Will to Write" and "Putting Reality into Your Genre Fiction." **Previous agents/speakers attending include:** Alice Orr, Jennifer Jackson, Ricia Mainhardt, Christy Fletcher. Agents will be speaking and available for meetings with attendees.
**Costs:** $195 for advance registration, $220 for general registration (includes lunch on Friday and Saturday, awards banquet Saturday, hospitality room and get-acquainted mixer Thursday night).
**Accommodations:** Blocks of rooms are available at special conference rate at conference venue and at two nearby motels. Cost: $45/night (1998 price).
**Additional Information:** Brochures available late January 2002. Inquiries by e-mail and fax OK.

☑ **NATIONAL WRITERS ASSOCIATION FOUNDATION CONFERENCE**, 3140 S. Peoria, #295, Aurora CO 80014. (303)841-0246. Fax: (303)841-2607. E-mail: sandywrter@aol.com. Website: www.nationalwriters.com. **Contact:** Sandy Whelchel, executive director. Estab. 1926. Annual. Conference held June 7-9, 2002. Conference held in Denver, CO. Conference duration: 3 days. Average attendance: 200-300. General writing and marketing.
**Costs:** $200 (approx.).
**Additional Information:** Awards for previous contests will be presented at the conference. Conference brochures/guidelines are available for SASE.

☑ **THE NEW LETTERS WEEKEND WRITERS CONFERENCE**, University of Missouri-Kansas City, College of Arts and Sciences Continuing Ed. Division, 215 4825 Troost Bldg., 5100 Rockhill Rd., Kansas City MO 64110-2499. (816)235-2736. Fax: (816)235-2611. E-mail: newletters@umkc.edu. Website: www.umkc.edu/newletters. **Contact:** Mary Ellen Buck or Sharon Seaton, administrative associates. Estab. in the mid-70s as The Longboat Key Writers Conference. Annual. Conference held June. Conference duration is 3 weeks. Average attendance: 75. Fiction, nonfiction, scriptwriting, poetry, playwriting, journalism. "The New Letters Weekend Writers Conference brings together talented writers in many genres for lectures, seminars, readings, workshops and individual conferences. The emphasis is on craft and the creative process in poetry, fiction, screenwriting, playwriting and journalism; but the program also deals with matters of psychology, publications and marketing. The conference is appropriate for both advanced and beginning writers. The conference meets at the beautiful Diastole conference center of The University of Missouri-Kansas City."
**Costs:** Several options are available. Participants may choose to attend as a noncredit student or they may attend for 1 hour of college credit from the University of Missouri-Kansas City. Conference registration includes continental breakfasts, Saturday and Sunday lunch. For complete information, contact the University of Missouri-Kansas City.
**Accommodations:** Registrants are responsible for their own transportation, but information on area accommodations is made available.
**Additional Information:** Those registering for college credit are required to submit a ms in advance. Ms reading and critique is included in the credit fee. Those attending the conference for noncredit also have the option of having their ms critiqued for an additional fee. Conference brochures/guidelines are available for SASE after March. Inquiries by e-mail and fax OK.

☑ **NORTHEAST TEXAS COMMUNITY COLLEGE & NETWO ANNUAL CONFERENCE**, Continuing Education, Northeast Texas Community College, P.O. Box 1307, Mount Pleasant TX 75456-9991. (903)572-1911, ext. 241. Fax: (903)572-6712.E-mail: vcastleberry@ntcc.cc.tx.us. Website: www.ntcc.cc.tx.us/instruction/conted.html. **Contact:** Program Coordinator, Continuing Education. Estab. 1987. Annual. Conference held April. Conference duration: 1 day. Presenters include agents, writers, editors and publishers.

**Additional Information:** Write for additional information. Conference is co-sponsored by the Northeast Texas Writers Organization (NETWO).

**PIKES PEAK WRITERS CONFERENCE**, 5550 North Union Blvd., Colorado Springs CO 80918. E-mail: info@ppwc.net. Website: www.ppwc.net. Estab. 1994. Annual. Conference held May 3-5, 2002. Conference duration: Friday 11:30 am to Sunday 2 pm. Average attendance: 400. Commercial fiction. Held at the Wyndham Hotel. "Workshops, presentations and panels focus on writing and publishing genre fiction—romance, scifi and fantasy, suspense thrillers, action adventure, mysteries. Agents and editors are available for meetings with attendees.
**Costs:** $250 (includes all meals).
**Accommodations:** Wyndham Colorado Springs holds a block of rooms for conference attendees until March 30 at a special $75 rate (1-800-962-6982).
**Additional Information:** Readings with critique are available or Friday afternoon. One-on-one meetings with editors and agents available Saturday and Sunday. Brochures available in October. Inquiries by e-mail OK. Registration form available on website. Contest for unpublished writers; need not attend conference to enter contest. Deadline January 7, 2002.

**ROCKY MOUNTAIN BOOK FESTIVAL**, 2123 Downing St., Denver CO 80211-5210. (303)839-8320. Fax: (303)839-8319. E-mail: ccftb@compuserve.com. Website: www.coloradobook.org. **Contact:** Christiane Citron, executive director. Estab. 1991. Annual. Festival held March 2002. Festival duration: 2 days. Average attendance: 10,000. Festival promotes work published from all genres. Held at Denver Merchandise Mart in Denver. Offers a wide variety of panels. Approximately 200 authors are scheduled to speak each year. **Previous speakers have included:** Sherman Alexie, Dixie Carter, Dave Barry, Alice Walker, Dr. Andrew Weil, Jill Kerr Conway, Bill Moyers and Dava Sobel.
**Costs:** $4 adult; $2 child.
**Additional Information:** Please submit copy of book, bio and publicity material for consideration.

**ROCKY MOUNTAIN CHILDREN'S BOOK FESTIVAL**, 2123 Downing St., Denver CO 80205-5210. (303)839-8320. Fax: (303)839-8319. E-mail: ccftb@compuserve.com. Website: www.coloradobook.org. **Contact:** Christiane Citron, executive director. Estab. 1996. Annual festival held March or April; part of Rocky Mountain Book Festival. Festival duration: 2 days. Average attendance: 10,000. Fiction, nonfiction, screenwriting. Festival promotes published work for and about children/families. Held at Denver Merchandise Mart. Approximately 100 authors speak annually. **Previous speakers have included:** Ann M. Martin, Sharon Creech, Laura Numeroff, Jean Craighead George, the Kratt Brothers, Bruce Lansky and Jane Yolen.
**Costs:** None.
**Additional Information:** "For published authors of children's/family works only." Brochure/guidelines available for SASE.

**N: ROCKY MOUNTAIN FICTION WRITERS COLORADO GOLD**, P.O. Box 260244, Denver CO 80226-0244. (303)791-3941. Website: www.rmfw.org (includes contest, membership, conference, critique). Estab. 1983. Annual. Conference held weekend after Labor Day. Conference duration: 3 days. Average attendance: 250. For novel length fiction. The conference will be held in Denver. Themes included general novel length fiction, genre fiction, contemporary romance, mystery, sf/f, mainstream, history. **Guest speakers and panelists have included:** Terry Brooks, Dorothy Cannell, Patricia Gardner Evans, Diane Mott Davidson, Constance O'Day, Connie Willis, Clarissa Pinkola Estes and Michael Palmer; approximately 6 editors and 4 agents annually.
**Costs:** In 2001, cost was $169 early, $189 walk-in (includes conference, reception, banquet). Editor workshop $20 additional.
**Accommodations:** Information on overnight accommodations made available of area hotels. The conference will be at the Embassy Suites Denver Tech Center. Conference rates available.
**Additional Information:** Editor conducted workshops are limited to 10 participants for critique with auditing available. Workshops in science fiction, mainstream, mystery, historical, contemporary romance. Sponsors a contest. For 20-page mss and 8-page synopsis; categories mentioned above. First rounds are done by qualified members, published and nonpublished, with editors doing the final ranking; 2 copies need to be submitted without author's name. $20 entry only, $40 entry and (one) critique. Guidelines available for SASE. Deadline June 1.

**SHORT COURSE ON PROFESSIONAL WRITING**, University of Oklahoma, 860 Van Vleet Oval, Room 101, Norman OK 73071-0270. (405)325-2721. Fax: (405)325-7565. E-mail: jmadisondavis@ou.edu. Website: http://jmc.ou.edu. **Contact:** J. Madison Davis, professor of professional writing. Estab. 1938. Annual. Conference held in June. Conference duration: 3 days. Average attendance: 100-200. All areas of writing for publication, excluding poetry. Held in Norman, at the NCED Postal training center, a resort-like facility with recreational amenities. **Agents/speakers attending include:** Alison Bond, Lois de la Haba, Donald Maass, Betsey Lerner, Peter Rubie. Agents will be speaking and available for meetings with attendees.
**Costs:** $230 (includes banquet, all sessions) In addition: Private ms consultations for $45. Academic credit available for additional cost.
**Accommodations:** Special rates available with meals included.
**Additional Information:** "A warm, friendly and supportive conference." Brochures available April for SASE. Inquiries by e-mail and fax OK.

**N SOUTHWEST WRITERS WORKSHOP CONFERENCE**, 8200 Mountain Rd., NE, Suite 106, Albuquerque NM 87110. (505)265-9485. Fax: (505)265-9483. E-mail: swriters@aol.com. Website: www.southwestwriters.org. Estab. 1983. Annual. Conference held September 20-23, 2001. Average attendance: 350. "Conference concentrates on all areas of writing." Workshops and speakers include writers and editors of all genres for all levels from beginners to advanced. 1998 theme was "Master the Muse, Craft the Miracle." Keynote speaker was David Guterson, bestselling author of *Snow Falling on Cedars*. **Agents/speakers attending include:** Malachy McCourt, Robert Pinsky, Patricia Schroeder. **Costs:** $195-320 includes conference sessions, 2 luncheons, 2 banquets.
**Accommodations:** Usually have official airline and discount rates. Special conference rates are available at hotel. A list of other area hotels and motels is available.
**Additional Information:** Sponsors a contest judged by authors, editors and agents from New York, Los Angeles, etc., and from major publishing houses. Seventeen categories. Deadline: May 1. Entry fee is $29 (members) or $39 (nonmembers). Brochures/guidelines available for SASE. Inquiries by e-mail and fax OK. "An appointment (10 minutes, one-on-one) may be set up at the conference with editor or agent of your choice on a first-registered/first-served basis."

**☑ TAOS POETRY CIRCUS**, 5275 NDCBU, Taos NM 87571. (505)758-1800. E-mail: wpba@laplaza.org. Website: www.poetrycircus.org. **Contact:** Anne, director. Estab. 1982. Annual. Festival held June 8-16, 2002. Duration: 9 days. Average attendance: 2,000. Poetry. Held in Taos NM.
**Costs:** $3-75 per event.
**Accommodations:** Special room rates are available from $69-85/double. Special rental car rates available with Enterprise.
**Additional Information:** Festival includes readings, slams, seminars, a performance and poetics workshop, poetry video showing and free events. Main event is the World Heavyweight Championship Poetry Bout occurring on June 15, 2002. Brochures available March for SASE. Inquiries by e-mail OK.

**☑ WRITERS' LEAGUE OF TEXAS**, 1501 W. Fifth St., Suite E-2, Austin TX 78703. (512)499-8914. Fax: (512)499-0441. E-mail: awl@writersleague.org. Website: www.writersleague.org. **Contact:** Jim Bob McMillan, executive director. Estab. 1982. Conference held in July. Conference duration: varies according to program. Average attendance 200. Fiction, nonfiction. Programs held at AWL Resource Center/Library, other sites in Austin and Texas. Topics include: finding and working with agents and publishers; writing and marketing short fiction; dialogue; characterization; voice; research; basic and advanced fiction writing/focus on the novel; business of writing; also workshops for genres. **Agents/speakers attending include:** Ken Atchity, Sheree Bykofsky, Mary Evans, Felicia Eth, Michael Larsen, Elizabeth McHugh, Elizabeth Pomada, Nancy Stender, Andrew Whelchel, Tim Bent, Karen V. Haas, Kati Hesford, Ron Martirano. Agents will be speaking and available for meetings with attendees. In July the League holds its annual Agents! Agents! Agents! Conference which provides writers with the opportunity to meet top agents from New York and the West Coast.
**Costs:** Varies from $45-185, depending on program. Most classes, $80-200; workshops $50; conferences: $125-185.
**Accommodations:** Special rates given at some hotels for program participants.
**Additional Information:** Critique sessions offered at some programs. Individual presenters determine critique requirements. Those requirements are then made available through Writers' League office and in workshop promotion. Contests and awards programs are offered separately. Brochures/guidelines are available on request.

**WRITERS WORKSHOP IN SCIENCE FICTION**, English Department/University of Kansas, Lawrence KS 66045-2115. (785)864-3380. Fax: (785)864-4298. E-mail: jgunn@falcon.cc.ukans.edu. Website: http://falcon.cc.ukans.edu/~sfcenter/. **Contact:** James Gunn, professor. Estab. 1985. Annual. Conference held July 1-14, 2002. Average attendance: 15. Conference for writing and marketing science fiction. "Classes meet in university housing on the University of Kansas campus. Workshop sessions operate informally in a lounge." **Previous agents/speakers have included:** Frederick Pohl, Kij Johnson, Chris McKitterick.
**Costs:** Tuition: $400. Housing and meals are additional.
**Accommodations:** Housing information available. Several airport shuttle services offer reasonable transportation from the Kansas City International Airport to Lawrence. During past conferences, students were housed in a student dormitory at $12.50/day double, $23.50/day single.
**Additional Information:** "Admission to the workshop is by submission of an acceptable story. Two additional stories should be submitted by the middle of June. These three stories are copied and distributed to other participants for critiquing and are the basis for the first week of the workshop; one story is rewritten for the second week." Brochures/guidelines are available for SASE. "The Writers Workshop in Science Fiction is intended for writers who have just started to sell their work or need that extra bit of understanding or skill to become a published writer."

# West (AZ, CA, HI, NV, UT)

**☑ AMERICAN FOOD MEDIA CONFERENCE**, 2555 Main St., St. Helena CA 94574. Fax: (845)451-1066. E-mail: s_cussen@culinary.edu. Website: www.ciachef.edu. **Contact:** Sue Cussen, director of marketing. Estab. 1994. Annual. Conference held November 4-7, 2002. Conference duration: 4 days. Average attendance: 125. Fiction. Conference works to define the ever-evolving profession of communicating about food. Held at The Culinary Institute of

America's Greystone campus. "The Art & Craft of Food Writing," "Publishing & Marketing." **Agents/speakers attending include:** Doe Cover (The Doe Cover Agency). Agents will be speaking and available for meetings with attendees.
**Costs:** $695 (includes conference, seminar, lunches and breakfasts).
**Accommodations:** Limited on-site accommodations available. Single: $495. Rental car is needed for transportation to airport.
**Additional Information:** Brochures available in June for SASE or on website.

**IWWG EARLY SPRING IN CALIFORNIA CONFERENCE**, International Women's Writing Guild, P.O. Box 810, Gracie Station, New York NY 10028-0082. (212)737-7536. Fax: (212)737-9469. E-mail: iwwg@iwwg.com. Website: www.IWWG.com. **Contact:** Hannelore Hahn, executive director. Estab. 1982. Annual. Conference gennerally held on the 2nd weekend in March. Average attendance: 80. Conference to promote "creative writing, personal growth and empowerment." Site is a redwood forest mountain retreat in Santa Cruz, California.
**Costs:** $325 for weekend program with room and board, $150 for weekend program without room and board.
**Accommodations:** Accommodations are all at conference site.
**Additional Information:** Conference brochures/guidelines are available for SASE. Inquiries by e-mail and fax OK.

**MAUI WRITERS CONFERENCE**, P.O. Box 1118, Kihei HI 96753. (808)879-0061. Fax: (808)879-6233. E-mail: writers@maui.net. Website: www.mauiwriters.com (includes information covering all programs offered, writing competitions, presenters past and present, writers forum bulletin board, published attendees books, dates, price, hotel and travel information). **Contact:** Shannon and John Tullius. Estab. 1993. Annual. Conference held the end of August (Labor Day weekend). Conference duration: 4 days. Conference held at Outrigger Wailea Resort. Average attendance: 800. For fiction, nonfiction, poetry, children's, young adult, horror, mystery, romance, science fiction, journalism, screenwriting. **Previous agents/speakers have included:** Andrea Brown (Andrea Brown Literary Agency); Kimberley Cameron (The Reece Halsey Agency); Susan Crawford (Crawford Literary Agency); Laurie Horwitz (Creative Artists Agency); Amy Kossow (Linda Allen Literary Agency); Owen Laster (William Morris); Jillian Manus (Manus & Associates Literary Agency); Craig Nelson (The Craig Nelson Co.); Elizabeth Pomada (Larsen/Pomada Literary Agency); Susan Travis (Susan Travis Literary Agency). Agents will be speaking and available for consultations with attendees.
**Additional Information:** "We offer a comprehensive view of the business of publishing, with over 2,000 consultation slots with industry agents, editors and screenwriting professionals as well as workshops and sessions covering writing instruction." Write or call for additional information.

**N: MENDOCINO COAST WRITERS CONFERENCE**, 1211 Del Mar. Fort Bragg CA 95437. (707)964-6810. Fax: (707)961-1255. E-mail: mcwc@jps.org. Website: www.mcwcwritewhale.com. **Contact:** Jan Boyd, registrar. Estab. 1988. Annually. Conference held June 7-9. Conference duration: 3 days. Average attendance: 80. All areas of writing covered. Held at small community college campus on the northern Pacific Coast. **Agents/speakers attending include:** Esmond Harmsworth, Jim Dodge, Roy Parvin, John Lescroart, Maxine Schur, and others. Agents will be speaking and available for consultations with attendees.
**Costs:** $250-300 (includes one day intensive in one subject and two days of several short sessions; panels; meals; two socials with guest readers; one open to the public event. Kayak trip extra on Sunday.)
**Accommodations:** Information on overnight accommodations is made available. Special conference attendee accommodations made in some cases. Shared rides from San Francisco Airport are available.
**Additional Information:** Emphasis on writers who are also good teachers. Brochures available for SASE in January or on website now. Inquiries by e-mail and fax OK.

**☑ MOUNT HERMON CHRISTIAN WRITERS CONFERENCE**, P.O. Box 413, Mount Hermon CA 95041-0413. (831)335-4466. Fax: (831)335-9413. E-mail: dtalbot@mhcamps.org. Website: www.mounthermon.org. **Contact:** David R. Talbott, director of adult ministries. specialized programs. Estab. 1970. Annual. Conference held Friday-Tuesday over Palm Sunday weekend, March 22-26, 2002. Average attendance: 400. "We are a broad-ranging conference for all areas of Christian writing, including fiction, children's, poetry, nonfiction, magazines, inspirational and devotional writing, books, educational curriculum and radio and TV scriptwriting. This is a working, how-to conference, with many workshops within the conference involving on-site writing assignments. The conference is sponsored by and held at the 440-acre Mount Hermon Christian Conference Center near San Jose, California, in the heart of the coastal redwoods. The faculty/student ratio is about 1:6 or 7. The bulk of our faculty are editors and publisher representatives from major Christian publishing houses nationwide." **Agents/speakers attending include:** Janet Kobobel Grant, Elaine W. Colvin. Agents speaking and available for meetings with attendees.
**Costs:** Registration fees include tuition, conference sessions, resource notebook, refreshment breaks, room and board and vary from $600 (economy) to $895 (deluxe), double occupancy (2002 fees).
**Accommodations:** Registrants stay in hotel-style accommodations, and full board is provided as part of conference fees. Meals are taken family style, with faculty joining registrants. Airport shuttles are available from the San Jose International Airport. Housing is not required of registrants, but about 95% of our registrants use Mount Hermon's own housing facilities (hotel style double-occupancy rooms). Meals with the conference are required and are included in all fees.
**Additional Information:** "The residential nature of our conference makes this a unique setting for one-on-one interaction with faculty/staff. There is also a decided inspirational flavor to the conference, and general sessions with well-

known speakers are a highlight." Registrants may submit 2 works for critique in advance of the conference, then have personal interviews with critiquers during the conference. No advance work is required however. Conference brochures/ guidelines are available for SASE. Inquiries by e-mail and fax OK.

**PASADENA WRITERS' FORUM**, P.C.C. Extended Learning Center, 1570 E. Colorado Blvd., Pasadena CA 91106-2003. (626)585-7608. Fax: (626)796-5204. E-mail: pcclearn@webcom.com. **Contact:** Meredith Brucker, coordinator. Estab. 1954. Annual. Conference held in March 2002. Average attendance: 200. "For the novice as well as the professional writer in any field of interest: fiction or nonfiction, including scripts, children's, humor and poetry." Held on the campus of Pasadena City College. A panel discussion by agents, editors or authors is usually featured at the end of the day.
**Costs:** $100 (includes box lunch and coffee hour) for the one-day conference.
**Additional Information:** Brochure upon request, no SASE necessary. "Pasadena City College also periodically offers an eight-week class 'Writing for Publication.' "

**PIMA WRITERS' WORKSHOP**, Pima College, 2202 W. Anklam Rd., Tucson AZ 85709. (520)206-6974. Fax: (520)206-6020. E-mail: mfiles@pimacc.pima.edu. **Contact:** Meg Files, director. Estab. 1988. Annual. Conference held May 24-26, 2002. Conference duration 3 days. Average attendance 250. Fiction, nonfiction, scriptwriting. "For anyone interested in writing—beginning or experienced writer. The workshop offers sessions on writing short stories, novels, nonfiction articles and books, children's and juvenile stories, poetry and screenplays." Sessions are held in the Center for the Arts on Pima Community College's West Campus. **Previous agents/speakers have included:** Michael Blake, Ron Carlson, Gregg Levoy, Nancy Mairs, Linda McCarriston, Larry McMurty, Barbara Kingsolver, Jerome Stern, Connie Willis, Jack Heffron, Jeff Herman, Robert Morgan. Agents will be speaking and available for meetings with attendees.
**Costs:** $65 (can include ms critique). Participants may attend for college credit, in which case fees are $85 for Arizona residents and $215 for out-of-state residents. Meals and accommodations not included.
**Accommodations:** Information on local accommodations is made available, and special workshop rates are available at a specified motel close to the workshop site (about $60/night).
**Additional Information:** "The workshop atmosphere is casual, friendly, and supportive, and guest authors are very accessible. Readings and panel discussions are offered as well as talks and manuscript sessions." Participants may have up to 20 pages critiqued by the author of their choice. Mss must be submitted 3 weeks before the workshop. Conference brochure/guidelines available for SASE. Inquiries by e-mail OK.

☑ **SAN DIEGO STATE UNIVERSITY WRITERS' CONFERENCE**, SDSU College of Extended Studies, San Diego CA 92182-1920. (619)594-2517. Fax: (619)594-8566. E-mail: xtension@mail.sdsu.edu. Website: www.ces.sdsu.e du. **Contact:** Paula Pierce, coordinator, SDSU extension programs. Estab. 1984. Annual. Conference held the third weekend in January. Conference duration: 2 days. Average attendance: approximately 375. Fiction, nonfiction, scriptwriting, e-books. Held at the Doubletree Hotel, Mission Valley. "Each year the SDSU Writers Conference offers a variety of workshops for the beginner and the advanced writer. This conference allows the individual writer to choose which workshop best suits his/her needs. In addition to the workshops, editor/agent appointments and office hours are provided so attendees may meet with speakers, editors and agents in small, personal groups to discuss specific questions. A reception is offered Saturday immediately following the workshops where attendees may socialize with the faculty in a relaxed atmosphere. Keynote speaker is to be determined." **Agents/speakers attending include:** Betsy Amster, Loretta Barrett, Julie Castiglia, Laurie Horowitz, Jillian Manus, Angela Rinaldi. Agents will be speaking and available for meetings with attendees.
**Costs:** Approximately $250 (includes all conference workshops and office hours, coffee and pastries in the morning, lunch and reception Saturday evening).
**Accommodations:** Doubletree Hotel (800)222-TREE. Attendees must make their own travel arrangements.
**Additional Information:** Editor/agent appointments are private, one-on-one opportunities to meet with editors and agents to discuss your submission. To receive a brochure, e-mail, call or send a postcard with address to: SDSU Writers Conference, College of Extended Studies, 5250 Campanile Drive, San Diego State University, San Diego CA 92182-1920. No SASE required.

☑ **THE WILLIAM SAROYAN WRITERS' CONFERENCE**, P.O. Box 5331, Fresno CA 93755-5331. Phone/ fax: (559)224-2516. E-mail: law@pacbell.net. Website: www.homestead.com/winwinorg. **Contact:** Linda West. Estab. 1992. Annual. Conference held April 5-7, 2002. Conference duration: 3 days. Average attendance: 150. "This conference is designed to provide insights that could lift you out of the pack and into publication. You will learn from masters of the writing craft, you will discover current and future market trends, and you will meet and network with editors and agents who can sell, buy, or publish your manuscript." Fiction, nonfiction, scriptwriting. Held at the Piccadilly Inn Hotel across from the Fresno Airport. **Previous agents/speakers have included:** Leonard Bishop, David Brin, John Dunning, Marcia Preston, Andrea Brown, Kathleen Brenzel, Linda Mead, Nancy Ellis-Bell, Liz Pentacoff, Rita Robinson, Stephen Mattee. Agents will be speaking and available for meetings with attendees.
**Costs:** $225 for 3 days (includes some meals). Single day fees: $85 for Friday, $165 for Saturday, $50 for Sunday.
**Accommodations:** Special lodging rate at the Piccadilly Inn Hotel: $68 single, $78 double plus room tax. "Be sure to mention the William Saroyan Writers' Conference to obtain this special rate. Reservations must be made two weeks in advance to assure availability of room at the conference site."

## insider report

# The Perfect Pitch: One agent offers her advice on how to make the most of a writers' conference

Long before she appeared on the conference scene as a literary agent, Jandy Nelson had a passion for writing and books in all their many forms. Before joining Manus & Associates Literary Agency, Nelson worked in theater and film, as a creative writing professor, and was an award-winning poet. "My greatest enthusiasm has always been for words on the page," Nelson says. "I am crazy about books and always have been." She channels this love for books into her work. "As a literary agent, your life is all about finding and getting great writing out there."

Nelson excels in her role as agent, representing such books as *Catfish and Mandala*, by Whiting Award winner Andrew Pham, published by Farrar, Strauss & Giroux. *Catfish and Mandala*, a *New York Times* Notable Book of the Year, also won the prestigious

**Jandy Nelson**

Kiriyama Book Prize and the QPB award for best new nonfiction. Nelson also represented Lisa Huang Fleishman, author of *Dream of the Walled City*, published by Pocket Books. With Nelson's expertise on their side, many other successful writers have been published.

Helping new writers is just one rewarding aspect of being a literary agent, according to Nelson. She says there is also a more personal aspect to the process. "I know how much books have enriched my life, not only how much pleasure they have given me but also how much literature has guided me through difficult periods. I find it very exciting to be part of a community that is dedicated to publishing books that enrich and inspire."

Of course, a literary agent's life is not without disappointments. "A couple of years ago a manuscript came into the office that I fell in love with. I sent it out to editors and many responded as enthusiastically as I did. But time after time, the marketing departments at the publishing houses said there was no market for this type of novel.

"I found it very frustrating because I truly believed there was a big audience for this book." However, these difficulties can turn into the most triumphant part of agenting, as Nelson ultimately proved the marketing departments wrong. "It took a year to sell, but when the novel was published, it made the San Francisco bestseller list within two weeks and now has won a national prize and is doing phenomenally well."

One of the ways Nelson finds new projects to champion is through writers' conferences. "I always get very inspired by the writers I meet at conferences and return to the office with renewed excitement about the work we are all doing." Nelson also gives workshops at conferences, educating writers about the industry. She says it's important for writers to learn the business side of writing, such as "how to find an agent that is right for them, how to work with an editor, what the publishing process is actually like, how to market their work, and how the industry is changing."

For writers, the conferences also offer the opportunity to make contacts with agents, editors and other writers. Noting the excitement of connecting to the larger writing community through conferences, Nelson points out an additional benefit for attendees. "Ultimately writers will be inspired not only to get typing but to get their work in the mail!"

To have a successful experience at a conference, Nelson advises writers to attend as many lectures, readings, and workshops as possible, but most importantly to come prepared to meet with agents and editors. The "pitch," or the 10-15 minutes a writer might have to present their ideas, is crucial. "You want to make sure that you have your pitch down so that you don't waste that valuable time talking about the weather or your mother because you're nervous or unprepared.

"Practice your 'pitch' on friends or in the mirror or even write it down so by the time you pitch it, you're relaxed and confident. Sometimes people are shaking when they sit down for a meeting with me, but it's important to remember that agents are really excited to meet writers and hear about their work. We aren't scary at all—remember we are bookworms!"

Creating a pitch is easy according to Nelson. "For fiction, break your novel down to 1) a set up 2) a hook and 3) a resolution, which doesn't mean giving away the ending—don't do that." But what if your novel doesn't lend itself easily to a plot description? "If your novel is more literary or more character driven, try to distill the novel to its essence and convey in a few sentences the spirit of the work," Nelson advises. "Sometimes it's helpful to compare your book with others like it."

Nonfiction requires a slightly different approach, but nothing more difficult. She says the nonfiction pitch should cover four questions: "1) What is the angle and concept of the book; 2) Who is the audience and why do they need this book; 3) Why you are an authority; and 4) What differentiates this book from all other books on this topic that are out there." Nelson highlights two other key factors authors should keep in mind for the nonfiction pitch. "With nonfiction the title is very important, as well as the 'platform' of the author. The 'platform' is that author's access to an audience outside normal avenues of distribution—for instance a lecture circuit, radio show, TV show, or column in a newspaper."

Nelson points out some common blunders writers can avoid when making their pitch. For one, a writer should not sit down and tell the whole plot of their novel, scene by scene. Also, becoming hostile with an agent or editor if they offer critical feedback is not a good idea. "You want to open doors, not shut them!" The writer should not act too "kooky" either. Nelson recounts one story that happened to Jillian Manus at a writer's conference where a writer "pretended she was a turtle and crawled around on the floor!"

"Remember," she says, "PERFECT PITCH RESONATES."

Even though an author may be desperate for representation, Nelson reminds them to be discerning. While agents are looking to select writing they would represent, writers should also be looking for agents who seem like a good match. "It is crucial that an agent and writer like each other and get along well. It is a very significant relationship, especially these days with editors jumping around from publishing house to publishing house, an agent is sometimes the only stability a writer has in the industry."

> The most important element of this relationship "is that you share a common vision about the project at hand as well as the writer's long-term career goals. And of course, your agent should be wildly enthusiastic about your work and dedicated to getting it published well."
>
> After all, an agent has to retain her faith in your book to keep submitting despite a year of rejections. How else can she prove all those marketing departments wrong?
> —Joshua Easton

**Additional Information:** Offers "Persie" writing contest in connection with conference. Also offers a pre-conference ms critique service for fiction and nonfiction mss. Fees: $35/book chapter or short story, maximum length 20 pgs., double-spaced. Send SASE for brochure and guidelines. Fax and e-mail inquiries OK.

**SOCIETY OF CHILDREN'S BOOK WRITERS AND ILLUSTRATORS/NATIONAL CONFERENCE ON WRITING & ILLUSTRATING FOR CHILDREN**, 8271 Beverly Blvd., Los Angeles CA 90048-4515. (323)782-1010. Fax: (323)782-1892. E-mail: scbwi@juno.com. Website: www.scbwi.org. **Contact:** Stephen Mooser, president. Estab. 1972. Annual. Conference held in August. Conference duration: 4 days. Average attendance: 500. Writing and illustrating for children. Held at the Century Plaza Hotel in Los Angeles. **Previous agents/speakers have included:** Andrea Brown, Steven Malk, Scott Treimel (agents), Ashley Bryan, Bruce Coville, Karen Hesse, Harry Mazer, Lucia Monfried and Russell Freedman. Agents will be speaking and available for meetings with attendees.
**Costs:** $320 (members); $350 (late registration, members); $415 (nonmembers). Cost does not include hotel room.
**Accommodations:** Information on overnight accommodations made available.
**Additional Information:** Ms and illustration critiques are available. Conference brochures/guidelines are available June with SASE.

**☑ SOCIETY OF SOUTHWESTERN AUTHORS WRITERS' CONFERENCE—WRANGLING WITH WRITING**, P.O. Box 30355, Tucson AZ 85751-0355. (520)546-9382. Fax: (520)296-0409. E-mail: wporter202@aol.com. Website: www.azstarnet.com/nonprofit/ssa. **Contact:** Penny Porter, conference chair. Estab. 1972. Annual. Two-day conference held January 18-19, 2002. Maximum attendance: 400. Fiction, nonfiction, screenwriting, poetry. Conference offers 36 workshops covering all genres of writing; pre-scheduled one-on-one interviews with agents, editors and publishers. **Agents/speakers attending include:** Editors: Bob Early, Harvey Starbrough. Agents: Mark Ryan, Donald Maass, Barbara Gislason. Keynote speakers for 2002: Ray Bradbury (author); Jacqueline Mitchard; Elmore Leonard, Alan Dean Foster.
**Costs:** $250 (general); $200 (member).
**Additional Information:** Conference brochures/guidelines are available for SASE.

**☑ SOUTHERN CALIFORNIA WRITERS' CONFERENCE**, 4406 Park Blvd., Suite E, San Diego CA 92116. Phone/fax: (619)282-2983. E-mail: wewrite@writersconference.com. Website: www.writersconference.com. **Contact:** Michael Steven Gregory, executive director. Estab. 1986. Annually. Conference held February 15-18, 2002. Conference duration: 3 days. Average attendance: 250. Fiction and nonfiction, with particular emphasis on reading and critiquing. Held at Holiday Inn Hotel and Suites located in Old Town, San Diego. "Extensive reading and critiquing workshops by working writers. Over 3 dozen 2-hour workshops and no time limit late-night sessions." Agents will be speaking and available for meetings with attendees.
**Costs:** $275 (includes all workshops and events, as well as Saturday evening banquet).
**Accommodations:** Discounted rates available at Holiday Inn. Complimentary shuttle service provided from airport and Amtrak.
**Additional Information:** Late-night read and critique workshops run until 3 or 4 a.m. Brochures available for SASE or on website. Inquiries by e-mail and fax OK.

**SQUAW VALLEY COMMUNITY OF WRITERS FICTION WORKSHOP**, P.O. Box 2352. Olympic Valley CA 96146-2352. (530)274-8551. E-mail: svcw@oro.net. Website: www.squawvalleywriters.org. **Contact:** Ms. Brett Hall Jones, executive director. Estab. 1969. Annual. Conference held August. Conference duration: 1 week. Average attendance: 125. Fiction, nonfiction. Held in Squaw Valley, California—the site of the 1960 Winter Olympics. The workshops are held in a ski lodge at the foot of this spectacular ski area. **Previous agents/speakers have included:** Betsy Amster, Michael Carlisle, Elyse Cheney, Christy Fletcher, B.J. Robbins. Agents will be speaking and available for meetings with attendees.
**Costs:** $625 (includes tuition, dinners). Housing is extra.
**Accommodations:** Rooms available. Single: $425/week. Double: $275/week per person. Multiple room: $175/week per person. Shuttle available for additional cost. Contact conference for more information.
**Additional Information:** Brochures available March for SASE or on website. Inquiries by e-mail OK.

☑ **UCLA EXTENSION WRITERS' PROGRAM**, 10995 Le Conte Ave., #440, Los Angeles CA 90024. (310)825-9415 or (800)388-UCLA. Fax: (310)206-7382. E-mail: rnoguchi@unex.ucla.edu. Website: www.uclaextension.org/writers. **Contact:** Rick Noguchi, program manager. Estab. 1891. Courses held year-round with one-day or intensive weekend workshops to 12-week courses. Conference held February 7-10, 2002. Fiction, nonfiction, scriptwriting. "The diverse offerings span introductory seminars to professional novel and script completion workshops. The annual Los Angeles Writers Conference and a number of 1, 2 and 4-day intensive workshops are popular with out-of-town students due to their specific focus and the chance to work with industry professionals. The most comprehensive and diverse continuing education writing program in the country, offering over 500 courses a year including: screenwriting, fiction, writing for young people, poetry, nonfiction, playwriting, publishing and writing for interactive multimedia. Courses are offered in Los Angeles on the UCLA campus and Universal City as well as online over the Internet. Adult learners in the UCLA Extension Writers' Program study with professional screenwriters, fiction writers, playwrights, poets, nonfiction writers, and interactive multimedia writers, who bring practical experience, theoretical knowledge, and a wide variety of teaching styles and philosophies to their classes." Online courses are also available. Call for details.
**Costs:** Vary from $85-425.
**Accommodations:** Students make own arrangements. The program can provide assistance in locating local accommodations.
**Additional Information:** "Some advanced-level classes have manuscript submittal requirements; instructions are always detailed in the quarterly UCLA Extension course catalog." Screenwriting prize, the Diane Thomas Award, is given annually. Contact program for details. Conference brochures/guidelines are available in the Fall. Inquiries by e-mail and fax OK.

☑ **WATERSIDE PUBLISHING CONFERENCE**, 2191 San Elijo Ave., Cardiff CA 92007. (760)632-9190. Fax: (760)632-9295. E-mail: admin@waterside.com. Website: www.waterside.com. **Contact:** Kimberly Valentini. Estab. 1990 Annually. Conference held January 31-February 2, 2002. Conference duration: 3 days. Average attendance: 200. Focused on computer and technology, books and their writers and publishers. Issues in the industry that affect the genre. Held at Hilton Beach and Tennis Resort, San Diego, CA. A bayside hotel with full amenities and beautiful view. Past themes: Digital Delivery; Ask the Buyer; Author Taxes, Branding, Contracts. **Previous agents/speakers have included:** Paul Hilts (*Publishers Weekly*); Carla Bayha (Borders Books); Bob Ipsen (John Wiley & Sons); Microsoft; MightyWords.com. Agents will be speaking and available for meetings with attendees.
**Costs:** In 2002: $500 general; $250 for authors (includes all sessions and parties, meals, coffee breaks). Conference attendees get a discounted room rate at the Hilton.
**Accommodations:** Other hotels are in the area if conference hotel is booked or too expensive.
**Additional Information:** Brochures available via fax or e-mail, or call.

# Northwest (AK, ID, MT, OR, WA, WY)

**FLATHEAD RIVER WRITERS CONFERENCE**, P.O. Box 7711, Whitefish MT 59904-7711. (406)755-7272. Fax: (406)862-4839. E-mail: thehows@digisys.net. **Contact:** Jake How, chairman. Estab. 1990. Annual. Conference held early October. Conference duration: 3 days. Average attendance: 110. "We provide several small, intense three-day workshops on a wide variety of subjects every year, including fiction, nonfiction, screenwriting, and working with editors and agents." Held at Grouse Mountain Lodge. Workshops, panel discussions and speakers focus on novels, nonfiction, screenwriting, short stories, magazine articles, and the writing industry. **Previous agents/speakers have included:** Rob Simbeck, Marcela Landres, Amy Rennert, Ben Mikaelsen, Sandra West, Terry Borst, Ron Carlson. Agents will be speaking and available for meetings with attendees.
**Costs:** $135 (includes breakfast and lunch, but does not include lodging).
**Accommodations:** Rooms available at discounted rates: $85/night. Whitefish is a resort town, and less expensive lodging can be arranged.
**Additional Information:** "By limiting attendance to 110 people, we assure a quality experience and informal, easy access to the presentors and other attendees." Brochures available June. Inquiries by e-mail OK.

Ⓝ **JACKSON HOLE WRITERS CONFERENCE**, University of Wyoming, Box 3972, Laramie WY 82071-3972. (877)733-3618, #2. Fax: (307)766-3914. E-mail: kguille@uwyo.edu. Website: luci.uwyo.edu/conferences/jackson.htm. Conference Coordinator: Barbara Barnes. Estab. 1991. Annual. Conference held in July. Conference duration: 4 days. Average attendance: 70. For fiction, creative nonfiction, screenwriting. Offers critiques from authors, agents and editors. Write for additional information or visit website.

☑ **WHIDBEY ISLAND WRITERS' CONFERENCE**, P.O. Box 1289, Langley WA 98260. (360)331-6714. E-mail: writers@whidbey.com. Website: www.whidbey.com/writers. **Contact:** Celeste Mergens, director. Annual. Conference held first week in March. Conference duration: 3 days. Average attendance: 250 people. Fiction, nonfiction, screenwriting, writing for children, poetry, travel and naturalist. Conference held at conference hall, and break-out fireside chats in local homes near sea. Panels include: "Meeting the Challenges of Writing," "The Art of Revision."

**Agents/speakers attending include:** Catherine Coulter, Dale Furutani, Craig Lesley (fiction), Dan Millman, Dan Pynter, Eva Shaw (nonfiction), Marvin Bell, David Lee, Paggy Schumacher (poetry), Jandy Nelson (agent), Damaris Rowland (agent), Esmond Harmsworth (agent).
**Costs:** $258 before November 30; $308 after. Volunteer discounts available; early registration encouraged.
**Accommodations:** Information available for SASE. Shuttles to conference from airport can be arranged.
**Additional Information:** "If registrant desires an agent/editor consultation, pre-submission of first 5 pages and a synopsis is encouraged." Brochures available for SASE or on website. Inquiries by e-mail OK.

**WILLAMETTE WRITERS CONFERENCE**, 9045 SW Barbur, Suite 5-A, Portland OR 97219. (503)452-1592. Fax: (503)452-0372. E-mail: wilwrite@willamettewriters.com. Website: www.willamettewriters.com. **Contact:** Bill Johnson. Estab. 1968. Annual. Conference held August 2002. Average attendance: 320. Fiction, nonfiction, scriptwriting. "Willamette Writers is open to all writers, and we plan our conference accordingly. We offer workshops on all aspects of fiction, nonfiction, marketing, scriptwriting, the creative process, etc. Also we invite top notch inspirational speakers for key note addresses. Recent theme was 'Writing Your Future.' We always include at least one agent or editor panel and offer a variety of topics of interest to both fiction, screenwriters and nonfiction writers." **Previous editors/agents have included:** Mark Ryan, agent; Claire Eddy, Tor/Forge Books; Rachel Kahen, Crown Publishers; Mira Son, Avalon Books; Frederick Levy, Marty Katz Productions; Julian Fowles, Asparza-Katz Productions; Christopher Vogler, *The Writer's Journey*. Agents will be speaking and available for meetings with attendees.
**Costs:** Cost for full conference including meals is $210 members; $246 nonmembers.
**Accomodations:** If necessary, these can be made on an individual basis. Some years special rates are available.
**Additional Information:** Conference brochures/guidelines are available for catalog-size SASE.

## Canada

**THE FESTIVAL OF THE WRITTEN ARTS**, Box 2299, Sechelt, British Columbia V0N 3A0 Canada. (800)565-9631 or (604)885-9631. Fax: (604)885-3967. E-mail: written_arts@sunshine.net. Website: www.sunshine.net/rockwood. **Contact:** Gail Bull, festival producer. Estab. 1983. Annual. Festival held August 8-11, 2002. Average attendance: 3,500. To promote "all writing genres." Festival held at the Rockwood Centre. "The Centre overlooks the town of Sechelt on the Sunshine Coast. The lodge around which the Centre was organized was built in 1937 as a destination for holidayers arriving on the old Union Steamship Line; it has been preserved very much as it was in its heyday. A new twelve-bedroom annex was added in 1982, and in 1989 the Festival of the Written Arts constructed a 500-seat Pavilion for outdoor performances next to the annex. The festival does not have a theme. Instead, it showcases 25 or more Canadian writers in a wide variety of genres each year." **Previous agents/speakers have included:** Marilyn Bowering, Pat Carney, Lynn Coady, Roy Forbes, Mark Forsythe, Daniel Francis, Catherine Gildiner, Alison Gordon, Naomi Klein, Myrna Kostash, Dennis Lee, Annabel Lyon, Rita Moir, Donna Morrissey, David Adams Richards, Fred Stenson, Gwen Southin, Howard White, Jack Whyte. Agents will be speaking.
**Costs:** $12 per event or $175 for a four-day pass (Canadian).
**Accommodations:** Lists of hotels and bed/breakfast available.
**Additional Information:** The festival runs contests during the 3½ days of the event. Prizes are books donated by publishers. Brochures/guidelines are available.

**FESTIVAL OF WORDS**, 88 Saskatchewan St. E., Moose Jaw, Saskatchewan S6H 0V4 Canada. (306)691-0557. Fax: (306)693-2994. E-mail: word.festival@sk.sympatico.ca. Website: www.3.sk.sympatico.ca/praifes. **Contact:** Gary Hyland, coordinator; or Lori Dean, operations manager. Estab. 1997. Annual. Festival held July 25-28, 2002. Festival duration: 4 days. The festival celebrates the imaginative uses of language, and features fiction and nonfiction writers, screenwriters, poets, children's authors, songwriters, dramatists and film makers. Held at the Moose Jaw Public Library/Art Museum complex and in Crescent Park. **Previous agents/speakers have included:** Jane Urquhart, Susan Musgrave, M.T. Kelly, Terry Jordan, Sharon Butala, Maryann Kovalski, Allan Fotheringham, Pamela Wallin, Bonnie Burnard, Erika Ritter, Wayson Choy, Koozma Tarasoff, Lorna Crozier, Sheree Fitch, Nino Ricci.
**Costs:** $110 for 2001 (includes 3 meals).
**Accommodations:** Motels, hotels, campgrounds, bed and breakfasts.
**Additional Information:** "Our festival is an ideal meeting ground for people who love words to meet and mingle, promote their books and meet their fans." Brochures available for SASE. Inquiries by e-mail and fax OK.

**MARITIME WRITERS' WORKSHOP**, Extension & Summer Session, UNB Box 4400, Fredericton, New Brunswick E3B 5A3 Canada. Phone/fax: (506)474-1144. E-mail: K4JC@unb.ca. Website: www.unb.ca/web/coned/writers/writers.htm. **Contact:** Rhona Sawlor, coordinator. Estab. 1976. Annual. Conference held annually in July. Average attendance: 50. "Workshops in four areas: fiction, poetry, nonfiction, writing for children." Site is University of New Brunswick, Fredericton campus.
**Costs:** In 2001: $350, tuition; $135 meals; $125/double room; $145/single room (Canadian).
**Accommodations:** On-campus accommodations and meals.

**Additional Information:** "Participants must submit 10-20 manuscript pages which form a focus for workshop discussions." Must be at least 18 years old. Brochures are available after March. No SASE necessary. Inquiries by e-mail and fax OK.

**SAGE HILL WRITING EXPERIENCE**, Box 1731, Saskatoon, Saskatchewan S7K 2Z4 Canada. Phone/fax: (306)652-7395. E-mail: sage.hill@sk.sympatico.ca. Website: www.lights.com/sagehill (features complete program, including application and scholarship information). **Contact:** Steven Ross Smith, executive director. Annual. Workshops held in August and November. Workshop duration 10-21 days. Attendance: limited to 40-50. "Sage Hill Writing Experience offers a special working and learning opportunity to writers at different stages of development. Top quality instruction, low instructor-student ratio and the beautiful Sage Hill settings offer conditions ideal for the pursuit of excellence in the arts of fiction, nonfiction, poetry and playwriting." The Sage Hill location features "individual accommodation, in-room writing area, lounges, meeting rooms, healthy meals, walking woods and vistas in several directions." Seven classes are held: Introduction to Writing Fiction & Poetry; Fiction Workshop; Nonfiction Workshop; Writing Young Adult Fiction Workshop; Poetry Workshop; Poetry Colloquium; Fiction Colloquium; Playwriting Lab; Fall Poetry Colloquium. 2002 Application deadlines are: April 25, July 30. **Previous agents/speakers have included:** Bonnie Burnard, Elizabeth Philips, Dennis Cooley, Daniel David Moses, Dianne Warren and Tim Lilburn.
**Costs:** $675 (Canadian) includes instruction, accommodation, meals and all facilities. Fall Poetry Colloquium: $975.
**Accommodations:** On-site individual accommodations located at Lumsden 45 kilometers outside Regina. Fall Colloquium is at Muenster, Saskatchewan, 150 kilometers east of Saskatoon.
**Additional Information:** For Introduction to Creative Writing: A five-page sample of your writing or a statement of your interest in creative writing; list of courses taken required. For workshop and colloquium program: A résumé of your writing career and a 12-page sample of your work plus 5 pages of published work required. Guidelines are available for SASE. Inquiries by e-mail and fax OK. Scholarships and bursaries are available.

**THE VANCOUVER INTERNATIONAL WRITERS FESTIVAL**, 1398 Cartwright St., Vancouver, British Columbia V6H 3R8 Canada. (604)681-6330. Fax: (604)681-6400. E-mail: viwf@writersfest.bc.ca. Website: www.writersfest.bc.ca (includes information on festival). **Contact:** Jane Davidson, general manager. Estab. 1988. Annual. Held October 2002. Average attendance: 11,000. "This is a festival for readers and writers. The program of events is diverse and includes readings, panel discussions, seminars. Lots of opportunities to interact with the writers who attend." Held on Granville Island—in the heart of Vancouver. Two professional theaters are used as well as Performance Works (an open space). "We try to avoid specific themes. Programming takes place between February and June each year and is by invitation." **Previous agents/speakers have included:** Margaret Atwood, Maeve Binchy, J.K. Rowling.
**Costs:** Tickets are $6-20 (Canadian).
**Accommodations:** Local tourist info can be provided when necessary and requested.
**Additional Information:** Brochures/guidelines are available for SASE after August. Inquiries by e-mail and fax OK. "A reminder—this is a festival, a celebration, not a conference or workshop."

**WINNIPEG INTERNATIONAL WRITERS FESTIVAL**, 624-100 Arthur St., Winnipeg, Manitoba R3B 1H3 Canada. (204)927-7323. Fax: (204)927-7320. E-mail: info@winnipegwords.com. Website: www.winnipegwords.com. **Contact:** Kathleen Darby, executive director/producer. Estab. 1997. Annual. Conference held last week of September. Conference duration: 6 days. Average attendance: 10,000. Fiction, nonfiction, scriptwriting. All areas of written/spoken word. Previous themes: Words of Wisdom, Home. **Previous speakers/agents have included:** Michael Ondaatje, P.K. Page, Esta Spaldina. Agents will be speaking.
**Costs:** $10-30.
**Additional Information:** Brochures available on website. Inquiries by e-mail or fax OK.

**A WRITER'S W\*O\*R\*L\*D**, Surrey Writers' Conference, 10707 146th St., Surrey, British Columbia V3R 1T5 Canada. (604)589-2221. Fax: (604)588-9286. E-mail: ikmason@bc.sympatico.ca. Website: www.surreywritersconference.BC.ca. Principal: Bonnie Deren. Estab. 1992. Annual. Conference held October 18-20, 2002. Conference duration: 3 days. Average attendance: 400. Conference for fiction (romance/science fiction/fantasy/mystery—changes focus depending upon speakers and publishers scheduled), nonfiction, scriptwriting and poetry. "For everyone from beginner to professional." Conference held at Sheraton Guildford. **Agent/speakers attending have included:** Meredith Bernstein (Meredith Bernstein Literary Agency), Charlotte Gusay (Charlotte Gusay Literary Agency), Donald Maass (Donald Maass Literary Agency), Denise Marcil (Denise Marcil Literary Agency), Anne Sheldon and Michael Vidor (The Hardy Agency). Agents will be speaking and available for meetings with attendees.
**Costs:** Approximately $399.
**Accommodations:** On request will provide information on hotels and B&Bs. Conference rate: $109 (1999). Attendee must make own arrangements for hotel and transportation. For accomodations, call (800)661-2818.
**Additional Information:** Writer's contest entries must be submitted about 1 month early. Length: 1,000 words fiction, nonfiction, poetry, young writers (19 or less). Cash prizes awarded. Contest is judged by a qualified panel of writers and educators. Write, call or e-mail for additional information.

# Resources
## Professional Organizations

### ORGANIZATIONS FOR AGENTS

**Association of Authors' Representatives (AAR)**, P.O. Box 237201, Ansonia Station, New York NY 10023. Website: www.aar-online.org. A list of member agents is available for $7 and SAE with 99¢ postage.

**Association of Authors' Agents**, 62 Grafton Way, London W1P 5LD, England. (011) 44 7387 2076.

### ORGANIZATIONS FOR WRITERS

The following professional organizations publish newsletters and hold conferences and meetings at which they often share information on agents. Organizations with an asterisk (*) have members who are liaisons to the AAR

**Academy of American Poets**, 584 Broadway, Suite 1208, New York NY 10012-3250. (212)274-0343. Website: www.poets.org/index.cfm.

**American Medical Writers Association**, 40 W. Gude Dr., Suite 101, Rockville MD 20850-1192. (301)294-5303. Website: www.amwa.org.

**\*American Society of Journalists & Authors**, 1501 Broadway, Suite 302, New York NY 10036. (212)997-0947. Website: www.asja.org.

**American Translators Association**, 225 Reinekers Lane, Suite 590, Alexandria VA 22314. (703)683-6100. Website: www.atanet.org.

**Asian American Writers' Workshop**, 16 W. 32nd St., Suite 10A, New York NY 10001. (212)494-0061. Website: www.aaww.org

**\*Associated Writing Programs**, The Tallwood House, Mail stop 1E3, George Mason University, Fairfax VA 22030. (703)993-4301. Website: www.awpwriter.org.

**\*The Authors Guild Inc.**, 330 W. 42nd St., 29th Floor, New York NY 10036. (212)563-5904. Website: www.authorsguild.org.

**The Authors League of America, Inc.**, 330 W. 42nd St., New York NY 10036. (212)564-8350.

**Council of Writers Organizations**, 12724 Sagamore Rd., Leawood KS 66209. (913)451-9023. Website: www.councilofwriters.com.

**\*The Dramatists Guild**, 1501 Broadway, Suite 701, New York NY 10036. (212)398-9366.

**Education Writers Association**, 1331 H. St. NW, Suite 307, Washington DC 20005. (202)637-9700. Website: www.ewa.org.

**\*Horror Writers Association**, S.P. Somtow, President, P.O. Box 50577, Palo Alto CA 94303. Website: www.horror.org.

**International Association of Crime Writers Inc.**, North American Branch, P.O. Box 8674, New York NY 10016. (212)243-8966.

**International Television Association**, 9202 N. Meridian St., Suite 200, Indianapolis IN 46260. (317)816-6269. Website: www.itva.org.

**The International Women's Writing Guild**, P.O. Box 810, Gracie Station, New York NY 10028-0082. (212)737-7536. Website: www.iwwg.com. Provides a literary agent list to members and holds "Meet the Agents and Editors" in April and October.

**\*Mystery Writers of America (MWA)**, 17 E. 47th St., 6th Floor, New York NY 10017. (212)888-8171. Website: www.mysterywriters.net.

**National Association of Science Writers**, Box 294, Greenlawn NY 11740. (631)757-5664. Website: www.nasw.org.

**National League of American Pen Women**, 1300 17th St. NW, Washington DC 20036-1973. (202)785-1997. Website: http://members.aol.com/penwomen/pen.htm.

**National Writers Association**, 3140 S. Peoria, Suite 295, Aurora CO 80014. (303)841-0246. Website: www.nationalwriters.com. In addition to agent referrals, also operates an agency for members.

**\*National Writers Union**, 113 University Place, 6th Floor, New York NY 10003-4527. (212)254-0279. Website: www.nwu.org. A trade union, this organization has an agent database available to members.

**\*PEN American Center**, 568 Broadway, New York NY 10012-3225. (212)334-1660. Website: www.pen.org.

**\*Poets & Writers**, 72 Spring St., Suite 301, New York NY 10012. (212)226-3586. Website: www.pw.org. Operates an information line, taking calls from 11-3 EST Monday through Friday.

**Poetry Society of America**, 15 Gramercy Park, New York NY 10003. (212)254-9628. Website: www.poetrysociety.org.

**\*Romance Writers of America**, 3707 F.M. 1960 West, Suite 555, Houston TX 77068. (281)440-6885. Website: www.rwanational.com. Publishes an annual agent list for members for $10.

**\*Science Fiction and Fantasy Writers of America**, P.O. Box 171, Unity ME 04988-0171. Website: www.sfwa.org.

**Society of American Business Editors & Writers**, University of Missouri, School of Journalism, 76 Gannett Hall, Columbia MO 65211. (573)882-7862. Website: www.sabew.org.

**Society of American Travel Writers**, 4101 Lake Boone Trail, Suite 201, Raleigh NC 27607. (919)787-5181. Website: www.satw.org.

**\*Society of Children's Book Writers & Illustrators**, 8271 Beverly Blvd., Los Angeles CA 90048. (323)782-1010. Website: www.scbwi.org.

**Volunteer Lawyers for the Arts**, One E. 53rd St., 6th Floor, New York NY 10022. (212)319-2787. Website: www.vlany.org.

**Washington Independent Writers**, 220 Woodward Bldg., 733 15th St. NW, Washington DC 20005. (202)347-4973. Website: www.washwriter.org/.

**Western Writers of America**, 1012 Fair St., Franklin TN 37064. (615)791-1444. Website: www.imt.net/~gedison.

**Writers Guild of Alberta**, Main Floor, Percy Page Centre, 11759 Groat Rd., Edmonton, Alberta T5M 3K6 Canada. (780)422-8174. Website: http://writersguild.ab.ca.

**\*Writers Guild of America-East**, 555 W. 57th St., New York NY 10019. (212)767-7800. Website: www.wgaeast.org/. Provides list of WGA signatory agents for $1.29.

**Writers Guild of America-West**, 7000 W. Third St., Los Angeles CA 90048. (323)951-4000. Website: www.wga.org. Provides a list of WGA signatory agents for $2.50 and SASE sent to Agency Department.

# Websites of Interest

## WRITING

**Delphi Forums** (www.delphi.com)
This site hosts forums on many topics including writing and publishing. Just type "writing" in the search bar, and you'll find pages where you can talk about your craft.

**Zuzu's Petals Literary Resource** (www.zuzu.com)
Contains 7,000 organized links to helpful resources for writers, artists, performers, and researchers. Zuzu's Petals also publishes an electronic quarterly.

**Writer's Exchange** (http://writerexchange.about.com)
This site, hosted by writer Susan Molthrop, is a constantly updated resource devoted to the business of writing. Molthrop's goal is to include "everything I can discover to make your writing better, easier, and more fun."

**Inkspot** (www.inkspot.com)
This site by the publishers of *Inklings*, a free biweekly newsletter for writers, includes market information, writing tips, interviews, and networking opportunities.

## AGENTS

**WritersNet** (www.writers.net)
This site includes a bulletin board where writers can discuss their experiences with agents.

**Agent Research and Evaluation** (www.agentresearch.com)
This is the website of AR&E, a company that specializes in keeping tabs on literary agents. For a fee you can order their varied services to learn more about a specific agent.

**The Query Guild** (www.queryguild.com)
A working tool where writers can post queries for samples or receive feedback from other authors.

**Writer Beware** (www.sfwa.org/beware)
The Science Fiction Writers of America's page of warnings about agents and subsidy publishers.

**Writer's Market** (www.writersmarket.com)
This giant, searchable database includes agents and publishers, and offers daily updates tailored to your individual needs.

## SCREENWRITING

**The Hollywood Reporter** (www.hollywoodreporter.com)
Online version of print magazine for screenwriters. Get the buzz on the movie biz.

**Hollywood Creative Directory** (www.hcdonline.com)
By joining this website, you'll have access to listings of legitimate players in the film, television, and new media industry.

**MovieBytes** (www.moviebytes.com)
Subscribe to **MovieBytes'** Who's Buying What to learn which agencies and managers have sold which screenplays to which studios and production companies.

**Daily Variety** (http://nt.excite.com/142/variety)
This site archives the top stories from Daily Variety. Check here for the latest scoop on the movie and TV biz.

**Samuel French, Inc.** (www.samuelfrench.com/index.html)
This is the website of play publisher Samuel French that includes an index of authors and titles.

**Screenwriter's Heaven** (www.impactpc.freeserve.co.uk)
This is a page of links to many resources for screenwriters from workshops and competitions to scripts and software.

**Done Deal** (www.scriptsales.com)
The most useful features of this screenwriting site include descriptions of recently sold scripts, a list of script agents, and a list of production companies.

## MARKETING AND PUBLICISTS

**BookTalk** (www.booktalk.com)
This site "offers authors an opportunity to announce and market new releases to millions of viewers across the globe."

**Book Marketing Update** (http://bookmarket.com)
This website by John Kremer, author of *1001 Ways to Market Your Book*, offers helpful tips for marketing books and many useful links to publishing websites. Also offers an e-newsletter so writers may share their marketing success stories.

**Guerrilla Marketing** (www.gmarketing.com)
The writers of *Guerrilla Marketing for Writers* provide many helpful resources to help you successfully market your book.

**About Publishing** (http://publishing.about.com)
This website provides a wide range of information about publishing, including several articles on independent publicists.

**Authorlink** (www.authorlink.com)
"The news, information and marketing community for editors, literary agents and writers." Showcases manuscripts of experienced and beginning writers.

**BookWire** (www.bookwire.com)
BookWire bills itself as the book industry's most comprehensive online information source. The site includes industry news, features, reviews, fiction, events, interviews, and links to other book sites.

**Publishers Lunch** (www.publisherslunch.com)
This site allows you to sign up for the free newsletter, which offers daily updates on what's going on in the wonderful world of publishing. It's a good way to keep on top of the market.

**Writer's Digest** (www.writersdigest.com)
This site includes information about writing books and magazines from Writer's Digest. It also has a huge, searchable database of writer's guidelines from thousands of publishers.

## ORGANIZATIONS

**The Association of Authors' Representatives** (www.aar-online.org)
This association page includes a list of member agents, their newsletter and their canon of ethics.

**National Writer's Union** (www.nwu.org/)
Site of the National Writer's Union—the trade union for freelance writers of all genres publishing in the U.S.

**PEN American Center** (www.pen.org)
Site of the organization of writers and editors that seek to defend the freedom of expression and promote contemporary literature.

**Writer's Guild of America** (www.wga.org)
The WGA site includes advice and information on the art and craft of professional screenwriting for film, television, and interactive projects. This site offers script registration and a list of WGA signatory agencies.

---

## TABLE OF ACRONYMS

The organizations and their acronyms listed below are frequently referred to in the listings and are widely used in the industries of agenting and writing.

| | |
|---|---|
| AAA | Association of Authors' Agents |
| AAP | American Association of Publishers |
| AAR | Association of Authors' Representatives |
| ABA | American Booksellers Association |
| ABWA | Associated Business Writers of America |
| AEB | Association of Editorial Businesses |
| AFTRA | American Federation of TV and Radio Artists |
| AGVA | American Guild of Variety Artists |
| AMWA | American Medical Writer's Association |
| ASJA | American Society of Journalists and Authors |
| ATA | Association of Talent Agents |
| AWA | Aviation/Space Writers Association |
| CAA | Canadian Authors Association |
| DGA | Director's Guild of America |
| GWAA | Garden Writers Association of America |
| HWA | Horror Writers of America |
| IACP | International Association of Culinary Professionals |
| MOW | Movie of the Week |
| MWA | Mystery Writers of America, Inc. |
| NASW | National Association of Science Writers |
| NLAPW | National League of American Pen Women |
| NWA | National Writers Association |
| OWAA | Outdoor Writers Association of America, Inc. |
| RWA | Romance Writers of America |
| SAG | Screen Actor's Guild |
| SATW | Society of American Travel Writers |
| SCBWI | Society of Children's Book Writers & Illustrators |
| SFRA | Science Fiction Research Association |
| SFWA | Science Fiction and Fantasy Writers of America |
| SPWA | South Plains Writing Association |
| WGA | Writers Guild of America |
| WIA | Women in the Arts Foundation, Inc. |
| WIF | Women in Film |
| WICI | Women in Communications, Inc. |
| WIW | Washington Independent Writers |
| WMG | Women's Media Group |
| WNBA | Women's National Book Association |
| WRW | Washington Romance Writers (chapter of RWA) |
| WWA | Western Writers of America |

# Glossary

**Above the line.** A budgetary term for movies and TV. The line refers to money budgeted for creative talent, such as actors, writers, directors, and producers.

**Advance.** Money a publisher pays a writer prior to book publication, usually paid in installments, such as one-half upon signing the contract; one-half upon delivery of the complete, satisfactory manuscript. An advance is paid against the royalty money to be earned by the book. Agents take their percentage off the top of the advance as well as from the royalties earned.

**Auction.** Publishers sometimes bid for the acquisition of a book manuscript with excellent sales prospects. The bids are for the amount of the author's advance, guaranteed dollar amounts, advertising and promotional expenses, royalty percentage, etc.

**Backlist.** Those books still in print from previous years' publication.

**Backstory.** The history of what has happened before the action in your script takes place, affecting a character's current behavior.

**Beat.** Major plot points of a story.

**Below the line.** A budgetary term for movies and TV, referring to production costs, including production manager, cinematographer, editor and crew members such as gaffers, grips, set designers, make-up, etc.

**Bible.** The collected background information on all characters and storylines of all existing episodes, as well as projections of future plots.

**Bio.** Brief (usually one page) background information about an artist, writer, or photographer. Includes work and educational experience.

**Boilerplate.** A standardized publishing contract. Most authors and agents make many changes on the boilerplate before accepting the contract.

**Book club rights.** Rights to sell a book through a book club.

**Book packager.** Draws elements of a book together, from the initial concept to writing and marketing strategies, then sells the book package to a book publisher and/or movie producer. Also known as book producer or book developer.

**Business-size envelope.** Also known as a #10 envelope.

**Castable.** A script with attractive roles for known actors.

**Category fiction.** A term used to include all various types of fiction. See *genre*.

**Client.** When referring to a literary or script agent, "client" is used to mean the writer whose work the agent is handling.

**Clips.** Writing samples, usually from newspapers or magazines, of your published work.

**Commercial novels.** Novels designed to appeal to a broad audience. These are often broken down into categories such as western, mystery, and romance. See also *genre*.

**Concept.** A statement that summarizes a screenplay or teleplay—before the outline or treatment is written.

**Contributor's copies.** Copies of the author's book sent to the author. The number of contributor's copies is often negotiated in the publishing contract.

**Co-agent.** See *subagent*.

**Co-publishing.** Arrangement where author and publisher share publication costs and profits of a book. Also known as cooperative publishing.

**Copyediting.** Editing of a manuscript for writing style, grammar, punctuation, and factual accuracy.

**Copyright.** A means to protect an author's work.

**Cover letter.** A brief descriptive letter sent with a manuscript submitted to an agent or publisher.

**Coverage.** A brief synopsis and analysis of a script, provided by a reader to a buyer considering purchasing the work.

**Critiquing service.** A service offered by some agents in which writers pay a fee for comments on the saleability or other qualities of their manuscript. Sometimes the critique includes suggestions on how to improve the work. Fees vary, as do the quality of the critiques. See also *editing service*.

**Curriculum vitae.** Short account of one's career or qualifications (i.e., résumé).

**D person.** Development person. Includes readers and story editors through creative executives who work in development and acquisition of properties for TV and movies.

**Deal memo.** The memorandum of agreement between a publisher and author that precedes the actual contract and includes important issues such as royalty, advance, rights, distribution, and option clauses.

**Development.** The process where writers present ideas to producers overseeing the developing script through various stages to finished product.

**Division.** An unincorporated branch of a company.

**Docudrama.** A fictional film rendition of recent newsmaking events or people.

**Editing service.** A service offered by some agents in which writers pay a fee—either lump sum or per-page—to have their manuscript edited. The quality and extent of the editing varies from agency to agency. See also *critiquing service*.

**Electronic rights.** Secondary or subsidiary rights dealing with electronic/multimedia formats (e.g., the Internet, CD-ROMs, electronic magazines).

**Elements.** Actors, directors, and producers attached to a project to make an attractive package.

**El-hi.** Elementary to high school. A term used to indicate reading or interest level.

**Episodic drama.** Hour-long continuing TV show, often shown at 10 p.m.

**Evaluation fees.** Fees an agent may charge to evaluate material. The extent and quality of this evaluation varies, but comments usually concern the saleability of the manuscript.

**Exclusive.** Offering a manuscript, usually for a set period of time, to just one agent and guaranteeing that agent is the only one looking at the manuscript.

**Film rights.** May be sold or optioned by author to a person in the film industry, enabling the book to be made into a movie.

**Flap copy.** The text which appears on the inside covers of a published book which briefly tell the book's premise. Also called jacket copy.

**Floor bid.** If a publisher is very interested in a manuscript he may offer to enter a floor bid when the book goes to auction. The publisher sits out of the auction, but agrees to take the book by topping the highest bid by an agreed-upon percentage (usually 10 percent).

**Foreign rights.** Translation or reprint rights to be sold abroad.

**Foreign rights agent.** An agent who handles selling the rights to a country other than that of the first book agent. Usually an additional percentage (about 5 percent) will be added on to the first book agent's commission to cover the foreign rights agent.

**Genre.** Refers to either a general classification of writing such as a novel, poem, or short story or to the categories within those classifications, such as problem novels or sonnets. Genre fiction is a term that covers various types of commercial novels such as mystery, romance, western, science fiction, or horror.

**Ghosting/ghostwriting.** A writer puts into literary form the words, ideas, or knowledge of another person under that person's name. Some agents offer this service; others pair ghostwriters with celebrities or experts.

**Green light.** To give the go-ahead to a movie or TV project.

**Half-hour.** A 30-minute TV show, also known as a *sitcom*.

**High concept.** A story idea easily expressed in a quick, one-line description.

**Hook.** Aspect of the work that sets it apart from others.

**Imprint.** The name applied to a publisher's specific line of books.

**IRC.** International Reply Coupon. Buy at a post office to enclose with material sent outside your country to cover the cost of return postage. The recipient turns them in for stamps in their own country.

**Log line.** A one-line description of a plot as it might appear in *TV Guide*.

**Long-form TV.** Movies of the week (MOW) or *miniseries*.

**Mainstream fiction.** Fiction on subjects or trends that transcend popular novel categories such as mystery or romance. Using conventional methods, this kind of fiction tells stories about people and their conflicts.

**Marketing fee.** Fee charged by some agents to cover marketing expenses. It may be used to cover postage, telephone calls, faxes, photocopying or any other expense incurred in marketing a manuscript.

**Mass market paperbacks.** Softcover book, usually around $4 \times 7$, on a popular subject directed at a general audience and sold in groceries and drugstores as well as bookstores.

**MFTS.** Made for TV series. A series developed for television. See also episodics.

**Middle reader.** The general classification of books written for readers 9-11 years old.

**Midlist.** Those titles on a publisher's list expected to have limited sales. Midlist books are mainstream, not literary, scholarly, or genre, and are usually written by new or relatively unknown writers.

**Miniseries.** A limited dramatic series written for television, often based on a popular novel.

**MOW.** Movie of the week. A movie script written especially for television, usually seven acts with time for commercial breaks. Topics are often contemporary, sometimes controversial, fictional accounts. Also known as a made-for-TV-movie.

**Multiple contract.** Book contract with an agreement for a future book(s).

**Net receipts.** One method of royalty payment based on the amount of money a book publisher receives on the sale of the book after the booksellers' discounts, special sales discounts and returned copies.

**Novelization.** A novel created from the script of a popular movie, usually called a movie "tie-in" and published in paperback.

**Novella.** A short novel or long short story, usually 7,000 to 15,000 words. Also called a novelette.

**One-time rights.** This right allows a short story or portions of a fiction or nonfiction book to be published. The work can be printed again without violating the contract.

**Option.** Also known as a script option. Instead of buying a movie script outright, a producer buys the right to a script for a short period of time (usually six months to one year) for a small down payment. At the end of the agreed time period, if the movie has not begun production and the producer does not wish to purchase the script, the rights revert back to the scriptwriter.

**Option clause.** A contract clause giving a publisher the right to publish an author's next book.

**Outline.** A summary of a book's contents in 5 to 15 double-spaced pages; often in the form of chapter headings with a descriptive sentence or two under each one to show the scope of the book. A script's outline is a scene-by-scene narrative description of the story (10-15 pages for a ½-hour teleplay; 15-25 pages for 1-hour; 25-40 pages for 90 minutes; and 40-60 pages for a 2-hour feature film or teleplay).

**Over-the-transom.** Slang for the path of an unsolicited manuscript into the slush pile.

**Packaging.** The process of putting elements together, increasing the chances of a project being made. See also *book packager*.

**Platform.** A writer's speaking experience, interview skills, website, and other abilities which helps form a following of potential buyers for that author's book.

**Picture book.** A type of book aimed at the preschool to 8-year-old that tells the story primarily or entirely with artwork. Agents and reps interested in selling to publishers of these books often handle both artists and writers.

**Pitch.** The process where a writer meets with a producer and briefly outlines ideas that could be developed if the writer is hired to write a script for the project.

**Proofreading.** Close reading and correction of a manuscript's typographical errors.

**Property.** Books or scripts forming the basis for a movie or TV project.

**Proposal.** An offer to an editor or publisher to write a specific work, usually a package consisting of an outline and sample chapters.

**Prospectus.** A preliminary, written description of a book, usually one page in length.

**Query.** A letter written to an agent or a potential market, to elicit interest in a writer's work.

**Reader.** A person employed by an agent or buyer to go through the slush pile of manuscripts and scripts and select those worth considering.

**Release.** A statement that your idea is original, has never been sold to anyone else, and that you are selling negotiated rights to the idea upon payment.

**Remainders.** Leftover copies of an out-of-print or slow-selling book purchased from the publisher at a reduced rate. Depending on the contract, a reduced royalty or no royalty is paid on remaindered books.

**Reporting time.** The time it takes the agent to get back to you on your query or submission.

**Reprint rights.** The rights to republish your book after its initial printing.

**Royalties.** A percentage of the retail price paid to the author for each copy of the book that is sold. Agents take their percentage from the royalties earned as well as from the advance.

**SASE.** Self-addressed, stamped envelope; should be included with all correspondence.

**Scholarly books.** Books written for an academic or research audience. These are usually heavily researched, technical, and often contain terms used only within a specific field.

**Screenplay.** Script for a film intended to be shown in theaters.

**Script.** Broad term covering teleplay, screenplay, or stage play. Sometimes used as a shortened version of the word "manuscript" when referring to books.

**Serial rights.** The right for a newspaper or magazine to publish sections of a manuscript.

**Simultaneous submission.** Sending a manuscript to several agents or publishers at the same time. Simultaneous queries are common; simultaneous submissions are unacceptable to many agents or publishers.

**Sitcom.** Situation comedy. Episodic comedy script for a television series. Term comes from the characters dealing with various situations with humorous results.

**Slush pile.** A stack of unsolicited submissions in the office of an editor, agent or publisher.

**Spec script.** A script written on speculation without confirmation of a sale.

**Standard commission.** The commission an agent earns on the sales of a manuscript or script. For literary agents, this commission percentage (usually between 10 and 20 percent) is taken from the advance and royalties paid to the writer. For script agents, the commission is taken from script sales; if handling plays, agents take a percentage from the box office proceeds.

**Story analyst.** See *reader.*

**Storyboards.** Series of panels which illustrates a progressive sequence or graphics and story copy for a TV commercial, film, or filmstrip.

**Subagent.** An agent handling certain subsidiary rights, usually working in conjunction with the agent who handled the book rights. The percentage paid the book agent is increased to pay the subagent.

**Subsidiary.** An incorporated branch of a company or conglomerate (e.g., Alfred Knopf, Inc. is a subsidiary of Random House, Inc.).

**Subsidiary rights.** All rights other than book publishing rights included in a book publishing contract, such as paperback rights, bookclub rights, movie rights. Part of an agent's job is to negotiate those rights and advise you on which to sell and which to keep.

**Syndication rights.** The right which allows a television station to rerun a sit-com or drama, even if the show appeared originally on a different network.

**Synopsis.** A brief summary of a story, novel. or play. As a part of a book proposal, it is a comprehensive summary condensed in a page or page and a half, single-spaced. See also *outline.*

**Tearsheet.** Published samples of your work, usually pages torn from a magazine.

**Teleplay.** Script for television.

**Terms.** Financial provisions agreed upon in a contract.

**Textbook.** Book used in a classroom on the elementary, high school, or college level.

**Trade book.** Either a hard cover or soft cover book; subject matter frequently concerns a special interest for a general audience; sold mainly in bookstores.

**Trade paperback.** A softbound volume, usually around $5 \times 8$, published and designed for the general public, available mainly in bookstores.

**Translation rights.** Sold to a foreign agent or foreign publisher.

**Treatment.** Synopsis of a television or film script (40-60 pages for a 2-hour feature film or teleplay).

**Turnaround.** When a script has been in development but not made in the time allotted, it can be put back on the market.

**Unsolicited manuscript.** An unrequested manuscript sent to an editor, agent, or publisher.

**Young adult.** The general classification of books written for readers age 12-18.

**Young reader.** Books written for readers 5-8 years old, where artwork only supports the text.

# Contributors to the Insider Reports

**ANNE BOWLING**
Anne Bowling is the editor for *Novel & Short Story Writer's Market* and a columnist on young adult literature for *Pages* magazine.

**NANCY BREEN**
Nancy Breen is the editor for *Poet's Market*, as well as a published poet and former senior writer at Gibson Greetings.

**DON PRUES**
Don Prues is a writer and editor whose work has appeared in *The New York Post* and *The Oregonian*, and numerous Writer Digest books. Don has been managing editor of Critics Inc., editor of *Guide to Literary Agents*, and assistant editor of *Writer's Market*. His recent projects include *An Expression of The Community: Cincinnati Public Schools' Legacy of Art and Architecture* (Managing Editor, Art League Press, 2001), *Formatting and Submitting Your Manuscript* (coauthor, with Jack Neff, Writer's Digest Books, 2000), and the forthcoming *The Setting Sourcebook* (Writer's Digest Books, 2003). He lives with his wife, Jennifer Lile, in Cincinnati.

**RODNEY A. WILSON**
Rodney A. Wilson (rodneywilsonac.com) is a professional freelance writer and editor. He currently lives in Kentucky with his beautiful wife Carla and their two cats, Whisper and Lany.

**JEFF HILLARD**
Jeff Hillard is a poet, journalist, novelist, and screenwriter who has written three books of poetry. Additionally, he is editor for Writer Online and is an associate professor of English at the College of Mount St. Joseph in Cincinnati, Ohio.

**WILL ALLISON**
Will Allison is editor at large for *Zoetrope: All-Story*, former executive editor of STORY, and former editor of *Novel & Short Story Writer's Market*. He is the recipient of an Ohio Arts Council grant for fiction, has published short stories in *American Short Fiction*, *Florida Review*, and *Kansas Quarterly/ Arkansas Review*, and owns an impressive collection of rejection slips.

**H.R. LOGAN**
H.R. Logan is a freelance writer and editor currently residing in Covington, Kentucky.

**CANDY LACE**
Candy Lace is the production editor and staff writer for *Artist's & Graphic Designer's Market* and *Children's Writer's & Illustrator's Market*. Her writings have been published in *Clamor*, *Art Papers*, *Alternative Cinema*, and *Sojouner: The Women's Forum*, among other venues.

**JOSHUA EASTON**
Joshua Easton, a native of Kentucky, is a law student at Tulane University in New Orleans.

# Literary Agents Specialties Index

The subject index is divided into fiction and nonfiction subject categories for Literary Agents. To find an agent interested in the type of manuscript you've written, see the appropriate sections under subject headings that best describe your work.

## FICTION

**Action/Adventure:** Acacia House Publishing Services Ltd. 76; Ahearn Agency, Inc., The 77; Alive Communications, Inc. 78; Allen Literary Agency, Linda 78; Allred and Allred Literary Agents 78; AMG/Renaissance 79; Amsterdam Agency, Marcia 80; Authentic Creations Literary Agency 81; Authors & Artists Group, Inc. 82; Baldi Literary Agency, Malaga 82; Barrett Books Inc., Loretta 83; Bial Agency, Daniel 84; Bova Literary Agency, The Barbara 88; Brandt & Hochman Literary Agents Inc. 88; Brown Ltd., Curtis 90; Browne Ltd., Pema 90; Buck Agency, Howard 91; Cambridge Literary 92; Congdon Associates Inc., Don 95; Crawford Literary Agency 97; Curtis Associates, Inc., Richard 97; Donovan Literary, Jim 101; Ducas, Robert 103; Dupree/Miller and Associates Inc. Literary 103; Dystel Literary Management, Inc., Jane 104; Elite Online 105; Elmo Agency Inc., Ann 106; Farber Literary Agency Inc. 111; Fernandez Agent/Attorney, Justin E. 112
Fort Ross Inc. Russian-American Publishing Projects 113; Goldfarb & Associates 117; Goodman Associates 118; Grace Literary Agency, Carroll 118; Greenburger Associates, Inc., Sanford J. 118; Gregory and Radice Authors' Agents 119; Gusay Literary Agency, The Charlotte 120; Halsey Agency, Reece 121; Halsey North, Reece 121; Hamilburg Agency, Mitchell J., The 122; Harris Literary Agency, Inc., The Joy 122; Hartline Literary Agency 122; Hawkins & Associates, Inc., John 122; Henshaw Group, Richard 123; Herner Rights Agency, Susan 124; Jabberwocky Literary Agency 128; JCA Literary Agency 129; Jellinek and Murray Literary Agency 130; Kleinman, Esq., of Graybill & English L.L.C., Jeffrey M. 133; Klinger, Inc., Harvey 133; Koster Literary Agency, LLC, Elaine 134; Kraas Agency, Irene 135; Kritzer Productions, Eddie 135; Lampack Agency, Inc., Peter 136; Larsen/Elizabeth Pomada Literary Agents, Michael 136; Lazear Agency Incorporated 137; Levine Literary Agency, Paul S. 138; Lewis & Company, Karen 139; Lincoln Literary Agency, Ray 140; Literary Group, The 141; Madsen Agency, Robert 144; Marshall Agency, The Evan 146; McBride Literary Agency, Margret 147; Morrison, Inc., Henry 149; Mura Enterprises, Inc., Dee 150; Naggar Literary Agency, Jean V. 151; National Writers Literary Agency 151; New Brand Agency Group, LLC 152; Norma-Lewis Agency, The 153; Paraview, Inc. 154; Picard, Literary Agent, Alison J. 157; Quicksilver Books Literary Agents 160; Rhodes Literary Agency, Jodie 164; RLR Associates, Ltd. 168; Rotrosen Agency, LLC, Jane 171; Rubie Literary Agency, The Peter 172; Russell and Volkening 172; Sanders & Associates, Victoria 173; Scherf, Inc., Literary Management 173; Sedgeband Literary Associates 176; Serendipity Literary Agency, LLC 176; Seymour Agency, The 177; Simmons Literary Agency, Jeffrey 178; Southern Literary Group 181; Sternig & Byrne Literary Agency 183; Treimel NY, Scott 187; Van Der Leun & Associates 188; Venture Literary 189; Vines Agency, Inc., The 189; Wald Associates, Inc., Mary Jack 190; Waxman Agency, Inc., Scott 192; Weiner Literary Agency, Cherry 192; Wonderland Press, Inc., The 194; Writers House 195

**Cartoon/Comic:** Bial Agency, Daniel 84; Brown Ltd., Curtis 90; Buck Agency, Howard 91; Congdon Associates Inc., Don 95; Curtis Associates, Inc., Richard 97; Fernandez Agent/Attorney, Justin E. 112
Goodman Associates 118; Gusay Literary Agency, The Charlotte 120; Hamilburg Agency, Mitchell J., The 122; Harris Literary Agency, Inc., The Joy 122; Hawkins & Associates, Inc., John 122; Jabberwocky Literary Agency 128; Lazear Agency Incorporated 137; Levine Literary Agency, Paul S. 138; Literary Group, The 141; Madsen Agency, Robert 144; Pevner, Inc., Stephen 157; Preskill Literary Agency, Robert 159; RLR Associates, Ltd. 168; Treimel NY, Scott 187; Van Der Leun & Associates 188; Writers House 195

**Confessional:** Allred and Allred Literary Agents 78; Barrett Books Inc., Loretta 83; Bial Agency, Daniel 84; Brown Ltd., Curtis 90; Buck Agency, Howard 91; Congdon Associates Inc., Don 95; Curtis Associates, Inc., Richard 97; Fernandez Agent/Attorney, Justin E. 112
Goodman Associates 118; Gusay Literary Agency, The Charlotte 120; Hamilburg Agency, Mitchell J., The 122; Harris Literary Agency, Inc., The Joy 122; Jellinek and Murray Literary Agency 130; Kritzer Productions, Eddie 135; Lazear Agency Incorporated 137; Levine Literary Agency, Paul S. 138; Madsen Agency, Robert 144; March Tenth, Inc. 145; New Brand Agency Group, LLC 152; Serendipity Literary Agency, LLC 176; Simmons Literary Agency, Jeffrey 178; Treimel NY, Scott 187; Van Der Leun & Associates 188; Writers House 195

**Contemporary Issues:** Ahearn Agency, Inc., The 77; Alive Communications, Inc. 78; Authentic Creations Literary Agency 81; Authors & Artists Group, Inc. 82; Baldi Literary Agency, Malaga 82; Barrett Books Inc.,

Loretta 83; Bernstein & Associates, Inc., Pam 84; Bial Agency, Daniel 84; Boates Literary Agency, Reid 86; BookEnds, LLC 86; Books & Such 87; Brandt Agency, The Joan 89; Brandt & Hochman Literary Agents Inc. 88; Brown Associates Inc., Marie 89; Brown Ltd., Curtis 90; Browne Ltd., Pema 90; Buck Agency, Howard 91; Castiglia Literary Agency 93; Clark Associates, William 94; Congdon Associates Inc., Don 95; Curtis Associates, Inc., Richard 97; Delbourgo Associates, Inc., Joélle 99; Doyen Literary Services, Inc. 102; Ducas, Robert 103; Dupree/Miller and Associates Inc. Literary 103; Dystel Literary Management, Inc., Jane 104; Elmo Agency Inc., Ann 106; Farber Literary Agency Inc. 111; Fernandez Agent/Attorney, Justin E. 112

Frenkel & Associates, James 115; Freymann Literary Agency, Sarah Jane 115; Goldfarb & Associates 117; Goodman Associates 118; Goodman-Andrew Agency, Inc. 118; Greenburger Associates, Inc., Sanford J. 118; Grosjean Literary Agency, Jill 120; Grosvenor Literary Agency, The 120; Gusay Literary Agency, The Charlotte 120; Halsey Agency, Reece 121; Hamilburg Agency, Mitchell J., The 122; Harris Literary Agency, Inc., The Joy 122; Hartline Literary Agency 122; Hawkins & Associates, Inc., John 122; Herner Rights Agency, Susan 124; Jabberwocky Literary Agency 128; JCA Literary Agency 129; Jellinek and Murray Literary Agency 130; Jenks Agency, Carolyn 130; Kidde, Hoyt & Picard 132; Kleinman, Esq., of Graybill & English L.L.C., Jeffrey M. 133; Koster Literary Agency, LLC, Elaine 134; Kouts, Literary Agent, Barbara S. 134; Kritzer Productions, Eddie 135; Larsen/Elizabeth Pomada Literary Agents, Michael 136; Lazear Agency Incorporated 137; Levine Communications, Inc., James 138; Levine Literary Agency, Paul S. 138; Lincoln Literary Agency, Ray 140; Literary Group, The 141; Litwest Group, LLC 141; Lowenstein Associates, Inc. 143; Madsen Agency, Robert 144; Markowitz Literary Agency, Barbara 146; McGrath, Helen 147; Michaels Literary Agency, Inc., Doris S. 148; Multimedia Product Development, Inc. 150; Mura Enterprises, Inc., Dee 150; Naggar Literary Agency, Jean V. 151; New Brand Agency Group, LLC 152; Paraview, Inc. 154; Pevner, Inc., Stephen 157; Picard, Literary Agent, Alison J. 157; Pinder Lane & Garon-Brooke Associates, Ltd. 158; Rees Literary Agency, Helen 160; Rhodes Literary Agency, Jodie 164; RLR Associates, Ltd. 168; Robbins Literary Agency, B.J. 169; Rosenberg Group, The 170; Sanders & Associates, Victoria 173; Schiavone Literary Agency, Inc. 174; Schulman, A Literary Agency, Susan 174; Sedgeband Literary Associates 176; Shepard Agency, The 177; Singer Literary Agency Inc., Evelyn 179; Skolnick Literary Agency, Irene 179; Southern Literary Group 181; Spectrum Literary Agency 181; Spitzer Literary Agency, Philip G. 181; Stauffer Associates, Nancy 182; Straus Agency, Inc., Robin 183; Swayze Literary Agency, Carolyn 184; Travis Literary Agency, Susan 186; Treimel NY, Scott 187; Van Der Leun & Associates 188; Venture Literary 189; Vines Agency, Inc., The 189; Wald Associates, Inc., Mary Jack 190; Wales, Literary Agency, Inc. 190; Watt & Associates, Sandra 191; Wecksler-Incomco 192; Weiner Literary Agency, Cherry 192; Wieser & Wieser, Inc. 194; Witherspoon & Associates, Inc. 194; Writers House 195; Zachary Shuster Harmsworth 197

**Detective/Police/Crime:** Acacia House Publishing Services Ltd. 76; Ahearn Agency, Inc., The 77; Alive Communications, Inc. 78; Allen Literary Agency, Linda 78; Allred and Allred Literary Agents 78; AMG/Renaissance 79; Amsterdam Agency, Marcia 80; Anubis Literary Agency 81; Appleseeds Management 81; Authentic Creations Literary Agency 81; Authors & Artists Group, Inc. 82; Baldi Literary Agency, Malaga 82; Barrett Books Inc., Loretta 83; Bial Agency, Daniel 84; Bleeker Street Associates, Inc. 85; BookEnds, LLC 86; Bova Literary Agency, The Barbara 88; Brandt Agency, The Joan 89; Brandt & Hochman Literary Agents Inc. 88; Brown Ltd., Curtis 90; Browne Ltd., Pema 90; Buck Agency, Howard 91; Collin Literary Agency, Frances 95; Congdon Associates Inc., Don 95; Core Creations 96; Curtis Associates, Inc., Richard 97; Delbourgo Associates, Inc., Joélle 99; DHS Literary, Inc. 100; Donovan Literary, Jim 101; Dorian Literary Agency 102; Ducas, Robert 103; Dupree/Miller and Associates Inc. Literary 103; Dystel Literary Management, Inc., Jane 104; Ellenberg Literary Agency, Ethan 106; Elmo Agency Inc., Ann 106; Fernandez Agent/Attorney, Justin E. 112

Fort Ross Inc. Russian-American Publishing Projects 113; Frenkel & Associates, James 115; Goldfarb & Associates 117; Goodman Associates 118; Grace Literary Agency, Carroll 118; Greenburger Associates, Inc., Sanford J. 118; Gregory and Radice Authors' Agents 119; Grosvenor Literary Agency, The 120; Gusay Literary Agency, The Charlotte 120; Halsey Agency, Reece 121; Hamilburg Agency, Mitchell J., The 122; Harris Literary Agency, Inc., The Joy 122; Hawkins & Associates, Inc., John 122; Henshaw Group, Richard 123; Herner Rights Agency, Susan 124; J de S Associates Inc. 128; Jabberwocky Literary Agency 128; JCA Literary Agency 129; Jellinek and Murray Literary Agency 130; Kern Literary Agency, Natasha 131; Kidde, Hoyt & Picard 132; Klinger, Inc., Harvey 133; Koster Literary Agency, LLC, Elaine 134; Kraas Agency, Irene 135; Kritzer Productions, Eddie 135; Lampack Agency, Inc., Peter 136; Larsen/Elizabeth Pomada Literary Agents, Michael 136; Lazear Agency Incorporated 137; Levine Literary Agency, Paul S. 138; Lewis & Company, Karen 139; Lincoln Literary Agency, Ray 140; Literary Group, The 141; Litwest Group, LLC 141; Lowenstein Associates, Inc. 143; Maass Literary Agency 143; Madsen Agency, Robert 144; Markowitz Literary Agency, Barbara 146; McBride Literary Agency, Margret 147; McGrath, Helen 147; Morrison, Inc., Henry 149; Multimedia Product Development, Inc. 150; Mura Enterprises, Inc., Dee 150; Naggar Literary Agency, Jean V. 151; New Brand Agency Group, LLC 152; Norma-Lewis Agency, The 153; Picard, Literary Agent, Alison J. 157; Pinder Lane & Garon-Brooke Associates, Ltd. 158; Pine Associates, Inc., Arthur 158; Preskill Literary Agency, Robert 159; Protter Literary Agent, Susan Ann 159; Rhodes Literary Agency, Jodie 164; RLR Associates, Ltd. 168; Robbins Literary Agency, B.J. 169; Rosenberg Group, The 170; Rotrosen Agency, LLC, Jane 171; Rubie Literary Agency, The Peter 172; Russell and Volkening 172; Schulman, A Literary Agency, Susan 174; Seligman, Literary Agent, Lynn 176; Seymour Agency, The 177; Simmons Literary Agency, Jeffrey 178; Southern Literary Group 181; Spitzer Literary Agency, Philip G. 181; Treimel NY, Scott 187; Van Der Leun & Associates 188; Venture Literary 189; Vines Agency, Inc., The

189; Wald Associates, Inc., Mary Jack 190; Ware Literary Agency, John A. 190; Watt & Associates, Sandra 191; Weiner Literary Agency, Cherry 192; Whittaker, Literary Agent, Lynn 193; Wieser & Wieser, Inc. 194; Witherspoon & Associates, Inc. 194; Writers House 195; Zachary Shuster Harmsworth 197; Zeckendorf Assoc. Inc., Susan 197

**Erotica:** Authors & Artists Group, Inc. 82; Baldi Literary Agency, Malaga 82; Bial Agency, Daniel 84; Bleeker Street Associates, Inc. 85; Brown Ltd., Curtis 90; Browne Ltd., Pema 90; Buck Agency, Howard 91; Congdon Associates Inc., Don 95; Curtis Associates, Inc., Richard 97; DHS Literary, Inc. 100; Fernandez Agent/Attorney, Justin E. 112
Goodman Associates 118; Gusay Literary Agency, The Charlotte 120; Hamilburg Agency, Mitchell J., The 122; Harris Literary Agency, Inc., The Joy 122; Jellinek and Murray Literary Agency 130; Lazear Agency Incorporated 137; Levine Literary Agency, Paul S. 138; Lewis & Company, Karen 139; Lowenstein Associates, Inc. 143; Madsen Agency, Robert 144; Marshall Agency, The Evan 146; New Brand Agency Group, LLC 152; Pevner, Inc., Stephen 157; Picard, Literary Agent, Alison J. 157; Treimel NY, Scott 187; Van Der Leun & Associates 188; Writers House 195

**Ethnic:** Ahearn Agency, Inc., The 77; Allen Literary Agency, Linda 78; Allred and Allred Literary Agents 78; Amster Literary Enterprises, Betsy 80; Authors & Artists Group, Inc. 82; Baldi Literary Agency, Malaga 82; Barrett Books Inc., Loretta 83; Bent Literary Agent, Harvey Klinger, Inc., Jenny 83; Bernstein & Associates, Inc., Pam 84; Bial Agency, Daniel 84; Bleeker Street Associates, Inc. 85; Book Deals, Inc. 86; BookEnds, LLC 86; Brandt & Hochman Literary Agents Inc. 88; Brown Associates Inc., Marie 89; Brown Ltd., Curtis 90; Browne Ltd., Pema 90; Buck Agency, Howard 91; Castiglia Literary Agency 93; Clark Associates, William 94; Cohen, Inc. Literary Agency, Ruth 94; Collin Literary Agency, Frances 95; Congdon Associates Inc., Don 95; Curtis Associates, Inc., Richard 97; Daves Agency, Joan 98; Dawson Associates, Liza 98; DeFiore and Company 99; DHS Literary, Inc. 100; Dijkstra Literary Agency, Sandra 100; Dunham Literary 103; Dupree/Miller and Associates Inc. Literary 103; Dystel Literary Management, Inc., Jane 104; Elmo Agency Inc., Ann 106; Eth Literary Agency, Felicia 110; Fernandez Agent/Attorney, Justin E. 112
Frenkel & Associates, James 115; Freymann Literary Agency, Sarah Jane 115; Goldfarb & Associates 117; Goodman Associates 118; Goodman-Andrew Agency, Inc. 118; Greenburger Associates, Inc., Sanford J. 118; Gusay Literary Agency, The Charlotte 120; Halsey Agency, Reece 121; Halsey North, Reece 121; Hamilburg Agency, Mitchell J., The 122; Harris Literary Agency, Inc., The Joy 122; Hawkins & Associates, Inc., John 122; Henshaw Group, Richard 123; Herner Rights Agency, Susan 124; Hill & Barlow Agency 124; Jabberwocky Literary Agency 128; Jellinek and Murray Literary Agency 130; Jenks Agency, Carolyn 130; Kern Literary Agency, Natasha 131; Kleinman, Esq., of Graybill & English L.L.C., Jeffrey M. 133; Knight Agency, The 134; Koster Literary Agency, LLC, Elaine 134; Larsen/Elizabeth Pomada Literary Agents, Michael 136; Lazear Agency Incorporated 137; Levine Literary Agency, Paul S. 138; Lewis & Company, Karen 139; Lincoln Literary Agency, Ray 140; Literary Group, The 141; Litwest Group, LLC 141; Lowenstein Associates, Inc. 143; Madsen Agency, Robert 144; March Tenth, Inc. 145; Markowitz Literary Agency, Barbara 146; Marshall Agency, The Evan 146; McBride Literary Agency, Margret 147; Multimedia Product Development, Inc. 150; Mura Enterprises, Inc., Dee 150; Naggar Literary Agency, Jean V. 151; New Brand Agency Group, LLC 152; Nine Muses and Apollo Inc. 153; Paraview, Inc. 154; Pevner, Inc., Stephen 157; Picard, Literary Agent, Alison J. 157; Rhodes Literary Agency, Jodie 164; RLR Associates, Ltd. 168; Robbins Literary Agency, B.J. 169; Rubie Literary Agency, The Peter 172; Russell and Volkening 172; Sanders & Associates, Victoria 173; Schiavone Literary Agency, Inc. 174; Sedgeband Literary Associates 176; Seligman, Literary Agent, Lynn 176; Serendipity Literary Agency, LLC 176; Seymour Agency, The 177; Singer Literary Agency Inc., Evelyn 179; Southern Literary Group 181; Swayze Literary Agency, Carolyn 184; Travis Literary Agency, Susan 186; Treimel NY, Scott 187; Van Der Leun & Associates 188; Venture Literary 189; Vines Agency, Inc., The 189; Wald Associates, Inc., Mary Jack 190; Wales, Literary Agency, Inc. 190; Whittaker, Literary Agent, Lynn 193; Witherspoon & Associates, Inc. 194; Writers House 195; Zachary Shuster Harmsworth 197; Zeckendorf Assoc. Inc., Susan 197

**Experimental:** Baldi Literary Agency, Malaga 82; Brown Ltd., Curtis 90; Buck Agency, Howard 91; Congdon Associates Inc., Don 95; Curtis Associates, Inc., Richard 97; Dupree/Miller and Associates Inc. Literary 103; Fernandez Agent/Attorney, Justin E. 112
Goodman Associates 118; Gusay Literary Agency, The Charlotte 120; Hamilburg Agency, Mitchell J., The 122; Harris Literary Agency, Inc., The Joy 122; Hawkins & Associates, Inc., John 122; Larsen/Elizabeth Pomada Literary Agents, Michael 136; Lazear Agency Incorporated 137; Levine Literary Agency, Paul S. 138; Madsen Agency, Robert 144; Mura Enterprises, Inc., Dee 150; New Brand Agency Group, LLC 152; Pevner, Inc., Stephen 157; Picard, Literary Agent, Alison J. 157; RLR Associates, Ltd. 168; Sedgeband Literary Associates 176; Treimel NY, Scott 187; Van Der Leun & Associates 188; Vines Agency, Inc., The 189; Wald Associates, Inc., Mary Jack 190; Whittaker, Literary Agent, Lynn 193; Writers House 195

**Family Saga:** Ahearn Agency, Inc., The 77; Alive Communications, Inc. 78; Allred and Allred Literary Agents 78; AMG/Renaissance 79; Authentic Creations Literary Agency 81; Barrett Books Inc., Loretta 83; Bleeker Street Associates, Inc. 85; Boates Literary Agency, Reid 86; BookEnds, LLC 86; Books & Such 87; Brandt Agency, The Joan 89; Brandt & Hochman Literary Agents Inc. 88; Brown Ltd., Curtis 90; Buck Agency, Howard 91; Collin Literary Agency, Frances 95; Congdon Associates Inc., Don 95; Curtis Associates, Inc., Richard 97;

Daves Agency, Joan 98; Dawson Associates, Liza 98; Delbourgo Associates, Inc., Joélle 99; Dorian Literary Agency 102; Doyen Literary Services, Inc. 102; Ducas, Robert 103; Dupree/Miller and Associates Inc. Literary 103; Dystel Literary Management, Inc., Jane 104; Ellenberg Literary Agency, Ethan 106; Elmo Agency Inc., Ann 106; Feigen/Parent Literary Management 111; Fernandez Agent/Attorney, Justin E. 112
Goodman Associates 118; Grace Literary Agency, Carroll 118; Greenburger Associates, Inc., Sanford J. 118; Grosvenor Literary Agency, The 120; Gusay Literary Agency, The Charlotte 120; Halsey Agency, Reece 121; Hamilburg Agency, Mitchell J., The 122; Harris Literary Agency, Inc., The Joy 122; Hartline Literary Agency 122; Hawkins & Associates, Inc., John 122; Henshaw Group, Richard 123; Herner Rights Agency, Susan 124; Hornfischer Literary Management, Inc. 125; Jabberwocky Literary Agency 128; JCA Literary Agency 129; Jellinek and Murray Literary Agency 130; Kleinman, Esq., of Graybill & English L.L.C., Jeffrey M. 133; Klinger, Inc., Harvey 133; Koster Literary Agency, LLC, Elaine 134; Kouts, Literary Agent, Barbara S. 134; Lampack Agency, Inc., Peter 136; Larsen/Elizabeth Pomada Literary Agents, Michael 136; Lazear Agency Incorporated 137; Levine Literary Agency, Paul S. 138; Lincoln Literary Agency, Ray 140; Literary Group, The 141; Litwest Group, LLC 141; Madsen Agency, Robert 144; March Tenth, Inc. 145; Morrison, Inc., Henry 149; Multimedia Product Development, Inc. 150; Mura Enterprises, Inc., Dee 150; Naggar Literary Agency, Jean V. 151; Norma-Lewis Agency, The 153; Picard, Literary Agent, Alison J. 157; Pinder Lane & Garon-Brooke Associates, Ltd. 158; Pine Associates, Inc., Arthur 158; Rhodes Literary Agency, Jodie 164; RLR Associates, Ltd. 168; Rotrosen Agency, LLC, Jane 171; Sanders & Associates, Victoria 173; Schiavone Literary Agency, Inc. 174; Shepard Agency, The 177; Simmons Literary Agency, Jeffrey 178; Spieler Agency, The 181; Straus Agency, Inc., Robin 183; Swayze Literary Agency, Carolyn 184; Treimel NY, Scott 187; Van Der Leun & Associates 188; Vines Agency, Inc., The 189; Wald Associates, Inc., Mary Jack 190; Watt & Associates, Sandra 191; Weiner Literary Agency, Cherry 192; Witherspoon & Associates, Inc. 194; Writers House 195

**Fantasy:** Ahearn Agency, Inc., The 77; Allred and Allred Literary Agents 78; AMG/Renaissance 79; Anubis Literary Agency 81; Brown Ltd., Curtis 90; Carvainis Agency, Inc., Maria 92; Collin Literary Agency, Frances 95; Congdon Associates Inc., Don 95; Curtis Associates, Inc., Richard 97; Dorian Literary Agency 102; Ellenberg Literary Agency, Ethan 106; Fernandez Agent/Attorney, Justin E. 112
Fleury Agency, B.R. 112; Fort Ross Inc. Russian-American Publishing Projects 113; Frenkel & Associates, James 115; Gislason Agency, The 116; Goodman Associates 118; Grace Literary Agency, Carroll 118; Gusay Literary Agency, The Charlotte 120; Hamilburg Agency, Mitchell J., The 122; Hawkins & Associates, Inc., John 122; Henshaw Group, Richard 123; Herner Rights Agency, Susan 124; Jabberwocky Literary Agency 128; Kern Literary Agency, Natasha 131; Kidd Agency, Inc. Virginia 132; Kleinman, Esq., of Graybill & English L.L.C., Jeffrey M. 133; Larsen/Elizabeth Pomada Literary Agents, Michael 136; Lazear Agency Incorporated 137; Lincoln Literary Agency, Ray 140; Literary Group, The 141; Maass Literary Agency 143; Madsen Agency, Robert 144; Mura Enterprises, Inc., Dee 150; Perkins Associates, L. 157; Pinder Lane & Garon-Brooke Associates, Ltd. 158; Rubie Literary Agency, The Peter 172; Sedgeband Literary Associates 176; Seligman, Literary Agent, Lynn 176; Spectrum Literary Agency 181; Sternig & Byrne Literary Agency 183; Treimel NY, Scott 187; Van Der Leun & Associates 188; Viciananza, Ltd., Ralph 189; Weiner Literary Agency, Cherry 192; Writers House 195

**Feminist:** A.L.P. Literary Agency 76; Ahearn Agency, Inc., The 77; Allen Literary Agency, Linda 78; Allred and Allred Literary Agents 78; Baldi Literary Agency, Malaga 82; Barrett Books Inc., Loretta 83; Bial Agency, Daniel 84; Bleecker Street Associates, Inc. 85; BookEnds, LLC 86; Brown Ltd., Curtis 90; Browne Ltd., Pema 90; Buck Agency, Howard 91; Congdon Associates Inc., Don 95; Curtis Associates, Inc., Richard 97; DHS Literary, Inc. 100; Dijkstra Literary Agency, Sandra 100; Dupree/Miller and Associates Inc. Literary 103; Elite Online 105; Elmo Agency Inc., Ann 106; Eth Literary Agency, Felicia 110; Feigen/Parent Literary Management 111; Fernandez Agent/Attorney, Justin E. 112
Frenkel & Associates, James 115; Goldfarb & Associates 117; Goodman Associates 118; Greenburger Associates, Inc., Sanford J. 118; Gusay Literary Agency, The Charlotte 120; Hamilburg Agency, Mitchell J., The 122; Harris Literary Agency, Inc., The Joy 122; Hawkins & Associates, Inc., John 122; Herner Rights Agency, Susan 124; Hill & Barlow Agency 124; Jellinek and Murray Literary Agency 130; Kern Literary Agency, Natasha 131; Kidd Agency, Inc. Virginia 132; Kidde, Hoyt & Picard 132; Kleinman, Esq., of Graybill & English L.L.C., Jeffrey M. 133; Koster Literary Agency, LLC, Elaine 134; Kouts, Literary Agent, Barbara S. 134; Larsen/Elizabeth Pomada Literary Agents, Michael 136; Lazear Agency Incorporated 137; Levine Literary Agency, Paul S. 138; Lincoln Literary Agency, Ray 140; Literary Group, The 141; Litwest Group, LLC 141; Lowenstein Associates, Inc. 143; Madsen Agency, Robert 144; Michaels Literary Agency, Inc., Doris S. 148; Mura Enterprises, Inc., Dee 150; Naggar Literary Agency, Jean V. 151; Paraview, Inc. 154; Picard, Literary Agent, Alison J. 157; Rhodes Literary Agency, Jodie 164; RLR Associates, Ltd. 168; Sanders & Associates, Victoria 173; Seligman, Literary Agent, Lynn 176; Singer Literary Agency Inc., Evelyn 179; Southern Literary Group 181; Spieler Agency, The 181; Treimel NY, Scott 187; Van Der Leun & Associates 188; Venture Literary 189; Vines Agency, Inc., The 189; Wald Associates, Inc., Mary Jack 190; Wales, Literary Agency, Inc. 190; Whittaker, Literary Agent, Lynn 193; Witherspoon & Associates, Inc. 194; Writers House 195; Zachary Shuster Harmsworth 197

**Glitz:** Ahearn Agency, Inc., The 77; Allen Literary Agency, Linda 78; Allred and Allred Literary Agents 78; Barrett Books Inc., Loretta 83; BookEnds, LLC 86; Bova Literary Agency, The Barbara 88; Brown Ltd., Curtis 90; Browne Ltd., Pema 90; Buck Agency, Howard 91; Castiglia Literary Agency 93; Congdon Associates Inc.,

Don 95; Curtis Associates, Inc., Richard 97; Dupree/Miller and Associates Inc. Literary 103; Elmo Agency Inc., Ann 106; Fernandez Agent/Attorney, Justin E. 112
Goldfarb & Associates 117; Goodman Associates 118; Greenburger Associates, Inc., Sanford J. 118; Gusay Literary Agency, The Charlotte 120; Hamilburg Agency, Mitchell J., The 122; Harris Literary Agency, Inc., The Joy 122; Hawkins & Associates, Inc., John 122; Henshaw Group, Richard 123; Herner Rights Agency, Susan 124; Jabberwocky Literary Agency 128; Jellinek and Murray Literary Agency 130; Kidd Agency, Inc. Virginia 132; Kidde, Hoyt & Picard 132; Kleinman, Esq., of Graybill & English L.L.C., Jeffrey M. 133; Klinger, Inc., Harvey 133; Koster Literary Agency, LLC, Elaine 134; Larsen/Elizabeth Pomada Literary Agents, Michael 136; Lazear Agency Incorporated 137; Levine Literary Agency, Paul S. 138; Madsen Agency, Robert 144; Multimedia Product Development, Inc. 150; Mura Enterprises, Inc., Dee 150; Pevner, Inc., Stephen 157; Picard, Literary Agent, Alison J. 157; Quicksilver Books Literary Agents 160; Rosenberg Group, The 170; Seymour Agency, The 177; Sternig & Byrne Literary Agency 183; Teal Literary Agency, Patricia 185; Treimel NY, Scott 187; Van Der Leun & Associates 188; Wald Associates, Inc., Mary Jack 190; Weiner Literary Agency, Cherry 192; Writers House 195

**Historical:** Ahearn Agency, Inc., The 77; Alive Communications, Inc. 78; Allred and Allred Literary Agents 78; Altair Literary Agency 79; AMG/Renaissance 79; Anubis Literary Agency 81; Baldi Literary Agency, Malaga 82; Barrett Books Inc., Loretta 83; Bernstein & Associates, Inc., Pam 84; Bleeker Street Associates, Inc. 85; BookEnds, LLC 86; Books & Such 87; Brandt & Hochman Literary Agents Inc. 88; Brown Ltd., Curtis 90; Browne Ltd., Pema 90; Buck Agency, Howard 91; Cambridge Literary 92; Carvainis Agency, Inc., Maria 92; Clark Associates, William 94; Cohen, Inc. Literary Agency, Ruth 94; Collin Literary Agency, Frances 95; Congdon Associates Inc., Don 95; Curtis Associates, Inc., Richard 97; Dawson Associates, Liza 98; Delbourgo Associates, Inc., Joëlle 99; DHS Literary, Inc. 100; Donovan Literary, Jim 101; Dorian Literary Agency 102; Doyen Literary Services, Inc. 102; Dupree/Miller and Associates Inc. Literary 103; Ellenberg Literary Agency, Ethan 106; Elmo Agency Inc., Ann 106; English, Elaine P. 110; Fernandez Agent/Attorney, Justin E. 112
Fogelman Literary Agency 113; Frenkel & Associates, James 115; Goodman Associates 118; Grace Literary Agency, Carroll 118; Greenburger Associates, Inc., Sanford J. 118; Gregory and Radice Authors' Agents 119; Grosjean Literary Agency, Jill 120; Grosvenor Literary Agency, The 120; Gusay Literary Agency, The Charlotte 120; Halsey Agency, Reece 121; Halsey North, Reece 121; Hamilburg Agency, Mitchell J., The 122; Harris Literary Agency, Inc., The Joy 122; Hartline Literary Agency 122; Hawkins & Associates, Inc., John 122; Henshaw Group, Richard 123; Herner Rights Agency, Susan 124; Hopkins Literary Associates 125; Hornfischer Literary Management, Inc. 125; J de S Associates Inc. 128; Jabberwocky Literary Agency 128; JCA Literary Agency 129; Jellinek and Murray Literary Agency 130; Jenks Agency, Carolyn 130; Kern Literary Agency, Natasha 131; Kidd Agency, Inc. Virginia 132; Kidde, Hoyt & Picard 132; Kleinman, Esq., of Graybill & English L.L.C., Jeffrey M. 133; Koster Literary Agency, LLC, Elaine 134; Kouts, Literary Agent, Barbara S. 134; Lampack Agency, Inc., Peter 136; Larsen/Elizabeth Pomada Literary Agents, Michael 136; Lazear Agency Incorporated 137; Levine Literary Agency, Paul S. 138; Lincoln Literary Agency, Ray 140; Litwest Group, LLC 141; Lowenstein Associates, Inc. 143; Maass Literary Agency 143; Madsen Agency, Robert 144; March Tenth, Inc. 145; Markowitz Literary Agency, Barbara 146; Marshall Agency, The Evan 146; McBride Literary Agency, Margret 147; McHugh Literary Agency 147; Morrison, Inc., Henry 149; Multimedia Product Development, Inc. 150; Mura Enterprises, Inc., Dee 150; Naggar Literary Agency, Jean V. 151; Norma-Lewis Agency, The 153; Picard, Literary Agent, Alison J. 157; Rees Literary Agency, Helen 160; Rhodes Literary Agency, Jodie 164; RLR Associates, Ltd. 168; Rosenberg Group, The 170; Rotrosen Agency, LLC, Jane 171; Rowland Agency, The Damaris 171; Rubie Literary Agency, The Peter 172; Schiavone Literary Agency, Inc. 174; Schulman, A Literary Agency, Susan 174; Seligman, Literary Agent, Lynn 176; Serendipity Literary Agency, LLC 176; Seymour Agency, The 177; Shepard Agency, The 177; Singer Literary Agency Inc., Evelyn 179; Skolnick Literary Agency, Irene 179; Southern Literary Group 181; Spectrum Literary Agency 181; Straus Agency, Inc., Robin 183; Swayze Literary Agency, Carolyn 184; Toad Hall, Inc. 186; Travis Literary Agency, Susan 186; Treimel NY, Scott 187; Van Der Leun & Associates 188; Venture Literary 189; Vines Agency, Inc., The 189; Wald Associates, Inc., Mary Jack 190; Waxman Agency, Inc., Scott 192; Wecksler-Incomco 192; Weiner Literary Agency, Cherry 192; Whittaker, Literary Agent, Lynn 193; Wieser & Wieser, Inc. 194; Witherspoon & Associates, Inc. 194; Writers House 195; Wylie-Merrick Literary Agency 196; Zachary Shuster Harmsworth 197; Zeckendorf Assoc. Inc., Susan 197

**Horror:** Ahearn Agency, Inc., The 77; Allen Literary Agency, Linda 78; Allred and Allred Literary Agents 78; Amsterdam Agency, Marcia 80; Anubis Literary Agency 81; Authors & Artists Group, Inc. 82; Brown Ltd., Curtis 90; Cambridge Literary 92; Congdon Associates Inc., Don 95; Connor Literary Agency 96; Core Creations 96; Curtis Associates, Inc., Richard 97; Donovan Literary, Jim 101; Dorian Literary Agency 102; Elite Online 105; Fernandez Agent/Attorney, Justin E. 112
Fleury Agency, B.R. 112; Fort Ross Inc. Russian-American Publishing Projects 113; Goodman Associates 118; Grace Literary Agency, Carroll 118; Hamilburg Agency, Mitchell J., The 122; Harris Literary Agency, Inc., The Joy 122; Hawkins & Associates, Inc., John 122; Henshaw Group, Richard 123; Herner Rights Agency, Susan 124; Hornfischer Literary Management, Inc. 125; Jabberwocky Literary Agency 128; Jellinek and Murray Literary Agency 130; Kleinman, Esq., of Graybill & English L.L.C., Jeffrey M. 133; Lazear Agency Incorporated 137; Literary Group, The 141; Maass Literary Agency 143; Madsen Agency, Robert 144; Marshall Agency, The Evan 146; New Brand Agency Group, LLC 152; Norma-Lewis Agency, The 153; Perkins Associates, L. 157; Pevner,

Inc., Stephen 157; Picard, Literary Agent, Alison J. 157; RLR Associates, Ltd. 168; Rotrosen Agency, LLC, Jane 171; Schiavone Literary Agency, Inc. 174; Sedgeband Literary Associates 176; Seligman, Literary Agent, Lynn 176; Seymour Agency, The 177; Sternig & Byrne Literary Agency 183; Treimel NY, Scott 187; Venture Literary 189; Vines Agency, Inc., The 189; Writers House 195

**Humor:** A.L.P. Literary Agency 76; Ahearn Agency, Inc., The 77; Alive Communications, Inc. 78; Allred and Allred Literary Agents 78; AMG/Renaissance 79; Amsterdam Agency, Marcia 80; Authors & Artists Group, Inc. 82; Barrett Books Inc., Loretta 83; Bial Agency, Daniel 84; Brandt & Hochman Literary Agents Inc. 88; Brown Ltd., Curtis 90; Browne Ltd., Pema 90; Buck Agency, Howard 91; Congdon Associates Inc., Don 95; Curtis Associates, Inc., Richard 97; Dupree/Miller and Associates Inc. Literary 103; Elite Online 105; Fleury Agency, B.R. 112; Farber Literary Agency Inc. 111; Fernandez Agent/Attorney, Justin E. 112
Flannery Literary 112; Goodman Associates 118; Greenburger Associates, Inc., Sanford J. 118; Gregory and Radice Authors' Agents 119; Grosjean Literary Agency, Jill 120; Gusay Literary Agency, The Charlotte 120; H.W.A. Talent Representatives 121; Hamilburg Agency, Mitchell J., The 122; Harris Literary Agency, Inc., The Joy 122; Hawkins & Associates, Inc., John 122; Henshaw Group, Richard 123; International Creative Management 128; Jabberwocky Literary Agency 128; Jackson Agency, Melanie 129; Janklow & Nesbit Associates 129; Jellinek and Murray Literary Agency 130; Kidde, Hoyt & Picard 132; Kleinman, Esq., of Graybill & English L.L.C., Jeffrey M. 133; Kroll Literary Agency Inc., Edite 135; Larsen/Elizabeth Pomada Literary Agents, Michael 136; Lazear Agency Incorporated 137; Levine Literary Agency, Paul S. 138; Lincoln Literary Agency, Ray 140; Literary Group, The 141; Litwest Group, LLC 141; March Tenth, Inc. 145; Marshall Agency, The Evan 146; McBride Literary Agency, Margret 147; Madsen Agency, Robert 144; Markowitz Literary Agency, Barbara 146; Mura Enterprises, Inc., Dee 150; New Brand Agency Group, LLC 152; Norma-Lewis Agency, The 153; Pevner, Inc., Stephen 157; Picard, Literary Agent, Alison J. 157; RLR Associates, Ltd. 168; Schiavone Literary Agency, Inc. 174; Seligman, Literary Agent, Lynn 176; Shepard Agency, The 177; Spieler Agency, The 181; Swayze Literary Agency, Carolyn 184; Treimel NY, Scott 187; Van Der Leun & Associates 188; Venture Literary 189; Vines Agency, Inc., The 189; Writers House 195

**Juvenile:** Ahearn Agency, Inc., The 77; Alive Communications, Inc. 78; Allred and Allred Literary Agents 78; Books & Such 87; Briggs, M. Courtney 89; Brown Associates Inc., Marie 89; Brown Ltd., Curtis 90; Brown Literary Agency, Inc., Andrea 89; Browne Ltd., Pema 90; Cohen, Inc. Literary Agency, Ruth 94; Congdon Associates Inc., Don 95; Curtis Associates, Inc., Richard 97; Dunham Literary 103; Dwyer & O'Grady, Inc. 104; Ellenberg Literary Agency, Ethan 106; Elmo Agency Inc., Ann 106; Farber Literary Agency Inc. 111; Fernandez Agent/Attorney, Justin E. 112
Flannery Literary 112; Fort Ross Inc. Russian-American Publishing Projects 113; Gusay Literary Agency, The Charlotte 120; Hamilburg Agency, Mitchell J., The 122; Hawkins & Associates, Inc., John 122; J de S Associates Inc. 128; Kouts, Literary Agent, Barbara S. 134; Kroll Literary Agency Inc., Edite 135; Lazear Agency Incorporated 137; Lincoln Literary Agency, Ray 140; Litwest Group, LLC 141; Livingston Cooke 142; Madsen Agency, Robert 144; Markowitz Literary Agency, Barbara 146; Multimedia Product Development, Inc. 150; Mura Enterprises, Inc., Dee 150; National Writers Literary Agency 151; Norma-Lewis Agency, The 153; Picard, Literary Agent, Alison J. 157; Rhodes Literary Agency, Jodie 164; Schiavone Literary Agency, Inc. 174; Serendipity Literary Agency, LLC 176; Sternig & Byrne Literary Agency 183; Treimel NY, Scott 187; Van Der Leun & Associates 188; Wald Associates, Inc., Mary Jack 190; Wecksler-Incomco 192; Writers House 195; Wylie-Merrick Literary Agency 196

**Literary:** A.L.P. Literary Agency 76; Acacia House Publishing Services Ltd. 76; Ahearn Agency, Inc., The 77; Alive Communications, Inc. 78; Allen Literary Agency, Linda 78; Allred and Allred Literary Agents 78; Altair Literary Agency 79; Altshuler Literary Agency, Miriam 79; AMG/Renaissance 79; Amster Literary Enterprises, Betsy 80; Authentic Creations Literary Agency 81; Baldi Literary Agency, Malaga 82; Barrett Books Inc., Loretta 83; Bent Literary Agent, Harvey Klinger, Inc., Jenny 83; Bernstein Literary Agency, Meredith 84; Bial Agency, Daniel 84; Black Literary Agency, David 85; Bleeker Street Associates, Inc. 85; Book Deals, Inc. 86; BookEnds, LLC 86; Borchardt Inc., Georges 87; Brady Literary Management 88; Brandt Agency, The Joan 89; Brandt & Hochman Literary Agents Inc. 88; Brown Associates Inc., Marie 89; Brown Ltd., Curtis 90; Browne Ltd., Pema 90; Buck Agency, Howard 91; Bykofsky Associates, Inc., Sheree 91; Carlisle & Company 92; Carvainis Agency, Inc., Maria 92; Castiglia Literary Agency 93; Clark Associates, William 94; Cohen, Inc. Literary Agency, Ruth 94; Collin Literary Agency, Frances 95; Congdon Associates Inc., Don 95; Connor Literary Agency 96; Coover Agency, The Doe 96; Cornfield Literary Agency, Robert 97; Curtis Associates, Inc., Richard 97; Darhansoff & Verrill Literary Agency 98; Daves Agency, Joan 98; Dawson Associates, Liza 98; DeFiore and Company 99; Delbourgo Associates, Inc., Joélle 99; DH Literary, Inc. 100; DHS Literary, Inc. 100; Dijkstra Literary Agency, Sandra 100; Donnaud & Associates, Inc., Janis A. 101; Donovan Literary, Jim 101; Dorian Literary Agency 102; Doyen Literary Services, Inc. 102; Ducas, Robert 103; Dunham Literary 103; Dupree/Miller and Associates Inc. Literary 103; Dystel Literary Management, Inc., Jane 104; Ellenberg Literary Agency, Ethan 106; Ellison, Inc., Nicholas 106; Elmo Agency Inc., Ann 106; Eth Literary Agency, Felicia 110; Farber Literary Agency Inc. 111; Feigen/Parent Literary Management 111; Fernandez Agent/Attorney, Justin E. 112
Flannery Literary 112; Fleury Agency, B.R. 112; Fogelman Literary Agency 113; Franklin Associates, Ltd., Lynn C. 114; Freymann Literary Agency, Sarah Jane 115; Gelfman Schneider Literary Agents, Inc. 116; Goldfarb & Associates 117; Goodman Associates 118; Goodman–Andrew Agency, Inc. 118; Grace Literary Agency, Carroll

# Get the 2003 EDITION at this year's price!

You already know an agent can be the key to selling your work. But, how do you know when you're ready to sign on with one? And, how do you select an agent that's right for you? To make such crucial decisions you need the most up-to-date information on the agents out there and what they can offer you. That's exactly what you'll find in *Guide to Literary Agents*.

Through this special offer, you can get a jump on next year today! If you order now, you'll get the *2003 Guide to Literary Agents* at the 2002 price—just $22.99—no matter how much the regular price may increase!

**Completely Updated Each Year**

## Guide to Literary Agents

**570+ AGENTS WHO SELL WHAT YOU WRITE**

450+ new markets
500+ book publishers
700+ literary magazines
600+ genre markets
300+ electric markets

*Includes independent publicists*

*2003 Guide to Literary Agents* will be published and ready for shipment in January 2003.

## More books to help you write & sell your work

---

**■ Yes!** I want next year's edition of *Guide to Literary Agents*. Please send me the 2003 edition at the 2002 price—$22.99. (NOTE: *2003 Guide to Literary Agents* will be ready for shipment in January 2003.) #10811-K

| # 10811-K | $ 22.99 |

Additional books from the back of this card:

| Book | Price |
|------|-------|
| # | $ |
| # | $ |
| # | $ |
| # | $ |
| Subtotal | $ |
| Postage & Handling | $ |

Payment in U.S. funds must accompany this order. In the U.S., please add $3.95 s&h for the first book, $1.95 for each additional book. In Ohio, New York and Colorado, please add applicable state tax. In Canada, add US$5.00 for the first book, US$3.00 for each additional book, and 7% GST.

| Total | $ |

*Credit Card orders call*
**TOLL FREE 1-800-221-5831**
or visit
www.writersdigest.com/catalog

☐ Payment enclosed $_____ (or)

Charge my: ☐ VISA ☐ MasterCard ☐ AmEx

Exp._____

Account #_____

Signature_____

Name_____

Address_____

City_____

State/Prov._____ ZIP/PC _____

☐ Check here if you do not want your name added to our mailing list.

| 30-Day Money Back Guarantee on every book you buy! |

ZAL01B3

**Visit the Web site for additional information: www.writersdigest.com/catalog**

**Mail to: Writer's Digest Books • PO Box 9274 • Central Islip, NY 11722-9274**

# Write Better & Sell More
## with help from these Writer's Digest Books!

**Writer's Market FAQs**
You'll find fast answers on how to get published more easily, more often and for more money. With tips on how to succeed with traditional publishing houses as well as in the wired world of e-publishing. Plus, how to protect your work, handle agents and editors and more!
#10754-K/$18.99/240p/pb

**The Writer's Market Companion**
Complementing the "where-to" information in *Writer's Market*, this handy "how-to" guide features an easy-to-use reference format where you'll find guidelines on countless writing issues. You'll find advice for successful networking, pricing and researching, even how to define your writing goals and save time.
#10653-K/$19.99/272p/pb

**Writer's Online Marketplace**
Discover more than 250 paying Internet markets, and get advice on the unique marketing and writing techniques needed to succeed in the wired world. Includes interviews with online editors, and a list of agents who handle e-work.
#10697-K/$17.99/240p/pb

**Guerrilla Marketing for Writers**
Packed with more than 100 low-cost weapons to help you sell your books, before and after they're finished. You'll also get insider insight into how the publishing industry works to help you develop a complete, professional promotion plan.
#10667-K/$14.99/224p/pb

**The Insider's Guide to Getting an Agent**
Getting an agent is sometimes crucial to getting published. Find out the best ways to research and contact your perfect agent. Includes advice on query letters, proposals, synopses, plot outlines, cover letters and more!
#10630-K/$16.99/240p/pb

**Formatting & Submitting Your Manuscript**
Dozens of charts, lists and models will show you how to format your manuscripts correctly, no matter what you write. From screenplays to stage scripts, novels to articles, you'll discover the secrets of professional submission. Successful agents and editors share dozens of visual examples of formatting do's and don'ts.
#10618-K/$18.99/208 pgs/pb

**Books are available at your local bookstore, or directly from the publisher using the order card on the reverse.**

118; Gregory and Radice Authors' Agents 119; Greenburger Associates, Inc., Sanford J. 118; Grosjean Literary Agency, Jill 120; Grosvenor Literary Agency, The 120; Gusay Literary Agency, The Charlotte 120; Halsey Agency, Reece 121; Halsey North, Reece 121; Hamilburg Agency, Mitchell J., The 122; Harris Literary Agency, Inc., The Joy 122; Hartline Literary Agency 122; Hawkins & Associates, Inc., John 122; Henshaw Group, Richard 123; Herner Rights Agency, Susan 124; Hill & Barlow Agency 124; Hill Bonnie Nadell, Inc., Frederick 124; Hornfischer Literary Management, Inc. 125; J de S Associates Inc. 128; Jabberwocky Literary Agency 128; JCA Literary Agency 129; Jellinek and Murray Literary Agency 130; Jenks Agency, Carolyn 130; Kidd Agency, Inc. Virginia 132; Kidde, Hoyt & Picard 132; Kleinman, Esq., of Graybill & English L.L.C., Jeffrey M. 133; Klinger, Inc., Harvey 133; Knight Agency, The 134; Koster Literary Agency, LLC, Elaine 134; Kouts, Literary Agent, Barbara S. 134; Lampack Agency, Inc., Peter 136; Larsen/Elizabeth Pomada Literary Agents, Michael 136; Lazear Agency Incorporated 137; Levine Communications, Inc., James 138; Levine Literary Agency, Inc., Ellen 138; Levine Literary Agency, Paul S. 138; Lewis & Company, Karen 139; Lincoln Literary Agency, Ray 140; Litwest Group, LLC 141; Livingston Cooke 142; Lowenstein Associates, Inc. 143; Maass Literary Agency 143; Madsen Agency, Robert 144; Mann Agency, Carol 144; Manus & Associates Literary Agency, Inc. 145; March Tenth, Inc. 145; Marshall Agency, The Evan 146; McBride Literary Agency, Margret 147; McGrath, Helen 147; Michaels Literary Agency, Inc., Doris S. 148; Multimedia Product Development, Inc. 150; Mura Enterprises, Inc., Dee 150; Naggar Literary Agency, Jean V. 151; Nine Muses and Apollo Inc. 153; Paraview, Inc. 154; Paton Literary Agency, Kathi J. 154; Perkins Associates, L. 157; Pevner, Inc., Stephen 157; Picard, Literary Agent, Alison J. 157; Pinder Lane & Garon-Brooke Associates, Ltd. 158; Pine Associates, Inc., Arthur 158; Preskill Literary Agency, Robert 159; Rees Literary Agency, Helen 160; Rein Books, Inc., Jody 164; Rhodes Literary Agency, Jodie 164; Rinaldi Literary Agency, Angela 165; Rittenberg Literary Agency, Inc., Ann 165; RLR Associates, Ltd. 168; Robbins Literary Agency, B.J. 169; Robbins Office, Inc., The 169; Rosenberg Group, The 170; Ross Literary Agency, The Gail 170; Rowland Agency, The Damaris 171; Rubie Literary Agency, The Peter 172; Russell and Volkening 172; Sanders & Associates, Victoria 173; Sandum and Associates 173; Scherf, Inc., Literary Management 173; Schiavone Literary Agency, Inc. 174; Schulman, A Literary Agency, Susan 174; Sedgeband Literary Associates 176; Seligman, Literary Agent, Lynn 176; Serendipity Literary Agency, LLC 176; Shepard Agency, The 177; Sherman Associates, Inc., Wendy 178; Simmons Literary Agency, Jeffrey 178; Singer Literary Agency Inc., Evelyn 179; Skolnick Literary Agency, Irene 179; Slopen Literary Agency, Beverley 179; Southern Literary Group 181; Spieler Agency, The 181; Spitzer Literary Agency, Philip G. 181; Stauffer Associates, Nancy 182; Straus Agency, Inc., Robin 183; Susijn Agency, The 183; Swayze Literary Agency, Carolyn 184; Talbot Agency, The John 185; Travis Literary Agency, Susan 186; Treimel NY, Scott 187; Van Der Leun & Associates 188; Venture Literary 189; Viciananza, Ltd., Ralph 189; Vines Agency, Inc., The 189; Wald Associates, Inc., Mary Jack 190; Wales, Literary Agency, Inc. 190; Watkins Loomis Agency, Inc. 191; Waxman Agency, Inc., Scott 192; Wecksler-Incomco 192; Weingel-Fidel Agency, The 193; Whittaker, Literary Agent, Lynn 193; Wieser & Wieser, Inc. 194; Witherspoon & Associates, Inc. 194; Wonderland Press, Inc., The 194; Writers House 195; Writers' Representatives, Inc. 196; Zachary Shuster Harmsworth 197; Zeckendorf Assoc. Inc., Susan 197

**Mainstream:** Acacia House Publishing Services Ltd. 76; Ahearn Agency, Inc., The 77; Alive Communications, Inc. 78; Allen Literary Agency, Linda 78; Allred and Allred Literary Agents 78; Altshuler Literary Agency, Miriam 79; AMG/Renaissance 79; Amsterdam Agency, Marcia 80; Authentic Creations Literary Agency 81; Authors & Artists Group, Inc. 82; Baldi Literary Agency, Malaga 82; Barrett Books Inc., Loretta 83; Bent Literary Agent, Harvey Klinger, Inc., Jenny 83; Bernstein & Associates, Inc., Pam 84; Black Literary Agency, David 85; Boates Literary Agency, Reid 86; Book Deals, Inc. 86; BookEnds, LLC 86; Books & Such 87; Brady Literary Management 88; Brandt Agency, The Joan 89; Brandt & Hochman Literary Agents Inc. 88; Briggs, M. Courtney 89; Brown Associates Inc., Marie 89; Brown Ltd., Curtis 90; Browne Ltd., Pema 90; Buck Agency, Howard 91; Bykofsky Associates, Inc., Sheree 91; Cambridge Literary 92; Carlisle & Company 92; Carvainis Agency, Inc., Maria 92; Castiglia Literary Agency 93; Clark Associates, William 94; Cohen, Inc. Literary Agency, Ruth 94; Collin Literary Agency, Frances 95; Congdon Associates Inc., Don 95; Connor Literary Agency 96; Coover Agency, The Doe 96; Curtis Associates, Inc., Richard 97; Daves Agency, Joan 98; DeFiore and Company 99; Delbourgo Associates, Inc., Joélle 99; DH Literary, Inc. 100; DHS Literary, Inc. 100; Dijkstra Literary Agency, Sandra 100; Donovan Literary, Jim 101; Dorian Literary Agency 102; Doyen Literary Services, Inc. 102; Ducas, Robert 103; Dunham Literary 103; Dupree/Miller and Associates Inc. Literary 103; Dystel Literary Management, Inc., Jane 104; Ellenberg Literary Agency, Ethan 106; Ellison, Inc., Nicholas 106; Elmo Agency Inc., Ann 106; English, Elaine P. 110; Eth Literary Agency, Felicia 110; Farber Literary Agency Inc. 111; Fernandez Agent/Attorney, Justin E. 112

Flannery Literary 112; Fogelman Literary Agency 113; Franklin Associates, Ltd., Lynn C. 114; Frenkel & Associates, James 115; Freymann Literary Agency, Sarah Jane 115; Gelfman Schneider Literary Agents, Inc. 116; Goldfarb & Associates 117; Goodman Associates 118; Goodman-Andrew Agency, Inc. 118; Grace Literary Agency, Carroll 118; Greenburger Associates, Inc., Sanford J. 118; Gregory and Radice Authors' Agents 119; Grosjean Literary Agency, Jill 120; Grosvenor Literary Agency, The 120; Gusay Literary Agency, The Charlotte 120; Halsey Agency, Reece 121; Halsey North, Reece 121; Hamilburg Agency, Mitchell J., The 122; Harris Literary Agency, Inc., The Joy 122; Hawkins & Associates, Inc., John 122; Henshaw Group, Richard 123; Herner Rights Agency, Susan 124; Hill & Barlow Agency 124; Hill Bonnie Nadell, Inc., Frederick 124; Hopkins Literary Associates 125; Hornfischer Literary Management, Inc. 125; J de S Associates Inc. 128; Jabberwocky Literary Agency 128; JCA Literary Agency 129; Jellinek and Murray Literary Agency 130; Jenks Agency, Carolyn 130;

**Multicultural:** Brown Ltd., Curtis 90; Buck Agency, Howard 91; Congdon Associates Inc., Don 95; Curtis Associates, Inc., Richard 97; Delbourgo Associates, Inc., Joélle 99; Fernandez Agent/Attorney, Justin E. 112 Goodman Associates 118; Gusay Literary Agency, The Charlotte 120; Hamilburg Agency, Mitchell J., The 122; Harris Literary Agency, Inc., The Joy 122; Hawkins & Associates, Inc., John 122; Kleinman, Esq., of Graybill & English L.L.C., Jeffrey M. 133; Lazear Agency Incorporated 137; Madsen Agency, Robert 144; Treimel NY, Scott 187; Van Der Leun & Associates 188; Writers House 195

**Multimedia:** Brown Ltd., Curtis 90; Buck Agency, Howard 91; Congdon Associates Inc., Don 95; Curtis Associates, Inc., Richard 97; Fernandez Agent/Attorney, Justin E. 112 Goodman Associates 118; Gusay Literary Agency, The Charlotte 120; Hamilburg Agency, Mitchell J., The 122; Harris Literary Agency, Inc., The Joy 122; Hawkins & Associates, Inc., John 122; Kleinman, Esq., of Graybill & English L.L.C., Jeffrey M. 133; Lazear Agency Incorporated 137; Madsen Agency, Robert 144; Treimel NY, Scott 187; Van Der Leun & Associates 188; Writers House 195

**Mystery/Suspense:** Acacia House Publishing Services Ltd. 76; Ahearn Agency, Inc., The 77; Alive Communications, Inc. 78; Allen Literary Agency, Linda 78; Allred and Allred Literary Agents 78; AMG/Renaissance 79; Amsterdam Agency, Marcia 80; Appleseeds Management 81; Authentic Creations Literary Agency 81; Axelrod Agency, The 82; Baldi Literary Agency, Malaga 82; Barrett Books Inc., Loretta 83; Bernstein & Associates, Inc., Pam 84; Bernstein Literary Agency, Meredith 84; Bleeker Street Associates, Inc. 85; BookEnds, LLC 86; Bova Literary Agency, The Barbara 88; Brandt Agency, The Joan 89; Brandt & Hochman Literary Agents Inc. 88; Brown Ltd., Curtis 90; Browne Ltd., Pema 90; Buck Agency, Howard 91; Carlisle & Company 92; Carvainis Agency, Inc., Maria 92; Castiglia Literary Agency 93; Cohen, Inc. Literary Agency, Ruth 94; Collin Literary Agency, Frances 95; Congdon Associates Inc., Don 95; Connor Literary Agency 96; Crawford Literary Agency 97; Curtis Associates, Inc., Richard 97; Darhansoff & Verrill Literary Agency 98; Dawson Associates, Liza 98; DeFiore and Company 99; Delbourgo Associates, Inc., Joélle 99; DH Literary, Inc. 100; DHS Literary, Inc. 100; Dijkstra Literary Agency, Sandra 100; Donovan Literary, Jim 101; Dorian Literary Agency 102; Ducas, Robert 103; Dunham Literary 103; Dupree/Miller and Associates Inc. Literary 103; Dystel Literary Management, Inc., Jane 104; Ellenberg Literary Agency, Ethan 106; Elmo Agency Inc., Ann 106; Farber Literary Agency Inc. 111; Fernandez Agent/Attorney, Justin E. 112 Flannery Literary 112; Fort Ross Inc. Russian-American Publishing Projects 113; Frenkel & Associates, James 115; Freymann Literary Agency, Sarah Jane 115; Gelfman Schneider Literary Agents, Inc. 116; Gislason Agency, The 116; Goldfarb & Associates 117; Goodman Associates 118; Grace Literary Agency, Carroll 118; Greenburger Associates, Inc., Sanford J. 118; Grosjean Literary Agency, Jill 120; Grosvenor Literary Agency, The 120; Gusay Literary Agency, The Charlotte 120; Halsey Agency, Reece 121; Halsey North, Reece 121; Hamilburg Agency, Mitchell J., The 122; Harris Literary Agency, Inc., The Joy 122; Hartline Literary Agency 122; Hawkins & Associates, Inc., John 122; Henshaw Group, Richard 123; Herner Rights Agency, Susan 124; J de S Associates Inc. 128; JCA Literary Agency 129; Jellinek and Murray Literary Agency 130; Jenks Agency, Carolyn 130; Kern

Literary Agency, Natasha 131; Kidd Agency, Inc. Virginia 132; Kidde, Hoyt & Picard 132; Klinger, Inc., Harvey 133; Koster Literary Agency, LLC, Elaine 134; Kouts, Literary Agent, Barbara S. 134; Kraas Agency, Irene 135; Lampack Agency, Inc., Peter 136; Larsen/Elizabeth Pomada Literary Agents, Michael 136; Lazear Agency Incorporated 137; Lescher & Lescher Ltd. 138; Levine Communications, Inc., James 138; Levine Literary Agency, Inc., Ellen 138; Levine Literary Agency, Paul S. 138; Lewis & Company, Karen 139; Lincoln Literary Agency, Ray 140; Lipkind Agency, Wendy 140; Litwest Group, LLC 141; Literary Group, The 141; Love Literary Agency, Nancy 142; Lowenstein Associates, Inc. 143; Maass Literary Agency 143; Madsen Agency, Robert 144; Manus & Associates Literary Agency, Inc. 145; Markowitz Literary Agency, Barbara 146; Marshall Agency, The Evan 146; McBride Literary Agency, Margret 147; McGrath, Helen 147; McHugh Literary Agency 147; Multimedia Product Development, Inc. 150; Mura Enterprises, Inc., Dee 150; Naggar Literary Agency, Jean V. 151; National Writers Literary Agency 151; New Brand Agency Group, LLC 152; Norma-Lewis Agency, The 153; Picard, Literary Agent, Alison J. 157; Pinder Lane & Garon-Brooke Associates, Ltd. 158; Protter Literary Agent, Susan Ann 159; Quicksilver Books Literary Agents 160; Rees Literary Agency, Helen 160; Rhodes Literary Agency, Jodie 164; RLR Associates, Ltd. 168; Robbins Literary Agency, B.J. 169; Roghaar Literary Agency, Inc., Linda 169; Rosenberg Group, The 170; Rotrosen Agency, LLC, Jane 171; Russell and Volkening 172; Scherf, Inc., Literary Management 173; Schulman, A Literary Agency, Susan 174; Sedgeband Literary Associates 176; Seligman, Literary Agent, Lynn 176; Seymour Agency, The 177; Sherman Associates, Inc., Wendy 178; Simmons Literary Agency, Jeffrey 178; Singer Literary Agency Inc., Evelyn 179; Slopen Literary Agency, Beverley 179; Southern Literary Group 181; Spectrum Literary Agency 181; Spitzer Literary Agency, Philip G. 181; Sternig & Byrne Literary Agency 183; Swayze Literary Agency, Carolyn 184; Talbot Agency, The John 185; Teal Literary Agency, Patricia 185; Toad Hall, Inc. 186; Treimel NY, Scott 187; Van Der Leun & Associates 188; Venture Literary 189; Vines Agency, Inc., The 189; Wald Associates, Inc., Mary Jack 190; Ware Literary Agency, John A. 190; Watt & Associates, Sandra 191; Waxman Agency, Inc., Scott 192; Weiner Literary Agency, Cherry 192; Whittaker, Literary Agent, Lynn 193; Wieser & Wieser, Inc. 194; Witherspoon & Associates, Inc. 194; Writers House 195; Zachary Shuster Harmsworth 197; Zeckendorf Assoc. Inc., Susan 197

**Occult:** Brown Ltd., Curtis 90; Buck Agency, Howard 91; Congdon Associates Inc., Don 95; Curtis Associates, Inc., Richard 97; Doyen Literary Services, Inc. 102; Fernandez Agent/Attorney, Justin E. 112
Goodman Associates 118; Gusay Literary Agency, The Charlotte 120; Hamilburg Agency, Mitchell J., The 122; Harris Literary Agency, Inc., The Joy 122; Hawkins & Associates, Inc., John 122; Lazear Agency Incorporated 137; Madsen Agency, Robert 144; Treimel NY, Scott 187; Van Der Leun & Associates 188; Vines Agency, Inc., The 189; Writers House 195

**Picture Book:** Books & Such 87; Briggs, M. Courtney 89; Brown Ltd., Curtis 90; Browne Ltd., Pema 90; Cohen, Inc. Literary Agency, Ruth 94; Congdon Associates Inc., Don 95; Curtis Associates, Inc., Richard 97; Dunham Literary 103; Dupree/Miller and Associates Inc. Literary 103; Dwyer & O'Grady, Inc. 104; Ellenberg Literary Agency, Ethan 106; Flannery Literary 112; Goodman Associates 118; Gusay Literary Agency, The Charlotte 120; Hamilburg Agency, Mitchell J., The 122; Harris Literary Agency, Inc., The Joy 122; Hawkins & Associates, Inc., John 122; Jellinek and Murray Literary Agency 130; Kouts, Literary Agent, Barbara S. 134; Kroll Literary Agency Inc., Edite 135; Lazear Agency Incorporated 137; Litwest Group, LLC 141; Madsen Agency, Robert 144; Multimedia Product Development, Inc. 150; Norma-Lewis Agency, The 153; Picard, Literary Agent, Alison J. 157; Russell and Volkening 172; Serendipity Literary Agency, LLC 176; Tobias, A Literary Agency for Chilren's Books, Ann 186; Treimel NY, Scott 187; Van Der Leun & Associates 188; Wald Associates, Inc., Mary Jack 190; Wecksler-Incomco 192; Writers House 195; Wylie-Merrick Literary Agency 196

**Psychic/Supernatural:** Ahearn Agency, Inc., The 77; Allen Literary Agency, Linda 78; Allred and Allred Literary Agents 78; Authors & Artists Group, Inc. 82; Barrett Books Inc., Loretta 83; Bleeker Street Associates, Inc. 85; Brown Ltd., Curtis 90; Browne Ltd., Pema 90; Buck Agency, Howard 91; Collin Literary Agency, Frances 95; Congdon Associates Inc., Don 95; Curtis Associates, Inc., Richard 97; Doyen Literary Services, Inc. 102; Dupree/Miller and Associates Inc. Literary 103; Elits Online 105; Elmo Agency Inc., Ann 106; Fernandez Agent/Attorney, Justin E. 112
Fleury Agency, B.R. 112; Goodman Associates 118; Grace Literary Agency, Carroll 118; Greenburger Associates, Inc., Sanford J. 118; Gusay Literary Agency, The Charlotte 120; H.W.A. Talent Representatives 121; Hamilburg Agency, Mitchell J., The 122; Harris Literary Agency, Inc., The Joy 122; Hawkins & Associates, Inc., John 122; Henshaw Group, Richard 123; Hornfischer Literary Management, Inc. 125; International Creative Management 128; Jabberwocky Literary Agency 128; Jackson Agency, Melanie 129; Janklow & Nesbit Associates 129; Jellinek and Murray Literary Agency 130; Kleinman, Esq., of Graybill & English L.L.C., Jeffrey M. 133; Larsen/Elizabeth Pomada Literary Agents, Michael 136; Lazear Agency Incorporated 137; Levine Literary Agency, Paul S. 138; Lincoln Literary Agency, Ray 140; Literary Group, The 141; Maass Literary Agency 143; Madsen Agency, Robert 144; McGrath, Helen 147; Mura Enterprises, Inc., Dee 150; Naggar Literary Agency, Jean V. 151; New Brand Agency Group, LLC 152; Pevner, Inc., Stephen 157; Picard, Literary Agent, Alison J. 157; Rhodes Literary Agency, Jodie 164; Sedgeband Literary Associates 176; Simmons Literary Agency, Jeffrey 178; Sternig & Byrne Literary Agency 183; Treimel NY, Scott 187; Van Der Leun & Associates 188; Vines Agency, Inc., The 189; Weiner Literary Agency, Cherry 192; Writers House 195

**Regional:** A.L.P. Literary Agency 76; Ahearn Agency, Inc., The 77; Allen Literary Agency, Linda 78; Allred and Allred Literary Agents 78; Baldi Literary Agency, Malaga 82; Brandt & Hochman Literary Agents Inc. 88; Brown Ltd., Curtis 90; Buck Agency, Howard 91; Collin Literary Agency, Frances 95; Congdon Associates Inc., Don 95; Curtis Associates, Inc., Richard 97; Dawson Associates, Liza 98; Elmo Agency Inc., Ann 106; Fernandez Agent/Attorney, Justin E. 112

Goodman Associates 118; Greenburger Associates, Inc., Sanford J. 118; Grosjean Literary Agency, Jill 120; Gusay Literary Agency, The Charlotte 120; Hamilburg Agency, Mitchell J., The 122; Harris Literary Agency, Inc., The Joy 122; Hartline Literary Agency 122; Hawkins & Associates, Inc., John 122; Jabberwocky Literary Agency 128; Jellinek and Murray Literary Agency 130; Kern Literary Agency, Natasha 131; Kleinman, Esq., of Graybill & English L.L.C., Jeffrey M. 133; Koster Literary Agency, LLC, Elaine 134; Lazear Agency Incorporated 137; Levine Literary Agency, Paul S. 138; Lincoln Literary Agency, Ray 140; Madsen Agency, Robert 144; Mura Enterprises, Inc., Dee 150; New Brand Agency Group, LLC 152; Paraview, Inc. 154; Picard, Literary Agent, Alison J. 157; Rhodes Literary Agency, Jodie 164; Shepard Agency, The 177; Singer Literary Agency Inc., Evelyn 179; Southern Literary Group 181; Stauffer Associates, Nancy 182; Treimel NY, Scott 187; Van Der Leun & Associates 188; Vines Agency, Inc., The 189; Wales, Literary Agency, Inc. 190; Watt & Associates, Sandra 191; Writers House 195

**Religious/Inspirational:** A.L.P. Literary Agency 76; Alive Communications, Inc. 78; Allred and Allred Literary Agents 78; Authors & Artists Group, Inc. 82; Barrett Books Inc., Loretta 83; Books & Such 87; Brown Ltd., Curtis 90; Browne Ltd., Pema 90; Buck Agency, Howard 91; Congdon Associates Inc., Don 95; Curtis Associates, Inc., Richard 97; Dupree/Miller and Associates Inc. Literary 103; Fernandez Agent/Attorney, Justin E. 112

Goodman Associates 118; Gusay Literary Agency, The Charlotte 120; Hamilburg Agency, Mitchell J., The 122; Harris Literary Agency, Inc., The Joy 122; Hartline Literary Agency 122; Hawkins & Associates, Inc., John 122; Hornfischer Literary Management, Inc. 125; Kern Literary Agency, Natasha 131; Larsen/Elizabeth Pomada Literary Agents, Michael 136; Lazear Agency Incorporated 137; Levine Literary Agency, Paul S. 138; Litwest Group, LLC 141; Madsen Agency, Robert 144; Marshall Agency, The Evan 146; Multimedia Product Development, Inc. 150; New Brand Agency Group, LLC 152; Picard, Literary Agent, Alison J. 157; Scherf, Inc., Literary Management 173; Seymour Agency, The 177; Treimel NY, Scott 187; Van Der Leun & Associates 188; Watt & Associates, Sandra 191; Waxman Agency, Inc., Scott 192; Writers House 195

**Romance:** A.L.P. Literary Agency 76; Ahearn Agency, Inc., The 77; Allred and Allred Literary Agents 78; Amsterdam Agency, Marcia 80; Authentic Creations Literary Agency 81; Axelrod Agency, The 82; Barrett Books Inc., Loretta 83; Bent Literary Agent, Harvey Klinger, Inc., Jenny 83; Bernstein & Associates, Inc., Pam 84; Bernstein Literary Agency, Meredith 84; Bleeker Street Associates, Inc. 85; BookEnds, LLC 86; Books & Such 87; Brandt & Hochman Literary Agents Inc. 88; Brown Ltd., Curtis 90; Browne Ltd., Pema 90; Buck Agency, Howard 91; Cambridge Literary 92; Carvainis Agency, Inc., Maria 92; Collin Literary Agency, Frances 95; Congdon Associates Inc., Don 95; Connor Literary Agency 96; Curtis Associates, Inc., Richard 97; Dorian Literary Agency 102; Ellenberg Literary Agency, Ethan 106; Elmo Agency Inc., Ann 106; English, Elaine P. 110; Feigenbaum Publishing Consultants, Inc. 111; Fernandez Agent/Attorney, Justin E. 112

Fogelman Literary Agency 113; Fort Ross Inc. Russian-American Publishing Projects 113; Gislason Agency, The 116; Goodman Associates 118; Grace Literary Agency, Carroll 118; Gregory and Radice Authors' Agents 119; Grosjean Literary Agency, Jill 120; Grosvenor Literary Agency, The 120; Harris Literary Agency, Inc., The Joy 122; Hartline Literary Agency 122; Henshaw Group, Richard 123; Herner Rights Agency, Susan 124; Hopkins Literary Associates 125; Jenks Agency, Carolyn 130; Kern Literary Agency, Natasha 131; Kidde, Hoyt & Picard 132; Knight Agency, The 134; Larsen/Elizabeth Pomada Literary Agents, Michael 136; Lazear Agency Incorporated 137; Levine Literary Agency, Paul S. 138; Lincoln Literary Agency, Ray 140; Literary Group, The 141; Lowenstein Associates, Inc. 143; Maass Literary Agency 143; Madsen Agency, Robert 144; Manus & Associates Literary Agency, Inc. 145; Marshall Agency, The Evan 146; McGrath, Helen 147; McHugh Literary Agency 147; Multimedia Product Development, Inc. 150; Mura Enterprises, Inc., Dee 150; New Brand Agency Group, LLC 152; Norma-Lewis Agency, The 153; Paraview, Inc. 154; Picard, Literary Agent, Alison J. 157; Pinder Lane & Garon-Brooke Associates, Ltd. 158; Pine Associates, Inc., Arthur 158; Rosenberg Group, The 170; Rotrosen Agency, LLC, Jane 171; Rowland Agency, The Damaris 171; Sedgeband Literary Associates 176; Seligman, Literary Agent, Lynn 176; Serendipity Literary Agency, LLC 176; Seymour Agency, The 177; Sherman Associates, Inc., Wendy 178; Southern Literary Group 181; Spectrum Literary Agency 181; Steele-Perkins Literary Agency 182; Teal Literary Agency, Patricia 185; Toad Hall, Inc. 186; Travis Literary Agency, Susan 186; Treimel NY, Scott 187; Van Der Leun & Associates 188; Vines Agency, Inc., The 189; Waxman Agency, Inc., Scott 192; Weiner Literary Agency, Cherry 192; Wieser & Wieser, Inc. 194; Writers House 195

**Science Fiction:** Ahearn Agency, Inc., The 77; Allred and Allred Literary Agents 78; AMG/Renaissance 79; Amsterdam Agency, Marcia 80; Anubis Literary Agency 81; Bova Literary Agency, The Barbara 88; Brown Ltd., Curtis 90; Cambridge Literary 92; Collin Literary Agency, Frances 95; Congdon Associates Inc., Don 95; Core Creations 96; Curtis Associates, Inc., Richard 97; Dorian Literary Agency 102; Elite Online 105; Ellenberg Literary Agency, Ethan 106; Fernandez Agent/Attorney, Justin E. 112

Fleury Agency, B.R. 112; Fort Ross Inc. Russian-American Publishing Projects 113; Frenkel & Associates, James 115; Gislason Agency, The 116; Goodman Associates 118; Halsey Agency, Reece 121; Halsey North, Reece 121; Hamilburg Agency, Mitchell J., The 122; Hawkins & Associates, Inc., John 122; Henshaw Group, Richard 123; Herner Rights Agency, Susan 124; Jabberwocky Literary Agency 128; Kidd Agency, Inc. Virginia 132;

Kleinman, Esq., of Graybill & English L.L.C., Jeffrey M. 133; Kraas Agency, Irene 135; Lazear Agency Incorporated 137; Lewis & Company, Karen 139; Maass Literary Agency 143; Madsen Agency, Robert 144; Marshall Agency, The Evan 146; McGrath, Helen 147; Mura Enterprises, Inc., Dee 150; National Writers Literary Agency 151; New Brand Agency Group, LLC 152; Perkins Associates, L. 157; Pinder Lane & Garon-Brooke Associates, Ltd. 158; Protter Literary Agent, Susan Ann 159; Rubie Literary Agency, The Peter 172; Schiavone Literary Agency, Inc. 174; Sedgeband Literary Associates 176; Seligman, Literary Agent, Lynn 176; Serendipity Literary Agency, LLC 176; Spectrum Literary Agency 181; Sternig & Byrne Literary Agency 183; Toad Hall, Inc. 186; Treimel NY, Scott 187; Viciananza, Ltd., Ralph 189; Vines Agency, Inc., The 189; Weiner Literary Agency, Cherry 192; Writers House 195

**Sports:** Allred and Allred Literary Agents 78; Authentic Creations Literary Agency 81; Barrett Books Inc., Loretta 83; Brandt & Hochman Literary Agents Inc. 88; Brown Ltd., Curtis 90; Buck Agency, Howard 91; Cambridge Literary 92; Congdon Associates Inc., Don 95; Curtis Associates, Inc., Richard 97; DHS Literary, Inc. 100; Donovan Literary, Jim 101; Ducas, Robert 103; Dupree/Miller and Associates Inc. Literary 103; Fernandez Agent/Attorney, Justin E. 112
Goodman Associates 118; Greenburger Associates, Inc., Sanford J. 118; Gusay Literary Agency, The Charlotte 120; Hamilburg Agency, Mitchell J., The 122; Harris Literary Agency, Inc., The Joy 122; Hawkins & Associates, Inc., John 122; Henshaw Group, Richard 123; Jabberwocky Literary Agency 128; JCA Literary Agency 129; Lazear Agency Incorporated 137; Levine Literary Agency, Paul S. 138; Lincoln Literary Agency, Ray 140; Literary Group, The 141; Litwest Group, LLC 141; Madsen Agency, Robert 144; Markowitz Literary Agency, Barbara 146; Multimedia Product Development, Inc. 150; Mura Enterprises, Inc., Dee 150; National Writers Literary Agency 151; Picard, Literary Agent, Alison J. 157; Rhodes Literary Agency, Jodie 164; RLR Associates, Ltd. 168; Robbins Literary Agency, B.J. 169; Rosenberg Group, The 170; Russell and Volkening 172; Shepard Agency, The 177; Spitzer Literary Agency, Philip G. 181; Treimel NY, Scott 187; Van Der Leun & Associates 188; Venture Literary 189; Vines Agency, Inc., The 189; Waxman Agency, Inc., Scott 192; Whittaker, Literary Agent, Lynn 193; Writers House 195

**Thriller/Espionage:** Acacia House Publishing Services Ltd. 76; Ahearn Agency, Inc., The 77; Alive Communications, Inc. 78; Allen Literary Agency, Linda 78; Allred and Allred Literary Agents 78; Altshuler Literary Agency, Miriam 79; AMG/Renaissance 79; Amsterdam Agency, Marcia 80; Authentic Creations Literary Agency 81; Authors & Artists Group, Inc. 82; Baldi Literary Agency, Malaga 82; Barrett Books Inc., Loretta 83; Bernstein & Associates, Inc., Pam 84; Bleeker Street Associates, Inc. 85; Boates Literary Agency, Reid 86; BookEnds, LLC 86; Bova Literary Agency, The Barbara 88; Brandt Agency, The Joan 89; Brandt & Hochman Literary Agents Inc. 88; Brown Ltd., Curtis 90; Buck Agency, Howard 91; Cambridge Literary 92; Carlisle & Company 92; Carvainis Agency, Inc., Maria 92; Congdon Associates Inc., Don 95; Connor Literary Agency 96; Crawford Literary Agency 97; Curtis Associates, Inc., Richard 97; Dawson Associates, Liza 98; DeFiore and Company 99; Delbourgo Associates, Inc., Joélle 99; DH Literary, Inc. 100; DHS Literary, Inc. 100; Dijkstra Literary Agency, Sandra 100; Donovan Literary, Jim 101; Dorian Literary Agency 102; Ducas, Robert 103; Dunham Literary 103; Dupree/Miller and Associates Inc. Literary 103; Dystel Literary Management, Inc., Jane 104; Ellenberg Literary Agency, Ethan 106; Elmo Agency Inc., Ann 106; Eth Literary Agency, Felicia 110; Farber Literary Agency Inc. 111; Fernandez Agent/Attorney, Justin E. 112
Fleury Agency, B.R. 112; Fort Ross Inc. Russian-American Publishing Projects 113; Frenkel & Associates, James 115; Freymann Literary Agency, Sarah Jane 115; Gislason Agency, The 116; Goldfarb & Associates 117; Goodman Associates 118; Grace Literary Agency, Carroll 118; Greenburger Associates, Inc., Sanford J. 118; Gregory and Radice Authors' Agents 119; Grosjean Literary Agency, Jill 120; Grosvenor Literary Agency, The 120; Gusay Literary Agency, The Charlotte 120; Halsey Agency, Reece 121; Hamilburg Agency, Mitchell J., The 122; Harris Literary Agency, Inc., The Joy 122; Hartline Literary Agency 122; Hawkins & Associates, Inc., John 122; Henshaw Group, Richard 123; Herner Rights Agency, Susan 124; Hornfischer Literary Management, Inc. 125; Jabberwocky Literary Agency 128; JCA Literary Agency 129; Jellinek and Murray Literary Agency 130; Jenks Agency, Carolyn 130; Kern Literary Agency, Natasha 131; Kidde, Hoyt & Picard 132; Kleinman, Esq., of Graybill & English L.L.C., Jeffrey M. 133; Klinger, Inc., Harvey 133; Koster Literary Agency, LLC, Elaine 134; Kraas Agency, Irene 135; Lampack Agency, Inc., Peter 136; Lawyer's Literary Agency, Inc. 137; Lazear Agency Incorporated 137; Levine Communications, Inc., James 138; Levine Literary Agency, Inc., Ellen 138; Levine Literary Agency, Paul S. 138; Lewis & Company, Karen 139; Lincoln Literary Agency, Ray 140; Literary Group, The 141; Litwest Group, LLC 141; Love Literary Agency, Nancy 142; Lowenstein Associates, Inc. 143; Maass Literary Agency 143; Madsen Agency, Robert 144; Manus & Associates Literary Agency, Inc. 145; Markowitz Literary Agency, Barbara 146; McBride Literary Agency, Margret 147; McGrath, Helen 147; McHugh Literary Agency 147; Multimedia Product Development, Inc. 150; Mura Enterprises, Inc., Dee 150; Naggar Literary Agency, Jean V. 151; New Brand Agency Group, LLC 152; Norma-Lewis Agency, The 153; Pevner, Inc., Stephen 157; Picard, Literary Agent, Alison J. 157; Pine Associates, Inc., Arthur 158; Preskill Literary Agency, Robert 159; Protter Literary Agent, Susan Ann 159; Quicksilver Books Literary Agents 160; Rees Literary Agency, Helen 160; Rhodes Literary Agency, Jodie 164; RLR Associates, Ltd. 168; Robbins Literary Agency, B.J. 169; Rotrosen Agency, LLC, Jane 171; Rubie Literary Agency, The Peter 172; Russell and Volkening 172; Sanders & Associates, Victoria 173; Scherf, Inc., Literary Management 173; Serendipity Literary Agency, LLC 176; Shepard Agency, The 177; Simmons Literary Agency, Jeffrey 178; Singer Literary Agency Inc., Evelyn 179; Southern Literary Group 181; Spitzer Literary Agency, Philip G. 181; Sternig & Byrne Literary Agency 183;

Treimel NY, Scott 187; Van Der Leun & Associates 188; Venture Literary 189; Viciananza, Ltd., Ralph 189; Vines Agency, Inc., The 189; Wald Associates, Inc., Mary Jack 190; Ware Literary Agency, John A. 190; Watt & Associates, Sandra 191; Weiner Literary Agency, Cherry 192; Wieser & Wieser, Inc. 194; Witherspoon & Associates, Inc. 194; Wonderland Press, Inc., The 194; Writers House 195; Zachary Shuster Harmsworth 197; Zeckendorf Assoc. Inc., Susan 197

**Translation:** Brown Ltd., Curtis 90; Buck Agency, Howard 91; Congdon Associates Inc., Don 95; Curtis Associates, Inc., Richard 97; Fernandez Agent/Attorney, Justin E. 112
Goodman Associates 118; Gusay Literary Agency, The Charlotte 120; Hamilburg Agency, Mitchell J., The 122; Harris Literary Agency, Inc., The Joy 122; Hawkins & Associates, Inc., John 122; Lazear Agency Incorporated 137; Madsen Agency, Robert 144; Treimel NY, Scott 187; Van Der Leun & Associates 188; Writers House 195

**Westerns/Frontier:** Ahearn Agency, Inc., The 77; Alive Communications, Inc. 78; Allred and Allred Literary Agents 78; Amsterdam Agency, Marcia 80; Brown Ltd., Curtis 90; Buck Agency, Howard 91; Cambridge Literary 92; Congdon Associates Inc., Don 95; Curtis Associates, Inc., Richard 97; Donovan Literary, Jim 101; Fernandez Agent/Attorney, Justin E. 112
Frenkel & Associates, James 115; Goodman Associates 118; Grace Literary Agency, Carroll 118; Gusay Literary Agency, The Charlotte 120; Hamilburg Agency, Mitchell J., The 122; Hawkins & Associates, Inc., John 122; J de S Associates Inc. 128; Jellinek and Murray Literary Agency 130; Jenks Agency, Carolyn 130; Kern Literary Agency, Natasha 131; Lazear Agency Incorporated 137; Levine Literary Agency, Paul S. 138; Literary Group, The 141; Madsen Agency, Robert 144; Marshall Agency, The Evan 146; McBride Literary Agency, Margret 147; McHugh Literary Agency 147; Mura Enterprises, Inc., Dee 150; Norma-Lewis Agency, The 153; Seymour Agency, The 177; Treimel NY, Scott 187; Van Der Leun & Associates 188; Vines Agency, Inc., The 189; Weiner Literary Agency, Cherry 192; Writers House 195

**Women's:** Axelrod Agency, The 82; Book Deals, Inc. 86; Brown Ltd., Curtis 90; Buck Agency, Howard 91; Castiglia Literary Agency 93; Congdon Associates Inc., Don 95; Connor Literary Agency 96; Curtis Associates, Inc., Richard 97; English, Elaine P. 110; Fernandez Agent/Attorney, Justin E. 112
Halsey Agency, Reece 121; Harris Literary Agency, Inc., The Joy 122; Hawkins & Associates, Inc., John 122; Hopkins Literary Associates 125; Knight Agency, The 134; Lazear Agency Incorporated 137; Levine Communications, Inc., James 138; Levine Literary Agency, Inc., Ellen 138; Maass Literary Agency 143; Madsen Agency, Robert 144; Manus & Associates Literary Agency, Inc. 145; Moran Agency, Maureen 149; Paraview, Inc. 154; Rhodes Literary Agency, Jodie 164; Rotrosen Agency, LLC, Jane 171; Treimel NY, Scott 187; Van Der Leun & Associates 188; Vines Agency, Inc., The 189; Writers House 195

**Young Adult:** Alive Communications, Inc. 78; Allred and Allred Literary Agents 78; Amsterdam Agency, Marcia 80; BookEnds, LLC 86; Books & Such 87; Brandt & Hochman Literary Agents Inc. 88; Briggs, M. Courtney 89; Brown Literary Agency, Inc., Andrea 89; Brown Ltd., Curtis 90; Browne Ltd., Pema 90; Cambridge Literary 92; Carvainis Agency, Inc., Maria 92; Cohen, Inc. Literary Agency, Ruth 94; Congdon Associates Inc., Don 95; Curtis Associates, Inc., Richard 97; Dorian Literary Agency 102; Dunham Literary 103; Dwyer & O'Grady, Inc. 104; Ellenberg Literary Agency, Ethan 106; Elmo Agency Inc., Ann 106; Farber Literary Agency Inc. 111; Fernandez Agent/Attorney, Justin E. 112
Flannery Literary 112; Fort Ross Inc. Russian-American Publishing Projects 113; Frenkel & Associates, James 115; Gusay Literary Agency, The Charlotte 120; Hamilburg Agency, Mitchell J., The 122; Harris Literary Agency, Inc., The Joy 122; Hawkins & Associates, Inc., John 122; J de S Associates Inc. 128; Kidd Agency, Inc. Virginia 132; Kouts, Literary Agent, Barbara S. 134; Lazear Agency Incorporated 137; Lincoln Literary Agency, Ray 140; Literary Group, The 141; Litwest Group, LLC 141; Madsen Agency, Robert 144; Markowitz Literary Agency, Barbara 146; Mura Enterprises, Inc., Dee 150; National Writers Literary Agency 151; New Brand Agency Group, LLC 152; Norma-Lewis Agency, The 153; Picard, Literary Agent, Alison J. 157; Rhodes Literary Agency, Jodie 164; Schiavone Literary Agency, Inc. 174; Schulman, A Literary Agency, Susan 174; Southern Literary Group 181; Sternig & Byrne Literary Agency 183; Tobias, A Literary Agency for Chilren's Books, Ann 186; Treimel NY, Scott 187; Van Der Leun & Associates 188; Wald Associates, Inc., Mary Jack 190; Watt & Associates, Sandra 191; Writers House 195; Wylie-Merrick Literary Agency 196

# NONFICTION

**Agriculture/Horticulture:** A.L.P. Literary Agency 76; Baldi Literary Agency, Malaga 82; Barrett Books Inc., Loretta 83; Brown Ltd., Curtis 90; Buck Agency, Howard 91; Bykofsky Associates, Inc., Sheree 91; Cassel-man Literary Agency, Martha 93; Congdon Associates Inc., Don 95; Curtis Associates, Inc., Richard 97; Doyen Literary Services, Inc. 102; Dupree/Miller and Associates Inc. Literary 103; Gartenberg, Literary Agent, Max 116; Goldfarb & Associates 117; Goodman Associates 118; Goodman-Andrew Agency, Inc. 118; Greenburger Associates, Inc., Sanford J. 118; Gusay Literary Agency, The Charlotte 120; Hamilburg Agency, Mitchell J., The 122; Hawkins & Associates, Inc., John 122; Kleinman, Esq., of Graybill & English L.L.C., Jeffrey M. 133; Lazear Agency Incorporated 137; Lieberman Associates, Robert 139; Limelight Management 140; Madsen Agency, Robert 144; McHugh Literary Agency 147; Multimedia Product Development, Inc. 150; Mura Enterprises, Inc., Dee 150; Paraview, Inc. 154; Seymour Agency, The 177; Shepard Agency, The 177; Snell Literary Agency, Michael 180; Treimel NY, Scott 187; Watt & Associates, Sandra 191

**Animals:** A.L.P. Literary Agency 76; Acacia House Publishing Services Ltd. 76; Ahearn Agency, Inc., The 77; Baldi Literary Agency, Malaga 82; Balkin Agency, Inc. 83; Barrett Books Inc., Loretta 83; Bent Literary Agent, Harvey Klinger, Inc., Jenny 83; Bernstein Literary Agency, Meredith 84; Bial Agency, Daniel 84; Bleeker Street Associates, Inc. 85; Boates Literary Agency, Reid 86; BookEnds, LLC 86; Boston Literary Group, The 87; Brandt & Hochman Literary Agents Inc. 88; Briggs, M. Courtney 89; Brown Literary Agency, Inc., Andrea 89; Brown Ltd., Curtis 90; Buck Agency, Howard 91; Bykofsky Associates, Inc., Sheree 91; Castiglia Literary Agency 93; Congdon Associates Inc., Don 95; Cornfield Literary Agency, Robert 97; Curtis Associates, Inc., Richard 97; Delbourgo Associates, Inc., Joélle 99; DH Literary, Inc. 100; Doyen Literary Services, Inc. 102; Ducas, Robert 103; Dupree/Miller and Associates Inc. Literary 103; Dystel Literary Management, Inc., Jane 104; Eth Literary Agency, Felicia 110; Fredericks Literary Agency, Jeanne 115; Freymann Literary Agency, Sarah Jane 115; Gartenberg, Literary Agent, Max 116; Gislason Agency, The 116; Goldfarb & Associates 117; Goodman Associates 118; Greenburger Associates, Inc., Sanford J. 118; Grosvenor Literary Agency, The 120; Gusay Literary Agency, The Charlotte 120; Hamilburg Agency, Mitchell J., The 122; Hawkins & Associates, Inc., John 122; Henshaw Group, Richard 123; Jellinek and Murray Literary Agency 130; Jenks Agency, Carolyn 130; Kern Literary Agency, Natasha 131; Kleinman, Esq., of Graybill & English L.L.C., Jeffrey M. 133; Kritzer Productions, Eddie 135; Lazear Agency Incorporated 137; Levine Communications, Inc., James 138; Lincoln Literary Agency, Ray 140; Literary Group, The 141; Lowenstein Associates, Inc. 143; Madsen Agency, Robert 144; Marshall Agency, The Evan 146; McHugh Literary Agency 147; Multimedia Product Development, Inc. 150; Mura Enterprises, Inc., Dee 150; National Writers Literary Agency 151; Nine Muses and Apollo Inc. 153; Paraview, Inc. 154; Parks Agency, The Richard 154; Picard, Literary Agent, Alison J. 157; Rhodes Literary Agency, Jodie 164; RLR Associates, Ltd. 168; Roghaar Literary Agency, Inc., Linda 169; Rosenkranz Literary Agency, Rita 170; Rowland Agency, The Damaris 171; Schiavone Literary Agency, Inc. 174; Seymour Agency, The 177; Shepard Agency, The 177; Snell Literary Agency, Michael 180; Straus Agency, Inc., Robin 183; Teal Literary Agency, Patricia 185; Toad Hall, Inc. 186; Treimel NY, Scott 187; Venture Literary 189; Wales, Literary Agency, Inc. 190; Ware Literary Agency, John A. 190; Watt & Associates, Sandra 191; Whittaker, Literary Agent, Lynn 193; Writers House 195; Zachary Shuster Harmsworth 197

**Americana:** A.L.P. Literary Agency 76; Barrett Books Inc., Loretta 83; Brown Ltd., Curtis 90; Buck Agency, Howard 91; Bykofsky Associates, Inc., Sheree 91; Congdon Associates Inc., Don 95; Curtis Associates, Inc., Richard 97; Doyen Literary Services, Inc. 102; Dupree/Miller and Associates Inc. Literary 103; Goldfarb & Associates 117; Goodman Associates 118; Greenburger Associates, Inc., Sanford J. 118; Gusay Literary Agency, The Charlotte 120; Hamilburg Agency, Mitchell J., The 122; Hawkins & Associates, Inc., John 122; Lazear Agency Incorporated 137; Madsen Agency, Robert 144; McHugh Literary Agency 147; Paraview, Inc. 154; Seymour Agency, The 177; Snell Literary Agency, Michael 180; Treimel NY, Scott 187

**Anthropology/Archaeology:** A.L.P. Literary Agency 76; Allen Literary Agency, Linda 78; Allred and Allred Literary Agents 78; Altair Literary Agency 79; Authentic Creations Literary Agency 81; Baldi Literary Agency, Malaga 82; Balkin Agency, Inc. 83; Barrett Books Inc., Loretta 83; Bial Agency, Daniel 84; Bleeker Street Associates, Inc. 85; Boates Literary Agency, Reid 86; Borchardt Inc., Georges 87; Boston Literary Group, The 87; Brandt & Hochman Literary Agents Inc. 88; Brown Literary Agency, Inc., Andrea 89; Brown Ltd., Curtis 90; Buck Agency, Howard 91; Bykofsky Associates, Inc., Sheree 91; Casselman Literary Agency, Martha 93; Castiglia Literary Agency 93; Collin Literary Agency, Frances 95; Congdon Associates Inc., Don 95; Coover Agency, The Doe 96; Cornfield Literary Agency, Robert 97; Curtis Associates, Inc., Richard 97; Darhansoff & Verrill Literary Agency 98; Delbourgo Associates, Inc., Joélle 99; DH Literary, Inc. 100; Dijkstra Literary Agency, Sandra 100; Doyen Literary Services, Inc. 102; Dunham Literary 103; Dupree/Miller and Associates Inc. Literary 103; Dystel Literary Management, Inc., Jane 104; Educational Design Services, Inc. 105; Elek Associates, Peter 105; Elmo Agency Inc., Ann 106; Eth Literary Agency, Felicia 110; Fredericks Literary Agency, Jeanne 115; Freymann Literary Agency, Sarah Jane 115; Goldfarb & Associates 117; Goodman Associates 118; Goodman-Andrew Agency, Inc. 118; Greenburger Associates, Inc., Sanford J. 118; Grosvenor Literary Agency, The 120; Gusay Literary Agency, The Charlotte 120; Hamilburg Agency, Mitchell J., The 122; Hawkins & Associates, Inc., John 122; Herner Rights Agency, Susan 124; Hill & Barlow Agency 124; Hochmann Books, John L. 125; Hornfischer Literary Management, Inc. 125; James Peter Associates, Inc. 129; JCA Literary Agency 129; Jellinek and Murray Literary Agency 130; Kellock Company Inc., The 131; Kern Literary Agency, Natasha 131; Kleinman, Esq., of Graybill & English L.L.C., Jeffrey M. 133; Lampack Agency, Inc., Peter 136; Larsen/Elizabeth Pomada Literary Agents, Michael 136; Lazear Agency Incorporated 137; Levine Literary Agency, Inc., Ellen 138; Lieberman Associates, Robert 139; Lincoln Literary Agency, Ray 140; Literary Group, The 141; Lowenstein Associates, Inc. 143; Lownie Literary Agency Ltd., Andrew 143; Madsen Agency, Robert 144; Mann Agency, Carol 144; McHugh Literary Agency 147; Miller Agency, The 149; Morrison, Inc., Henry 149; Multimedia Product Development, Inc. 150; Mura Enterprises, Inc., Dee 150; Paraview, Inc. 154; Parks Agency, The Richard 154; Picard, Literary Agent, Alison J. 157; Quicksilver Books Literary Agents 160; Rabiner, Literary Agent, Inc., Susan 160; Rhodes Literary Agency, Jodie 164; RLR Associates, Ltd. 168; Roghaar Literary Agency, Inc., Linda 169; Rosenkranz Literary Agency, Rita 170; Ross Literary Agency, The Gail 170; Russell and Volkening 172; Schiavone Literary Agency, Inc. 174; Schulman, A Literary Agency, Susan 174; Seligman, Literary Agent,

Lynn 176; Seymour Agency, The 177; Singer Literary Agency Inc., Evelyn 179; Slopen Literary Agency, Beverley 179; Snell Literary Agency, Michael 180; Straus Agency, Inc., Robin 183; Toad Hall, Inc. 186; Treimel NY, Scott 187; United Tribes 188; Venture Literary 189; Ware Literary Agency, John A. 190; Watt & Associates, Sandra 191; Witherspoon & Associates, Inc. 194

**Art/Architecture/Design:** A.L.P. Literary Agency 76; Allen Literary Agency, Linda 78; Allred and Allred Literary Agents 78; Altair Literary Agency 79; Authors & Artists Group, Inc. 82; Baldi Literary Agency, Malaga 82; Barrett Books Inc., Loretta 83; Boates Literary Agency, Reid 86; Boston Literary Group, The 87; Brandt & Hochman Literary Agents Inc. 88; Brown Associates Inc., Marie 89; Brown Literary Agency, Inc., Andrea 89; Brown Ltd., Curtis 90; Buck Agency, Howard 91; Bykofsky Associates, Inc., Sheree 91; Clark Associates, William 94; Congdon Associates Inc., Don 95; Cornfield Literary Agency, Robert 97; Curtis Associates, Inc., Richard 97; Donnaud & Associates, Inc., Janis A. 101; Doyen Literary Services, Inc. 102; Dunham Literary 103; Dupree/Miller and Associates Inc. Literary 103; Elmo Agency Inc., Ann 106; Forthwrite Literary Agency 114; Freymann Literary Agency, Sarah Jane 115; Gartenberg, Literary Agent, Max 116; Goldfarb & Associates 117; Goodman Associates 118; Goodman-Andrew Agency, Inc. 118; Greenburger Associates, Inc., Sanford J. 118; Grosjean Literary Agency, Jill 120; Grosvenor Literary Agency, The 120; Gusay Literary Agency, The Charlotte 120; Hamilburg Agency, Mitchell J., The 122; Hawkins & Associates, Inc., John 122; Heacock Literary Agency, Inc. 123; Hochmann Books, John L. 125; James Peter Associates, Inc. 129; Jellinek and Murray Literary Agency 130; Kellock Company Inc., The 131; Kidde, Hoyt & Picard 132; Kleinman, Esq., of Graybill & English L.L.C., Jeffrey M. 133; Lampack Agency, Inc., Peter 136; Larsen/Elizabeth Pomada Literary Agents, Michael 136; Lazear Agency Incorporated 137; Levine Communications, Inc., James 138; Levine Literary Agency, Paul S. 138; Lieberman Associates, Robert 139; Limelight Management 140; Lincoln Literary Agency, Ray 140; Madsen Agency, Robert 144; Mann Agency, Carol 144; McHugh Literary Agency 147; Millard Literary Agency, Martha 148; Miller Agency, The 149; Norma-Lewis Agency, The 153; Paraview, Inc. 154; Parks Agency, The Richard 154; Picard, Literary Agent, Alison J. 157; Preskill Literary Agency, Robert 159; RLR Associates, Ltd. 168; Rosenkranz Literary Agency, Rita 170; Russell and Volkening 172; Seligman, Literary Agent, Lynn 176; Seymour Agency, The 177; Snell Literary Agency, Michael 180; Straus Agency, Inc., Robin 183; Treimel NY, Scott 187; United Tribes 188; Van Der Leun & Associates 188; Waterside Productions, Inc. 191; Watkins Loomis Agency, Inc. 191; Watt & Associates, Sandra 191; Wecksler-Incomco 192; Weingel-Fidel Agency, The 193; Wonderland Press, Inc., The 194; Wray Literary Agency, Pamela D. 195; Writers House 195

**Biography/Autobiography:** A.L.P. Literary Agency 76; Acacia House Publishing Services Ltd. 76; Ahearn Agency, Inc., The 77; Alive Communications, Inc. 78; Allen Literary Agency, Linda 78; Allred and Allred Literary Agents 78; Altair Literary Agency 79; Altshuler Literary Agency, Miriam 79; AMG/Renaissance 79; Amster Literary Enterprises, Betsy 80; Andrews & Associates, Bart 80; Authentic Creations Literary Agency 81; Authors & Artists Group, Inc. 82; Baldi Literary Agency, Malaga 82; Balkin Agency, Inc. 83; Barrett Books Inc., Loretta 83; Bent Literary Agent, Harvey Klinger, Inc., Jenny 83; Bial Agency, Daniel 84; Black Literary Agency, David 85; Bleeker Street Associates, Inc. 85; Boates Literary Agency, Reid 86; BookEnds, LLC 86; Borchardt Inc., Georges 87; Boston Literary Group, The 87; Bova Literary Agency, The Barbara 88; Brandt & Hochman Literary Agents Inc. 88; Briggs, M. Courtney 89; Brown Associates Inc., Marie 89; Brown Literary Agency, Inc., Andrea 89; Brown Ltd., Curtis 90; Buck Agency, Howard 91; Bykofsky Associates, Inc., Sheree 91; Cambridge Literary 92; Carlisle & Company 92; Carvainis Agency, Inc., Maria 92; Casselman Literary Agency, Martha 93; Castiglia Literary Agency 93; Clark Associates, William 94; Clausen, Mays & Tahan, LLC 94; Collin Literary Agency, Frances 95; Congdon Associates Inc., Don 95; Coover Agency, The Doe 96; Curtis Associates, Inc., Richard 97; Cyper, The Cypher Agency, James R. 98; Daves Agency, Joan 98; Dawson Associates, Liza 98; DeFiore and Company 99; Delbourgo Associates, Inc., Joélle 99; DHS Literary, Inc. 100; Donnaud & Associates, Inc., Janis A. 101; Donovan Literary, Jim 101; Doyen Literary Services, Inc. 102; Ducas, Robert 103; Dunham Literary 103; Dupree/Miller and Associates Inc. Literary 103; Dystel Literary Management, Inc., Jane 104; Ellenberg Literary Agency, Ethan 106; Elmo Agency Inc., Ann 106; Eth Literary Agency, Felicia 110; Feigen/Parrent Literary Management 111; Fogelman Literary Agency 113; Fort Ross Inc. Russian-American Publishing Projects 113; Forthwrite Literary Agency 114; Franklin Associates, Ltd., Lynn C. 114; Fredericks Literary Agency, Jeanne 115; Frenkel & Associates, James 115; Freymann Literary Agency, Sarah Jane 115; Gartenberg, Literary Agent, Max 116; Goldfarb & Associates 117; Goodman Associates 118; Goodman-Andrew Agency, Inc. 118; Greenburger Associates, Inc., Sanford J. 118; Gregory and Radice Authors' Agents 119; Grosvenor Literary Agency, The 120; Gusay Literary Agency, The Charlotte 120; Halsey Agency, Reece 121; Halsey North, Reece 121; Hamilburg Agency, Mitchell J., The 122; Hawkins & Associates, Inc., John 122; Heacock Literary Agency, Inc. 123; Henshaw Group, Richard 123; Herner Rights Agency, Susan 124; Hill & Barlow Agency 124; Hill Bonnie Nadell, Inc., Frederick 124; Hochmann Books, John L. 125; Hornfischer Literary Management, Inc. 125; J de S Associates Inc. 128; Jabberwocky Literary Agency 128; James Peter Associates, Inc. 129; JCA Literary Agency 129; Jellinek and Murray Literary Agency 130; Jenks Agency, Carolyn 130; Jordan Literary Agency, Lawrence 130; Kellock Company Inc., The 131; Kern Literary Agency, Natasha 131; Ketz Agency, Louise B. 132; Kidde, Hoyt & Picard 132; Kleinman, Esq., of Graybill & English L.L.C., Jeffrey M. 133; Klinger, Inc., Harvey 133; Knight Agency, The 134; Koster Literary Agency, LLC, Elaine 134; Kouts, Literary Agent, Barbara S. 134; Kritzer Productions, Eddie 135; Lampack Agency, Inc., Peter 136; Larsen/Elizabeth Pomada Literary Agents, Michael 136; Lawyer's Literary Agency, Inc. 137; Lazear Agency Incorporated 137; Levine Communications, Inc., James 138; Levine Literary Agency, Inc., Ellen 138; Levine Literary

Agency, Paul S. 138; Lincoln Literary Agency, Ray 140; Lipkind Agency, Wendy 140; Literary and Creative Artists, Inc. 141; Literary Group, The 141; Litwest Group, LLC 141; Livingston Cooke 142; Love Literary Agency, Nancy 142; Lowenstein Associates, Inc. 143; Lownie Literary Agency Ltd., Andrew 143; Madsen Agency, Robert 144; Mann Agency, Carol 144; Manus & Associates Literary Agency, Inc. 145; March Tenth, Inc. 145; Markowitz Literary Agency, Barbara 146; McBride Literary Agency, Margret 147; McGrath, Helen 147; McHugh Literary Agency 147; Michaels Literary Agency, Inc., Doris S. 148; Millard Literary Agency, Martha 148; Miller Agency, The 149; Morrison, Inc., Henry 149; Multimedia Product Development, Inc. 150; Mura Enterprises, Inc., Dee 150; Naggar Literary Agency, Jean V. 151; National Writers Literary Agency 151; New England Publishing Associates Inc. 152; Nine Muses and Apollo Inc. 153; Norma-Lewis Agency, The 153; Paraview, Inc. 154; Parks Agency, The Richard 154; Pevner, Inc., Stephen 157; Picard, Literary Agent, Alison J. 157; Pinder Lane & Garon-Brooke Associates, Ltd. 158; Preskill Literary Agency, Robert 159; Protter Literary Agent, Susan Ann 159; Quicksilver Books Literary Agents 160; Rabiner, Literary Agent, Inc., Susan 160; Rees Literary Agency, Helen 160; Rhodes Literary Agency, Jodie 164; Rinaldi Literary Agency, Angela 165; Rittenberg Literary Agency, Inc., Ann 165; RLR Associates, Ltd. 168; Robbins Literary Agency, B.J. 169; Robbins Office, Inc., The 169; Roghaar Literary Agency, Inc., Linda 169; Rosenberg Group, The 170; Rosenkranz Literary Agency, Rita 170; Ross Literary Agency, The Gail 170; Rotrosen Agency, LLC, Jane 171; Russell and Volkening 172; Sanders & Associates, Victoria 173; Schiavone Literary Agency, Inc. 174; Schulman, A Literary Agency, Susan 174; Sebastian Literary Agency 175; Sedgeband Literary Associates 176; Seligman, Literary Agent, Lynn 176; Seymour Agency, The 177; Shepard Agency, The 177; Simmons Literary Agency, Jeffrey 178; Singer Literary Agency Inc., Evelyn 179; Skolnick Literary Agency, Irene 179; Slopen Literary Agency, Beverley 179; Smith Literary Agency Ltd., Robert 180; Snell Literary Agency, Michael 180; Spieler Agency, The 181; Spitzer Literary Agency, Philip G. 181; Stauffer Associates, Nancy 182; Straus Agency, Inc., Robin 183; Susijn Agency, The 183; Swayze Literary Agency, Carolyn 184; Teal Literary Agency, Patricia 185; Treimel NY, Scott 187; Two M Communications Ltd. 187; United Tribes 188; Van Der Leun & Associates 188; Venture Literary 189; Viciananza, Ltd., Ralph 189; Vines Agency, Inc., The 189; Wald Associates, Inc., Mary Jack 190; Wales, Literary Agency, Inc. 190; Ware Literary Agency, John A. 190; Waterside Productions, Inc. 191; Watkins Loomis Agency, Inc. 191; Wecksler-Incomco 192; Weingel-Fidel Agency, The 193; Whittaker, Literary Agent, Lynn 193; Witherspoon & Associates, Inc. 194; Wonderland Press, Inc., The 194; Wray Literary Agency, Pamela D. 195; Writers House 195; Zachary Shuster Harmsworth 197; Zeckendorf Assoc. Inc., Susan 197

**Business:** A.L.P. Literary Agency 76; Ahearn Agency, Inc., The 77; Alive Communications, Inc. 78; Allen Literary Agency, Linda 78; Altair Literary Agency 79; Amster Literary Enterprises, Betsy 80; Authors & Artists Group, Inc. 82; Baldi Literary Agency, Malaga 82; Barrett Books Inc., Loretta 83; Bernstein Literary Agency, Meredith 84; Bial Agency, Daniel 84; Black Literary Agency, David 85; Bleeker Street Associates, Inc. 85; Boates Literary Agency, Reid 86; Book Deals, Inc. 86; BookEnds, LLC 86; Boston Literary Group, The 87; Brown Associates Inc., Marie 89; Brown Ltd., Curtis 90; Browne Ltd., Pema 90; Buck Agency, Howard 91; Bykofsky Associates, Inc., Sheree 91; Carlisle & Company 92; Carvainis Agency, Inc., Maria 92; Castiglia Literary Agency 93; Congdon Associates Inc., Don 95; Connor Literary Agency 96; Coover Agency, The Doe 96; Curtis Associates, Inc., Richard 97; Dawson Associates, Liza 98; DeFiore and Company 99; Delbourgo Associates, Inc., Joélle 99; DHS Literary, Inc. 100; Dijkstra Literary Agency, Sandra 100; Donovan Literary, Jim 101; Doyen Literary Services, Inc. 102; Ducas, Robert 103; Dunham Literary 103; Dupree/Miller and Associates Inc. Literary 103; Dystel Literary Management, Inc., Jane 104; Educational Design Services, Inc. 105; Ellenberg Literary Agency, Ethan 106; Elmo Agency Inc., Ann 106; Eth Literary Agency, Felicia 110; Feigen/Parrent Literary Management 111; Fogelman Literary Agency 113; Forthwrite Literary Agency 114; Fredericks Literary Agency, Jeanne 115; Freymann Literary Agency, Sarah Jane 115; Goldfarb & Associates 117; Goodman Associates 118; Goodman-Andrew Agency, Inc. 118; Greenburger Associates, Inc., Sanford J. 118; Grosvenor Literary Agency, The 120; Gusay Literary Agency, The Charlotte 120; Hamilburg Agency, Mitchell J., The 122; Hartline Literary Agency 122; Hawkins & Associates, Inc., John 122; Henshaw Group, Richard 123; Herman Agency LLC, The Jeff 124; Herner Rights Agency, Susan 124; Hill & Barlow Agency 124; Hornfischer Literary Management, Inc. 125; J de S Associates Inc. 128; Jabberwocky Literary Agency 128; James Peter Associates, Inc. 129; JCA Literary Agency 129; Jellinek and Murray Literary Agency 130; Jordan Literary Agency, Lawrence 130; Kellock Company Inc., The 131; Kern Literary Agency, Natasha 131; Ketz Agency, Louise B. 132; Kleinman, Esq., of Graybill & English L.L.C., Jeffrey M. 133; Knight Agency, The 134; Konner Literary Agency, Linda 134; Koster Literary Agency, LLC, Elaine 134; Kritzer Productions, Eddie 135; Lampack Agency, Inc., Peter 136; Larsen/Elizabeth Pomada Literary Agents, Michael 136; Lazear Agency Incorporated 137; Levine Communications, Inc., James 138; Levine Literary Agency, Paul S. 138; Lieberman Associates, Robert 139; Lincoln Literary Agency, Ray 140; Literary and Creative Artists, Inc. 141; Literary Group, The 141; Litwest Group, LLC 141; Livingston Cooke 142; Lowenstein Associates, Inc. 143; Madsen Agency, Robert 144; Mann Agency, Carol 144; Manus & Associates Literary Agency, Inc. 145; Marshall Agency, The Evan 146; McBride Literary Agency, Margret 147; McGrath, Helen 147; McHugh Literary Agency 147; Menza Literary Agency, Claudia 148; Michaels Literary Agency, Inc., Doris S. 148; Millard Literary Agency, Martha 148; Miller Agency, The 149; Moore Literary Agency 149; Multimedia Product Development, Inc. 150; Mura Enterprises, Inc., Dee 150; New Brand Agency Group, LLC 152; New England Publishing Associates Inc. 152; Nine Muses and Apollo Inc. 153; Paraview, Inc. 154; Parks Agency, The Richard 154; Paton Literary Agency, Kathi J. 154; Picard, Literary Agent, Alison J. 157; Pine Associates, Inc., Arthur 158; Preskill Literary Agency, Robert 159; Quicksilver Books Literary

Agents 160; Rabiner, Literary Agent, Inc., Susan 160; Rees Literary Agency, Helen 160; Rein Books, Inc., Jody 164; Rhodes Literary Agency, Jodie 164; Rinaldi Literary Agency, Angela 165; RLR Associates, Ltd. 168; Rosenberg Group, The 170; Rosenkranz Literary Agency, Rita 170; Ross Literary Agency, The Gail 170; Roth, Literary Representation, Carol Susan 171; Rotrosen Agency, LLC, Jane 171; Russell and Volkening 172; Scherf, Inc., Literary Management 173; Sebastian Literary Agency 175; Seligman, Literary Agent, Lynn 176; Serendipity Literary Agency, LLC 176; Seymour Agency, The 177; Shepard Agency, The 177; Shepard Agency, The Robert 177; Singer Literary Agency Inc., Evelyn 179; Slopen Literary Agency, Beverley 179; Snell Literary Agency, Michael 180; Spieler Agency, The 181; Spitzer Literary Agency, Philip G. 181; Swayne Agency Literary Management & Consulting, Inc., The 184; Toad Hall, Inc. 186; Travis Literary Agency, Susan 186; Treimel NY, Scott 187; United Tribes 188; Venture Literary 189; Viciananza, Ltd., Ralph 189; Vines Agency, Inc., The 189; Waterside Productions, Inc. 191; Waxman Agency, Inc., Scott 192; Wecksler-Incomco 192; Whittaker, Literary Agent, Lynn 193; Wieser & Wieser, Inc. 194; Witherspoon & Associates, Inc. 194; Wray Literary Agency, Pamela D. 195; Writers House 195; Zachary Shuster Harmsworth 197

**Child Guidance/Parenting:** A.L.P. Literary Agency 76; Ahearn Agency, Inc., The 77; Alive Communications, Inc. 78; Allen Literary Agency, Linda 78; Amster Literary Enterprises, Betsy 80; Amsterdam Agency, Marcia 80; Authentic Creations Literary Agency 81; Authors & Artists Group, Inc. 82; Barrett Books Inc., Loretta 83; Bent Literary Agent, Harvey Klinger, Inc., Jenny 83; Bernstein Literary Agency, Meredith 84; Bial Agency, Daniel 84; Bleeker Street Associates, Inc. 85; Boates Literary Agency, Reid 86; Book Deals, Inc. 86; BookEnds, LLC 86; Books & Such 87; Boston Literary Group, The 87; Brandt & Hochman Literary Agents Inc. 88; Brown Ltd., Curtis 90; Browne Ltd., Pema 90; Buck Agency, Howard 91; Bykofsky Associates, Inc., Sheree 91; Castiglia Literary Agency 93; Charlton Associates, James 93; Congdon Associates Inc., Don 95; Connor Literary Agency 96; Coover Agency, The Doe 96; Curtis Associates, Inc., Richard 97; DeFiore and Company 99; Delbourgo Associates, Inc., Joélle 99; DH Literary, Inc. 100; DHS Literary, Inc. 100; Dijkstra Literary Agency, Sandra 100; Donnaud & Associates, Inc., Janis A. 101; Donovan Literary, Jim 101; Doyen Literary Services, Inc. 102; Dupree/Miller and Associates Inc. Literary 103; Dystel Literary Management, Inc., Jane 104; Educational Design Services, Inc. 105; Elek Associates, Peter 105; Ellenberg Literary Agency, Ethan 106; Elmo Agency Inc., Ann 106; Eth Literary Agency, Felicia 110; Farber Literary Agency Inc. 111; Fogelman Literary Agency 113; Forthwrite Literary Agency 114; Fredericks Literary Agency, Jeanne 115; Freymann Literary Agency, Sarah Jane 115; Gartenberg, Literary Agent, Max 116; Goldfarb & Associates 117; Goodman Associates 118; Goodman-Andrew Agency, Inc. 118; Greenburger Associates, Inc., Sanford J. 118; Grosvenor Literary Agency, The 120; Gusay Literary Agency, The Charlotte 120; Hamilburg Agency, Mitchell J., The 122; Hartline Literary Agency 122; Hawkins & Associates, Inc., John 122; Henshaw Group, Richard 123; Herner Rights Agency, Susan 124; Hill & Barlow Agency 124; Hornfischer Literary Management, Inc. 125; James Peter Associates, Inc. 129; Jellinek and Murray Literary Agency 130; Kellock Company Inc., The 131; Kern Literary Agency, Natasha 131; Kleinman, Esq., of Graybill & English L.L.C., Jeffrey M. 133; Knight Agency, The 134; Konner Literary Agency, Linda 134; Koster Literary Agency, LLC, Elaine 134; Kouts, Literary Agent, Barbara S. 134; Lazear Agency Incorporated 137; Levine Communications, Inc., James 138; Levine Literary Agency, Paul S. 138; Lincoln Literary Agency, Ray 140; Literary Group, The 141; Litwest Group, LLC 141; Livingston Cooke 142; Love Literary Agency, Nancy 142; Lowenstein Associates, Inc. 143; Madsen Agency, Robert 144; Mann Agency, Carol 144; Manus & Associates Literary Agency, Inc. 145; Marshall Agency, The Evan 146; McBride Literary Agency, Margret 147; McHugh Literary Agency 147; Millard Literary Agency, Martha 148; Miller Agency, The 149; Multimedia Product Development, Inc. 150; Mura Enterprises, Inc., Dee 150; Naggar Literary Agency, Jean V. 151; National Writers Literary Agency 151; New Brand Agency Group, LLC 152; New England Publishing Associates Inc. 152; Norma-Lewis Agency, The 153; Paraview, Inc. 154; Parks Agency, The Richard 154; Paton Literary Agency, Kathi J. 154; Picard, Literary Agent, Alison J. 157; Pinder Lane & Garon-Brooke Associates, Ltd. 158; Quicksilver Books Literary Agents 160; Rein Books, Inc., Jody 164; Rhodes Literary Agency, Jodie 164; Rinaldi Literary Agency, Angela 165; RLR Associates, Ltd. 168; Robbins Literary Agency, B.J. 169; Rosenberg Group, The 170; Rosenkranz Literary Agency, Rita 170; Rotrosen Agency, LLC, Jane 171; Schiavone Literary Agency, Inc. 174; Schulman, A Literary Agency, Susan 174; Sebastian Literary Agency 175; Seligman, Literary Agent, Lynn 176; Seymour Agency, The 177; Shepard Agency, The 177; Singer Literary Agency Inc., Evelyn 179; Snell Literary Agency, Michael 180; Spieler Agency, The 181; Straus Agency, Inc., Robin 183; Swayze Literary Agency, Carolyn 184; Teal Literary Agency, Patricia 185; Toad Hall, Inc. 186; Travis Literary Agency, Susan 186; Treimel NY, Scott 187; Two M Communications Ltd. 187; United Tribes 188; Waterside Productions, Inc. 191; Wray Literary Agency, Pamela D. 195; Writers House 195; Zeckendorf Assoc. Inc., Susan 197

**Computers/Electronics:** A.L.P. Literary Agency 76; Allen Literary Agency, Linda 78; Authors & Artists Group, Inc. 82; Barrett Books Inc., Loretta 83; Bleeker Street Associates, Inc. 85; Brown Ltd., Curtis 90; Buck Agency, Howard 91; Bykofsky Associates, Inc., Sheree 91; Congdon Associates Inc., Don 95; Curtis Associates, Inc., Richard 97; Doyen Literary Services, Inc. 102; Dupree/Miller and Associates Inc. Literary 103; Elmo Agency Inc., Ann 106; Goldfarb & Associates 117; Goodman Associates 118; Greenburger Associates, Inc., Sanford J. 118; Gusay Literary Agency, The Charlotte 120; Hamilburg Agency, Mitchell J., The 122; Henshaw Group, Richard 123; Herman Agency LLC, The Jeff 124; Jellinek and Murray Literary Agency 130; Kleinman, Esq., of Graybill & English L.L.C., Jeffrey M. 133; Kritzer Productions, Eddie 135; Lazear Agency Incorporated 137; Levine Communications, Inc., James 138; Levine Literary Agency, Paul S. 138; Lieberman Associates,

Robert 139; Madsen Agency, Robert 144; McHugh Literary Agency 147; Moore Literary Agency 149; Mura Enterprises, Inc., Dee 150; Paraview, Inc. 154; Rhodes Literary Agency, Jodie 164; Rosenkranz Literary Agency, Rita 170; Serendipity Literary Agency, LLC 176; Seymour Agency, The 177; Shepard Agency, The 177; Snell Literary Agency, Michael 180; Swayne Agency Literary Management & Consulting, Inc., The 184; Treimel NY, Scott 187; Venture Literary 189; Waterside Productions, Inc. 191; Wray Literary Agency, Pamela D. 195; Wylie-Merrick Literary Agency 196

**Cooking/Food/Nutrition:** A.L.P. Literary Agency 76; Agents Incorporated for Medical and Mental Health Professionals 76; Allred and Allred Literary Agents 78; Authors & Artists Group, Inc. 82; Baldi Literary Agency, Malaga 82; Barrett Books Inc., Loretta 83; Bial Agency, Daniel 84; Bleeker Street Associates, Inc. 85; Book Deals, Inc. 86; BookEnds, LLC 86; Brandt & Hochman Literary Agents Inc. 88; Brown Ltd., Curtis 90; Browne Ltd., Pema 90; Buck Agency, Howard 91; Bykofsky Associates, Inc., Sheree 91; Cambridge Literary 92; Carlisle & Company 92; Casselman Literary Agency, Martha 93; Castiglia Literary Agency 93; Charlton Associates, James 93; Clausen, Mays & Tahan, LLC 94; Congdon Associates Inc., Don 95; Connor Literary Agency 96; Coover Agency, The Doe 96; Cornfield Literary Agency, Robert 97; Curtis Associates, Inc., Richard 97; DeFiore and Company 99; Delbourgo Associates, Inc., Joélle 99; DHS Literary, Inc. 100; Dijkstra Literary Agency, Sandra 100; Donnaud & Associates, Inc., Janis A. 101; Doyen Literary Services, Inc. 102; Dupree/Miller and Associates Inc. Literary 103; Dystel Literary Management, Inc., Jane 104; Ellenberg Literary Agency, Ethan 106; Elmo Agency Inc., Ann 106; Farber Literary Agency Inc. 111; Forthwrite Literary Agency 114; Fredericks Literary Agency, Jeanne 115; Freymann Literary Agency, Sarah Jane 115; Goldfarb & Associates 117; Goodman Associates 118; Goodman-Andrew Agency, Inc. 118; Greenburger Associates, Inc., Sanford J. 118; Gusay Literary Agency, The Charlotte 120; Hamilburg Agency, Mitchell J., The 122; Hartline Literary Agency 122; Hawkins & Associates, Inc., John 122; Henshaw Group, Richard 123; Herner Rights Agency, Susan 124; Hill Bonnie Nadell, Inc., Frederick 124; Hochmann Books, John L. 125; Jabberwocky Literary Agency 128; Jellinek and Murray Literary Agency 130; Kleinman, Esq., of Graybill & English L.L.C., Jeffrey M. 133; Klinger, Inc., Harvey 133; Konner Literary Agency, Linda 134; Koster Literary Agency, LLC, Elaine 134; Kritzer Productions, Eddie 135; Larsen/Elizabeth Pomada Literary Agents, Michael 136; Lazear Agency Incorporated 137; Lescher & Lescher Ltd. 138; Levine Communications, Inc., James 138; Levine Literary Agency, Paul S. 138; Limelight Management 140; Lincoln Literary Agency, Ray 140; Literary and Creative Artists, Inc. 141; Literary Group, The 141; Love Literary Agency, Nancy 142; Madsen Agency, Robert 144; Marshall Agency, The Evan 146; McBride Literary Agency, Margret 147; McHugh Literary Agency 147; Millard Literary Agency, Martha 148; Miller Agency, The 149; Multimedia Product Development, Inc. 150; Nolan Literary Agency, Betsy 153; Norma-Lewis Agency, The 153; Paraview, Inc. 154; Parks Agency, The Richard 154; Picard, Literary Agent, Alison J. 157; Quicksilver Books Literary Agents 160; Rhodes Literary Agency, Jodie 164; Rinaldi Literary Agency, Angela 165; RLR Associates, Ltd. 168; Rosenkranz Literary Agency, Rita 170; Rotrosen Agency, LLC, Jane 171; Rowland Agency, The Damaris 171; Rubie Literary Agency, The Peter 172; Russell and Volkening 172; Seligman, Literary Agent, Lynn 176; Seymour Agency, The 177; Shepard Agency, The 177; Smith Literary Agency Ltd., Robert 180; Snell Literary Agency, Michael 180; Spieler Agency, The 181; Straus Agency, Inc., Robin 183; Swayze Literary Agency, Carolyn 184; Toad Hall, Inc. 186; Travis Literary Agency, Susan 186; Treimel NY, Scott 187; United Tribes 188; Van Der Leun & Associates 188; Wieser & Wieser, Inc. 194; Wray Literary Agency, Pamela D. 195; Writers House 195

**Crafts/Hobbies:** A.L.P. Literary Agency 76; Allred and Allred Literary Agents 78; Authentic Creations Literary Agency 81; Authors & Artists Group, Inc. 82; Barrett Books Inc., Loretta 83; BookEnds, LLC 86; Brown Ltd., Curtis 90; Buck Agency, Howard 91; Bykofsky Associates, Inc., Sheree 91; Congdon Associates Inc., Don 95; Connor Literary Agency 96; Curtis Associates, Inc., Richard 97; Doyen Literary Services, Inc. 102; Dupree/Miller and Associates Inc. Literary 103; Forthwrite Literary Agency 114; Fredericks Literary Agency, Jeanne 115; Goldfarb & Associates 117; Goodman Associates 118; Greenburger Associates, Inc., Sanford J. 118; Gusay Literary Agency, The Charlotte 120; Hamilburg Agency, Mitchell J., The 122; Hawkins & Associates, Inc., John 122; Kellock Company Inc., The 131; Kleinman, Esq., of Graybill & English L.L.C., Jeffrey M. 133; Lazear Agency Incorporated 137; Levine Literary Agency, Paul S. 138; Limelight Management 140; Lincoln Literary Agency, Ray 140; Literary Group, The 141; Lowenstein Associates, Inc. 143; Madsen Agency, Robert 144; McHugh Literary Agency 147; Multimedia Product Development, Inc. 150; Norma-Lewis Agency, The 153; Paraview, Inc. 154; Parks Agency, The Richard 154; Rosenkranz Literary Agency, Rita 170; Seymour Agency, The 177; Shepard Agency, The 177; Snell Literary Agency, Michael 180; Toad Hall, Inc. 186; Treimel NY, Scott 187; Watt & Associates, Sandra 191

**Creative Nonfiction:** A.L.P. Literary Agency 76; Barrett Books Inc., Loretta 83; Bernstein Literary Agency, Meredith 84; Brown Ltd., Curtis 90; Buck Agency, Howard 91; Bykofsky Associates, Inc., Sheree 91; Congdon Associates Inc., Don 95; Curtis Associates, Inc., Richard 97; Donnaud & Associates, Inc., Janis A. 101; Doyen Literary Services, Inc. 102; Dupree/Miller and Associates Inc. Literary 103; Goldfarb & Associates 117; Goodman Associates 118; Greenburger Associates, Inc., Sanford J. 118; Gusay Literary Agency, The Charlotte 120; Hamilburg Agency, Mitchell J., The 122; Hawkins & Associates, Inc., John 122; Kellock Company Inc., The 131; Kleinman, Esq., of Graybill & English L.L.C., Jeffrey M. 133; Lazear Agency Incorporated 137; Levine Literary Agency, Inc., Ellen 138; Levine Literary Agency, Paul S. 138; Lincoln Literary Agency, Ray 140; Literary Group, The 141; Lowenstein Associates, Inc. 143; Madsen Agency, Robert 144; Manus & Associates Literary Agency,

Inc. 145; McHugh Literary Agency 147; Multimedia Product Development, Inc. 150; Paraview, Inc. 154; Rein Books, Inc., Jody 164; Rubie Literary Agency, The Peter 172; Russell and Volkening 172; Sebastian Literary Agency 175; Seymour Agency, The 177; Snell Literary Agency, Michael 180; Stauffer Associates, Nancy 182; Talbot Agency, The John 185; Treimel NY, Scott 187; Van Der Leun & Associates 188; Wecksler-Incomco 192

**Current Affairs:** A.L.P. Literary Agency 76; Ahearn Agency, Inc., The 77; Allred and Allred Literary Agents 78; Authentic Creations Literary Agency 81; Authors & Artists Group, Inc. 82; Baldi Literary Agency, Malaga 82; Balkin Agency, Inc. 83; Barrett Books Inc., Loretta 83; Bial Agency, Daniel 84; Bleeker Street Associates, Inc. 85; Boates Literary Agency, Reid 86; BookEnds, LLC 86; Borchardt Inc., Georges 87; Boston Literary Group, The 87; Brandt & Hochman Literary Agents Inc. 88; Brown Literary Agency, Inc., Andrea 89; Brown Ltd., Curtis 90; Buck Agency, Howard 91; Bykofsky Associates, Inc., Sheree 91; Cambridge Literary 92; Castiglia Literary Agency 93; Clark Associates, William 94; Congdon Associates Inc., Don 95; Connor Literary Agency 96; Curtis Associates, Inc., Richard 97; Cyper, The Cypher Agency, James R. 98; Delbourgo Associates, Inc., Joélle 99; DHS Literary, Inc. 100; Donnaud & Associates, Inc., Janis A. 101; Donovan Literary, Jim 101; Doyen Literary Services, Inc. 102; Ducas, Robert 103; Dunham Literary 103; Dupree/Miller and Associates Inc. Literary 103; Dystel Literary Management, Inc., Jane 104; Educational Design Services, Inc. 105; Ellenberg Literary Agency, Ethan 106; Elmo Agency Inc., Ann 106; Eth Literary Agency, Felicia 110; Feigen/Parrent Literary Management 111; Fogelman Literary Agency 113; Forthwrite Literary Agency 114; Franklin Associates, Ltd., Lynn C. 114; Freymann Literary Agency, Sarah Jane 115; Gartenberg, Literary Agent, Max 116; Goldfarb & Associates 117; Goodman Associates 118; Goodman-Andrew Agency, Inc. 118; Greenburger Associates, Inc., Sanford J. 118; Grosvenor Literary Agency, The 120; Gusay Literary Agency, The Charlotte 120; Halsey Agency, Reece 121; Halsey North, Reece 121; Hamilburg Agency, Mitchell J., The 122; Hawkins & Associates, Inc., John 122; Henshaw Group, Richard 123; Herner Rights Agency, Susan 124; Hill & Barlow Agency 124; Hill Bonnie Nadell, Inc., Frederick 124; Hochmann Books, John L. 125; Hornfischer Literary Management, Inc. 125; J de S Associates Inc. 128; Jabberwocky Literary Agency 128; James Peter Associates, Inc. 129; JCA Literary Agency 129; Jellinek and Murray Literary Agency 130; Kellock Company Inc., The 131; Kern Literary Agency, Natasha 131; Ketz Agency, Louise B. 132; Kidde, Hoyt & Picard 132; Kleinman, Esq., of Graybill & English L.L.C., Jeffrey M. 133; Knight Agency, The 134; Koster Literary Agency, LLC, Elaine 134; Kouts, Literary Agent, Barbara S. 134; Kritzer Productions, Eddie 135; Lampack Agency, Inc., Peter 136; Larsen/Elizabeth Pomada Literary Agents, Michael 136; Lazear Agency Incorporated 137; Levine Literary Agency, Inc., Ellen 138; Levine Literary Agency, Paul S. 138; Lincoln Literary Agency, Ray 140; Lipkind Agency, Wendy 140; Literary Group, The 141; Litwest Group, LLC 141; Livingston Cooke 142; Love Literary Agency, Nancy 142; Lowenstein Associates, Inc. 143; Lownie Literary Agency Ltd., Andrew 143; Madsen Agency, Robert 144; Mann Agency, Carol 144; Manus & Associates Literary Agency, Inc. 145; March Tenth, Inc. 145; Markowitz Literary Agency, Barbara 146; McBride Literary Agency, Margret 147; McGrath, Helen 147; McHugh Literary Agency 147; Menza Literary Agency, Claudia 148; Michaels Literary Agency, Inc., Doris S. 148; Millard Literary Agency, Martha 148; Miller Agency, The 149; Multimedia Product Development, Inc. 150; Mura Enterprises, Inc., Dee 150; Naggar Literary Agency, Jean V. 151; Nine Muses and Apollo Inc. 153; Norma-Lewis Agency, The 153; Paraview, Inc. 154; Parks Agency, The Richard 154; Picard, Literary Agent, Alison J. 157; Pine Associates, Inc., Arthur 158; Preskill Literary Agency, Robert 159; Quicksilver Books Literary Agents 160; Rabiner, Literary Agent, Inc., Susan 160; Rees Literary Agency, Helen 160; Rein Books, Inc., Jody 164; Rhodes Literary Agency, Jodie 164; Rinaldi Literary Agency, Angela 165; RLR Associates, Ltd. 168; Robbins Literary Agency, B.J. 169; Rosenberg Group, The 170; Rosenkranz Literary Agency, Rita 170; Rotrosen Agency, LLC, Jane 171; Rubie Literary Agency, The Peter 172; Russell and Volkening 172; Sanders & Associates, Victoria 173; Schiavone Literary Agency, Inc. 174; Schulman, A Literary Agency, Susan 174; Sebastian Literary Agency 175; Seligman, Literary Agent, Lynn 176; Seymour Agency, The 177; Shepard Agency, The 177; Shepard Agency, The Robert 177; Simmons Literary Agency, Jeffrey 178; Singer Literary Agency Inc., Evelyn 179; Skolnick Literary Agency, Irene 179; Slopen Literary Agency, Beverley 179; Snell Literary Agency, Michael 180; Southern Literary Group 181; Spieler Agency, The 181; Spitzer Literary Agency, Philip G. 181; Stauffer Associates, Nancy 182; Straus Agency, Inc., Robin 183; Swayne Agency Literary Management & Consulting, Inc., The 184; Treimel NY, Scott 187; United Tribes 188; Van Der Leun & Associates 188; Venture Literary 189; Vines Agency, Inc., The 189; Wald Associates, Inc., Mary Jack 190; Wales, Literary Agency, Inc. 190; Ware Literary Agency, John A. 190; Watkins Loomis Agency, Inc. 191; Watt & Associates, Sandra 191; Wecksler-Incomco 192; Whittaker, Literary Agent, Lynn 193; Wieser & Wieser, Inc. 194; Witherspoon & Associates, Inc. 194; Wray Literary Agency, Pamela D. 195; Zachary Shuster Harmsworth 197

**Education:** A.L.P. Literary Agency 76; Allred and Allred Literary Agents 78; Authors & Artists Group, Inc. 82; Barrett Books Inc., Loretta 83; Brown Ltd., Curtis 90; Buck Agency, Howard 91; Bykofsky Associates, Inc., Sheree 91; Congdon Associates Inc., Don 95; Curtis Associates, Inc., Richard 97; Delbourgo Associates, Inc., Joélle 99; Doyen Literary Services, Inc. 102; Dunham Literary 103; Dupree/Miller and Associates Inc. Literary 103; Dystel Literary Management, Inc., Jane 104; Educational Design Services, Inc. 105; Elmo Agency Inc., Ann 106; Fogelman Literary Agency 113; Goldfarb & Associates 117; Goodman Associates 118; Goodman-Andrew Agency, Inc. 118; Greenburger Associates, Inc., Sanford J. 118; Gusay Literary Agency, The Charlotte 120; Hamilburg Agency, Mitchell J., The 122; Hawkins & Associates, Inc., John 122; Hill & Barlow Agency 124; Kellock Company Inc., The 131; Kleinman, Esq., of Graybill & English L.L.C., Jeffrey M. 133; Lazear Agency Incorporated 137; Levine Literary Agency, Paul S. 138; Lieberman Associates, Robert 139; Literary

Group, The 141; Lowenstein Associates, Inc. 143; Madsen Agency, Robert 144; McHugh Literary Agency 147; Menza Literary Agency, Claudia 148; Millard Literary Agency, Martha 148; Mura Enterprises, Inc., Dee 150; National Writers Literary Agency 151; Paraview, Inc. 154; Picard, Literary Agent, Alison J. 157; Rhodes Literary Agency, Jodie 164; RLR Associates, Ltd. 168; Roghaar Literary Agency, Inc., Linda 169; Ross Literary Agency, The Gail 170; Russell and Volkening 172; Schiavone Literary Agency, Inc. 174; Schulman, A Literary Agency, Susan 174; Seligman, Literary Agent, Lynn 176; Serendipity Literary Agency, LLC 176; Seymour Agency, The 177; Snell Literary Agency, Michael 180; Treimel NY, Scott 187; United Tribes 188; Wray Literary Agency, Pamela D. 195

**Ethnic/Cultural Interests:** A.L.P. Literary Agency 76; Ahearn Agency, Inc., The 77; Allen Literary Agency, Linda 78; Allred and Allred Literary Agents 78; Altair Literary Agency 79; Altshuler Literary Agency, Miriam 79; Amster Literary Enterprises, Betsy 80; Authors & Artists Group, Inc. 82; Baldi Literary Agency, Malaga 82; Barrett Books Inc., Loretta 83; Bent Literary Agent, Harvey Klinger, Inc., Jenny 83; Bial Agency, Daniel 84; Bleeker Street Associates, Inc. 85; Boates Literary Agency, Reid 86; Book Deals, Inc. 86; BookEnds, LLC 86; Boston Literary Group, The 87; Brandt & Hochman Literary Agents Inc. 88; Brown Associates Inc., Marie 89; Brown Literary Agency, Inc., Andrea 89; Brown Ltd., Curtis 90; Browne Ltd., Pema 90; Buck Agency, Howard 91; Bykofsky Associates, Inc., Sheree 91; Castiglia Literary Agency 93; Clark Associates, William 94; Cohen, Inc. Literary Agency, Ruth 94; Congdon Associates Inc., Don 95; Connor Literary Agency 96; Coover Agency, The Doe 96; Curtis Associates, Inc., Richard 97; Cyper, The Cypher Agency, James R. 98; Delbourgo Associates, Inc., Joélle 99; DH Literary, Inc. 100; DHS Literary, Inc. 100; Dijkstra Literary Agency, Sandra 100; Doyen Literary Services, Inc. 102; Dunham Literary 103; Dupree/Miller and Associates Inc. Literary 103; Dystel Literary Management, Inc., Jane 104; Educational Design Services, Inc. 105; Eth Literary Agency, Felicia 110; Fogelman Literary Agency 113; Freymann Literary Agency, Sarah Jane 115; Goldfarb & Associates 117; Goodman Associates 118; Goodman-Andrew Agency, Inc. 118; Greenburger Associates, Inc., Sanford J. 118; Gusay Literary Agency, The Charlotte 120; Hamilburg Agency, Mitchell J., The 122; Hawkins & Associates, Inc., John 122; Herner Rights Agency, Susan 124; Hill & Barlow Agency 124; J de S Associates Inc. 128; James Peter Associates, Inc. 129; Jellinek and Murray Literary Agency 130; Jenks Agency, Carolyn 130; Kellock Company Inc., The 131; Kern Literary Agency, Natasha 131; Kidde, Hoyt & Picard 132; Kleinman, Esq., of Graybill & English L.L.C., Jeffrey M. 133; Knight Agency, The 134; Koster Literary Agency, LLC, Elaine 134; Kouts, Literary Agent, Barbara S. 134; Larsen/Elizabeth Pomada Literary Agents, Michael 136; Lazear Agency Incorporated 137; Levine Literary Agency, Paul S. 138; Lewis & Company, Karen 139; Lincoln Literary Agency, Ray 140; Literary Group, The 141; Litwest Group, LLC 141; Love Literary Agency, Nancy 142; Lowenstein Associates, Inc. 143; Madsen Agency, Robert 144; Mann Agency, Carol 144; Manus & Associates Literary Agency, Inc. 145; McBride Literary Agency, Margret 147; McHugh Literary Agency 147; Menza Literary Agency, Claudia 148; Michaels Literary Agency, Inc., Doris S. 148; Millard Literary Agency, Martha 148; Miller Agency, The 149; Multimedia Product Development, Inc. 150; Mura Enterprises, Inc., Dee 150; New Brand Agency Group, LLC 152; Nine Muses and Apollo Inc. 153; Norma-Lewis Agency, The 153; Paraview, Inc. 154; Parks Agency, The Richard 154; Pevner, Inc., Stephen 157; Picard, Literary Agent, Alison J. 157; Quicksilver Books Literary Agents 160; Rabiner, Literary Agent, Inc., Susan 160; Rein Books, Inc., Jody 164; Rhodes Literary Agency, Jodie 164; RLR Associates, Ltd. 168; Robbins Literary Agency, B.J. 169; Rosenberg Group, The 170; Rosenkranz Literary Agency, Rita 170; Ross Literary Agency, The Gail 170; Rubie Literary Agency, The Peter 172; Russell and Volkening 172; Sanders & Associates, Victoria 173; Schiavone Literary Agency, Inc. 174; Schulman, A Literary Agency, Susan 174; Sedgeband Literary Associates 176; Seligman, Literary Agent, Lynn 176; Serendipity Literary Agency, LLC 176; Seymour Agency, The 177; Shepard Agency, The Robert 177; Singer Literary Agency Inc., Evelyn 179; Snell Literary Agency, Michael 180; Spitzer Literary Agency, Philip G. 181; Stauffer Associates, Nancy 182; Straus Agency, Inc., Robin 183; Swayne Agency Literary Management & Consulting, Inc., The 184; Swayze Literary Agency, Carolyn 184; Travis Literary Agency, Susan 186; Treimel NY, Scott 187; Two M Communications Ltd. 187; United Tribes 188; Van Der Leun & Associates 188; Venture Literary 189; Vines Agency, Inc., The 189; Wald Associates, Inc., Mary Jack 190; Wales, Literary Agency, Inc. 190; Waterside Productions, Inc. 191; Watkins Loomis Agency, Inc. 191; Waxman Agency, Inc., Scott 192; Whittaker, Literary Agent, Lynn 193; Witherspoon & Associates, Inc. 194; Wonderland Press, Inc., The 194

**Gardening:** A.L.P. Literary Agency 76; Amster Literary Enterprises, Betsy 80; Barrett Books Inc., Loretta 83; Brown Ltd., Curtis 90; Buck Agency, Howard 91; Bykofsky Associates, Inc., Sheree 91; Congdon Associates Inc., Don 95; Curtis Associates, Inc., Richard 97; Doyen Literary Services, Inc. 102; Dupree/Miller and Associates Inc. Literary 103; Fredericks Literary Agency, Jeanne 115; Goldfarb & Associates 117; Goodman Associates 118; Greenburger Associates, Inc., Sanford J. 118; Grosjean Literary Agency, Jill 120; Gusay Literary Agency, The Charlotte 120; Hamilburg Agency, Mitchell J., The 122; Hawkins & Associates, Inc., John 122; Kern Literary Agency, Natasha 131; Lazear Agency Incorporated 137; Levine Communications, Inc., James 138; Limelight Management 140; Lincoln Literary Agency, Ray 140; Madsen Agency, Robert 144; McHugh Literary Agency 147; Paraview, Inc. 154; Parks Agency, The Richard 154; Rittenberg Literary Agency, Inc., Ann 165; Seymour Agency, The 177; Snell Literary Agency, Michael 180; Treimel NY, Scott 187; Van Der Leun & Associates 188

**Gay/Lesbian Issues:** A.L.P. Literary Agency 76; Ahearn Agency, Inc., The 77; Allen Literary Agency, Linda 78; Altair Literary Agency 79; Authors & Artists Group, Inc. 82; Baldi Literary Agency, Malaga 82; Barrett Books Inc., Loretta 83; Bent Literary Agent, Harvey Klinger, Inc., Jenny 83; Bial Agency, Daniel 84; Bleeker

Street Associates, Inc. 85; BookEnds, LLC 86; Brandt & Hochman Literary Agents Inc. 88; Brown Ltd., Curtis 90; Browne Ltd., Pema 90; Buck Agency, Howard 91; Bykofsky Associates, Inc., Sheree 91; Cambridge Literary 92; Congdon Associates Inc., Don 95; Core Creations 96; Curtis Associates, Inc., Richard 97; Cyper, The Cypher Agency, James R. 98; Daves Agency, Joan 98; DeFiore and Company 99; Doyen Literary Services, Inc. 102; Ducas, Robert 103; Dunham Literary 103; Dupree/Miller and Associates Inc. Literary 103; Dystel Literary Management, Inc., Jane 104; Eth Literary Agency, Felicia 110; Feigen/Parrent Literary Management 111; Freymann Literary Agency, Sarah Jane 115; Goldfarb & Associates 117; Goodman Associates 118; Goodman-Andrew Agency, Inc. 118; Greenburger Associates, Inc., Sanford J. 118; Gusay Literary Agency, The Charlotte 120; Hamilburg Agency, Mitchell J., The 122; Hawkins & Associates, Inc., John 122; Henshaw Group, Richard 123; Herner Rights Agency, Susan 124; Hill & Barlow Agency 124; Hochmann Books, John L. 125; Jabberwocky Literary Agency 128; James Peter Associates, Inc. 129; Jellinek and Murray Literary Agency 130; Jenks Agency, Carolyn 130; Kidde, Hoyt & Picard 132; Kleinman, Esq., of Graybill & English L.L.C., Jeffrey M. 133; Konner Literary Agency, Linda 134; Larsen/Elizabeth Pomada Literary Agents, Michael 136; Lazear Agency Incorporated 137; Levine Communications, Inc., James 138; Levine Literary Agency, Paul S. 138; Lewis & Company, Karen 139; Lincoln Literary Agency, Ray 140; Literary Group, The 141; Livingston Cooke 142; Lowenstein Associates, Inc. 143; Madsen Agency, Robert 144; McBride Literary Agency, Margret 147; McHugh Literary Agency 147; Miller Agency, The 149; Mura Enterprises, Inc., Dee 150; New Brand Agency Group, LLC 152; Paraview, Inc. 154; Parks Agency, The Richard 154; Pevner, Inc., Stephen 157; Picard, Literary Agent, Alison J. 157; Pinder Lane & Garon-Brooke Associates, Ltd. 158; Rabiner, Literary Agent, Inc., Susan 160; Rhodes Literary Agency, Jodie 164; RLR Associates, Ltd. 168; Rosenkranz Literary Agency, Rita 170; Ross Literary Agency, The Gail 170; Russell and Volkening 172; Sanders & Associates, Victoria 173; Schiavone Literary Agency, Inc. 174; Schulman, A Literary Agency, Susan 174; Seymour Agency, The 177; Shepard Agency, The Robert 177; Snell Literary Agency, Michael 180; Spieler Agency, The 181; Treimel NY, Scott 187; Two M Communications Ltd. 187; United Tribes 188; Wales, Literary Agency, Inc. 190; Whittaker, Literary Agent, Lynn 193; Witherspoon & Associates, Inc. 194; Zachary Shuster Harmsworth 197

**Government/Politics/Law:** A.L.P. Literary Agency 76; Allen Literary Agency, Linda 78; Baldi Literary Agency, Malaga 82; Barrett Books Inc., Loretta 83; Bernstein Literary Agency, Meredith 84; Bial Agency, Daniel 84; Black Literary Agency, David 85; Bleeker Street Associates, Inc. 85; Boates Literary Agency, Reid 86; Boston Literary Group, The 87; Brandt & Hochman Literary Agents Inc. 88; Brown Ltd., Curtis 90; Buck Agency, Howard 91; Bykofsky Associates, Inc., Sheree 91; Congdon Associates Inc., Don 95; Connor Literary Agency 96; Curtis Associates, Inc., Richard 97; Cyper, The Cypher Agency, James R. 98; Delbourgo Associates, Inc., Joélle 99; DH Literary, Inc. 100; Dijkstra Literary Agency, Sandra 100; Doyen Literary Services, Inc. 102; Ducas, Robert 103; Dunham Literary 103; Dupree/Miller and Associates Inc. Literary 103; Dystel Literary Management, Inc., Jane 104; Educational Design Services, Inc. 105; Eth Literary Agency, Felicia 110; Feigen/Parrent Literary Management 111; Fogelman Literary Agency 113; Goldfarb & Associates 117; Goodman Associates 118; Goodman-Andrew Agency, Inc. 118; Greenburger Associates, Inc., Sanford J. 118; Gregory and Radice Authors' Agents 119; Grosvenor Literary Agency, The 120; Gusay Literary Agency, The Charlotte 120; Hamilburg Agency, Mitchell J., The 122; Hawkins & Associates, Inc., John 122; Henshaw Group, Richard 123; Herman Agency LLC, The Jeff 124; Herner Rights Agency, Susan 124; Hill & Barlow Agency 124; Hill Bonnie Nadell, Inc., Frederick 124; Hochmann Books, John L. 125; Hornfischer Literary Management, Inc. 125; J de S Associates Inc. 128; Jabberwocky Literary Agency 128; James Peter Associates, Inc. 129; JCA Literary Agency 129; Jellinek and Murray Literary Agency 130; Kellock Company Inc., The 131; Kleinman, Esq., of Graybill & English L.L.C., Jeffrey M. 133; Kroll Literary Agency Inc., Edite 135; Lampack Agency, Inc., Peter 136; Larsen/Elizabeth Pomada Literary Agents, Michael 136; Lawyer's Literary Agency, Inc. 137; Lazear Agency Incorporated 137; Levine Literary Agency, Paul S. 138; Lincoln Literary Agency, Ray 140; Literary and Creative Artists, Inc. 141; Literary Group, The 141; Love Literary Agency, Nancy 142; Lowenstein Associates, Inc. 143; Lownie Literary Agency Ltd., Andrew 143; Madsen Agency, Robert 144; Mann Agency, Carol 144; Marshall Agency, The Evan 146; McBride Literary Agency, Margret 147; McHugh Literary Agency 147; Morrison, Inc., Henry 149; Mura Enterprises, Inc., Dee 150; Naggar Literary Agency, Jean V. 151; National Writers Literary Agency 151; New England Publishing Associates Inc. 152; Norma-Lewis Agency, The 153; Paraview, Inc. 154; Parks Agency, The Richard 154; Picard, Literary Agent, Alison J. 157; Preskill Literary Agency, Robert 159; Rabiner, Literary Agent, Inc., Susan 160; Rees Literary Agency, Helen 160; Rein Books, Inc., Jody 164; Rhodes Literary Agency, Jodie 164; RLR Associates, Ltd. 168; Robbins Office, Inc., The 169; Rosenberg Group, The 170; Rosenkranz Literary Agency, Rita 170; Ross Literary Agency, The Gail 170; Russell and Volkening 172; Sanders & Associates, Victoria 173; Schiavone Literary Agency, Inc. 174; Schulman, A Literary Agency, Susan 174; Seligman, Literary Agent, Lynn 176; Seymour Agency, The 177; Shepard Agency, The Robert 177; Simmons Literary Agency, Jeffrey 178; Singer Literary Agency Inc., Evelyn 179; Snell Literary Agency, Michael 180; Spieler Agency, The 181; Spitzer Literary Agency, Philip G. 181; Straus Agency, Inc., Robin 183; Treimel NY, Scott 187; United Tribes 188; Venture Literary 189; Whittaker, Literary Agent, Lynn 193; Witherspoon & Associates, Inc. 194; Wray Literary Agency, Pamela D. 195; Zachary Shuster Harmsworth 197

**Health/Medicine:** A.L.P. Literary Agency 76; Agents Incorporated for Medical and Mental Health Professionals 76; Ahearn Agency, Inc., The 77; Allred and Allred Literary Agents 78; Altair Literary Agency 79; Amster Literary Enterprises, Betsy 80; Authors & Artists Group, Inc. 82; Baldi Literary Agency, Malaga 82; Balkin Agency, Inc. 83; Barrett Books Inc., Loretta 83; Bent Literary Agent, Harvey Klinger, Inc., Jenny 83; Bernstein

& Associates, Inc., Pam 84; Bernstein Literary Agency, Meredith 84; Bleeker Street Associates, Inc. 85; Boates Literary Agency, Reid 86; Book Deals, Inc. 86; BookEnds, LLC 86; Boston Literary Group, The 87; Brandt & Hochman Literary Agents Inc. 88; Briggs, M. Courtney 89; Brown Ltd., Curtis 90; Browne Ltd., Pema 90; Buck Agency, Howard 91; Bykofsky Associates, Inc., Sheree 91; Cambridge Literary 92; Carlisle & Company 92; Carvainis Agency, Inc., Maria 92; Casselman Literary Agency, Martha 93; Castiglia Literary Agency 93; Charlton Associates, James 93; Clausen, Mays & Tahan, LLC 94; Collin Literary Agency, Frances 95; Congdon Associates Inc., Don 95; Connor Literary Agency 96; Coover Agency, The Doe 96; Curtis Associates, Inc., Richard 97; Cyper, The Cypher Agency, James R. 98; Darhansoff & Verrill Literary Agency 98; Dawson Associates, Liza 98; DeFiore and Company 99; Delbourgo Associates, Inc., Joélle 99; DH Literary, Inc. 100; Dijkstra Literary Agency, Sandra 100; Donnaud & Associates, Inc., Janis A. 101; Donovan Literary, Jim 101; Doyen Literary Services, Inc. 102; Ducas, Robert 103; Dunham Literary 103; Dupree/Miller and Associates Inc. Literary 103; Dystel Literary Management, Inc., Jane 104; Ellenberg Literary Agency, Ethan 106; Elmo Agency Inc., Ann 106; Eth Literary Agency, Felicia 110; Feigen/Parrent Literary Management 111; Fleury Agency, B.R. 112; Fogelman Literary Agency 113; Forthwrite Literary Agency 114; Franklin Associates, Ltd., Lynn C. 114; Fredericks Literary Agency, Jeanne 115; Freymann Literary Agency, Sarah Jane 115; Gartenberg, Literary Agent, Max 116; Gislason Agency, The 116; Goldfarb & Associates 117; Goodman Associates 118; Goodman-Andrew Agency, Inc. 118; Greenburger Associates, Inc., Sanford J. 118; Grosvenor Literary Agency, The 120; Gusay Literary Agency, The Charlotte 120; Hamilburg Agency, Mitchell J., The 122; Hawkins & Associates, Inc., John 122; Henshaw Group, Richard 123; Herman Agency LLC, The Jeff 124; Herner Rights Agency, Susan 124; Hill & Barlow Agency 124; Hochmann Books, John L. 125; Hornfischer Literary Management, Inc. 125; J de S Associates Inc. 128; Jabberwocky Literary Agency 128; James Peter Associates, Inc. 129; JCA Literary Agency 129; Jellinek and Murray Literary Agency 130; Jordan Literary Agency, Lawrence 130; Kellock Company Inc., The 131; Kern Literary Agency, Natasha 131; Kleinman, Esq., of Graybill & English L.L.C., Jeffrey M. 133; Klinger, Inc., Harvey 133; Knight Agency, The 134; Konner Literary Agency, Linda 134; Koster Literary Agency, LLC, Elaine 134; Kouts, Literary Agent, Barbara S. 134; Kritzer Productions, Eddie 135; Lampack Agency, Inc., Peter 136; Larsen/Elizabeth Pomada Literary Agents, Michael 136; Lazear Agency Incorporated 137; Levine Communications, Inc., James 138; Levine Literary Agency, Inc., Ellen 138; Levine Literary Agency, Paul S. 138; Lieberman Associates, Robert 139; Limelight Management 140; Lincoln Literary Agency, Ray 140; Lipkind Agency, Wendy 140; Literary and Creative Artists, Inc. 141; Literary Group, The 141; Litwest Group, LLC 141; Livingston Cooke 142; Love Literary Agency, Nancy 142; Lowenstein Associates, Inc. 143; Madsen Agency, Robert 144; Mann Agency, Carol 144; Manus & Associates Literary Agency, Inc. 145; March Tenth, Inc. 145; Marshall Agency, The Evan 146; McBride Literary Agency, Margret 147; McGrath, Helen 147; McHugh Literary Agency 147; Menza Literary Agency, Claudia 148; Michaels Literary Agency, Inc., Doris S. 148; Millard Literary Agency, Martha 148; Miller Agency, The 149; Multimedia Product Development, Inc. 150; Mura Enterprises, Inc., Dee 150; Naggar Literary Agency, Jean V. 151; New England Publishing Associates Inc. 152; Nine Muses and Apollo Inc. 153; Norma-Lewis Agency, The 153; Paraview, Inc. 154; Parks Agency, The Richard 154; Picard, Literary Agent, Alison J. 157; Pinder Lane & Garon-Brooke Associates, Ltd. 158; Pine Associates, Inc., Arthur 158; Protter Literary Agent, Susan Ann 159; Quicksilver Books Literary Agents 160; Rees Literary Agency, Helen 160; Rein Books, Inc., Jody 164; Rhodes Literary Agency, Jodie 164; Rinaldi Literary Agency, Angela 165; RLR Associates, Ltd. 168; Robbins Literary Agency, B.J. 169; Rosenberg Group, The 170; Rosenkranz Literary Agency, Rita 170; Ross Literary Agency, The Gail 170; Roth, Literary Representation, Carol Susan 171; Rotrosen Agency, LLC, Jane 171; Rowland Agency, The Damaris 171; Russell and Volkening 172; Schiavone Literary Agency, Inc. 174; Schulman, A Literary Agency, Susan 174; Sebastian Literary Agency 175; Seligman, Literary Agent, Lynn 176; Seymour Agency, The 177; Shepard Agency, The 177; Singer Literary Agency Inc., Evelyn 179; Smith Literary Agency Ltd., Robert 180; Snell Literary Agency, Michael 180; Spitzer Literary Agency, Philip G. 181; Straus Agency, Inc., Robin 183; Teal Literary Agency, Patricia 185; Toad Hall, Inc. 186; Travis Literary Agency, Susan 186; Treimel NY, Scott 187; Two M Communications Ltd. 187; United Tribes 188; Venture Literary 189; Ware Literary Agency, John A. 190; Waterside Productions, Inc. 191; Waxman Agency, Inc., Scott 192; Wieser & Wieser, Inc. 194; Witherspoon & Associates, Inc. 194; Wonderland Press, Inc., The 194; Wray Literary Agency, Pamela D. 195; Writers House 195; Zachary Shuster Harmsworth 197; Zeckendorf Assoc. Inc., Susan 197

**History:** A.L.P. Literary Agency 76; Ahearn Agency, Inc., The 77; Allen Literary Agency, Linda 78; Allred and Allred Literary Agents 78; Altair Literary Agency 79; Altshuler Literary Agency, Miriam 79; AMG/Renaissance 79; Amster Literary Enterprises, Betsy 80; Authentic Creations Literary Agency 81; Authors & Artists Group, Inc. 82; Baldi Literary Agency, Malaga 82; Balkin Agency, Inc. 83; Barrett Books Inc., Loretta 83; Bent Literary Agent, Harvey Klinger, Inc., Jenny 83; Bial Agency, Daniel 84; Black Literary Agency, David 85; Bleeker Street Associates, Inc. 85; Boates Literary Agency, Reid 86; Book Deals, Inc. 86; Borchardt Inc., Georges 87; Boston Literary Group, The 87; Brandt & Hochman Literary Agents Inc. 88; Brown Associates Inc., Marie 89; Brown Literary Agency, Inc., Andrea 89; Brown Ltd., Curtis 90; Buck Agency, Howard 91; Bykofsky Associates, Inc., Sheree 91; Cambridge Literary 92; Carlisle & Company 92; Castiglia Literary Agency 93; Clark Associates, William 94; Clausen, Mays & Tahan, LLC 94; Collin Literary Agency, Frances 95; Congdon Associates Inc., Don 95; Coover Agency, The Doe 96; Curtis Associates, Inc., Richard 97; Cyper, The Cypher Agency, James R. 98; Darhansoff & Verrill Literary Agency 98; Dawson Associates, Liza 98; Delbourgo Associates, Inc., Joélle 99; DH Literary, Inc. 100; Dijkstra Literary Agency, Sandra 100; Donovan Literary, Jim 101; Doyen

Literary Agents 160; Rein Books, Inc., Jody 164; Rhodes Literary Agency, Jodie 164; Robbins Literary Agency, B.J. 169; Rosenberg Group, The 170; Rosenkranz Literary Agency, Rita 170; Rotrosen Agency, LLC, Jane 171; Scherf, Inc., Literary Management 173; Schiavone Literary Agency, Inc. 174; Schulman, A Literary Agency, Susan 174; Seligman, Literary Agent, Lynn 176; Serendipity Literary Agency, LLC 176; Seymour Agency, The 177; Singer Literary Agency Inc., Evelyn 179; Snell Literary Agency, Michael 180; Swayne Agency Literary Management & Consulting, Inc., The 184; Teal Literary Agency, Patricia 185; Toad Hall, Inc. 186; Travis Literary Agency, Susan 186; Treimel NY, Scott 187; United Tribes 188; Vines Agency, Inc., The 189; Watt & Associates, Sandra 191; Wonderland Press, Inc., The 194; Wray Literary Agency, Pamela D. 195; Wylie-Merrick Literary Agency 196; Zachary Shuster Harmsworth 197

**Humor:** A.L.P. Literary Agency 76; Allred and Allred Literary Agents 78; Amsterdam Agency, Marcia 80; Authors & Artists Group, Inc. 82; Barrett Books Inc., Loretta 83; Bial Agency, Daniel 84; Bleeker Street Associates, Inc. 85; BookEnds, LLC 86; Books & Such 87; Brown Ltd., Curtis 90; Buck Agency, Howard 91; Bykofsky Associates, Inc., Sheree 91; Charlton Associates, James 93; Clausen, Mays & Tahan, LLC 94; Congdon Associates Inc., Don 95; Connor Literary Agency 96; Core Creations 96; Curtis Associates, Inc., Richard 97; Delbourgo Associates, Inc., Joélle 99; Donnaud & Associates, Inc., Janis A. 101; Doyen Literary Services, Inc. 102; Dupree/Miller and Associates Inc. Literary 103; Dystel Literary Management, Inc., Jane 104; Ellenberg Literary Agency, Ethan 106; Fleury Agency, B.R. 112; Goldfarb & Associates 117; Goodman Associates 118; Greenburger Associates, Inc., Sanford J. 118; Grosjean Literary Agency, Jill 120; Gusay Literary Agency, The Charlotte 120; Hamilburg Agency, Mitchell J., The 122; Hawkins & Associates, Inc., John 122; Henshaw Group, Richard 123; Hornfischer Literary Management, Inc. 125; Jabberwocky Literary Agency 128; Kellock Company Inc., The 131; Kleinman, Esq., of Graybill & English L.L.C., Jeffrey M. 133; Kritzer Productions, Eddie 135; Larsen/Elizabeth Pomada Literary Agents, Michael 136; Lazear Agency Incorporated 137; Levine Literary Agency, Paul S. 138; Literary Group, The 141; Litwest Group, LLC 141; Lowenstein Associates, Inc. 143; Madsen Agency, Robert 144; March Tenth, Inc. 145; McHugh Literary Agency 147; Multimedia Product Development, Inc. 150; Mura Enterprises, Inc., Dee 150; New Brand Agency Group, LLC 152; Paraview, Inc. 154; Parks Agency, The Richard 154; Pevner, Inc., Stephen 157; Picard, Literary Agent, Alison J. 157; Preskill Literary Agency, Robert 159; Rein Books, Inc., Jody 164; RLR Associates, Ltd. 168; Robbins Literary Agency, B.J. 169; Rosenkranz Literary Agency, Rita 170; Ross Literary Agency, The Gail 170; Rotrosen Agency, LLC, Jane 171; Sanders & Associates, Victoria 173; Schiavone Literary Agency, Inc. 174; Seligman, Literary Agent, Lynn 176; Seymour Agency, The 177; Snell Literary Agency, Michael 180; Swayze Literary Agency, Carolyn 184; Treimel NY, Scott 187; Vines Agency, Inc., The 189; Waterside Productions, Inc. 191; Watt & Associates, Sandra 191

**Interior Design/Decorating:** A.L.P. Literary Agency 76; Allred and Allred Literary Agents 78; Authors & Artists Group, Inc. 82; Baldi Literary Agency, Malaga 82; Barrett Books Inc., Loretta 83; Brandt & Hochman Literary Agents Inc. 88; Brown Ltd., Curtis 90; Buck Agency, Howard 91; Bykofsky Associates, Inc., Sheree 91; Congdon Associates Inc., Don 95; Connor Literary Agency 96; Curtis Associates, Inc., Richard 97; Delbourgo Associates, Inc., Joélle 99; Doyen Literary Services, Inc. 102; Dupree/Miller and Associates Inc. Literary 103; Forthwrite Literary Agency 114; Fredericks Literary Agency, Jeanne 115; Freymann Literary Agency, Sarah Jane 115; Goldfarb & Associates 117; Goodman Associates 118; Greenburger Associates, Inc., Sanford J. 118; Grosjean Literary Agency, Jill 120; Gusay Literary Agency, The Charlotte 120; Hamilburg Agency, Mitchell J., The 122; Hawkins & Associates, Inc., John 122; Kellock Company Inc., The 131; Kleinman, Esq., of Graybill & English L.L.C., Jeffrey M. 133; Larsen/Elizabeth Pomada Literary Agents, Michael 136; Lazear Agency Incorporated 137; Levine Literary Agency, Paul S. 138; Limelight Management 140; Lincoln Literary Agency, Ray 140; Madsen Agency, Robert 144; McHugh Literary Agency 147; Paraview, Inc. 154; Preskill Literary Agency, Robert 159; RLR Associates, Ltd. 168; Rosenkranz Literary Agency, Rita 170; Seligman, Literary Agent, Lynn 176; Seymour Agency, The 177; Shepard Agency, The 177; Snell Literary Agency, Michael 180; Treimel NY, Scott 187; Wonderland Press, Inc., The 194; Writers House 195

**Juvenile Nonfiction:** A.L.P. Literary Agency 76; Ahearn Agency, Inc., The 77; Allred and Allred Literary Agents 78; Barrett Books Inc., Loretta 83; Bleeker Street Associates, Inc. 85; Books & Such 87; Briggs, M. Courtney 89; Brown Associates Inc., Marie 89; Brown Literary Agency, Inc., Andrea 89; Brown Ltd., Curtis 90; Browne Ltd., Pema 90; Bykofsky Associates, Inc., Sheree 91; Congdon Associates Inc., Don 95; Curtis Associates, Inc., Richard 97; Doyen Literary Services, Inc. 102; Dunham Literary 103; Dupree/Miller and Associates Inc. Literary 103; Dwyer & O'Grady, Inc. 104; Elek Associates, Peter 105; Ellenberg Literary Agency, Ethan 106; Elmo Agency Inc., Ann 106; Flannery Literary 112; Goldfarb & Associates 117; Greenburger Associates, Inc., Sanford J. 118; Gusay Literary Agency, The Charlotte 120; Hamilburg Agency, Mitchell J., The 122; Hawkins & Associates, Inc., John 122; Kouts, Literary Agent, Barbara S. 134; Lazear Agency Incorporated 137; Lewis & Company, Karen 139; Lincoln Literary Agency, Ray 140; Literary Group, The 141; Litwest Group, LLC 141; Madsen Agency, Robert 144; Markowitz Literary Agency, Barbara 146; McHugh Literary Agency 147; Millard Literary Agency, Martha 148; Morrison, Inc., Henry 149; Multimedia Product Development, Inc. 150; Mura Enterprises, Inc., Dee 150; Naggar Literary Agency, Jean V. 151; New Brand Agency Group, LLC 152; Norma-Lewis Agency, The 153; Paraview, Inc. 154; Picard, Literary Agent, Alison J. 157; Rhodes Literary Agency, Jodie 164; Schiavone Literary Agency, Inc. 174; Schulman, A Literary Agency, Susan 174; Serendipity Literary Agency, LLC 176; Seymour Agency, The 177; Shepard Agency, The 177; Singer Literary Agency Inc., Evelyn 179; Snell Literary Agency, Michael 180; Sternig & Byrne Literary Agency 183; Tobias, A Literary

Agency for Chilren's Books, Ann 186; Treimel NY, Scott 187; Wald Associates, Inc., Mary Jack 190; Wecksler-Incomco 192; Writers House 195; Wylie-Merrick Literary Agency 196

**Language/Literature/Criticism:** A.L.P. Literary Agency 76; Acacia House Publishing Services Ltd. 76; Allred and Allred Literary Agents 78; Altshuler Literary Agency, Miriam 79; Baldi Literary Agency, Malaga 82; Balkin Agency, Inc. 83; Barrett Books Inc., Loretta 83; Bent Literary Agent, Harvey Klinger, Inc., Jenny 83; Bial Agency, Daniel 84; Boates Literary Agency, Reid 86; Brandt & Hochman Literary Agents Inc. 88; Brown Ltd., Curtis 90; Buck Agency, Howard 91; Bykofsky Associates, Inc., Sheree 91; Castiglia Literary Agency 93; Congdon Associates Inc., Don 95; Connor Literary Agency 96; Coover Agency, The Doe 96; Cornfield Literary Agency, Robert 97; Curtis Associates, Inc., Richard 97; Cyper, The Cypher Agency, James R. 98; Darhansoff & Verrill Literary Agency 98; Delbourgo Associates, Inc., Joélle 99; DH Literary, Inc. 100; Dijkstra Literary Agency, Sandra 100; Doyen Literary Services, Inc. 102; Dunham Literary 103; Dupree/Miller and Associates Inc. Literary 103; Educational Design Services, Inc. 105; Goldfarb & Associates 117; Goodman Associates 118; Goodman-Andrew Agency, Inc. 118; Greenburger Associates, Inc., Sanford J. 118; Grosvenor Literary Agency, The 120; Gusay Literary Agency, The Charlotte 120; Halsey Agency, Reece 121; Halsey North, Reece 121; Hamilburg Agency, Mitchell J., The 122; Hawkins & Associates, Inc., John 122; Herner Rights Agency, Susan 124; Hill & Barlow Agency 124; Hill Bonnie Nadell, Inc., Frederick 124; Jabberwocky Literary Agency 128; James Peter Associates, Inc. 129; JCA Literary Agency 129; Jenks Agency, Carolyn 130; Kidde, Hoyt & Picard 132; Kleinman, Esq., of Graybill & English L.L.C., Jeffrey M. 133; Lazear Agency Incorporated 137; Levine Literary Agency, Paul S. 138; Lincoln Literary Agency, Ray 140; Literary Group, The 141; Lowenstein Associates, Inc. 143; Madsen Agency, Robert 144; March Tenth, Inc. 145; Marshall Agency, The Evan 146; McHugh Literary Agency 147; Miller Agency, The 149; New England Publishing Associates Inc. 152; Nine Muses and Apollo Inc. 153; Paraview, Inc. 154; Parks Agency, The Richard 154; Pevner, Inc., Stephen 157; Preskill Literary Agency, Robert 159; Quicksilver Books Literary Agents 160; RLR Associates, Ltd. 168; Robbins Office, Inc., The 169; Rosenkranz Literary Agency, Rita 170; Russell and Volkening 172; Sanders & Associates, Victoria 173; Schiavone Literary Agency, Inc. 174; Seligman, Literary Agent, Lynn 176; Seymour Agency, The 177; Shepard Agency, The 177; Simmons Literary Agency, Jeffrey 178; Snell Literary Agency, Michael 180; Spitzer Literary Agency, Philip G. 181; Straus Agency, Inc., Robin 183; Treimel NY, Scott 187; United Tribes 188; Venture Literary 189; Wald Associates, Inc., Mary Jack 190; Ware Literary Agency, John A. 190; Watt & Associates, Sandra 191; Whittaker, Literary Agent, Lynn 193; Wonderland Press, Inc., The 194; Zachary Shuster Harmsworth 197

**Memoirs:** A.L.P. Literary Agency 76; Acacia House Publishing Services Ltd. 76; Altshuler Literary Agency, Miriam 79; Authors & Artists Group, Inc. 82; Baldi Literary Agency, Malaga 82; Barrett Books Inc., Loretta 83; Bial Agency, Daniel 84; Black Literary Agency, David 85; Bleeker Street Associates, Inc. 85; BookEnds, LLC 86; Borchardt Inc., Georges 87; Brown Ltd., Curtis 90; Buck Agency, Howard 91; Bykofsky Associates, Inc., Sheree 91; Cambridge Literary 92; Carlisle & Company 92; Carvainis Agency, Inc., Maria 92; Clark Associates, William 94; Clausen, Mays & Tahan, LLC 94; Congdon Associates Inc., Don 95; Coover Agency, The Doe 96; Curtis Associates, Inc., Richard 97; Cyper, The Cypher Agency, James R. 98; Dawson Associates, Liza 98; Delbourgo Associates, Inc., Joélle 99; Doyen Literary Services, Inc. 102; Ducas, Robert 103; Dupree/Miller and Associates Inc. Literary 103; Feigen/Parrent Literary Management 111; Fort Ross Inc. Russian-American Publishing Projects 113; Franklin Associates, Ltd., Lynn C. 114; Goldfarb & Associates 117; Goodman Associates 118; Greenburger Associates, Inc., Sanford J. 118; Gusay Literary Agency, The Charlotte 120; Halsey North, Reece 121; Hamilburg Agency, Mitchell J., The 122; Hawkins & Associates, Inc., John 122; Hornfischer Literary Management, Inc. 125; James Peter Associates, Inc. 129; JCA Literary Agency 129; Jellinek and Murray Literary Agency 130; Jordan Literary Agency, Lawrence 130; Kidde, Hoyt & Picard 132; Larsen/Elizabeth Pomada Literary Agents, Michael 136; Lazear Agency Incorporated 137; Levine Literary Agency, Inc., Ellen 138; Levine Literary Agency, Paul S. 138; Lieberman Associates, Robert 139; Literary and Creative Artists, Inc. 141; Literary Group, The 141; Litwest Group, LLC 141; Love Literary Agency, Nancy 142; Lowenstein Associates, Inc. 143; Lownie Literary Agency Ltd., Andrew 143; Madsen Agency, Robert 144; Manus & Associates Literary Agency, Inc. 145; McHugh Literary Agency 147; Millard Literary Agency, Martha 148; Multimedia Product Development, Inc. 150; Mura Enterprises, Inc., Dee 150; Naggar Literary Agency, Jean V. 151; New Brand Agency Group, LLC 152; Paraview, Inc. 154; Parks Agency, The Richard 154; Pevner, Inc., Stephen 157; Picard, Literary Agent, Alison J. 157; Pinder Lane & Garon-Brooke Associates, Ltd. 158; Preskill Literary Agency, Robert 159; Protter Literary Agent, Susan Ann 159; Quicksilver Books Literary Agents 160; Rhodes Literary Agency, Jodie 164; Rittenberg Literary Agency, Inc., Ann 165; RLR Associates, Ltd. 168; Robbins Literary Agency, B.J. 169; Robbins Office, Inc., The 169; Rosenberg Group, The 170; Serendipity Literary Agency, LLC 176; Seymour Agency, The 177; Simmons Literary Agency, Jeffrey 178; Smith Literary Agency Ltd., Robert 180; Snell Literary Agency, Michael 180; Spieler Agency, The 181; Susijn Agency, The 183; Swayze Literary Agency, Carolyn 184; Treimel NY, Scott 187; Two M Communications Ltd. 187; United Tribes 188; Van Der Leun & Associates 188; Venture Literary 189; Vines Agency, Inc., The 189; Wales, Literary Agency, Inc. 190; Watt & Associates, Sandra 191; Weingel-Fidel Agency, The 193; Whittaker, Literary Agent, Lynn 193; Witherspoon & Associates, Inc. 194; Wray Literary Agency, Pamela D. 195; Zachary Shuster Harmsworth 197

**Military/War:** A.L.P. Literary Agency 76; Acacia House Publishing Services Ltd. 76; Allred and Allred Literary Agents 78; Barrett Books Inc., Loretta 83; Bial Agency, Daniel 84; Black Literary Agency, David 85; Bleeker

Street Associates, Inc. 85; Boston Literary Group, The 87; Brown Ltd., Curtis 90; Browne Ltd., Pema 90; Buck Agency, Howard 91; Bykofsky Associates, Inc., Sheree 91; Cambridge Literary 92; Charlton Associates, James 93; Congdon Associates Inc., Don 95; Curtis Associates, Inc., Richard 97; Delbourgo Associates, Inc., Joélle 99; Dijkstra Literary Agency, Sandra 100; Donovan Literary, Jim 101; Doyen Literary Services, Inc. 102; Ducas, Robert 103; Dupree/Miller and Associates Inc. Literary 103; Dystel Literary Management, Inc., Jane 104; Educational Design Services, Inc. 105; Gartenberg, Literary Agent, Max 116; Goldfarb & Associates 117; Goodman Associates 118; Greenburger Associates, Inc., Sanford J. 118; Grosvenor Literary Agency, The 120; Gusay Literary Agency, The Charlotte 120; Hamilburg Agency, Mitchell J., The 122; Hawkins & Associates, Inc., John 122; Henshaw Group, Richard 123; Hochmann Books, John L. 125; Hornfischer Literary Management, Inc. 125; J de S Associates Inc. 128; Jabberwocky Literary Agency 128; James Peter Associates, Inc. 129; JCA Literary Agency 129; Jellinek and Murray Literary Agency 130; Kellock Company Inc., The 131; Ketz Agency, Louise B. 132; Lazear Agency Incorporated 137; Levine Literary Agency, Paul S. 138; Literary Group, The 141; Litwest Group, LLC 141; Lownie Literary Agency Ltd., Andrew 143; Madsen Agency, Robert 144; Marshall Agency, The Evan 146; McGrath, Helen 147; McHugh Literary Agency 147; Mura Enterprises, Inc., Dee 150; New England Publishing Associates Inc. 152; Paraview, Inc. 154; Parks Agency, The Richard 154; Picard, Literary Agent, Alison J. 157; Pinder Lane & Garon-Brooke Associates, Ltd. 158; Preskill Literary Agency, Robert 159; Rabiner, Literary Agent, Inc., Susan 160; Rhodes Literary Agency, Jodie 164; Rosenkranz Literary Agency, Rita 170; Russell and Volkening 172; Schiavone Literary Agency, Inc. 174; Seymour Agency, The 177; Snell Literary Agency, Michael 180; Spitzer Literary Agency, Philip G. 181; Swayze Literary Agency, Carolyn 184; Treimel NY, Scott 187; Venture Literary 189; Vines Agency, Inc., The 189; Wray Literary Agency, Pamela D. 195; Writers House 195

**Money/Finance/Economics:** A.L.P. Literary Agency 76; Altair Literary Agency 79; Amster Literary Enterprises, Betsy 80; Authors & Artists Group, Inc. 82; Baldi Literary Agency, Malaga 82; Barrett Books Inc., Loretta 83; Bial Agency, Daniel 84; Black Literary Agency, David 85; Bleeker Street Associates, Inc. 85; Book Deals, Inc. 86; BookEnds, LLC 86; Boston Literary Group, The 87; Brown Ltd., Curtis 90; Browne Ltd., Pema 90; Buck Agency, Howard 91; Bykofsky Associates, Inc., Sheree 91; Castiglia Literary Agency 93; Clausen, Mays & Tahan, LLC 94; Congdon Associates Inc., Don 95; Connor Literary Agency 96; Coover Agency, The Doe 96; Curtis Associates, Inc., Richard 97; Cyper, The Cypher Agency, James R. 98; DeFiore and Company 99; Delbourgo Associates, Inc., Joélle 99; DH Literary, Inc. 100; Dijkstra Literary Agency, Sandra 100; Donovan Literary, Jim 101; Doyen Literary Services, Inc. 102; Ducas, Robert 103; Dupree/Miller and Associates Inc. Literary 103; Dystel Literary Management, Inc., Jane 104; Educational Design Services, Inc. 105; Elmo Agency Inc., Ann 106; Feigen/Parrent Literary Management 111; Fleury Agency, B.R. 112; Fredericks Literary Agency, Jeanne 115; Gartenberg, Literary Agent, Max 116; Goldfarb & Associates 117; Goodman Associates 118; Greenburger Associates, Inc., Sanford J. 118; Grosvenor Literary Agency, The 120; Gusay Literary Agency, The Charlotte 120; Hamilburg Agency, Mitchell J., The 122; Hartline Literary Agency 122; Hawkins & Associates, Inc., John 122; Henshaw Group, Richard 123; Hill & Barlow Agency 124; Hornfischer Literary Management, Inc. 125; Jabberwocky Literary Agency 128; James Peter Associates, Inc. 129; JCA Literary Agency 129; Jellinek and Murray Literary Agency 130; Kellock Company Inc., The 131; Kern Literary Agency, Natasha 131; Ketz Agency, Louise B. 132; Kleinman, Esq., of Graybill & English L.L.C., Jeffrey M. 133; Knight Agency, The 134; Konner Literary Agency, Linda 134; Koster Literary Agency, LLC, Elaine 134; Lampack Agency, Inc., Peter 136; Larsen/Elizabeth Pomada Literary Agents, Michael 136; Lazear Agency Incorporated 137; Levine Communications, Inc., James 138; Levine Literary Agency, Paul S. 138; Lieberman Associates, Robert 139; Lincoln Literary Agency, Ray 140; Literary Group, The 141; Litwest Group, LLC 141; Lowenstein Associates, Inc. 143; Madsen Agency, Robert 144; Mann Agency, Carol 144; Manus & Associates Literary Agency, Inc. 145; Marshall Agency, The Evan 146; McBride Literary Agency, Margret 147; McHugh Literary Agency 147; Michaels Literary Agency, Inc., Doris S. 148; Millard Literary Agency, Martha 148; Multimedia Product Development, Inc. 150; Mura Enterprises, Inc., Dee 150; New England Publishing Associates Inc. 152; Paraview, Inc. 154; Parks Agency, The Richard 154; Paton Literary Agency, Kathi J. 154; Picard, Literary Agent, Alison J. 157; Pine Associates, Inc., Arthur 158; Preskill Literary Agency, Robert 159; Rabiner, Literary Agent, Inc., Susan 160; Rees Literary Agency, Helen 160; Rhodes Literary Agency, Jodie 164; Rinaldi Literary Agency, Angela 165; RLR Associates, Ltd. 168; Rosenberg Group, The 170; Rosenkranz Literary Agency, Rita 170; Ross Literary Agency, The Gail 170; Roth, Literary Representation, Carol Susan 171; Rotrosen Agency, LLC, Jane 171; Russell and Volkening 172; Scherf, Inc., Literary Management 173; Schulman, A Literary Agency, Susan 174; Sebastian Literary Agency 175; Seligman, Literary Agent, Lynn 176; Serendipity Literary Agency, LLC 176; Seymour Agency, The 177; Shepard Agency, The 177; Shepard Agency, The Robert 177; Singer Literary Agency Inc., Evelyn 179; Snell Literary Agency, Michael 180; Spieler Agency, The 181; Treimel NY, Scott 187; United Tribes 188; Venture Literary 189; Vines Agency, Inc., The 189; Waterside Productions, Inc. 191; Waxman Agency, Inc., Scott 192; Whittaker, Literary Agent, Lynn 193; Wieser & Wieser, Inc. 194; Witherspoon & Associates, Inc. 194; Wray Literary Agency, Pamela D. 195; Writers House 195; Zachary Shuster Harmsworth 197

**Music/Dance:** A.L.P. Literary Agency 76; Acacia House Publishing Services Ltd. 76; Ahearn Agency, Inc., The 77; Allen Literary Agency, Linda 78; Allred and Allred Literary Agents 78; Altair Literary Agency 79; Altshuler Literary Agency, Miriam 79; Andrews & Associates, Bart 80; Authors & Artists Group, Inc. 82; Baldi Literary Agency, Malaga 82; Balkin Agency, Inc. 83; Barrett Books Inc., Loretta 83; Bial Agency, Daniel 84; Brandt & Hochman Literary Agents Inc. 88; Brown Associates Inc., Marie 89; Brown Ltd., Curtis 90; Buck

Agency, Howard 91; Bykofsky Associates, Inc., Sheree 91; Clark Associates, William 94; Congdon Associates Inc., Don 95; Cornfield Literary Agency, Robert 97; Curtis Associates, Inc., Richard 97; Cyper, The Cypher Agency, James R. 98; Delbourgo Associates, Inc., Joélle 99; Donovan Literary, Jim 101; Doyen Literary Services, Inc. 102; Dunham Literary 103; Dupree/Miller and Associates Inc. Literary 103; Elmo Agency Inc., Ann 106; Farber Literary Agency Inc. 111; Gartenberg, Literary Agent, Max 116; Goldfarb & Associates 117; Goodman Associates 118; Goodman-Andrew Agency, Inc. 118; Greenburger Associates, Inc., Sanford J. 118; Grosvenor Literary Agency, The 120; Gusay Literary Agency, The Charlotte 120; Hamilburg Agency, Mitchell J., The 122; Hawkins & Associates, Inc., John 122; Heacock Literary Agency, Inc. 123; Henshaw Group, Richard 123; Hill & Barlow Agency 124; Hochmann Books, John L. 125; Jabberwocky Literary Agency 128; James Peter Associates, Inc. 129; JCA Literary Agency 129; Kellock Company Inc., The 131; Kleinman, Esq., of Graybill & English L.L.C., Jeffrey M. 133; Knight Agency, The 134; Kouts, Literary Agent, Barbara S. 134; Lampack Agency, Inc., Peter 136; Larsen/Elizabeth Pomada Literary Agents, Michael 136; Lazear Agency Incorporated 137; Levine Literary Agency, Paul S. 138; Lieberman Associates, Robert 139; Lincoln Literary Agency, Ray 140; Literary Group, The 141; Lowenstein Associates, Inc. 143; Lownie Literary Agency Ltd., Andrew 143; Madsen Agency, Robert 144; March Tenth, Inc. 145; Markowitz Literary Agency, Barbara 146; Marshall Agency, The Evan 146; McBride Literary Agency, Margret 147; McHugh Literary Agency 147; Menza Literary Agency, Claudia 148; Michaels Literary Agency, Inc., Doris S. 148; Millard Literary Agency, Martha 148; Norma-Lewis Agency, The 153; Paraview, Inc. 154; Parks Agency, The Richard 154; Pevner, Inc., Stephen 157; Picard, Literary Agent, Alison J. 157; Pinder Lane & Garon-Brooke Associates, Ltd. 158; Preskill Literary Agency, Robert 159; Rein Books, Inc., Jody 164; Rhodes Literary Agency, Jodie 164; RLR Associates, Ltd. 168; Robbins Literary Agency, B.J. 169; Rosenkranz Literary Agency, Rita 170; Rubie Literary Agency, The Peter 172; Russell and Volkening 172; Sanders & Associates, Victoria 173; Schulman, A Literary Agency, Susan 174; Seligman, Literary Agent, Lynn 176; Seymour Agency, The 177; Shepard Agency, The 177; Simmons Literary Agency, Jeffrey 178; Smith Literary Agency Ltd., Robert 180; Snell Literary Agency, Michael 180; Spieler Agency, The 181; Spitzer Literary Agency, Philip G. 181; Straus Agency, Inc., Robin 183; Treimel NY, Scott 187; Two M Communications Ltd. 187; United Tribes 188; Venture Literary 189; Wald Associates, Inc., Mary Jack 190; Ware Literary Agency, John A. 190; Wecksler-Incomco 192; Weingel-Fidel Agency, The 193; Witherspoon & Associates, Inc. 194; Writers House 195; Zachary Shuster Harmsworth 197; Zeckendorf Assoc. Inc., Susan 197

**Nature/Environment:** A.L.P. Literary Agency 76; Acacia House Publishing Services Ltd. 76; Allen Literary Agency, Linda 78; Altair Literary Agency 79; Altshuler Literary Agency, Miriam 79; Authors & Artists Group, Inc. 82; Baldi Literary Agency, Malaga 82; Balkin Agency, Inc. 83; Barrett Books Inc., Loretta 83; Bial Agency, Daniel 84; Bleeker Street Associates, Inc. 85; Boates Literary Agency, Reid 86; Boston Literary Group, The 87; Brandt & Hochman Literary Agents Inc. 88; Brown Literary Agency, Inc., Andrea 89; Brown Ltd., Curtis 90; Browne Ltd., Pema 90; Buck Agency, Howard 91; Bykofsky Associates, Inc., Sheree 91; Castiglia Literary Agency 93; Collin Literary Agency, Frances 95; Congdon Associates Inc., Don 95; Coover Agency, The Doe 96; Curtis Associates, Inc., Richard 97; Cyper, The Cypher Agency, James R. 98; Darhansoff & Verrill Literary Agency 98; Delbourgo Associates, Inc., Joélle 99; DH Literary, Inc. 100; Dijkstra Literary Agency, Sandra 100; Donovan Literary, Jim 101; Doyen Literary Services, Inc. 102; Ducas, Robert 103; Dunham Literary 103; Dupree/Miller and Associates Inc. Literary 103; Elek Associates, Peter 105; Eth Literary Agency, Felicia 110; Forthwrite Literary Agency 114; Fredericks Literary Agency, Jeanne 115; Freymann Literary Agency, Sarah Jane 115; Gartenberg, Literary Agent, Max 116; Goldfarb & Associates 117; Goodman Associates 118; Goodman-Andrew Agency, Inc. 118; Greenburger Associates, Inc., Sanford J. 118; Grosjean Literary Agency, Jill 120; Grosvenor Literary Agency, The 120; Gusay Literary Agency, The Charlotte 120; Hamilburg Agency, Mitchell J., The 122; Hawkins & Associates, Inc., John 122; Heacock Literary Agency, Inc. 123; Henshaw Group, Richard 123; Herner Rights Agency, Susan 124; Hill & Barlow Agency 124; Hornfischer Literary Management, Inc. 125; Jabberwocky Literary Agency 128; JCA Literary Agency 129; Jellinek and Murray Literary Agency 130; Jenks Agency, Carolyn 130; Kellock Company Inc., The 131; Kern Literary Agency, Natasha 131; Kleinman, Esq., of Graybill & English L.L.C., Jeffrey M. 133; Koster Literary Agency, LLC, Elaine 134; Kouts, Literary Agent, Barbara S. 134; Larsen/Elizabeth Pomada Literary Agents, Michael 136; Lazear Agency Incorporated 137; Levine Communications, Inc., James 138; Levine Literary Agency, Paul S. 138; Lieberman Associates, Robert 139; Limelight Management 140; Lincoln Literary Agency, Ray 140; Literary Group, The 141; Love Literary Agency, Nancy 142; Lowenstein Associates, Inc. 143; Madsen Agency, Robert 144; Manus & Associates Literary Agency, Inc. 145; Markowitz Literary Agency, Barbara 146; Marshall Agency, The Evan 146; McHugh Literary Agency 147; Michaels Literary Agency, Inc., Doris S. 148; Multimedia Product Development, Inc. 150; Mura Enterprises, Inc., Dee 150; New England Publishing Associates Inc. 152; Norma-Lewis Agency, The 153; Paraview, Inc. 154; Parks Agency, The Richard 154; Paton Literary Agency, Kathi J. 154; Picard, Literary Agent, Alison J. 157; Preskill Literary Agency, Robert 159; Quicksilver Books Literary Agents 160; Rabiner, Literary Agent, Inc., Susan 160; Rein Books, Inc., Jody 164; Rhodes Literary Agency, Jodie 164; RLR Associates, Ltd. 168; Roghaar Literary Agency, Inc., Linda 169; Rosenberg Group, The 170; Rosenkranz Literary Agency, Rita 170; Ross Literary Agency, The Gail 170; Rotrosen Agency, LLC, Jane 171; Rowland Agency, The Damaris 171; Russell and Volkening 172; Schiavone Literary Agency, Inc. 174; Schulman, A Literary Agency, Susan 174; Seligman, Literary Agent, Lynn 176; Seymour Agency, The 177; Shepard Agency, The 177; Singer Literary Agency Inc., Evelyn 179; Snell Literary Agency, Michael 180; Spieler Agency, The 181; Spitzer Literary Agency, Philip G. 181; Straus Agency, Inc., Robin 183; Swayze Literary Agency, Carolyn 184; Toad Hall, Inc. 186; Treimel NY,

Scott 187; United Tribes 188; Venture Literary 189; Vines Agency, Inc., The 189; Wald Associates, Inc., Mary Jack 190; Wales, Literary Agency, Inc. 190; Ware Literary Agency, John A. 190; Waterside Productions, Inc. 191; Watkins Loomis Agency, Inc. 191; Watt & Associates, Sandra 191; Wecksler-Incomco 192; Whittaker, Literary Agent, Lynn 193; Wieser & Wieser, Inc. 194; Writers House 195

**New Age/Metaphysics:** A.L.P. Literary Agency 76; Allred and Allred Literary Agents 78; Authors & Artists Group, Inc. 82; Barrett Books Inc., Loretta 83; Bial Agency, Daniel 84; Bleeker Street Associates, Inc. 85; BookEnds, LLC 86; Brown Ltd., Curtis 90; Browne Ltd., Pema 90; Buck Agency, Howard 91; Bykofsky Associates, Inc., Sheree 91; Castiglia Literary Agency 93; Congdon Associates Inc., Don 95; Curtis Associates, Inc., Richard 97; Delbourgo Associates, Inc., Joélle 99; Doyen Literary Services, Inc. 102; Dupree/Miller and Associates Inc. Literary 103; Dystel Literary Management, Inc., Jane 104; Ellenberg Literary Agency, Ethan 106; Fleury Agency, B.R. 112; Franklin Associates, Ltd., Lynn C. 114; Gislason Agency, The 116; Goldfarb & Associates 117; Goodman Associates 118; Greenburger Associates, Inc., Sanford J. 118; Grosvenor Literary Agency, The 120; Gusay Literary Agency, The Charlotte 120; Hamilburg Agency, Mitchell J., The 122; Hawkins & Associates, Inc., John 122; Henshaw Group, Richard 123; Herner Rights Agency, Susan 124; Hill & Barlow Agency 124; J de S Associates Inc. 128; Jellinek and Murray Literary Agency 130; Kern Literary Agency, Natasha 131; Koster Literary Agency, LLC, Elaine 134; Larsen/Elizabeth Pomada Literary Agents, Michael 136; Lazear Agency Incorporated 137; Levine Communications, Inc., James 138; Levine Literary Agency, Paul S. 138; Lewis & Company, Karen 139; Limelight Management 140; Literary Group, The 141; Love Literary Agency, Nancy 142; Lowenstein Associates, Inc. 143; Madsen Agency, Robert 144; McHugh Literary Agency 147; Millard Literary Agency, Martha 148; Miller Agency, The 149; Naggar Literary Agency, Jean V. 151; New Brand Agency Group, LLC 152; Paraview, Inc. 154; Pevner, Inc., Stephen 157; Picard, Literary Agent, Alison J. 157; Quicksilver Books Literary Agents 160; Rosenkranz Literary Agency, Rita 170; Roth, Literary Representation, Carol Susan 171; Schulman, A Literary Agency, Susan 174; Serendipity Literary Agency, LLC 176; Seymour Agency, The 177; Smith Literary Agency Ltd., Robert 180; Snell Literary Agency, Michael 180; Toad Hall, Inc. 186; Treimel NY, Scott 187; Vines Agency, Inc., The 189; Watt & Associates, Sandra 191

**Philosophy:** A.L.P. Literary Agency 76; Barrett Books Inc., Loretta 83; Brown Ltd., Curtis 90; Buck Agency, Howard 91; Bykofsky Associates, Inc., Sheree 91; Congdon Associates Inc., Don 95; Curtis Associates, Inc., Richard 97; Doyen Literary Services, Inc. 102; Dupree/Miller and Associates Inc. Literary 103; Goldfarb & Associates 117; Goodman Associates 118; Greenburger Associates, Inc., Sanford J. 118; Gusay Literary Agency, The Charlotte 120; Hamilburg Agency, Mitchell J., The 122; Hawkins & Associates, Inc., John 122; Lazear Agency Incorporated 137; Literary and Creative Artists, Inc. 141; Madsen Agency, Robert 144; McHugh Literary Agency 147; Paraview, Inc. 154; Seymour Agency, The 177; Snell Literary Agency, Michael 180; Treimel NY, Scott 187

**Photography:** A.L.P. Literary Agency 76; Allred and Allred Literary Agents 78; Altair Literary Agency 79; Authors & Artists Group, Inc. 82; Baldi Literary Agency, Malaga 82; Barrett Books Inc., Loretta 83; Boston Literary Group, The 87; Brown Literary Agency, Inc., Andrea 89; Brown Ltd., Curtis 90; Buck Agency, Howard 91; Bykofsky Associates, Inc., Sheree 91; Congdon Associates Inc., Don 95; Connor Literary Agency 96; Curtis Associates, Inc., Richard 97; Delbourgo Associates, Inc., Joélle 99; Doyen Literary Services, Inc. 102; Dunham Literary 103; Dupree/Miller and Associates Inc. Literary 103; Elmo Agency Inc., Ann 106; Fredericks Literary Agency, Jeanne 115; Goldfarb & Associates 117; Goodman Associates 118; Greenburger Associates, Inc., Sanford J. 118; Grosvenor Literary Agency, The 120; Gusay Literary Agency, The Charlotte 120; Hamilburg Agency, Mitchell J., The 122; Hawkins & Associates, Inc., John 122; Kleinman, Esq., of Graybill & English L.L.C., Jeffrey M. 133; Larsen/Elizabeth Pomada Literary Agents, Michael 136; Lazear Agency Incorporated 137; Levine Literary Agency, Paul S. 138; Limelight Management 140; Madsen Agency, Robert 144; McHugh Literary Agency 147; Menza Literary Agency, Claudia 148; Millard Literary Agency, Martha 148; Norma-Lewis Agency, The 153; Paraview, Inc. 154; Pevner, Inc., Stephen 157; RLR Associates, Ltd. 168; Rosenkranz Literary Agency, Rita 170; Russell and Volkening 172; Seligman, Literary Agent, Lynn 176; Seymour Agency, The 177; Snell Literary Agency, Michael 180; Treimel NY, Scott 187; Vines Agency, Inc., The 189; Wald Associates, Inc., Mary Jack 190; Wecksler-Incomco 192; Wonderland Press, Inc., The 194

**Popular Culture:** A.L.P. Literary Agency 76; Ahearn Agency, Inc., The 77; Allen Literary Agency, Linda 78; Allred and Allred Literary Agents 78; Altair Literary Agency 79; Altshuler Literary Agency, Miriam 79; Amsterdam Agency, Marcia 80; Authors & Artists Group, Inc. 82; Balkin Agency, Inc. 83; Barrett Books Inc., Loretta 83; Bent Literary Agent, Harvey Klinger, Inc., Jenny 83; Bernstein & Associates, Inc., Pam 84; Bial Agency, Daniel 84; Bleeker Street Associates, Inc. 85; Book Deals, Inc. 86; Brown Literary Agency, Inc., Andrea 89; Brown Ltd., Curtis 90; Browne Ltd., Pema 90; Buck Agency, Howard 91; Bykofsky Associates, Inc., Sheree 91; Carlisle & Company 92; Charlton Associates, James 93; Clark Associates, William 94; Congdon Associates Inc., Don 95; Connor Literary Agency 96; Curtis Associates, Inc., Richard 97; Cyper, The Cypher Agency, James R. 98; Daves Agency, Joan 98; DeFiore and Company 99; Delbourgo Associates, Inc., Joélle 99; DHS Literary, Inc. 100; Donovan Literary, Jim 101; Dorian Literary Agency 102; Doyen Literary Services, Inc. 102; Dunham Literary 103; Dupree/Miller and Associates Inc. Literary 103; Dystel Literary Management, Inc., Jane 104; Elek Associates, Peter 105; Ellenberg Literary Agency, Ethan 106; Elmo Agency Inc., Ann 106; Eth Literary Agency, Felicia 110; Fogelman Literary Agency 113; Goldfarb & Associates 117; Goodman Associates 118; Goodman-

Andrew Agency, Inc. 118; Greenburger Associates, Inc., Sanford J. 118; Grosvenor Literary Agency, The 120; Gusay Literary Agency, The Charlotte 120; Halsey Agency, Reece 121; Halsey North, Reece 121; Hamilburg Agency, Mitchell J., The 122; Hawkins & Associates, Inc., John 122; Henshaw Group, Richard 123; Herner Rights Agency, Susan 124; Hill & Barlow Agency 124; Hornfischer Literary Management, Inc. 125; Jabberwocky Literary Agency 128; James Peter Associates, Inc. 129; JCA Literary Agency 129; Jellinek and Murray Literary Agency 130; Kellock Company Inc., The 131; Kern Literary Agency, Natasha 131; Kidde, Hoyt & Picard 132; Kleinman, Esq., of Graybill & English L.L.C., Jeffrey M. 133; Knight Agency, The 134; Konner Literary Agency, Linda 134; Koster Literary Agency, LLC, Elaine 134; Lampack Agency, Inc., Peter 136; Larsen/Elizabeth Pomada Literary Agents, Michael 136; Lazear Agency Incorporated 137; Levine Literary Agency, Inc., Ellen 138; Levine Literary Agency, Paul S. 138; Literary Group, The 141; Litwest Group, LLC 141; Livingston Cooke 142; Love Literary Agency, Nancy 142; Lowenstein Associates, Inc. 143; Lownie Literary Agency Ltd., Andrew 143; Madsen Agency, Robert 144; Manus & Associates Literary Agency, Inc. 145; March Tenth, Inc. 145; Markowitz Literary Agency, Barbara 146; McBride Literary Agency, Margret 147; McHugh Literary Agency 147; Millard Literary Agency, Martha 148; Multimedia Product Development, Inc. 150; National Writers Literary Agency 151; New Brand Agency Group, LLC 152; Norma-Lewis Agency, The 153; Paraview, Inc. 154; Parks Agency, The Richard 154; Perkins Associates, L. 157; Pevner, Inc., Stephen 157; Picard, Literary Agent, Alison J. 157; Preskill Literary Agency, Robert 159; Quicksilver Books Literary Agents 160; Rein Books, Inc., Jody 164; Rhodes Literary Agency, Jodie 164; Rinaldi Literary Agency, Angela 165; RLR Associates, Ltd. 168; Robbins Literary Agency, B.J. 169; Roghaar Literary Agency, Inc., Linda 169; Rosenberg Group, The 170; Rosenkranz Literary Agency, Rita 170; Rotrosen Agency, LLC, Jane 171; Rubie Literary Agency, The Peter 172; Russell and Volkening 172; Sanders & Associates, Victoria 173; Scherf, Inc., Literary Management 173; Schiavone Literary Agency, Inc. 174; Schulman, A Literary Agency, Susan 174; Seligman, Literary Agent, Lynn 176; Serendipity Literary Agency, LLC 176; Seymour Agency, The 177; Shepard Agency, The Robert 177; Simmons Literary Agency, Jeffrey 178; Smith Literary Agency Ltd., Robert 180; Snell Literary Agency, Michael 180; Southern Literary Group 181; Spitzer Literary Agency, Philip G. 181; Straus Agency, Inc., Robin 183; Susijn Agency, The 183; Swayne Agency Literary Management & Consulting, Inc., The 184; Swayze Literary Agency, Carolyn 184; Toad Hall, Inc. 186; Travis Literary Agency, Susan 186; Treimel NY, Scott 187; United Tribes 188; Venture Literary 189; Vicinanza, Ltd., Ralph 189; Vines Agency, Inc., The 189; Wales, Literary Agency, Inc. 190; Ware Literary Agency, John A. 190; Waterside Productions, Inc. 191; Watkins Loomis Agency, Inc. 191; Watt & Associates, Sandra 191; Whittaker, Literary Agent, Lynn 193; Wonderland Press, Inc., The 194

**Psychology:** A.L.P. Literary Agency 76; Agents Incorporated for Medical and Mental Health Professionals 76; Allen Literary Agency, Linda 78; Allred and Allred Literary Agents 78; Altair Literary Agency 79; Altshuler Literary Agency, Miriam 79; Amster Literary Enterprises, Betsy 80; Authors & Artists Group, Inc. 82; Baldi Literary Agency, Malaga 82; Barrett Books Inc., Loretta 83; Bent Literary Agent, Harvey Klinger, Inc., Jenny 83; Bernstein & Associates, Inc., Pam 84; Bernstein Literary Agency, Meredith 84; Bial Agency, Daniel 84; Bleeker Street Associates, Inc. 85; Boates Literary Agency, Reid 86; Book Deals, Inc. 86; BookEnds, LLC 86; Boston Literary Group, The 87; Brandt & Hochman Literary Agents Inc. 88; Brown Ltd., Curtis 90; Browne Ltd., Pema 90; Buck Agency, Howard 91; Bykofsky Associates, Inc., Sheree 91; Carlisle & Company 92; Castiglia Literary Agency 93; Clausen, Mays & Tahan, LLC 94; Congdon Associates Inc., Don 95; Coover Agency, The Doe 96; Core Creations 96; Curtis Associates, Inc., Richard 97; Cyper, The Cypher Agency, James R. 98; Dawson Associates, Liza 98; DeFiore and Company 99; Delbourgo Associates, Inc., Joélle 99; DH Literary, Inc. 100; Dijkstra Literary Agency, Sandra 100; Donnaud & Associates, Inc., Janis A. 101; Doyen Literary Services, Inc. 102; Dunham Literary 103; Dupree/Miller and Associates Inc. Literary 103; Dystel Literary Management, Inc., Jane 104; Ellenberg Literary Agency, Ethan 106; Elmo Agency Inc., Ann 106; Eth Literary Agency, Felicia 110; Farber Literary Agency Inc. 111; Feigen/Parrent Literary Management 111; Fogelman Literary Agency 113; Fort Ross Inc. Russian-American Publishing Projects 113; Forthwrite Literary Agency 114; Franklin Associates, Ltd., Lynn C. 114; Fredericks Literary Agency, Jeanne 115; Freymann Literary Agency, Sarah Jane 115; Gartenberg, Literary Agent, Max 116; Gislason Agency, The 116; Goldfarb & Associates 117; Goodman Associates 118; Goodman-Andrew Agency, Inc. 118; Greenburger Associates, Inc., Sanford J. 118; Grosvenor Literary Agency, The 120; Gusay Literary Agency, The Charlotte 120; Hamilburg Agency, Mitchell J., The 122; Hawkins & Associates, Inc., John 122; Heacock Literary Agency, Inc. 123; Henshaw Group, Richard 123; Herman Agency LLC, The Jeff 124; Herner Rights Agency, Susan 124; Hill & Barlow Agency 124; Hornfischer Literary Management, Inc. 125; James Peter Associates, Inc. 129; Jellinek and Murray Literary Agency 130; Kellock Company Inc., The 131; Kern Literary Agency, Natasha 131; Kidde, Hoyt & Picard 132; Kleinman, Esq., of Graybill & English L.L.C., Jeffrey M. 133; Klinger, Inc., Harvey 133; Knight Agency, The 134; Konner Literary Agency, Linda 134; Koster Literary Agency, LLC, Elaine 134; Kouts, Literary Agent, Barbara S. 134; Larsen/Elizabeth Pomada Literary Agents, Michael 136; Lazear Agency Incorporated 137; Levine Communications, Inc., James 138; Levine Literary Agency, Inc., Ellen 138; Levine Literary Agency, Paul S. 138; Lieberman Associates, Robert 139; Lincoln Literary Agency, Ray 140; Literary Group, The 141; Litwest Group, LLC 141; Love Literary Agency, Nancy 142; Lowenstein Associates, Inc. 143; Madsen Agency, Robert 144; Mann Agency, Carol 144; Manus & Associates Literary Agency, Inc. 145; Marshall Agency, The Evan 146; McBride Literary Agency, Margret 147; McGrath, Helen 147; McHugh Literary Agency 147; Menza Literary Agency, Claudia 148; Millard Literary Agency, Martha 148; Miller Agency, The 149; Multimedia Product Development, Inc. 150; Naggar Literary Agency, Jean V. 151; New Brand Agency Group, LLC 152; New England Publishing Associates Inc.

152; Nine Muses and Apollo Inc. 153; Paraview, Inc. 154; Parks Agency, The Richard 154; Paton Literary Agency, Kathi J. 154; Picard, Literary Agent, Alison J. 157; Pinder Lane & Garon-Brooke Associates, Ltd. 158; Pine Associates, Inc., Arthur 158; Preskill Literary Agency, Robert 159; Protter Literary Agent, Susan Ann 159; Quicksilver Books Literary Agents 160; Rabiner, Literary Agent, Inc., Susan 160; Rein Books, Inc., Jody 164; Rhodes Literary Agency, Jodie 164; Rinaldi Literary Agency, Angela 165; RLR Associates, Ltd. 168; Robbins Literary Agency, B.J. 169; Rosenberg Group, The 170; Rosenkranz Literary Agency, Rita 170; Ross Literary Agency, The Gail 170; Rotrosen Agency, LLC, Jane 171; Russell and Volkening 172; Sanders & Associates, Victoria 173; Scherf, Inc., Literary Management 173; Schiavone Literary Agency, Inc. 174; Schulman, A Literary Agency, Susan 174; Sebastian Literary Agency 175; Seligman, Literary Agent, Lynn 176; Serendipity Literary Agency, LLC 176; Seymour Agency, The 177; Shepard Agency, The 177; Sherman Associates, Inc., Wendy 178; Singer Literary Agency Inc., Evelyn 179; Slopen Literary Agency, Beverley 179; Snell Literary Agency, Michael 180; Spitzer Literary Agency, Philip G. 181; Straus Agency, Inc., Robin 183; Teal Literary Agency, Patricia 185; Travis Literary Agency, Susan 186; Treimel NY, Scott 187; United Tribes 188; Venture Literary 189; Vines Agency, Inc., The 189; Ware Literary Agency, John A. 190; Waterside Productions, Inc. 191; Watt & Associates, Sandra 191; Weingel-Fidel Agency, The 193; Wieser & Wieser, Inc. 194; Wonderland Press, Inc., The 194; Writers House 195; Zachary Shuster Harmsworth 197; Zeckendorf Assoc. Inc., Susan 197

**Recreation:** A.L.P. Literary Agency 76; Barrett Books Inc., Loretta 83; Brown Ltd., Curtis 90; Buck Agency, Howard 91; Bykofsky Associates, Inc., Sheree 91; Congdon Associates Inc., Don 95; Curtis Associates, Inc., Richard 97; Doyen Literary Services, Inc. 102; Dupree/Miller and Associates Inc. Literary 103; Goldfarb & Associates 117; Goodman Associates 118; Greenburger Associates, Inc., Sanford J. 118; Gusay Literary Agency, The Charlotte 120; Hamilburg Agency, Mitchell J., The 122; Hawkins & Associates, Inc., John 122; Heacock Literary Agency, Inc. 123; Lazear Agency Incorporated 137; Madsen Agency, Robert 144; McHugh Literary Agency 147; Paraview, Inc. 154; Seymour Agency, The 177; Snell Literary Agency, Michael 180; Treimel NY, Scott 187

**Regional:** A.L.P. Literary Agency 76; Barrett Books Inc., Loretta 83; Brown Ltd., Curtis 90; Buck Agency, Howard 91; Bykofsky Associates, Inc., Sheree 91; Congdon Associates Inc., Don 95; Curtis Associates, Inc., Richard 97; Doyen Literary Services, Inc. 102; Dupree/Miller and Associates Inc. Literary 103; Goldfarb & Associates 117; Goodman Associates 118; Greenburger Associates, Inc., Sanford J. 118; Gusay Literary Agency, The Charlotte 120; Hamilburg Agency, Mitchell J., The 122; Hawkins & Associates, Inc., John 122; Lazear Agency Incorporated 137; Madsen Agency, Robert 144; McHugh Literary Agency 147; Paraview, Inc. 154; Seymour Agency, The 177; Snell Literary Agency, Michael 180; Treimel NY, Scott 187

**Religious/Inspirational:** A.L.P. Literary Agency 76; Alive Communications, Inc. 78; Allred and Allred Literary Agents 78; Authors & Artists Group, Inc. 82; Barrett Books Inc., Loretta 83; Bent Literary Agent, Harvey Klinger, Inc., Jenny 83; Bernstein & Associates, Inc., Pam 84; Bial Agency, Daniel 84; Bleeker Street Associates, Inc. 85; Book Deals, Inc. 86; BookEnds, LLC 86; Books & Such 87; Brown Associates Inc., Marie 89; Brown Ltd., Curtis 90; Browne Ltd., Pema 90; Buck Agency, Howard 91; Bykofsky Associates, Inc., Sheree 91; Castiglia Literary Agency 93; Clark Associates, William 94; Clausen, Mays & Tahan, LLC 94; Congdon Associates Inc., Don 95; Crawford Literary Agency 97; Curtis Associates, Inc., Richard 97; DeFiore and Company 99; Delbourgo Associates, Inc., Joélle 99; Doyen Literary Services, Inc. 102; Dupree/Miller and Associates Inc. Literary 103; Dystel Literary Management, Inc., Jane 104; Ellenberg Literary Agency, Ethan 106; Forthwrite Literary Agency 114; Franklin Associates, Ltd., Lynn C. 114; Freymann Literary Agency, Sarah Jane 115; Goldfarb & Associates 117; Goodman Associates 118; Greenburger Associates, Inc., Sanford J. 118; Grosvenor Literary Agency, The 120; Gusay Literary Agency, The Charlotte 120; Hamilburg Agency, Mitchell J., The 122; Hartline Literary Agency 122; Herner Rights Agency, Susan 124; Hill & Barlow Agency 124; Hornfischer Literary Management, Inc. 125; Jellinek and Murray Literary Agency 130; Jordan Literary Agency, Lawrence 130; Kern Literary Agency, Natasha 131; Knight Agency, The 134; Larsen/Elizabeth Pomada Literary Agents, Michael 136; Lazear Agency Incorporated 137; Levine Communications, Inc., James 138; Levine Literary Agency, Paul S. 138; Literary Group, The 141; Litwest Group, LLC 141; Love Literary Agency, Nancy 142; Lowenstein Associates, Inc. 143; Madsen Agency, Robert 144; Marshall Agency, The Evan 146; McBride Literary Agency, Margret 147; McHugh Literary Agency 147; Multimedia Product Development, Inc. 150; Naggar Literary Agency, Jean V. 151; New Brand Agency Group, LLC 152; Paraview, Inc. 154; Paton Literary Agency, Kathi J. 154; Pevner, Inc., Stephen 157; Picard, Literary Agent, Alison J. 157; Quicksilver Books Literary Agents 160; Rein Books, Inc., Jody 164; RLR Associates, Ltd. 168; Roghaar Literary Agency, Inc., Linda 169; Rosenkranz Literary Agency, Rita 170; Ross Literary Agency, The Gail 170; Roth, Literary Representation, Carol Susan 171; Rowland Agency, The Damaris 171; Scherf, Inc., Literary Management 173; Schulman, A Literary Agency, Susan 174; Serendipity Literary Agency, LLC 176; Seymour Agency, The 177; Shepard Agency, The 177; Singer Literary Agency Inc., Evelyn 179; Snell Literary Agency, Michael 180; Toad Hall, Inc. 186; Treimel NY, Scott 187; United Tribes 188; Venture Literary 189; Viciananza, Ltd., Ralph 189; Vines Agency, Inc., The 189; Watt & Associates, Sandra 191; Waxman Agency, Inc., Scott 192; Wray Literary Agency, Pamela D. 195

**Science/Technology:** A.L.P. Literary Agency 76; Agents Incorporated for Medical and Mental Health Professionals 76; Allred and Allred Literary Agents 78; Altair Literary Agency 79; Authentic Creations Literary Agency 81; Authors & Artists Group, Inc. 82; Baldi Literary Agency, Malaga 82; Balkin Agency, Inc. 83; Barrett Books

Inc., Loretta 83; Bent Literary Agent, Harvey Klinger, Inc., Jenny 83; Bernstein Literary Agency, Meredith 84; Bial Agency, Daniel 84; Bleeker Street Associates, Inc. 85; Boates Literary Agency, Reid 86; Book Deals, Inc. 86; Boston Literary Group, The 87; Bova Literary Agency, The Barbara 88; Brandt & Hochman Literary Agents Inc. 88; Brown Literary Agency, Inc., Andrea 89; Brown Ltd., Curtis 90; Buck Agency, Howard 91; Bykofsky Associates, Inc., Sheree 91; Carlisle & Company 92; Carvainis Agency, Inc., Maria 92; Castiglia Literary Agency 93; Clark Associates, William 94; Congdon Associates Inc., Don 95; Curtis Associates, Inc., Richard 97; Cyper, The Cypher Agency, James R. 98; Darhansoff & Verrill Literary Agency 98; Delbourgo Associates, Inc., Joélle 99; DH Literary, Inc. 100; Dijkstra Literary Agency, Sandra 100; Doyen Literary Services, Inc. 102; Ducas, Robert 103; Dunham Literary 103; Dupree/Miller and Associates Inc. Literary 103; Dystel Literary Management, Inc., Jane 104; Educational Design Services, Inc. 105; Elek Associates, Peter 105; Ellenberg Literary Agency, Ethan 106; Eth Literary Agency, Felicia 110; Fredericks Literary Agency, Jeanne 115; Gartenberg, Literary Agent, Max 116; Gislason Agency, The 116; Goldfarb & Associates 117; Goodman Associates 118; Greenburger Associates, Inc., Sanford J. 118; Grosvenor Literary Agency, The 120; Gusay Literary Agency, The Charlotte 120; Hamilburg Agency, Mitchell J., The 122; Hawkins & Associates, Inc., John 122; Heacock Literary Agency, Inc. 123; Henshaw Group, Richard 123; Herner Rights Agency, Susan 124; Hill & Barlow Agency 124; Hornfischer Literary Management, Inc. 125; Jabberwocky Literary Agency 128; JCA Literary Agency 129; Jellinek and Murray Literary Agency 130; Jenks Agency, Carolyn 130; Jordan Literary Agency, Lawrence 130; Kern Literary Agency, Natasha 131; Ketz Agency, Louise B. 132; Kleinman, Esq., of Graybill & English L.L.C., Jeffrey M. 133; Klinger, Inc., Harvey 133; Larsen/Elizabeth Pomada Literary Agents, Michael 136; Lazear Agency Incorporated 137; Levine Communications, Inc., James 138; Levine Literary Agency, Inc., Ellen 138; Levine Literary Agency, Paul S. 138; Lieberman Associates, Robert 139; Lincoln Literary Agency, Ray 140; Lipkind Agency, Wendy 140; Literary Group, The 141; Livingston Cooke 142; Love Literary Agency, Nancy 142; Lowenstein Associates, Inc. 143; Madsen Agency, Robert 144; Manus & Associates Literary Agency, Inc. 145; Marshall Agency, The Evan 146; McBride Literary Agency, Margret 147; McHugh Literary Agency 147; Multimedia Product Development, Inc. 150; Mura Enterprises, Inc., Dee 150; National Writers Literary Agency 151; New England Publishing Associates Inc. 152; Paraview, Inc. 154; Parks Agency, The Richard 154; Picard, Literary Agent, Alison J. 157; Protter Literary Agent, Susan Ann 159; Quicksilver Books Literary Agents 160; Rabiner, Literary Agent, Inc., Susan 160; Rein Books, Inc., Jody 164; Rhodes Literary Agency, Jodie 164; RLR Associates, Ltd. 168; Rosenkranz Literary Agency, Rita 170; Ross Literary Agency, The Gail 170; Rubie Literary Agency, The Peter 172; Russell and Volkening 172; Schiavone Literary Agency, Inc. 174; Seligman, Literary Agent, Lynn 176; Serendipity Literary Agency, LLC 176; Seymour Agency, The 177; Shepard Agency, The Robert 177; Singer Literary Agency Inc., Evelyn 179; Snell Literary Agency, Michael 180; Straus Agency, Inc., Robin 183; Susijn Agency, The 183; Swayne Agency Literary Management & Consulting, Inc., The 184; Treimel NY, Scott 187; United Tribes 188; Venture Literary 189; Vicananza, Ltd., Ralph 189; Vines Agency, Inc., The 189; Wales, Literary Agency, Inc. 190; Ware Literary Agency, John A. 190; Watkins Loomis Agency, Inc. 191; Weingel-Fidel Agency, The 193; Whittaker, Literary Agent, Lynn 193; Witherspoon & Associates, Inc. 194; Wray Literary Agency, Pamela D. 195; Writers House 195; Zachary Shuster Harmsworth 197; Zeckendorf Assoc. Inc., Susan 197

**Self-Help/Personal Improvement:** A.L.P. Literary Agency 76; Agents Incorporated for Medical and Mental Health Professionals 76; Ahearn Agency, Inc., The 77; Alive Communications, Inc. 78; Allred and Allred Literary Agents 78; Altair Literary Agency 79; Amsterdam Agency, Marcia 80; Authentic Creations Literary Agency 81; Authors & Artists Group, Inc. 82; Barrett Books Inc., Loretta 83; Bent Literary Agent, Harvey Klinger, Inc., Jenny 83; Bernstein & Associates, Inc., Pam 84; Bial Agency, Daniel 84; Bleeker Street Associates, Inc. 85; Boates Literary Agency, Reid 86; Book Deals, Inc. 86; BookEnds, LLC 86; Books & Such 87; Bova Literary Agency, The Barbara 88; Briggs, M. Courtney 89; Brown Associates Inc., Marie 89; Brown Ltd., Curtis 90; Browne Ltd., Pema 90; Bykofsky Associates, Inc., Sheree 91; Castiglia Literary Agency 93; Congdon Associates Inc., Don 95; Connor Literary Agency 96; Crawford Literary Agency 97; Curtis Associates, Inc., Richard 97; Cyper, The Cypher Agency, James R. 98; Dawson Associates, Liza 98; DeFiore and Company 99; Delbourgo Associates, Inc., Joélle 99; Dorian Literary Agency 102; Doyen Literary Services, Inc. 102; Dupree/Miller and Associates Inc. Literary 103; Ellenberg Literary Agency, Ethan 106; Elmo Agency Inc., Ann 106; Feigen/Parrent Literary Management 111; Fleury Agency, B.R. 112; Fort Ross Inc. Russian-American Publishing Projects 113; Forthwrite Literary Agency 114; Franklin Associates, Ltd., Lynn C. 114; Fredericks Literary Agency, Jeanne 115; Frenkel & Associates, James 115; Freymann Literary Agency, Sarah Jane 115; Gartenberg, Literary Agent, Max 116; Gislason Agency, The 116; Goldfarb & Associates 117; Goodman Associates 118; Goodman-Andrew Agency, Inc. 118; Greenburger Associates, Inc., Sanford J. 118; Grosvenor Literary Agency, The 120; Gusay Literary Agency, The Charlotte 120; Hamilburg Agency, Mitchell J., The 122; Hartline Literary Agency 122; Hawkins & Associates, Inc., John 122; Heacock Literary Agency, Inc. 123; Henshaw Group, Richard 123; Herman Agency LLC, The Jeff 124; Herner Rights Agency, Susan 124; Hill & Barlow Agency 124; Hornfischer Literary Management, Inc. 125; J de S Associates Inc. 128; James Peter Associates, Inc. 129; Jellinek and Murray Literary Agency 130; Jordan Literary Agency, Lawrence 130; Kellock Company Inc., The 131; Kern Literary Agency, Natasha 131; Kidde, Hoyt & Picard 132; Kleinman, Esq., of Graybill & English L.L.C., Jeffrey M. 133; Klinger, Inc., Harvey 133; Knight Agency, The 134; Konner Literary Agency, Linda 134; Koster Literary Agency, LLC, Elaine 134; Kouts, Literary Agent, Barbara S. 134; Kritzer Productions, Eddie 135; Larsen/Elizabeth Pomada Literary Agents, Michael 136; Lazear Agency Incorporated 137; Levine Communications, Inc., James

138; Levine Literary Agency, Paul S. 138; Lewis & Company, Karen 139; Limelight Management 140; Lincoln Literary Agency, Ray 140; Literary Group, The 141; Litwest Group, LLC 141; Love Literary Agency, Nancy 142; Lowenstein Associates, Inc. 143; Madsen Agency, Robert 144; Mann Agency, Carol 144; Manus & Associates Literary Agency, Inc. 145; McBride Literary Agency, Margret 147; McGrath, Helen 147; McHugh Literary Agency 147; Menza Literary Agency, Claudia 148; Michaels Literary Agency, Inc., Doris S. 148; Millard Literary Agency, Martha 148; Miller Agency, The 149; Multimedia Product Development, Inc. 150; Mura Enterprises, Inc., Dee 150; Naggar Literary Agency, Jean V. 151; New Brand Agency Group, LLC 152; New England Publishing Associates Inc. 152; Norma-Lewis Agency, The 153; Paraview, Inc. 154; Parks Agency, The Richard 154; Picard, Literary Agent, Alison J. 157; Pinder Lane & Garon-Brooke Associates, Ltd. 158; Pine Associates, Inc., Arthur 158; Preskill Literary Agency, Robert 159; Quicksilver Books Literary Agents 160; Rein Books, Inc., Jody 164; Rinaldi Literary Agency, Angela 165; RLR Associates, Ltd. 168; Robbins Literary Agency, B.J. 169; Roghaar Literary Agency, Inc., Linda 169; Rosenberg Group, The 170; Rosenkranz Literary Agency, Rita 170; Ross Literary Agency, The Gail 170; Roth, Literary Representation, Carol Susan 171; Rotrosen Agency, LLC, Jane 171; Scherf, Inc., Literary Management 173; Schiavone Literary Agency, Inc. 174; Schulman, A Literary Agency, Susan 174; Sebastian Literary Agency 175; Seligman, Literary Agent, Lynn 176; Serendipity Literary Agency, LLC 176; Seymour Agency, The 177; Shepard Agency, The 177; Singer Literary Agency Inc., Evelyn 179; Smith Literary Agency Ltd., Robert 180; Snell Literary Agency, Michael 180; Swayze Literary Agency, Carolyn 184; Teal Literary Agency, Patricia 185; Toad Hall, Inc. 186; Travis Literary Agency, Susan 186; Treimel NY, Scott 187; Two M Communications Ltd. 187; United Tribes 188; Venture Literary 189; Vines Agency, Inc., The 189; Watt & Associates, Sandra 191; Weiner Literary Agency, Cherry 192; Witherspoon & Associates, Inc. 194; Wonderland Press, Inc., The 194; Wray Literary Agency, Pamela D. 195; Writers House 195; Wylie-Merrick Literary Agency 196; Zachary Shuster Harmsworth 197

**Sociology:** A.L.P. Literary Agency 76; Agents Incorporated for Medical and Mental Health Professionals 76; Allen Literary Agency, Linda 78; Allred and Allred Literary Agents 78; Altshuler Literary Agency, Miriam 79; Amster Literary Enterprises, Betsy 80; Authors & Artists Group, Inc. 82; Baldi Literary Agency, Malaga 82; Balkin Agency, Inc. 83; Barrett Books Inc., Loretta 83; Bernstein & Associates, Inc., Pam 84; Bial Agency, Daniel 84; Bleeker Street Associates, Inc. 85; Boston Literary Group, The 87; Brandt & Hochman Literary Agents Inc. 88; Brown Literary Agency, Inc., Andrea 89; Brown Ltd., Curtis 90; Buck Agency, Howard 91; Bykofsky Associates, Inc., Sheree 91; Castiglia Literary Agency 93; Clark Associates, William 94; Congdon Associates Inc., Don 95; Coover Agency, The Doe 96; Curtis Associates, Inc., Richard 97; Cyper, The Cypher Agency, James R. 98; Dawson Associates, Liza 98; Delbourgo Associates, Inc., Joélle 99; Dijkstra Literary Agency, Sandra 100; Doyen Literary Services, Inc. 102; Dunham Literary 103; Dupree/Miller and Associates Inc. Literary 103; Educational Design Services, Inc. 105; Eth Literary Agency, Felicia 110; Gislason Agency, The 116; Goldfarb & Associates 117; Goodman Associates 118; Goodman-Andrew Agency, Inc. 118; Greenburger Associates, Inc., Sanford J. 118; Grosvenor Literary Agency, The 120; Gusay Literary Agency, The Charlotte 120; Hamilburg Agency, Mitchell J., The 122; Hawkins & Associates, Inc., John 122; Henshaw Group, Richard 123; Herner Rights Agency, Susan 124; Hill & Barlow Agency 124; Hochmann Books, John L. 125; Hornfischer Literary Management, Inc. 125; J de S Associates Inc. 128; Jabberwocky Literary Agency 128; JCA Literary Agency 129; Jenks Agency, Carolyn 130; Kellock Company Inc., The 131; Kidde, Hoyt & Picard 132; Kleinman, Esq., of Graybill & English L.L.C., Jeffrey M. 133; Kroll Literary Agency Inc., Edite 135; Larsen/Elizabeth Pomada Literary Agents, Michael 136; Lazear Agency Incorporated 137; Levine Communications, Inc., James 138; Levine Literary Agency, Paul S. 138; Lieberman Associates, Robert 139; Lincoln Literary Agency, Ray 140; Literary Group, The 141; Litwest Group, LLC 141; Love Literary Agency, Nancy 142; Lowenstein Associates, Inc. 143; Madsen Agency, Robert 144; Mann Agency, Carol 144; McBride Literary Agency, Margret 147; McHugh Literary Agency 147; Multimedia Product Development, Inc. 150; Mura Enterprises, Inc., Dee 150; Naggar Literary Agency, Jean V. 151; New Brand Agency Group, LLC 152; New England Publishing Associates Inc. 152; Paraview, Inc. 154; Parks Agency, The Richard 154; Pevner, Inc., Stephen 157; Quicksilver Books Literary Agents 160; Rabiner, Literary Agent, Inc., Susan 160; Rein Books, Inc., Jody 164; Rinaldi Literary Agency, Angela 165; RLR Associates, Ltd. 168; Robbins Literary Agency, B.J. 169; Rosenberg Group, The 170; Ross Literary Agency, The Gail 170; Russell and Volkening 172; Schiavone Literary Agency, Inc. 174; Schulman, A Literary Agency, Susan 174; Sebastian Literary Agency 175; Seligman, Literary Agent, Lynn 176; Seymour Agency, The 177; Shepard Agency, The 177; Shepard Agency, The Robert 177; Simmons Literary Agency, Jeffrey 178; Slopen Literary Agency, Beverley 179; Snell Literary Agency, Michael 180; Spieler Agency, The 181; Spitzer Literary Agency, Philip G. 181; Straus Agency, Inc., Robin 183; Treimel NY, Scott 187; United Tribes 188; Vines Agency, Inc., The 189; Wald Associates, Inc., Mary Jack 190; Waterside Productions, Inc. 191; Weiner Literary Agency, Cherry 192; Weingel-Fidel Agency, The 193; Wray Literary Agency, Pamela D. 195; Zeckendorf Assoc. Inc., Susan 197

**Sports:** A.L.P. Literary Agency 76; Agents Incorporated for Medical and Mental Health Professionals 76; Alive Communications, Inc. 78; Allred and Allred Literary Agents 78; Altair Literary Agency 79; Authentic Creations Literary Agency 81; Authors & Artists Group, Inc. 82; Barrett Books Inc., Loretta 83; Bial Agency, Daniel 84; Black Literary Agency, David 85; Bleeker Street Associates, Inc. 85; Boates Literary Agency, Reid 86; Brandt & Hochman Literary Agents Inc. 88; Brown Literary Agency, Inc., Andrea 89; Brown Ltd., Curtis 90; Browne Ltd., Pema 90; Buck Agency, Howard 91; Bykofsky Associates, Inc., Sheree 91; Cambridge Literary 92; Charlton Associates, James 93; Congdon Associates Inc., Don 95; Connor Literary Agency 96; Curtis Associates, Inc.,

Richard 97; Cyper, The Cypher Agency, James R. 98; DeFiore and Company 99; Delbourgo Associates, Inc., Joélle 99; DHS Literary, Inc. 100; Dijkstra Literary Agency, Sandra 100; Donovan Literary, Jim 101; Doyen Literary Services, Inc. 102; Ducas, Robert 103; Dunham Literary 103; Dupree/Miller and Associates Inc. Literary 103; Fogelman Literary Agency 113; Fredericks Literary Agency, Jeanne 115; Gartenberg, Literary Agent, Max 116; Goldfarb & Associates 117; Goodman Associates 118; Goodman-Andrew Agency, Inc. 118; Greenburger Associates, Inc., Sanford J. 118; Gusay Literary Agency, The Charlotte 120; Hamilburg Agency, Mitchell J., The 122; Hawkins & Associates, Inc., John 122; Henshaw Group, Richard 123; Hornfischer Literary Management, Inc. 125; J de S Associates Inc. 128; Jabberwocky Literary Agency 128; JCA Literary Agency 129; Jordan Literary Agency, Lawrence 130; Kellock Company Inc., The 131; Ketz Agency, Louise B. 132; Klinger, Inc., Harvey 133; Larsen/Elizabeth Pomada Literary Agents, Michael 136; Lazear Agency Incorporated 137; Levine Communications, Inc., James 138; Levine Literary Agency, Paul S. 138; Limelight Management 140; Lincoln Literary Agency, Ray 140; Literary Group, The 141; Litwest Group, LLC 141; Lowenstein Associates, Inc. 143; Madsen Agency, Robert 144; Markowitz Literary Agency, Barbara 146; McBride Literary Agency, Margret 147; McGrath, Helen 147; McHugh Literary Agency 147; Michaels Literary Agency, Inc., Doris S. 148; Miller Agency, The 149; Multimedia Product Development, Inc. 150; Mura Enterprises, Inc., Dee 150; National Writers Literary Agency 151; Paraview, Inc. 154; Preskill Literary Agency, Robert 159; Quicksilver Books Literary Agents 160; Rhodes Literary Agency, Jodie 164; RLR Associates, Ltd. 168; Robbins Literary Agency, B.J. 169; Rosenberg Group, The 170; Rosenkranz Literary Agency, Rita 170; Ross Literary Agency, The Gail 170; Rotrosen Agency, LLC, Jane 171; Russell and Volkening 172; Serendipity Literary Agency, LLC 176; Seymour Agency, The 177; Shepard Agency, The 177; Shepard Agency, The Robert 177; Simmons Literary Agency, Jeffrey 178; Snell Literary Agency, Michael 180; Spitzer Literary Agency, Philip G. 181; Steele-Perkins Literary Agency 182; Swayze Literary Agency, Carolyn 184; Treimel NY, Scott 187; Venture Literary 189; Vines Agency, Inc., The 189; Ware Literary Agency, John A. 190; Waterside Productions, Inc. 191; Watt & Associates, Sandra 191; Waxman Agency, Inc., Scott 192; Whittaker, Literary Agent, Lynn 193; Wieser & Wieser, Inc. 194; Wray Literary Agency, Pamela D. 195; Zachary Shuster Harmsworth 197

**Theater/Film:** A.L.P. Literary Agency 76; Acacia House Publishing Services Ltd. 76; Ahearn Agency, Inc., The 77; Allred and Allred Literary Agents 78; Altshuler Literary Agency, Miriam 79; AMG/Renaissance 79; Andrews & Associates, Bart 80; Baldi Literary Agency, Malaga 82; Barrett Books Inc., Loretta 83; Bial Agency, Daniel 84; Brandt & Hochman Literary Agents Inc. 88; Brown Associates Inc., Marie 89; Brown Ltd., Curtis 90; Buck Agency, Howard 91; Bykofsky Associates, Inc., Sheree 91; Clark Associates, William 94; Congdon Associates Inc., Don 95; Curtis Associates, Inc., Richard 97; Cyper, The Cypher Agency, James R. 98; Doyen Literary Services, Inc. 102; Dupree/Miller and Associates Inc. Literary 103; Elmo Agency Inc., Ann 106; Farber Literary Agency Inc. 111; Feigen/Parrent Literary Management 111; Forthwrite Literary Agency 114; Gartenberg, Literary Agent, Max 116; Goldfarb & Associates 117; Goodman Associates 118; Goodman-Andrew Agency, Inc. 118; Greenburger Associates, Inc., Sanford J. 118; Grosvenor Literary Agency, The 120; Gusay Literary Agency, The Charlotte 120; Hamilburg Agency, Mitchell J., The 122; Hawkins & Associates, Inc., John 122; Hochmann Books, John L. 125; Jabberwocky Literary Agency 128; James Peter Associates, Inc. 129; JCA Literary Agency 129; Jenks Agency, Carolyn 130; Kellock Company Inc., The 131; Kleinman, Esq., of Graybill & English L.L.C., Jeffrey M. 133; Knight Agency, The 134; Kouts, Literary Agent, Barbara S. 134; Lampack Agency, Inc., Peter 136; Larsen/Elizabeth Pomada Literary Agents, Michael 136; Lazear Agency Incorporated 137; Levine Literary Agency, Paul S. 138; Lieberman Associates, Robert 139; Lincoln Literary Agency, Ray 140; Literary Group, The 141; Lowenstein Associates, Inc. 143; Lownie Literary Agency Ltd., Andrew 143; Madsen Agency, Robert 144; March Tenth, Inc. 145; Markowitz Literary Agency, Barbara 146; McHugh Literary Agency 147; Menza Literary Agency, Claudia 148; Millard Literary Agency, Martha 148; Norma-Lewis Agency, The 153; Paraview, Inc. 154; Parks Agency, The Richard 154; Pinder Lane & Garon-Brooke Associates, Ltd. 158; Rein Books, Inc., Jody 164; Rhodes Literary Agency, Jodie 164; Robbins Literary Agency, B.J. 169; Rosenkranz Literary Agency, Rita 170; Rubie Literary Agency, The Peter 172; Russell and Volkening 172; Sanders & Associates, Victoria 173; Schulman, A Literary Agency, Susan 174; Seligman, Literary Agent, Lynn 176; Seymour Agency, The 177; Shepard Agency, The 177; Simmons Literary Agency, Jeffrey 178; Smith Literary Agency Ltd., Robert 180; Snell Literary Agency, Michael 180; Spieler Agency, The 181; Spitzer Literary Agency, Philip G. 181; Straus Agency, Inc., Robin 183; Treimel NY, Scott 187; Two M Communications Ltd. 187; United Tribes 188; Wald Associates, Inc., Mary Jack 190; Wecksler-Incomco 192; Witherspoon & Associates, Inc. 194; Writers House 195

**Translations:** A.L.P. Literary Agency 76; Balkin Agency, Inc. 83; Barrett Books Inc., Loretta 83; Brown Ltd., Curtis 90; Buck Agency, Howard 91; Bykofsky Associates, Inc., Sheree 91; Clark Associates, William 94; Congdon Associates Inc., Don 95; Curtis Associates, Inc., Richard 97; Daves Agency, Joan 98; Doyen Literary Services, Inc. 102; Dupree/Miller and Associates Inc. Literary 103; Goldfarb & Associates 117; Goodman Associates 118; Greenburger Associates, Inc., Sanford J. 118; Grosvenor Literary Agency, The 120; Gusay Literary Agency, The Charlotte 120; Hamilburg Agency, Mitchell J., The 122; J de S Associates Inc. 128; JCA Literary Agency 129; Jenks Agency, Carolyn 130; Kleinman, Esq., of Graybill & English L.L.C., Jeffrey M. 133; Lazear Agency Incorporated 137; Madsen Agency, Robert 144; McHugh Literary Agency 147; Paraview, Inc. 154; Picard, Literary Agent, Alison J. 157; RLR Associates, Ltd. 168; Sanders & Associates, Victoria 173; Schulman, A Literary Agency, Susan 174; Seligman, Literary Agent, Lynn 176; Seymour Agency, The 177; Simmons

Literary Agency, Jeffrey 178; Snell Literary Agency, Michael 180; Treimel NY, Scott 187; United Tribes 188; Vines Agency, Inc., The 189; Wald Associates, Inc., Mary Jack 190

**True Crime/Investigative:** A.L.P. Literary Agency 76; Ahearn Agency, Inc., The 77; Allred and Allred Literary Agents 78; AMG/Renaissance 79; Appleseeds Management 81; Authentic Creations Literary Agency 81; Authors & Artists Group, Inc. 82; Baldi Literary Agency, Malaga 82; Balkin Agency, Inc. 83; Barrett Books Inc., Loretta 83; Bernstein & Associates, Inc., Pam 84; Bial Agency, Daniel 84; Bleeker Street Associates, Inc. 85; Boates Literary Agency, Reid 86; Boston Literary Group, The 87; Bova Literary Agency, The Barbara 88; Brandt & Hochman Literary Agents Inc. 88; Brown Ltd., Curtis 90; Browne Ltd., Pema 90; Buck Agency, Howard 91; Bykofsky Associates, Inc., Sheree 91; Cambridge Literary 92; Collin Literary Agency, Frances 95; Congdon Associates Inc., Don 95; Connor Literary Agency 96; Coover Agency, The Doe 96; Core Creations 96; Curtis Associates, Inc., Richard 97; Cyper, The Cypher Agency, James R. 98; Delbourgo Associates, Inc., Joëlle 99; DHS Literary, Inc. 100; Donovan Literary, Jim 101; Doyen Literary Services, Inc. 102; Ducas, Robert 103; Dupree/Miller and Associates Inc. Literary 103; Dystel Literary Management, Inc., Jane 104; Elek Associates, Peter 105; Ellenberg Literary Agency, Ethan 106; Elmo Agency Inc., Ann 106; Eth Literary Agency, Felicia 110; Fleury Agency, B.R. 112; Fogelman Literary Agency 113; Fort Ross Inc. Russian-American Publishing Projects 113; Frenkel & Associates, James 115; Gartenberg, Literary Agent, Max 116; Goldfarb & Associates 117; Goodman Associates 118; Goodman-Andrew Agency, Inc. 118; Grace Literary Agency, Carroll 118; Greenburger Associates, Inc., Sanford J. 118; Grosvenor Literary Agency, The 120; Gusay Literary Agency, The Charlotte 120; Halsey Agency, Reece 121; Halsey North, Reece 121; Hamilburg Agency, Mitchell J., The 122; Hawkins & Associates, Inc., John 122; Henshaw Group, Richard 123; Herner Rights Agency, Susan 124; Hornfischer Literary Management, Inc. 125; Jabberwocky Literary Agency 128; JCA Literary Agency 129; Jellinek and Murray Literary Agency 130; Kleinman, Esq., of Graybill & English L.L.C., Jeffrey M. 133; Klinger, Inc., Harvey 133; Kritzer Productions, Eddie 135; Lampack Agency, Inc., Peter 136; Larsen/Elizabeth Pomada Literary Agents, Michael 136; Lawyer's Literary Agency, Inc. 137; Lazear Agency Incorporated 137; Levine Literary Agency, Paul S. 138; Literary Group, The 141; Litwest Group, LLC 141; Love Literary Agency, Nancy 142; Lownie Literary Agency Ltd., Andrew 143; Madsen Agency, Robert 144; McBride Literary Agency, Margret 147; McHugh Literary Agency 147; Millard Literary Agency, Martha 148; Multimedia Product Development, Inc. 150; Mura Enterprises, Inc., Dee 150; New Brand Agency Group, LLC 152; New England Publishing Associates Inc. 152; Norma-Lewis Agency, The 153; Paraview, Inc. 154; Picard, Literary Agent, Alison J. 157; Pinder Lane & Garon-Brooke Associates, Ltd. 158; Preskill Literary Agency, Robert 159; Quicksilver Books Literary Agents 160; Rhodes Literary Agency, Jodie 164; Rinaldi Literary Agency, Angela 165; RLR Associates, Ltd. 168; Robbins Literary Agency, B.J. 169; Ross Literary Agency, The Gail 170; Rotrosen Agency, LLC, Jane 171; Russell and Volkening 172; Scherf, Inc., Literary Management 173; Schiavone Literary Agency, Inc. 174; Schulman, A Literary Agency, Susan 174; Sedgeband Literary Associates 176; Seligman, Literary Agent, Lynn 176; Seymour Agency, The 177; Simmons Literary Agency, Jeffrey 178; Slopen Literary Agency, Beverley 179; Smith Literary Agency Ltd., Robert 180; Snell Literary Agency, Michael 180; Spitzer Literary Agency, Philip G. 181; Swayze Literary Agency, Carolyn 184; Teal Literary Agency, Patricia 185; Treimel NY, Scott 187; Venture Literary 189; Vines Agency, Inc., The 189; Wald Associates, Inc., Mary Jack 190; Ware Literary Agency, John A. 190; Watkins Loomis Agency, Inc. 191; Watt & Associates, Sandra 191; Wieser & Wieser, Inc. 194; Witherspoon & Associates, Inc. 194; Writers House 195; Zachary Shuster Harmsworth 197

**Women's Issues/Women's Studies:** A.L.P. Literary Agency 76; Ahearn Agency, Inc., The 77; Alive Communications, Inc. 78; Allen Literary Agency, Linda 78; Allred and Allred Literary Agents 78; Altair Literary Agency 79; Altshuler Literary Agency, Miriam 79; Amster Literary Enterprises, Betsy 80; Authentic Creations Literary Agency 81; Authors & Artists Group, Inc. 82; Baldi Literary Agency, Malaga 82; Barrett Books Inc., Loretta 83; Bent Literary Agent, Harvey Klinger, Inc., Jenny 83; Bernstein & Associates, Inc., Pam 84; Bial Agency, Daniel 84; Bleeker Street Associates, Inc. 85; Boates Literary Agency, Reid 86; BookEnds, LLC 86; Books & Such 87; Borchardt Inc., Georges 87; Boston Literary Group, The 87; Bova Literary Agency, The Barbara 88; Brandt & Hochman Literary Agents Inc. 88; Brown Associates Inc., Marie 89; Brown Ltd., Curtis 90; Browne Ltd., Pema 90; Buck Agency, Howard 91; Bykofsky Associates, Inc., Sheree 91; Cambridge Literary 92; Carvainis Agency, Inc., Maria 92; Casselman Literary Agency, Martha 93; Castiglia Literary Agency 93; Clausen, Mays & Tahan, LLC 94; Cohen, Inc. Literary Agency, Ruth 94; Congdon Associates Inc., Don 95; Connor Literary Agency 96; Coover Agency, The Doe 96; Crawford Literary Agency 97; Curtis Associates, Inc., Richard 97; Cyper, The Cypher Agency, James R. 98; Daves Agency, Joan 98; Dawson Associates, Liza 98; Delbourgo Associates, Inc., Joëlle 99; DH Literary, Inc. 100; Dijkstra Literary Agency, Sandra 100; Doyen Literary Services, Inc. 102; Dunham Literary 103; Dupree/Miller and Associates Inc. Literary 103; Dystel Literary Management, Inc., Jane 104; Educational Design Services, Inc. 105; Elmo Agency Inc., Ann 106; Eth Literary Agency, Felicia 110; Feigen/Parrent Literary Management 111; Fogelman Literary Agency 113; Forthwrite Literary Agency 114; Fredericks Literary Agency, Jeanne 115; Freymann Literary Agency, Sarah Jane 115; Gartenberg, Literary Agent, Max 116; Goldfarb & Associates 117; Goodman Associates 118; Goodman-Andrew Agency, Inc. 118; Grace Literary Agency, Carroll 118; Greenburger Associates, Inc., Sanford J. 118; Grosjean Literary Agency, Jill 120; Grosvenor Literary Agency, The 120; Gusay Literary Agency, The Charlotte 120; Halsey Agency, Reece 121; Halsey North, Reece 121; Hamilburg Agency, Mitchell J., The 122; Hartline Literary Agency 122; Hawkins & Associates, Inc., John 122; Heacock Literary Agency, Inc. 123; Henshaw Group, Richard 123; Herner Rights Agency, Susan 124; Hill & Barlow Agency 124; Hill Bonnie Nadell, Inc., Frederick 124; Jabber-

# Agents Specialties Index: Script

This subject index is divided into script subject categories. To find an agent interested in the type of screenplay you've written, see the appropriate sections under subject headings that best describe your work.

## Comedy

## Contemporary Issues

## Detective/Police/ Crime

## Fantasy

## Feminist

## Gay/Lesbian

## Glitz

## Historical

Bohrman Agency, The 233
Brown Agency, Bruce 234
Gage Group, The 239
Kerin-Goldberg Associates 243
Lake Agency, The Candace 244
Luedtke Agency, The 245
Miller Co., The Stuart M. 246
Omniquest Entertainment 247
Picture of You, A 249
Robins & Associates, Michael D. 250
Sherman & Associates, Ken 251
Soloway Grant Kopaloff & Associates 252
Stone Manners Agency 254
Suite A Management Talent & Literary Agency 254
Visionary Entertainment 255
Wardlow and Associates 256
Windfall Management 257
Writers & Artists Agency 258

## Myetery/Suspense

Abrams Artists Agency 231
Acme Talent & Literary 231
Agency, The 232
Alpern Group, The 232
Artists Agency, The 232
Baskow Agency 233
Bohrman Agency, The 233
Brown Agency, Bruce 234
Cedar Grove Agency Entertainment 235
Chadwick & Gros Literary Agency 235
Client First-a/k/a/ Leo P. Haffey Agency 236
Douroux & Co. 237
Epstein-Wyckoff and Associates 237
Esq. Management 237
Filmwriters Literary Agency 238
French, Inc., Samuel 239
Gage Group, The 239
Geddes Agency 239
Greene, Arthur B. 240
Gurman Agency, The Susan 240
H.W.A. Talent Representatives 240
Hayes & Associates, Gil 241
Hudson Agency 242
International Leonards Corp. 242
Jaret Entertainment 242
Kerin-Goldberg Associates 243
Kerwin Agency, William 243
Ketay Agency, The Joyce 243
Kohner, Inc., Paul 244
Lake Agency, The Candace 244
Larchmont Literary Agency 244
Luedtke Agency, The 245
Major Clients Agency 245
Miller Co., The Stuart M. 246
Momentum Marketing 246
Monteiro Rose Agency 247
Niad Management 247

Omniquest Entertainment 247
Palmer, Dorothy 248
Panda Talent 248
Perelman Agency, Barry 248
Picture of You, A 249
Redler Entertainment, Dan 249
Redwood Empire Agency 250
Robins & Associates, Michael D. 250
Robinson Talent and Literary Management 250
Scagnetti Talent & Literary Agency, Jack 251
Shapiro-Lichtman 251
Sherman & Associates, Ken 251
Silver Screen Placements 252
Soloway Grant Kopaloff & Associates 252
Sorice Agency, Camille 253
Stars, The Agency 253
Stein Agency 253
Stone Manners Agency 254
Suite A Management Talent & Literary Agency 254
Sydra Techniques Corp. 254
Talent Source 254
Talesmyth Entertainment, Inc. 255
Visionary Entertainment 255
Wardlow and Associates 256
Windfall Management 257
Wright Representatives, Ann 257
Writer Store 257
Writers & Artists Agency 258

## Psychic/Supernatural

Acme Talent & Literary 231
Agency, The 232
Alpern Group, The 232
Bohrman Agency, The 233
Brown Agency, Bruce 234
Communications Management Associates 236
Esq. Management 237
Filmwriters Literary Agency 238
Gage Group, The 239
Geddes Agency 239
H.W.A. Talent Representatives 240
Jaret Entertainment 242
Kay Agency, Charlene 243
Kerin-Goldberg Associates 243
Ketay Agency, The Joyce 243
Lake Agency, The Candace 244
Larchmont Literary Agency 244
Luedtke Agency, The 245
Momentum Marketing 246
Monteiro Rose Agency 247
Niad Management 247
Omniquest Entertainment 247
Picture of You, A 249
Redler Entertainment, Dan 249
Robins & Associates, Michael D. 250
Robinson Talent and Literary Management 250

Sherman & Associates, Ken 251
Soloway Grant Kopaloff & Associates 252
Stein Agency 253
Stone Manners Agency 254
Suite A Management Talent & Literary Agency 254
Talesmyth Entertainment, Inc. 255
Visionary Entertainment 255
Wardlow and Associates 256
Wright Representatives, Ann 257
Writer Store 257
Writers & Artists Agency 258

## Regional

Acme Talent & Literary 231
Alpern Group, The 232
Bohrman Agency, The 233
Brown Agency, Bruce 234
Gage Group, The 239
Kerin-Goldberg Associates 243
Lake Agency, The Candace 244
Luedtke Agency, The 245
Picture of You, A 249
Robins & Associates, Michael D. 250
Sherman & Associates, Ken 251
Soloway Grant Kopaloff & Associates 252
Stone Manners Agency 254
Suite A Management Talent & Literary Agency 254
Visionary Entertainment 255
Wardlow and Associates 256
Writer Store 257
Writers & Artists Agency 258

## Religious/Inspirational

Acme Talent & Literary 231
Alpern Group, The 232
Baskow Agency 233
Bohrman Agency, The 233
Brown Agency, Bruce 234
Bulger and Associates, Kelvin C. 234
Communications Management Associates 236
Esq. Management 237
Gage Group, The 239
Kerin-Goldberg Associates 243
Lake Agency, The Candace 244
Luedtke Agency, The 245
Momentum Marketing 246
Picture of You, A 249
Robins & Associates, Michael D. 250
Robinson Talent and Literary Management 250
Sherman & Associates, Ken 251
Soloway Grant Kopaloff & Associates 252
Stone Manners Agency 254

## Westerns/Frontier

# Script Agents Format Index:

This subject index will help you determine agencies interested in handling scripts for particular types of movies or TV programs. These formats are delineated into ten categories; animation, documentary; episodic drama; feature film; miniseries; movie of the week (MOW); sitcom; soap opera; stage play; variety show.

## Variety Show

# Agencies Indexed by Openness to Submissions

We've ranked the agencies and independent publicists according to their openness to submissions. Check this index to find an agent or independent publicist who is appropriate for your level of experience. Some companies are listed under more than one category.

World Class Speakers & Entertainers

Zegarek Public Relations, Inc., Meryl

## ◐ AGENCIES PREFERRING TO WORK WITH ESTABLISHED WRITERS, MOSTLY OBTAIN NEW CLIENTS THROUGH REFERRALS

### Literary agents

AMG/Renaissance
Authentic Creations Literary Agency
Authors & Artists Group, Inc.
Axelrod Agency, The
Black Literary Agency, David
Bleeker Street Associates, Inc.
Boates Literary Agency, Reid
Books & Such
Borchardt Inc., Georges
Boston Literary Group, The
Bova Literary Agency, The Barbara
Brady Literary Management
Buck Agency, Howard
Casselman Literary Agency, Martha
Clark Associates, William
Collin Literary Agent, Frances
Communications and Entertainment, Inc.
Congdon Associates Inc., Don
Cornfield Literary Agency, Robert
Curtis Associates, Inc., Richard
DH Literary, Inc.
Donnaud & Associates, Inc., Janis A.
Doyen Literary Services, Inc.
Elmo Agency Inc., Ann
Farber Literary Agency Inc.
Feigenbaum Publishing Consultants, Inc.
Fogelman Literary Agency
Fort Ross Inc. Russian-American Publishing Projects
Freymann Literary Agency, Sarah Jane
Gartenberg, Literary Agent, Max
Goldfarb & Associates
Goodman Associates
Grayson Literary Agency, Ashley
Greene, Arthur B.
Gregory, Inc. Blanche C.
Grosvenor Literary Agency, The
Halsey Agency, Reece
Hartline Literary Agency
Hawkins & Associates, Inc., John
Henshaw Group, Richard
Hill & Barlow Agency
Hochmann Books, John L.
Hogenson Agency, Barbara
J de S Associates Inc.

Kellock Company, Inc., The
Kidd Agency, Inc., Virginia
Koster Literary Agency, LLC, Elaine
Lampack Agency, Inc., Peter
Lawyer's Literary Agency, Inc.
Lescher & Lescher Ltd.
Levine Communications, Inc., James
Levine Literary Agency, Inc., Ellen
Lieberman Associates, Robert
Limelight Management
Lincoln Literary Agency, Ray
Lipkind Agency, Wendy
Literary and Creative Artists, Inc.
Mann Agency, Carol
March Tenth, Inc.
McGrath, Helen
Michaels Literary Agency, Inc., Doris S.
Millard Literary Agency, Martha
Miller Agency, The
Moran Agency, Maureen
Morris Agency, Inc., William
Morrison, Inc., Henry
Multimedia Product Development, Inc.
Naggar Literary Agency, Jean V.
Oscard Agency, Inc., Fifi
Paraview, Inc.
Parks Agency, The Richard
Pine Associates, Inc., Arthur
Preskill Literary Agency, Robert
Protter Literary Agent, Susan Ann
Rein Books, Inc., Jody
Rittenberg Literary Agency, Inc., Ann
Riverside Literary Agency
Robbins Office, Inc., The
Robinson Talent and Literary Management
Ross Literary Agency, The Gail
Rowland Agency, The Damaris
Ryan Publishing Enterprises, Inc., Regina
Schulman, A Literary Agency, Susan
Scovil Chichak Galen Literary Agency
Sebastian Literary Agency
Shukat Company Ltd., The
Siegel, International Literary Agency, Inc., Rosalie
Singer Literary Agency Inc., Evelyn
Slopen Literary Agency, Beverley
Spitzer Literary Agency, Philip G.
Stauffer Associates, Nancy
Swayne Agency Literary Management & Consulting, Inc., The
Talbot Agency, The John

Targ Literary Agency, Inc., Roslyn
Teal Literary Agency, Patricia
Tiersten Literary Agency, Irene
Weingel-Fidel Agency, The
Wieser & Wieser, Inc.
Wright Representatives, Ann
Writers' Representatives, Inc.
Wylie-Merrick Literary Agency

### Script agents

Above the Line Agency
Acme Talent & Literary Agency, The
AMG/Renaissance Literary Agency
Baskow Agency
Bennett Agency, The
Berman Boals and Flynn Inc.
Bohrman Agency, The
Brodie Representation, Alan
Brown Agency, Bruce
Buchwald and Associates, Inc. Don
Cameron Agency, The Marshall
Cedar Grove Agency Entertainment
Communications and Entertainment, Inc.
Epstein-Wyckoff and Associates
Fran Literary Agency
Freed Co., The Barry
French, Inc., Samuel
Greene, Arthur B.
Gurman Agency, The Susan
Hayes & Assoc., Gil
Hodges Agency, Carolyn
Hogenson Agency, Barbara
International Creative Management
Kallen Agency, Leslie
Major Clients Agency
Monteiro Rose Agency
Niad Management
Omniquest Entertainment
Palmer, Dorothy
Partos Company, The
Preminger Agency, Jim
Redler Entertainment, Dan
Robins & Associates, Michael D.
Robinson Talent and Literary Management
Scagnetti Talent & Literary Agency, Jack
Schulman, A Literary Agency, Susan
Shapiro-Lichtman
Sherman & Associates, Ken
Soloway Grant Kopaloff & Associates
Stein Agency
Toomey Associates, Jeanne
Visionary Entertainment
Windfall Management
Writers & Artists Agency

*Publicists*
Brody Public Relations
Greater Talent Network, Inc.
Carlton, Inc., Royce
Warwick Associates
Write Publicist & Co., The

## ⊚ AGENCIES HANDLING ONLY CERTAIN TYPES OF WORK OR WORK BY WRITERS UNDER CERTAIN CIRCUMSTANCES

*Literary agents*
Andrews & Associates Inc., Bart
Books & Such
Brown Literary Agency, Inc., Andrea
Casselman Literary Agency, Martha
Dwyer & O'Grady, Inc.
Educational Design Services, Inc.
Flannery Literary
Ghosts & Collaborators International
Hopkins Literary Associates
Kidd Agency, Inc., Virginia
Kirchoff/Wohlberg, Inc., Authors' Representation Division
Paraview, Inc.
Roth, Literary Representation, Carol Susan
Schulman, A Literary Agency, Susan
Tobias—A Literary Agency for Children's Books, Ann
Treimel NY, Scott
Valcourt Agency, Inc., The Richard R.

*Script agents*
Camejo & Assoc., Suzanna
Dramatic Publishing
Kohner, Inc., Paul

Momentum Marketing
Schulman, A Literary Agency, Susan

*Publicists*
Brody Public Relations
Event Management Services
KSB Promotions
Leondar Public Relations, Gail
Raab Associates

## ⊘ AGENCIES NOT CURRENTLY SEEKING NEW CLIENTS

*Literary agents*
A.L.P. Literary Agency
Abel Literary Agent, Carole
Bach Literary Agency, Julian
Basch, Margaret
Bijur, Vicky
Brann Agency, Inc., The Helen
Broadway Play Publishing
Brown Associates Inc., Marie
Burger Associates, Ltd., Knox
Chelius Literary Agency, Jane
Cole, Literary Agent, Joanna Lewis
Columbia Literary Associates, Inc.
Dijkstra Literary Agency, Sandra
Dolger Agency, The Jonathan
Dorian Literary Agency
Dunow Literary Agency, Henry
Dwyer & O'Grady, Inc.
Edelstein Literary Agency, Anne
Fallon Literary Agency
Foley Literary Agency, The
Fox Chase Agency, Inc.
Goldin, Frances
Groffsky Literary Agency, Maxine
Hanson Literary Agency, Jeanne K.
Harden Curtis Associates
International Creative Management
Jackson Agency, Melanie
Janklow & Nesbit Associates
Krichevsky Literary Agency, Inc.

Lazin, Sarah
Leavitt Agency, The Ned
Marcil Literary Agency, Inc., The Denise
Marshall Agency, The Evan
Marton Agency Inc., The
Matson Co. Inc., Harold
Mattes, Inc., Jed
McCauley, Gerard
McClellan Associates, Anita D.
Merrill, Ltd., Helen
Morhaim Literary Agency, Howard
Roberts, Flora
Rosenstone/Wender
Sheedy Agency, Charlotte
Smith-Skolnik Literary
Stuhlmann, Author's Representative, Gunther
Van Duren Agency, Annette
Viciananza, Ltd., Ralph
Vigliano Literary Agency, David
Wald Associates, Inc., Mary Jack
Wasserman Literary Agency, Harriet
Watt & Associates, Sandra
Weil Agency, Inc., The Wendy
Weiner Literary Agency, Cherry
Weyr Agency, Rhoda
Wolf Literary Agency, Audrey A.
Writers' Productions
Yost Associates, Inc., Mary

*Script agents*
Baranski Literary Agency, Joseph A.
Communications Management Associates
Filmwriters Literary Agency
French's
International Leonards Corp.
Momentum Marketing
Panda Talent
Quillco Agency, The
Redwood Empire Agency
Stone Manners Agency
Van Duren Agency, Annette

# Geographic Index

Some writers prefer to work with an agent or independent publicist in their vicinity. If you're such a writer, this index offers you the opportunity to easily select agents closest to home. Agencies and independent publicists are separated by state. We've also arranged them according to the sections in which they appear in the book (Nonfee-charging agents, Script agents or Publicists). Once you find the agency you're interested in, refer to the Listing Index for the page number.

GEOGRAPHIC INDEX

## UTAH
*Publicists*
Firstword Agency

## VERMONT
*Literary agents*
Brady Literary Management

## VIRGINIA
*Script agents*
Filmwriters Literary Agency

*Publicists*
Gray Communications, Cameron

## WASHINGTON
*Literary agents*
Wales, Literary Agency, Inc.

*Script agents*
Cedar Grove Agency
    Entertainment

*Publicists*
Acheson-Greub, Inc.
Talion.com

## WISCONSIN
*Literary agents*
Frenkel & Associates, James
Sternig & Byrne Literary Agency

## CANADA
*Literary agents*
Acacia House Publishing
    Services Ltd.
Livingston Cooke
Slopen Literary Agency,
    Beverley
Swayze Literary Agency, Carolyn

*Script agents*
Kay Agency, Charlene
Livingston Cooke

## INTERNATIONAL
*Literary agents*
Anubis Literary Agency
Dorian Literary Agency
Gregory And Radice Authors'
    Agents
Limelight Management
Lownie Literary Agency Ltd.,
    Andrew
Simmons Literary Agency,
    Jeffrey
Smith Literary Agency Ltd.,
    Robert
Susijn Agency, The

*Script agents*
Brodie Representation, Alan

# Agents Index

This index of agent names can help you locate agents you may have read or heard about even when you do not know which agency for which they work. Agent names are listed with their agencies' names.

# Listing Index

Agencies that appeared in the 2001 *Guide to Literary Agents* but are not included this year are identified by a two-letter code explaining why the agency is not listed: **ED**)—Editorial Decision, (**NS**)—Not Accepting Submissions/Too Many Queries, (**NR**)—No (or Late) Response to Listing Request, (**OB**)—Out of Business, (**RR**)—Removed by Agency's Request, (**UF**)—Uncertain Future, (**UC**)—Unable to Contact, (**RP**)—Business Restructured or Sold.

LISTING INDEX